# Benchmark Papers in Electrical Engineering and Computer Science

**Series Editor: John B. Thomas**
**Princeton University**

**PUBLISHED VOLUMES**

SYSTEM SENSITIVITY ANALYSIS
*J. B. Cruz, Jr.*
RANDOM PROCESSES, Part I: Multiplicity Theory and Canonical Decompositions
*Anthony Ephremides and John B. Thomas*
ALGEBRAIC CODING THEORY: History and Development
*Ian F. Blake*
PATTERN RECOGNITION: Introduction and Foundations
*Jack Sklansky*
COMPUTER-AIDED CIRCUIT DESIGN: Simulation and Optimization
*S. W. Director*
ENVIRONMENTAL MODELING: Analysis and Management
*Douglas Daetz and Richard H. Pantell*
AUTOMATIC CONTROL: Classical Linear Theory
*George J. Thaler*
CIRCUIT THEORY: Foundations and Classical Contributions
*M. E. Van Valkenburg*
DATA COMMUNICATION: Fundamentals of Baseband Transmission
*L. E. Franks*
NONLINEAR SYSTEMS: Processing of Random Signals—Classical Analysis
*A. H. Haddad*
RANDOM PROCESSES, PART II: Poisson and Jump-Point Processes
*Anthony Ephremides*
DIGITAL FILTERS AND THE FAST FOURIER TRANSFORM
*Bede Liu*
DETECTION AND ESTIMATION: Applications to Radar
*Simon S. Haykin*
NONLINEAR SYSTEMS: Stability Analysis
*J. K. Aggarwal and M. Vidyasagar*
LINEAR LEAST-SQUARES ESTIMATION
*Thomas Kailath*
OPTICAL COMMUNICATION THEORY
*R. O. Harger*

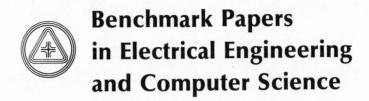

Benchmark Papers
in Electrical Engineering
and Computer Sciences / 18

A BENCHMARK® Books Series

# OPTICAL COMMUNICATION THEORY

Edited by

**R. O. HARGER**
**University of Maryland**

Dowden, Hutchinson
& Ross, Inc.
STROUDSBURG, PENNSYLVANIA

Benchmark Papers in Electrical Engineering and Computer Sciences, Volume 18
Library of Congress Catalog Card Number: 77–2360
ISBN: 0–87933–286–7



79 78 77 1 2 3 4 5
Manufactured in the United States of America.

LIBRARY OF CONGRESS CATALOGING IN PUBLICATION DATA

Main entry under title:
Optical communication theory.
(Benchmark papers in electrical engineering and computer science; 18)
Includes index.
1. Optical communications—Addresses, essays, lectures. I. Harger, R.O.
TK5103.59.067 621.38'0414 77–2360
ISBN 0–87933–286–7

Exclusive Distributor: **Halsted Press**
A Division of John Wiley & Sons, Inc.
ISBN: 0-470-99228-x

# SERIES EDITOR'S FOREWORD

This Benchmark Series in Electrical Engineering and Computer Science is aimed at sifting, organizing, and making readily accessible the vast literature that has accumulated on the subject. Although the series is not intended as a complete substitute for a study of this literature, it will serve at least three major critical purposes. In the first place, it provides a practical point of entry into a given area of research. Each volume offers an expert's selection of the critical papers on a given topic as well as his views on its structure, development, and present status. In the second place, the series provides a convenient and time-saving means for study in areas related to but not contiguous with one's principal interests. Last but by no means least, the series allows the collection, in a particularly compact and convenient form, of the major works on which present research activities and interests are based.

Each volume in the series has been collected, organized, and edited by an authority in a particular area. To present a unified view of the area, the volume editor has prepared an introduction to the subject, included his comments on each article, and provided a subject index to facilitate access to the papers.

We believe that this series will provide a manageable working library of the most important technical articles in electrical engineering and computer science. We hope that it will be equally valuable to students, teachers, and researchers.

This volume, *Optical Communication Theory*, has been edited by R. O. Harger of the University of Maryland. It contains 23 papers, with editorial comments, on the theoretical foundations of optical communications. As would be expected, most of the papers in this volume have appeared in the last 10 years. Professor Harger has been strongly involved in the development of this area. His editorial comments are unusually complete and should serve as a valuable adjunct to the papers themselves.

JOHN B. THOMAS

# PREFACE

Light has always been importantly and variedly instrumental in human communication; and the progressing understanding of the physics of light, especially its dual nature as wave and particle, has provided many triumphs. Heretofore the source, usually the sun, emitted a chaotic, or incoherent, radiation ill suited to information transmission for most modern technological purposes. During this century, regular, or coherent, radiation sources have been developed at continually increasing frequencies—the application to communications continuing apace—and about 15 years ago, light frequencies were attained with the laser. Prototype optical communication systems now carry common carrier traffic, an application to be routine in a few years, and exemplifying important realizations of the laser's promise for efficient, high-capacity communication.

Among many challenging problems posed by optical communications, paramount are those centered on light's dual nature as wave and particle. That is, at light frequencies fundamental limitations are imposed by quantum mechanical restraints on measurement, and communication inextricably involves measurement. Ultimately required is the replacement of the Kolmogoroff probability structure that has heretofore underlain communication theory: it results that optimal receivers can be strikingly nonclassical. This development of an understanding of these limitations is a central theme of this volume.

There of course remains much interesting elaboration and application of a rich theory of optical communications, required to inform and be informed by the future engineering of an elegant, efficient new means of communication whose future is now assured.

R. O. HARGER

# CONTENTS

## PART II: POISSON PROCESS MODELS



## PART III: OPTICAL CHANNELS



## PART IV: QUANTUM COMMUNICATION THEORY SINCE 1971

# CONTENTS BY AUTHOR

# INTRODUCTION

For nearly two decades, the laser has held obvious promise for efficient use in communication applications: its temporal and spatial coherence, very great frequency, and possible high power seemed to offer enormous capacity. During these years, myriad research and development problems have been solved, and the promise is beginning to be realized practically, even in the competitive common carrier network. The engineering analysis and design of optical communication systems has required the contributions of several disciplines to form a rational base: the understanding of modulators, demodulators, and fiber channels requires mastery of the subject of quantum electronics and related materials science; the modeling and analysis of optical channels requires mastery of electromagnetic theory, especially as applied to guided optical fields; and understanding fundamental limitations and finding optimal optical communication signals, receivers, and transmitters requires communication theory. Each of these subjects required extension and specialization for this application, but none so fundamentally as communication theory.

The extension and application of communication theory to, e.g., the fiber and atmospheric turbulent channels to account for spatial effects and quantum effects as modeled by "shot processes" is a significant recent accomplishment. The truly striking work to determine optical communication system limitations in a most fundamental way, however, required the complete revamping of the subject, discarding the Kolmogoroff probability theory basis that is insufficiently general to account for quantum mechanics. At heart, communication is measurement: at optical frequencies the photon energy is sufficiently large that quantum mechanical limitations on measurement must be considered. In turn, in its mature form (see, e.g., Jauch [1]), this subject is an elegant mathematical theory representing one of the set pieces of twentieth-century physics. The relevant methods of statistical inference must account for quantum mechanics. As has happened before, the mathematical theory required by communication theory far outstrips the mathematical theory available in classical methods of statistical inference.

In short, the communication theorist could hardly ask for a more challenging research area, and the communication engineer could hardly ask for a more promising development area. Perhaps surprisingly, the existing theory of quantum mechanical measurement, in an important sense, has required extension: optimal measurements have been shown to embody the adjoining of an auxiliary apparatus to the original system—a strikingly nonclassical procedure—resulting in appropriate "approximate joint measurement" of noncommuting observables. The evolution of this idea is a central theme in this collection of papers.

Optical communication systems (see Figure 1) are primarily special in their form of transmitter—laser, light emitting diode—and receiver—e.g., photodiode, photomultiplier—and also channel—e.g., optical, clear (turbulent) atmosphere or optical fiber—and this special nature of course reflects ultimately on appropriate signal waveforms and coding. The channel transmits an electromagnetic field and must be described ab initio spatio-temporally, including the transitions between fields and electrical, temporal waveforms in the transmitter and receiver. The extension of "standard" communication theory to account for spatial effects classically encounters no difficulties in principle though the electromagnetic theory may be very involved; rather satisfactory descriptions have now been developed for the optical fiber channel, but the theory for the clear-air turbulent channel remains only partially developed. Quantum mechanics enters into the description of the transitions between radiation and matter at the transmitter and

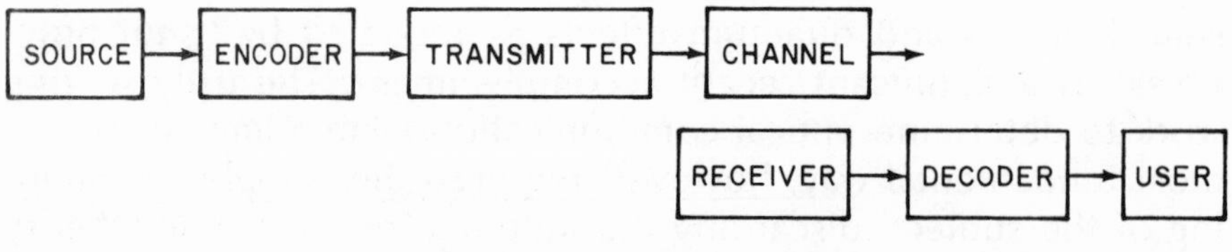


**Figure 1** A typical optical communication system

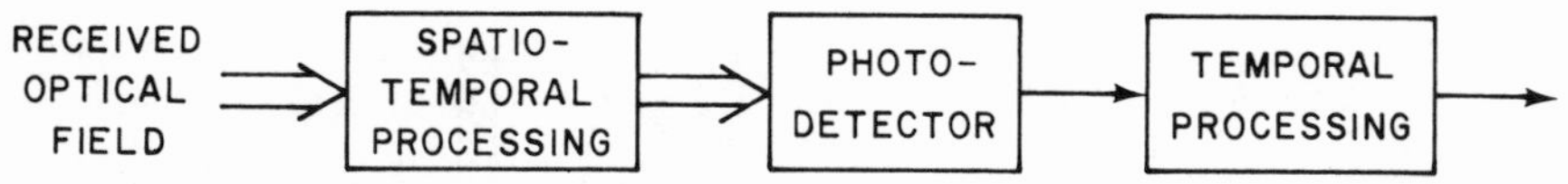


**Figure 2** Optical receiver

receiver. Thus far quantum optical communication theory has, rather naturally, been concerned almost exclusively with the latter transition.

The optical receiver can be described conceptually as in Figure 2. A very simple receiver would have a lens to focus the received light onto a photodetector and might have a counter for processing the photodetector's output (see Figure 3).

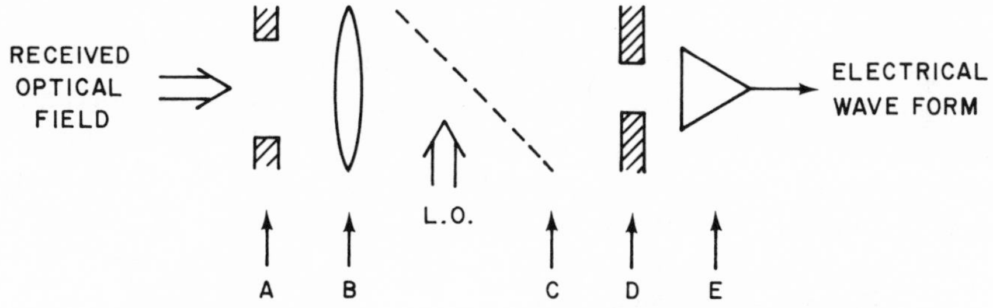

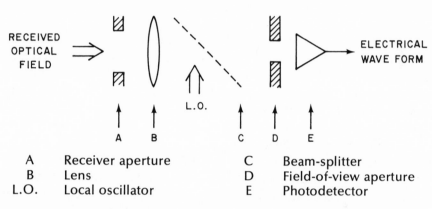

| | | | |
|---|---|---|---|
| A | Receiver aperture | C | Beam-splitter |
| B | Lens | D | Field-of-view aperture |
| L.O. | Local oscillator | E | Photodetector |

**Figure 3** Simple receiver

If the local oscillator has a frequency appropriately different from the center frequency of the received light field, this receiving structure is called a "heterodyne receiver"; if the frequency difference is zero, a "homodyne receiver"; and if no local oscillator is used, a "direct-detection receiver." For such receiver configurations, the Kirchhoff–Huygens diffraction theory—see, e.g., Goodman [2]—is sufficient to calculate the classical field impinging on the photodetector, which in turn determines the intensity function of a Poisson point process basic to describing the resultant electrical waveform according to the "semiclassical method of quantum mechanics": communication theory can begin at this point.

The optimization of classical models of such optical communication systems for the clear-air turbulent channel established that more sophisticated spatio-temporal processing was required and

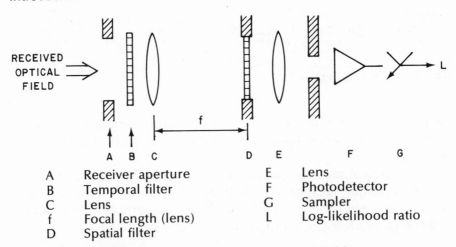

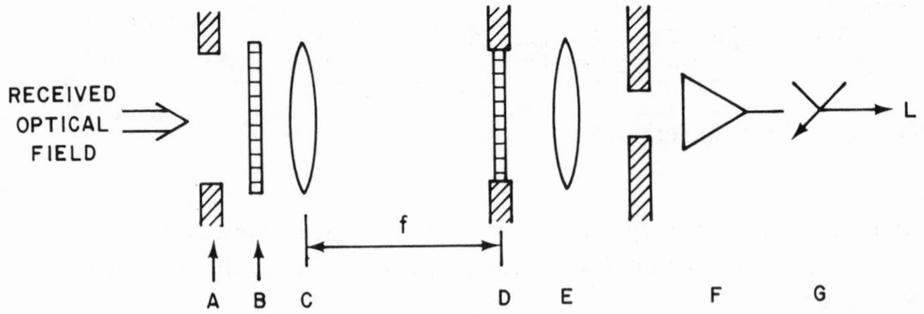


| | | | |
|---|---|---|---|
| A | Receiver aperture | E | Lens |
| B | Temporal filter | F | Photodetector |
| C | Lens | G | Sampler |
| f | Focal length (lens) | L | Log-likelihood ratio |
| D | Spatial filter | | |

**Figure 4** Optimal structure for Gaussian received fields

clearly suggested its ad hoc incorporation. For example, the structure shown in Figure 4 is optimal for Gaussian received fields and, in limiting cases, for lognormal fields [3, 4]. Its operation has several interpretations. For example, it can be shown to sum the received field over correlated subareas coherently and to sum all such contributions incoherently—hence meriting the name "mixed-integrator receiver."

Communication theorists would like to minimize a priori structural assumptions, of course, and this was one motivation to go to a more basic quantum mechanical treatment. By assuming merely a cavity receiver or, even better, just the presence of the field in a time-space region, a modal decomposition and mode quantization results in an assemblage of harmonic oscillators whose quantum mechanical treatment has been well developed. At this point communication theory can begin relatively free of a priori structural assumptions and can develop truly fundamental limitations.

The area of optical communications is expanding very rapidly, and even the subject of optical communication theory cannot be completely covered within the limitations of a single volume. We have chosen to stress the unique aspect of this subject—quantum communication theory. The "semiclassical" theory accounts for quantum effects with Poisson process–based models and is more accessible for immediate application at the cost of a priori structural assumptions and less generality. Some of the more theoretical and recent developments of "point process" theory have not yet found application in this subject and are adequately included in another volume in this series [5]. A recent book by Snyder [6] also gives many optical communication applications. We have had to restrict coverage of optical channels rather severely. The atmospheric, clear-air turbulent channel figured prominently into the early 1970s, being eclipsed, it seems fair to say, for attention recently by the optical fiber channel. Communication theory was successfully applied to the investigation of the atmospheric channel, suggesting appealing receiving structures, not conceived in earlier practice, whose practical realizations—under still continuing study—were reasonable. The communication theory analysis of the fiber channel is now getting underway; a large body of electromagnetic theory results are now available for this in tractable form [7].

Another measure of the maturity of optical communication theory is the appearance of a number of books. In addition to the early background books of Ross [8] and Pratt [9] and the abovementioned book by Snyder [6], there is *Optical Communications* by Gagliardi and Karp [10], *Quantum Detection and Estimation Theory* by Helstrom [11], and *Fundamentals of Optical Fiber Communications*, edited by Barnoski [12]. The October 1970 issue of the *Proceedings of the IEEE* was devoted to optical communication and contained review articles on quantum [13], atmospheric channel [14], free-space (Poisson process–based) [15], and scattering channel [16] communication theories.

This collection of papers allows a natural division into those emphasizing quantum communication theory (Parts I and IV), the semiclassical, or Poisson process–based, communication theory (Part II), and optical communication channels (Part III). Of course, the more mature and comprehensive papers tend to resist this classification. Further, the period near 1971 represents the end of a formative period for much of this theory, especially quantum communication theory, and hence the papers included on this latter subject are divided accordingly. The reader interested in the more fundamental theoretical aspects may wish to begin with Part I, while the reader interested in the more immediately useful theory may wish to begin with Part II. Part III can be read independently of the other parts. The understanding of Part IV (and its motivation) is aided by some familiarity with Part I, though the mathematically inclined reader may well prefer to begin with Holevo's papers.

## REFERENCES

1. Jauch, J. M. *Foundations of Quantum Mechanics*. Reading, Mass., Addison-Wesley, 1968.
2. Goodman, J. W. *Introduction to Fourier Optics*. New York: McGraw-Hill, 1968.
3. Harger, R. O. "On processing optical images propagated through the atmosphere." *IEEE Trans. Aerosp. Electron. Syst.* **AES-3:**819–828 (Sept. 1967).
4. Harger, R. O. "Maximum Likelihood and Optimized Coherent Heterodyne Receivers for Strongly Scattered Gaussian Fields." *Optica Acta* **16**:745–760 (Dec. 1969).
5. Ephremides, A., ed. *Random Processes, Part II: Poisson and Jump Point Processes*. Benchmark Papers in Electrical Engineering and Computer Sciences, vol. 11. Stroudsburg, Pa.: Dowden, Hutchinson & Ross, 1975.
6. Snyder, D. L. *Random Point Processes*. New York: John Wiley & Sons, 1975.
7. Gloge, D., ed. *Optical Fiber Technology*. New York: IEEE Press, 1976.
8. Ross, M. *Laser Receivers*. New York: John Wiley & Sons, 1966.
9. Pratt, W. K. *Laser Communication Systems*. New York: John Wiley & Sons, 1969.
10. Gagliardi, R. M., and S. Karp. *Optical Communications*. New York: John Wiley & Sons, 1976.
11. Helstrom, C. W. *Quantum Detection and Estimation Theory*. New York: Academic Press, 1976.
12. Barnoski, M. K., ed. *Fundamentals of Optical Fiber Communications*. New York: Academic Press, 1976.
13. Helstrom, C. W., J. W. S. Liu, and J. P. Gordon. "Quantum Mechanical Communication Theory." *IEEE Proc.* **58**:1578–1598 (Oct. 1970).
14. Hoversten, E. V., R. O. Harger, and S. J. Halme. "Communication Theory for the Turbulent Atmosphere." *IEEE Proc.* **58**:1626–1650 (Oct. 1970).
15. Karp, S., E. L. O'Neill, and R. M. Gagliardi. "Communication Theory for the Free Space Optical Channel." *IEEE Proc.* **58**:1611–1626 (Oct. 1970).
16. Kennedy, R. S. "Communication Through Optical Scattering Channels: An Introduction." *IEEE Proc.* **58**:1651–1665 (Oct. 1970).

Part I

# QUANTUM COMMUNICATION THEORY TO 1971

# Editor's Comments on Papers 1 Through 8

1 **GORDON**
*Quantum Effects in Communications Systems*

2A **HELSTROM**
Excerpts from *Detection Theory and Quantum Mechanics*

2B **HELSTROM**
Excerpts from *Detection Theory and Quantum Mechanics (II)*

3 **LIU**
*Reliability of Quantum-Mechanical Communication Systems*

4 **HELSTROM**
*The Minimum Variance of Estimates in Quantum Signal Detection*

5 **PERSONICK**
*Application of Quantum Estimation Theory to Analog Communication Over Quantum Channels*

6 **ARTHURS and KELLY**
*On the Simultaneous Measurement of a Pair of Conjugate Observables*

7 **SHE**
*Quantum Electrodynamics of a Communication Channel*

8 **HELSTROM, LIU, and GORDON**
*Quantum-Mechanical Communication Theory*

It has been known since the turn of the twentieth century that Maxwell's electrodynamics describing the electromagnetic field led to certain difficulties (e.g., the "ultraviolet catastrophe") when describing the interaction of the electromagnetic field and matter. The resolution involved Planck's conclusion that energy is radiated and absored in quanta (photons) of energy $h\nu$, where $h = 6.624 \times 10^{-34}$ J·s is Planck's constant and $\nu$ is the frequency of the electromagnetic field.

This "photoelectric effect" can be easily observed in a simple optical communication system comprising an amplitude-modulated laser transmitter, a short clear-air propagation path, and a photodiode receiver. As the received light power is decreased, the photodiode output, viewed on an oscilloscope, will depart from a continuous waveform approximately replicating the transmitted modulation and become a sequence of similar, pulselike waveforms occurring at apparently random times, the rate of occurrences proportional to the light power. These random times, or points, can be associated with those of a Poisson process: this "shot" effect can be attributed directly to the quantization of permissible energy states of electrons in a material. It is convenient to regard the received light wave as consisting of quanta (photons), whose arrival times at the receiver are those of a Poisson process and whose energy is $h\nu$, that in the photodiode elevate an electron to the conduction band with probability $\eta$, the "quantum efficiency" of the particular photodiode. Roughly, if the received light wave has a modulation bandwidth $B$ Hz and power $P$ when $P/B$ is comparable to or smaller than $h\nu$, quantum effects will be observable. Also, again roughly speaking, when $h\nu B$ is comparable to or larger than the unavoidably present thermal noise power $kTB$, one may expect "quantum noise" to be as important an effect in an optical communication system as thermal noise.

Using a "shot noise" model for the detection process, one can begin to gain insight by analyzing specific optical communication system configurations using an SNR (signal-to-noise-ratio) criterion defined as the ratio of the squared mean photoelectron current to the mean-square photoelectron current. Oliver [1] gave an early analysis that includes a very readable review of some relevant physics including the important topic of modal decomposition of the electromagnetic field. Oliver shows that a balanced heterodyne receiver has SNR $= \eta P/h\nu B$, as if an additive input noise with spectral density $h\nu/\eta$ were present, and that a homodyne receiver can have SNR $= 2\eta P/h\nu B$. For comparison, the added noise of an "ideal amplifier" is asserted to be $h\nu$. As thermal noise has a spectral density $h\nu/(\exp h\nu/kT - 1)$, where $k = 1.38 \times 10^{-23}$ J/deg is Boltzmann's constant and $T$ the absolute temperature, there are distinct frequency regions: a "thermal-noise-dominant region" where $h\nu/kT < 1$ and the overall "noise" spectral density is $kT$, and a "quantum-noise-dominated region" where $h\nu/kT > 1$ and the overall "noise" spectral density is $h\nu$ for the homodyne receiver with unit quantum efficiency. Such analyses of "shot noise" models with an SNR criterion can be carried out for many specific configurations (see, e.g., Pratt [2, Ch. 10], where it is shown that a direct detection receiver can attain a "noise level" of $2h\nu$).

Oliver's argument to support the assertion that the noise level $h\nu$ is the least achievable by a linear amplifier is quite different, applying the "principal of complementarity" to the joint measurement of the amplitude and phase of a light wave—the argument was given earlier by Heffner [3]—strongly suggesting that eventually a much more fundamental theory must be employed to establish basic limitations on optical communications, which can account for restrictions on "simultaneous measurements" and allow for use of more basic optimality criteria—e.g., Bayes optimality criteria. It evolved that a decade would be required for the development of a satisfactory foundation.

A remarkably prescient article by James P. Gordon of Bell Laboratories is the first paper in this collection. Entitled "Quantum Effects in Communications Systems," it attempts to establish the ultimate capacity of a single-transmission-mode, optical channel and compare it to that achieved by specific structures: ideal amplifier, heterodyne and homodyne receivers, and quantum counter.

The ultimate capacity is derived by first considering the "entropy of white noise": the "state" of any mode is determined by assigning it $m$ photons with probability $p(m)$: the entropy $-\Sigma p(m)\log p(m)$ is then maximized subject to an average excitation energy restraint $\bar{m}h\nu$, where $\bar{m}$ is the average "mode occupation number"; the result is an exponential distribution. The maximum entropy per mode is then calculated and, using the concept of "rate of arrival of independent modes," the rate of arrival of entropy. The quantum mechanics involved here is actually not at all deep: the discrete arrival of modes corresponds to sampling and transmitting a classical source, and the enforced quantum mechanical quantization corresponds to classical quantization. The optimization performed is then interpretable as a best choice of source distribution as in the "noiseless coding theorem." It remains unclear exactly what the significance of this entropy is. In Gordon's words, "It is not obvious . . . that all of this entropy can be prescribed as signal. . . . We . . . do not know the answer to this problem." The ultimate capacity is then set equal to the entropy of the signal-plus-noise waveform minus the entropy of the noise-alone waveform. Gordon's development proceeds in a style very reminiscent of Shannon's classic work [4] and seems to leave at least as many questions for uninitiated readers. It would be necessary to establish a definite theory of quantum mechanical measurement, extend as necessary methods of statistical inference, and calculate—or more likely bound with error-rate-type functions—the probability of error to fully understand and place these results: this program is only partially completed after 10 years.

In contrast, Gordon's calculation of the capacity of a channel with a quantum counter is clear. He considers two limiting cases of $h\nu B$ large and small relative to signal power. In the former case he considers the transmission of a binary source with constant amplitude pulses: the mutual information of the resulting binary unsymmetric channel is maximized under an average power restraint. Also computed for comparison is the capacity of optical channels using heterodyne and homodyne receivers; a variety of assumptions tend to obscure the significance of these calculations. Also stated is the capacity of an optical channel using an ideal amplifier receiver that is assumed to add a Gaussian noise proportional to $h\nu B$—thus the classical Gaussian channel capacity of Shannon can be used directly. A summary in Figure 4 of the paper shows that in specific situations each one of these receivers can be relatively optimal, which of course disagrees with the results under the SNR criterion where a homodyne reciever is always best. It was implicit in this work that the optimum receiver configuration and its performance would depend on signal waveform selection.

Carl Helstrom's "Quantum Limitations on the Detection of Coherent and Incoherent Signals" was an early influential paper; it was the first serious attempt to comprehensively apply detection theory accounting for quantum mechanical restraints. The paper was also valuable in joining many of the applicable concepts of quantum optics: the receiver idealized as a cavity; geometrical aspects of coupling and modal decomposition; quantization of the electromagnetic field; "pure," "mixed," and "coherent" states; the *P*-representation of density operators; and product Hilbert spaces. The paper assumed specific quantum mechanical measurements seemingly reasonable for the two signal types. In the case of an incoherent signal, the selected measurement, the "number operator," was later shown to be in fact optimal. Once a "complete set of commuting observables" [5, p. 47] is chosen, the detection problem is entirely classical, the distribution of the measurement outcomes being known. A likelihood ratio can be formed and, e.g., a Bayes strategy determined. (The treatment of the coherent case was marred by an asserted joint distribution not permitted by quantum mechanics, as later became clear.)

The removal of assumptions about the specificity of quantum measurements requires their general characterization. In quantum mechanics it is customary [6, Sec. 8.5], [7] to represent a measurement by a self-adjoint operator—say, $A$—on a Hilbert space $\mathcal{H}$ and to incorporate the a priori statistical knowledge with a density operator—say, $\rho$—a self-adjoint, positive definite, unit trace operator on $\mathcal{H}$. To take the simplest case, if $A$ has a discrete spectrum of characteristic values $\alpha_n$ of unit multiplicity, the probability that a measurement represented by $A$ has outcome $\alpha_n$ is $Tr\{\rho E_n\}$, where $E_n$ is the projection onto the one-dimensional subspace of $\mathcal{H}$ spanned by the characteristic function associated with $\alpha_n$: an entirely classical discrete distribution.

With such a distribution function, a study of the usual statistical procedures such as Bayes inference can be initiated. Recalling the idea of the classical "single experiment statistical game" [8, p. 82], which lies at the heart of statistical inference and hence classical communication theory, if the set $\Omega$ of states of nature $\theta$ is the real line and so too the space of actions $\tilde{A}$, then the real line can be taken as the space $S$ of outcomes of the observable represented by an operator $A$ on a Hilbert space $\mathcal{H}$. The a priori quantum state could be represented by a density operator $\rho_\theta$, defined on $\mathcal{H}$ and dependent on the state of nature $\theta$. It is easily argued that the decision mapping $d{:}S \rightarrow \tilde{A}$ is simply equivalent to another observable $A' \equiv d(A)$. The average risk assumes the form $R(A) = E_\Omega Tr\{\rho(\theta)W(\theta,A)\}$, where $W$ is a specified loss function, and the problem is to choose the observable $A$, a self-adjoint operator, that minimizes $R(A)$.

This formulation allows study of a limited, but interesting, set of problems including binary detection (Papers 2A and 2B) and single-parameter estimation (Paper 5) and also certain $M$-ary detection problems—e.g., those in which the density operators, describing the a priori statistics under the separate hypotheses, commute (Paper 3) [9].

In both papers discussing "Detection Theory and Quantum Mechanics" (Papers 2A and 2B), Carl Helstrom achieved a considerably more advanced statement of the binary detection problem that allowed optimal choice of quantum measurement. He brought together many of the ideas of quantum optics and statistical inference and firmly established a level and direction for future work. The optimum observable is shown to be a projection operator and the reduction to the classical likelihood ratio test is noted when the two density operators (corresponding to the two hypotheses) commute: when such is not true, a general solution is not known even now and special cases are resorted to—here a certain "threshold" situation and the choice between pure states, applicable to the detection of "noiseless" coherent states. (A more concise statement of some of these and other results is given in Helstrom [13].) Helstrom shows that the average risk has the form $R(\pi_0) = (1 - \zeta)[1 - Tr\{[\pi(H_1) - \lambda\rho(H_0)]\pi_0\}]$ where $\lambda \equiv C\zeta/(1 - \zeta), \zeta$ is the a priori probability of $H_0$, $C$ is a cost, and $\pi_0$ is a projection operator. Thus the problem of choosing the quantum measurement best by the Bayes criterion is the problem of maximizing $Tr\{[\rho(H_1) - \lambda\rho(H_0)]\pi\}$ over choice of the projection operator $\pi_0$. Helstrom solves this problem assuming the self-adjoint operator $[\rho(H_1) - \lambda\rho(H_0)]$ is compact.

Following the Introduction, in Section I Helstrom sets up the decision problem as a choice between two density operators; conventional (Bayes and Neymann–Pearson) strategies are formulated and the optimum detection operator is shown to be a projection determined by the operator $\rho(H_1) - \lambda\rho(H_0)$. (All operators are assumed to have discrete, simple spectra.) Spin detection is exemplified and the case of $\rho(H_0)$ and $\rho(H_1)$ commuting is noted. In Section II Helmstrom studies the detection of a signal occupying a single mode of an electromagnetic field, along with thermal noise, and he introduces the attendant concepts from quantum optics. He considers three signal types of practical significance: incoherent, coherent with unknown phase, and coherent with known phase. In the first two cases $\rho(H_0)$ and $\rho(H_1)$ commute with the so-called number operator, and it follows that the latter's measurement, interpretable as ideal photon counting, provides a sufficient statistic for the detection problem. In the third case no solution is obtained: $\rho(H_0)$ and $\rho(H_1)$ do not commute.

In Part II (Paper 2B), Helmstrom pursues the optimal detection of a known signal further, but in the absence of thermal noise. This leads him to a consideration of a decision between pure states (Section 8) prior to this application (Section 9). The analysis shows that the optimum quantum measurement is markedly superior to photon counting and homodyne detection (Figure 1). Although a later analysis by Helstrom showed this advantage to be very sensitive to thermal noise, it was a first result that showed quantum communication theory could provide novel, significantly superior receivers.

(Because of certain page and copyright restrictions, I have not included some sections of these two papers that, though interesting, are less central to the subject's development. Sections 3 through 5 develop the ad hoc notion of a "threshold receiver" and apply it to single- and multiple-mode receivers with the above three signal types. Section 7 reviews Part I, and Sections 10 and 11 discuss the extension of "sufficiency." Also omitted were lists of symbols from both papers and Appendix B of Part I, which discusses a generating function of the Laguerre distribution function.)

The next paper, Jane Liu's "Reliability of Quantum-Mechanical Communication Systems," considers the *M*-ary detection problem and, assuming that the *M* density operators commute, brings the results to the interesting application of communicating orthogonal signals over the random phase and incoherent (Rayleigh fading) channels, deriving probability of error bounds, error exponents, and channel capacities in the style [15, Ch. 5] of such derivations in the classical case. For the random phase channel, the density operators commute with the number operator and the optimum quantum measurement is photon counting in each mode, the largest count being decisive. The structure of the receiver is given (Figure 3) and compared to the classical receiver (Figure 4), and it is shown that as the additive noise goes to zero, so does the probability of error while the capacity and transmitted power increase without bound. Under a more meaningful average energy restraint, e.g., no results were obtained.

The problem of parameter estimation in the quantum context received one of the first treatments in another paper by Carl Helstrom, "The Minimum Variance of Estimates in Quantum Signal Detection." Helstrom obtained Cramer–Rao bounds and applied the results to estimating parameters of coherent and incoherent signals. In the problem formulation, the precise class of measurements was not explicitly set down. This led later to some consternation in determining the significance of the bounds. The basic estimation error variance bounds were obtained by applying an operator form of the Schwarz inequality with no assumption on the collection of operators representing the quantum measurements except boundedness. Since the existence and explicit form of such "efficient" estimators are generally unknown, commutation relations are generally unknown and hence it was not known whether or not they could be measured simultaneously or would have to be measured on separate systems, at least conceptually. In the specific case of incoherent signals, however, an efficient quantum estimator can be found explicitly and is the number operator, realized essentially by photon counting; the subsequent multimode extension and the comparison with the classical limit has clear meaning. Somewhat later Holevo [16] discussed more rigorously the generalization of Cramer–Rao bounds.

This work of Helstrom has been extended by Stewart Personick to consider the estimation of random parameters in Paper 5, "Application to Quantum Estimation Theory to Analog Communication Over Quantum Channels." A Cramer–Rao bound was established, and the interesting relation $\eta V + V\eta = 2\delta$ is given for the minimum mean square error observable represented by the self-adjoint operator $V$; here $\eta \equiv E_x\{\rho(x)\}$, $\delta \equiv E_x\{x\rho(x)\}$ and $x$ is the random variable to be estimated. The reduction to classical conditional expectation when $\eta$ and $\delta$ commute is noted. Very interesting applications are made to estimation (demodulation) of linearly modulated (optical) waveforms where the optimum measurement is shown to be proportional to $(\mathbf{a} + \mathbf{a}^+)$ where $\mathbf{a}$ is the annihilation operator associated with the harmonic oscillator and $\mathbf{a}^+$ is its adjoint. In the thesis underlying this paper, Personick gives the significant realization of this measurement as an idealized homodyne receiver. The bounds are also used to compare optimal and specific estimators, for various modulation formats and even fading channels that operated at or near the bounds, perhaps asymptotically. For example, for pulse-position modulation with real pulses, homodyning with a strong local oscillator followed by matched filter processing, and also direct detection, can be asymptotically efficient.

As this basic quantum measurement optimization problem was being recognized, an interesting paper by Arthurs and Kelly discussed an apparently quite different measurement procedure. Prior to measurement, an adjunct apparatus, in a prepared (pure) state, is allowed to interact with the receiver system; then at a specified time, a measurement, represented by two commuting operators, is made on this adjunct apparatus. In their paper, "On the Simultaneous Measurement of a Pair of Conjugate Observables," the observables are the position ($q$) and momentum ($p$) operators of the harmonic osciallator, which of course do not commute. In brief, Arthurs and Kelly established that by coupling—the degree of coupling parameterized by $b$—two "one-dimensional" adjunct systems in prepared states to the "original" system, allowing interaction for an appropriate time, and then making two measurements ($X$ and $Y$) on the two meter systems—$X$ and $Y$ necessarily thereby commuting—an approximate measurement can be made of the two noncommuting observables defined on the original system. They derived the joint distribution of the outcomes $x$ and $y$ and showed, e.g., that the means $E(x) = q$ and $E(y) = p$ and that the variances $\sigma_x^2 = \sigma_q^2 + b/2$ and $\sigma_y^2 = \sigma_y^2 + 1/2b$ from which they deduced that $\sigma_x\sigma_y \geq 1$. As the authors note, "The uncertainty principle [that yields $\sigma_p\sigma_q \geq 1/2$], of course, does not directly address this [simultaneous measurement] problem, since it is a statement about the variances of two hypothetical ideal measurements."

Arthurs and Kelly state that "Just as Von Neumann [10] uses an ideal measurement together with an interaction to explain an indirect observation, we shall use ideal measurements together with interactions to explain the simultaneous measurement of an observable and its conjugate," a clue to the genesis of a clever idea. It was hardly clear at that time that measurements employing adjunct apparatus could, in any statistical inference problem, be more desirable than commuting quantum measurements on the original Hilbert space: nevertheless this eventually proved to be true.

In the late sixties it was observed in the work of Gordon and Louisell [11], Personick [12, Sec. 4], and others that this novel type of measurement implicitly defined so-called overcomplete sets on the original (receiver) Hilbert space and that with them one could associate a corresponding "ideal measurement," on the latter space, whose "measurement" yielded the same probability distributions. By such an "ideal measurement" it was meant that each possible outcome $(\alpha)$ is associated with a member $(\psi_\alpha)$ of the overcomplete set, has probability proportional to $|(\psi_\alpha, \psi)|^2$ when the system state prior to measurement was $\psi$, and the system is left in state $\psi_\alpha$. As the sum of all such probabilities is unity, the $\{\psi_\alpha\}$ necessarily form a possibly unaccountable, or "overcomplete," basis for the Hilbert space associated with the quantum system.

A specific overcomplete set had been in use in quantum optics for some time—the characteristic functions of the annhilation operator **a** of the harmonic oscillator—denoted $|\alpha\rangle$, $\alpha$ any complex number, in the Dirac notation; their desirability in quantum optics is emphasized by Glauber [18]. In much work in this field the non-self-adjoint operator **a** is treated implicitly as an observable, in apparent violation of the customary formulation of quantum mechanics. The work of Arthurs and Kelly and of Gordon and Louisell [11] indicates that such an observable might be approximately measureable; further, Personick [12] shows that the approximate measurement is achieved by an idealized heterodyne detector.

She's "Quantum Electrodynamics of a Communication Channel" (Paper 7) is interesting for its explicit use of the quantum mechanical dynamical equations of motion and the use of a specific "ideal measurement." The paper begins with a cogent critique of the "uncertainty principle." Again a quantized single mode of a transmission line was considered and Heisenberg's equations of motion for the annhilation and creation operators (**a** and $\mathbf{a}^{+}$, respectively) of the mode were solved explicitly. Since the ideal measurement outcome determines the resultant quantum state and the measurement outcome sequence is Gaussian as a result of the specific "Gaussian" density operator and measurements assumed, the classical information theory analysis of the Gauss–Markov (discrete time) channel can be applied to determine channel capacity. A related article by She and Heffner [14] complements this paper.

The status of quantum communication theory up to 1971 is admirably reviewed—along with some of the necessary physics background—by Carl Helstrom, Jane Liu, and James Gordon in the final paper of this part, "Quantum Mechanical Communication Theory." While very interesting results, particularly in *M*-ary communication, were available by the time of their writing, the lack of a sufficiently general characterization of quantum measurements is especially noticeable in the estimation discussion where even conceptual problem formulation is impeded.

Another summary [17] incorporates an analysis of amplification and notes that it is generally not an optimum receiver/measurement in quantum detection systems.

## REFERENCES


1. Oliver, B. M. "Thermal and Quantum Noise." *Proc. of the IEEE* **53**:436–454 (May 1965).
2. Pratt, W. K. *Laser Communication Systems*. New York: John Wiley & Sons, 1969.
3. Heffner, H. "The Fundamental Noise Limit of Linear Amplifiers." *IRE Proc.* **50**:1604–1608 (July 1962).
4. Shannon, C. E., and W. Weaver. *The Mathematical Theory of Communication*. Urbana: University of Illinois Press, 1949.
5. Dirac, P. A. M. *The Principles of Quantum Mechanics,* 4th ed. Oxford: Clarendon Press, 1958.
6. Jauch, J. M. *Foundations of Quantum Mechanics*. Reading, Mass.: Addison-Wesley, 1968.
7. Prugovecki, E. *Quantum Mechanics in Hilbert Space*. New York: Academic Press, 1971.
8. Blackwell, D., and M. A. Girshick. *Theory of Games and Statistical Decisions*. New York: John Wiley & Sons, 1954.
9. Gudder, S. "Axiomatic Quantum Mechanics and Generalized Probability Theory," in *Probabilistic Methods in Applied Mathematics*, edited by A. T. Bharucha-Reid. New York: Academic Press, 1970.
10. Von Neumann, J. *Mathematical Foundations of Quantum Mechanics*. Princeton, N.J.: Princeton University Press, 1955.

11. Gordon, J. P., and W. H. Louisell. "Simultaneous Measurement of Noncommuting Observables," in *Physics of Quantum Electronics*, edited by P. L. Kelley, B. Lax, and P. E. Tannernwald. New York: McGraw-Hill, 1966.
12. Personick, S. D. "Efficient Analog Communication over Quantum Channels." Cambridge, Mass.: M.I.T. Res. Lab. Electron. Technol. Rep. 477.
13. Helstrom, C. W. "Fundamental Limitations on the Detection of Electromagnetic Signals." *Int. J. Theor. Phys.* **1**(1):37–50 (1968).
14. She, C. V., and H. Heffner. "Simultaneous measurement of noncommuting observables." *Phys. Rev.* **152**:1003–1110 (Dec. 1966).
15. Gallagher, R. G. *Information Theory and Reliable Communication*. New York: John Wiley & Sons, 1968.
16. Holevo, A. S. "A Generalization of the Rao–Cramer Inequality." *Theory Probab. and Appl.* **18**:359–362 (1973).
17. Helstrom, C. W. "Quantum Detection Theory," in *Progress in Optics*, vol. 10, edited by E. Wolf. Amsterdam: North-Holland, 1972.
18. Glauber, R. J. "Coherent and Incoherent States of the Radiation Field." *Phys. Rev.* **131**:2766–2788 (1963).

# 1



Reprinted from *IRE Proc.* **50**:1898–1908 (Sept. 1962)

# Quantum Effects in Communications Systems*

J. P. GORDON†

*Summary*—The information capacity of various communications systems is considered. Quantum effects are taken fully into account. The entropy of an electromagnetic wave having the quantum statistical properties of white noise in a single transmission mode is found, and from it the information efficiency of various possible systems may be derived. The receiving systems considered include amplifiers, heterodyne and homodyne converters and quantum counters. In the limit of high signal or noise power (compared to $h\nu B$, where $h$ is Planck's constant and $\nu$ and $B$ are, respectively, the center frequency and bandwidth of the channel) the information efficiency of an amplifier can approach unity. In the limit of low powers the amplifier becomes inefficient, while the efficiency of the quantum counter can approach unity. The amount of information that can be incorporated in a wave drops off rather rapidly when the power drops below $h\nu B$.

## I. Introduction

With the advent of the possibility of broad-band communications at frequencies in the infrared and optical range, it has become important to investigate the effects of the quantization of radiation on the capacity of electromagnetic waves to transmit information. Unlike the situation prevailing in the microwave range, where thermal noise generally provides an ultimate limit to our ability to transmit information, in the infrared and optical range this limit is provided by what may be called quantum noise.

Our work stems principally from the classic work of Shannon[1] on discrete and continuous information channels. Gabor[2,3] introduced the concept of quantization into electromagnetic communication channels and coined the term "quantum noise." In consideration of the problem of field measurements by a receiver, he used an electron beam probe. The shot noise in the beam influenced his results in an important and, in the light of present knowledge, unnecessary way. Stern[4,5] has considered information rates in "photon channels." His conclusion[5] that the information efficiency of a linear amplifier can be no greater than 50 per cent conflicts with the results presented here. The major difference may be traced to the fact that he takes no account of the information that may be stored in the signal phase; and phase information approaches 50 per cent of the total possible information in the large signal-to-noise case where the quantum theory and the classical theory approach one another. Lasher[6,7] has also obtained expressions for information capacity based on quantum mechanical principles. His results agree qualitatively with ours; the quantitative differences presumably arise from the approximate methods which he used. We[8] have previously discussed some of the ideas which are utilized in this paper. In other recent work the important question of the statistical properties of quantum noise in linear amplifiers has been studied.[9,10,11]

Our ruminations will be limited to waves existing in a transmission system for which only a single transmission mode of the field is utilized. That is, the polarization and distribution of the field over any plane perpendicular to the direction of propagation are considered invariant. This situation is typical of transmisssion in a coaxial line or in a waveguide. It will also very likely be true for long-distance broad-band optical communication systems. A possible departure from such a single-mode system would involve the use of the two orthogonal field polarizations to provide two independent channels.

During the course of passage from transmitter to receiver, the signal is presumed to suffer a large attenuation and, in general, to be supplemented by some amount of additive white[12] noise power. At the receiver

* Received March 22, 1962; revised manuscript received June 7, 1962.

† Bell Telephone Laboratories, Murray Hill, N. J.

[1] C. E. Shannon and W. Weaver, "The Mathematical Theory of Communication," University of Illinois Press, Urbana, Ill.; 1949.

[2] D. Gabor, "Communication theory and physics," *Phil. Mag.*, vol. 41, pp. 1161–1187; 1950.

[3] D. Gabor, "Lectures on Communication Theory," Res. Lab. of Electronics, M.I.T., Cambridge, Mass., Tech. Rept. No. 238; April 3, 1952.

[4] T. E. Stern, "Some quantum effects in information channels," IRE Trans. on Information Theory, vol. IT-6, pp. 435–440; September, 1960.

[5] T. E. Stern, "Information rates in photon channels and photon amplifiers," 1960 IRE International Convention Record, pt. 4, pp. 182–188.

[6] G. J. Lasher, "A quantum statistical treatment of the channel capacity problem of information theory," in "Advances in Quantum Electronics," J. R. Singer, Ed., Columbia University Press, New York, N. Y., pp. 520–536; 1961.

[7] G. J. Lasher, "Channel capacity of optical frequencies," presented at the NATO-SADTC Symp. on Technical and Military Applications of Laser Techniques, The Hague, Netherlands; April, 1962.

[8] J. P. Gordon, "Information capacity of a communications channel in the presence of quantum effects," in "Advances in Quantum Electronics," J. R. Singer, Ed., Columbia University Press, New York, N. Y., pp. 509–519; 1961.

[9] W. H. Wells, "Quantum formalism adapted to radiation in a coherent field," *Ann. Phys. (N. Y.)*, vol. 12, pp. 1–40; January, 1961.

[10] J. P. Gordon, W. H. Louisell, and L. R. Walier, "Quantum fluctuations and noise in parametric processes. II," to be published.

[11] J. P. Gordon, W. H. Louisell, and L. R. Walker, "Quantum statistics of maser amplifiers and attenuators," to be published.

[12] Since we are concerned with a very broad range of frequencies, neither thermal noise nor quantum noise is truly "white," as this would imply a uniform spectral density. Rather, the noise is "colored"; its spectral density is generally a function of frequency. Since, however, the systems we consider are all narrow band, in the sense that the bandwidth is always much smaller than the carrier frequency, the noise may be considered to be white within the bandwidth. Cases in which the spectral density of the noise varies appreciably across the band may be treated by dividing the band up into smaller segments, and treating each such segment as an independent channel.

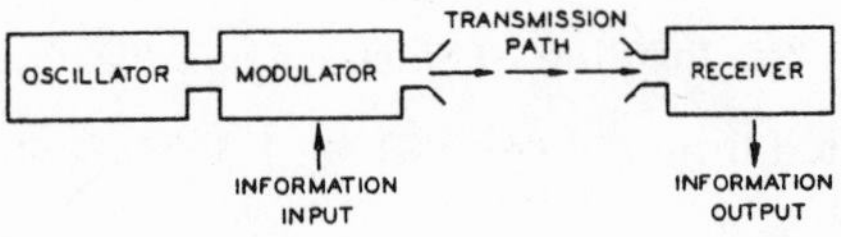


Fig. 1—Typical communication system.

as much as possible of the information remaining in the received wave is extracted. The receiver may incorporate an amplifier at the carrier frequency or it may not. We will investigate both of these cases. Fig. 1 shows a typical communications channel such as we have described.

So long as the electromagnetic waves may be described classically, *i.e.*, without quantization, Shannon[1] has shown that the information capacity $C$ of a signal of average power $S$ in the presence of additive white noise power $N$ in a channel of bandwidth $B$ is given by

$$C = B \log\left(1 + \frac{S}{N}\right) \tag{1}$$

If the logarithm is taken to the base 2, $C$ is in units of bits per second. To realize this capacity the signal must be modulated in such a way as to have also the statistical randomness of white noise.

In deriving (1) Shannon noted that information and entropy were closely allied quantities. In fact he identified information as *prescribed* entropy. He was able to show that the entropy rate $R$ of a continuous wave, having the statistical properties of narrow-band white noise and average power $P$, could be expressed as

$$R = B \log\left(\frac{P}{P_0}\right) \tag{2}$$

where the constant $P_0$ is arbitrary. To obtain (1) he subtracted the entropy rate for the noise alone from the entropy rate for the combined signal and noise. The latter also has the statistical properties of white noise when both signal and noise have these properties independently. Thus the constant is cancelled out and

$$C = B \log\left(\frac{S + N}{P_0}\right) - B \log\left(\frac{N}{P_0}\right) = B \log\left(1 + \frac{S}{N}\right).$$

$C$ is the additional entropy occasioned by the presence of the signal. Since the signal is completely prescribed, the added entropy is prescribed entropy, or information.

Eq. (1) says that the information capacity approaches infinity as the signal-to-noise ratio approaches infinity. This is because as the noise decreases we can make more and more accurate measurements of the state of the signal field. However, the uncertainty principle of quantum mechanics tells us that in fact we cannot measure a field to arbitrary accuracy, and so as $N \to 0$, fundamental quantum limitations on information capacity make their appearance.

## II. Entropy of White Noise

The fact that an electromagnetic wave is quantized allows us to obtain an absolute value for its entropy without the arbitrary constant of (2). Consider the wave in a transmission line traveling toward the receiver. Assume that the wave velocity is $v$ and that there is no dispersion. Then, in time $t$, the receiver measures the field which had previously occupied a length $L = vt$ of the line. To describe this field we can expand it into a series of orthogonal modes, and then measure the state of excitation of each mode as well as possible. A commonly used expansion is a spatial Fourier series. For this expansion the $q$th mode varies with distance and time according to the exponential factor

$$\exp\left[jq \frac{2\pi}{L}(z - vt)\right].$$

The condition for orthogonality of the modes is that the different values of $q$ differ by integers. It is also clear from the above expression that the mode $q$ has frequency $qv/L$. Thus the frequency separation between adjacent modes is $\Delta\nu = v/L$. In a bandwidth $B$ there are $B/\Delta\nu = BL/v$ orthogonal modes. Since $L = vt$ we see that in time $t$ the receiver measures the state of excitation of $Bt$ such modes. The rate of arrival of independent field modes at the receiver is therefore $B$.

The complete description of the field requires measurement of the state of excitation of each mode. Classically this would involve independent simultaneous measurements of the amplitude and phase of each mode, or equivalently simultaneous measurement of the electric and magnetic fields associated with each mode. Thus, classically, we make $2B$ independent measurements per second to identify the wave. In quantum mechanics the measurements of electric and magnetic fields are not independent, so we must consider that we make only $B$ independent measurements per second, each measurement specifying the state of one particular field mode.

Now we know that a white noise wave must have the most random possible excitation of the various modes consistent with the average power in the wave. This allows us to calculate the entropy of such a wave. Let us specify the state of each mode by assigning to it exactly $m$ photons, *i.e.*, an excitation energy $mh\nu$. From statistical mechanics[13] we know that the entropy per mode for a large number of modes is given by the expression

$$H = -\sum_m p(m) \log p(m)$$

where $p(m)$ is the probability that a mode will contain just $m$ photons. The average energy per mode is given by

$$\bar{E} = h\nu\bar{m} = h\nu \sum_m m p(m)$$

and of course since $p(m)$ is a probability, the $p(m)$'s must fulfill the requirement that

$$\sum_m p(m) = 1.$$

To find the most random possible excitation consistent with a given average power, we must maximize $H$ by varying the probabilities $p(m)$ while keeping $\Sigma p(m)$ and $\Sigma m p(m)$ constant. This is a simple problem in the calculus of variations. The set of $p(m)$ which maximize $H$ are

$$p(m) = \frac{1}{1+\bar{m}}\left(\frac{\bar{m}}{1+\bar{m}}\right)^m.$$

The average power $P$ in this wave is

$$P = EB = \bar{m}h\nu B$$

since $E = \bar{m}h\nu$ is the average energy per mode and $B$ modes per second are incident on the receiver. This exponential probability distribution for the excitation of the modes is consistent with the exponential power distribution which we know is characteristic of white noise. The entropy per mode for white noise is thus

$$\begin{aligned} H &= -\sum p(m) \log p(m) \\ &= \sum p(m)\left[\log(1+\bar{m}) + m \log\left(\frac{1+\bar{m}}{\bar{m}}\right)\right] \\ &= \log(1+\bar{m}) + \bar{m}\log\left(1+\frac{1}{\bar{m}}\right). \end{aligned} \qquad (3)$$

Since $\bar{m} = P/h\nu B$ where $P$ is the average power in the wave, we may express the entropy per mode as

$$H = \log\left(1+\frac{P}{h\nu B}\right) + \frac{P}{h\nu B}\log\left(1+\frac{h\nu B}{P}\right).$$

One may object that the specification of the excitation of each mode in terms of exact numbers of photons is not the only possible way. However, the number of distinguishable excitations within an energy range from $E$ to $E+\Delta E$ should be independent of the quantities used for the field specification, and so we are free to choose the most convenient specification, as we have done. Finally we note that the rate of arrival of entropy at the receiver for a white noise wave is

$$R = HB = B\log\left(1+\frac{P}{h\nu B}\right) + \frac{P}{h\nu}\log\left(1+\frac{h\nu B}{P}\right). \qquad (4)$$

Eq. (4) is the quantum equivalent of (2).

Of the terms in (4) the first has a form quite similar to the classical expression and predominates when the average number of photons per mode is large compared to unity. We can call it the mode entropy. It is equal to the rate of arrival of modes, $B$, times the logarithm of $\bar{m}+1$, which may be thought of rather loosely as the number of frequently occurring mode occupation numbers in a typical noise wave. By mode occupation number we mean the number of photons in the mode.

The second term of (4) is of fundamental quantum origin. It is the predominant term at power levels less than $h\nu B$ where the mean occupation number $\bar{m}$ becomes less than unity. We can call it the photon entropy. It is equal to the rate of arrival of photons, $P/h\nu$, times the logarithm of the number of frequently occurring intervals (*i.e.*, modes) for each photon. We shall see that at least part of this entropy can take the form of information which is recoverable if we use a photocell or some other energy-sensitive device as a receiver.

If we approach classical theory by the frequently used artifice of supposing that $h$ becomes very small, it may be seen that (4) approaches (2) with the arbitrary constant evaluated as

$$P_0 = h\nu B/e$$

where $e$ is the Naperian base for natural logarithms. Since the arbitrary constant contains $h$, it is clear that it could not be determined from a classical description.

### III. Entropy and Information

In Section II we found an absolute expression for the entropy of white noise, utilizing a particular quantum mechanical description of the possible excitations of the field modes. It is not obvious, however, that all of this entropy can be prescribed as a signal, and so constitute information. This is not to say that we cannot modulate a CW carrier wave in such a way as to give the resulting wave the statistical properties of white noise in the prescribed bandwidth $B$, but rather that there is very likely some part of the resulting entropy which is essentially irretrievable as information. We must confess that we do not know at present the answer to this problem. In any event the entropy of the wave is certainly an upper limit to the amount of information it may contain, and as such it is a useful quantity.

[13] R. C. Tolman, "The principles of statistical mechanics," Oxford University Press, Oxford, England, 1938. See also Shannon and Weaver.[1]

## IV. Information Capacity in the Presence of Additive Noise

Suppose we have a signal with average power $S$ accompanied by additive white noise with average power $N$. Following the ideas of Shannon we note that the information in the wave can be no greater than the entropy of the combination of signal plus noise less the uninformative entropy of the noise alone. The entropy of the combined signal and noise is maximized when the total wave has the statistics of white noise. Quantum mechanically as well as classically, this implies that the signal alone should also have the characteristics of white noise. The entropy rate for the combined wave is then given by (4) with $P=S+N$, while the entropy rate for noise alone has $P=N$. The upper limit to the information in the wave, which we will label $C_{\text{wave}}$, for a signal of average power $S$ in the presence of white noise of average power $N$ is thus given by

$$C_{\text{wave}} = R_{(P=S+N)} - R_{(P=N)}$$

or

$$C_{\text{wave}} = B\log\left(1+\frac{S}{N+h\nu B}\right) + \frac{S+N}{h\nu}\log\left(1+\frac{h\nu B}{S+N}\right) - \frac{N}{h\nu}\log\left(1+\frac{h\nu B}{N}\right). \quad (5)$$

For a bandwidth of $10^9$ cps and an additive noise power $N$ taken as arising from a black body at 290°K, *i.e.*,

$$N = h\nu B\left[\exp\left(\frac{h\nu}{290k}\right)-1\right]^{-1},$$

the information limit, $C_{\text{wave}}$, is plotted in Fig. 2 as a function of frequency for power levels ranging from $10^{-7}$ to $10^{-13}$ watt.

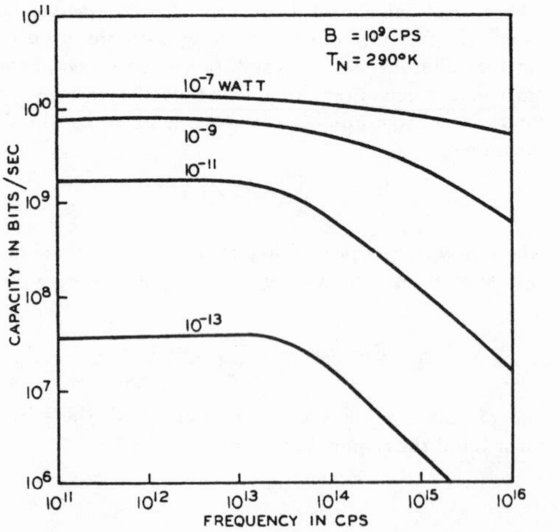


Fig. 2—Upper limit to the information that may be incorporated into an electromagnetic wave in a single transmission mode. Thermal noise, as originating from a black body at 290°K, is assumed to accompany the wave.

### A. Classical Limit

If the noise power $N$ is considerably greater than $h\nu B$, we have a situation where a classical description of the wave should be adequate. Expansion of (5) to first order in the small quantities $h\nu B/N$ and $(h\nu B)/(S+N)$ yields

$$C_{\text{wave}} = B\left[\log\left(1+\frac{S}{N}\right) - \frac{h\nu BS}{2N(S+N)}\log e \cdots\right].$$

Under the assumed condition $N \gg h\nu B$, the second term is always much smaller than the first, independent of the value of $S/N$, so the classical description which results in (2) is quite good.

If there is no additive noise, but the signal is much larger than $h\nu B$, we find

$$C_{\text{wave}} = B\left[\log\left(1+\frac{S}{h\nu B}\right) + \log e + \cdots\right].$$

In the limit of very high signal power this expression is nearly the same as one would obtain from the classical expression (1), by assuming the presence of an equivalent "zero-point" noise power $h\nu B/e$. Note, however, that this equivalence is not exact.

## V. Information Capacity After Transmission

As our transmitted signal travels toward the receiver, it is attenuated and usually some noise power is added to it. If we assume that the added noise is white then the information capacity of the received wave is limited by (5) where $S$ is the received signal power and $N$ the added noise power.

## VI. Information Capacity After Coherent Amplification

Suppose now that the first element of the receiver is an amplifier at the carrier frequency. This could be a maser, a nondegenerate parametric amplifier or any other type of linear amplifier. Assume that the amplifier has high gain. There is always internal white noise generated in such an amplifier which, referred to the input, may be described by an effective input noise, $N_{\text{eff}}$. In the case of the maser this noise is known to be

$$N_{\text{eff}} = Kh\nu B,$$

where $K=n_2/(n_2-n_1)$ and $n_2$ and $n_1$ are, respectively, the densities of upper-state and lower-state atoms in the active medium. In terms of a negative temperature of the active medium $T_m$, we have

$$K = \left[1-\exp\left(-\frac{h\nu}{k|T_m|}\right)\right]^{-1}.$$

For the parametric amplifier $N_{eff}$ may be written in a similar way, with $K$ also greater than or equal to unity.[14] After much amplification the additive noise, given by the gain times the sum of the incident noise plus the effective input noise,[15] is *always* much greater than $h\nu B$ and so the classical formula applies for the information capacity. We find, therefore, that after much amplification the information capacity of the wave is reduced to

$$C_{\text{amplifier}} = B \log \left(1 + \frac{S}{N + Kh\nu B}\right) \tag{6}$$

where $S$ is the incident signal, $N$ is the incident noise and $K \geq 1$. Thus the best possible amplifier, for which $K = 1$, retains only the first term in the incident wave information limit, (5). We now can define the information efficiency of an amplifier as $C_{\text{amplifier}}/C_{\text{wave}}$. For the interesting case of a perfect amplifier this is plotted for various values of signal strength in Fig. 3. The incident noise is assumed the same as for Fig. 2.

After much amplification we may assume that all of the information remaining in the wave can be extracted, so (6) also gives the information capacity of a system using a high gain coherent amplifier at the carrier frequency as the first element of the receiver.[16] For small $N$ the efficiency drops off for signal levels less than about $h\nu B$, indicating a substantial loss of information in this region for such a system.

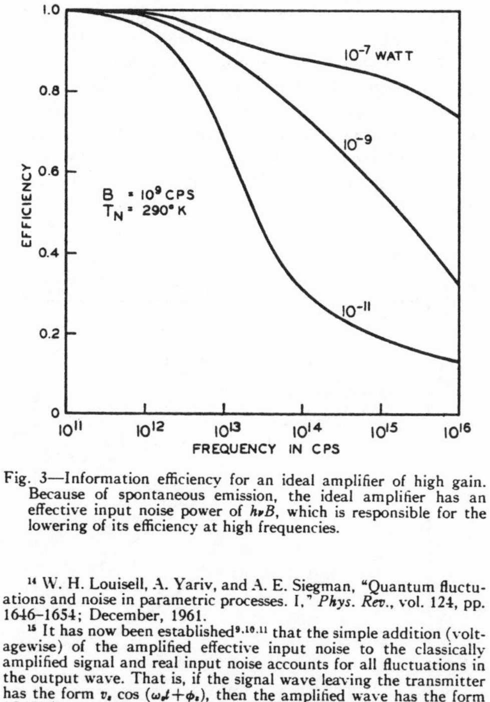


Fig. 3—Information efficiency for an ideal amplifier of high gain. Because of spontaneous emission, the ideal amplifier has an effective input noise power of $h\nu B$, which is responsible for the lowering of its efficiency at high frequencies.

## VII. The Heterodyne Receiver

Instead of amplifying the wave we might immediately make use of a photoelectric device in a heterodyne receiver.[17,18] To do this we might let the signal and power from a CW local oscillator fall simultaneously on a photosensitive element.

Then the photocurrent is proportional to the instantaneous power $P_{\text{inst}}$ incident on the element. If the quantum efficiency of the photosensitive device is $\epsilon$, the current is given by

$$I = \frac{\epsilon P_{\text{inst}}}{h\nu} q$$

where $q$ is the electronic charge. Let the signal frequency be $\omega_{\text{sig}}$ and the local oscillator frequency be $\omega_{\text{local}}$. If the local oscillator power is much greater than the signal power, the instantaneous power will have the form

$$P_{\text{inst}} \approx P_{\text{local}} + 2\sqrt{P_{\text{sig}}P_{\text{local}}} \cos (\omega_{\text{sig}} - \omega_{\text{local}})t + \cdots$$

where $P_{\text{sig}}$ is the instantaneous input signal power and $P_{\text{local}}$ is the local oscillator power. The photocurrent thus consists of a dc component

$$I_0 = \frac{\epsilon q}{h\nu} P_{\text{local}}$$

and a signal current at the intermediate frequency whose mean square is

$$\overline{I_{\text{sig}}^2} = 2\left(\frac{\epsilon q}{h\nu}\right)^2 S P_{\text{local}}$$

where $S$ is the average input signal power. Because of the dc current there will be shot noise, whose mean square is

$$\overline{I_N^2} = 2qI_0B = 2\left(\frac{\epsilon}{h\nu}\right) q^2 P_{\text{local}} B.$$

[14] W. H. Louisell, A. Yariv, and A. E. Siegman, "Quantum fluctuations and noise in parametric processes. I," *Phys. Rev.*, vol. 124, pp. 1646–1654; December, 1961.

[15] It has now been established[9,10,11] that the simple addition (voltagewise) of the amplified effective input noise to the classically amplified signal and real input noise accounts for all fluctuations in the output wave. That is, if the signal wave leaving the transmitter has the form $v_s \cos(\omega_s t + \phi_s)$, then the amplified wave has the form $(G/L)^{1/2} v_s \cos(\omega t + \phi_s) + G^{1/2} v_n \cos(\omega t + \phi_n)$, where $G$ and $L$ are the gain and loss of the amplifier and attenuator, respectively, and where the added term in the amplified wave is the fluctuating white noise voltage. This is rigorously true no matter how small, in terms of quanta per mode, the signal may be at the amplifier input. We are of course assuming that the gain and loss are not subject to fluctuations caused by such things as variations in the density of attenuating or amplifying particles, variations in pumping of a parametric amplifier, etc.

[16] It might appear that we are departing somewhat from common usage here by speaking of the information capacity of a system using a specific receiver. The reason for it is that in quantum mechanics the properties of the measuring apparatus (*i.e.*, the receiver) inevitably influence to some extent the quantities to be measured. Thus, while we can obtain from entropy considerations an upper limit to the capacity of *any* system, from which we may derive "efficiencies" for particular systems, this upper limit cannot be termed a capacity. It would seem that we cannot obtain any expression which might properly be called a channel capacity unless we include as an essential part of the channel such elements of the receiver as are necessary to insure that subsequent measurement can be performed with no further appreciable reaction back on the channel itself.

[17] A. Javan and R. Kompfner, private communication.

[18] B. M. Oliver, "Signal-to-noise ratios in photoelectric mixing," Proc. IRE, vol. 49, pp. 1960–1961; December, 1961.

The ratio $\overline{I_{sig}^2}/\overline{I_N^2}$ is the signal-to-noise ratio at the IF, which comes out to be simply $\epsilon S/h\nu B$. This implies an information capacity for the IF signal of

$$C_{\text{heterodyne}} = B \log \left(1 + \epsilon \frac{S}{h\nu B}\right).$$

It is not difficult to include the effect of incident additive noise coming in with the signal. This simply reduces the signal-to-noise ratio at the IF to

$$\frac{S}{N + \frac{1}{\epsilon} h\nu B}$$

and the information capacity to

$$C_{\text{heterodyne}} = B \log \left\{1 + \frac{S}{N + \frac{1}{\epsilon} h\nu B}\right\}.$$

The information capacity of a system using a heterodyne receiver thus has the same form as that of a system using a coherent amplifier, with $K$ replaced by $\epsilon^{-1}$.

## VIII. The Homodyne Receiver

It was pointed out by B. M. Oliver[18,19] that the homodyne receiver has quite interesting properties. In this case we confine the modulation to *amplitude* modulation, along with an allowed phase shift of $\pi$, and then use a local oscillator in the receiver which has exactly the same frequency and phase as the signal carrier. Since $\cos(\omega_{sig} - \omega_{local})t$ is then always equal to $\pm 1$, the instantaneous power incident on the photocell is

$$P = P_{\text{local}} + 2\sqrt{P_{sig}}\sqrt{P_{\text{local}}} + \cdots,$$

where the quantity $\sqrt{P_{sig}}$ may range through positive and negative values according to the modulation amplitude and phase. The dc component of the photocurrent is again

$$I_0 = \frac{\epsilon q}{h\nu} P_{\text{local}}.$$

For this case, however, the signal current is at baseband and has bandwidth $B/2$, where $B$ is the high-frequency band used for transmission. The mean-square shot current at baseband is therefore

$$\overline{I_N^2} = 2qI_0(B/2) = \left(\frac{\epsilon}{h\nu}\right) q^2 P_{\text{local}} B,$$

while the mean-square signal current is now

$$\overline{I_{sig}^2} = 4\left(\frac{\epsilon q}{h\nu}\right)^2 S P_{\text{local}}$$

where again $S$ is the average signal power, *i.e.*, the average of $P_{sig}$. The signal-to-noise ratio is therefore

$$\overline{I_{sig}^2}/\overline{I_N^2} = 4\frac{\epsilon S}{h\nu B},$$

and so the information capacity of the baseband signal is

$$C_{\text{homodyne}} = \frac{B}{2} \log \left(1 + 4\frac{\epsilon S}{h\nu B}\right).$$

As in the heterodyne case we may include incident noise without too much difficulty. The result is

$$C_{\text{homodyne}} = \frac{B}{2} \log \left\{1 + \frac{2S}{N + \frac{1}{2\epsilon} h\nu B}\right\}$$

where $N$ is the average received noise in the high-frequency band $B$.

Oliver pointed out that in this case the equivalent input quantum noise is only half as large as that occurring in the heterodyne receiver or in the equivalent maser. At first sight this is somewhat curious. In fact it simply indicates that perhaps one cannot always deduce the effects of quantum noise simply on the assumption of some fixed equivalent input noise which is the same in all situations. In no case is the capacity of a system using a homodyne receiver greater than the capacity limit, (5), of a wave of average power $S$ in the presence of the average incident noise $N$. Such a result would be truly surprising. In Fig. 4 the information efficiency for

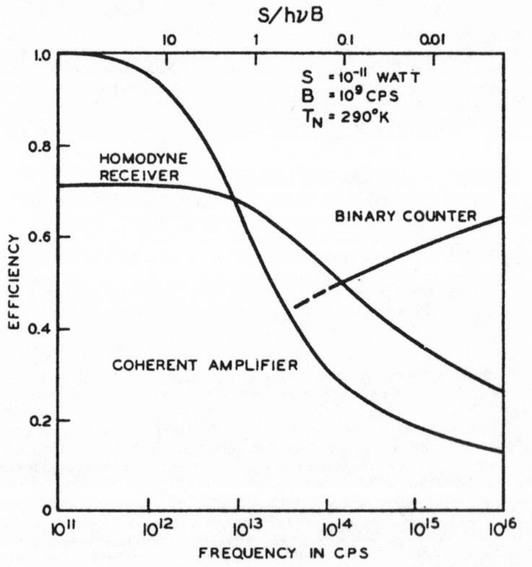


Fig. 4—Information efficiency for various receivers for an average received signal power of $10^{-11}$ w, a bandwidth of $10^9$ cps, and an external noise temperature of 290°K. Note that at the higher frequencies the coherent amplifier is not as good as the other types of receivers.

[19] B. M. Oliver, "Comments on 'Noise in photoelectric mixing,'" Proc. IRE (*Correspondence*), vol. 50, pp. 1545–1546; June, 1962.

an ideal ($\epsilon = 1$) homodyne system is also plotted against frequency, for a signal power of $10^{-11}$ w and an external noise temperature of 290°K. For comparison the information efficiency of an ideal amplifier is plotted also, as well as that of an ideal detector using a binary quantum counter (see Section IX-A, and note that for frequencies of $10^{14}$ cps or greater the external noise may be completely neglected).

## IX. The Quantum Counter

Instead of using any of the aforementioned receivers, we might simply allow the signal to fall on some photoelectric device and count the photoelectrons as they are produced. If we could do this with unity quantum efficiency and with perfect discrimination between different numbers of photoelectrons, we would surely have an ideal power-sensitive receiver. The information capacity for this general case can in principle be found since the probability distribution for the various numbers of received photons resulting from the transmission of some known number of photons has been computed.[20] Unfortunately, attempts to calculate the information capacity of a communication system using such a receiver encounter rather great computational difficulties. Nevertheless in some simple cases the problem can be solved approximately. When $S/h\nu B$ is either much larger or much smaller than unity, we may obtain approximately correct values for the capacity.

### A. *The Binary Counter*

For the case $S \ll h\nu B$, the average number of photons per independent field mode is much smaller than unity, so that only the two events, no photon received or one photon received, have appreciable probabilities. Consider, then, the following communication system. The transmitted signal consists of a series of pulses, each of duration $1/B$ and of constant amplitude. The pulses occur in a statistically random sequence with the probability $Q$ of sending a pulse in any particular time interval. A typical transmitted message would then appear as in Fig. 5. The average power in the signal is $Q$ times the pulse power, or if the energy in each pulse is $E$ the average power is $QEB$. The receiver measures the number of received photons in each time interval $1/B$; thus it makes $B$ measurements per second, which is consistent with the notion that there are $B$ independent field modes received per second. If the receiver simply distinguishes between no photons received or some photons received, we will have a system which should do nearly as well as possible when the average number of photons received per interval is much smaller than unity but of course is rather inefficient for larger average numbers of photons. This system has the advantage that one can compute its information capacity exactly, and we shall now proceed to do this.

Fig. 6 shows the communications channel under consideration. In each time interval $1/B$ the transmitter either emits a pulse or it does not. The probability of occurrence of a pulse in any particular time interval is $Q$. If the receiver detects at least one photon in any time interval, it records a 1; if not, it records a 0. To simplify matters, let us assume that the quantum efficiency of the receiver is unity, and at first let us assume that there is no noise in the channel. In this case if the transmitter does not send a pulse, the receiver definitely records a 0. This is indicated in Fig. 6. On the other hand if the transmitter sends a pulse, the receiver does not definitely record a 1. There is a finite probability that no photons reach the receiver even when the pulse is sent. This probability is known, however. So long as the number of photons in the transmitted pulse is reasonably well known, the probability distribution $q(m)$ for the various numbers $m$ of photons received after large transmission loss is a Poisson distribution, from which

$$q(m) = \frac{s^m}{m!} e^{-s}.$$

Here the average or expected number of received photons in the pulse is labeled $s$. Thus the probability of receiving no photons is $e^{-s}$, and the probability of receiving at least one is of course $1-e^{-s}$. These probabilities are also indicated on Fig. 6.

Now to compute information capacity we must use some further results of Shannon's work.[1] He showed that the information $I$ per symbol (*i.e.*, time interval)

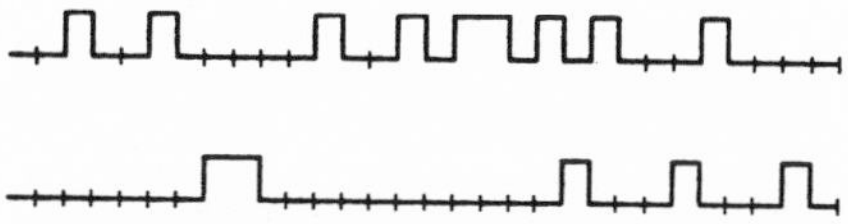

Fig. 5—Typical sequence of pulses in a message suitable for a binary communication system. The statistical probability for the occurrence of a pulse is 0.25 in this message.

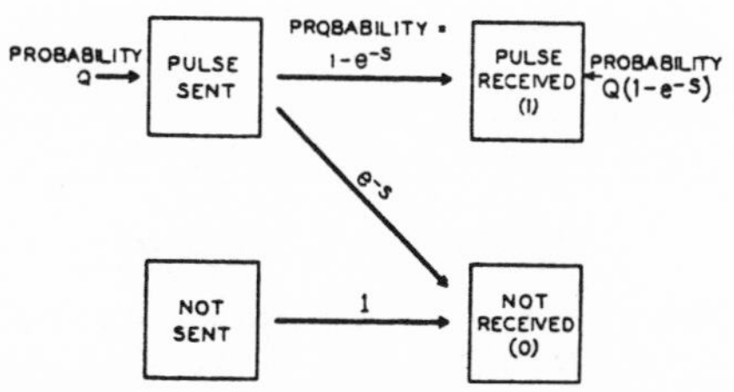


Fig. 6—Schematic diagram for a noiseless binary channel. The various probabilities necessary for the solution of the information problem are indicated on the diagram.

[20] K. Shimoda, H. Takahasi, and C. H. Townes, "Fluctuations in the amplification of quanta with applications to maser amplifiers," *J. Phys. Soc. Japan*, vol. 12, pp. 686–700; June, 1957.

for such a discrete communication channel is given by

$$I = H(y) - H_x(y)$$

where $H(y)$ is the entropy per symbol of the received message, given by

$$H(y) = -\sum p(y) \log p(y)$$

summed over the probabilities $p(y)$ for the possible received symbols $y$, while $H_x(y)$ is the conditional entropy of the received message, given by

$$H_x(y) = -\sum_x p(x) \sum_y p_x(y) \log p_x(y).$$

Here the quantities

$$\left[-\sum_y p_x(y) \log p_x(y)\right]$$

are the entropy per symbol of the received message when the transmitted symbol $(x)$ is known, and $H_x(y)$ is this entropy averaged over the probability distribution $p(x)$ for transmitted symbols. Thus $H(y)$ is the total received entropy, while $H_x(y)$ is that part of the received entropy which does not contain information.

With the help of these formulas we are able to compute the information capacity of the channel. For a probability $Q$ of sending a pulse, the total probabilities for receiving a 1 or a 0 are

$$p(1) = Q(1 - e^{-s}); \qquad p(0) = 1 - Q(1 - e^{-s})$$

while the conditional probabilities are

$$P_{\text{pulse}}(0) = e^{-s}; \; P_{\text{pulse}}(1) = 1 - e^{-s}, \; P_{\text{no pulse}}(0) = 1,$$

$$P_{\text{no pulse}}(1) = 0.$$

The received entropy is then

$$H(y) = -Q(1 - e^{-s}) \log [Q(1 - e^{-s})] - [1 - Q(1 - e^{-s})] \log [1 - Q(1 - e^{-s})]$$

and the conditional entropy is

$$H_x(y) = -Q[e^{-s} \log e^{-s} + (1 - e^{-s}) \log (1 - e^{-s})] - (1 - Q)[0].$$

Subtracting the two, we find

$$I = -Q(1 - e^{-s}) \log Q - [1 - Q(1 - e^{-s})] \cdot \log [1 - Q(1 - e^{-s})] + Qe^{-s} \log e^{-s}.$$

To find the maximum information per symbol we must maximize $I$ with respect to $Q$, under the constraint that the average power remain constant. Now since $s$ is the average number of received photons per pulse, and $Q$ the probability of sending a pulse, the average number of photons per time interval is $Qs$. This is the quantity which must remain constant and was called $\bar{m}$ in Section I. If we therefore substitute $Q = \bar{m}/s$, where $\bar{m}$ is a constant, into $I$, differentiate with respect to $s$ and set the result equal to 0, we obtain the condition for maximum $I$. This is

$$\log_e \left[\frac{s}{\bar{m}} + e^{-s} - 1\right] = \frac{s}{\left(\dfrac{e^s}{s+1} - 1\right)} \cdot$$

To find $I_{\max}$ this transcendental equation must be solved for $s$, assuming some value of $\bar{m}$, and then the result used to evaluate $I$. In Fig. 7, $s$ is plotted against $\bar{m}$. It may be seen that $s$ does not drop off very rapidly for small $\bar{m}$. Finally $I_{\max}$ can then be calculated, and the information capacity of this system

$$C_{\text{binary}} = I_{\max} B$$

may be compared to the information limit for a noiseless wave of the same average power (*i.e.*, $\bar{m}h\nu B$) at the receiver input. The efficiency of the system

$$C_{\text{binary}}/C_{\text{wave}}$$

is plotted in Fig. 4. It may be seen to approach unity slowly at small signal levels. One can in fact show that at very very small signal levels, *i.e.*, for $\log_e(1/\bar{m}) \gg 1$, the information per symbol approaches

$$I_{\max} \rightarrow \bar{m} \log \frac{1}{\bar{m}} \cdot$$

This may be compared to $H$ of (3).

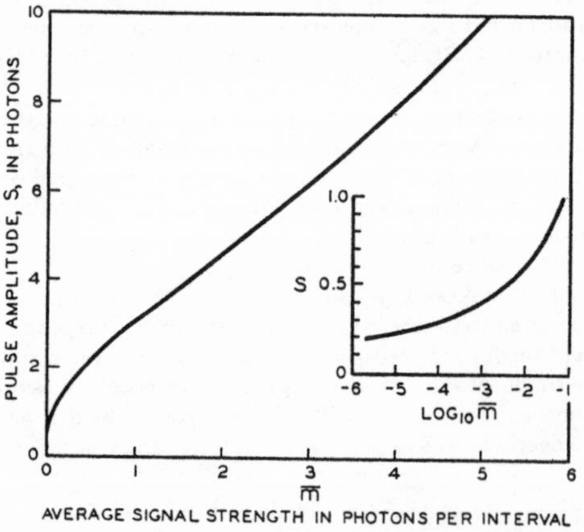


Fig. 7—Optimized average received pulse amplitude for the noiseless binary channel as a function of the average number of received photons per available time interval. The probability of sending a pulse is given by $Q = \bar{m}/s$.

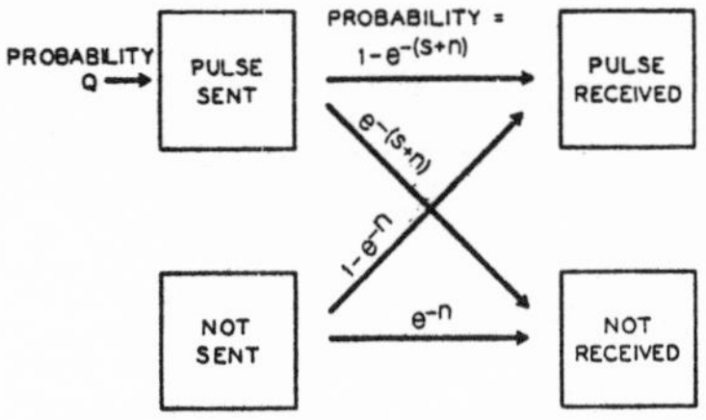


Fig. 8—Schematic diagram for a noisy binary channel.

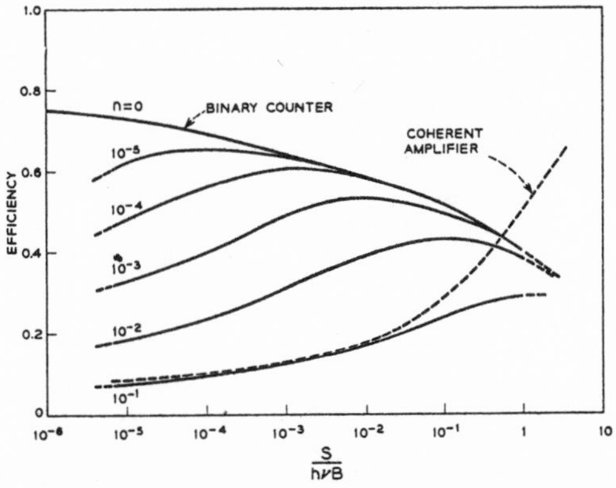


Fig. 9—Information efficiency of a binary counter perturbed by various amounts of incoherent noise. The numbers $n$ represent the average number of noise photoelectrons per pulse interval $B^{-1}$. Note that the efficiency drops off when $nh\nu B > S$, and that for $n$ greater than 0.1, the efficiency of the binary counter is always less than that of the coherent amplifier.

From this fairly simple example the mathematical complexity of the quantum counter system is reasonably evident. However, the case of the binary counter with noise is also simple enough to be calculated. There are two cases of possible interest involving noise. The first is when the noise in the counter results from noise power in the transmission mode accompanying the signal. It is then important to consider the effects of interference between noise and signal. However, there seems little use in calculating information capacities for this case since, for a given noise temperature, the number of noise photons per interval $1/B$, as a function of frequency, is for the greater part of the frequency range either greater than one—when $h\nu < kT$, or much less than one—when $h\nu > kT$. In the former case the binary counter is clearly not the most efficient receiver, in the latter the noise may be ignored so long as it is much less than the signal.

The second case involving noise in the counter is when the noise and signal are statistically independent. This would occur if the noise results from dark current in the photodetector, or from the effects of stray light incident in the receiver from modes other than the transmission mode or at frequencies outside of the useful band. If we assume that the noise photoelectrons arise from a large number of statistically independent causes, then the probability distribution of noise photoelectrons is also a Poisson. From this the conditional probabilities given in Fig. 8 follow. The results of a calculation of $I_{\max}$ for these probabilities, based on the equations of the previous section, are given in Fig. 9. For comparison, $I_{\max}$ for the noiseless case, is plotted there also.

### *B. The Quantum Counter When $S \gg h\nu B$*

In the previous subsection we considered a particular communication system using a quantum counter for which the capacity could be calculated exactly, but which approximates an ideal receiver only when $S+N \ll h\nu B$. We can also obtain an approximate result for an ideal quantum counter system which is valid at high power levels. We assume again that the transmitter sends out a sequence of pulses, each of duration $1/B$, but with varying amplitudes. We suppose that the receiver tells the exact number of photons it receives in each such time interval, and we may assume that in the great majority of intervals it receives a reasonably large number of photons.

The calculation is carried out in the Appendix and gives the results that an exponential probability distribution for the energy of the transmitted pulses is approximately optimum, and that for this distribution and no noise the information capacity of the counter system is [see (13)]

$$C_{\text{counter}} \doteq \tfrac{1}{2}C_{\text{wave}} - B[\log\sqrt{2\pi} + 0.289\log e]. \quad (7)$$

In the limit of very high power the constant term can be neglected, and the quantum counter then extracts half of the information in the wave. It is likely that when the wave capacity is small enough so that the second term begins to be significant, the exponential distribution is no longer optimum.

Having gone this far we perhaps should go on to add noise to the wave and again calculate the information capacity. In fact one can do so using similar approximate methods. Again one finds that in the limit of high power the counter system achieves half the capacity of the wave. The calculation is much like that in the Appendix, and in order not to bore the reader excessively, we shall omit it here.

The fact that a system using an energy-sensitive receiver has a capacity no greater than half of the wave capacity in the limit of high power (*i.e.*, high signal-to-noise ratio) is just what we might expect. In this limit the classical theory should give an adequate description of physical phenomena. Classically, when the signal-to-noise ratio is high, then equal amounts of information may be obtained from measurements of amplitude and measurements of phase; and the energy sensitive receiver automatically rejects all phase information.

## X. Summary

We have found an expression for the absolute rate at which entropy is carried by an electromagnetic wave having the statistical properties of white noise, in a transmission medium which supports a single transmission mode. Further, we have found an upper limit for the information capacity of a wave consisting of signal with average power $S$ in the presence of white noise with average power $N$. We have investigated the information capacity of a number of communication systems. The results of this investigation may be summarized as follows:

1) When the received signal or noise power is much larger than $h\nu B$, where $\nu$ is the center frequency of the wave and $B$ its bandwidth, a receiver using an ideal coherent amplifier or an ideal heterodyne converter can extract essentially all the information that can be incorporated in the wave, while an ideal energy-sensitive receiver is limited to about half the capacity of the wave. The ideal homodyne converter is intermediate between these two.
2) When the total received power is much less than $h\nu B$, a binary quantum counter can extract essentially all the information that can be incorporated in the wave, while the other types of receivers become increasingly less efficient.
3) For a given power and bandwidth, the upper limit to the information which can be incorporated in an electromagnetic wave begins to drop off fairly rapidly when $\nu$ increases beyond $P/hB$. Viewed from another angle, for a given frequency and bandwidth there is a kind of threshold for received power below which the information capacity of a communications channel drops off rapidly. When external noise is absent, this power level is about $h\nu B$.

## Appendix

### The Quantum Counter When $S \gg h\nu B$

Our first step will be to calculate the conditional entropy $H_x(y)$. If the transmitter sends a pulse of $M$ photons in a particular interval with any reasonably small uncertainty and there is no additive noise, the probability distribution for received photons is, as before, known to be a Poisson; that is, the probability of reception of $m$ photons when $M$ were sent is

$$P_M(m) = \frac{(\bar{m})^m e^{-\bar{m}}}{m!}\cdot$$

Here $\bar{m}$ is the expected number of received photons. $\bar{m}$ is of course $MT$, where $T$ is the transmission coefficient of the transmission line. By supposition, $T$ is much less than unity. The conditional entropy of the received signal, $H_M(m)$, may then be written as

$$H_M(m) = -\sum_M p(M) \sum_m P_M(m) \log P_M(m).$$

Now

$$\log P_M(m) = m \log \bar{m} - \bar{m} \log e - \log (m!)$$

and since we assume $m$ is large in the great majority of instances we may use Stirling's approximation for $\bar{m}!$, which is

$$\log m! \approx (m + \tfrac{1}{2}) \log m - m \log e + \log \sqrt{2\pi}.$$

Using this relation we find

$$\log P_M(m) \approx \log \bar{m} - (m + \tfrac{1}{2}) \log m - (m - \bar{m}) \log e - \log \sqrt{2\pi},$$

whence

$$\sum_m P_M(m) \log P_M(m) = \bar{m} \log \bar{m} - \log \sqrt{2\pi} - \sum_m P_M(m)(m + \tfrac{1}{2}) \log m.$$

It remains to evaluate the last term. To do this we expand $\log m$ in a power series in $(m - \bar{m})/\bar{m}$, according to the prescription

$$\log m = \log \bar{m} + \log \left[1 + \frac{m - \bar{m}}{\bar{m}}\right] = \log \bar{m} + \left[\frac{m - \bar{m}}{\bar{m}} - \frac{1}{2}\,\frac{(m - \bar{m})^2}{\bar{m}^2} + \cdots\right] \log e.$$

We can then make the necessary summation in terms of the moments of the Poisson distribution $P_M(m)$, for which we know that

$$\sum_m P_M(m)(m - \bar{m}) = 0, \qquad \sum_m P_M(m)(m - \bar{m})^2 = \bar{m}$$
$$\sum_m P_M(m)(m - \bar{m})^3 = \bar{m}, \qquad \text{etc.}$$

Doing this we find that

$$\sum_m P_M(m)(m + \tfrac{1}{2}) \log m = (\bar{m} + \tfrac{1}{2}) \log \bar{m} + \tfrac{1}{2} \log e + O(1/\bar{m}).$$

Substituting this in (8) we find the relation

$$-\sum_m P_M(m) \log P_M(m) = \tfrac{1}{2} \log (2\pi e \bar{m}) + O\left(\frac{1}{\bar{m}}\right),$$

and so the conditional entropy is given very nearly by

$$H_M(m) = \frac{1}{2} \sum_M p(M) \log (2\pi e \bar{m}).$$

Since $M$ is exceedingly large over most of its significant range, we can replace this summation by an integral, thus

$$H_M(m) \approx \frac{1}{2} \int_0^\infty dM p(M) \log (2\pi e \bar{m})$$

and finally since $\bar{m}$ is a known function of $M$, we have

$$H_M(m) \approx \frac{1}{2} \int_0^\infty d\bar{m} p(\bar{m}) \log (2\pi e \bar{m}) \tag{9}$$

where $p(\bar{m})$ is the probability distribution of the expected value of the number of photons incident on the receiver and $p(\bar{m})d\bar{m}=p(M)dM$.

Now let us ask how the conditional entropy varies with the choice of the expected signal distribution $p(\bar{m})$. We must know this in order to maximize the information content of the signal. As before we can expand $\log(2\pi e\bar{m})$ in a power series in $\bar{m}-\bar{\bar{m}}$, where $\bar{\bar{m}}$ is the average value of $\bar{m}$ over the distribution $p(\bar{m})$. Thus

$$\log 2\pi e\bar{m}$$
$$= \log 2\pi e\bar{\bar{m}} + \log\left(1+\frac{\bar{m}-\bar{\bar{m}}}{\bar{\bar{m}}}\right)$$
$$= \log 2\pi e\bar{\bar{m}} + \log e \cdot\left[\left(\frac{\bar{m}-\bar{\bar{m}}}{\bar{\bar{m}}}\right)-\frac{1}{2}\left(\frac{\bar{m}-\bar{\bar{m}}}{\bar{\bar{m}}}\right)^2+\frac{1}{3}\left(\frac{\bar{m}-\bar{\bar{m}}}{\bar{\bar{m}}}\right)^3-\cdots\right]$$

where

$$\bar{\bar{m}} = \int_0^\infty \bar{m}p(\bar{m})d\bar{m}.$$

Substituting this in (9), we find

$$H_M(m) \cong \tfrac{1}{2}\log 2\pi e\bar{\bar{m}} + \tfrac{1}{2}(\log e)\cdot\int_0^\infty\left[-\frac{(\bar{m}-\bar{\bar{m}})^2}{2\bar{\bar{m}}^2}+\frac{1}{3}\frac{(\bar{m}-\bar{\bar{m}})^3}{\bar{\bar{m}}^3}-\cdots\right]p(\bar{m})d\bar{m}. \quad (10)$$

It is clear from (10) that if $\bar{\bar{m}}$ is large, and if the distribution $p(\bar{m})$ is any reasonably sharp distribution, the conditional entropy is very nearly given by the first term alone; *i.e.*,

$$H_M(m) \approx \tfrac{1}{2}\log(2\pi e\bar{\bar{m}})$$

and thus is dependent only on the average signal power. Thus the problem of maximizing the information in the signal subject to a given average power (therefore, a given value of $\bar{\bar{m}}$) reduces simply to the problem of maximizing the received entropy. This we already know how to do. It requires an exponential probability distribution for received photons. For this distribution the received entropy is given by (3) with $\bar{\bar{m}}$ replacing $\bar{m}$, and for large $\bar{\bar{m}}$ may be approximated by

$$H(m) \cong \log\bar{\bar{m}} + \log e = \log(e\bar{\bar{m}}). \quad (11)$$

The most straightforward way to obtain an exponential probability distribution at the receiver is to generate an exponential probability distribution at the transmitter. Our final task is then to check whether our result for the conditional entropy at the receiver is valid for this very broad distribution as well as for narrow ones. For the exponential distribution with a reasonably large average, the probability distribution for the expected number of received photons may be assumed to be very nearly continuous and given by

$$p(\bar{m}) = \frac{1}{\bar{\bar{m}}}\exp\left(-\frac{\bar{m}}{\bar{\bar{m}}}\right).$$

For this distribution the series expansion (10), for the conditional probability converges embarrassingly slowly, so we must go back to the integral form (9). Doing this we obtain for the conditional entropy

$$H_M(m) \approx \frac{1}{2}\int_0^\infty d\bar{m}\left(\frac{1}{\bar{\bar{m}}}\right)\exp\left(-\frac{\bar{m}}{\bar{\bar{m}}}\right)\log(2\pi e\bar{m}).$$

Substituting $x=\bar{m}/\bar{\bar{m}}$ we find

$$H_M(m) \approx \frac{1}{2}\log(2\pi e\bar{\bar{m}}) + \frac{1}{2}\int_0^\infty dx\exp(-x)\log x.$$

The integral evaluates to 0.577 log $e$, so that

$$H_M(m) = \tfrac{1}{2}\log(2\pi e\bar{\bar{m}}) + 0.289\log e. \quad (12)$$

Comparison of this result with (10) shows that by going to the broad exponential distribution we have slightly increased the conditional entropy, but probably not enough to invalidate the conclusion that for large $\bar{\bar{m}}$ the exponential distribution is the optimum one.

Finally, we obtain for the information per symbol obtained by the ideal quantum counter,

$$I = H(m) - H_M(m)$$

where $H_M(m)$ is given by (12) and $H(m)$ by (11). We can express this as

$$I = \tfrac{1}{2}H(m) - (\tfrac{1}{2}\log 2\pi + 0.289\log e).$$

Since $BH(m)$ for thise case is just the information capacity of the wave, $C_{\text{wave}}$, we find for the information capacity of the ideal quantum counter, at high power levels, the expression

$$C_{\text{counter}} = BI \approx \tfrac{1}{2}C_{\text{wave}} - B(\tfrac{1}{2}\log 2\pi + 0.289\log e). \quad (13)$$

ACKNOWLEDGMENT

The author is pleased to acknowledge the able assistance of Mrs. C. A. Lambert in carrying out the necessary numerical computations; and many thanks to J. R. Pierce, for his continuing interest in the whole subject.

# 2A



Reprinted from pp. 254, 257–271, 287–289, 290–291 of *Inf. and Control*
**10**:254–291 (1967)

## Detection Theory and Quantum Mechanics

Carl W. Helstrom

*Westinghouse Research Laboratories, Pittsburgh, Pennsylvania 15235**

Statistical signal detection is formulated quantum-mechanically in terms of choosing one of two density operators as the better description of the state of an ideal receiver after exposure to a field in which a signal may or may not be present. The optimum decision procedure is expressed as a projection operator on the state-space of the receiver. Examples involving the single-mode detection of coherent and incoherent signals are given. Threshold detection as an approximation to optimum detection for weak signals is also defined quantum-mechanically, and threshold detectors for coherent and incoherent fields occupying many modes of a receiver cavity are worked out. The noise in all cases is taken to be thermal radiation described by the Planck law.

[*Editor's Note:* The list of symbols has been omitted.]

* Present address: Department of Applied Electrophysics, University of California, San Diego, La Jolla, Calif. 92037.

## INTRODUCTION

The development of communication and radar systems using laser beams has stimulated interest in the efficient detection of signals of optical frequencies and in the properties of channels utilizing such signals. (Gordon, 1962, 1964; Jelsma and Bolgiano, 1965; Takahasi, 1965; Lebedev and Levitin, 1966). The reliability of detectors of optical signals is limited not only by the random noise accompanying the signals and generated in the detectors, but also by the quantum nature of the signals themselves, which introduces an additional stochastic element to the detection process. The fundamental limitations on the detectability of signals in ordinary radar and communication systems have been delineated by the statistical theory of signal detection (Peterson *et al.* 1954; Middleton and Van Meter, 1955a; Middleton, 1960, 1965), and it is appropriate to ask what the theory can say about detecting signals of optical frequencies.

Before the limitations on signal detectability can be analyzed, it is necessary to adopt some model for an ideal receiver. This model should involve a minimum of assumptions about the way information is to be extracted from the incident electromagnetic radiation. The usual instruments for detecting optical signals admit the radiation through an aperture into a system that processes it in some way. The radiation may be focused on a sensitive cell or a photographic plate, it may be transmitted to photomultipliers or photon counters, or, when it is coherent, it may be heterodyned with a locally generated coherent beam through some material nonlinearity. Whatever is done to the radiation happens in a limited region of space behind the aperture of the optical system.

A natural idealization of a receiver of optical signals, therefore, is a box or a cavity, initially empty, that is exposed to the source of the signals by opening an aperture during the time when a signal, if transmitted, is expected to arrive. At the end of this time the aperture is closed, and an observer measures the field inside the cavity as extensively as he can in order to extract all the information relevant to a decision whether a signal was present or not in the external electromagnetic field (Takahasi, 1965).

At the low frequencies with which communication theory has in the past been concerned, classical physics adequately describes the electromagnetic fields of signal and noise. It permits the electromagnetic field in the cavity to be measured in as great a detail as necessary, and signal-detection theory has been able to presume that this field is in principle completely known to the observer. At optical frequencies, however, it is necessary to describe the field quantum-mechanically, and quantum mechanics places certain limitations on the precision with which the field can be measured both temporally and spatially. Detection theory must now prescribe not only how the measurements of the field shall be processed, but also what measurements shall be made.

The electromagnetic field in the cavity of our ideal receiver will not be in a pure quantum-mechanical state, but in a statistical mixture of states. Such mixtures are described by density operators (von Neumann, 1932; Fano, 1957). If there was no signal present in the external field during the time when the aperture was open, the field in the cavity after the aperture was closed resulted only from the stochastic background radiation and is represented by a density operator $\rho_0$. If a signal arrived while the aperture was open, the field is represented by some other density operator $\rho_1$. The task of the observer is to choose one or the other of these density operators as the more consistent with as much as he can measure of the cavity field.

The first section of this paper reformulates detection theory in terms of such a choice between density operators, preserving the standard goals of minimizing the average cost of operation or, for a fixed false-alarm probability, maximizing the probability of detection. The optimum procedure for deciding between two hypotheses about the cavity field is characterized as the measurement of a certain projection operator. When the two density operators commute, the usual likelihood-ratio strategy appears. Examples are presented in Section 2.

In important cases, however, the density operators between which a choice must be made do not commute. The mathematical problem of finding the optimum projection operator in those cases is a formidable one, and as a means of avoiding it we investigate the common threshold approximation that the signal is weak. In Section 3 a quantum-mechanical form of the optimum threshold detector is defined as the measurement of the operator yielding the greatest equivalent signal-to-noise ratio. An equation for this operator in terms of the density operators $\rho_0$ and $\rho_1$ is given. Section 4 derives the threshold detector for a coherent signal of random phase, such as an ideal laser pulse, received in the presence of thermal background radiation. In Section 5 the reception of an incoherent, noise-like signal is treated on the same basis. In both cases the maximum equivalent signal-to-noise ratios reduce at low frequencies to the familiar forms.

## 1. THE DETECTION OPERATOR

(i) *The Decision Problem in Quantum Mechanics.* Detection in quantum mechanics involves deciding which of two density operators $\rho_0$ or $\rho_1$ describes a system. These operators are presumed to be known functions of the operators for the dynamical variables of the system. The hypothesis that $\rho_0$ applies we denote by $H_0$, the hypothesis that $\rho_1$ applies by $H_1$. The decision between them is to be based on the outcome of a measurement of some dynamical variable $X$, which is represented by an operator that will also be called $X$.

This operator $X$ may stand for a set or $n$-tuple of commuting and hence simultaneously measurable operators. It possesses a set of eigenkets $|x_k\rangle$ corresponding to the eigenvalues $x_k$ :

$$X|x_k\rangle = x_k|x_k\rangle, \tag{1.1}$$

and this set will be assumed to be complete, so that any state of the system can be expressed as a linear combination of the eigenkets $|x_k\rangle$. We shall assume that the eigenvalues form a discrete set and are all distinct. That the eigenvalues, which may also be $n$-tuples, are distinct means that all degeneracies have been resolved by introducing additional commuting operators, as when the degenerate energy eigenstates of the hydrogen atom are resolved into simultaneous eigenstates of the angular momentum and its component along an arbitrary axis. If the eigenvalues form a continuous set, the usual modifications, involving the replacement of sums by integrals, can be made (Dirac, 1947).

The outcome of a measurement of $X$ is one of the eigenvalues of $X$, say the $m$th, $x_m$ ; and the system is left in the associated eigenstate $|x_m\rangle$. No further measurements will be of any help in deciding which of the density operators originally described the system. The observer needs a strategy for choosing one or the other density operator on the basis of the outcome $x_m$ .

A randomized strategy assigns a probability $\pi_m$ to each outcome $x_m$ and directs the observer to choose hypothesis $H_1$ with probability $\pi_m$—and $H_0$ with probability $1 - \pi_m$—when that outcome occurs, perhaps by tossing a properly biased coin. In effect he measures not $X$, in whose value he is not really interested, but a dynamical variable corresponding to the operator

$$\Pi = \sum_k |x_k\rangle \pi_k \langle x_k|, \tag{1.2}$$

which we shall call the "detection operator." The states $|x_k\rangle$ are eigenstates of $\Pi$ with eigenvalues $\pi_k$ , and the measurement of $\Pi$ gives the observer the probability with which he should choose hypothesis $H_1$ .

The detection operator $\Pi$ is a Hermitian operator, and as shown in Appendix A, its matrix elements $\Pi_{mn}$ in any representation are equal to or less in absolute value than 1, and its diagonal elements $\Pi_{mm}$ are nonnegative real numbers:

$$| \Pi_{mn} | \leqq 1, \qquad 0 \leqq \Pi_{mm} \leqq 1. \tag{1.3}$$

There is an infinity of such detection operators $\Pi$, and the problem now is to find the best one.

(ii) *The Detection Criteria.* According to detection theory, receivers should be designed to meet one of two principal criteria, the Bayes criterion or the Neyman-Pearson criterion. The former directs us to minimize the average cost of operation, the latter to maximize the probability of detecting the signal while maintaining a fixed false-alarm probability (Middleton, 1960, Chapt. 19; Helstrom, 1960, Chapt. 3).

The false-alarm probability $Q_0$ is the probability of choosing hypothesis $H_1$ when hypothesis $H_0$ is true. The probability under hypothesis $H_0$ that a measurement of $X$ or $\Pi$ will leave the system in the $m$th state $|x_m\rangle$ is equal to $\langle x_m| \rho_0 |x_m\rangle$, and the total probability that hypothesis $H_1$ will be selected is

$$Q_0 = \sum_m \pi_m \langle x_m| \rho_0 |x_m\rangle = \mathrm{Tr}\ (\rho_0 \Pi), \tag{1.4}$$

where "Tr" stands for the trace of the operator written after it. The probability of detection $Q_d$ is the probability of choosing $H_1$ when $H_1$ is true and is similarly given by

$$Q_d = \text{Tr}\,(\rho_1\Pi). \tag{1.5}$$

Let the prior probabilities of hypotheses $H_0$ and $H_1$ be $\zeta$ and $(1 - \zeta)$, respectively, and let $C_{ij}$ be the cost of choosing hypothesis $H_i$ when $H_j$ is true $(i, j = 0, 1)$. Then the average cost of each decision is

$$\begin{aligned}\bar{C} &= \zeta[C_{00}(1 - Q_0) + C_{10}Q_0] + (1 - \zeta)[C_{01}(1 - Q_d) + C_{11}Q_d] \\ &= \zeta C_{00} + (1 - \zeta)C_{01} - (1 - \zeta)(C_{01} - C_{11})(Q_d - \lambda Q_0),\end{aligned} \tag{1.6}$$

where

$$\lambda = \frac{\zeta}{1 - \zeta}\left(\frac{C_{10} - C_{00}}{C_{01} - C_{11}}\right). \tag{1.7}$$

If we remember that $C_{01} > C_{11}$, $C_{10} > C_{00}$, we see that we must pick as our detection operator one that maximizes the quantity

$$Q_d - \lambda Q_0 = \text{Tr}\,[(\rho_1 - \lambda\rho_0)\Pi]. \tag{1.8}$$

To meet the Neyman-Pearson criterion we must maximize $Q_d$ for a fixed value of $Q_0$. By introducing the Lagrange multiplier $\lambda$, we find that it is again the quantity $Q_d - \lambda Q_0$ that is to be maximized. The resulting detection operator $\Pi$ will be a function of $\lambda$, which must be determined afterward in such a way that the false-alarm probability $Q_0$ takes on its pre-assigned value.

(iii) *The Optimum Strategy.* We adopt a representation in which the matrix of the operator $\rho_1 - \lambda\rho_0$ is diagonal, and we denote its eigenvalues by $\eta_k$ and its associated eigenstates by $|\eta_k\rangle$:

$$\rho_1 - \lambda\rho_0 = \sum_k |\eta_k\rangle\eta_k\langle\eta_k|. \tag{1.9}$$

If in that representation the matrix elements of $\Pi$ are $\Pi_{mn}$, we are to maximize the quantity

$$\text{Tr}\,[(\rho_1 - \lambda\rho_0)\Pi] = \sum_m \eta_m\Pi_{mm}.$$

Since the diagonal elements $\Pi_{mm}$ are positive real numbers between 0 and 1, this quantity is largest if we take $\Pi_{nn} = 1$ for $\eta_n \geqq 0$ and $\Pi_{nn} = 0$ for $\eta_n < 0$. The relation

$$\sum_k |\Pi_{nk}|^2 \leqq 1$$

(Appendix A, Eq. (A.4)) then requires the off-diagonal elements $\Pi_{mn}$ to vanish in those rows $m$ and columns $n$ for which either $\Pi_{mm} = 1$ or $\Pi_{nn} = 1$. In the rest of the matrix they vanish by virtue of the relation $| \Pi_{mn} | \leqq \Pi_{mm}\Pi_{nn}$ (Eq. (A.6)), for there both $\Pi_{mm} = 0$ and $\Pi_{nn} = 0$. Hence the matrix $\| \Pi_{mn} \|$ is diagonal with eigenvalues 0 and 1.

The optimum detection operator is therefore a projection operator on to the manifold spanned by the eigenkets of the operator $\rho_1 - \lambda\rho_0$ with non-negative eigenvalues:

$$\Pi = \sum_{k:\eta_k \geqq 0} |\eta_k\rangle\langle\eta_k|. \tag{1.10}$$

As in ordinary choices between simple alternatives, the observer can adopt a nonrandomized strategy. He measures the dynamical variable whose operator is $\rho_1 - \lambda\rho_0$, and if the outcome of his measurement is non-negative, he chooses hypothesis $H_1$, otherwise $H_0$. The false-alarm and detection probabilities attaining the minimum Bayes cost are given by

$$Q_0 = \sum_{k:\eta_k \geqq 0} \langle\eta_k| \rho_0 |\eta_k\rangle, \qquad Q_d = \sum_{k:\eta_k \geqq 0} \langle\eta_k| \rho_1 |\eta_k\rangle, \tag{1.11}$$

and in order to calculate them it is necessary to be able to find the eigenvalues and eigenstates of $\rho_1 - \lambda\rho_0$.

(iv) *The Choice Between Two Directions of Spin.* The optimum detection operator $\Pi$ can seldom be easily calculated when the density operators $\rho_0$ and $\rho_1$ do not commute. Here is an example whose only value is simplicity and instructiveness. Someone is sending a beam of spin-$\frac{1}{2}$ particles, such as sodium atoms, along the $y$-axis, preparing it in such a way that each particle has its spin parallel either to the $z$-axis (hypothesis $H_0$) or to the $x$-axis (hypothesis $H_1$). For each particle the observer is to choose between these hypotheses.

In terms of the Pauli spin matrices

$$\sigma_x = \begin{pmatrix} 0 & 1 \\ 1 & 0 \end{pmatrix}, \quad \sigma_y = \begin{pmatrix} 0 & -i \\ i. & 0 \end{pmatrix}, \quad \sigma_z = \begin{pmatrix} 1 & 0 \\ 0 & -1 \end{pmatrix} \tag{1.12}$$

(Dirac, 1947, p. 149), the two density operators between which one is to decide are

$$\rho_0 = \tfrac{1}{2}(\mathbf{I} + \sigma_z), \qquad \rho_1 = \tfrac{1}{2}(\mathbf{I} + \sigma_x) \tag{1.13}$$

where $\mathbf{I}$ is the $2 \times 2$ density matrix. These density operators do not commute. The optimum detection operator $\Pi$, which maximizes

$$\mathrm{Tr}\,[(\rho_1 - \lambda\rho_0)\Pi] = \tfrac{1}{2}\,\mathrm{Tr}\,\{[(1-\lambda)\mathrm{I} + \sigma_x - \lambda\sigma_z]\Pi\},$$

can be shown to be

$$\Pi = \tfrac{1}{2}(\mathrm{I} - \sigma_z \cos\psi + \sigma_x \sin\psi), \tag{1.14}$$

where the angle $\psi$ is defined by $\lambda = \cot\psi$ and lies between 0 and $\pi/2$.

The eigenvalues of $\rho_1 - \lambda\rho_0$ are

$$\eta_1 = \tfrac{1}{2}[1 - \cot(\psi/2)] \leqq 0, \tag{1.15}$$

$$\eta_2 = \tfrac{1}{2}[1 + \tan(\psi/2)] > 0,$$

and the eigenstates, in a representation in which, as in Eq. (1.12), $\sigma_z$ is diagonal, are

$$|\eta_1\rangle = \begin{pmatrix} \cos(\psi/2) \\ -\sin(\psi/2) \end{pmatrix}, \qquad |\eta_2\rangle = \begin{pmatrix} \sin(\psi/2) \\ \cos(\psi/2) \end{pmatrix}. \tag{1.16}$$

We leave the calculations to the reader.

Both the operator $\rho_1 - \lambda\rho_0$ and the detection operator $\Pi$ involve the spins only through the operator

$$\sigma_\psi = \sigma_z \cos\psi - \sigma_x \sin\psi, \tag{1.17}$$

whose only eigenvalues are $+1$ and $-1$. This operator can be measured for each particle by passing the beam through an inhomogeneous magnetic field directed at an angle $\psi + \pi/2$ with respect to the $x$-axis. This field splits the beam into two components. For the particles of one component $\sigma_\psi$ has the eigenvalue $+1$, and these, one decides, were originally spinning in the $z$-direction. For the particles of the other component, the eigenvalue of $\sigma_\psi$ is $-1$, and to them one assigns hypothesis $H_1$.

The false-alarm and detection probabilities are

$$Q_0 = \mathrm{Tr}\,(\rho_0\Pi) = \tfrac{1}{2}(1 - \cos\psi) \tag{1.18}$$

$$Q_d = \mathrm{Tr}\,(\rho_1\Pi) = \tfrac{1}{2}(1 + \sin\psi) \tag{1.19}$$

as can be easily calculated from Eqs. (1.13), (1.14) if one remembers the rules for the spin matrices,

$$\sigma_x^2 = \sigma_y^2 = \sigma_z^2 = \mathrm{I}, \qquad \sigma_z\sigma_x = i\sigma_y,$$

$$\mathrm{Tr}\,\sigma_x = \mathrm{Tr}\,\sigma_y = \mathrm{Tr}\,\sigma_z = 0, \qquad \mathrm{Tr}\,\mathrm{I} = 2.$$

Thus

$$Q_d = \tfrac{1}{2} + [Q_0(1 - Q_0)]^{1/2}, \qquad 0 \leqq Q_0 \leqq \tfrac{1}{2},\ \tfrac{1}{2} \leqq Q_d \leqq 1. \tag{1.20}$$

A value $Q_0 = 0$ corresponds to $\psi = 0$. The magnetic field is then directed along the $z$-axis, and whenever the particle is spinning in the $z$-direction, it goes into the component beam with the eigenvalue of $\sigma_\psi$ equal to 1, and hypothesis $H_0$ is correctly chosen. If it is spinning in the $x$-direction, it will give the eigenvalues $+1$ and $-1$ with equal probabilities, and hypothesis $H_1$ is correctly chosen with probability $Q_d = \frac{1}{2}$. For $Q_0 = \frac{1}{2}$, $Q_d = 1$, the field lies in the $x$-direction. The best orientation of the field is determined, under the Bayes criterion, by the value of $\lambda = \cot \psi$ given by Eq. (1.7). Under the Neyman-Pearson criterion the angle $\psi$ is determined by the pre-assigned false-alarm probability through Eq. (1.18).

For problems of any real interest, unfortunately, it seems to be very difficult to diagonalize the operator $\rho_1 - \lambda\rho_0$ when $\rho_0$ and $\rho_1$ do not commute; and unless this can be done, the optimum detection operator cannot be found. We therefore examine in Section 3 an alternative based on the presumption that the signal to be detected is relatively weak.

(v) *Commuting Density Operators.* Matters are much simpler when the density operators $\rho_1$ and $\rho_0$ commute, for it is then necessary to measure only one or the other or, if available, a dynamical variable $X$ whose operator commutes with both. Two commuting density operators possess a common set of eigenkets, which we denote by $|k\rangle$, and they can be written as

$$\rho_i = \sum_k |k\rangle P_{ik} \langle k|, \qquad i = 0, 1, \tag{1.21}$$

where $P_{ik}$ is the probability that the system is in the state $|k\rangle$ under hypothesis $H_i$ $(i = 0, 1)$. The eigenvalues of $\rho_1 - \lambda\rho_0$ are now

$$\eta_k = P_{1k} - \lambda P_{0k}, \tag{1.22}$$

and the optimum strategy is to choose hypothesis $H_1$ if a measurement of $\rho_0$, $\rho_1$, or $X$ leaves the system in a state $|k\rangle$ for which

$$P_{1k}/P_{0k} \geqq \lambda. \tag{1.23}$$

This is the familiar likelihood-ratio strategy of detection theory. If the common eigenstates of the density operators $\rho_0$ and $\rho_1$ form a continuous rather than a discrete set, the probabilities $P_{0k}$ and $P_{1k}$ are replaced by probability density functions.

(vi) *Multiple Choices and Parameter Estimation.* The question how best to choose among more than two hypotheses can be formulated in a similar way. Denote the hypotheses by $H_1, H_2, \cdots, H_r$ and define $r$ commuting operators $\Pi_1, \Pi_2, \cdots, \Pi_r$ whose sum is the identity operator,

$$\Pi_1 + \Pi_2 + \cdots + \Pi_r = \mathbf{1}.$$

These operators are simultaneously measured for the system, and the outcomes give the probabilities with which the corresponding hypotheses should be adopted, again by means of a chance device. If $\zeta_i$ is the prior probability of hypothesis $H_i$ and $C_{ij}$ is the cost of choosing hypothesis $H_i$ when $H_j$ is true, the average cost is

$$\bar{C} = \sum_{i=1}^{r} \sum_{j=1}^{r} \zeta_j C_{ij} \operatorname{Tr} (\rho_j \Pi_i), \tag{1.24}$$

where $\rho_j$ is the density operator of the system under hypothesis $H_j$. The operators $\Pi_j$, $j = 1, 2, \cdots, r$, must be selected to minimize this average cost. If the density operators $\rho_i$ commute, any one of them, or a sufficient statistic $X$ commuting with all of them, can be measured, and the treatment of the outcome is the same as in ordinary multi-hypothesis decision theory (Middleton and Van Meter, 1955b).

In the quantum-mechanical counterpart of the problem of parameter estimation, the density operator of a system is of a known functional form, but depends on an unknown parameter $\theta$. The statement that the value of $\theta$ lies in the interval $(\theta, \theta + d\theta)$ is what von Neumann (1932) calls a "property" ("Eigenschaft") of the system and identifies with a projection operator $dE(\theta)$: $\int dE(\theta) = \mathbf{1}$. If the true values $\theta_0$ of the parameter have a prior probability density function $z(\theta_0)$, and if $C(\theta, \theta_0)$ is the cost of assigning the value $\theta$ to the parameter when its true value is $\theta_0$, the Bayes cost of estimating $\theta$ by means of a particular "resolution of the identity" $dE(\theta)$ is

$$\bar{C} = \iint z(\theta_0) C(\theta, \theta_0) \operatorname{Tr} [\rho(\theta_0)\, dE(\theta)]\, d\theta_0 . \tag{1.25}$$

One must find the set $dE(\theta)$ of infinitesimal projection operators that minimizes this average cost. If $X$ is the best dynamical variable to measure, and if its operator has the continuous eigenvalues $x$ and the eigenkets $|x\rangle$,

$$dE(\theta) = \int_{dR(\theta)} |x\rangle\langle x|\, dx, \tag{1.26}$$

where $dR(\theta)$ is the region in the space of outcomes $x$ leading to an estimate of the parameter in the range $(\theta, \theta + d\theta)$.

## 2. DETECTION IN A SINGLE MODE

(i) *The Harmonic Oscillator.* Some simple examples to illustrate the ideas of the previous section can be put forth by considering the field in the cavity of our ideal receiver to have a single mode that can be excited by coupling with the external electromagnetic field. In quantum mechanics this mode can be treated as a simple harmonic oscillator of frequency $\omega$ and unit mass. The co-ordinate $q$ and the momentum $p$ of the oscillator are expressed in terms of an "annihilation operator" $a$ and a "creation operator," the adjoint $a^+$ of $a$:

$$q = (\hbar/2\omega)^{1/2}(a^+ + a), \qquad p = i(\hbar\omega/2)^{1/2}(a^+ - a), \tag{2.1}$$

where $\hbar$ is Planck's constant $h/2\pi$. The operator $a$ and its adjoint $a^+$ are subject to the commutation relations

$$aa^+ - a^+a = 1. \tag{2.2}$$

The operator $n = a^+a$ is called the "number operator." We denote its eigenstates by $|m\rangle$.

$$n|m\rangle = m|m\rangle. \tag{2.3}$$

It is customary to say that when the oscillator or the mode is in the state $|m\rangle$, it contains $m$ "photons"; and a representation of the state in terms of the eigenstates $|m\rangle$ of the number operator $n = a^+a$ is called the "number representation." Since the Hamiltonian of the oscillator is

$$H = \tfrac{1}{2}(p^2 + \omega^2 q^2) = (\hbar\omega/2)(aa^+ + a^+a) = \hbar\omega(n + \tfrac{1}{2}), \tag{2.4}$$

the eigenstates of the number operator $n$ are stationary states of the harmonic oscillator. The effects of the annihilation and creation operators on such an eigenstate $|m\rangle$ are given by the equations

$$a|m\rangle = m^{1/2}|m - 1\rangle, \qquad a^+|m\rangle = (m + 1)^{1/2}|m + 1\rangle. \tag{2.5}$$

Thus the action of $a$ is to decrease the number of photons by 1, and the action of $a^+$ is to increase it by 1, whence the names of these operators.

R. J. Glauber (1963) has developed a useful calculus for dealing with the states of a harmonic oscillator in terms of the right eigenkets of the operator $a$, which are denoted by $|\alpha\rangle$:

$$a|\alpha\rangle = \alpha|\alpha\rangle. \tag{2.6}$$

The $\alpha$'s are complex numbers ranging over the entire complex plane, and the set of eigenkets $|\alpha\rangle$ is overcomplete. Nevertheless any state of the oscillator can be represented as a superposition of these eigenkets by virtue of the representation of the identity,

$$\mathbf{1} = \pi^{-1} \int |\alpha\rangle\langle\alpha| \, d^2\alpha, \tag{2.7}$$

in which the integration is taken over the plane of $\alpha = \alpha_x + i\alpha_y$, and $d^2\alpha = d\alpha_x \, d\alpha_y$. These states $|\alpha\rangle$ in the co-ordinate representation are Gaussian wave-packets of minimum uncertainty $\Delta p \Delta q$. When $|\alpha|$ is large, they exhibit the features of a classical oscillating field of frequency $\omega$, and they can be considered as the counterparts of coherent signals in classical electromagnetism. The average energy of the state $|\alpha\rangle$ is

$$\langle\alpha| H |\alpha\rangle = \hbar\omega(|\alpha|^2 + \tfrac{1}{2}). \tag{2.8}$$

We shall suppose that when there is no signal present, the oscillator is in a mixture of states characteristic of thermal radiation. Its density operator $\rho_0$ can then be written as

$$\begin{aligned} \rho_0 = (1 - e^{-w})e^{-wn} &= \sum_{k=0}^{\infty} P_{0k} |k\rangle\langle k| \\ &= (\pi N)^{-1} \int \exp(-|\alpha|^2/N) \, |\alpha\rangle\langle\alpha| \, d^2\alpha, \end{aligned} \tag{2.9}$$

where $N$ is the mean number of photons in the mode,

$$N = v_0/(1 - v_0), \qquad v_0 = N/(N + 1) = e^{-w} \tag{2.10}$$

(Louisell, 1964, p. 243; Glauber, 1963, p. 2780). The eigenvalues $P_{0k}$ of the density operator are given by the geometrical distribution

$$P_{0k} = (1 - v_0)v_0^k. \tag{2.11}$$

In thermal equilibrium at absolute temperature $\mathfrak{J}$ the mean number $N$ is determined by the Planck formula,

$$N = (e^w - 1)^{-1}, \qquad w = \hbar\omega/K\mathfrak{J} \tag{2.12}$$

with $K$ the Boltzmann constant.

(ii) *An Incoherent Signal.* By an "incoherent signal" we mean one that superimposes on the distribution of states given by $\rho_0$ another distribution of the same kind, but with a mean number of photons $N_s$.

The density operator $\rho_1$ under hypothesis $H_1$ has the same form as that in Eq. (2.9), except that $N$ is replaced by $N' = N + N_s$, and $v_0$ is replaced by $v_1 = N'/(N' + 1)$.[1]

The two density operators $\rho_0$ and $\rho_1$ commute and possess the simultaneous eigenstates $|m\rangle$, for both are functions only of the number operator $n$, which can be considered as a sufficient statistic. A decision about the presence or absence of the signal can be based on the outcome of a measurement of $n$. If the outcome of this measurement exceeds a decision level $n_0$, hypothesis $H_1$ is chosen. Under the Bayes criterion,

$$n_0 = \frac{\ln [\lambda(1 - v_0)/(1 - v_1)]}{\ln (v_1/v_0)}. \tag{2.13}$$

The false-alarm and detection probabilities are

$$Q_0 = v_0^{n_0'}, \qquad Q_d = v_1^{n_0'}, \tag{2.14}$$

where $n_0'$ is the least integer greater than $n_0$.

(iii) *A Coherent Signal of Known Phase.* Let us suppose that when a coherent signal of known phase impinges on our cavity, the single mode with which we are dealing is excited into a coherent state $|\mu\rangle$, which as we mentioned before is a right eigenstate of the annihilation operator $a$ corresponding to the complex eigenvalue $\mu$. If there is also background radiation of the type described by the density operator $\rho_0$ of Eq. (2.9), the combined fields of the signal and the background are distributed among the possible states of the mode oscillator in accordance with the density operator

$$\begin{aligned} \rho_1 &= (1 - e^{-w})e^{-w(a^+ - \mu^*)(a - \mu)} \\ &= (\pi N)^{-1} \int \exp(-|\alpha - \mu|^2/N)\, |\alpha\rangle\langle\alpha|\, d^2\alpha \end{aligned} \tag{2.15}$$

(Louisell, 1964, p. 246). The mean number of signal photons is now $N_s = |\mu|^2$.

This density operator $\rho_1$ does not commute with the density operator $\rho_0$ of Eq. (2.9), and there exists no set of simultaneous eigenstates. To describe and evaluate the optimum detector, it is necessary to diagonalize

[1] The signal is superposed on the noise in the manner outlined by Glauber (1963, p. 2778). The noise can be thought of as having been turned on first, bringing the system to a mixture of states described by $\rho_0$ of Eq. (2.9), after which the signal is turned on and the mixture described by $\rho_1$ results.

the operator $\rho_1 - \lambda\rho_0$ for arbitrary values of $\lambda$ between 0 and $\infty$, and this appears to be a formidable problem.

The matrix elements $\rho_{1nm} = \langle n|\,\rho_1\,|m\rangle$ of the density operator $\rho_1$ in the number representation can be obtained from the generating function

$$\begin{aligned} R_1(\alpha^*, \beta) &= \sum_{n=0}^{\infty}\sum_{m=0}^{\infty} \frac{\rho_{1nm}(\alpha^*)^n\beta^m}{\sqrt{n!\,m!}} \\ &= (1 - v_0)\exp\,[v_0\,\alpha^*\beta + (1 - v_0)(\alpha^*\mu + \beta\mu^* - |\,\mu\,|^2)]. \end{aligned} \tag{2.16}$$

In Glauber's representation the eigenstates $|\eta_k\rangle$ of the operator $\rho_1 - \lambda\rho_0$ might be determined by solving the integral equation

$$\int [R_1(\alpha^*, \beta) - \lambda R_0(\alpha^*, \beta)]e^{-|\beta|^2}F_k(\beta^*)\,d^2\beta/\pi = \eta_k\,F_k(\alpha^*), \tag{2.17}$$

where $R_0(\alpha^*, \beta)$ is obtained by setting $\mu = 0$ in Eq. (2.16), and

$$\begin{aligned} F_k(\alpha^*) &= \langle\alpha\,|\,\eta_k\rangle\,e^{|\alpha|^2/2}, \\ |\,\eta_k\rangle &= \int |\,\alpha\rangle\,F_k(\alpha^*)e^{-|\alpha|^2/2}\,d^2\alpha/\pi. \end{aligned} \tag{2.18}$$

Solving the integral equation (2.17) is equivalent to diagonalizing the infinite matrix $\rho_{1nm} - \lambda\rho_{0nm}$, $\rho_{0nm} = (1 - v_0)v_0^{\,m}\delta_{nm}$.

(iv) *A Coherent Signal of Unknown Phase.* It is unlikely that the receiver will know in advance the phase of a coherent optical signal, for a shift in the relative positions of transmitter and receiver through a distance of the order of a wavelength will alter the phase by a considerable fraction of $2\pi$. When the phase of the complex parameter $\mu$ in Eq. (2.15) is completely unknown, it should be assigned the least favorable prior distribution, which is uniform over the interval $(0, 2\pi)$. The density operator under hypothesis $H_1$ is then obtained by averaging Eq. (2.15) with respect to that distribution of $\arg\mu = \psi$:

$$\begin{aligned} \rho_1 &= (\pi N)^{-1}\int_0^{2\pi}\frac{d\psi}{2\pi}\int \exp\,[-(|\,\alpha\,|^2 - 2\,|\,\alpha\,|\,|\,\mu\,|\cos(\psi - \theta) \\ &\qquad + |\,\mu\,|^2)/N]\cdot|\,\alpha\rangle\langle\alpha\,|\,d^2\alpha \\ &= (\pi N)^{-1}\int \exp\,[-(|\,\alpha\,|^2 + |\,\mu\,|^2)/N]I_0(2\,|\,\alpha\,|\,|\,\mu\,|/N)|\alpha\rangle\langle\alpha|\,d^2\alpha, \end{aligned} \tag{2.19}$$

where $\theta = \arg\alpha$ and $I_0(x)$ is the modified Bessel function. The density operator $\rho_0$ for the field in the absence of a signal is still given by Eq. (2.9).

Both density operators $\rho_0$ and $\rho_1$ are diagonal in the number representation, for the integrands in Eqs. (2.9), (2.19) depend on $\alpha$ only through its modulus $|\alpha|$. The observer can therefore base his decision about the presence or absence of a signal on a measurement of the number $n$ of photons in the mode. Under hypothesis $H_0$ this number is distributed according to the geometrical distribution in Eq. (2.11). When a signal is present, the "Laguerre distribution" applies (Lachs, 1965),

$$P_{1k} = (N+1)^{-1} \exp[-N_s/(N+1)] v_0^k L_k[-N_s/N(N+1)] \qquad v_0 = N/(N+1), \tag{2.20}$$

where $L_k(x)$ is the $k$th Laguerre polynomial and $N_s = |\mu|^2$ is the average number of photons in the component of the field due to the signal.

The observer chooses hypothesis $H_1$ whenever the likelihood ratio $\exp[-N_s/(N+1)]L_k[-N_s/N(N+1)]$ exceeds a decision level $\lambda$. If $n_0'$ is the smallest integer $k$ for which this is possible, the false-alarm probability is $Q_0 = v_0^{n_0'}$. The detection probability

$$Q_d = \sum_{k=n_0'}^{\infty} P_{1k}$$

cannot apparently be expressed in any simple form.

The moments of the distribution in Eq. (2.20) can be obtained from the moment-generating function

$$\sum_{k=0}^{\infty} P_{1k}u^k = (1-v_0)(1-v_0u)^{-1} \cdot \exp[-N_s(1-v_0)(1-u)(1-v_0u)^{-1}]. \tag{2.21}$$

In particular the mean and the variance of $n$ are

$$\mathrm{E}(n \mid H_1) = N + N_s, \qquad \mathrm{Var}_1\, n = N(N+1) + (2N+1)N_s. \tag{2.22}$$

When the expected number of photons in the mode is large, the distribution $P_{1k}$ can be written in the approximate form (Erdélyi *et al.*, 1953, Vol. 1, p. 280, Eq. [6.13 (15)])

$$P_{1k} \cong N^{-1} \exp[-(k+N_s)/N] I_0(2\sqrt{N_s k}/N), \tag{2.23}$$

which is the noncentral Rayleigh or Rice distribution that appears in the theory of detecting a signal of unknown phase in the presence of

Gaussian random noise (Helstrom, 1960, Chapt. V). The power signal-to-noise ratio is then

$$d^2 \cong 2N_s/N, \tag{2.24}$$

which in the limit $\hbar\omega \ll K\mathfrak{T}$ becomes, by Eq. (2.12), $d^2 \doteq 2E/K\mathfrak{T}$, where $E = N_s\hbar\omega$ is the energy of the signal component of the field. When Eq. (2.23) applies, the probability of detection can be expressed approximately in terms of the $Q$-function,[2]

$$Q_d \cong Q(\sqrt{2N_s/N}, \sqrt{2n_0/N}),$$
$$Q(\alpha, \beta) = \int_\beta^\infty x \exp[-(x^2 + \alpha^2)/2] I_0(\alpha x)\, dx. \tag{2.25}$$

At high frequencies, $\omega \gg K\mathfrak{T}/\hbar$, $v_0 = e^{-w} \ll 1$, and the Laguerre distribution becomes approximately the Poisson distribution for the number of signal photons in the mode,

$$P_{1k} = N_s^k \exp(-N_s)/k!, \tag{2.26}$$

as can be shown by keeping only the highest power in the Laguerre polynomial. If $v_0$ is less than the pre-assigned value of the false-alarm probability, $n_0' = 1$, and the receiver declares a signal present whenever it counts any photons at all in the mode. The probability of detection is less than 1 only because of the stochastic nature of the signal itself.

[*Editor's Note:* Material has been omitted at this point.]

## 6. CONCLUSION

The task of realizing the threshold receivers of Sections 4 and 5 remains. The cavity must be designed in such a way as to maximize the probability of detection attainable by the threshold receiver, and a physical means of combining the mode amplitudes as directed by Eqs. (4.23) and (5.6) must be discovered, but these are problems in electromagnetism. Signal detection theory can only specify the measurements to be made on the receiver and their subsequent treatment for the purpose of decision.

Much more is yet to be done. The structure and properties of the optimum detection operator put forth in Section 1 should be explored in

[2] As shown in Appendix B, the $Q$-function also provides a generating function for the cumulative Laguerre distribution.

situations where the two density operators $\rho_0$ and $\rho_1$ do not commute. Parameter estimation, as formulated in Eq. (1.16), should be studied, and the quantum-mechanical counterparts of minimum-mean-square and maximum-likelihood estimation worked out and evaluated. The optimum forms of special detectors, such as those employing photosensitive surfaces and counters, should be derived and compared with the ideal receiver.[3] The multifarious special problems of optical radar and communication systems, arising from the vagaries of the transmitting medium and the sources of the radiation, provide further opportunities for applying the methods of signal-detection theory and should not be neglected.

## APPENDIX A. PROPERTIES OF THE DETECTION OPERATOR

In the representation in which the matrix of the detection operator $\Pi$ is diagonal, as given in Eq. (1.2), its diagonal elements are the eigenvalues $\pi_k$, which lie between 0 and 1, $0 \leqq \pi_k \leqq 1$. Let another representation be obtained by a transformation specified by the unitary matrix $\mathbf{U} = \| U_{km} \|$. The new matrix elements of $\Pi$ are

$$\Pi_{km} = \sum_{n,p} U_{kn}\pi_n\delta_{np}U^{+}_{pm} = \sum_n \pi_n U_{kn} U^{*}_{mn} . \qquad (A.1)$$

In particular the diagonal elements are

$$\Pi_{kk} = \sum_n \pi_n | U_{kn} |^2 \leqq \sum_n | U_{kn} |^2 = 1, \qquad (A.2)$$

in which the final step follows from the unitarity of $\mathbf{U}$. The $\pi_n$'s being all positive, $\Pi_{kk}$ must be positive, and we have shown that

$$0 \leqq \Pi_{kk} \leqq 1. \qquad (A.3)$$

The operator $\Pi^2$ has eigenvalues $\pi_m^2$, and since $0 \leqq \pi_m^2 \leqq 1$, $\Pi^2$ is an operator of the same kind as $\Pi$. In any representation its diagonal elements lie between 0 and 1:

$$0 \leqq (\Pi^2)_{mm} = \sum_k \Pi_{mk}\Pi_{km} = \sum_k | \Pi_{km} |^2 \leqq 1, \qquad (A.4)$$

where we have used the Hermiticity of $\Pi$. This equation shows that all the matrix elements of $\Pi$ have absolute values less than or equal to 1:

$$| \Pi_{km} | \leqq 1. \qquad (A.5)$$

[3] Two recent papers (Helstrom, 1964, 1967) represent a start in this direction.

If we now write Eq. (A.1) as

$$\Pi_{km} = \sum_n \pi_n^{1/2} U_{kn} \cdot \pi_n^{1/2} U_{mn}^*$$

and apply Schwarz's inequality, we find, using Eq. (A.2),

$$|\Pi_{km}|^2 \leqq \sum_n \pi_n |U_{kn}|^2 \cdot \sum_n \pi_n |U_{mn}|^2 = \Pi_{kk}\Pi_{mm}. \qquad (A.6)$$

Hence any off-diagonal element $\Pi_{km}$ has an absolute value less than or equal to the geometric mean of the diagonal elements of $\Pi$ in its row and column. If either of these diagonal elements is 0, the off-diagonal element must also vanish.

[*Editor's Note:* Appendix B on a generating function for the cumulative Laguerre distribution has been omitted.]

## REFERENCES

CAPON, J. (1961), On the asymptotic efficiency of locally optimum detectors. *Trans. IRE* **IT-7,** 67–71.

DIRAC, P. A. M. (1947), "Quantum Mechanics," 3rd ed. Oxford Univ. Press, London.

ERDÉLYI, A., MAGNUS, W., OBERHETTINGER, F., AND TRICOMI, F. G. (1953), "Higher Transcendental Functions." McGraw-Hill, New York.

FANO, U. (1957), Description of states in quantum mechanics by density matrix and operator techniques. *Rev. Mod. Phys.* **29,** 74–93.

GORDON, J. P. (1962), Quantum effects in communication systems. *Proc. IRE* **50,** 1898–1908.

GORDON, J. P. (1964), Quantum noise in communication channels, *In* "3rd International Congress on Quantum Electronics," pp. 55–64. Columbia Univ. Press, New York.

GLAUBER, R. J. (1963), Coherent and incoherent states of the radiation field. *Phys. Rev.* **131,** 2766–2788.

GLAUBER, R. J. (1965), Optical coherence and photon statistics. *In* "Quantum Optics and Electronics" (C. de Witt *et al.*, eds.) pp. 63–185. Gordon and Breach, New York.

HELSTROM, C. W. (1960), "Statistical Theory of Signal Detection," Pergamon Press, London.

HELSTROM, C. W. (1964), The detection and resolution of optical signals. *Trans. IEEE* **IT-10,** 275–287.

HELSTROM, C. W. (1965), Quantum limitations on the detection of coherent and incoherent signals. *Trans. IEEE*, **IT-11,** 482–490.

HELSTROM, C. W. (1966), Quasi-classical analysis of coupled oscillators. *J. Math. Phys.*, in press.

HELSTROM C. W. (1967), Detectability of coherent optical signals in a heterodyne receiver. *J. Opt. Soc. Am.*, in press.

JELSMA, L. F., AND BOLGIANO, L. P. (1965), A quantum field description of communication systems. *IEEE Ann. Commun. Conv. Record*, pp. 635–642.

KELLER, E. F. (1965), Statistics of the thermal radiation field. *Phys. Rev.* **139,** B202–B211.

LACHS, G. (1965), Theoretical aspects of mixtures of thermal and coherent radiation. *Phys. Rev.* **138,** B1012–B1016.

LEBEDEV, D. S., AND LEVITIN, L. B. (1966), Information transmission by electromagnetic field. *Inform. Control* **9,** 1–22.

LOUISELL, W. H. (1964), "Radiation and Noise in Quantum Electronics." McGraw-Hill, New York.

MIDDLETON, D., AND VAN METER, D. (1955a), Detection and extraction of signals in noise from the point of view of statistical decision theory. *J. Soc. Ind. Appl. Math.* **3,** 192–253.

MIDDLETON, D., AND VAN METER, D. (1955b), On optimum multiple-alternative detection of signals in noise. *Trans. IRE* **IT-1,** 1–9.

MIDDLETON, D. (1960), "An Introduction to Statistical Communication Theory." McGraw-Hill, New York.

MIDDLETON, D. (1965), "Topics in Communication Theory." McGraw-Hill, New York.

MIDDLETON, D. (1966), Canonically optimum threshold detection. *Trans. IEEE* **IT-12,** 230–243.

NEUMANN, J. VON (1932), "Mathematical Foundations of Quantum Mechanics," Springer, Berlin. [Translated by R. T. Beyer, Princeton Univ. Press, Princeton, N. J. (1955).]

PETERSON, W. W., BIRDSALL, T. G., AND FOX, W. C. (1954), The theory of signal detectability. *Trans. IRE* **PGIT-4,** 171–212.

RUDNICK, P. (1962). A signal-to-noise property of binary decisions. *Nature* **193,** 604–605.

TAKAHASI, H. (1965), Information theory of quantum-mechanical channels. *Advan. Commun. Systems* **1,** 227–310.

# 2B



Reprinted from pp. 156, 160, 161–164, 171 of *Inf. and Control*
**13**(2):156–171 (1968)

## Detection Theory and Quantum Mechanics (II)

CARL W. HELSTROM

*Department of Applied Electrophysics, University of California, San Diego, La Jolla, California 92037 and Institute for Radiation Physics and Aerodynamics**

The detection of a coherent radiative signal of known phase in the absence of background noise is treated in the framework of the quantum-mechanical form of detection theory. The error probabilities of the optimum detector assess the effects of quantum-mechanical uncertainly alone on the detectability of such a signal; they are compared with those attained by a quasi-classical threshold detector and by a detector that counts the number of photons. The question of sufficient statistics in quantum detection and estimation is discussed.

[*Editor's Note:* Material has been omitted at this point.]

* This research was supported in part by the Advanced Research Projects Agency (Project DEFENDER) and was monitored by the U. S. Army Research Office—Durham under Contract DA-31-124-ARO-D-257.

## 8. CHOICES BETWEEN PURE STATES

An extreme case of quantum detection is that in which the receiver is in one pure state $| \psi_0 \rangle$ under hypothesis $H_0$ and in another pure state $| \psi_1 \rangle$ under $H_1$. Such a condition would arise, for instance, if the observer had to decide which of two coherent signals is present in the ideal receiver, background radiation being negligible or absent. This decision may be liable to error owing to the quantum-mechanical uncertainties in the specification of the two signals, whose wave-packets may overlap.

The density operators are now

$$\rho_0 = | \psi_0 \rangle \langle \psi_0 | , \rho_1 = | \psi_1 \rangle \langle \psi_1 | , \tag{8.1}$$

and in order to find the detection operator $\Pi$ we must solve the characteristic equation (7.2). There are only two eigenstates with nonzero eigenvalues, and we label them $| \eta_1 \rangle$ and $| \eta_0 \rangle$. They are linear combinations of $| \psi_0 \rangle$ and $| \psi_1 \rangle$,

$$| \eta_k \rangle = z_{k0} | \psi_0 \rangle + z_{k1} | \psi_1 \rangle, \quad k = 0, 1, \tag{8.2}$$

where $z_{k0}$ and $z_{k1}$ are constants to be determined. Substituting into (7.2) and equating coefficients of $| \psi_0 \rangle$ and $| \psi_1 \rangle$, we obtain the simultaneous equations

$$\begin{aligned} z_{k1} + \gamma z_{k0} &= \eta_k z_{k1} , \\ -\lambda\gamma^* z_{k1} - \lambda z_{k0} &= \eta_k z_{k0} , \\ \gamma &= \langle \psi_1 | \psi_0 \rangle. \end{aligned} \tag{8.3}$$

The two eigenvalues $\eta_k$ for which these equations possess nonvanishing solutions are the roots of the determinantal equation

$$\begin{vmatrix} 1 - \eta & \gamma \\ -\lambda\gamma^* & - \lambda' - \eta \end{vmatrix} = 0,$$

and are given by

$$\eta_1 = \tfrac{1}{2}(1 - \lambda) + R > 0, \eta_0 = \tfrac{1}{2}(1 - \lambda) - R < 0, \tag{8.4}$$

$$R = \{[\tfrac{1}{2}(1 - \lambda)]^2 + \lambda q\}^{\frac{1}{2}}, q = 1 - | \gamma |^2. \tag{8.5}$$

The parameter $q$ equals the square of the sine of the angle between the state vectors $|\psi_0\rangle$ and $|\psi_1\rangle$ in Hilbert space; when $q = 1$, they are orthogonal.

The coefficients $z_{k1}$, $z_{k0}$ are given by

$$z_{k1} = -\gamma A_k, \; z_{k0} = (1 - \eta_k)A_k, \tag{8.6}$$

and some tedious algebra shows that $A_k$, determined by the normalization $\langle \eta_k | \eta_k \rangle = 1$, is given by

$$|A_k|^{-2} = 2R(\eta_k - q), \quad k = 0, 1, \tag{8.7}$$

within an inconsequential phase factor.

Any other eigenstates $|\eta_k\rangle$ must be orthogonal to both $|\eta_0\rangle$ and $|\eta_1\rangle$, and hence also to both $|\psi_0\rangle$ and $|\psi_1\rangle$. Their eigenvalues are therefore 0, and on measurement of $\Pi$ they occur with zero probability under both hypotheses,

$$|\langle \psi_0 | \eta_k \rangle|^2 = |\langle \psi_1 | \eta_k \rangle|^2 = 0, \quad k \neq 0, 1.$$

The optimum detection operator can be taken simply as

$$\Pi = |\eta_1\rangle \langle \eta_1| . \tag{8.8}$$

The false-alarm and detection probabilities are, by (7.4) and (7.5),

$$\begin{aligned} Q_0 &= \langle \eta_1 | \rho_0 | \eta_1 \rangle = |\langle \eta_1 | \psi_0 \rangle|^2 \\ &= |\gamma^* z_{11} + z_{10}|^2 = (\eta_1 - q)/2R, \end{aligned} \tag{8.9}$$

$$\begin{aligned} Q_d &= \langle \eta_1 | \rho_1 | \eta_1 \rangle = |\langle \eta_1 | \psi_1 \rangle|^2 \\ &= |z_{11} + \gamma z_{10}|^2 = (\eta_1 + \lambda q)/2R. \end{aligned} \tag{8.10}$$

If the receiver is to meet the Neyman–Pearson criterion, the parameter $\lambda$ is determined so that $Q_0$ in (8.9) equals the pre-assigned value. The detection probability is then calculated from (8.10).

If, in particular, the states $|\psi_0\rangle$ and $|\psi_1\rangle$ are orthogonal,

$$|\gamma| = 0, q = 1, R = \tfrac{1}{2}(1 + \lambda), \eta_1 = 1, \eta_0 = -\lambda;$$

and $Q_0 = 0$, $Q_d = 1$. Orthogonal states can be distinguished with zero probability of error. The problem of deciding between two orientations of the spin of a particle, treated in Part I, Section 1 (iv), is another special case of the present analysis, $q$ being there equal to $\frac{1}{2}$.

## 9. NOISELESS DETECTION OF RADIATIVE SIGNALS

The electromagnetic field of the receiver will be described in terms of normal modes as outlined in Section 4, part I. The coherent states of this field are simultaneously right-eigenstates of the set of annihilation operators $a_{\mathrm{m}}$ for the modes, and we denote them by $|\,\boldsymbol{\alpha}\rangle$,

$$a_{\mathrm{m}}\,|\,\boldsymbol{\alpha}\rangle = \alpha_{\mathrm{m}}\,|\,\boldsymbol{\alpha}\rangle, \tag{9.1}$$

where $\boldsymbol{\alpha}$ is the column vector of the right-eigenvalues $\alpha_{\mathrm{m}}$. The $\alpha_{\mathrm{m}}$ are the mean complex amplitudes of the modes, and the expected value of the positive-frequency part of the electric intensity is, by (4.2),

$$\langle \boldsymbol{\varepsilon}^{+}(\mathbf{r}, t)\rangle = i\sum_{\mathrm{m}} (\hbar\omega_{\mathrm{m}}/2)^{\frac{1}{2}}\alpha_{\mathrm{m}}\mathbf{u}_{\mathrm{m}}(\mathbf{r}) \exp(-i\omega_{\mathrm{m}}t). \tag{9.2}$$

In the classical limit this is the positive-frequency part of the electric intensity itself, and it corresponds to the classical analytic signal.

Suppose that an observer is to decide whether the field in the receiver is in the coherent state $|\,\boldsymbol{\alpha}\rangle$ (hypothesis $H_0$) or in the coherent state $|\,\boldsymbol{\beta}\rangle$ (hypothesis $H_1$). When this decision is made in the best possible way, the probabilities, under the two hypotheses, of choosing $H_1$ are given by (8.9) and (8.10), in which the parameter $q$ is[3]

$$q = 1 - |\langle\boldsymbol{\alpha}\,|\,\boldsymbol{\beta}\rangle|^2 = 1 - \exp\Big(-\sum_{\mathrm{m}} |\,\alpha_{\mathrm{m}} - \beta_{\mathrm{m}}\,|^2\Big). \tag{9.3}$$

It depends on the states of the fields of the two signals and the degree to which they are orthogonal.

In particular, if the decision is between an empty receiver ($\alpha_{\mathrm{m}} \equiv 0$) and one with a signal represented by the coherent state $|\,\boldsymbol{\beta}\rangle$, the false-alarm and detection probabilities are given by (8.9) and (8.10) with

$$q = 1 - \exp(-N_s), \tag{9.4}$$

where

$$N_s = \sum_{\mathrm{m}} |\,\beta_{\mathrm{m}}\,|^2 \tag{9.5}$$

is the average total number of photons in the field of the signal. For a narrowband signal whose spectrum is centered at an angular frequency $\Omega$, $N_s = E/\hbar\Omega$, where $E$ is the expected value of the energy of the signal. The operating characteristic of the optimum detector, the graph of $Q_d$ versus $Q_0$, is plotted in Fig. 1 for $N_s = 1$ as the curve marked "optimum".

In Section 3, part I, the threshold detector of a signal was defined as one that in effect measures an operator $\Pi_0$ for which a certain signal–

[3] Glauber (1963), Eq. (3.33), p. 2771 and Section IX, pp. 2781–2784.

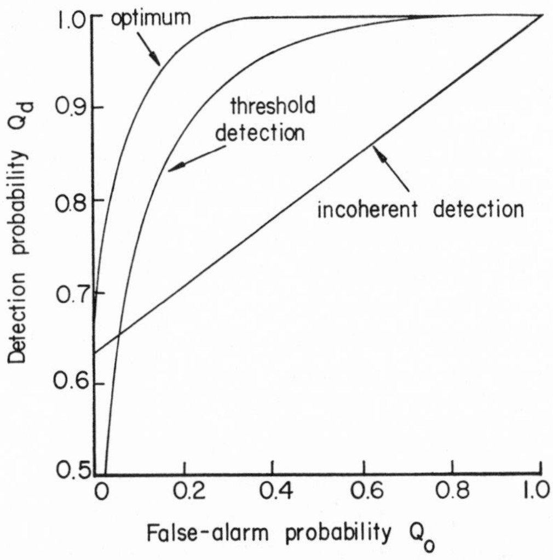


FIG. 1. Operating characteristics for detection of a signal of known phase in the absence of background noise; $N_s = 1$. For the optimum detector $Q_d \equiv 1$, exp $(-N_s) = 0.368 \leqq Q_0 \leqq 1$.

to–noise ratio, (3.11), is maximum. As a direct extension of (3.22) to a receiver with many modes, the threshold operator for deciding whether the signal $|\beta\rangle$ is present or not in the midst of thermal noise is given by

$$\Pi_0 = \sum_{\mathrm{m}} (\beta_{\mathrm{m}}{}^* a_{\mathrm{m}} + \beta_{\mathrm{m}} a_{\mathrm{m}}{}^+), \tag{9.6}$$

when the noise components of the modes are uncorrelated and have the same average number $N$ of photons. This threshold operator corresponds to the matched filter for ordinary detection in Gaussian noise.

The false-alarm and detection probabilities for the threshold detector are (Helstrom, 1965)

$$\begin{aligned} Q_0 &= \operatorname{erfc} x = (2\pi)^{-\frac{1}{2}} \int_x^\infty \exp(-t^2/2)\, dt, \\ Q_d &= 1 - \operatorname{erfc}(D - x), \end{aligned} \tag{9.7}$$

where the signal–to–noise ratio $D^2$ is

$$D^2 = 4N_s/(2N + 1), \tag{9.8}$$

and erfc $x$ is the error–function integral. The curve marked "threshold detection" in Fig. 1 displays the operating characteristic of the threshold receiver when background noise is absent and $D^2 = 4N_s$, again for $N_s = 1$.

Incoherent detection, the mere counting of photons, has been considered superior to coherent detection of optical signals (Goodman, 1966). As shown in Section 2(iv), the optimum detector of a coherent signal of unknown phase in a single mode of the ideal receiver indeed compares the number of photons in the mode with a decision level. Phase information can be used, however, when available, to attain a greater probability of detecting a signal.

If the receiver simply counts the number of photons in the modes, it might decide that a signal is present whenever any photons are observed, hypothesis $H_0$ being chosen only when no photons at all are counted. When background radiation is absent, the number of photons is governed under hypothesis $H_1$ by the Poisson distribution with mean value $N_s$. The probability of detection is $Q_d = 1 - \exp(-N_s)$, and the false-alarm probability is zero. By randomization, however, a greater probability of detection can be attained if the possibility of false alarms is accepted. The observer chooses hypothesis $H_1$ whenever he counts a positive number of photons; when he counts none, he chooses $H_1$ with probability $Q_0$ by, for instance, tossing a properly biased coin. The false-alarm probability is then $Q_0$, and the probability of detection is

$$\begin{aligned} Q_d &= Q_0 \exp(-N_s) + 1 - \exp(-N_s) \\ &= 1 - (1 - Q_0) \exp(-N_s). \end{aligned} \tag{9.9}$$

This is plotted for $N_s = 1$ as the straight line marked "incoherent detection" in Fig. 1. The optimum detector, which uses knowledge of the phase of the signal, is superior to both the threshold and the incoherent detector.

[*Editor's Note:* Material has been omitted at this point.]

## REFERENCES

CRAMÉR, H. (1946), "Mathematical Methods of Statistics," chapter 32, pp. 473–497, Princeton University Press, Princeton, New Jersey.

GLAUBER, R. J. (1963), Coherent and incoherent states of the radiation field. *Phys. Rev.* **131,** 2766–2788.

GOODMAN, J. W. (1966), Comparative performance of optical-radar detection techniques. *Trans. IEEE,* **AES-2,** 526–535.

HELSTROM, C. W. (1965), Quantum limitations on the detection of coherent and incoherent signals. *Trans. IEEE,* **IT-11,** 482–490.

HELSTROM, C. W. (1967a), Detection theory and quantum mechanics, *Inform. Control* **10,** 254–291.

HELSTROM, C. W. (1967b), Minimum mean-squared error of estimates in quantum statistics. *Phys. Letters,* **25A,** 101–102.

HELSTROM, C. W. (1967c), Quasi-classical analysis of coupled oscillators. *J. Math. Phys.* **8,** 37–42.

HELSTROM, C. W. (1968a), The minimum variance of estimates in quantum signal detection. *Trans. IEEE,* **IT-14,** 234–242.

HELSTROM, C. W. (1968b), Fundamental limitations on the detectability of electromagnetic signals. *Int. J. Theor. Phys.* **1,** no. 1, 37–50.

MESSIAH, A. (1961), "Quantum Mechanics," vol. I. North-Holland Publishing Co., Amsterdam.

RAO, C. R. (1945), Information and accuracy attainable in the estimation of statistical parameters. *Bull. Calcutta Math. Soc.* **37,** 81–91.

# 3



Reprinted from *IEEE Trans. Inf. Theory* **IT-16**(3):319–329 (1970)

# Reliability of Quantum-Mechanical Communication Systems

JANE W. S. LIU

***Abstract*—We are concerned with the detection of a set of $M$ messages that are transmitted over a channel disturbed by chaotic thermal noise when quantum effects in the communication systems are taken into account. Our attention is restricted to the special case in which the density operators specifying the state of the received field are commutative. In particular, the performance of two special communication systems is evaluated. For a system in which orthogonal signals with known amplitudes and random phases are transmitted over an additive white Gaussian channel, the structure of an optimum receiver is found. Expressions for the system reliability function and channel capacity are derived. For a system in which orthogonal signals are transmitted over a Rayleigh fading channel, the optimum performance is obtained. The optimum degree of diversity for an equal-strength diversity system is found numerically as a function of the average thermal-noise energy and information rate.**

## I. Introduction

Interest in quantum effects in communication systems has been stimulated in recent years by the development of optical communication systems. In such systems, the electromagnetic fields of signal and noise, as well as the receivers, can only be adequately described quantum mechanically. The laws of quantum mechanics limit both the knowledge that the receiver has about the signal field and the precision with which the received fields can be measured. While the effects of these limitations on the reliability of a communication system are negligible at microwave frequencies, they are often more prominent than that of the background noise at optical frequencies.

Most previous work is concerned with derivation of channel capacities of communication systems modeled quantum mechanically. Emphasis has been placed on the dependence of channel capacity on the type of receiver used in the system; therefore, specific receivers are included as parts of the channels. Stern [1], [2], Gordon [3], Hagfors [4], and others investigated the effects of Planck's quantization of radiant energy on the maximum entropy of an electromagnetic wave and the information capacity of a communication system. In their studies, continuous channels are replaced by equivalent discrete ones usually called photon channels. For photon channels with various probability distributions of noises and propagation losses, expressions for channel capacities have been derived. As we would expect, capacities of photon channels remain finite as the thermal-noise energy approaches zero. Gordon [3] and She [5] also derived capacities of communication systems using various receivers, for example, linear amplifiers, heterodyne receivers, and homodyne receivers. Quantum-mechanical limitations on the accuracy of measurements made by receivers are taken into account by modeling the receivers as noisy ones. Noises introduced by these receiving systems are found to be additive and Gaussian with energy of the order of $hf$ ($h$ is Planck's constant) when the signal frequency is $f$. Therefore, the energy of the effective noise in the system is always nonzero.

The statistical signal detection theory taking into account laws of quantum mechanics was formulated by Helstrom [6]–[9]. The problem of deciding whether a signal has been transmitted becomes that of selecting the one of two possible density operators that can better describe the state of the electromagnetic field at the receiver. It has been found that the optimum receiver under the Bayes criterion of minimum average cost measures a dynamical variable represented by a projection operator whose null space is the subspace spanned by the eigenvectors corresponding to the positive eigenvalues of the operator $\rho_1 - d\rho_2$. $\rho_1$ and $\rho_2$ are density operators specifying the states of the field at the receiver when the signal is present and when the signal is not present, respectively, and $d$ is a constant depending on the cost function to be minimized and the probability that the signal is present. The optimum receiver decides that the signal is present if the outcome of the measurement is zero. It has been shown that the presence of a background noise is not the only limiting factor on the detectability of signals generated by all known practical sources. Because of the fundamental quantum-mechanical limitations, the effective signal-to-noise ratio does not become infinite, as in the classical case when the noise energy approaches zero.

We shall investigate the problem of detecting a set of $M$ messages transmitted over a channel disturbed by chaotic noise when quantum effects are taken into consideration. Our attention is restricted to the special case in which density operators specifying the states of the electromagnetic field at the receiver are commutative. In Section II, a quantum-mechanical model of communication systems is described. The structure and performance of a quantum-mechanical optimum receiver for detecting signals specified by commuting density operators are described. In Sections III and IV,

Manuscript received April 11, 1969; revised September 22, 1969. This work was supported by the National Aeronautics and Space Administration under Grant NGL 22-009-013.

The author is with the Department of Electrical Engineering and Research Laboratory of Electronics, Massachusetts Institute of Technology, Cambridge, Mass. 02139.

we use these results in studies of two special systems.

In Section III, an optimum receiver is found for the reception of orthogonal signals that are in coherent states of known amplitudes and random phases, and the background thermal-noise field is in a completely incoherent state.[1] In the classical limit, these signals have known orthogonal waveforms but unknown phases,[2] and are transmitted over an additive white Gaussian channel. The minimum attainable error probability in the form $\exp[-\tau C E(R)]$ is derived. The system reliability function $E(R)$ is a function of the information rate $R$ of the system, $\tau$ is the time allotted for the transmission of a message, and $C$ is the capacity of the system. Expressions for the system reliability function and channel capacity are obtained.

In Section IV, the optimum performance of a system in which orthogonal signals are transmitted over a Rayleigh fading channel is found. The optimum degree of diversity for an equal-strength diversity system is obtained numerically as a function of the average thermal-noise energy and information rate.

## II. Quantum-Mechanical Model of Communication Systems

A model of typical communication systems is shown in Fig. 1. The input to the system in a given signaling interval of duration $\tau$ is one of $M$ input symbols denoted $m_1, m_2, \cdots, m_M$. For simplicity, it is assumed that the $M$ input symbols occur with equal probabilities, and input symbols transmitted in different signaling intervals are statistically independent. Correspondingly, in every signaling interval, the output $\hat{m}$ of the system is also one of $M$ symbols, which is the estimate of the transmitted input $m$. Therefore, the information rate of the system, in nats per second, is

$$R = (\ln M)/\tau . \tag{1}$$

Our objective is to design the receiver so that the probability of error $P(\epsilon)$ defined to be

$$P(\epsilon) = \Pr[\hat{m} \neq m], \tag{2}$$

is minimized.

Without loss of generality, let us assume that each input symbol is represented by a time-limited signal field of finite beam width. At any time, the average instantaneous power associated with such a field is nonzero only in a finite region in space. In other words, the transmitted signal field forms a wave packet. Hence, for convenience, the receiver can be idealized as a lossless cavity

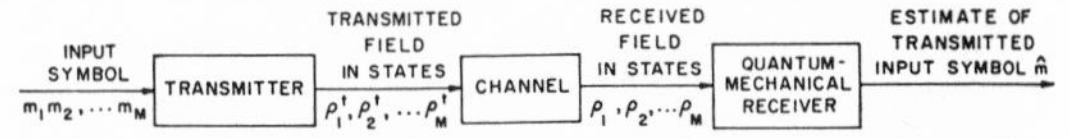


Fig. 1. Quantum-mechanical model of a communication system.

of a volume identical to that occupied by the signal.[3] The cavity, initially empty, is exposed to the signal source through an aperture for the duration within which the signal is expected to arrive. When the signal is inside the cavity, the aperture is closed, and a measurement (or several simultaneous measurements) is made on the field inside the cavity (the received field). On the basis of this measurement, the receiver decides which one of the $M$ symbols is transmitted. (It can be shown [7] that the probability of error $P(\epsilon)$ is independent of the exact time after the closure of the aperture at which the measurement is made.) Such an idealization of the receiver allows us to speak of receiver measurements over the region in which the signal is expected to be present. That such measurements are equivalent to measurements made by most optical frequency receivers on the received field as it propagates through an input aperture will be evident in Sections III and IV, where physical implementations of specific receivers are presented.

We shall assume that the measurement (or simultaneous measurements) made by the receiver is ideal. An ideal measurement is one in which the state of the field after the measurement depends on the outcome of the measurement, but not on the initial state of the field. It follows that the probability distribution of the outcome of any subsequent measurement does not depend on the transmitted input symbol. That is, any measurement made after an ideal measurement yields no information relevant to the optimum estimation of the transmitted input symbol.

It has been shown [10] that an ideal measurement whose possible outcomes are $n$-tuples of parameters $\boldsymbol{x}_k$ can be characterized by a complete set of measurement state vectors $\{|\boldsymbol{x}_k\rangle\}$.[4] By completeness, we mean

$$\sum_k |\boldsymbol{x}_k\rangle\langle\boldsymbol{x}_k| = \boldsymbol{I}, \tag{3}$$

where $\boldsymbol{I}$ is the identity operator. For simplicity, we assume that the parameters $\boldsymbol{x}_k$, as well as the eigenspectra of all operators, are discrete. It is obvious that this assumption

[1] By state, we mean either a pure state or a statistical mixture of states. There is no need to make such distinction here.

[2] It should be pointed out that in classical communication theory a signal with a known amplitude but an unknown absolute phase is sometimes called an incoherent signal. In the quantum-mechanical limit, such signal fields are in coherent states. Here, we shall use the quantum-mechanical meaning of "coherence."

[3] It can be shown [11] that the background noise field inside the cavity is statistically independent of that outside the cavity. That is, the outcomes of any measurements made on the two regions are statistically independent. Therefore, the noise field outside of the space occupied by the signal contains only irrelevant information.

[4] Clearly, a simultaneous measurement of several quantum-mechanical observables [12] represented by commutative Hermitian operators is an ideal measurement. In this particular case, the associated measurement state vectors are the simultaneous eigenstates of the commutative Hermitian operators. Hence $\{|\boldsymbol{x}_k\rangle\}$ is not only a complete set, but also an orthogonal one. As another example, a noisy simultaneous measurement of the amplitude and the phase of a field is ideal when the uncertainty in the outcomes is minimum possible according to quantum theory ([12], p. 98). The associated measurement state vectors are all the coherent states [5].

imposes no real restriction, since all discussions can be generalized by replacing the sums with integrals and probability distributions by their corresponding probability density functions. We also assume that associated with any given vector $|x_k\rangle$ there is a unique $n$-tuple of parameters $x_k$.

In the absence of a background noise field, the electromagnetic field at the receiver is in a state specified by the density operator $\rho_j^t$ when the input symbol is $m_j$. Therefore, the signal source, if acting alone, generates a field that is in one of the $M$ states specified by the density operators $\rho_1^t, \rho_2^t, \cdots, \rho_M^t$ at the receiver. Because of the presence of the background thermal noise, the total field is in one of the $M$ states specified by density operators $\rho_1, \rho_2, \cdots, \rho_M$ in a given signaling interval. Our attention will be restricted to the case in which these density operators are commutative,

$$\rho_i\rho_j = \rho_j\rho_i \qquad \text{for all } i, j = 1, 2, \cdots, M.$$

It can be shown [10] that when the field is in the state specified by the density operator $\rho_j$, the probability that the outcome of the ideal measurement associated with the set $\{|x_k\rangle\}$ is $x_k$ is given by

$$P(x_k \mid \rho_j) = P(x_k \mid m_j) = \langle x_k \mid \rho_j \mid x_k\rangle. \tag{4}$$

Let $p_{jk}$ be the probability that the transmitted input symbol is estimated to be $m_j$ by the receiver when the outcome of the measurement is $x_k$. It follows from (4) that the probability of error defined in (2) for the set of equiprobable messages characterized by density operators $\rho_j$ is

$$P(\epsilon) = 1 - \frac{1}{M}\sum_{j=1}^{M}\sum_k p_{jk}\langle x_k|\ \rho_j\ |x_k\rangle. \tag{5}$$

Hence, the structure of an optimum receiver is specified by a complete set of measurement state vectors $\{|x_k\rangle\}$ and the probabilities $p_{jk}$, which are chosen to minimize $P(\epsilon)$.

*Structure and Performance of Optimum Receiver*

Let $|\gamma_i\rangle$ denote the simultaneous eigenstates of the density operators $\rho_j$. Since the density operators are commutative, the vectors $|\gamma_i\rangle$ form a complete set (see [12], p. 49). By expanding the operators $\rho_j$ in terms of $|\gamma_i\rangle$ and by substituting the completeness relation (3) in (5), we found [11] that $P(\epsilon)$ is bounded from below by

$$P(\epsilon) \geq 1 - \frac{1}{M}\sum_i \left(\max_{1\leq j\leq M} \gamma_{ji}\right). \tag{6}$$

In this expression,

$$\left(\max_{1\leq j\leq M} \gamma_{ji}\right)$$

denotes the largest of the $M$ eigenvalues $\gamma_{1i}, \gamma_{2i}, \cdots, \gamma_{Mi}$ of the operators $\rho_1, \rho_2, \cdots, \rho_M$, respectively, corresponding to a given eigenstate $|\gamma_i\rangle$.

The lower bound of $P(\epsilon)$ in (6) can be achieved by choosing the set of measurement state vectors to be $\{|\gamma_i\rangle\}$. Let the outcome associated with $|\gamma_i\rangle$ be denoted by $x_i$. $p_{ik}$ is chosen to be 1 if

$$P(x_k \mid m_j) \geq P(x_k \mid m_i); \qquad \text{for} \quad i, j = 1, 2, \cdots, M, \tag{7}$$

and $p_{ik}$ equals zero for all other $i \neq j$.[5] But this is just the maximum-likelihood decision rule. Moreover, the receiver specified by $\{|\gamma_i\rangle\}$ and $p_{ik}$ given by (7) is identical to the one found by Helstrom ([7], p. 265), which is optimum over a smaller class of receivers. Measurements made by the receivers considered in [7] can be characterized by orthogonal measurement state vectors.

*Description of the Signal and Noise Fields*

We shall now discuss those constraints imposed on the signal field for both systems considered in Sections III and IV. For simplicity, the signal field is assumed to be linearly polarized and not modulated spatially. Since the additive thermal-noise field has statistically independent polarization components [11], the relevant component of the electric-field operator can be expanded in terms of plane wave normal-mode functions[6] and Fourier components in a signaling-time interval

$$E(r, t) = i\sum_k \sqrt{\frac{\hbar\omega_k}{2c\tau}}\left\{\mathfrak{a}_k \exp\left[i\omega_k\left(\frac{z}{c} - t\right)\right] - \mathfrak{a}_k^+ \exp\left[-i\omega_k\left(\frac{z}{c} - t\right)\right]\right\} \tag{8}$$

when the signal field propagates along the $z$ axis. In (8), $\mathfrak{a}_k$ and $\mathfrak{a}_k^+$ are the annihilation and creation operators of the $k$th normal mode, respectively, with natural frequency $\omega_k$ [13].

We shall further assume that the signals are narrow band and orthogonal. By orthogonal, we mean that the classical waveforms of the signals form an orthogonal set. Specifically, let $s_jV_j(r, t)$ be the classical complex amplitude of the signal at the receiver and time $t$ when input symbol $m_j$ is transmitted. That is

$$\mathrm{Tr}\,[\rho_j^t E(r, t)] = s_jV_j(r, t) + s_j^*V_j^*(r, t); \qquad j = 1, 2, \cdots, M, \tag{9}$$

where the parameter $s_j$ is either a known constant or a random variable. If we write

$$V_j(r, t) = \sum_{k=0}^{\infty} V_{jk} \exp\left[-i\omega_k\left(\frac{z}{c} - t\right)\right],$$

the coefficients $V_{jk}$ satisfy the condition

[5] This rule becomes ambiguous whenever (7) is satisfied for more than one value of $j$; however, the ambiguity can be easily resolved. Furthermore, the minimum value of $P(\epsilon)$ is not affected by the way in which this ambiguity is resolved.

[6] These are the transversal normal-mode functions of the receiver cavity with length $c\tau$. Without loss of generality, the cross-sectional area of the cavity, which is equal to that of the input aperture, is taken to be 1.

[7] The signal field is strictly time limited. It is approximately bandlimited in the sense that its energy outside of a finite bandwidth is nearly zero [14].

$$\sum_{k=0}^{\infty} V_{jk}V_{j'k}^{*} = \delta_{jj'}; \qquad j, j' = 1, 2, \cdots, M. \tag{10}$$

In particular, we shall be concerned with the set of orthogonal signals corresponding to that in a frequency-position modulation system. This set of signal waveforms also satisfies the condition

$$V_{jk}V_{j'k}^{*} = |V_{jk}|^2 \, \delta_{jj'}. \tag{11}$$

It is evident that the orthogonality condition is equivalent to the requirement that different normal modes be excited by the signal source when different input symbols are transmitted.

Just as in a classical communication system, the orthogonality constraint on the signal is a stringent one when the available bandwidth is limited. When the bandwidth for transmission is unlimited, however, orthogonal waveforms yield the best possible performance of classical systems. In our study, this constraint is imposed so that analysis in Section IV will be tractable. In Section III it is possible to find the structure and performance of an optimum receiver for orthogonal coherent signals only.

By additive thermal noise, we mean the background radiation of thermal nature that is also present at the receiver. The classical amplitude of the electric field associated with the thermal noise is a zero-mean stationary Gaussian random process. At thermal equilibrium and in the absence of the signal, the field is in the state specified by the density operator $\rho^{(n)}$, which in the $P$-representation [13], [15] is given by

$$\rho^{(n)} = \int \prod_k \exp\left[-|\alpha_k|^2/\bar{n}_k\right] |\alpha_k\rangle\langle\alpha_k| \, (d^2\alpha_k)/\pi\bar{n}_k. \tag{12}$$

Such a density operator specifies a completely incoherent state.[8] In expression (12), $|\alpha_k\rangle$ are the right eigenstates of annihilation operators $\mathfrak{a}_k$ in (8), $d^2\alpha_k$ stands for the differential $(d \operatorname{Re}[\alpha_k])(d \operatorname{Im}[\alpha_k])$, and the integrals are taken over the entire complex $\alpha$ planes. The parameter $\bar{n}_k$ is the average number of photons in the $k$th normal mode in the noise field. At background temperature $T$, it is given by

$$\bar{n}_k = \left[\exp\left(\frac{\hbar\omega_k}{kT}\right) - 1\right]^{-1}.$$

We shall also assume that the frequency range of interest is small so that these average numbers are approximately equal,

$$\bar{n}_k \approx \bar{n}; \qquad \text{for all } k. \tag{13}$$

## III. Orthogonal Signals With Known Amplitudes and Random Phases

A simple communication system of practical interest that has been studied in classical communication theory is one in which all characteristics of the received signal are known except its absolute phase. When the signal field is not modulated spatially, its classical amplitude at the receiver can be described by the function

$$2 \operatorname{Re}\left[S(t) \exp\left\{i\omega\left(\frac{z}{c} - t\right) + i\phi\right\}\right]. \tag{14}$$

$S(t)$ is one of a set of orthogonal time functions $\{S_j(t)\}$ depending on the transmitted input symbol, and $\phi$ is a random variable uniformly distributed over the interval $(0, 2\pi)$. The randomness of the parameter $\phi$ corresponds to the uncertainty in the phase of the received signal, as is often the case for signals at optical frequencies.

To describe the received field quantum mechanically, we expand the electric-field operator as in (8). When the transmitted input symbol is $m_j$, the field at the receiver in the absence of the noise field is in a state specified by the density operator

$$\rho_j^t = \int_0^{2\pi} \frac{d\phi}{2\pi} \int \prod_k \delta^{(2)}(\alpha_k - \sigma_{jk}e^{i\phi}) \, |\alpha_k\rangle\langle\alpha_k| \, d^2\alpha_k \tag{15}$$

in the $P$ representation. In other words, the signal field at the receiver is in one of the coherent states $\prod_k |\sigma_{jk}e^{i\phi}\rangle$. Again, $|\alpha_k\rangle$ are the right eigenstates of the annihilation operators $\mathfrak{a}_k$. The $\sigma_{jk}$ are known complex quantities, while $\phi$ is a random variable evenly distributed over the interval $(0, 2\pi)$. Moreover, $\sigma_{jk}$ satisfy the condition in (11), that is

$$\sigma_{jk}\sigma_{j'k}^{*} = |\sigma_{jk}|^2 \, \delta_{jj'}; \qquad \text{for all } k \quad \text{and} \quad j, j' = 1, 2, \cdots, M,$$

since the signals are orthogonal, as in frequency-position modulation systems. In the classical limit, these signals are just those given by (14) if the $\sigma_{jk}$ are such that

$$S_j(t) = \sum_k (\hbar\omega_k/2c\tau)^{1/2} i\sigma_{jk} \exp\left[i(\omega_k - \omega)\left(\frac{z}{c} - t\right)\right]; \qquad j = 1, 2, \cdots, M.$$

In the presence of an additive noise field of the type described by the density operator $\rho^{(n)}$ in (12), the total received field is in a state specified by the density operators

$$\rho_j = \int_0^{2\pi} \frac{d\phi}{2\pi} \prod_k \int \exp\left[-|\alpha_k - \sigma_{jk}e^{i\phi}|^2/\bar{n}\right] |\alpha_k\rangle\langle\alpha_k| \, d^2\alpha_k/\pi\bar{n} \tag{16}$$

when the input symbol $m_j$ is transmitted. An easy computation shows that the density operators $\rho_j$ are commutative; hence, the results of Section II can be applied here.

A simple example of coherent signals described above are unmodulated signals. When the transmitted input symbol is $m_j$, only the $j$th mode of the signal field is excited, while the other modes remain in their vacuum states. (Here we denote the $M$ relevant modes of the field as 1st, 2nd, and $M$th.) It can be shown [11] that the outcomes in measuring dynamical variables of two different modes of the noise are statistically independent.

[8] The different modes of the noise field are uncorrelated; i.e., $\operatorname{Tr}[\rho^{(n)}\mathfrak{a}_k^{+}\mathfrak{a}_{k'}] = \langle n_k\rangle\delta_{kk'}$. When the classical amplitude of this noise electric field $n(\mathbf{r}, t)$ is expanded in terms of an arbitrary orthogonal set, the expansion coefficients are statistically independent Gaussian random variables. This condition is satisfied by the white Gaussian noise field.

Therefore, we only need to consider the first $M$ modes of the received field. The states of the relevant modes are specified by the density operators

$$\rho_j = \int_0^{2\pi} \frac{d\phi}{2\pi} (\pi \bar{n})^{-M} \cdot \int \prod_{\substack{k \neq j \\ k=1}}^{M} \exp\left[-|\alpha_k|^2/\bar{n}\right] \exp\left[-|\alpha_j - \sigma_j e^{i\phi}|^2/\bar{n}\right] \cdot \prod_{k=1}^{M} |\alpha_k\rangle\langle\alpha_k| \, d^2\alpha_k \qquad j = 1, 2, \cdots, M. \tag{17}$$

A complete set of simultaneous eigenstates of the density operators $\rho_j$ in (17) is that of the number operators of the individual normal modes. Let $|n_1, n_2, \cdots, n_M\rangle$ denote the simultaneous eigenstates of the number operators $\mathfrak{a}_1^+\mathfrak{a}_1$, $\mathfrak{a}_2^+\mathfrak{a}_2$, $\cdots$, $\mathfrak{a}_M^+\mathfrak{a}_M$ corresponding to the eigenvalues $n_1$, $n_2$, $\cdots$, $n_M$, respectively. According to the results in Section II, the measurement made by an optimum receiver for the reception of these $M$ signals is characterized by the state vectors $|n_1, n_2, \cdots, n_M\rangle$ for all nonnegative integer values of $n_1, n_2, \cdots, n_M$. That is, the optimum receiver measures the numbers of photons in each of the $M$ modes [11].

It follows from (4) and (17) that the joint conditional probability distribution of the observed photon numbers $n_1, n_2, \cdots, n_M$ in modes $1, 2, \cdots, M$, respectively, when $m_j$ is transmitted, is[9]

$$P(n_1, n_2, \cdots, n_M \mid m_j) = \left(\frac{1}{1+\bar{n}}\right)^M \left(\frac{\bar{n}}{1+\bar{n}}\right)^{n_1+n_2+\cdots n_M} \cdot \sum_{r=0}^{n_j} \binom{n_j}{r} \frac{1}{r!} \left[\frac{|\sigma_j|^2}{\bar{n}(1+\bar{n})}\right]^r \exp\left[-\frac{|\sigma_j|^2}{1+\bar{n}}\right]. \tag{18}$$

The receiver estimates that the transmitted input symbol is $m_j$ if the conditional probability $P(n_1, n_2, \cdots, n_M \mid m_j)$ is maximum over all $j$. According to (18), the maximization of $P(n_1, n_2, \cdots, n_M \mid m_j)$ amounts to the maximization of the quantity

$$f_j = \sum_{r=0}^{n_j} \binom{n_j}{r} \frac{1}{r!} \left[\frac{|\sigma_j|^2}{\bar{n}(1+\bar{n})}\right]^r \exp\left[-\frac{|\sigma_j|^2}{1+\bar{n}}\right]. \tag{19}$$

For simplicity, we shall further assume that the complex quantities $\sigma_j$ have equal magnitudes

$$|\sigma_j|^2 = |\sigma|^2 = p\tau. \tag{20}$$

Since the average number of signal photons when $m_j$ is transmitted is $|\sigma_j|^2$, (20) implies that the average number of photons in the signal field is independent of the transmitted input symbol. In this case, the quantity $f_j$ in (19) is the largest among all $j$ if and only if $n_j$ is the largest. Therefore, an optimum receiver for this simple signal set is the direct detection system shown in Fig. 2.

It can be shown that the minimum attainable error probability in the reception of the narrow-band frequency-orthogonal signals given in (15) equals that of the unmodulated signal set. To show this, let

$$\sum_k |\sigma_{jk}|^2 = |\sigma_j|^2; \qquad \text{for } j = 1, 2, \cdots, M.$$

Let us consider a unitary transformation $V$, which relate a set of new annihilation operators $\{b_k\}$ to the set o annihilation operators $\{\mathfrak{a}_k\}$,

$$b_j = \sum_k V_{jk}\mathfrak{a}_k.$$

In particular, the elements of $V$ are so chosen that fo all $j = 1, 2, \cdots, M$

$$V_{jm} = \sigma_j^{-1}\sigma_{jm}^*, \; V_{mj}^+ = \sigma_j^{-1}\sigma_{jm}; \qquad \text{for all } m \text{ such that } \sigma_{jm} \neq 0 \tag{21}$$

$$V_{jm} = 0; \qquad \text{for all } m \text{ such that } \sigma_{jm} = 0.$$

The rows of the matrix $V$ defined in (21) clearly satisf the unitary condition

$$\sum_k V_{mk}V_{kn}^+ = \delta_{mn}. \tag{22}$$

The other rows of the matrix $V$ can be chosen arbitrarily provided that the resultant matrix $V$ is unitary. Expandin the density operators $\rho_j$ in (16) in terms of the righ eigenvectors $\{|\beta_j\rangle\}$ of the operators $b_j$, we obtain

$$\rho_j = \int_0^{2\pi} \frac{d\phi}{2\pi} \int \exp\left[-|\beta_j - \sigma_j e^{i\phi}|^2/\bar{n} - \sum_{k\neq j} |\beta_k|^2/\bar{n}\right] \cdot \prod_k |\beta_k\rangle\langle\beta_k| \, d^2\beta_k/\pi\bar{n}$$

From this expression, it is clear that the optimum per formance in the reception of this set of signals is identica to that of the unmodulated signals.

The direct detection system shown in Fig. 2 is, howeve no longer an optimum receiver. According to Section I an optimum receiver should measure simultaneousl dynamical variables represented by operators $b_1^+b$, $b_2^+b_2$, $\cdots$, $b_M^+b_M$. Let us again denote the outcomes c the measurement of $b_1^+b_1, b_2^+b_2, \cdots, b_M^+b_M$ by $n_1, n_2, \cdots$ $n_M$, respectively. The receiver estimates that $m_j$ is trans mitted if $n_j$ is the largest among all $n_i$. An idealize quantum optimum receiver is shown in Fig. 3. Th function of the mode-transformation filters is simila to that of an optical matched filter [11]. At the outpu of the $j$th filter, only the normal mode whose annihilatio operator is $b_j$ is excited.

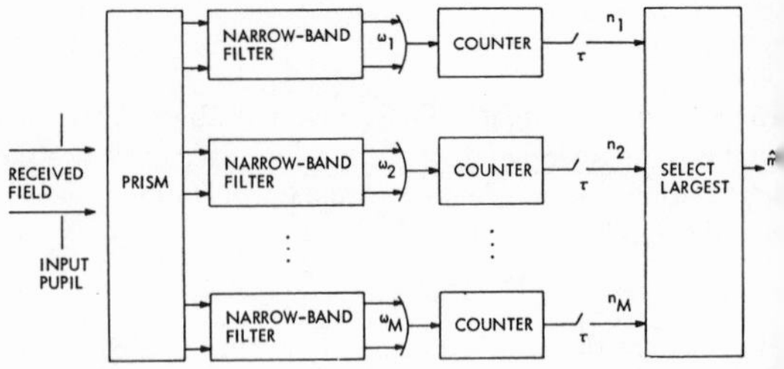

Fig. 2. Optimum receiver for equal-strength unmodulated signa with random phases.

[9] The derivation of this equation is similar to that of (3.9) in [16].

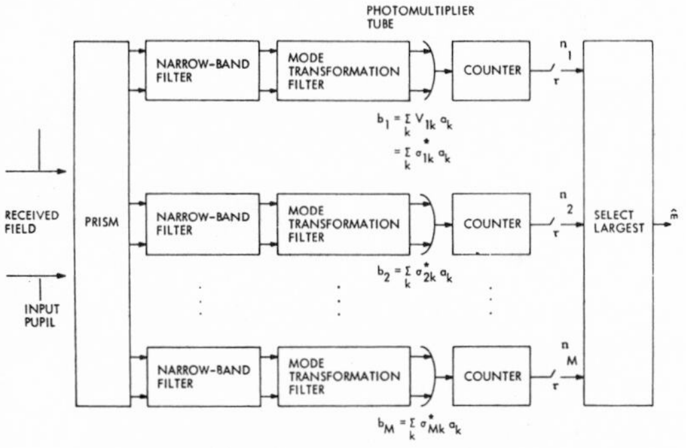


Fig. 3. Quantum-mechanical optimum receiver for orthogonal signals in coherent states with random phases.

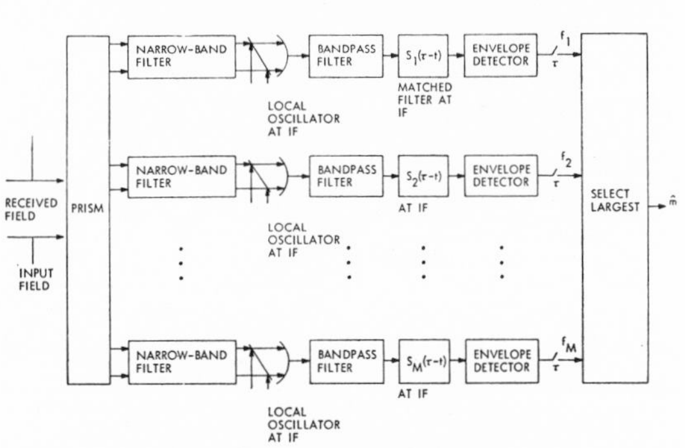


Fig. 4. Classical optimum receiver for orthogonal signals with random phases.

In the classical limit, one may consider $\sigma_{jk}$ and $\mathcal{A}_k$ as complex amplitudes of Fourier components of the signal $S_j(t)$ and the received electric field $\epsilon(r, t)$, respectively. Hence, according to Parseval's theorem, the variable $b_j^+ b_j$ is the quantity

$$f_j = \Big|\sum_k \sigma_{jk}^* \mathcal{A}_k\Big|^2 = \left|\left\{\int_0^\tau \left\{\int \epsilon(r, t)\, dr\right\} S_j^*(t)\, dt\right|^2; \qquad j = 1, 2, \cdots, M.$$

An implementation of the classical optimum receiver is shown in Fig. 4. But this receiver is not optimum in the quantum limit. When quantum effects in the system are taken into account; a semiclassical analysis [17] shows that the effective noise energy in the system is increased from $\frac{1}{2}\eta_0$ to $\frac{1}{2}(\eta_0 + \frac{1}{2}\hbar\omega)$ while the $f_j$ remain Rayleigh random variables. $\eta_0 = \bar{n}\hbar\omega$ is the average energy in each mode of the noise field. Hence, the system reliability function is the same as that for the classical additive white Gaussian channel (see Fig. 5).

Our objective is to find bounds to the error probability $P(\epsilon)$ of the form

$$P(\epsilon) \leq K_1 \exp\,[-\,\tau C E(R)], \tag{23a}$$

$$P(\epsilon) \geq K_2 \exp\,[-\,\tau C E(R)], \tag{23b}$$

where the information rate $R$ is given by (1). The coefficients $K_1$ and $K_2$ are not exponential functions of $\tau$. That is,

$$\lim_{C\tau\to\infty} \ln\,[P(\epsilon)/\tau C] = \lim_{C\tau\to\infty}\,[-E(R)]. \tag{24}$$

The channel capacity $C$ is found [11] to be

$$C = p \ln\left(\frac{1 + \bar{n}}{\bar{n}}\right), \tag{25}$$

where $p$, given by (20), is the average number of photons in the signal field at the receiver per unit time. We note that $C$ can also be expressed as

$$C = \frac{P}{2\eta_z} \ln\left(\frac{2\eta_z + \eta_0}{\eta_0}\right).$$

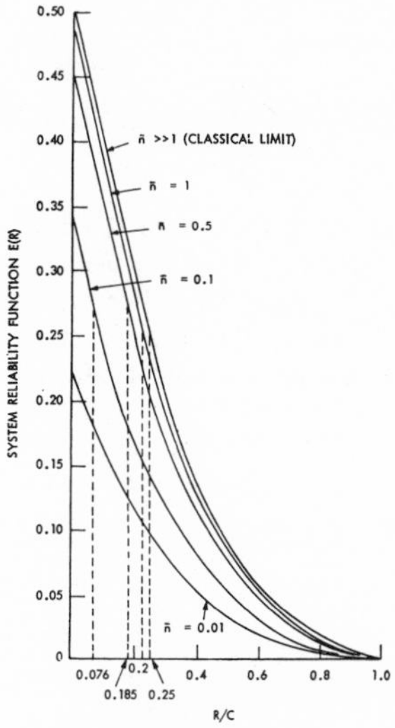


Fig. 5. System reliability function (for orthogonal signals in coherent states).

$P = p\hbar\omega$ is the average received signal power in the system, and $\eta_z = \frac{1}{2}\hbar\omega$ is usually called the zero-point fluctuation energy in the received field. As before, $\eta_0 = \bar{n}\hbar\omega$ is the average thermal energy.

The derivation of the system reliability function $E(R)$ is too lengthy to be included here. It has been found in [11] that for rates $R$ in the range $0 \leq R \leq R_c$, where $R_c$ is given by

$$\frac{R_c}{C} = \frac{\bar{n}(1 + \bar{n})}{(1 + 2\bar{n})^2}, \tag{26a}$$

the system reliability function $E(R)$ is bounded from below by

$$E(R) \geq \left[(1 + 2\bar{n}) \ln\left(\frac{1 + \bar{n}}{\bar{n}}\right)\right]^{-1} - \frac{R}{C}. \tag{26b}$$

For rates $R$ in the range $R_c \leq R \leq C$, the reliability function $E(R)$ is given by

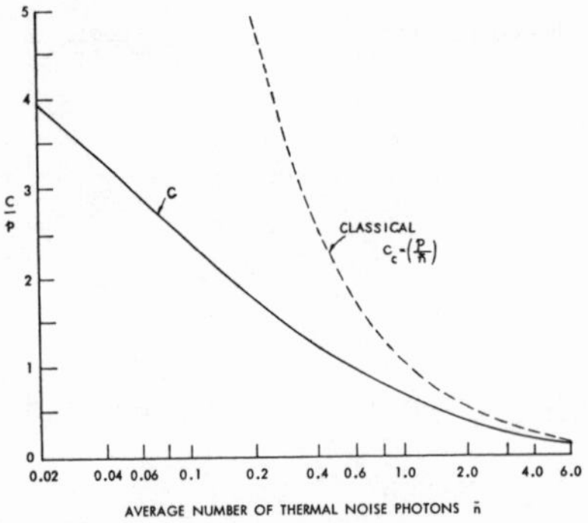


Fig. 6. Channel capacity as a function of noise levels.

$$E(R) = \frac{p}{C}\left\{\frac{1 + 2\bar{n}R/C - [1 + 4\bar{n}(1 + \bar{n})R/C]^{1/2}}{\bar{n} - \bar{n}[1 + 4\bar{n}(1 + \bar{n})R/C]^{1/2}}\right.$$

$$\left. - \frac{R}{C}\ln\left\{\frac{1 + 2\bar{n}(1 + \bar{n})R/C + [1 + 4\bar{n}(1 + \bar{n})R/C]^{1/2}}{2(1 + \bar{n})^2 R/C}\right\}\right\}.$$

A quick computation shows that the system reliability function $E(R)$ is positive for all values of $R$ less than $C$ when $\bar{n}$ is nonzero. Its general behavior for several different values of $\bar{n}$ is shown in Fig. 5. In contrast to the corresponding classical additive white Gaussian channel, $E(R)$ depends not only on $R/C$ but also on the average noise level $\bar{n}$. For large $\bar{n}$, $E(R)$ approaches as a limit the classical reliability function of a white Gaussian channel with infinite bandwidth

$$\begin{aligned} E_c(R) &= \tfrac{1}{2} - R/C\,, & 0 \leq R/C \leq \tfrac{1}{4}, \\ &= 1 - (R/C)^{1/2}, & \tfrac{1}{4} \leq R/C \leq 1. \end{aligned} \tag{27}$$

Clearly, when $\bar{n} \gg 1$, the channel capacity $C$ is approximately equal to $C_c = p/\bar{n} = P/\eta_0$, the capacity of the classical white Gaussian channel with no bandwidth constraint. Fig. 6 shows the values of $C$ and $C_c$ per unit average signal photon as functions of $\bar{n}$.

In Fig. 7 the exponent factor $CE(R)$ is plotted as a function of $R$ for several values of $p$ and $\bar{n}$. The corresponding value of $C_cE_c(R)$ is also shown for comparison. The exponent factor $C_cE_c(R)$ is obtained when quantum effects are completely ignored. The performance of the classical optimum receiver shown in Fig. 4 when quantum effects are considered is also shown in Fig. 7.

When $\bar{n} = 0$, the capacity $C$ becomes infinite. One is tempted to conclude from this fact that arbitrarily small probability of error can be achieved at any information rate $R$ by increasing the parameters $\tau$ and $M$ while keeping the average signal power fixed whenever $\bar{n} = 0$. Such a conclusion is not valid, since for very small $\bar{n}$

$$E(R) \approx \left\{\left(1 - \frac{R}{C}\right) - \frac{R}{C}\ln\left(\frac{C}{R} + 2\bar{n}\right)\right\}[-\ln(\bar{n})]^{-1}. \tag{28}$$

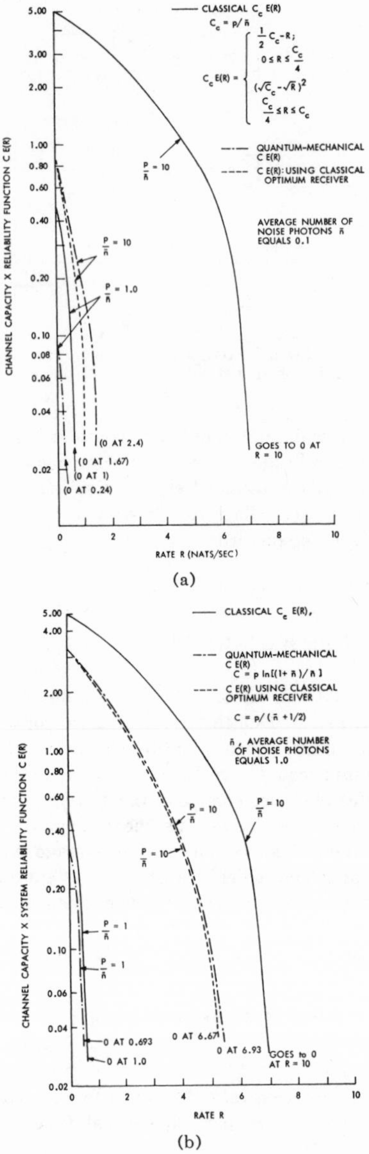


Fig. 7. System reliability function × channel capacity.

As $\bar{n}$ approaches 0, the right-hand side of this equation also approaches 0 as a limit for all $R$.

As a matter of fact, when the average number of noise photons $\bar{n}$ is equal to 0, the error probability becomes

$$P(\epsilon) = \exp(-\tau p).$$

That $P(\epsilon)$ is independent of the number $M$ of input symbols when $\bar{n}$ equals 0 implies that arbitrarily small probability of error can still be achieved at arbitrarily large information rate for the transmission of a fixed number $p$ of photons per second in the signal field. Since the signals are orthogonal, however, holding the average number of photons per second constant in the signal fields makes the average power in the signal field grow linearly with the number of input symbols $M$. Hence, the small error probability is achieved only by an accompanying increase in the power of the transmitted signal.

In practice, one usually holds the average (or peak) signal power fixed. Therefore, it is more meaningful to derive the system reliability functions under the assumption that the average energy in the signal fields is independent of the transmitted input symbols. That is,

$$|\sigma_i|^2\hbar\omega_i = E_i = E; \qquad j = 1, 2, \cdots, M.$$

Unfortunately, an analytical result cannot be obtained in this case.

## IV. Orthogonality Signals in Completely Incoherent States

We shall now find the structure and performance of an optimum receiver when the signal field at the receiver is also in completely incoherent states. Let us again expand the electric-field operator in terms of its Fourier components and plane-wave mode functions as in (8). When the transmitted input symbol is $m_i$, the received field in the presence of a thermal radiation field of the type described by the density operator $\rho^{(n)}$ in (12) is in a state specified by the density operator

$$\rho_i = |\det K_i|^{-1} \int \cdots \int \exp\,[-\sum_m \sum_n \alpha_m^*[K_i]_{mn}^{-1}\alpha_n] \cdot \prod_m |\alpha_m\rangle\langle\alpha_m|\, d^2\alpha_m/\pi. \tag{29}$$

In this expression, $K_i$ is the mode-correlation matrix whose elements are

$$[K_i]_{mn} = \mathrm{Tr}\,[\rho_i \mathfrak{a}_m^+ \mathfrak{a}_n].$$

Since the signal source and the noise source are independent, $[K_i]_{mn}$ are given by

$$[K_i]_{mn} = [K_i^{(t)}]_{mn} + \bar{n}\delta_{mn}, \qquad \text{for all } m \text{ and } n, \tag{30}$$

where the $[K_i^{(t)}]_{mn}$ are elements of the mode-correlation matrices when no noise is present. At thermal equilibrium, when the mode-correlation matrix $K_i$ is diagonal, the element $[K_i]_{kk}$ is equal to the average number of photons in the $k$th mode of the received field passing through the receiving aperture in a signaling interval.

The mode-correlation matrices $K_1, K_2, \cdots, K_M$ commute when the signals are orthogonal. The commutativity of these matrices implies the existence of a unitary transformation matrix $V$ such that the matrices

$$R_i = V^+K_iV, \qquad j = 1, 2, \cdots, M,$$

are diagonalized. When the elements of the $K_i$ are given by (30), the $(kk)$ element of the matrix $R_i$ can be written

$$[R_i]_{kk} = \bar{n} + s_{ik}, \tag{31}$$

where

$$s_{ik} = [V^+K_i^{(t)}V]_{kk}. \tag{32}$$

In the following discussions, we shall consider only frequency-orthogonal signals. In this case, the elements $V_{kn}$ of the matrix $V$ also satisfy the condition given by (11). Let $|\beta_k\rangle$ be the right eigenstate of the operator

$$b_k = \sum_n V_{kn}\mathfrak{a}_n. \tag{33}$$

Let us assume that only $J$ modes are excited by the signal source in any given signaling-time interval.[10] When the input symbol $m_i$ is transmitted, the excited $J$ modes are those whose annihilation operators are $b_{(j-1)\Delta+1}, b_{(j-1)\Delta+2}, \cdots, b_{(j-1)\Delta+J}$ where $\Delta$ is an integer larger than $J$. For the sake of clarity, let us denote by $b_{ik}$ and $|\beta_{ik}\rangle$ the operator $b_{(j-1)\Delta+k}$ and the coherent state $|\beta_{(j-1)\Delta+k}\rangle$, respectively. When the electric-field operator is expanded in terms of $b_{jk}$ and $b_{jk}^+$, the density operator $\rho_i$ specifying the states of relevant modes of the received field can be written

$$\rho_i = \left\{\int \exp\left[-\sum_{k=1}^{J} \frac{|\beta_{ik}|^2}{\bar{n} + s_{ik}}\right] \prod_{k=1}^{J} |\beta_{ik}\rangle\langle\beta_{ik}|\, \frac{d^2\beta_{ik}}{\pi(\bar{n} + s_{ik})}\right\} \cdot \left\{\int \exp\left[-\sum_{\substack{j'\neq j\\ j'=1}}^{M} \sum_{k=1}^{J} \frac{|\beta_{j'k}|^2}{\bar{n}}\right] \prod_{k=1}^{J} \prod_{\substack{j'\neq j\\ j'=1}}^{M} |\beta_{j'k}\rangle\langle\beta_{j'k}|\, \frac{d^2\beta_{j'k}}{\pi\bar{n}}\right\}. \tag{34}$$

That is, the received field in the absence of noise is in the state specified by

$$\rho_i^{(t)} = \left\{\int \exp\left[-\sum_{k=1}^{J} \frac{|\beta_{ik}|^2}{s_{ik}}\right] \prod_{k=1}^{J} |\beta_{ik}\rangle\langle\beta_{ik}|\, \frac{d^2\beta_{ik}}{\pi s_{ik}}\right\} \cdot \left\{\int \prod_{\substack{j'\neq j\\ j'=1}}^{M} \prod_{k=1}^{J} \delta^{(2)}(\beta_{j'k})\, |\beta_{j'k}\rangle\langle\beta_{j'k}|\, d^2\beta_{j'k}\right\}. \tag{35}$$

*Corresponding Classical Communication System*

The type of signals characterized by the density operators $\rho_i^{(t)}$ in (35) can be generated by natural light sources, which can be considered as consisting of a very large number of independently radiating atoms. Such random and chaotic excitation is characteristic of all incoherent macroscopic sources, for example, gas discharges, incandescent radiators, etc. The density operators $\rho_i^{(t)}$ also describe the state of the received field, in the absence of an additive noise field, in a Rayleigh fading channel.

When the transmitted input symbol is $m_i$, the transmitted electric field has a classical waveform in a frequency-position modulation system

$$\epsilon_{ci}^{(t)}(r, t) = \mathrm{Re}\left\{S_i v_{i1}(r, t) \exp\left[-i\omega_i\left(\frac{z}{c} - t\right)\right]\right\}; \qquad j = 1, 2, \cdots, M, \tag{36}$$

[10] It will become evident that there is no loss of generality in making this assumption.

where $\omega_j = 2\pi[k_0 + (j - 1)\Delta]/\tau$ for some integer $k_0$, and the complex envelopes $v_{j1}(r, t)$ constitute a set of orthonormal waveforms. The waveform of the received electric field in the absence of additive noise is

$$\epsilon_{cj}(r, t) = \text{Re}\left\{xS_j v_{j1}(r, t) \exp\left[-i\omega_j\left(\frac{z}{c} - t\right) - i\phi\right]\right\}, \quad (37)$$

where $x$ is a Rayleigh-distributed random variable, and $\phi$ is uniformly distributed over the interval $(0, 2\pi)$. Here, we have assumed that $x$ and $\phi$ vary so slowly that they can be regarded as constants over a signaling-time interval. Similarly, they are considered as constants in space over the beamwidth. In the quantum-mechanical limit, the state of the received field in the absence of an additive noise field is specified by the density operator $\rho_j^{(t)}$ in (35) with $J = 1$. The annihilation operator of the normal mode is $b_{j1}$, with mode function $v_{j1}(r, t)$.

It has been shown [18], [19] that the error probability in transmitting one of $M$ equally likely orthogonal signals over a Rayleigh fading channel can be reduced by circumventing the high probability of a deep fade on a single transmission by means of diversity transmissions. In a diversity system, several transmissions are made for each input symbol. These transmissions are spaced either in time, space, or frequency in such a way that the fadings experienced by each transmission are statistically independent.

Without loss of generality, we shall confine our discussion to frequency-diversity systems. Let $J$ denote the number of diversity transmissions. In the absence of additive noise, the transmitted waveform and the received waveform are, respectively,

$$\epsilon_{cj}^{(t)}(r, t) = \text{Re}\left\{\sum_{k=1}^{J} s'_{jk} v_{jk}(r, t) \exp\left[-i\omega_j\left(\frac{z}{c} - t\right)\right]\right\}$$

$$\epsilon_{cj}(r, t) = \text{Re}\left\{\sum_{k=1}^{J} x_{jk} s'_{jk} v_{jk}(r, t) \exp\left[-i\omega_j\left(\frac{z}{c} - t\right) - i\phi_{jk}\right]\right\}$$

when $m_j$ is transmitted. The $x_{jk}$ and $\phi_{jk}$ are statistically independent Rayleigh distributed and uniformly distributed random variables, respectively. The narrow-band orthogonal functions $v_{jk}(r, t)$ are such that the frequency spectra of $v_{jk}(r, t) \exp[-i\omega_j t]$ are disjoint for different $j$ and $k$. In the quantum-mechanical limit, the relevant modes of the received field are in the state given by the density operator in (35) when no noise is present and $m_j$ is transmitted. Although in the discussion above our attention was confined to the classical diversity system, it is evident that the density operators in (35) also specify the states of received field in the more general fading dispersive channel, since a fading dispersive channel can be represented canonically as a classical diversity system [19].

*Optimum Receiver*

Let $\prod_{j=1}^{M}\prod_{k=1}^{J} \mid n_{jk}\rangle$ denote the simultaneous eigenstate of the operators $b_{11}^+b_{11}, b_{12}^+b_{12}, \cdots, b_{MJ}^+b_{MJ}$ corresponding to eigenvalues $n_{11}, n_{12}, \cdots, n_{MJ}$. In terms of these eigenstates, the density operator $\rho_i$ can be expanded as

$$\rho_i = (1 - q_0)^{(M-1)J} \cdot \sum_{n_{11}=0}^{\infty} \sum_{n_{12}=0}^{\infty}, \cdots, \sum_{n_{MJ}=0}^{\infty} \prod_{k=1}^{J} \left\{\prod_{\substack{j'\neq j\\ j'=1}}^{M} q_0^{n_{j'k}}(1 - q_{jk})q_{jk}^{n_{jk}}\right\} \cdot \left\{\prod_{j=1}^{M} |n_{jk}\rangle\langle n_{jk}|\right\}.$$

where

$$q_{jk} = (\bar{n} + s_{jk})/(1 + \bar{n} + s_{jk}) \quad (38a)$$

$$q_0 = \bar{n}/(1 + \bar{n}). \quad (38b)$$

Therefore, according to Section II, the measurement made by the optimum receiver is characterized by the state vectors $\prod_{j=1}^{M} \mid n_{jk}\rangle$ for all nonnegative integer values of the $n_{jk}$. In other words, the optimum receiver measures simultaneously the dynamical variables $b_{11}^+b_{11}, b_{12}^+b_{12}, \cdots, b_{MJ}^+b_{MJ}$.

When the variables $b_{jk}^+b_{jk}$ are measured simultaneously, the probability distribution of the outcome being the $MJ$-tuple $\mathbf{n} = (n_{11}, n_{12}, \cdots, n_{1J}, \cdots, n_{MJ})$, providing the density operator of the received field is $\rho_j$, is

$$P(\mathbf{n} \mid m_j) = (1 - q_0)^{(M-1)J} \prod_{k=1}^{J} \left\{\prod_{\substack{j'\neq j\\ j'=1}}^{M} q_0^{n_{j'k}}(1 - q_{jk})q_{jk}^{n_{jk}}\right\}. \quad (39)$$

It is clear that the value of $j$, which maximizes $P(\mathbf{n} \mid m_j)$, also maximizes the quantity

$$f_j = \sum_{k=1}^{J}\left\{n_{jk} \ln\left(\frac{q_{jk}}{q_0}\right) + \ln(1 - q_{jk})\right\}. \quad (40)$$

Hence the optimum receiver needs only to evaluate the quantities $f_j$. The transmitted input symbol is estimated as $m_j$ if

$$f_j \geq f_i; \quad i \neq j, i, j = 1, 2, \cdots, M.$$

Unfortunately, it is difficult to evaluate the performance of such a system. We shall consider the case in which the numbers of signal photons $s_{jk}$ are equal, i.e.,

$$s_{jk} \equiv s, j = 1, 2, \cdots, M; \quad k = 1, 2, \cdots. \quad (41)$$

For the narrow-band signals considered here, (41) also implies that the energies in all of the $J$ modes ($J$ diversity paths) of the signal field are equal, as in equal-strength diversity systems. It has been shown [19] classically that the system performance is optimized when the energies in the diversity paths are equal. Here we shall not try to prove the optimality of the equal-strength diversity system. For this special case, the structure of the optimum receiver simplifies to that shown in Fig. 8.

*Performance of the Optimum Receiver*

Just as in Section III, the bounds of the error probability $P(\epsilon)$ will be expressed as

$$K_1 \exp[-\tau CE(R)] \leq P(\epsilon) \leq K_2 \exp[-\tau CE(R)].$$

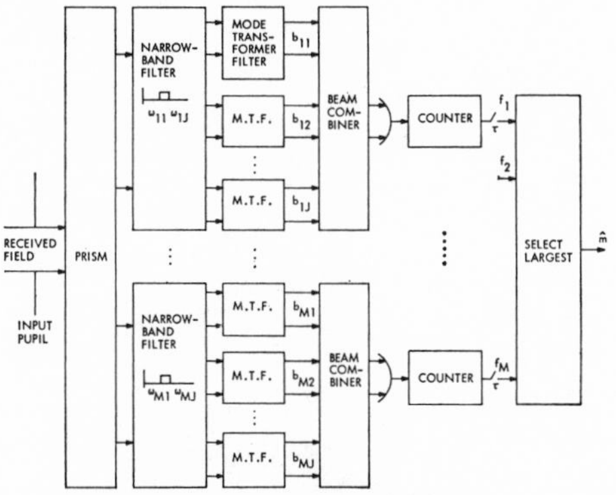


Fig. 8. Optimum receiver for equal-strength orthogonal signals in completely incoherent states.

The quantity $C$ given by (25) is the capacity of the system in which signals are in coherent states with $p = S/\tau$. In this expression, $S$ is the total number of photons transmitted through $J$ diversity paths,

$$S = Js. \tag{42}$$

Our attention will again be focused upon the reliability function $E(R)$, which can be used to characterize the system, since coefficients $K_1$ and $K_2$ are not exponential functions of $\tau$. The detailed derivation of $E(R)$, which is too lengthy to be included here, can be found in [11].

Let

$$q_s = (\bar{n} + s)/(1 + \bar{n} + s) \tag{43}$$

For $0 \leq R \leq R_c$, where

$$\frac{R_c}{C} = \frac{J}{\tau}\{\ln[1 - (q_0 q_s)^{1/2}] - \ln(1 - q_0) + \{(q_0 q_s)^{1/2}/2[1 - (q_0 q_s)^{1/2}]\}\ln(q_s/q_0)\}, \tag{44a}$$

the reliability function $E(R)$ is given by

$$E(R) = \frac{2J}{\tau C}\{\ln[1 - (q_0 q_s)^{1/2}] - \tfrac{1}{2}\ln[(1 - q_0)(1 - q_s)]\} - \frac{R}{C}. \tag{44b}$$

For rates $R$ in the range $(R_c, C_g)$, where

$$C_g = \frac{J}{\tau}\left[(s + \bar{n})\ln\left(1 + \frac{s}{\bar{n}}\right) - (1 + \bar{n} + s)\ln\left(1 + \frac{s}{1 + \bar{n}}\right)\right], \tag{45}$$

the reliability function $E(R)$ satisfies the parametric equation

$$\frac{R}{C} = \frac{J}{C\tau}\left\{[S + \ln(q_s/q_0)]\frac{q_s e^S}{1 - q_s e^S} - \ln\frac{1 - q_0}{1 - q_s e^S}\right\} \tag{46a}$$

$$E(R) = \frac{J}{C\tau}\{Sq_s e^S/(1 - q_s e^S) + \ln[(1 - q_s e^S)/(1 - q_s)]\}. \tag{46b}$$

Alternatively, the reliability function is the solution to the following maximization problem:

$$E(R) = \max_{0 \leq \delta \leq 1}\{e_0(\delta) - \delta R/C\} \tag{47a}$$

$$e_0(\delta) = \frac{J(1 + \delta)}{C\tau}\ln\{1 - q_s(q_0/q_s)^{\delta/1+\delta}\} - \frac{\delta J}{C\tau}\ln(1 - q_0) - \frac{J}{C\tau}\ln(1 - q_s). \tag{47b}$$

It can be shown [11] from (47) that in the limit of large $\bar{n}$ (the classical limit) the reliability function of the system becomes

$$E(R) = \max_{0 \leq \delta \leq 1}\frac{\bar{n}}{S}\left\{J(1 + \delta)\ln\left(1 + \frac{\delta}{1 + \delta}\frac{S}{\bar{n}J}\right) - J\delta\ln\left(1 + \frac{S}{J\bar{n}}\right) - \delta R\right\}. \tag{48}$$

Equation (48) is just the reliability function for a classical fading channel when the number of equal-strength diversity paths is $J$[19].

As in the case of coherent signals discussed in Section III, the reliability function depends not only on the signal-to-noise ratio $S/\bar{n}$, but also on the average noise level $\bar{n}$ and the number of diversity paths $J$. The optimum reliability function $E^0(R)$ is obtained by maximizing the function $E(R)$ in (47) with respect to $J$ or, alternatively, with respect to $s$. That is,

$$E^0(R) = \max_{s \geq 0}[\max_{0 \leq \delta \leq 1}\{e_0(\delta) - \delta R/C\}].$$

The function $e_0(\delta)$ given by (47b) can be written in terms of $s$ and $\delta$.

$$e_0(\delta, s) = \left[s\ln\left(\frac{1 + \bar{n}}{\bar{n}}\right)\right]^{-1} \cdot\left\{-\delta\ln[1 + s/(1 + \bar{n})] + (1 + \delta)\ln \cdot\left\{1 + (\bar{n} + s)\left[1 - \left(\frac{\bar{n}}{1 + \bar{n}}\frac{1 + \bar{n} + s}{s + \bar{n}}\right)^{\delta/1+\delta}\right]\right\}\right\}. \tag{49}$$

Let $s^0$ denote the value of $s$ that maximizes the function $e_0(\delta)$. Then

$$E^0(R) = \max_{0 \leq \delta \leq 1}[e_0(\delta, s^0) - \delta R/C] \tag{50a}$$

if the value of $s^0$ does not exceed $S$. When $s^0$ is larger than $S$, we have

$$E^0(R) = \max_{0 \leq \delta \leq 1}[e_0(\delta, S) - \delta R/C]. \tag{50b}$$

The values of $E^0$ and $s^0$ as functions of $R/C$ and $\bar{n}$ have been determined numerically [11]. The results are shown in Fig. 9, where the optimum average number $s^0$ of signal photons per diversity path is plotted as a function of $R/C$ for $\bar{n} = 0.1$, and $\bar{n} = 10$. Also shown in Fig. 9 is the value of $s^0$ in the classical limit [19]. The values of $s^0/\bar{n}$ for rates $R$ less than $R_c^0$ are independent of $R/C$, but they are functions of the noise level $\bar{n}$. It is interesting to note that if the effective noise in the system is taken to be $(\bar{n} + \frac{1}{2})$, the optimum ratio $s^0/(\bar{n} + \frac{1}{2})$ is roughly 3 for $R \leq R_c^0$ independently of the value of $\bar{n}$.

For rates greater than $R_c^0$, the value of $s^0$ increases rapidly with $R/C$. That is, for a fixed value of $S$, the optimum number of equal-strength diversity paths decreases at higher information rates. From Fig. 9, it is clear that for increasing $R/C$, $s^0$ increases without bound. Hence, when the average number of transmitted photons is fixed at $S$, a point where the value of $s^0$ is equal to $S$ will eventually be reached, i.e., the optimum value of $J$ is equal to 1. The rate at which $S = s^0$ is called the threshold rate for the given value of $S$.

Let us assume for the moment that, for any given value of $R/C$, $S$ is so large that $S/s^0$ is larger than 1. For this limiting case, the general behavior of $E^0(R)$ is given by Fig. 10 for different thermal-noise levels. The reliability function for the optimum classical fading channel is also shown for comparison.

When the value of $S$ is finite and fixed, the threshold effects should be considered. At rates such that $S \geq s^0$, the optimum value of $J$ is equal to $S/s^0$. At rates such that $s^0 \geq S$, the optimum value of $J$ is equal to 1. Hence, for rates less than threshold rate, the optimum reliability function $E^0(R)$ is identical to that derived under the supposition that $S$ is extremely large. For rates greater than the threshold, the optimum value of $E$ as a function of $s$ is given by (50b).

ACKNOWLEDGMENT

The author is indebted to Prof. R. S. Kennedy for his guidance and suggestions. Thanks are also due to Profs. P. Elias and H. A. Haus, who have offered many helpful comments.

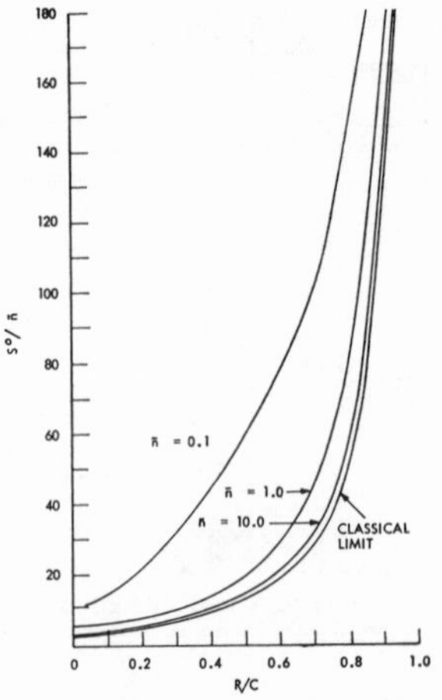


Fig. 9. Optimum average number of signal photons per diversity path/average number of thermal-noise photons versus $R/C$ (classical limit taken from [19] and $R_c^0/C \approx 0.04$).

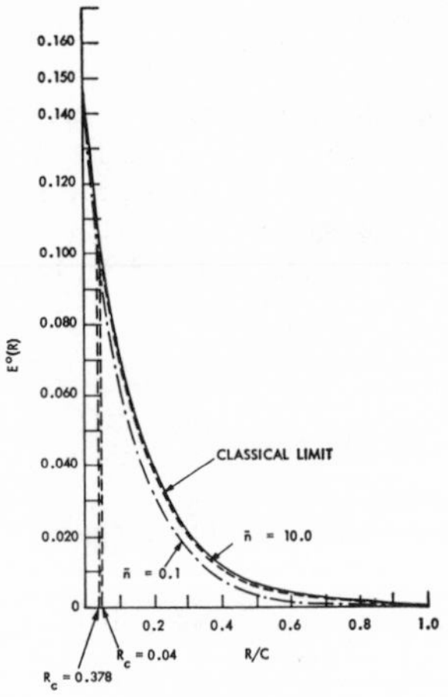


Fig. 10. Optimum system reliability function (classical limit taken from [19]).

REFERENCES

[1] T. E. Stern, "Some quantum effects in information channels," *IRE Trans. Information Theory*, vol. IT-6, pp. 435–440, September 1960.
[2] ——, "Information rates in photon channels and photon amplifiers," *IRE Internatl. Conv. Rec.*, pt. 4, pp. 182–188, 1963.
[3] J. P. Gordon, "Quantum effects in communications systems," *Proc. IRE*, vol. 50, pp. 1898–1908, September 1962.
[4] T. Hagfors, "Information capacity and quantum effects in propagation circuits," Lincoln Lab., M.I.T., Lexington, Mass., Tech. Rept. 344, January 24, 1964.
[5] C. Y. She, "Quantum electrodynamics of a communication channel," *IEEE Trans. Information Theory*, vol. IT-14, pp. 32–37, January 1968.
[6] C. W. Helstrom, "Quantum limitations on the detection of coherent and incoherent signals," *IEEE Trans. Information Theory*, vol. IT-11, pp. 482–490, October 1965.
[7] ——, "Detection theory and quantum mechanics," *Inform. Control*, vol. 10, pp. 254–291, March 1968.
[8] ——, "Detection theory and quantum mechanics (II)," *Inform. Control*, vol. 13, pp. 156–171, August 1968.
[9] ——, "Fundamental limitations on the detectability of electromagnetic signals," *Internatl. J. Theoret. Phys.*, vol. 1, pp. 37–50, 1968.
[10] J. P. Gordon and W. H. Louisell, "Simultaneous measurements of noncommuting observables," in *Physics of Quantum Electronics*, P. L. Kelley, B. Lax, and P. E. Tannenwald, Eds. New York: McGraw-Hill, 1966, pp. 833–840.
[11] J. W. S. Liu, "Reliability of quantum-mechanical communication systems," Res. Lab. of Electron., M.I.T., Cambridge, Mass., Tech. Rept. 468, December 31, 1968.
[12] P. A. M. Dirac, *The Principle of Quantum Mechanics*. London: Oxford University Press, 1958.
[13] R. J. Glauber, "Coherent and incoherent states of the radiation field," *Phys. Rev.*, vol. 131, pp. 2766–2788, 1963.
[14] H. L. Landau and H. O. Pollak, "Prolate spheroidal wave functions, Fourier analysis and uncertainty—III: The dimension of the space and essentially time- and band-limited signals," *Bell Sys. Tech. J.*, vol. 41, pp. 1295–1336, July 1962.
[15] R. J. Glauber, "Quantum optics and electronics, lecture notes, Session of the Summer School of Theoretical Physics, University of Grenoble, Les Houches, France, 1964.
[16] G. Lachs, "Theoretical aspects of mixtures of thermal and coherent radiation," *Phys. Rev.*, vol. 138B, pp. 1012–1016, May 1965.
[17] R. S. Kennedy, unpublished class notes, course 6.575, Massachusetts Institute of Technology, Cambridge, Mass., 1968.
[18] J. M. Wozencraft and I. M. Jacobs, *Principles of Communication Engineering*. New York: Wiley, 1965, pp. 533–550.
[19] R. S. Kennedy, *Performance Limitations of Fading Dispersive Channels*. New York: Wiley, 1969.

# 4



Reprinted from *IEEE Trans. Inf. Theory* **IT-14**(2):234–242 (1968)

# The Minimum Variance of Estimates in Quantum Signal Detection

CARL W. HELSTROM, SENIOR MEMBER, IEEE

***Abstract*—A quantum-mechanical form of the Cramér–Rao inequality is derived, setting a lower bound to the variance of an unbiased estimate of a parameter of a density operator. It is applied to the estimates of parameters such as amplitude, arrival time, and carrier frequency of a coherent signal as picked up by an ideal receiver in the presence of thermal noise. The estimation of parameters of a noise-like signal is also treated.**

## I. Signal Estimation and the Ideal Receiver

The ACCURACY with which signal parameters such as arrival time, frequency, and amplitude can be estimated in the presence of noise has been investigated by Slepian,[1] Swerling,[2] Bello,[3] Kelly,[4] and others. A typical result of the theory of estimation is the statement that the minimum variance of an unbiased estimate of the carrier frequency of a signal received in white Gaussian noise is inversely proportional to the signal-to-noise ratio and to the mean-square duration of the signal. The analysis is based on the classical assumptions that the input to the receiver, consisting of signal and noise, can be measured as precisely and in as fine a detail as necessary, and that it can be described by an array of probability density functions.

The advent of the laser and the development of optical communication and radar techniques raise the question how accurately can parameters of signals at optical frequencies be estimated. Such signals must be described quantum-mechanically, in terms, for instance, of photons; and it is known that quantum mechanics imposes certain limitations on the extent to which the electromagnetic field of the signal and noise can be measured. The probability density functions of conventional detection and estimation theory no longer apply, and an approach taking into account the laws of quantum mechanics must be sought.

To study the fundamental limitations on the estimation of signal parameters it is expedient to consider an ideal receiver that is as free as possible from special assumptions about how the signal and the noise are to be processed. Most receivers of optical signals admit the radiation through an aperture into a device in which it may be focused on to a photoelectric surface or a photographic plate, or be heterodyned with a locally generated coherent signal through some material nonlinearity. As the ideal receiver of an electromagnetic signal of very high frequency it is, therefore, natural to imagine a large box or cavity having lossless walls and initally empty. While the signal is arriving, an aperture is opened to admit it with the inevitably accompanying background radiation. After the signal has passed in, the aperture is closed, and the observer proceeds to make whatever measurements he can on the field within the cavity.

According to classical physics the observer can in principle measure the field as precisely as he wishes and in complete detail. Ordinary signal-detection and estimation theory presumes this ability and shows how the resulting data are best processed to detect a signal with minimum probability of a mistake or to estimate its parameters with the smallest possible average error. In the domain of quantum physics such a presumption is unwarranted, and it is necessary not only to inquire how the data should be processed, but in the first place to decide what measurements had best be made.

The field of the cavity after the aperture is closed will be found not in a pure quantum-mechanical state but, owing to the noise, in a mixture of states specified by a density operator[5] $\rho$. The density operator will differ when there is a signal present from what it is in the absence of the signal, and signal detection can be treated as a choice between two density operators $\rho_0$ and $\rho_1$ for the field.[6] The density operator replaces the joint probability density functions of the usual theory.

When a signal is known to be present, but depends on certain unknown parameters such as its amplitude $A$, its arrival time $\tau$, or its carrier frequency $\Omega$, these parameters will appear in the density operator $\rho$. Let us denote

Manuscript received March 26, 1967. This paper was presented at the 1967 International Symposium on Information Theory, San Remo, Italy. The research was performed at the Institute for Radiation Physics and Aerodynamics and was supported by the Advanced Research Projects Agency (Project DEFENDER) and was monitored by the US Army Research Office, Durham, N. C., under Contract DA-31-124-ARO-D-257.

The author is with the Department of Applied Electrophysics, University of California, at San Diego, La Jolla, Calif. 92037

[1] D. Slepian, "Estimation of signal parameters in the presence of noise," *IRE Trans. Information Theory*, vol. PGIT-3, pp. 68–89, March 1954.

[2] P. Swerling, "Parameter estimation for waveforms in additive Gaussian noise," *J. SIAM*, vol. 7, pp. 152–166, June 1959.

[3] P. Bello, "Joint estimation of delay, Doppler, and Doppler rate," *IRE Trans. Information Theory*, vol. IT-6, pp. 330–341, June 1960.

[4] E. J. Kelly, "The radar measurement of range, velocity, and acceleration," *IRE Trans. Military Electronics*, vol. MIL-6, pp. 51–57, April 1961.

[5] W. H. Louisell, *Radiation and Noise in Quantum Electronics*. New York: McGraw-Hill, 1964, ch. 6, pp. 220–252.

[6] C. W. Helstrom, "Detection theory and quantum mechanics," *Information and Control*, vol. 10, pp. 254–291, March 1967.

them by $\theta_1, \theta_2, \cdots, \theta_m$, which we collect into the vector $\boldsymbol{\theta}$ of a suitable parameter space. The density operator is a function $\rho(\boldsymbol{\theta})$ of the parameters.

Estimation of the parameters involves measuring certain dynamical variables $X_1, X_2, \cdots, X_m$ of the electromagnetic field, and dynamical variables in quantum mechanics are represented by operators. Each $X$ may be a function of a set of commuting operators that are measured simultaneously and combined in a fixed manner to form the estimate of the associated parameter $\theta$. One would like to employ such operators $X_1, \cdots, X_m$ as yield estimates $\hat{\theta}_1, \cdots, \hat{\theta}_m$ of the parameters that are as accurate as possible in some sense. Criteria of the goodness of estimators have been extensively treated in books on statistics, and there is no need to repeat the discussions here. In the main one wishes the estimates to be unbiased, and their mean-square errors should be as small as possible.

Classical statistics sets a limit to how small the variance of an unbiased estimate can be. It is given by the Cramér–Rao inequality,[7,8] which for estimation of a single parameter $\theta$ is

$$\operatorname{Var} \hat{\theta} \geq \left\{ \mathrm{E}\left[\frac{\partial}{\partial \theta} \ln p(\mathbf{x}; \theta)\right]^2 \right\}^{-1}, \tag{1}$$

where $p(\mathbf{x}; \theta)$ is the joint probability density function of the data $\mathbf{x} = (x_1, x_2, \cdots, x_n)$ on which the estimate is based, as a function of the unknown parameter $\theta$, and $\mathrm{E}$ denotes the statistical expectation. The lower limit can be attained only by such an estimator $\hat{\theta}$ that

$$\frac{\partial}{\partial \theta} \ln p(\mathbf{x}; \theta) = k(\theta)[\hat{\theta}(\mathbf{x}) - \theta], \tag{2}$$

where $k(\theta)$ depends on $\theta$, but not on the data $\mathbf{x}$. It is also necessary that $\hat{\theta}(\mathbf{x})$ be a sufficient statistic. Such an estimate, when it exists, is said to be "efficient." For joint estimates of a number of parameters, inequalities corresponding to (1) can be set down.[7,8]

The question arises whether estimates of the parameters of a density operator are subject to similar lower bounds on their variances, and in response a counterpart of the Cramér–Rao inequality will be derived. It will be applied to estimates of parameters of coherent and incoherent signals received in thermal noise.

## II. The Basic Inequality

### A. *The Derivation*

The density operator $\rho$ of a quantum-mechanical system depends on $m$ unknown parameters $\theta_1, \theta_2, \cdots, \theta_m$; $\rho = \rho(\boldsymbol{\theta})$. The estimate $\hat{\theta}_k$ of the $k$th parameter is defined as the outcome of a measurement of a dynamical variable $X_k$, represented quantum-mechanically by the operator $X_k$. The expected value of the outcome of the measurement is the trace $\operatorname{Tr} \rho X_k$; and if the estimate is unbiased,

$$\mathrm{E}(\hat{\theta}_k) = \operatorname{Tr} \rho X_k = \theta_k. \tag{3}$$

For the sake of efficiency we shall derive the counterpart of the Cramér–Rao inequality for an arbitrary number $m$ of estimates, specializing at the end to the estimation of a single parameter. We first differentiate (3) with respect to the parameter $\theta_n$

$$\delta_{nk} = \operatorname{Tr}\left(\frac{\partial \rho}{\partial \theta_n} X_k\right), \qquad k, n = 1, 2, \cdots, m. \tag{4}$$

The relation $\operatorname{Tr} \rho = 1$ yields upon differentiation $\operatorname{Tr}(\partial \rho / \partial \theta_n) = 0$, and

$$0 = \operatorname{Tr}\left(\frac{\partial \rho}{\partial \theta_n} \theta_k\right). \tag{5}$$

Subtracting (5) from (4), we obtain

$$\delta_{nk} = \operatorname{Tr}\left[\frac{\partial \rho}{\partial \theta_n}(X_k - \theta_k)\right] = \operatorname{Tr}\left(\frac{\partial \rho}{\partial \theta_n} X_k'\right),$$
$$X_k' = X_k - \theta_k. \tag{6}$$

We define a set of $m$ Hermitian operators $L_n$ as the solutions of the equations

$$\frac{\partial \rho}{\partial \theta_n} = \tfrac{1}{2}(\rho L_n + L_n \rho), \qquad n = 1, \cdots, m. \tag{7}$$

Here $L_n$ is the symmetrized logarithmic derivative (SLD) of the density operator with respect to the parameter $\theta_n$. For a parameter $\theta$ representing the strength of a signal in our ideal receiver, the SLD $L$ corresponds, in the limit $\theta \rightarrow 0$, to the threshold detection operator defined previously.[9] We can now write (6) as

$$\delta_{nk} = \tfrac{1}{2} \operatorname{Tr}[(\rho L_n + L_n \rho) X_k']. \tag{8}$$

We introduce the row vectors

$$\tilde{\mathbf{Z}} = (z_1, z_2, \cdots, z_m), \qquad \tilde{\mathbf{Y}} = (y_1, y_2, \cdots, y_m),$$

whose components are real numbers; the corresponding column vectors are $\mathbf{Z}$ and $\mathbf{Y}$. We can combine the $m^2$ equations in (8) into one by writing

$$\sum_{n=1}^{m} \sum_{k=1}^{m} z_n \, \delta_{nk} y_k = \sum_{k=1}^{m} z_k y_k = \tilde{\mathbf{Z}}\mathbf{Y}$$
$$= \tfrac{1}{2} \operatorname{Tr} \sum_{n=1}^{m} \sum_{k=1}^{m} z_n(\rho L_n + L_n \rho) X_k' y_k$$
$$= \tfrac{1}{2} \operatorname{Tr}(\rho \zeta \eta + \eta \zeta \rho) = \operatorname{Rl} \operatorname{Tr} \rho \zeta \eta, \tag{9}$$

where $\zeta$ and $\eta$ are the Hermitian operators

$$\zeta = \sum_{n=1}^{m} z_n L_n, \qquad \eta = \sum_{k=1}^{m} y_k X_k', \tag{10}$$

and 'Rl' stands for "the real part of."

For any two operators $P$ and $Q$ there exists the equivalent of the Schwarz inequality[10]

[7] C. R. Rao, "Information and the accuracy attainable in the estimation of statistical parameters," *Bull. Calcutta Math. Soc.*, vol. 37, pp. 81–91, 1945.

[8] H. Cramér, *Mathematical Methods of Statistics*. Princeton, N. J.: Princeton University Press, 1946, p. 473ff.

[9] C. W. Helstrom,[6] sec. 3.

[10] This inequality can be derived by observing that $\operatorname{Tr}[(P - \lambda Q)(P^+ - \lambda^* Q^+)] \geq 0$ and minimizing the left-hand side with respect to the complex variable $\lambda$.

$$|\mathrm{Tr}\, PQ^+|^2 \le \mathrm{Tr}\, PP^+ \,\mathrm{Tr}\, QQ^+, \tag{11}$$

where $P^+ = \tilde{P}^*$ is the conjugate transpose of $P$, and $Q^+ = \tilde{Q}^*$. Equality obtains if and only if $P = cQ$ for some constant $c$. Applying (11) to (9) with $P = \rho^{1/2}\zeta$, $Q = \rho^{1/2}\eta$, we get

$$[\tilde{\mathbf{Z}}\mathbf{Y}]^2 = [\mathrm{Rl}\,\mathrm{Tr}\,\rho\zeta\eta]^2 \le |\mathrm{Tr}\,\rho\zeta\eta|^2 = |\mathrm{Tr}\,\rho^{1/2}\zeta\eta\rho^{1/2}|^2$$
$$\le \mathrm{Tr}\,\rho^{1/2}\zeta\zeta\rho^{1/2}\,\mathrm{Tr}\,\rho^{1/2}\eta\eta\rho^{1/2} = \mathrm{Tr}\,\rho\zeta^2\,\mathrm{Tr}\,\rho\eta^2,$$

since the operators are Hermitian. Hence,

$$\mathrm{Tr}\,\rho\eta^2 = \tilde{\mathbf{Y}}\mathbf{B}\mathbf{Y} \ge [\tilde{\mathbf{Z}}\mathbf{Y}]^2/\mathrm{Tr}\,\rho\zeta^2 = [\tilde{\mathbf{Z}}\mathbf{Y}]^2/\tilde{\mathbf{Z}}\mathbf{A}\mathbf{Z}, \tag{12}$$

where $\mathbf{A}$ and $\mathbf{B}$ are matrices whose elements are

$$A_{ij} = \tfrac{1}{2}\,\mathrm{Tr}\,\rho(L_iL_j + L_jL_i) = \mathrm{Tr}\,(\partial\rho/\partial\theta_i)L_j, \tag{13}$$

$$B_{ij} = \tfrac{1}{2}\,\mathrm{Tr}\,\rho(X_i'X_j' + X_j'X_i'), \tag{14}$$

the reality of the components of $\mathbf{Y}$ and $\mathbf{Z}$ having permitted the symmetrization.

*B. Estimation of a Single Parameter*

For an estimate $\hat{\theta}$ of a single parameter $\theta$ the quadratic forms in (12) each contain a single term, and we immediately find the inequality

$$\mathrm{Var}\,\hat{\theta} = \mathrm{Tr}\,\rho(X - \theta)^2$$
$$\ge [\mathrm{Tr}\,\rho L^2]^{-1} = \left[\mathrm{Tr}\left(\frac{\partial\rho}{\partial\theta}L\right)\right]^{-1}, \tag{15}$$

where the SLD $L$ is defined by

$$2\frac{\partial\rho}{\partial\theta} = \rho L + L\rho. \tag{16}$$

The variance of an unbiased estimate of $\theta$ is at least as great as the right-hand side of (15).

Equality obtains in (15) if and only if the SLD $L$ is proportional to $X - \theta$,

$$L = k(\theta)(X - \theta), \tag{17}$$

where $k(\theta)$ may be a function of the parameter $\theta$, but not of the operator $X$. Such an operator $X$ may be said to provide an efficient estimate of $\theta$; some examples will appear in the next section.

*C. Estimation of Multiple Parameters*

If the estimators $X_k$ are commuting operators, the measurements of the $X_k$ can be performed on a single system, simultaneously or consecutively. The matrix element $B_{ij}$ in (14) can then be identified with the covariance of the estimates $\hat{\theta}_i$ and $\hat{\theta}_j$ in the usual statistical sense,

$$B_{ij} = \mathrm{cov}\,(\hat{\theta}_i, \hat{\theta}_j)$$
$$= \iint (\hat{\theta}_i - \theta_i)(\hat{\theta}_j - \theta_j)p(\hat{\theta}_i, \hat{\theta}_j)\,d\hat{\theta}_i\,d\hat{\theta}_j, \tag{18}$$

where $p(\hat{\theta}_i, \hat{\theta}_j)$ is the joint probability density function (PDF) of the estimates.

If we write (12) as

$$\tilde{\mathbf{Z}}\mathbf{A}\mathbf{Z} \ge (\tilde{\mathbf{Z}}\mathbf{Y})^2/\tilde{\mathbf{Y}}\mathbf{B}\mathbf{Y}$$

and, to obtain the most effective bound, maximize the right-hand side with respect to the components of $\mathbf{Y}$, we find by the Schwarz inequality

$$\frac{(\tilde{\mathbf{Z}}\mathbf{Y})^2}{\tilde{\mathbf{Y}}\mathbf{B}\mathbf{Y}} = \frac{(\tilde{\mathbf{Z}}\mathbf{B}^{-1/2}\mathbf{B}^{1/2}\mathbf{Y})^2}{\tilde{\mathbf{Y}}\mathbf{B}\mathbf{Y}} \le \tilde{\mathbf{Z}}\mathbf{B}^{-1}\mathbf{Z},$$

and hence

$$\tilde{\mathbf{Z}}\mathbf{B}^{-1}\mathbf{Z} \le \tilde{\mathbf{Z}}\mathbf{A}\mathbf{Z}. \tag{19}$$

The equation $\tilde{\mathbf{Z}}\mathbf{B}^{-1}\mathbf{Z} = m + 2$ defines the "concentration ellipsoid"[11] of the estimates $\hat{\theta}_j$, and (19) shows that it lies outside the ellipsoid $\tilde{\mathbf{Z}}\mathbf{A}\mathbf{Z} = m + 2$, whose matrix $\mathbf{A}$ is given by (13). The concentration ellipsoid is most readily visualized by pretending that the estimates $\hat{\theta}_j$ are Gaussian random variables. Then the ellipsoid

$$\sum_{i=1}^{m}\sum_{j=1}^{m}(\hat{\theta}_i - \theta_i)(\mathbf{B}^{-1})_{ij}(\hat{\theta}_j - \theta_j) = K$$

for arbitrary positive $K$, defines a contour surface of constant joint probability density, and the smaller this ellipsoid, the more "peaked" is the PDF $p(\hat{\boldsymbol{\theta}})$ at its center. The inequality (19) states that this contour surface lies outside the ellipsoid

$$\sum_{i=1}^{m}\sum_{j=1}^{m}(\hat{\theta}_i - \theta_i)A_{ij}(\hat{\theta}_j - \theta_j) = K,$$

which limits the concentration of the joint probability density function $p(\hat{\boldsymbol{\theta}})$ of the estimates about the point $\hat{\boldsymbol{\theta}}$ representing their expected values.

Alternatively, one can pick the vector $\mathbf{Z}$ in (12) to maximize the right-hand side, and one finds the inequality.

$$\tilde{\mathbf{Y}}\mathbf{B}\mathbf{Y} \ge \tilde{\mathbf{Y}}\mathbf{A}^{-1}\mathbf{Y}. \tag{20}$$

The choice of special values of the components of $\mathbf{Y}$ furnishes a lower bound to a particular element or combination of elements of the covariance matrix $\mathbf{B}$.

The operators $X_k$ have been left unspecified beyond the assumption (3) that they are unbiased. If a pair, say $X_1$ and $X_2$, do not commute, it is difficult in the framework of quantum mechanics to give a meaning to the quantity

$$B_{12} = \tfrac{1}{2}\,\mathrm{Tr}\,\rho(X_1'X_2' + X_2'X_1').$$

Margenau and Hill[12] show that an interpretation of $B_{12}$ as a covariance in the sense of (18) leads in certain cases to negative joint probabilities $p(\hat{\theta}_1, \hat{\theta}_2)$.

The diagonal elements of the matrix $\mathbf{B}$ retain their validity as variances

$$B_{jj} = \mathrm{Var}\,\hat{\theta}_j = \mathrm{Tr}\,\rho(X_j - \theta_j)^2,$$

[11] L. Schmetterer, *Mathematische Statistik*. New York: Springer-Verlag, 1966, p. 63.

[12] H. Margenau and R. N. Hill, "Corelation between measurements in quantum theory," *Progr. Theoret. Phys.* (Kyoto), vol. 26, pp. 722–738, November 1961.

but it is necessary to assume, when the operators $X_i$ do not commute, that the measurements of their associated dynamical variables are made on separate systems, all prepared in such a way that the same density operator pertains.

The nonvanishing of off-diagonal elements $B_{ij}$, $i \neq j$, is not necessarily related to noncommutativity of the operators $X_i$, $X_j$. We shall see an example in which two operators $X_1$, $X_2$ yielding efficient estimates do not commute, yet the cross-term $B_{12}$ vanishes. The cross-term may, on the other hand, not vanish in a case where the operators remain unspecified and are hence not necessarily noncommutative, as with the measurement of arrival time and frequency of a coherent signal.

## III. Single-Mode Estimation

### A. Incoherent Signals

To find simple applications of the inequality (15) let us consider an ideal receiver whose cavity has only a single mode of its electromagnetic field coupled with the external field when the aperture is open. The mode can be represented as a simple harmonic oscillator whose energy levels are integral multiples of $\hbar\omega$, where $\hbar$ is Planck's constant $h/2\pi$ and $\omega$ is the angular frequency of the mode.[13]

In thermal equilibrium at absolute temperature $T$ the density operator of such a mode is[14]

$$\rho = (1 - e^{-w}) \exp(-wa^+a), \qquad w = \hbar\omega/KT, \tag{21}$$

where $K$ is Boltzmann's constant, and $a$ and $a^+$ are the annihilation and creation operators for the mode oscillator. These operators do not commute,

$$aa^+ - a^+a = 1.$$

The operator $n = a^+a$ is called the "number operator"; its eigenvalues are the numbers of photons in the energy eigenstates of the oscillator. The mean number $N$ of photons in the mode is given by the Planck formula[15]

$$N = \mathbf{E}(n) = \mathrm{Tr}\, \rho a^+a = (e^w - 1)^{-1}, \tag{22}$$

and it is a parameter of the density operator $\rho = \rho(N)$.

Estimating the mean number $N$ is equivalent, for instance, to measuring the temperature of the cavity. If the receiver has picked up an incoherent signal with the same characteristics as thermal noise, the mean number $N$ will equal $N_0 + N_s$, where $N_0 = (e^w - 1)^{-1}$ is the average number of photons due to the noise and $N_s$ is the average number contributed by the signal. Estimating $N$ is then tantamount to measuring the strength of the signal if $N_0$ is known.

Letting the parameter $\theta$ stand for the mean number $N$, we find, by differentiating (21) and using (22),

$$\partial\rho/\partial N = [N(N + 1)]^{-1}(a^+a - N), \tag{23}$$

and the SLD of $\rho$ with respect to $N$ is

$$L = [N(N + 1)]^{-1}(a^+a - N), \tag{24}$$

which happens to commute with $\rho$. From (15) we find that for any unbiased estimate $\hat{N}$ of the mean number $N$,

$$\mathrm{Var}\, \hat{N} \geq [N(N + 1)]^2[\mathrm{Tr}\, \rho(a^+a - N)^2]^{-1} = N(N + 1). \tag{25}$$

The trace here is most easily evaluated in the diagonal representation of $\rho$

$$\rho = \sum_{k=0}^{\infty} |k\rangle P_k \langle k|, \qquad P_k = (1 - e^{-w})e^{-kw}, \tag{26}$$

where $|k\rangle$ is the eigenvector ("ket") corresponding to a state with exactly $k$ photons.[16] Thus

$$\mathrm{Tr}\, \rho(a^+a - N)^2 = \sum_{k=0}^{\infty} (k - N)^2 P_k = N^2 + N.$$

The SLD $L$ is here proportional to the operator $(n - N)$, and $n = a^+a$ is an unbiased linear estimator of $N$ actually attaining the minimum variance $N(N + 1)$.

### B. Coherent Signals

If the mode of the field in the receiver contains a coherent signal superimposed on thermal noise, the density operator $\rho$ is[17]

$$\rho = (1 - e^{-w}) \exp[-w(a^+ - A\mu^*)(a - A\mu)], \tag{27}$$

where $A$ is a real quantity specifying the amplitude of the signal, and $\mu$ is a complex phase factor, $|\mu| = 1$. The average number of signal photons in the mode equals $A^2$, and $E = \hbar\omega A^2$ equals the energy of the signal,

$$\mathrm{Tr}\, \rho a^+a = N + A^2, \qquad N = (e^w - 1)^{-1}. \tag{28}$$

We first analyze the estimation of the signal amplitude $A$.

As shown in the Appendix, the derivative of the density operator with respect to $A$ is

$$\partial\rho/\partial A = N^{-1}[\mu^*(a - A\mu)\rho + \rho\mu(a^+ - A\mu^*)]. \tag{29}$$

The SLD of $\rho$ with respect to $A$ is

$$L = (N + \tfrac{1}{2})^{-1}[\mu(a^+ - A\mu^*) + \mu^*(a - A\mu)], \tag{30}$$

for substitution of (30) into (7) and use of operational rules given by Louisell[18] lead to (29). Then

$$\mathrm{Tr}\left(\frac{\partial\rho}{\partial A} L\right) = 2(N + \tfrac{1}{2})^{-1},$$

and by (15)

$$\mathrm{Var}\, \hat{A} \geq \tfrac{1}{2}(N + \tfrac{1}{2}).$$

The relative variance of the estimate of amplitude is bounded by

[13] W. H. Louisell,[5] ch. 2, pt. 1, pp. 71–85.
[14] *Ibid.*, sec. 6.6, pp. 228–233.
[15] *Ibid.*, p. 231, p. 264.
[16] *Ibid.*, eq. (6.111), p. 243.
[17] *Ibid.*, eq. (6.128), p. 246.
[18] *Ibid.*, eq. (3.47), p. 111.

$$(\text{Var } \hat{A})/A^2 \geq (N + \tfrac{1}{2})/2A^2 = \tfrac{1}{2}\hbar\omega(N + \tfrac{1}{2})/E = d^{-2}, \quad (31)$$

where

$$d^2 = \frac{2E}{\hbar\omega(N + \frac{1}{2})} = \frac{4E}{\hbar\omega} \tanh (\hbar\omega/2KT). \quad (32)$$

The quantity $d^2$ is the signal-to-noise ratio for detecting a coherent signal of energy $E$ in the presence of thermal background radiation.[19] At low frequencies, $\hbar\omega \ll KT$, $d^2$ reduces to $2E/KT$, and (31) becomes equivalent to the result obtained by ordinary estimation theory.[20] For $\hbar\omega \gg KT$, $d^2 \doteq 4E/\hbar\omega$, and the accuracy of estimating the amplitude $A$ is limited by the random properties of the signal itself.

The operator $X = \frac{1}{2}(\mu a^+ + \mu^* a)$ is an unbiased and efficient estimator of the amplitude $A$, and the SLD is

$$L = 4(X - A)/(2N + 1)$$

which accords with (17). For this estimator (31) becomes an equality.

If one asks for estimates of the real and imaginary parts, $m_x$ and $m_y$, of the complex amplitude $A\mu = m_x + im_y$ of the signal, one finds by a similar calculation the SLDs

$$L_x = (N + \tfrac{1}{2})^{-1}(a^+ + a - 2m_x),$$
$$L_y = (N + \tfrac{1}{2})^{-1}i(a^+ - a + 2im_y)$$

and the elements of the matrix $\mathbf{A}$ in (13) are

$$A_{xx} = A_{yy} = \text{Tr } \rho L_x^2 = \text{Tr } \rho L_y^2 = 2(N + \tfrac{1}{2})^{-1}$$
$$A_{xy} = A_{yx} = \tfrac{1}{2} \text{Tr } \rho(L_xL_y + L_yL_x) = 0.$$

The matrix $\mathbf{A}^{-1}$ has the elements

$$(\mathbf{A}^{-1})_{xx} = (\mathbf{A}^{-1})_{yy} = \tfrac{1}{2}(N + \tfrac{1}{2}), \ (\mathbf{A}^{-1})_{xy} = 0,$$

which by (20) permit bounding the variances of estimates of $m_x$ and $m_y$. Efficient estimates of the parameters are provided by the operators

$$\hat{m}_x = \tfrac{1}{2}(a^+ + a), \qquad \hat{m}_y = (i/2)(a^+ - a).$$

Although these do not commute and must be measured on separate systems, the cross-term $A_{xy}$ vanishes.

To $m_x$ corresponds the oscillator coordinate $q = (2\hbar/\omega)^{1/2}m_x$, and to $m_y$ the conjugate momentum $p = (2\hbar\omega)^{1/2}m_y$. The minimum variances of their estimates are thus

$$\text{Var } \hat{q} \geq \hbar(N + \tfrac{1}{2})/\omega, \qquad \text{Var } \hat{p} \geq \hbar\omega(N + \tfrac{1}{2})$$

and

$$(\text{Var } \hat{q} \text{ Var } \hat{p})^{1/2} \geq \hbar(N + \tfrac{1}{2}),$$

which in the absence of background noise ($N = 0$) is similar to the uncertainty principle for a coherent state of the harmonic oscillator.[21]

## IV. Estimation of the Parameters of a Coherent Signal

A coherent signal is admitted along with background radiation into a receiver whose cavity is initially empty. After the aperture is closed, the parameters $\boldsymbol{\theta}$ of the signal are to be estimated on the basis of measurements of certain dynamical variables $X_j$. We wish to apply the basic inequality of Section II to determine lower bounds on the variances of such estimates.

The operator for the electric field at a point $\mathbf{r}$ in the cavity can be expressed in terms of the normal modes by[22]

$$\mathbf{E}(\mathbf{r}, t) = \mathbf{E}^{(+)}(\mathbf{r}, t) + \mathbf{E}^{(-)}(\mathbf{r}, t),$$
$$\mathbf{E}^{(-)}(\mathbf{r}, t) = [\mathbf{E}^{(+)}(\mathbf{r}, t)]^+, \quad (33)$$
$$\mathbf{E}^{(+)}(\mathbf{r}, t) = i \sum_{\mathbf{m}} (\tfrac{1}{2}\hbar\omega_{\mathbf{m}})^{1/2} a_{\mathbf{m}} \mathbf{u}_{\mathbf{m}}(\mathbf{r}) \exp(-i\omega_{\mathbf{m}}t),$$

where $\mathbf{u}_{\mathbf{m}}(\mathbf{r})$ is a mode eigenfunction with frequency $\omega_{\mathbf{m}}$, the solution of the vector Helmholtz equation with proper boundary conditions at the walls of the cavity. The mode functions are orthonormal over the volume of the cavity. The annihilation operator $a_{\mathbf{m}}$ for mode $\mathbf{m}$ and its conjugate, the creation operator $a_{\mathbf{m}}^+$, obey the standard commutation rules, and the operators for different modes commute. The operator $n_{\mathbf{m}} = a_{\mathbf{m}}^+ a_{\mathbf{m}}$ corresponds to the number of photons in mode $\mathbf{m}$.

The mode index $\mathbf{m}$ is, in general, a set of four numbers. For a rectilinear cavity, for instance, with periodic boundary conditions at the walls, the mode functions have the form[23]

$$\mathbf{u}_{\mathbf{m}}(\mathbf{r}) = V^{-1/2} \boldsymbol{\varepsilon}_\delta \exp[-i(m_1x + m_2y + m_3z)]$$
$$m_i = 2\pi n_i/L_i, \qquad i = 1, 2, 3; \quad \delta = 1, 2,$$

where $L_1$, $L_2$, $L_3$ are the lengths of the edges of the cavity, $V = L_1L_2L_3$ is its volume, $n_1$, $n_2$, $n_3$ are integers, and $\boldsymbol{\varepsilon}_1$, $\boldsymbol{\varepsilon}_2$ are unit vectors perpendicular to each other and to the propagation vector $(m_1, m_2, m_3)$. Here $\mathbf{m}$ can be taken as the quadruplet $(m_1, m_2, m_3, \delta)$, with $\delta$ specifying the polarization of the mode.

A coherent signal is defined as one creating in the receiver a field that, in the absence of noise, is coherent to all orders.[24] Such a field is a right-eigenstate of the positive-frequency part $\mathbf{E}^{(+)}(\mathbf{r}, t)$ of the electric field operator, and the associated eigenvalue is

$$\mathbf{E}_s^{(+)}(\mathbf{r}, t; \boldsymbol{\theta}) = i \sum_{\mathbf{m}} (\tfrac{1}{2}\hbar\omega_{\mathbf{m}})\mu_{\mathbf{m}}(\theta)\mathbf{u}_{\mathbf{m}}(\mathbf{r}) \exp(-i\omega_{\mathbf{m}}t), \quad (34)$$

[19] C. W. Helstrom, "Quantum limitations on the detection of coherent and incoherent signals," *IEEE Trans. Information Theory*, vol. IT-11, pp. 482–490, October 1965.

[20] C. W. Helstrom, *Statistical Theory of Signal Detection*. New York: Pergamon, 1960, p. 202.

[21] The "simultaneous measurement" of such variables in a single system has been treated by C. Y. She and H. Heffner, "Simultaneous measurement of noncommuting observables," *Phys. Rev.*, vol. 152, pp. 1103–1110, December 23, 1966.

[22] W. H. Louisell,[5] sec. 4.4, pp. 148–156.

[23] *Ibid.*, pp. 153–156.

[24] R. J. Glauber, "Coherent and incoherent states of the radiation field," *Phys. Rev.*, vol. 131, pp. 2766–2788, September 15, 1963.

where the c-number $\mu_{\mathbf{m}}(\boldsymbol{\theta})$ corresponds to the classical field amplitude and is so normalized that $|\mu_{\mathbf{m}}|^2$ is the expected number of signal photons in the mode $\mathbf{m}$. We have indicated the dependence of the field on the signal parameters $\boldsymbol{\theta}$, which might include the amplitude of the signal, its arrival time at the receiver, and its carrier frequency. Such a coherent field is the quantum-mechanical counterpart of a classical coherent signal, one that would be produced by a current distribution in, say, an antenna suffering no unpredictable reaction from the electromagnetic field. It may serve as a model of the field generated by an ideal laser oscillator.[25]

When such a coherent signal is superimposed on Gaussian noise, the field in the cavity is in a mixture of quantum-mechanical states described by a density operator that in Glauber's notation can be written as[24,26]

$$\rho(\boldsymbol{\theta}) = |\det \boldsymbol{\phi}|^{-1} \cdot \int \cdots \int \exp\left[-\sum_{\mathbf{k}}\sum_{\mathbf{m}} (\alpha_{\mathbf{k}}^* - \mu_{\mathbf{k}}^*)(\boldsymbol{\phi}^{-1})_{\mathbf{km}}(\alpha_{\mathbf{m}} - \mu_{\mathbf{m}})\right] \cdot \prod_{\mathbf{k}} |\alpha_{\mathbf{k}}\rangle\langle\alpha_{\mathbf{k}}| \, (d^2\alpha_{\mathbf{k}}/\pi) \qquad (35)$$

in terms of the mode correlation matrix $\boldsymbol{\phi}$, whose elements are

$$\phi_{\mathbf{km}} = \mathrm{Tr}\,[\rho(a_{\mathbf{m}}^+ - \mu_{\mathbf{m}}^*)(a_{\mathbf{k}} - \mu_{\mathbf{k}})]. \qquad (36)$$

The inverse of this matrix is $\boldsymbol{\phi}^{-1}$; its determinant is $\det \boldsymbol{\phi}$. In (35) $|\alpha_{\mathbf{m}}\rangle$ is the right-eigenket of the operator $a_{\mathbf{m}}$ with the eigenvalue $\alpha_{\mathbf{m}} = \alpha_{\mathbf{m}x} + i\alpha_{\mathbf{m}y}$; and $d^2\alpha_{\mathbf{m}} = d\alpha_{\mathbf{m}x}\, d\alpha_{\mathbf{m}y}$ is the element of integration in the complex plane, the integral being carried out over the entire plane.

For the purpose of working out the SLDs $L_i$ associated with the parameters $\theta_i$ and evaluating the elements $A_{ij}$ of the matrix in (13), we shall suppose the modes to have been chosen so that the matrix $\boldsymbol{\phi}$ is diagonal

$$\phi_{\mathbf{km}} = N_{\mathbf{m}}\, \delta_{\mathbf{km}}, \qquad (37)$$

where $N_{\mathbf{m}}$ is the average number of background photons in mode $\mathbf{m}$. This diagonalization can be effected at any time $t$ by a unitary transformation[27] of the mode operators $a_{\mathbf{k}}$. The calculation can be executed without this diagonalization, but the mathematics is more cumbersome. We therefore write the density operator as

$$\rho(\boldsymbol{\theta}) = \int \cdots \int \exp\left[-\sum_{\mathbf{k}} |\alpha_{\mathbf{k}} - \mu_{\mathbf{k}}(\boldsymbol{\theta})|^2/N_{\mathbf{k}}\right] \cdot \prod_{\mathbf{k}} |\alpha_{\mathbf{k}}\rangle\langle\alpha_{\mathbf{k}}| \, (d^2\alpha_{\mathbf{k}}/\pi N_{\mathbf{k}})$$

$$= \prod_{\mathbf{k}} [1 - \exp(-w_{\mathbf{k}})] \cdot \exp\{-w_{\mathbf{k}}[a_{\mathbf{k}}^+ - \mu_{\mathbf{k}}^*(\theta)][a_{\mathbf{k}} - \mu_{\mathbf{k}}(\boldsymbol{\theta})]\},$$

$$N_{\mathbf{k}} = (\exp w_{\mathbf{k}} - 1)^{-1}.$$

The derivative of $\rho(\boldsymbol{\theta})$ with respect to a parameter $\theta_i$ is obtained as in (29) and the Appendix,

$$\partial\rho/\partial\theta_i = \sum_{\mathbf{k}} N_{\mathbf{k}}^{-1}\left[\frac{\partial\mu_{\mathbf{k}}^*}{\partial\theta_i}(a_{\mathbf{k}} - \mu_{\mathbf{k}})\rho + \rho\frac{\partial\mu_{\mathbf{k}}}{\partial\theta_i}(a_{\mathbf{k}}^+ - \mu_{\mathbf{k}}^*)\right], \qquad (38)$$

and the SLD $L_i$ satisfying (7) is

$$L_i = \sum_{\mathbf{k}} (N_{\mathbf{k}} + \tfrac{1}{2})^{-1}\left[\frac{\partial\mu_{\mathbf{k}}^*}{\partial\theta_i}(a_{\mathbf{k}} - \mu_{\mathbf{k}}) + \frac{\partial\mu_{\mathbf{k}}}{\partial\theta_i}(a_{\mathbf{k}}^+ - \mu_{\mathbf{k}}^*)\right], \qquad (39)$$

which corresponds directly to (30) when $\theta_i$ is the amplitude of the signal and only a single mode is excited. From (38) and (39) we can then calculate the trace

$$A_{ij} = \mathrm{Tr}\left(\frac{\partial\rho}{\partial\theta_i} L_j\right) = 2\sum_{\mathbf{k}} (N_{\mathbf{k}} + \tfrac{1}{2})^{-1}\,\mathrm{Rl}\left(\frac{\partial\mu_{\mathbf{k}}^*}{\partial\theta_i}\frac{\partial\mu_{\mathbf{k}}}{\partial\theta_j}\right). \qquad (40)$$

Returning to the original set of modes, we obtain

$$A_{ij} = \mathrm{Tr}\left(\frac{\partial\rho}{\partial\theta_i} L_j\right) = 2\,\mathrm{Rl}\sum_{\mathbf{k},\mathbf{m}} \frac{\partial\mu_{\mathbf{k}}^*}{\partial\theta_i}[(\tfrac{1}{2}\mathbf{I} + \boldsymbol{\phi})^{-1}]_{\mathbf{km}}\frac{\partial\mu_{\mathbf{m}}}{\partial\theta_j}, \qquad (41)$$

where $\mathbf{I}$ is the identity matrix.

When, for example, the parameter $\theta$ is the amplitude $A$ of the signal, we can put $\mu_{\mathbf{k}} = A\bar{\mu}_{\mathbf{k}}$, where the $\bar{\mu}_{\mathbf{k}}$'s are fixed. Denoting by $\mathbf{M}$ the column vector of the $\bar{\mu}_{\mathbf{k}}$'s and by $\mathbf{M}^+$ its conjugate transpose row vector, we find for the SLD

$$L = \mathbf{M}^+(\tfrac{1}{2}\mathbf{I} + \boldsymbol{\phi})^{-1}(\boldsymbol{a} - A\mathbf{M}) + (\boldsymbol{a}^+ - A\mathbf{M}^+)(\tfrac{1}{2}\mathbf{I} + \boldsymbol{\phi})^{-1}\mathbf{M},$$

where $\boldsymbol{a}$ is the column vector of the $a_{\mathbf{k}}$'s. The variance of an estimate of the amplitude is bounded below by

$$\mathrm{Var}\,\hat{A} \geq A_{11}^{-1},$$
$$A_{11} = 2\mathbf{M}^+(\tfrac{1}{2}\mathbf{I} + \boldsymbol{\phi})^{-1}\mathbf{M},$$

and the minimum variance is attained by the efficient linear estimator

$$\hat{A} = A_{11}^{-1}[\mathbf{M}^+(\tfrac{1}{2}\mathbf{I} + \phi)^{-1}\boldsymbol{a} + \boldsymbol{a}^+(\tfrac{1}{2}\mathbf{I} + \phi)^{-1}\mathbf{M}]$$

in terms of which the SLD is

$$L = A_{11}(\hat{A} - A)$$

in accordance with (17).

The mode amplitudes $\mu_{\mathbf{k}}(\boldsymbol{\theta})$ and the mode correlation matrix $\boldsymbol{\phi}$ can be determined from the external field of the coherent signal and from the distributions of the background radiation impinging on the aperture. The calculation is a purely classical one and involves the coupling coefficients between the modes of the internal and external fields.[26,27] We shall suppose that the ap-

[25] R. J. Glauber, "Optical coherence and photon statistics," in *Quantum Optics and Electronics*, C. DeWitt *et al.* Eds. New York: Gordon and Breach, 1965, pp. 65–185.
[26] C. W. Helstrom,[6] sec. 4.
[27] C. W. Helstrom, "Quasi-classical analysis of coupled oscillators," *J. Math. Phys.*, vol. 8, pp. 37–42. January 1967.

erture of the cavity is open long enough for the thermal radiation inside it to have acquired the equilibrium distribution corresponding to an absolute temperature $T$. The mode correlation matrix is then diagonal, as in (37), and the average number $N_{\mathbf{k}}$ of photons in mode $\mathbf{k}$ is given by the Planck law

$$N_{\mathbf{k}} = (\exp w_{\mathbf{k}} - 1)^{-1}, \qquad w_{\mathbf{k}} = \hbar\omega_{\mathbf{k}}/KT. \tag{42}$$

A coherent signal ordinarily occupies a band of frequencies so narrow that $N_{\mathbf{k}}$ is the same for all the modes excited, and we can set $N_{\mathbf{k}}$ equal to $N = (e^{w} - 1)^{-1}$ with $w = \hbar\Omega/KT$, where $\Omega$ is the carrier frequency of the signal. Then the matrix element in (40) becomes

$$A_{ij} = 2(N + \tfrac{1}{2})^{-1}\mathrm{Rl} \sum_{\mathbf{k}} \frac{\partial\mu_{\mathbf{k}}^*}{\partial\theta_i}\frac{\partial\mu_{\mathbf{k}}}{\partial\theta_j}. \tag{43}$$

In particular, the variance of an estimate of a single parameter $\theta$ of the signal is bounded by

$$\mathrm{Var}\,\hat{\theta} \geq \tfrac{1}{2}(N + \tfrac{1}{2})[\sum_{\mathbf{k}} |\partial\mu_{\mathbf{k}}/\partial\theta|^2]^{-1}. \tag{44}$$

The energy of the signal in the cavity is

$$E_s = \sum_{\mathbf{k}} \hbar\omega_{\mathbf{k}} |\mu_{\mathbf{k}}|^2 \doteq \hbar\Omega \sum_{\mathbf{k}} |\mu_{\mathbf{k}}|^2, \tag{45}$$

so that

$$\mathrm{Var}\,\hat{\theta} \geq d^{-2} \sum_{\mathbf{k}} |\mu_{\mathbf{k}}|^2 / \sum_{\mathbf{k}} |\partial\mu_{\mathbf{k}}/\partial\theta|^2, \tag{46}$$

where

$$d^2 = \frac{2E_s}{\hbar\Omega(N + \frac{1}{2})} = \frac{4E_s}{\hbar\Omega}\tanh(\hbar\Omega/2KT) \tag{47}$$

is the signal-to-noise ratio for detecting the signal in thermal noise. When the parameter $\theta$ is the amplitude $A$ of the signal, we obtain the same result as in (31).

The lower bound in (46) has the same form as would result from applying the Cramér–Rao inequality to the estimate of a signal parameter $\theta$ in the presence of Gaussian noise within the realm of ordinary signal estimation theory, with the sole exception that the signal-to-noise ratio has the quantum-mechanical form in (47) in place of the classical $2E_s/KT$.

If we consider a plane-polarized narrowband signal moving in the $x$-direction through a rectilinear cavity, the amplitudes $\mu_{\mathbf{k}}$ will vanish except for those modes specified by the quadruplets $\mathbf{k} = (k, 0, 0, \delta)$ for, say, $\delta = 1$. For these modes $\mu_{\mathbf{k}}$ is proportional to the positive-frequency part $S_+(\omega_k)$ of the spectrum of the signal, $\omega_{\mathbf{k}} = kc$. The mode frequencies are separated by $\Delta\omega = c\Delta k = 2\pi c/L_1$; and if the cavity is large enough that summation over the mode indices can be approximated by integration over frequency $\omega$,

$$\sum_{\mathbf{k}} |\mu_{\mathbf{k}}|^2 = C \int_{-\infty}^{\infty} |S_+(\omega)|^2\, d\omega \tag{48}$$

for some constant $C$.

Let the parameter $\theta$ represent the carrier frequency $\Omega$ of the narrowband signal, which might be unknown because of relative motion between the transmitter and the receiver. The positive-frequency part of the spectrum of such a signal has the form

$$S_+(\omega) = f(\omega - \Omega),$$

and $\partial\mu_{\mathbf{k}}/\partial\Omega$ is proportional to the derivative $f'(\omega - \Omega)$. Thus the inequality in (46) becomes

$$\mathrm{Var}\,\hat{\Omega} \geq d^{-2} \int_{-\infty}^{\infty} |f(\omega)|^2\, d\omega \Big/ \int_{-\infty}^{\infty} |f'(\omega)|^2\, d\omega$$
$$= d^{-2}(\Delta t)^{-2},$$

where $\Delta t^2$ is the mean-square duration of the signal.[28]

In speaking of the arrival time $\tau$ of a signal, it is generally the complex envelope of the signal that is referred to. In the density operator $\rho = \rho(\tau, \Psi)$ the mode amplitudes of the signal have the form

$$\mu_{\mathbf{k}} = \bar{\mu}_{\mathbf{k}} \exp[i(\omega_{\mathbf{k}} - \Omega)\tau + i\Psi],$$

where $\bar{\mu}_{\mathbf{k}}$ is known and $\Psi$ is a common phase that is unknown but inconsequential. Now

$$\partial\mu_{\mathbf{k}}/\partial\tau = i(\omega_{\mathbf{k}} - \Omega)\mu_{\mathbf{k}} \propto (\omega_{\mathbf{k}} - \Omega)f(\omega_{\mathbf{k}} - \Omega).$$

With a fixed common phase $\Psi$, (46) gives for the variance of an estimate of the arrival time $\tau$ the lower bound

$$\mathrm{Var}\,\hat{\tau}$$
$$\geq d^{-2} \int_{-\infty}^{\infty} |f(\omega - \Omega)|^2\, d\omega \Big/ \int_{-\infty}^{\infty} (\omega - \Omega)^2 |f(\omega - \Omega)|^2\, d\omega$$
$$= d^{-2} \int_{-\infty}^{\infty} |f(\omega)|^2\, d\omega \Big/ \int_{-\infty}^{\infty} \omega^2 |f(\omega)|^2\, d\omega$$
$$= d^{-2}(\Delta\omega)^{-2}, \tag{50}$$

where $\Delta\omega^2$ is the mean-square bandwidth of the signal.[28] As the lower bound is independent of the phase $\Psi$, it must apply even when the phase is unknown.

If we let $\theta_1 = \tau$, $\theta_2 = \Omega$, the elements of the matrix $\mathbf{A}$ in (13) are found by the same reasoning to be given by

$$A_{11} = d^2\,\Delta\omega^2, \qquad A_{22} = d^2\,\Delta t^2, \qquad A_{12} = d^2\,\Delta(\omega t), \tag{51}$$

where

$$\Delta(\omega t) = \mathrm{Rl}\, i \int \omega f^*(\omega) f'(\omega)\, d\omega \Big/ \int |f(\omega)|^2\, d\omega \tag{52}$$

is the cross moment of time and frequency of the narrowband signal.[28] For a purely amplitude-modulated signal, $\Delta(\omega t)$ and $A_{12}$ are zero. The remarks at the end of Section II concerning the significance of the matrix $\mathbf{A}$ apply here.

This theory only sets lower bounds on the variances of estimates of arrival time and frequency, and it reveals no way of determining what dynamical variables should be measured in order to attain them. In this respect it

[28] C. W. Helstrom,[19] ch. 1, sec. 5, pp. 18–22.

can go no farther than the classical estimation theory, which tells us only that at high signal-to-noise ratios the lower bound can be approached by a receiver incorporating a large bank of parallel filters matched to signals with a dense set of carrier frequencies in the expected range of values of $\Omega$. To estimate the signal frequency and arrival time, the rectified outputs of these filters must be observed to determine which exhibits the largest peak value and when that peak value occurs.[29] The optimum estimation of the arrival time and frequency of a quantum-mechanical signal can hardly be expected to be any simpler.

## V. Estimation of the Parameters of an Incoherent Signal

By an incoherent signal we mean one for which the net field in the cavity of the ideal receiver has a density operator of the general Gaussian form

$$\rho = |\det \phi|^{-1} \int \cdots \int \exp\left[-\sum_k \sum_m \alpha_k^* (\phi^{-1})_{km} \alpha_m\right] \cdot \prod_k |\alpha_k\rangle\langle\alpha_k|^2 (d\,\alpha_k/\pi), \tag{53}$$

where $\phi = \phi_0 + \phi_s(\theta)$ is the mode correlation matrix, composed of a term $\phi_0$ for the background radiation and a term $\phi_s(\theta)$ for the incoherent signal.[30] The signal matrix $\phi_s$ may depend on certain unknown parameters $\theta$ such as a power level or a mean carrier frequency.

The calculation of the SLD $L_i$ is quite similar to the derivation of the threshold detector of an incoherent signal, and for brevity we omit it.[30] The SLDs are quadratic forms involving the creation and annihilation operators of the modes

$$L_i = \sum_k \sum_m L_{km}^{(i)} a_k^+ a_m + C_i, \tag{54}$$

where the matrix $\Lambda_i = ||L_{km}^{(i)}||$ and the constant $C_i$ are given by the equations

$$2\,\partial\phi_s/\partial\theta_i = \phi\Lambda_i(I + \phi) + (I + \phi)\Lambda_i\phi, \tag{55}$$

$$C_i = -\mathrm{Tr}\left[(I + \phi)^{-1}\frac{\partial\phi_s}{\partial\theta_i}\right]. \tag{56}$$

In terms of the matrices $\Lambda_i$, which must be determined by solving (55), the elements of the matrix $A$ in (13) are

$$A_{ij} = \mathrm{Tr}\,\rho L_i L_j = \mathrm{Tr}\,\Lambda_i\phi\Lambda_j(I + \phi) = \mathrm{Tr}\,\Lambda_i(\partial\phi_s/\partial\theta_j). \tag{57}$$

In a representation in which the mode correlation matrix $\phi$ is diagonal, $\phi = ||N_k\,\delta_{km}||$,

$$A_{ij} = \sum_k \sum_m [\tfrac{1}{2}(N_k + N_m) + N_k N_m]^{-1} \cdot \left(\frac{\partial\phi_s}{\partial\theta_i}\right)_{km}\left(\frac{\partial\phi_s}{\partial\theta_j}\right)_{mk}. \tag{58}$$

The lower bound of the variance of an unbiased estimate of a parameter $\theta$ is

$$\mathrm{Var}\,\hat{\theta} \geq D_\theta^{-2},$$

$$D_\theta^2 = \sum_k \sum_m [\tfrac{1}{2}(N_k + N_m) + N_k N_m]^{-1} \cdot [(\partial\phi_s/\partial\theta)_{km}]^2. \tag{59}$$

When, for instance, $\theta$ stands for the power level $P$ of the signal, we can write $\phi = \phi_0 + P\phi_s'$, and we find

$$(\mathrm{Var}\,P)/P^2 \geq P^{-2}\{\sum_k \sum_m [\tfrac{1}{2}(N_k + N_m) + N_k N_m]^{-1} \cdot [(\varphi_s')_{km}]^2\}^{-1} = D^{-2}. \tag{60}$$

In the limit $P \to 0$, $D^2$ is the signal-to-noise ratio of the quantum-mechanical threshold detector of the incoherent signal.[30]

When the mode correlation matrix $\phi$ is diagonal for all values of the parameter $\theta$, we can put for all modes $\mathbf{k}$

$$N_k = N_{0k} + N_{sk}(\theta),$$

and the expression for $D_\theta^2$ in (59) becomes

$$D_\theta^2 = \sum_k [N_k(N_k + 1)]^{-1}(\partial N_{sk}/\partial\theta)^2 \geq \sum_k [N_{0k}(N_{0k} + 1)]^{-1}(\partial N_{sk}/\partial\theta)^2.$$

If signal and noise are moving in the $x$-direction through a rectilinear cavity

$$N_k = \frac{2\pi c}{\hbar\omega_k L_1}\Phi(\omega_k)$$

for those modes $\mathbf{k}$ that are excited, where $\Phi(\omega)\Delta\omega$ is the energy at frequencies between $\omega$ and $\omega + \Delta\omega$. The sum over $\mathbf{k}$ can be approximated by an integral by the correspondence

$$\sum_k \to \frac{L_1}{2\pi c}\int d\omega$$

when the cavity is long enough for these modes to be separated by frequency intervals $2\pi c/L_1$ much smaller than those over which the energy density $\Phi(\omega)$ changes significantly.

In the classical limit $N_k \gg 1$, the expression for $D_\theta^2$ becomes

$$D_\theta^2 = \frac{L_1}{c}\int_{-\infty}^{\infty}\{\partial[\ln\Phi(\omega)]/\partial\theta\}^2\,d\omega/2\pi,$$

and if we identify $L_1/c$, the time required for the radiation to fill the cavity, with the observation time $T$, we find the bound

$$\mathrm{Var}\,\hat{\theta} \geq \left\{T\int_{-\infty}^{\infty}\{\partial[\ln\Phi(\omega)]/\partial\theta\}^2\,d\omega/2\pi\right\}^{-1}$$

[29] *Ibid.*, ch. 8, sec. 4, pp. 223–231.
[30] C. W. Helstrom,[6] sec. 5.

as given by Levin, who analyzed the estimation of parameters such as center frequency and amplitude of noise-like signals.[31]

At optical frequencies, on the other hand, for radiation of the thermal variety, $N_k \ll 1$, and we find

$$\text{Var}\ \hat{\theta} \geq \left[\int_{-\infty}^{\infty} \frac{(\partial\Phi/\partial\theta)^2}{\hbar\omega\Phi(\omega)}\, d\omega\right]^{-1} \geq \left[\int_{-\infty}^{\infty} \frac{(\partial\Phi_s/\partial\theta)^2}{\hbar\omega\Phi_0(\omega)}\, d\omega\right]^{-1}$$

when $\Phi(\omega) = \Phi_0(\omega) + \Phi_s(\omega; \theta)$, where $\Phi_s(\omega; \theta)$ and $\Phi_0(\omega)$ represent the energy densities of signal and background radiation, respectively. If, as is often the case, the signal occupies a much narrower spectral band than the noise and is centered at a frequency $\Omega$, the lower bound on $\text{Var}\ \hat{\theta}$ can be approximated by

$$\text{Var}\ \hat{\theta} \geq \hbar\Omega\Phi_0(\Omega)\left[\int_{-\infty}^{\infty} [\partial\Phi_s/\partial\theta]^2\, d\omega\right]^{-1}.$$

[31] M. J. Levin, "Power spectrum parameter estimation," *IEEE Trans. Information Theory*, vol. IT-11, pp. 100–107, January 1965.

## Appendix

To derive (29) the simplest method seems to be to write the density operator of (27) in Glauber's notation[32]

$$\rho = \int \exp\left(-\ |\alpha - A\mu|^2/N\right)\ |\alpha\rangle\langle\alpha|\ d^2\alpha/\pi N.$$

Differentiation with respect to $A$ yields

$$\begin{aligned}\partial\rho \mid \partial A &= N^{-1} \int [\mu^*(\alpha - A\mu) + \mu(\alpha^* - A\mu^*)] \\ &\quad \cdot \exp\left(-\ |\alpha - A\mu|^2/N\right)\ |\alpha\rangle\langle\alpha|\ d^2\alpha/\pi N \\ &= N^{-1}[\mu^*(a - A\mu)\rho + \mu\rho(a^+ - A\mu^*)],\end{aligned}$$

where we have used the definition of the eigenkets $|\alpha\rangle$

$$a/\alpha\rangle = \alpha\ |\alpha\rangle, \qquad \langle\alpha|\ a^+ = \langle\alpha|\ \alpha^*.$$

[32] R. J. Glauber,[24] sec. 8, pp. 2777–2781.

# 5



Reprinted from *IEEE Trans. Inf. Theory* **IT-17**(3):240–246 (1971)

# Application of Quantum Estimation Theory to Analog Communication Over Quantum Channels

STEWART D. PERSONICK, MEMBER, IEEE

*Abstract*—**Recent inquiries into optical communication have raised questions as to the validity of classical detection and estimation theory for weak light fields. Helstrom [1] proposed that the axioms of quantum mechanics be incorporated into a quantum approach to optical estimation and detection. In this paper, we discuss two important results, the quantum equivalent of the minimum-mean-square-error (MMSE) estimator and the quantum Cramér–Rao bound for estimation of the parameters of an electromagnetic field. The first result, a new one, is applied to linear modulation. We show that homodyning is the optimal demodulation scheme in that case. Parallels to the classical MMSE estimator are drawn. The Cramér–Rao bound, first derived in the quantum case by Helstrom [1], is applied to specific estimation problems. Details are left to the references, but interesting results are presented.**

## Introduction

RECENT inquiries into the feasibility of optical communication have raised questions as to the validity of classical detection and estimation theory for weak light fields. Helstrom [1] proposed that the axioms of quantum mechanics be incorporated into a quantum approach to estimation. In this paper, we shall discuss two important results on quantum estimation. The first, a new result, is a quantum equivalent to the conditional-mean minimum-mean-square-error (MMSE) estimator of classical estimation theory. The second is the quantum Cramér–Rao bound, originally proposed by Helstrom [1] and applied here to the estimation of parameters and waveforms embedded in the mean or covariance of the quantum Gaussian random field.

The MMSE results will be applied to linear modulation and parallels to the classical case will be drawn. The Cramér–Rao bound will be applied to a number of single-parameter and waveform problems.

Manuscript received August 14, 1970; revised November 5, 1970. This work was partially supported by Bell Telephone Laboratories, Inc.

The author is with Bell Telephone Laboratories, Inc., Holmdel, N.Y. 07733.

## I. Quantum Theory of Measurements

Suppose we start with a physical system upon which we wish to perform measurements. The outcome of any given measurement depends upon the quantum state of the system. To use the axioms of quantum mechanics, we must find a Hilbert space $\Omega$ that is appropriate for the system we wish to study, in that it allows us to represent the system state by a unit-length (normed) element $|x\rangle$ of the space [2]. With each physical measurement that can be performed upon the system, we associate an Hermitian operator[1] $M$ that maps the above Hilbert space into itself. Hermitian operators have sets of orthonormal eigenvectors and associated real eigenvalues. (We consider here only operators with countable sets of eigenvectors, leaving operators with uncountable sets as a generalization [2, pp. 179–191]. We can write an Hermitian operator as follows:

$$M = \sum m_j \, |m_j\rangle\langle m_j| \quad (1)$$

where $m_j$ is real, $M \mid m_j\rangle = m_j \mid m_j\rangle$ for all $j$ and $\langle m_j \mid m_k\rangle = \delta_{kj}$ (Kronecker delta).

[1] Strictly speaking, operators are associated with dynamical variables of the system. We perform measurements of the dynamical variables.

If a physical measurement[2] $M$ with associated Hermitian operator with eigenvectors $|m_j\rangle$ and eigenvalues $m_j$ is performed on a system with mathematical state $|x\rangle$, the outcome of the measurement is a random variable. It must assume a value equal to an eigenvalue of the Hermitian operator $M$, and the probability that it assumes, the particular value $m_k$, is given by

$$\Pr(m_k | \text{ state } = |x\rangle) = \langle m_k \mid x\rangle\langle x \mid m_k\rangle. \quad (2)$$

Suppose a measurement $M$ with associated Hermitian operator $M$ is performed upon a system whose state is known only statistically. That is, the state is known to be a member of a set $\{|x_k\rangle\}$. The probability that the state is $|x_j\rangle$ is $p_j$. We can then use the axioms to write the probability that the outcome of measurement $M$ is the particular eigenvalue $m_j$,

$$\Pr(m_k | \text{ statistical state knowledge})$$
$$\triangleq \Pr(m_k) = \sum p_j[\langle m_k \mid x_j\rangle\langle x_j \mid m_k\rangle]. \quad (3)$$

Define the Hermitian operator $\rho$ as follows:

$$\rho = \sum p_j|x_j\rangle\langle x_j| = \sum \rho_j|\rho_j\rangle\langle\rho_j| \quad (4)$$

where

$$\langle\rho_j \mid \rho_k\rangle = \delta_{kj}, \qquad \rho_j \geq 0, \sum\rho_j = 1.$$

(On the right, we have written $\rho$ in terms of its eigenvectors and eigenvalues. Note that the $|x_k\rangle$ are not necessarily orthogonal.) We call this the density operator. Then from (3), it is clear that

$$\Pr(m_k) = \langle m_k|\rho|m_k\rangle.$$

Finally, it is straightforward to show that if $f(t)$ is analytic (i.e., it has a power series expansion about $t = 0$), then the expected value of $f$(outcome of measurement $M$) is

$$E\{f(\text{outcome})\} = \sum f(m_k)\Pr(m_k) = \operatorname{tr}[\rho f(M)] \quad (5)$$

where tr $(\cdot)$ signifies the operation "trace" and $f(M)$ is the power series expansion of $f$ using powers of $M$.

## II. Application to Estimation Theory

In the above section, we discussed the concept of a density operator as a summary of *a priori* knowledge of the state of a quantum system. Suppose we have a parameter $s$ that is coupled to the system state in a statistical way. That is, given the value $s$, we may not know the system state $|x\rangle$, but we establish a statistical distribution over the possible states that depends upon $s$. We have a conditional density operator $\rho^s$, which is defined for each $s$. The outcome of a measurement is now a random variable with outcome probabilities conditional upon the value $s$. That is, if we measure $M$ with corresponding Hermitian operator $M$, the probability that outcome is the eigenvalue $m_j$, given the value of the parameter is $s$, is

$$\Pr(m_j \mid s) = \langle m_j|\rho^s|m_j\rangle. \quad (6)$$

Our estimation problem is to make measurements upon a system whose state depends statistically upon a parameter $s$ and to use the outcome to estimate $s$, which is not known *a priori*. The parameter may be a real unknown parameter or an assumed value of a random variable whose *a priori* density $p(s)$ is given.

As a final point, suppose we measure $M$ with corresponding Hermitian operator $M$, and we deterministically transform the outcome of the measurement $m_j$ into a real number $\hat{s}(m_j)$, which is an estimate of the parameter $s$. This is equivalent to measurement $\hat{S}$ with corresponding Hermitian operator $\hat{S}$ whose eigenvectors are the eigenvectors of $M$ and whose eigenvalues are the transformed eigenvalues $\hat{s}(m_j)$. The process of making a measurement and a real transformation upon the outcome is therefore equivalent to a single operation of measurement and has an associated Hermitian operator.

## III. MMSE Estimator

Suppose we have a random variable $S$ that takes on values $s$ with probability density $p(s)$. This random variable is coupled to the state of a quantum system through the conditional density operator $\rho^s$. We wish to perform a measurement $\hat{S}$ with associated Hermitian operator $\hat{S}$ upon the quantum system, the outcome of which is an estimate of the value $s$. We wish to minimize the mean-square error (MSE) between the measurement outcome and the value $s$ assumed by the random variable $S$, which is

$$C(\hat{S}) = \int p(s)\{\operatorname{tr}[\rho^s(\hat{S} - sI)^2]\}\, ds. \quad (7)$$

The approach is to first find the Hermitian operator that minimizes $C(\hat{S})$. We define this operator as the MMSE estimator. We find the measurement associated with the MMSE estimator after we find the estimator (operator).

*Theorem:* If we make the definitions,

$$\Gamma = \int p(s)\rho^s\, ds, \quad (8)$$

$$\eta = \int sp(s)\rho^s\, ds, \quad (9)$$

the MMSE estimator must satisfy

$$\Gamma\hat{S}_{\text{opt}} + \hat{S}_{\text{opt}}\Gamma = 2\eta. \quad (10)$$

Further, if $\Gamma$ is positive definite, the solution of (10) is unique and Hermitian, and is given explicitly by

$$\hat{S}_{\text{opt}} = 2\int_0^\infty \exp(-\Gamma\alpha)\eta\exp(-\Gamma\alpha)\, d\alpha. \quad (11)$$

*Proof:* First we must apply the calculus of variations to obtain a necessary condition on the MMSE estimator.

[2] Throughout this paper, we shall use the same upper-case letter to refer to a measurement and to represent the operator associated with the measurement.

Let $\varepsilon$ be a real number and $H$ any Hermitian operator. Let $\hat{S}_{\rm opt}$ be the MMSE estimator, not yet shown to be unique. We must have $C(\hat{S}_{\rm opt} + \varepsilon H) \geq C(\hat{S}_{\rm opt})$ since the sum of two Hermitian operators is an Hermitian operator. Writing this out using (8) and (9), we obtain

$$C(\hat{S}_{\rm opt}) \leq C(\hat{S}_{\rm opt}) + \varepsilon \,{\rm tr}\,[H(\Gamma \hat{S}_{\rm opt} + \hat{S}_{\rm opt}\Gamma - 2\eta)] + \varepsilon^2 \,{\rm tr}\,[\Gamma H^2] \quad (12)$$

for all $\varepsilon$ and Hermitian $H$.

Differentiating with respect to $\varepsilon$, we obtain the necessary condition,

$${\rm tr}\,[H(\Gamma \hat{S}_{\rm opt} + \hat{S}_{\rm opt}\Gamma - 2\eta)] = 0 \quad (13)$$

for all Hermitian $H$.

We next show that an Hermitian solution to (13) must satisfy (10). Define $G$ as

$$G = \Gamma \hat{S}_{\rm opt} + \hat{S}_{\rm opt}\Gamma - 2\eta. \quad (14)$$

Since $\Gamma$ and $\eta$ are Hermitian, and since $\hat{S}$ is Hermitian, $G$ must be Hermitian. Let $|g_i\rangle$ be an eigenvector of $G$ with eigenvalue $g_i$. If we let $H$ equal the Hermitian operator $|g_i\rangle\langle g_i|$, we have

$${\rm tr}\,[G|g_i\rangle\langle g_i|] = \langle g_i|G|g_i\rangle = g_i = 0. \quad (15)$$

Thus all the eigenvalues of $G$ are zero, and $G$ is the zero operator. Thus an Hermitian solution to (13) must satisfy (10).

Next, make the condition that $\Gamma$ is positive definite. Let a general operator $\hat{S}$ be a hypothesized solution to (10). We can rewrite $\hat{S}$ as follows:

$$\hat{S} = \frac{\hat{S} + \hat{S}^+}{2} + i\left(\frac{\hat{S} - \hat{S}^+}{2i}\right) = T + iV. \quad (16)$$

The operators $T$ and $V$ are both Hermitian. Let $|v_i\rangle$ be an eigenvector of $V$ with eigenvalue $v_i$. From (10) we must have

$$\langle v_i|(\Gamma T + T\Gamma)|v_i\rangle + i\langle v_i|(\Gamma V + V\Gamma)|v_i\rangle = 2\langle v_i|\eta|v_i\rangle. \quad (17)$$

But the only imaginary quantities in the equation are on the left side. That is, we must have

$$\langle v_i|\Gamma V + V\Gamma|v_i\rangle = 2v_i\langle v_i|\Gamma|v_i\rangle = 0. \quad (18)$$

But $\Gamma$ is positive definite, $[\langle v_i|\Gamma|v_i\rangle] > 0$. Thus the eigenvalues of $V$ are all zero and $\hat{S}$ is therefore Hermitian. Thus a solution to (10) must be Hermitian.

Now we must show that there is at most one Hermitian solution to (10). Set $\hat{S}_1$ and $\hat{S}_2$ to be two Hermitian solutions to (10). Call the difference $\hat{S}_1 - \hat{S}_2 = \hat{S}_d$. $\hat{S}_d$ is Hermitian and must satisfy

$$\hat{S}_d\Gamma + \Gamma\hat{S}_d = 0. \quad (19)$$

Examining (17), (18), we see that $\hat{S}_d$ must be the zero operator by the same reasoning that showed $V$ to be the zero operator.

Finally, we must show that if $\hat{S}_{\rm opt}$ is given by (11), it satisfies (10). To do this, multiply (11) by $\Gamma$ and integrate by parts,

$$\begin{aligned}\Gamma\hat{S}_{\rm opt} &= 2\Gamma\int_0^\infty \exp(-\Gamma\alpha)\eta\exp(-\Gamma\alpha)\,d\alpha\\ &= -2\exp(-\Gamma\alpha)\eta\exp(-\Gamma\alpha)\Big|_0^\infty - 2\int_0^\infty \exp(-\Gamma\alpha)\eta\exp(-\Gamma\alpha)\,d\alpha\Gamma\\ &= 2\eta - \hat{S}_{\rm opt}\Gamma. \end{aligned} \quad (20)$$

The cost $C(\hat{S}_{\rm opt})$ is given by

$$\begin{aligned}C(\hat{S}_{\rm opt}) &= [E(s)]^2 + {\rm tr}\,[\Gamma\hat{S}_{\rm opt}{}^2] - 2\,{\rm tr}\,[\eta\hat{S}_{\rm opt}]\\ &= E(s^2) - {\rm tr}\,[\eta\hat{S}_{\rm opt}].\end{aligned} \quad (21)$$

It is interesting to show the relationship between quantum and classical MMSE estimators. Suppose $\Gamma$ and $\eta$ commute. Then the solution of (10) also satisfies

$$\Gamma\hat{S}_{\rm opt} = \eta \quad (22)$$

when $\Gamma\eta = \eta\Gamma$, i.e., we have

$$\left[\int p(s)\rho^s\,ds\right]\hat{S}_{\rm opt} = \int sp(s)\rho^s\,ds.$$

Classically, if we have a data vector $\boldsymbol{r}$ that is statistically dependent upon $s$ through the conditional density $p(\boldsymbol{r} \mid s)$, and if we wish to transform $\boldsymbol{r}$ into an estimate $\hat{S}_{\rm opt}(\boldsymbol{r})$ of $s$ that minimizes the average-square-estimation error, then we have this MMSE estimator given by the equation [3],

$$\left[\int p(s)p(\boldsymbol{r} \mid s)\,ds\right]\hat{S}_{\rm opt}(\boldsymbol{r}) = \int sp(s)p(\boldsymbol{r} \mid s)\,ds \quad (23)$$

i.e., $S_{\rm opt}(\boldsymbol{r}) = \int sp(s \mid \boldsymbol{r})\,ds$ the conditional mean of $s$. Comparing (23) with (22) we see that $\rho^s$ the conditional density operator plays a role analogous to $p(\boldsymbol{r} \mid s)$, the classical conditional density.

## IV. Cramér–Rao Bounds

Helstrom [1] proposed the following inequality (25), which is equivalent to the classical Cramér–Rao bound [3, pp. 66–77] for unbiased estimation of a parameter.

*Theorem:* Suppose $s$ is a real parameter coupled to some quantum system through a known conditional density operator $\rho^s$, defined on the appropriate Hilbert space in which the system state lies. Let $\hat{S}$ be an Hermitian operator associated with some measurement $\hat{S}$. The outcome of the measurement is to be an estimate of parameter $s$. If we have the following condition, which means that the estimate is unbiased for $s$ in some interval about the point $s_0$,

$$E(\hat{S}_{\rm outcome} - s) = {\rm tr}\,\rho^s(\hat{S} - sI) = 0, \quad |s - s_0| < \varepsilon, \varepsilon > 0, \quad (24)$$

then the variance of the difference between the estimate and the true value of $s$ must satisfy the inequality when $s = s_0$,

$${\rm var}\,(\hat{S}_{\rm outcome} - s_0) = {\rm tr}\,[\rho^{s_0}(S - s_0I)^2] \geq J^{-1} \quad (25)$$

where

$$J = {\rm tr}\,[\rho^{s_0}(L(s_0))^2] \quad (26)$$

and $L(s)$ satisfies

$$\frac{\partial}{\partial s}\rho^s = \tfrac{1}{2}[L(s)\rho^s + \rho^s L(s)].$$

*Corollary:* Let $S$ be a random variable which has *a priori* probability density $p(s)$. The values $s$ assumed are coupled to a quantum system as above through $\rho^s$. If a measurement $S$ with associated Hermitian operator $\hat{S}$ satisfies the weak bias condition,

$$p(s)E[\hat{S}_{\text{outcome}} - s]\big|_{s=\pm\infty} = p(s)\,\text{tr}\,\rho^s(\hat{S} - sI)\big|_{s=\pm\infty} = 0, \quad (27)$$

then we have for the MSE between the measurement outcome and the value assumed by $S$ the inequality,

$$E(\hat{S}_{\text{outcome}} - s)^2 \geq K^{-1}, \quad (28)$$

where

$$K = E(J) + E\left[\left(\frac{\partial}{\partial s}\ln p(s)\right)^2\right]$$

and $J$ is given in (26) (expectation with respect to the density $p(s)$ of $S$). Multiple parameter and waveform estimation bounds can be obtained as straightforward extensions of the above single parameter estimation bounds [3],[5].

The definition of the logarithmic derivative $L(s)$ in the above symmetrized manner results in the tightest bound of the Cramér–Rao type. That is, if we define $L(s)$ as $(\partial/\partial s)\rho^s = \frac{1}{2}[L(s)\rho^s + \rho^s L^+(s)]$, and we use Helstrom's approach to obtain a bound, then the Hermitian solution gives the tightest bound.

## V. Quantized Electromagnetic Field

In order to apply the above results to estimation of parameters embedded in a quantum field, we must define the appropriate Hilbert space, system states, and density operators. We shall consider a single polarization of a one-dimensional (plane wave) field for simplicity [5]. Classically, we can expand such a field in a finite interval of length $L$; its extent is infinite in two dimensions and finite in the dimension $z$.

$$\varepsilon(z) = i\sum_j (\hbar\omega_j/2L)^{\frac{1}{2}}[\varepsilon_j \exp(ik_j z) - \varepsilon_j^* \exp(-ik_j z)], \quad z \in [0,L], \quad (29)$$

where $k_j = 2\pi j/L$ for $j = \cdots,-2,-1,0,1,2,\cdots,\omega_j = k_j/c$, $c$ = speed of light in appropriate units, $\hbar$ = Planck's constant/$2\pi$, and $\varepsilon_k$ = a complex number that we shall call the amplitude of mode $k$. Classically, the coefficients $\{\varepsilon_j\}$ can be statistically dependent upon a parameter $s$ with a joint conditional density $p(\{\varepsilon_j\} \mid s)$ defined.

Now define a quantum $E$-field operator as [5],[6]

$$E(z) = i\sum_j (\hbar\omega_j/2L)^{\frac{1}{2}}[a_j \exp(ik_j z) - a_j^+ \exp(-ik_j z)]. \quad (30)$$

The $a_k$ are called annihilation operators. Their adjoints $a_k^+$ are called creation operators. They satisfy the commutation rules,

$$[a_k,a_j] = 0, \qquad [a_k,a_j^+] = \delta_{k,j}. \quad (31)$$

Each of the operators $a_k$ is defined on a Hilbert space. The field state lies in the Cartesian product of these spaces. The operators $a_k$ have nonorthogonal right eigenvectors and complex associated eigenvalues. These eigenvectors form over-complete sets in their associated spaces. We obtain an over-complete set of nonorthogonal vectors for the Hilbert space that contains the field state from the simultaneous eigenvectors of the operators $a_k$. That is, such a vector would satisfy the condition,

$$a_k|x\rangle = \alpha_k|x\rangle, \quad (32)$$

$\alpha_k$ a complex number.

We could write such a vector as

$$|x\rangle = |\alpha_1,\alpha_2,\alpha_3,\cdots\rangle = \prod_k |\alpha_k\rangle_k$$

where

$$a_k|\alpha_k\rangle_k = \alpha_k|\alpha_k\rangle_k, \qquad |{}_k\langle\alpha_k \mid \beta_k\rangle_k|^2 = \exp(-|\alpha_k - \beta_k|^2).$$

The density operator of the field can be expanded in the form [7],

$$\rho = \int p(\{\alpha_k\}) \prod_k |\alpha_k\rangle_{kk}\langle\alpha_k|\, d^2\alpha_k. \quad (33)$$

For the fields we shall discuss, the function $p(\{\alpha_k\})$ can be considered a probability density, perhaps dependent on a parameter $s$.

## VI. Application: MMSE Estimator for Linear Modulation

Suppose we consider only one mode of an electromagnetic plane-wave field and assume it is the only mode coupled to a parameter $s$. We write the single mode field classically as

$$\varepsilon(z) = i(\hbar\omega/2L)^{\frac{1}{2}}[\varepsilon \exp(ikz) - \varepsilon^* \exp(-ikz)], \qquad z \in [0,L]. \quad (34)$$

We shall assume that $\varepsilon = \lambda s + n$ where $\lambda$ is a real constant, $s$ is a parameter to be estimated, and $n$ is a complex Gaussian random variable with

$$E(nn) = 0, \qquad E[nn^*] = N_0. \quad (35)$$

The density operator, given the value of $s$, associated with the quantum field having the above classical representation is

$$\rho^s = (\pi N_0)^{-1} \int \exp(-|\alpha - \lambda s|^2/N_0)|\alpha\rangle\langle\alpha|\, d^2\alpha, \quad (36)$$

where $|\alpha\rangle$ is an eigenvector of the annihilation operator $a$ for the field mode under discussion.

Suppose now that the parameter $s$ is the value assumed by a random variable $S$ with density $p(s)$. The density is assumed to be Gaussian, i.e.,

$$p(s) = (2\pi)^{-\frac{1}{2}} \exp(-s^2/2). \quad (37)$$

If we approached the problem classically, using (34) and (35) and trying to find an estimate of $s$ based upon the received field, we would find that the classical MMSE estimator [3, pp. 271–273] has a performance given by

$$\text{MMSE} = E[(\hat{S}_{\text{opt}}(\varepsilon(z)) - s)^2] = \frac{\lambda^2 N_0/2}{\lambda^2 + N_0/2} \quad (38)$$

where $\hat{S}_{\text{opt}}\{\varepsilon(z)\}$ is the MMSE classical estimate of $s$ based upon $\varepsilon(z)$.

For optical fields, we must use the quantum approach. Using (36) and (37), we can find $\Gamma$ and $\eta$ of (8) and (9),

$$\Gamma = \int (\pi N_0)^{-\frac{1}{2}}(\pi[N_0 + 2\lambda^2])^{-\frac{1}{2}} \exp[-(\text{Re}\,\alpha)^2/(N_0 + 2\lambda^2)] \times \exp[-(\text{Im}\,\alpha)^2/N_0]\, |\alpha\rangle\langle\alpha|\, d^2\alpha, \quad (39)$$

where Re $(\cdot)$ means real part of $(\cdot)$, and Im $(\cdot)$ means imaginary part of $(\cdot)$.

$$\eta = \text{Re} \int \frac{(\alpha\lambda^2)}{N_0/2 + \lambda^2}, \quad [\text{integrand of } \Gamma \text{ in (39)}]\, d^2\alpha. \quad (40)$$

From (10) we obtain

$$\hat{S}_{\text{opt}} = [(a + a^+)/2] \frac{\lambda}{\lambda + N_0/2 + \frac{1}{4}} \quad (41)$$

$$C(\hat{S}) = E(\hat{S}_{\text{opt outcome}} - s)^2 = \frac{\lambda^2[\frac{1}{2}N_0 + \frac{1}{4}]}{\lambda^2 + \frac{1}{2}N_0 + \frac{1}{4}}. \quad (42)$$

Comparing (42) with (38), we see that the quantum MSE is larger than the classically predicted error, but approaches the classical error when $N_0 \gg \frac{1}{2}$. As a quantitative comment, the relationship between $N_0$ and $\hbar\omega$ when $N_0$ is associated with the noise of a medium in equilibrium at temperature $\theta$ is

$$N_0 = [e^{\hbar\omega/k\theta} - 1]^{-1}$$

where $k$ = Boltzmann's constant. If $\theta = 300°\ K$, $\omega = 2\pi(3 \times 10^{14})$ (a wavelength of 1 $\mu$), then $\hbar\omega/k\theta = 50$.

We have not yet specified what the operator of (41) corresponds to physically. It can be shown that the operator corresponds to a homodyne measurement [4],[7] of the real part of the mode amplitude. Homodyning will be discussed in Section VIII.

## VII. Cramér–Rao Bounds for Known and Fading Channels

Consider the following two classically represented fields impinging upon an aperture,

1) $$\varepsilon(\rho,t,s) = 2\,\text{Re}\,[f(\rho,t,s)\exp(i\Omega t) + n(\rho,t)\exp(i\Omega t)] \quad (43)$$

2) $$\varepsilon(\rho,t,s) = 2\,\text{Re}\,[c(\rho,t)f(\rho,t,s)\exp(i\Omega t) + n(\rho,t)\exp(i\Omega t)] \quad (44)$$

where $f(\rho,t,s)$ is a known function dependent upon a parameter $s$, $\rho$ is the position in the planar aperture upon which the field impinges, $t$ is time limited to some interval $[0,T]$, and $n(\rho,t)$ is a complex Gaussian random process with covariance,

$$E[n(\rho,t)n^*(\rho',t')] = K_n(\rho,\rho',t,t') = N_0\delta(\rho - \rho')\delta(t - t') \quad (45)$$

(Dirac delta) and where

$$E[n(\rho,t)n(\rho',t')] = 0.$$

Here $c(\rho,t)$ is a complex Gaussian random process with covariance $K_c(\rho,\rho',t,t') = E[c(\rho,t)c^*(\rho't')]$.

We shall assume that the field impinging upon the aperture is narrow-band about the carrier frequency $\Omega$ and is composed of plane waves, all of whose propagation vectors are approximately normal to the aperture plane. We then can use the quantum representation of the field to obtain the quantum Cramér–Rao bounds [4] given in (25) and (28). For field 1), we have

$$J = 2[N_0 + (\hbar\Omega/4c)]^{-1} \int_0^T \int_{\text{aperture}} \left|\frac{\partial}{\partial s} f(\rho,t,s)\right|^2 d^2\rho\, dt; \quad (46)$$

for field 2), we have

$$J = (2c/\hbar\Omega)^2 \int T(\rho_1,t_1,\cdots,\rho_4,t_4)K_c(\rho_2,\rho_3,t_2,t_3) \cdot K_c(\rho_4,\rho_1,t_4,t_1)\frac{\partial}{\partial s}[f(\rho_2,t_2,s)f^*(\rho_3,t_3,s)] \cdot \frac{\partial}{\partial s}[f(\rho_4,t_4,s)f^*(\rho_1,t_1,s)]\, d^2\rho_1,\cdots,dt_4, \quad (47)$$

where if $x \equiv \{\rho,t\}$, $T(x_1,x_2,x_3,x_4)$ is the solution of

$$\int T(x_1,x_2,x_3,x_4)T^{-1}(x_2,x_5,x_4,x_6)\, dx_2\, dx_4 = \delta(x_1 - x_5)\delta(x_3 - x_6)$$

and

$$T^{-1}(x_1,x_2,x_3,x_4) = (2c/\hbar\Omega)^2 K_g(x_1,x_2)K_g(x_3,x_4) + (2c/\hbar\Omega)K_g(x_1,x_2)\delta(x_3 - x_4) + (2c/\hbar\Omega)K_g(x_3,x_4)\delta(x_1 - x_2)$$

where

$$K_g(x_1,x_2) = K_c(\rho_1,\rho_2,t_1,t_2)f(\rho_1,t_1,s)f^*(\rho_2,t_2,s) + N_0\delta(\rho_1 - \rho_2)\delta(t_1 - t_2).$$

The bounds determined (46), (47) reduce to the classical bounds for fields 1) and 2) [3, pp. 273–275],[8] when $N_0 \gg \hbar\Omega$.

## VIII. Applications of Cramér–Rao Bounds

We wish to show that it is possible to find receivers whose performance is close to the quantum Cramér–Rao bound under some circumstances. The approach in finding classical receivers that operate near the classical Cramér–Rao bound is to use the concept of the maximum-likelihood estimator [3, pp. 63–65], which is linked with the bound [3, pp. 67–68]. Unfortunately, there is no general quantum equivalent maximum-likelihood estimator. The approach in the quantum case is to postulate an intuitively reasonable measurement and then use classical techniques to process the outcome. It is hoped that the calculated performance is close to the quantum Cramér–Rao bound. Thus, in the absence of a quantum version of the maximum-likelihood estimator, we can only use the quantum Cramér–Rao bound as a standard against which we can evaluate proposed receivers. Receivers that operate at or near the Cramér–Rao bound have been obtained for a variety of modulation schemes in known, fixed, and random fading channels [4]. Some interesting examples are presented below.

### *A. Real Envelope, No Fading*

Suppose we consider field 1) given in (43), with condition

$$f(\rho,t,s) = f_1(\rho)f_2(t,s) \tag{48}$$

where $f_2(t,s)$ is real valued for all $t$ and $s$. Now suppose we add to the field of (43) the following strong local oscillator field,

$$\varepsilon_{lo}(\rho,t) = \sqrt{2}\,\mathrm{Re}\,\{Af_1(\rho)\exp(i\Omega t)\} \tag{49}$$

where $A$ is a large real number.

We let the sum of these fields impinge upon an ideal photon counter. It has been shown [4],[7] that the output of the counter, after normalization and subtraction of a constant, is given by the current,

$$v(t) = f_2(t,s) + w(t) \tag{50}$$

where $w(t)$ is a real Gaussian random process with covariance

$$E(w(t)w(t')) = \tfrac{1}{2}(N_0 + (\hbar\Omega/4c))\left[\int_{\text{aperture}} |f_1(\rho)|^2\, d^2\rho\right]^{-1} \delta(t - t').$$

Now ask what the Cramér–Rao bound to the classical problem of estimating $s$ from $v(t)$ is. It is well known [2] that for this simple signal in Gaussian white noise, the bounds for unbiased estimation of a real parameter $s$ or estimation of a random variable with probability density $p(s)$ are given by (25) and (28) with $J$ identical to (46).

We can conclude the following. Call the operation of adding the local oscillator and using the ideal photon counter to obtain $v(t)$ homodyning. If an asymptotically efficient receiver [3, p. 71] exists for estimating $s$ from the classical signal $v(t)$ of (50) (asymptotically efficient with respect to the classical Cramér–Rao bound), a quantum receiver asymptotically efficient with respect to the quantum bound can be obtained by homodyning to obtain $v(t)$ and processing $v(t)$ with the classical receiver. It is important to note that we required $f_2(t,s)$ to be real so that we could homodyne. Heterodyning to an intermediate frequency will not admit an efficient or asymptotically efficient receiver [4],[7]. We must heterodyne to baseband, i.e., homodyne.

If we neglect the noise $n(\rho,t)$ in (43), as it is often reasonable to do at optical frequencies, we can use another approach to obtain an asymptotically efficient receiver. Allow the field given in (43) with the assumption of (48) to impinge upon an ideal photon counter. We use no local oscillator. This is called direct detection. The output of the counter is a Poisson process [9] with mean number of counts per unit time given by

$$\lambda(t,s) = (2c/\hbar\Omega)P(f_2(s,t))^2 \tag{51}$$

where

$$P = \int_{\text{aperture}} |f_1(\rho)|^2\, d\rho.$$

We must estimate $s$ by observing the number of counts $N$ and their arrival times $t_1 \cdots t_N$.

The probability density of receiving $N$ counts at times $t_k$ is

$$p(N,\{t_k\}) = [\exp(-\Lambda)/N!]\prod_{k=1}^{N}\lambda(t_k) \tag{52}$$

where

$$\Lambda = \int_0^T \lambda(t,s)\, dt.$$

The classical Cramér–Rao bounds for real-parameter and random-variable estimation are given by (25) and (28), respectively, with $J$ replaced by the following.

$$J = \sum_{N=0}^{\infty}\int [\exp(-\Lambda)/N!]\prod_{k=1}^{N}\lambda(t_k)\left[\frac{\partial}{\partial s}\ln p(N,\{t_k\})\right]^2 dt_k. \tag{53}$$

It is straightforward to show that $J$ of (53) is equal to $J$ of (46) with $N_0$ set to zero. Thus once again, the classical bound to the estimation of $s$ from the classical data equals the quantum bound. The comments above concerning classical and quantum asymptotically efficient estimators for the homodyne receiver also apply to the direct detection receiver.

The above arguments concerned asymptotically efficient receivers. No statement is made about the optimality of homodyning or direct detection followed by classical optimal processing in minimizing the MSE in general. We simply say that these receivers are nearly optimal in the limit of strong signals.

*Example—Pulse-Position Modulation:* If we have pulse-position modulation $f_2(t,s) = f(t - s)$, it is straightforward to show [3, pp. 276–286],[4], that homodyning followed by classical matched filter processing is asymptotically efficient. It can also be shown [4] that direct detection can lead to an asymptotically efficient receiver. If the pulse is Gaussian in shape, for instance, the classical processing simply involves taking the mean arrival time of the output counts.

### *B. Pulse-Frequency Modulation, No Fading*

We can obtain an interesting receiver for pulse-frequency modulation in the absence of background noise. Here, the modulation envelope $f(\rho,s,t)$ of (43) is assumed to be of the form of (48), but $f_2(t,s)$ is not real valued. It is given by

$$f_2(t,s) = \exp(i\beta st)f_3(t) \tag{54}$$

where $\beta$ is a real number, and $f_3(t)$ is some smooth pulse shape, e.g., Gaussian.

We allow the field to impinge upon a prism that disperses the almost plane-wave incident field into a field composed of plane waves whose propagation vectors lie on a cone with axis at an angle to the original propagation direction proportional to the parameter $s$. This output field is focused with a lens onto a photon counter. Thus the position of the focused field on the counter depends upon $s$. We have converted the temporal frequency-modulation problem into a spatial position-modulation problem. The counter is assumed able to distinguish between different arrival positions of counts. This information (the number of counts and their arrival positions) is classically processed to estimate $s$. Analysis [4] indicates that for a sufficiently dispersive prism (or diffraction grating), the system is asymptotically efficient with respect to the quantum Cramér–Rao bound.

### C. Comments on Fading Channel Bound

The number $J$ given in the complicated equation (47) determines the Cramér–Rao bounds for the field of (44). Application of this bound is too tedious to present here. The bound and its waveform-estimation counterpart have been applied by this author [4], usually under the assumption that $c(\rho,t)$ is time independent. Asymptotically efficient receivers are usually only possible if the kernel $K_c(\rho,\rho')$ has sufficiently many approximately equal eigenvalues. That is, we require sufficient spatial diversity. In the limit of large diversity, the bound determined by (47) often approaches the bound determined by (46) with $f(\rho,t,s)$ multiplied by the rms value of $|c(\rho)|$.

### D. Comments on Continuous-Time Modulation

The quantum equivalents of the Cramér–Rao bound for the estimation of a Gaussian random process [3, pp. 437–444] embedded in the mean or covariance of a received process have been obtained [4]. It has been shown [4] that if the received field is of the form,

$$\varepsilon(\rho,t,s(t)) = 2\,\mathrm{Re}\,[f(\rho)s(t)\exp(i\Omega t) + n(t)\exp(i\Omega t)], \tag{55}$$

similarly to (43) and (45), where $s(t)$ is a real Gaussian random message process to be estimated, then homodyning followed by optimal linear filtering of the photon counter output will result in efficient estimation performance.

For a phase-modulated signal where

$$\varepsilon(\rho,t,s(t)) = 2\,\mathrm{Re}\,[f(\rho)\exp[i\beta s(t)]\exp(i\Omega t) + n(t)\exp(i\Omega t)], \tag{56}$$

an asymptotically efficient system employs a phase-locked loop, where the feedback signal and the incoming field are multiplied by letting the sum of these signals impinge upon a photon counter, which is a square-law device, followed by an unrealizable post-loop filter.

## Conclusions

The quantum equivalent of the MMSE estimator has been derived and the results applied to linear modulation. Helstrom's quantum equivalent of the Cramér–Rao bound has been applied to the estimation of parameters embedded in electromagnetic fields and approaches to finding asymptotically efficient receivers have been presented. Important tools missing from quantum estimation theory are an operator analog of the classical maximum-likelihood estimator and an algorithm for synthesizing physical receivers that are asymptotically efficient.

## Acknowledgment

The author wishes to thank Prof. R. S. Kennedy of the Massachusetts Institute of Technology who supervised the thesis upon which this manuscript is based.

## References

[1] C. W. Helstrom, "The minimum variance of estimates in quantum signal detection," *IEEE Trans. Inform. Theory*, vol. IT-14, Mar. 1968, pp. 234–242.
[2] A. Messiah, *Quantum Mechanics*, vol. 1. New York: Wiley, 1966, pp. 243–340.
[3] H. L. Van Trees, *Detection Estimation and Modulation*, vol. 1. New York: Wiley, 1968, p. 56.
[4] S. D. Personick, "Efficient analog communication over quantum channels," Res. Lab. Electron., M.I.T., Cambridge, Tech. Rep. 477, May 15, 1970.
[5] W. H. Louisell, *Radiation and Noise in Quantum Electronics*. New York: McGraw-Hill, 1964.
[6] R. J. Glauber, "Coherent and incoherent states of the radiation field," *Phys. Rev.*, vol. 131, Sept. 1963, pp. 2766–2788.
[7] B. M. Oliver, "Signal-to-noise ratios in photoelectric mixing," *Proc. IRE* (Lett.), vol. 49, Dec. 1961, p. 1960.
[8] H. L. Van Trees, *Detection Estimation and Modulation*, vol. 3, to be published.
[9] R. J. Glauber, *Quantum Optics and Electronics*, C. Dewitt *et al.*, Eds. New York: Gordon and Breach, 1965, pp. 65–185.

# 6



Reprinted from *Bell Syst. Tech. J.* **44**(4):725–729 (1965)

## On the Simultaneous Measurement of a Pair of Conjugate Observables

By E. ARTHURS and J. L. KELLY, JR.

(Manuscript received December 16, 1964)

A precise theory of the simultaneous measurement of a pair of conjugate observables is necessary for obtaining the classical limit from the quantum theory, for determining the limitations of coherent quantum mechanical amplifiers, etc. The uncertainty principle, of course, does not directly address this problem, since it is a statement about the variances of two hypothetical ideal measurements. We will adopt the approach that there exist instantaneous inexplicable ideal measurements of a single observable. Just as von Neumann[1] uses an ideal measurement together with an interaction to explain an indirect observation, we use ideal measurements together with interactions to explain the simultaneous measurement of an observable and its conjugate.

The joint measurement described below is complete in the sense that all pertinent past history is subsumed under the meter readings. A precise formula for the joint probability distribution of the results of the measurements is given. The variances given by these distributions satisfy an inequality like the uncertainty principle but with an extra factor or two. It is also shown that this inequality governs any conceivable joint measurement. The single measurement of an observable is a limiting case of the joint measurement when the variance of one of the measured variables is allowed to approach infinity.

Since we are trying to measure two observables, we will introduce two meters, that is, two one-dimensional systems which will be coupled to the object system. Since the two meter positions commute, we can make ideal simultaneous measurements of them. Our interpretation will be that these two measurements will constitute a simultaneous measurement of the two noncommuting observables of the object system. We will see that we cannot let the strength of our interaction become infinite, unlike the indirect measurement of Ref. 1, but must adjust it to a certain critical value. We will find that after the interaction and the measurement of the meter values that the system is left in a state which is completely determined by the meter readings and a certain parameter which we will call the "balance," having to do with how near our joint measurement is to either of two ideal measurements.

To effect the desired measurement, the coupling must be described by the following Hamiltonian:

$$H_{\text{int}} = K(qP_x + pP_y) \tag{1}$$

where $p,q$ are the positions and momentum we wish to be measured and $P_x$, $P_y$ are the momenta of the two single-degree-of-freedom systems we are using for meters. The positions of the two meters will be $x$ and $y$. In addition, we require that the meters initially be in the states $M(x)$ and $N(y)$, where

$$\begin{aligned} M(x) &= \left(\frac{2}{\pi b}\right)^{\frac{1}{4}} e^{-x^2/b} \\ N(y) &= \left(\frac{2b}{\pi}\right)^{\frac{1}{4}} e^{-by^2} \end{aligned} \tag{2}$$

and $b$ is the "balance." The strength of the interaction $K$ is assumed to be sufficiently large that other terms in the Hamiltonian can be ignored. Hence the Schrödinger equation will be ($\hbar = 1$)

$$\frac{\partial \varphi}{\partial t} = -K\left(q\frac{\partial \varphi}{\partial x} - i\frac{\partial^2 \varphi}{\partial q \partial y}\right) \tag{3}$$

with the initial condition

$$\varphi(q,x,y,0) = F(q)M(x)N(y) \tag{4}$$

where $F(q)$ is the state of the system to be measured and the system and the two meters are assumed to be independent prior to the interaction. Equation (3) is solved by Fourier transforming on $y$. The solution is

$$\varphi(q,x,y,t) = \int_{-\infty}^{\infty} F(q - wtk)\, M(x - qtk + \tfrac{1}{2}wt^2k^2) \cdot \frac{\exp - (w^2/4b)}{(4\pi b)^{\frac{1}{2}}} \exp(iwy)\, dw. \tag{5}$$

To obtain the results we desire it is necessary to make ideal measurements of $x$ and $y$ at $t = 1/K$. In the following, $t$ will be assumed to be equal to $1/K$ and the time will be suppressed in the notation.

The joint probability distribution for the commuting observables $x$ and $y$, $P(x,y)$ is given, of course, by

$$P(x,y) = \int_{-\infty}^{\infty} |\varphi|^2\, dq. \tag{6}$$

Then, using (5), we have

$$P(x,y) = \left(\frac{1}{4\pi^3 b}\right)^{\frac{1}{2}} \left| \int_{-\infty}^{\infty} F(q) \exp - \left[\frac{1}{2b} (x-q)^2\right] \cdot \exp - (iqy)\, dq \right|^2 \tag{7}$$

or, if $G(p)$ is the momentum wave function of the system

$$P(x,y) = \left(\frac{b}{4\pi^3}\right)^{\frac{1}{2}} \left| \int_{-\infty}^{\infty} G(p) \exp - \left[\frac{b}{2} (y-p)^2\right] \cdot \exp - (ixp)\, dp \right|^2 . \tag{8}$$

That is, the joint probability distribution is the Fourier spectrum of the wave function multiplied by a Gaussian window whose width is related to the balance of the measurement.

The new wave function for the system after the measurement is given by substituting the results of the meter readings in the wave function and renormalizing. If we denote the measured value of $x$ by $x_m$ and the measured value of $y$, $y_m$, the new state of the system is given by

$$F'(q) = \frac{\varphi(q, x_m, y_m)}{\int |\varphi(q, x_m, y_m)|^2\, dq} = \left(\frac{1}{\pi b}\right)^{\frac{1}{4}} \cdot \exp - \left[\frac{1}{2b} (q - x_m)^2 + iqy_m\right]. \tag{9}$$

Notice that the measurement is complete, in that the state of the system after the measurement is dependent only on the meter readings and not otherwise on the state of the system before measurement. We also notice that the system is left in a minimum Gaussian packet after the measurement, with mean position $x_m$ and mean momentum $y_m$, which is an intuitively satisfying result.

From (7) or (8) it is easy to verify that the expected value of $x$ is equal to the expected value of $q$ before the interaction and that the expected value of $y$ is equal to the expected value of $p$ before the interaction. The variances of $x$ and $y$ are related to the variances of $q$ and $p$ before the interaction by

$$\begin{aligned} \sigma_x^2 &= \sigma_q^2 + b/2 \\ \sigma_y^2 &= \sigma_p^2 + 1/2b. \end{aligned} \tag{10}$$

Hence the variances are individually larger than those of the wave function $F(q)$ due to the disturbances caused by the joint measurement. From

(7) and (10) it can be seen that in the limit $b \to 0$ distribution of $x$ is the same as that of an ideal measurement of position and the system is left in an eigenstate of position. Similarly, if $b \to \infty$ we have an ideal momentum measurement and the system is left in an eigenstate of momentum.

From (10) and the uncertainty principle

$$\sigma_q \sigma_p \geqq 1/2 \tag{11}$$

we can deduce

$$\sigma_x \sigma_y \geqq 1 \tag{12}$$

which is the proper uncertainty principle for the joint measurement. The minimum can actually be met when $F(q)$ is a minimum Gaussian packet and the balance $b$ is suitably adjusted. It is interesting that, when $F(q)$ is a minimum Gaussian packet, (8) shows that the meter readings are distributed as independent Gaussian random variables.

We will now show that the bound expressed by (12) is valid for any joint measurement that meets certain reasonable requirements.

Let us consider a joint measurement from a more general point of view. As before, we will have a meter (a system with at least two degrees of freedom) interact with our system. The initial wave function for the meter plus system will be the product of the system wave function $F(q)$ and the meter function $M(w_1 w_2, \ldots)$. After allowing the interaction to proceed for $t$ seconds we will measure two observables, say $x(t)$ and $y(t)$, which will hopefully measure the system position and momentum. In the Heisenberg representation we may write without loss of generality

$$\begin{aligned} x(t) &= q(0) + A \\ y(t) &= p(0) + B. \end{aligned} \tag{13}$$

If we normalize with a scale factor of unity on both measurements, it is natural to require that the expectations of $x(t)$ and $y(t)$ satisfy

$$\begin{aligned} \langle x(t) \rangle &= \langle q(o) \rangle \\ \langle y(t) \rangle &= \langle p(o) \rangle \end{aligned} \tag{14}$$

uniformly for *all* initial states of the system, i.e., for all $F(q)$. This implies that

$$\begin{aligned} \langle A \rangle &= 0 \\ \langle B \rangle &= 0 \end{aligned} \tag{15}$$

identically for all $F(q)$. From this and the fact that the initial wave function for the system plus meter factors, it can be shown

$$\begin{aligned} \langle qA \rangle = \langle Aq \rangle = \langle Bq \rangle = \langle qB \rangle = 0 \\ \langle pA \rangle = \langle Ap \rangle = \langle Bp \rangle = \langle pB \rangle = 0. \end{aligned} \tag{16}$$

Secondly, we require that $x(t)$ and $y(t)$ commute so that they may be simultaneously measured. From this and (13) we have

$$[B,A] = [q,p] + [q,B] + [A,p]. \tag{17}$$

Squaring both sides of (17) and taking expectations, it follows from (16) that

$$\langle -[A,B]^2 \rangle \geqq 1 \tag{18}$$

which implies

$$\langle A^2 \rangle \langle B^2 \rangle \geqq 1/4. \tag{19}$$

Using (13) and (16), we obtain

$$\sigma_x^2 \sigma_y^2 = \sigma_p^2 \sigma_q^2 + \langle A^2 \rangle \langle B^2 \rangle + \sigma_q^2 \langle B^2 \rangle + \sigma_p^2 \langle A^2 \rangle \tag{20}$$

where $\sigma_x^2 = \langle (x - \langle x \rangle)^2 \rangle$, etc.

From (11) and (19) it follows that

$$\sigma_x \sigma_y \geqq 1 \tag{21}$$

which is the desired result.

REFERENCES

1. von Neumann, J., *Mathematical Foundations of Quantum Mechanics*, Princeton University Press, Princeton, N. J., 1955.

# 7



Reprinted from *IEEE Trans. Inf. Theory* **IT-14**(1):32–37 (1968)

# Quantum Electrodynamics of a Communication Channel

CHIAO YAO SHE, MEMBER, IEEE

***Abstract*—A simple one-dimensional model is taken to illustrate the quantum effects of a narrowband communication system. The system is quantized, and its dynamics are discussed in terms of the Heisenberg equations for field operators. The detection process of a "coherent joint detector," whose compatibility with quantum physics was justified elsewhere, is discussed. The detector, which is capable of measuring the quadrature-modulating components at Nyquist rate with minimum possible uncertainty allowed by quantum theory and which is most suitable for a continuous channel, is used to determine the channel capacity. It is shown that the noise of the channel, due to both thermal and quantum fluctuations, is additive and Gaussian. The classical concepts and expressions for the average mutual information and channel capacity are still valid, provided that the quantum noise of one quantum is included properly. The results obtained approach straightforwardly Shannon's in the classical limit.**

## I. Introduction

Over the past few years, with the advent of optical masers, there has been a considerable interest in dealing with quantum effects in communication systems. This enthusiasm was perhaps derived from the awareness that, at optical frequencies, the dual (corpuscle-like and wave-like) nature of radiation is essential[1] and a quantum mechanical treatment of electromagnetic fields is inevitable. Most of the previous work stressed fundamental limitations to information transmission,[2],[3] the behavior of certain types of detectors,[3],[4] and the discreteness of the radiation energy.[4],[5] The problem was, however, rarely attacked from the viewpoint of quantum field theory.

In this paper, we discuss the quantum electrodynamics of a narrowband channel with bandwidth $W$ centered at a carrier frequency $\omega_0/2\pi$. The channel is constantly perturbed by its environmental thermal noise at temperature $T$. We differ from the previous works in two respects: 1) we restrict ourselves to an ideal quantum mechanical detection system[6] which measures repeatedly the quadrature modulating components at Nyquist rate $W$, and thus describe the narrowband channel in the same manner as Shannon[7] did in his classical theory; 2) we use quantum field theory from which all the quantum effects should be accounted for properly without overweighting either the particle picture or the wave picture of the radiation fields.

Even in the realm of classical physics there is inexactness in a measurement which arises from the discrepancies between the discreteness associated with a practical measuring process and the continuity associated with its idealized definition. This kind of inexactness is nonetheless conceptually known, and it can be eliminated in principle by imagining a certain, perhaps unrealizable, limiting situation. As a useful example, let us consider the measurement of the quadrature modulating components of a narrowband signal $x(t) = x_c(t) \cos \omega_0 t + x_s(t) \sin \omega_0 t$. For simplicity, we represent the detection process by a linear system. With a suitable choice of the impulse response $h(t)$, the output $y(t)$, examined at synchronism so that $\cos \omega_0 t = 1$ and $\sin \omega_0 t = 0$, approximates either $x_c(t)$ or $x_s(t)$ to a desirable accuracy. The function of synchronization can also be achieved by sending $y(t)$ and a local carrier into a multiplier followed by a finite time integrator. This situation is shown in Fig. 1. Two sets of impulse responses are considered at synchronism. The outputs $y_c(t)$ and $y_s(t)$, respectively, approximate $x_c(t)$ and $x_s(t)$ rather well if the parameter $\gamma$ of the linear system is such that $W \ll \gamma \ll \omega_0$. $W$ is the bandwidth and $\omega_0$ the carrier frequency of the narrowband signal $x(t)$. It is assumed that $W \ll 1/T \ll \omega_0$. Intuitively, the measuring time, approximately $1/\gamma$, must be long enough to average over several cycles of carrier frequency and short enough to resolve the quadrature-modulating components of the signal in sufficient detail if the measurement is to be more or less exact. This inexactness is of classical origin since it can be eliminated when the limiting condition, i.e., $W \ll \gamma \ll \omega_0$, for this example is approached.

There are, in addition, unavoidable uncertainties inherent in quantum mechanical principles that affect the accuracy of a measurement. These uncertainties are due to the fact that the dynamical variables describing a system are associated with noncommuting operators.[8] One of the quantum effects which is now well known is the zero-point fluctuation. In many cases, it may be regarded equivalently as an inherent noise source of the system under consideration.[8],[9] A less well-known fact is that the initial state of a measured system depends, according to quantum mechanics, on the outcome of the previous measurement; this is evidently important when repeated measurements are considered.[10] To account for all these effects, a simple communication system will be treated from the viewpoint of quantum field theory. In Section II, we will construct a simple model without investigating its implications in communication theory. The model will be quantized and its dynamics solved by quantum field theory. The statistics of repeated ideal simultaneous measurements[6] for a set of detection field

Manuscript received November 29, 1966; revised May 15, 1967. This work was supported by the National Science Foundation under Grant GK-252.

The author is with the Dept. of Elec. Engrg., University of Minnesota, Minneapolis, Minn.

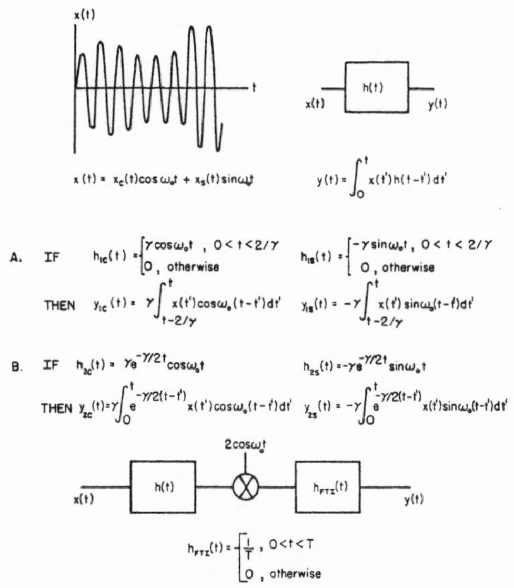


Fig. 1. A narrowband signal $x(t)$ is fed into a linear system with impulse response $h(t)$. The output $y(t)$ can be made to approximate the quadrature-modulating components of $x(t)$, either $x_c(t)$ or $x_s(t)$, by the arrangements shown.

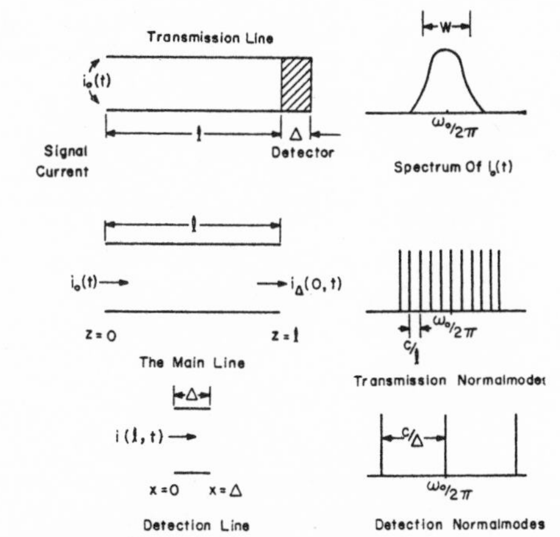


Fig. 2. A simple communication system. The system is broken into parts, and the source and sink current distributions for the main transmission line and the detector are indicated. The spectra of signal current, transmission, and detection system are shown.

variables $q$ and $p$ will be discussed in Section III. In Section IV we will point out that the model used and the statistics obtained are just what is needed to answer questions related to a communication problem. By stating the problem in a slightly different way and making a simple change of variables, we will have a communication system similar to Shannon's. The average mutual information and channel capacity can be obtained with the quantum effects accounted for in a natural manner.

## II. The Model and Its Dynamics

An extremely simple one-dimensional system as shown in Fig. 2 is to be treated quantum mechanically. A narrowband signal current $i_0(t) = i_c(t) \cos \omega_0 t + i_s(t) \sin \omega_0 t$ with bandwidth $W$ is fed into a very long transmission line from the left, and a physically small but finite detector is connected to the right to measure the incoming fields, which include the effects of both the fed signal and the noise associated with the line. The transmission line is embedded in a thermal bath at temperature $T$, which generates thermal noise. It is so long that its normal modes form nearly a continuum, and $c/l \ll W \ll \omega_0$ where $c$ is the velocity of the light. The detector is represented by a short line with the following characteristics: 1) it is matched to the main transmission line and has an ideal bandpass response in the frequency band of interest; 2) the length $\Delta$ of the line is so short that there is only one normal mode assumed to be centered in the band of width $W$ concerned, i.e., $W \ll c/\Delta \ll \omega_0/2\pi$; and 3) the conjugate field variables of the detector can be measured and recorded simultaneously to an accuracy limited only by the fundamental laws of quantum physics.[6]

Since the detector is a matched device and there is no reflection to worry about, one may write separate sets of equations of motion for the main transmission line and the detection line. When the boundary conditions are replaced by their equivalent source and sink distributions as shown in Fig. 2, classical equations to describe the dynamical behavior of the system are obtained as

$$\frac{\partial V}{\partial z} = -L \frac{\partial I}{\partial t};$$
$$\frac{\partial I}{\partial z} = -C \frac{\partial V}{\partial t} + i_0(t)\, \delta(z) - i_\Delta(0, t)\, \delta(z - l) \tag{1}$$

and

$$\frac{\partial V_\Delta}{\partial x} = -L \frac{\partial I_\Delta}{\partial t}; \quad \frac{\partial I_\Delta}{\partial x} = -C \frac{\partial V_\Delta}{\partial t} + i(l, t)\, \delta(x) \tag{2}$$

where the notation has usual meaning and the subscript $\Delta$ refers to the quantities of the detector. The system specified by (1) and (2) can be quantized by standard canonical procedures outlined in a previous paper.[11] Potential functions $\varphi(z, t)$ and $\varphi_\Delta(x, t)$ for the main transmission line and the detection line are introduced such that

$$V = L(\partial\varphi/\partial t), \qquad I = -\partial\varphi/\partial z$$
$$V_\Delta = L(\partial\varphi_\Delta/\partial t), \qquad I_\Delta = -\partial\varphi_\Delta/\partial x. \tag{3}$$

With the aid of (3), wave equations for both lines are constructed from which the total Hamiltonian of the system can be obtained as

$$\mathcal{H} = \int_0^l \left[\frac{c^2}{2L}\pi^2 + \frac{L}{2}\left(\frac{\partial\varphi}{\partial z}\right)^2\right] dz + \int_0^\Delta \left[\frac{c^2}{2L}\pi_\Delta^2 + \frac{L}{2}\left(\frac{\partial\varphi_\Delta}{\partial x}\right)^2\right] dx - L\int_0^l i_0(t)\varphi(z)\,\delta(z)\,dz + L\int_0^l i_\Delta(0, t)\varphi(z)\,\delta(z - l)\,dz - L\int_0^\Delta i(l, t)\varphi_\Delta(x)\,\delta(x)\,dx. \tag{4}$$

Here, $\varphi$, $\pi$ and $\varphi_\Delta$, $\pi_\Delta$ are canonically conjugate fields of the system which become operators when the commutation relations are imposed. When expressed in terms of the usual creation and annihilation operators, $a_k^\dagger$ and $a_k$, with the commutation relations $[a_k, a_{k'}^\dagger] = a_k a_{k'}^\dagger - a_{k'}^\dagger a_k = \delta_{kk'}$, the current operators take the form of

$$I(z) = ic(\hbar/2Ll)^{1/2} \sum_k k\omega_k^{-1/2}[a_k^\dagger \exp(-ikz) - a_k \exp(ikz)] \tag{5}$$

and

$$I_\Delta(x) = ick_0(\hbar/2\omega_0 L\Delta)^{1/2}[a_\Delta^\dagger \exp(-ik_0x) - a_\Delta \exp(ik_0x)] \tag{6}$$

where $\hbar$ is Planck's constant divided by $2\pi$. The transmission-line model is used to represent coherent plane waves at light frequencies. There are two independent polarizations for each wave vector, and the mode density per unit wave number is $(l/2\pi)$ (2). We also set up a matched system for signal propagation, and the signal interacts only with the forward waves which have positive wave vectors. In other words, the signal travels only from left to right, although there is thermal noise generated at every point of the main transmission line and running in both directions.

The electrodynamics of the system, according to quantum theory, may be described by the time evolution of the field operators by solving the pertinent Heisenberg equations of motion.[8] In our case, the coupled equations of the creation and annihilation operators for the normal modes of both the main transmission line and the detection line are

$$\frac{da_k}{dt} + i\omega_k a_k = i\frac{c}{\sqrt{2}}\sqrt{\frac{L}{l}}\frac{1}{\sqrt{\hbar\omega_k}}i_0(t) + \frac{c^2}{2}\frac{1}{\sqrt{l\Delta}}\frac{k_0}{\sqrt{\omega_k\omega_0}}(a_\Delta^\dagger - a_\Delta)e^{-ikl} \tag{7}$$

and

$$\frac{da_\Delta}{dt} + i\omega_0 a_\Delta = -\frac{c^2}{2}\frac{1}{\sqrt{l\Delta}}\sum_k \frac{k}{\sqrt{\omega_k\omega_0}}(a_k^\dagger e^{-ikl} - a_k e^{ikl}) \tag{8}$$

and their Hermitian adjoint equations. The terms in the right-hand side of (7) are zero for negative $k$, since the signal (source and sink) interacts only with the forward waves. Equation (7) may be integrated and substituted into (8), which yields

$$\frac{da_\Delta}{dt} + \left(\frac{\gamma}{2} + i\omega_0\right)a_\Delta - \frac{\gamma}{2}a_\Delta^\dagger = i\beta i_0\left(t - \frac{l}{c}\right) - \sum_k (\alpha_k^* e^{i\omega_k t} - \alpha_k e^{-i\omega_k t}) \tag{9}$$

where

$$\gamma = c/\Delta, \qquad \beta = c(L/2\hbar\omega_0\Delta)^{1/2},$$

and

$$\alpha_k = c^2k(4l\Delta\omega_k\omega_0)^{-1/2}a_k(0)\exp(ikl).$$

Equation (9) and its Hermitian adjoint are linear differential equations and can be solved exactly in a straightforward manner. The approximated solution for the case of interest, with $l \gg \Delta \gg c/\omega_0$, or $\omega_0 \gg \gamma$, turns out to be

$$a_\Delta(t) = a_\Delta(0)\exp\left[-\left(\frac{\gamma}{2} + i\omega_0\right)t\right] + i\beta \cdot \int_0^t \exp\left[-\frac{\gamma}{2}(t - t')\right]\exp[-i\omega_0(t - t')]i_0\left(t' - \frac{l}{c}\right)dt' - iK\sum_k \frac{k}{\sqrt{\omega_k}}\left[\frac{\exp[i\omega_k t] - \exp\left[-\left(\frac{\gamma}{2} + i\omega_0\right)t\right]}{\omega_k - \left(-\omega_0 + i\frac{\gamma}{2}\right)}e^{ikl}a_k^\dagger(0) + \frac{\exp[-i\omega_k t] - \exp\left[-\left(\frac{\gamma}{2} + i\omega_0\right)t\right]}{\omega_k - \left(\omega_0 - i\frac{\gamma}{2}\right)}e^{ikl}a_k(0)\right] \tag{10}$$

where $K = (c^2/2)(l\Delta\omega_0)^{-1/2}$. It is obvious from (10) that there are three different contributions to the detection field at time $t$, which is expressed in terms of $a_\Delta(t)$ and $a_\Delta^\dagger(t)$. The first term of (10) represents the effect of the previous detector condition and reflects the fact that a quantum mechanical measurement depends on its previous outcome. The third term depends on the initial noncommuting normal mode operators $a_k^\dagger(0)$ and $a_k(0)$ of the main transmission line at thermal equilibrium. The second term is due to the input narrowband signal, which is being retarded in an expected manner.

The effective exponential decay of the signal, which is characteristic of the couplings between one oscillation and many closely spaced oscillations,[12] reflects the finite memory of the detector.

## III. Statistics of Repeated Simultaneous Measurements

One of the principal interests of this paper is the transmission of information and the capacity for signal reconstruction of the communication channel. It is unfortunate that in quantum theory the solution to this problem depends intimately on the type of detector one uses to describe the channel.[3],[4] Here, we limit ourselves to what might be called the "coherent joint detector," which repeatedly measures, with maximum accuracy allowed by quantum mechanics, the conjugate field variables simultaneously at a proper rate. We are interested in obtaining the statistics of such measurement processes. The quadrature modulating components $i_c(t)$ and $i_s(t)$ may be regarded as the conjugate field variables of the signal current[13],[14], $i_0(t)$, while the conjugate field variables for the detection line are its electric field $q(t)$ and magnetic field[8],[13] $p(t)$,

$$\begin{aligned} q(t) &= (\hbar/2\omega_0)^{1/2}[a_\Delta^\dagger(t) + a_\Delta(t)] \\ p(t) &= i(\hbar\omega_0/2)^{1/2}[a_\Delta^\dagger(t) - a_\Delta(t)]. \end{aligned} \tag{11}$$

The "coherent joint detector" performs the ideal simultaneous measurements of $q$ and $p$ with minimum quantum uncertainties at the Nyquist rate. According to a previous paper,[6] the ideal simultaneous measurement at an instant may be defined as an observation that yields simultaneous knowledge about $q$ and $p$ with (understood) minimum uncertainty $\Delta q\ \Delta p = \hbar/2$. The system (detector in the present case) immediately after an ideal simultaneous measurement is left in a pure coherent state,[8] which is an eigenstate of the annihilation operator $a_\Delta$. It was shown[6] that a positive definite probability density can be obtained to describe the statistics of such a measurement. Furthermore, the conditional probability density of an ideal simultaneous measurement at time $t$ which yields the result $(q, p)$, given that a similar measurement made at an earlier time $t = 0$ yielded the result $(q_0, p_0)$, can also be determined. The characteristic function for the conditional probability density $P(q, p \mid q_0, p_0)$ of $(q, p)$ given $(q_0, p_0)$ was found to be [6],[13]

$$\begin{aligned} &C(\xi, \eta, q_0, p_0) \\ &= \mathrm{Tr}\,\{\rho(0) \exp[i\Omega^* a_\Delta(t)] \exp[i\Omega a_\Delta^\dagger(t)]\} \\ &= \exp[-|\Omega|^2/2]\,\mathrm{Tr}\,\{\rho(0) \exp i[\Omega a_\Delta^\dagger(t) + \Omega^* a_\Delta(t)]\} \end{aligned} \tag{12}$$

where $\Omega = (\hbar/2\omega_0)^{1/2}\xi + i(\hbar\omega_0/2)^{1/2}\eta$, $\Omega^* = (\hbar/2\omega_0)^{1/2}\xi - i(\hbar\omega_0/2)^{1/2}\eta$, and $\rho(0)$ is the density operator of the system at time $t = 0$ when the previous measurement was made with outcome $(q_0, p_0)$. The characteristic function $C(\xi, \eta, q_0, p_0)$ is defined as the two-dimensional Fourier transform [6],[13] of the conditional probability

$$P(q, p \mid q_0, p_0).$$

It should be pointed out that the characteristic function of (12) is not the Fourier transform of the well-known Wigner density[15],[16] which is Trace $\{\rho(0) \exp i[\Omega a_\Delta^\dagger(t) + \Omega^* a_\Delta(t)]\}$. The exponential factor $\exp[-|\Omega|^2/2]$ in (12) guarantees a positive definite inverse Fourier transform.[6],[17] Physically, the difference between the two arises from the fact that the Wigner density accounts for the unavoidable lack of precision in the state of a quantum system only, while the probability density associated with an ideal simultaneous measurement accounts not only for that, but also for the unavoidable perturbation introduced by the measuring process.[6] Thus, the difficulties of the probabilistic interpretation[18] of the Wigner density, which is not always positive definite, do not apply to the density functions associated with ideal simultaneous measurements.

For the purpose of present calculation, the density operator $\rho(0)$ for the system at $t = 0$, should be

$$\rho(0) = |q_0, p_0\rangle\langle q_0, p_0| \prod_k \left[1 - \exp\left(-\frac{\hbar\omega_k}{\kappa T}\right)\right] \cdot \exp\left[-\frac{\hbar\omega_k}{\kappa T}\, a_k^\dagger(0) a_k(0)\right]. \tag{13}$$

Here the density operator $|q_0, p_0\rangle\langle q_0, p_0|$ is a pure state, the state of the detector right after the previous measurement at time $t = 0$. It is a coherent state[8],[17] because the previous simultaneous measurement[6] yielding $q_0$ and $p_0$ was made at $t = 0$. The state of the main transmission line at the instant of the measurement is assumed to be thermal equilibrium. There are two reasons for this: 1) the interaction is to be momentarily turned off at the instant of measurement, and the state in the Heisenberg picture is independent of time corresponding to the unperturbed system; 2) no observation of the main transmission-line field is made, and hence no perturbation due to the simultaneous measurement is introduced to alter the state of the main transmission line. The density operator in the bracket of (13) is well known[6],[13] and represents the state of all transmission modes at thermal equilibrium at temperature $T$. In (13) $\kappa$ is the Boltzmann constant. Substituting (10) and (13) into (12), one obtains the following characteristic function after a considerable amount of calculation

$$C(\xi, \eta; q_0, p_0) = \exp[i\xi\bar{q} - \tfrac{1}{2}\xi^2\sigma_q^2] \exp[i\eta\bar{p} - \tfrac{1}{2}\eta^2\sigma_p^2]$$

where

$$\begin{aligned} \bar{q} &= \exp\left(-\frac{\gamma t}{2}\right)\left(q_0 \cos\omega_0 t + \frac{1}{\omega_0} p_0 \sin\omega_0 t\right) + \sqrt{\frac{2\hbar}{\omega_0}}\,\beta \\ &\quad \cdot \int_0^t \exp\left[-\frac{\gamma(t - t')}{2}\right] i_0\left(t' - \frac{l}{c}\right) \sin\omega_0(t - t')\, dt' \\ \bar{p} &= \exp\left(-\frac{\gamma t}{2}\right)(p_0 \cos\omega_0 t - \omega_0 q_0 \sin\omega_0 t) + \sqrt{2\hbar\omega_0}\,\beta \\ &\quad \cdot \int_0^t \exp\left[-\frac{\gamma(t - t')}{2}\right] i_0\left(t' - \frac{l}{c}\right) \cos\omega_0(t - t')\, dt' \\ \sigma_q^2 &= (\hbar/\omega_0)\{[\exp(\hbar\omega_0/\kappa T) - 1]^{-1}[1 - \exp(-\gamma t)] + 1\} \\ \sigma_p^2 &= \omega_0^2\sigma_q^2. \end{aligned} \tag{14}$$

The effect of the signal current $i_0(t)$ between two successive measurements is contained in the expression, as expected. Since the simultaneous measurement depends only on the outcomes of the preceding measurement, the process of the repeated simultaneous measurement would be Markovian, and the conditional probability density between two successive measurements specifies the detection process. This conditional probability of measuring $q_t$ and $p_t$ at time $t$ with the signal current $i_0(t)$ and the outcomes of the preceding measurement $q_{t-\tau}$ and $p_{t-\tau}$

at time $t - \tau$ specified can be obtained from (14) by a trivial extension. In fact, it is obtained by taking the inverse transform of (14) and replacing $t - 0$ by $\tau$ and 0 by $t - \tau$ where $\tau$ is the time interval between two successive measurements. The result is

$$P[q_t, p_t \mid q_{t-\tau}, p_{t-\tau}, i_0(t)] = \frac{1}{2\pi\sigma_{q_t}\sigma_{p_t}} \exp\left[-\frac{(q_t - \bar{q}_t)^2}{2\sigma_q^2} - \frac{(p_t - \bar{p}_t)^2}{2\sigma_{p_t}^2}\right] \quad (15)$$

with

$$\bar{q}_t = \exp\left(-\frac{\gamma\tau}{2}\right)\left(q_0 \cos\omega_0\tau + \frac{1}{\omega_0} p_0 \sin\omega_0 t\right) + \sqrt{\frac{2\hbar}{\omega_0}}\beta \cdot \int_{t-\tau}^{t} \exp\left[-\frac{\gamma(t-t')}{2}\right] i_0\left(t' - \frac{l}{c}\right) \sin\omega_0(t-t')\, dt'$$

$$\bar{p}_t = \exp\left(-\frac{\gamma\tau}{2}\right)(p_0 \cos\omega_0\tau - \omega_0 q_0 \sin\omega_0\tau) + \sqrt{2\hbar\omega_0}\,\beta \cdot \int_{t-\tau}^{t} \exp\left[-\frac{\gamma(t-t')}{2}\right] i_0\left(t' - \frac{l}{c}\right) \cos\omega_0(t-t')\, dt'$$

$$\sigma_{q_t}^2 = (\hbar/\omega_0)\{[\exp(\hbar\omega_0/\kappa T) - 1]^{-1}[1 - \exp(-\gamma\tau)] + 1\}$$

$$\sigma_{p_t}^2 = \omega_0^2\sigma_{q_t}^2.$$

The conditional probability of (15) is Gaussian, and the fluctuations depend on both the thermal excitations and the uncertainties of quantum mechanical origin. The total fluctuation (noise) energy is

$$E_{\text{noise}} = \tfrac{1}{2}[\sigma_{p_t}^2 + \omega_0^2\sigma_{q_t}^2] = \hbar\omega_0[(e^{\hbar\omega_0/\kappa T} - 1)^{-1}(1 - e^{-\gamma\tau}) + 1].$$

It is seen that there is a quantum fluctuation of energy $\hbar\omega_0$ in addition to the expected build-up of the thermal noise.[8],[12] It should be pointed out that the conditional probability function of (15) would be a random variable if $i_0(t)$ were a random process. In this case, the statistics of $i_0(t)$ can be specified over which the statistical averages may be taken.

## IV. The Communication Problem

We are now in a position to discuss problems related to communication theory. For this purpose, the model of Section II may be regarded as a simple communication system. The main transmission line is the channel with the signal current $i_0(t) = i_c(t) \cos\omega_0 t + i_s(t) \sin\omega_0 t$ as input. The detection line measures the output of the channel with an attempt to reconstruct the transmitted signal. Since $2W$ pieces of information per unit time are necessary to specify a narrowband signal[10] with bandwidth $W$, we need to perform the simultaneous measurements at an interval of $\tau = 1/W$. The conditional probability function of (15) is just what is needed for specifying the statistics of the measured output. As discussed in the Introduction, one would arrange the detection system so that its measuring time is long enough to average over a few cycles of the carrier and short enough to resolve the envelope in sufficient detail. In our case, we adjust the length of the detection line so that $W \ll c/\Delta \ll \omega_0$, since the measuring time is roughly $1/\gamma = \Delta/c$. Under this condition, it is fortunate that: 1) the quantum effect of measurement due to the previous outcome is negligible, since $\gamma\tau = c/\Delta W \to \infty$; and 2) at synchronism, the average values $\bar{q}_t$ and $\bar{p}_t$ are proportional to $i_s(t)$ and $i_c(t)$. Equation (15) reduces to the following simple form

$$P[q(t), p(t) \mid i_s(t), i_c(t)] = \frac{1}{2\pi\sigma_q\sigma_p} \exp\left[-\frac{(q(t) - \bar{q}(t))^2}{2\sigma_q^2} - \frac{(p(t) - \bar{p}(t))^2}{2\sigma_p^2}\right] \quad (16)$$

where

$$\sigma_q^2 = \frac{\hbar}{\omega_0}(n_{\text{th}} + 1), \qquad \sigma_p^2 = \hbar\omega_0(n_{\text{th}} + 1),$$

$$n_{\text{th}} = [\exp(\hbar\omega_0/\kappa T) - 1]^{-1}$$

$$\bar{q}(t) = \left(-\sqrt{\frac{2\hbar}{\omega_0}}\frac{\beta}{\gamma}\right) i_s\left(t - \frac{l}{c}\right) = -\frac{\sqrt{L\Delta}}{\omega_0} i_s\left(t - \frac{l}{c}\right)$$

$$\bar{p}(t) = \sqrt{2\hbar\omega_0}\,\frac{\beta}{\gamma}\, i_c\left(t - \frac{l}{c}\right) = \sqrt{L\Delta}\, i_c\left(t - \frac{l}{c}\right).$$

To facilitate our further discussion, let us make the following changes of variables, which enable the outputs of the channel to have the same physical meaning as their corresponding inputs, to

$$y_c(t) \equiv (L\Delta)^{-1/2} p(t), \qquad y_s(t) \equiv -\omega_0 (L\Delta)^{-1/2} q(t). \quad (17)$$

The conditional probability of the output $y_c(t)$ and $y_s(t)$ given the input $i_c(t)$ and $i_s(t)$ can be obtained easily from (16) as

$$P(y_c(t), y_s(t) \mid i_c(t), i_s(t)] = \frac{1}{2\pi\sigma_c\sigma_s} \exp\left[-\frac{(y_c(t) - i_c(t))^2}{2\sigma_c^2} - \frac{(y_s(t) - i_s(t))^2}{2\sigma_s^2}\right] \quad (18)$$

where $\sigma_c^2 = \sigma_s^2 = \hbar\omega_0(n_{\text{th}} + 1)/\Delta L \equiv \sigma^2$. The form of (18) suggests that we have a communication channel with additive[19] Gaussian noise. The situation is very similar to that treated by Shannon's classical theory although the fluctuations of noise contain both thermal and quantum mechanical contributions. Since the repeated measurements are independent under the ideal limiting condition of $W \ll c/\Delta \ll \omega_0$, we need calculate only the average mutual information for each event, i.e., an input pair and an output pair, and we obtain the total rate by multiplying it by the factor $W$. For a channel with additive noise, the mutual information of an event $I(y_c, y_s; i_c, i_s)$ equals the information of the output event $H(y_c, y_s)$ less the noise information[19] $H(n_c, n_s)$ where $n_c(t) = y_c(t) - i_c(t)$ and $n_s(t) = y_s(t) - i_s(t)$, i.e.,

$$I(y_c y_s; i_c, i_s) = H(y_c, y_s) - H(n_c, n_s). \quad (19)$$

$H(n_c, n_s)$ can be calculated with the aid of (18), while $H(y_c, y_s)$ depends on the statistics of the input signal, which determines its information content.

The maximum rate of the average mutual information is defined as the channel capacity. For additive noise, the mutual information is maximum if the output information content $H(y_c, y_s)$ is maximum. It can be shown that for given average signal energy and for additive Gaussian noise $n_c = y_c - i_c$, $n_s = y_s - i_s$ with the probability distribution of (18), $H(y_c, y_s)$ would be maximum if the statistics of the input signal were Gaussian.[13],[19] Under this condition, the statistics of $i_c(t)$ and $i_s(t)$ are independently Gaussian random process with equal variances, i.e., $\overline{i_c^2} = \overline{i_s^2} = \overline{i_0^2}$. The channel capacity, which is the maximum rate of mutual information, under the constraint of fixed average signal energy, can be shown to equal[13],[19]

$$C = W[H_{\max}(y_c, y_s) - H(n_c, n_s)]$$

$$= W\{\tfrac{1}{2} \log (2\pi)^2(\overline{i_c^2} + \sigma_c^2)(\overline{i_s^2} + \sigma_s^2) - \tfrac{1}{2} \log (2\pi)^2\sigma_c^2\sigma_s^2\}$$

$$= W \log \left[1 + \frac{\overline{i_0^2}}{\sigma^2}\right] = W \log \left[1 + \frac{S}{N}\right] \qquad (20)$$

where $S$ and $N$ are, respectively, the averaged signal and noise energy that the detector measures in a simultaneous measurement for which the effective signal measuring time is $\Delta/c$, i.e.,

$$\frac{S}{N} = \frac{\overline{i_0^2}\sqrt{\frac{L}{C}}\frac{\Delta}{c}}{\hbar\omega_0(n_{\text{th}} + 1)} = \frac{\overline{i_0^2}}{\hbar\omega_0(n_{\text{th}} + 1)/L\Delta} = \frac{\overline{i_0^2}}{\sigma^2}.$$

It is evident from (20) that Shannon's classical expression is still valid, provided that the quantum noise of one quantum is included. In the classical limit, the quantum effect vanishes, and $N$ approaches $\kappa T$ as $\hbar \to 0$.

## V. Conclusions

A simple model has been constructed to discuss the transmission of a narrowband signal from a quantum field point of view. Both the main transmission line (channel) and the measuring device (receiver) were quantized to account for the quantum effects due to both the zero-point fluctuations and the fact that the initial state of a measurement depends on the outcome of the preceding measurement. The memory of the measuring device discussed here decays exponentially with a characteristic time $\Delta/c$ that equals the time for an electromagnetic wave to go through the detector. It was pointed out that for an effective measurement, the memory $\Delta/c$ must be long enough to average over many cycles of carrier frequency and short enough to resolve the quadrature modulating components of the signal in sufficient detail. Under this condition, the rate of the repeated measurements is slow enough relative to the detection memory that the quantum effects due to the previous measurement are negligible or forgotten. It was shown that with a "coherent joint detector" that performs ideal simultaneous measurements at Nyquist rate, the detection process can be described by a simple Gaussian random process. The effective noise of the channel, due to both thermal and quantum fluctuations of total $(n_{\text{th}} + 1)$ quanta, is additive and Gaussian. If the statistics of the input signal are given or to be chosen with signal power limited to some value, the classical concepts and expressions for the average mutual information and channel capacity are still valid, provided that the quantum noise of one quantum is included properly.

It is also interesting to note the implication of the results when the temperature $T$ approaches zero. In this case, the unavoidable quantum effect of one noise quantum sets a fundamental limit to the accuracy of the well-known sampling theorem,[7],[19] and it also prevents an ideal channel from having infinite capacity.

## References


[1] W. Heisenberg, *The Physical Principles of the Quantum Theory.* Chicago, Ill.: University of Chicago Press, 1930.

[2] D. S. Lebedev and L. B. Levitan, "The maximum amount of information transmissible by an electromagnetic field," *Soviet Phys.—Doklady*, vol. 8, pp. 377–379, October 1963.

[3] C. W. Helstrom, "Quantum limitations on the detection of coherent and incoherent signals," *IEEE Trans. Information Theory*, vol. IT-11, pp. 482–490, October 1965.

[4] J. P. Gordon, "Quantum effects in communication systems," *Proc. IRE*, vol. 50, pp. 1898–1908, September 1962.

[5] T. E. Stern, "Some quantum effects in information channels," *IRE Trans. Information Theory*, vol. IT-6, pp. 435–440, September 1960.

[6] C. Y. She and H. Heffner, "Simultaneous measurement of noncommuting observables," *Phys. Rev.*, vol. 152, pp. 1103–1110, December 1966.

[7] C. E. Shannon and W. Weaver, *The Mathematical Theory of Communication.* Urbana, Ill.: University of Illinois Press, 1949, pp. 49–81.

[8] W. H. Louisell, *Radiation and Noise in Quantum Electronics.* New York: McGraw-Hill, 1964.

[9] W. H. Louisell, A. Yariv, and A. E. Siegman, "Quantum fluctuations and noise in parametric processes," *Phys. Rev.*, vol. 124, pp. 1646–1654, December 1961.

[10] R. P. Feynman, "Space-time approach to non-relativistic quantum mechanics," *Rev. Mod. Phys.*, vol. 20, pp. 367–387, April 1948.

[11] C. Y. She, "Quantum descriptions of an infinite lossless transmission line," *J. Appl. Phys.*, vol. 36, pp. 3784–3788, December 1965.

[12] J. P. Gordon, L. R. Walker, and W. H. Louisell, "Quantum statistics of masers and attenuators," *Phys. Rev.*, vol. 130, pp. 806–812, April 1963.

[13] C. Y. She, "Quantum descriptions on communication theory," Stanford Electronics Lab., Stanford University, Stanford, Calif., Rept. 64-074, 1964.

[14] T. Hagfors, "Information capacity and quantum effects in propagation circuits," M.I.T. Lincoln Lab., Lexington, Mass., Rept. 344, 1964.

[15] G. J. Lasher, "A quantum statistical treatment of the channel capacity problem of information theory," *Advances in Quantum Electronics*, Jay R. Singer, Ed. New York: Columbia University Press, 1961, pp. 520–536.

[16] L. F. Jelsma and L. P. Bolgiano, "A quantum field description of communication systems," *1st IEEE Annual Communications Conf. Rec.*, pp. 635–642, June 1965.

[17] R. J. Glauber, "Coherent and incoherent states of the radiation field," *Phys. Rev.*, vol. 131, pp. 2766–2788, September 1963.

[18] H. Margenau and R. N. Hill, "Correlation between measurements in quantum theory," *Prog. Theoret. Phys.*, vol. 26, pp. 722–738, November 1961.

[19] R. M. Fano, *Transmission of Information.* Cambridge, Mass: M.I.T. Press and New York: Wiley, 1961, ch. 5.

# 8



Reprinted from *IEEE Proc.* **58**(10):1578–1598 (1970)

# Quantum-Mechanical Communication Theory

CARL W. HELSTROM, SENIOR MEMBER, IEEE, JANE W. S. LIU, AND JAMES P. GORDON

**Abstract—This paper is concerned with the problem of finding the structure and performance of the receiver that yields the best performance in the reception of signals that are described quantum-mechanically. The principles of statistical detection and estimation theory are discussed, with the laws of quantum mechanics taken into account. Several specific communication systems of practical interest are studied as examples of applying these principles. Basic concepts in quantum mechanics that are needed in these discussions are briefly reviewed.**

## I. Introduction

THE performance and structure of a receiver in a communication system depend on the form of the signals used to transmit messages and the nature of the random noise that accompanies the signals. For a given performance measure, the best structure of the receiver can be determined by the principles of detection and estimation theory, which views the receiver as an instrument for testing certain hypotheses about its input and applies the methods of statistical decision theory [1]–[4].

Although real receivers are perturbed by a variety of noises whose characteristics differ from one application to another, thermal noise is always present. Thermal noise is the type of noise that arises from the chaotic thermal agitation of the atoms and molecules composing the receiver and its surroundings [5], [6]. The upper limit to the receiver performance in the reception of a given set of signals can be ascertained by calling upon detection or estimation theory to determine the best receiver for receiving these signals when they are accompanied only by thermal noise.

In most treatments of ideal reception of signals at microwave frequencies, it is assumed that the electromagnetic fields of signal and noise, the receiver, and the interaction between them behave in accordance with the classical laws of electromagnetism. The noise generated by an ideal receiver can be accounted for in the thermal noise accompanying the signals at its input. The ideal receiver can examine its input in every detail in order to extract all information relevant to the optimum reception of the given signals without introducing more uncertainty about them. Usually, the input to the receiver is described by the waveforms of the electric field over the receiving aperture.

When the signals to be detected are composed of optical rather than microwave frequencies, the input fields and their interaction with matter can be described accurat[e]ly only by the laws of quantum mechanics. The postulate th[at] the ideal receiver can make use of every detail of its inp[ut] without introducing further uncertainty must be scr[u]tinized. By virtue of the uncertainty principle of quantu[m] mechanics, for instance, the amplitude and phase of t[he] input field cannot be determined simultaneously with ar[bi]trary accuracy. Indeed, an electric field having both preci[se] amplitude and phase cannot in principle be generate[d]. Whereas the limitations imposed by the laws of quantu[m] mechanics negligibly affect the reliability of a communic[a]tion system at microwave frequencies, they are often mo[re] influential than the thermal noise at optical frequencies.

In early studies of the quantum-mechanical aspects [of] communication systems, emphasis was placed on findi[ng] upper bounds to channel capacity and on evaluating pe[r]formance of systems incorporating specific receive[rs]. Channel capacities were derived for communication syste[ms] using known receivers, such as linear amplifiers, heter[o]dyne and homodyne receivers, and photon counters [7]–[13]. Quantum-mechanical limitations on the accuracy [of] measurements made by a phase-sensitive receiver are tak[en] into account by introducing at its input a frequency-depe[n]dent noise statistically similar to thermal noise. Quantu[m] limitations on the detection of known and random sign[als] in thermal noise were found when the receiver measures t[he] strength of the electric field as in a heterodyne receiver [14].

This paper is concerned with the problem of finding t[he] structure and performance of the receiver that yields t[he] best performance in the reception of signals that are d[e]scribed quantum-mechanically. In Section IV and Secti[on] V, the principles of statistical detection and estimati[on] theory, taking into account the laws of quantum mechani[cs] [15]–[18], are discussed. Several specific communicati[on] systems of practical interest are studied as examples [of] applying these principles. Basic concepts in quantum m[e]chanics needed in these discussions are briefly reviewed [in] Section II.

## II. Quantum Mechanics

A thorough introduction to quantum mechanics c[an] hardly be fitted into the compass of this paper; at most t[he] paper can present the basic rules and concepts. The reaso[ns] behind them and the techniques of applying them to phy[si]cal problems have been discussed in textbooks [19], [20]. We shall content ourselves with asserting that from the[se] principles a broad and accurate understanding of the phy[si]cal world in general, and of the properties of matter a[nd] radiation in particular, have been achieved.

To great accuracy, the behavior of all physical commun[i]cation systems is governed by the laws of quantum mecha[nics]

Manuscript received April 27, 1970. The research of C. W. Helstrom was supported by NASA Grant NGL-05-009-079. The research of J. W. S. Liu was supported by NASA Grant NGL-22-009-013.

C. W. Helstrom is with the Department of Applied Physics and Information Science, University of California at San Diego, La Jolla, Calif. 92037.

J. W. S. Liu is with the Research Laboratory of Electronics, Massachusetts Institute of Technology, Cambridge, Mass. 02139.

J. P. Gordon is with Bell Telephone Laboratories, Inc., Holmdel, N. J. 07733.

cs. Whereas the classical laws predict the behavior of communication systems operating at microwave frequencies or below with reasonable accuracy, the radiation fields and the receivers in communication systems at optical frequencies can only be adequately described quantum-mechanically. We shall call a system classical or quantum-mechanical depending on whether a sufficiently accurate description of its behavior requires classical or quantum-mechanical laws.

*State Vectors and Operators*

As in the case of a classical system, the condition of a quantum-mechanical system at any instant of time is completely specified by its *state*. Mathematically, the state of a quantum-mechanical system is described by a state vector $|\psi\rangle$ in a Hilbert space $\mathscr{H}$ over the field of complex numbers [21]. Any state vector $|\psi\rangle$ can be expressed in terms of a linear combination of vectors $|\phi_n\rangle$ in a basis—coordinate system—$\{|\phi_n\rangle\}$ in the Hilbert space $\mathscr{H}$ [22] as follows.

$$|\psi\rangle = \sum_{n=1}^{\infty} a_n|\phi_n\rangle.$$

Hence without loss of generality, $|\psi\rangle$ can be thought of as a column vector having an infinite number of components that are the complex numbers $a_n$. State vectors can be combined linearly to form a new vector that also represents a possible state of the system. Associated with any $|\psi\rangle$ is a Hermitian conjugate $\langle\psi|$, which can be regarded as a row vector whose components are complex conjugates of those in $|\psi\rangle$.

The scalar product of two state vectors $|\phi\rangle$ and $|\psi\rangle$ is a complex number, written $\langle\phi|\psi\rangle$; in terms of the components $\{a_n\}$ and $\{b_n\}$ of these vectors,

$$\langle\phi|\psi\rangle = \sum_n a_n^* b_n. \tag{1}$$

Following Dirac, we call $|\psi\rangle$ a *ket*, and $\langle\phi|$ a *bra* because together they form a *bracket* $\langle\phi|\psi\rangle$. Although the components $a_n$ and $b_n$ of the kets $|\phi\rangle$ and $|\psi\rangle$ depend on the basis to which they are referred, the value of the scalar product $\langle\phi|\psi\rangle$ is independent thereof. The squared length of the ket $|\psi\rangle$ is $\langle\psi|\psi\rangle$. When it is finite, the ket is normalized to have unit length $\langle\psi|\psi\rangle = 1$. Not all state vectors in quantum mechanics can be assigned a finite length. Two kets differing only by a phase factor $e^{i\theta}$ common to all components describe physically identical states.

The kets $|\psi\rangle$ are transformed by linear operators. A linear operator $\Xi$ can be expressed in terms of the kets $|\phi_n\rangle$ in a basis $\{|\phi_n\rangle\}$ as

$$\Xi = \sum_{n=1}^{\infty}\sum_{m=1}^{\infty} |\phi_m\rangle\langle\phi_m|\Xi|\phi_n\rangle\langle\phi_n|.$$

When represented in terms of the basis $\{|\phi_n\rangle\}$, the operator is associated with a square matrix, albeit usually infinite in extent, whose elements are

$$\Xi_{mn} = \langle\phi_m|\Xi|\phi_n\rangle.$$

We can, therefore, regard a linear operator as a square matrix. An operator $\Xi$ is said to be Hermitian when its associated matrix equals the transpose conjugate matrix $\Xi^+$. The $\Xi^+$ is called the Hermitian adjoint of $\Xi$.

Suppose that a Hermitian operator $\Xi$ has a discrete set $(\xi_1, \xi_2, \cdots, \xi_n, \cdots)$ of eigenvalues. The associated eigenvectors $|\xi_1\rangle, |\xi_2, \cdots, |\xi_n\rangle, \cdots$, are defined by the eigenvalue equation

$$\Xi|\xi_n\rangle = \xi_n|\xi_n\rangle. \tag{2}$$

Because $\Xi$ is Hermitian, the eigenvalues $\xi_n$ are real. The eigenvectors are orthogonal. Being normalized to unit length, they have the scalar products

$$\langle\xi_n|\xi_m\rangle = \delta_{nm}, \tag{3}$$

where $\delta_{nm}$ is the Kronecker delta symbol. Our interest will be restricted to those Hermitian operators whose eigenvectors form a complete set,

$$\sum_{n=1}^{\infty} |\xi_n\rangle\langle\xi_n| = \mathbf{1}, \tag{4}$$

where $\mathbf{1}$ is the identity operator: $\mathbf{1}|\psi\rangle = |\psi\rangle$, for all $|\psi\rangle$. Having properties (3) and (4), the eigenvectors $|\xi_n\rangle$ form a basis in terms of which any ket $|\psi\rangle$ can be expressed as

$$|\psi\rangle = \sum_{n=1}^{\infty} c_n|\xi_n\rangle, \qquad c_n = \langle\xi_n|\psi\rangle. \tag{5}$$

If, on the other hand, a linear operator $Z$ has a continuum of eigenvalues $\zeta$,

$$Z|\zeta\rangle = \zeta|\zeta\rangle, \tag{6}$$

the eigenvectors $|\zeta\rangle$ have infinite length and are so normalized that

$$\langle\zeta'|\zeta''\rangle = \delta(\zeta' - \zeta''), \tag{7}$$

where $\delta(\zeta' - \zeta'')$ is the Dirac delta function. Their completeness relation now is

$$\int_{-\infty}^{\infty} |\zeta\rangle\langle\zeta|d\zeta = \mathbf{1}, \tag{8}$$

by virtue of which any ket $|\psi\rangle$ can be expressed as

$$|\psi\rangle = \int_{-\infty}^{\infty} \gamma(\zeta)|\zeta\rangle d\zeta, \qquad \gamma(\zeta) = \langle\zeta|\psi\rangle. \tag{9}$$

*Observables and Quantum-Mechanical Measurement*

Each measurable physical quantity, or *observable*, of the system, such as position, momentum, or angular momentum of a particle, is associated with a Hermitian operator that has a complete set of eigenvectors. The eigenvalues of such a Hermitian operator may form a discrete or a continuous set, or a combination of both [23]. Without loss of generality, we shall discuss observables and their operators as though their spectra were discrete. Modifications to cover those with a continuous spectrum of eigenvalues, or a combination of discrete and continuous spectra, will involve changing Kronecker deltas to Dirac deltas, and sums to integrations.

Quantum mechanics postulates that an exact measurement of an observable whose operator is $\Xi$ always yields as an outcome one or another of the eigenvalues $\xi_n$ of $\Xi$. Immediately after a measurement of $\Xi$ that yields the eigenvalue $\xi_k$, the measured system is in the corresponding eigenstate $|\xi_k\rangle$, and repeating the measurement immediately afterward on the same system would yield the same value $\xi_k$ [24].

Furthermore, if before measurement the system is in state $|\psi\rangle$, the probability that the measurement will yield the value $\xi_k$ is given by

$$\Pr(\xi_k) = |\langle \xi_k|\psi\rangle|^2 = |c_k|^2, \tag{10}$$

where $c_k$ is the coefficient in the expansion of $|\psi\rangle$ as in (5). By the closure relation (4), these probabilities sum to 1,

$$\sum_k \Pr(\xi_k) = \sum_k \langle\psi|\xi_k\rangle\langle\xi_k|\psi\rangle = \langle\psi|\psi\rangle = 1.$$

If the observable, as $Z$, has a continuous spectrum, $|\langle\zeta|\psi|^2\, d\zeta$ is the probability that the outcome of a measurement lies between $\zeta$ and $\zeta + d\zeta$. Hence $|\langle\zeta|\psi|^2$ is the probability density function of the outcome of the measurement. From (2) and (4), the expected value of the outcome of a measurement of $\Xi$ is

$$E[\Xi] = \sum_k \xi_k \Pr(\xi_k) = \langle\psi|\Xi|\psi\rangle, \tag{11}$$

when the system is in state $|\psi\rangle$. This expression for the expected value is independent of the coordinate system used to describe the ket $|\psi\rangle$.

The outcome of a measurement of the observable $\Xi$ answers the question, "What is the value of $\Xi$?" Instead, suppose that the weaker question is asked, "Does the value of $\Xi$ lie between $a$ and $b$?" and the actual value within the range $(a, b)$ is of no concern. While this question can also be answered by measuring $\Xi$ itself, it is sufficient to measure the observable represented by the operator

$$\Pi_{ab} = \sum_{R(a,b)} |\xi_n\rangle\langle\xi_n|, \tag{12}$$

where $R(a, b)$ is the set of eigenvalues $\xi_n$ of $\Xi$ lying within $(a, b)$. A complete set of eigenvectors of $\Pi_{ab}$ is the eigenvector $|\xi_n\rangle$ of $\Xi$. However, $\Pi_{ab}$ has only the two eigenvalues, 1 and 0. The outcome of the measurement of $\Pi_{ab}$ will be 1 if the value of $\Xi$ lies in $R(a, b)$ and 0 otherwise. If the state of the system before measurement is $|\psi\rangle$, the expected value of the outcome is

$$E[\Pi_{ab}] = \langle\psi|\Pi_{ab}|\psi\rangle = \sum_{R(a,b)} |\langle\xi_n|\psi\rangle|^2$$
$$= \Pr\{\xi \in R(a, b)\}, \tag{13}$$

which is the probability that the value $\xi$ of the observable $\Xi$ lies between $a$ and $b$.

The operator $\Pi_{ab}$ in (12) is a projection operator. It obeys the defining equation

$$\Pi_{ab}^2 = \Pi_{ab} \tag{14}$$

for projection operators, as can be seen by using (12) and the orthonormality of the kets $|\xi_n\rangle$ in (3). Since $\Pi_{ab}(\Pi_{ab} - \mathbf{1}) = 0$, the only eigenvalues of $\Pi_{ab}$ are 0 or 1, as we have already observed. The operator $\Pi_{ab}$ projects the ket $|\psi\rangle$ onto the linear subspace spanned by the kets $|\xi_n\rangle$ for which $\xi_n \in R(a, b)$. The statement that the value of the observable $\Xi$ lies between $a$ and $b$ is a proposition that is either true or false, and such propositions correspond in the logic of quantum mechanics to projection operators like $\Pi_{ab}$. The decisions among hypotheses treated in detection theory will be expressed in this form.

If two observables, say $\Xi$ and $\Upsilon$, are to be measured exactly and simultaneously on the same system, it must be left after the measurement in a state $|\xi_n, \upsilon_m\rangle$ that is an eigenstate of both operators $\Xi$ and $\Upsilon$ with eigenvalues $\xi_n$, $\upsilon_m$, respectively [25],

$$\Xi|\xi_n, \upsilon_m\rangle = \xi_n|\xi_n, \upsilon_m\rangle$$
$$\Upsilon|\xi_n, \upsilon_m\rangle = \upsilon_m|\xi_n, \upsilon_m\rangle, \tag{15}$$

and this must hold true for all possible outcomes $\xi_n$, $\upsilon_m$ of the measurement. It follows from (15) and the completeness of the states $|\xi_n, \upsilon_m\rangle$ that a necessary and sufficient condition is that the operators $\Xi$ and $\Upsilon$ commute,

$$\Xi\Upsilon = \Upsilon\Xi. \tag{16}$$

Two observables are said to be compatible when their corresponding operators commute. As an example, the three Cartesian coordinates $x$, $y$, and $z$ of a particle are compatible, for the three associated operators $X$, $Y$, and $Z$ commute.

*Uncertainty Principle*

When the two operators $\Xi$ and $\Upsilon$ do not commute, the corresponding observables cannot be measured simultaneously on the same system with complete precision. This is a crude statement of the Heisenberg uncertainty principle. To express this principle more precisely, suppose that the operators $\Xi$ and $\Upsilon$ satisfy the commutation relation,

$$[\Xi, \Upsilon] = \Xi\Upsilon - \Upsilon\Xi = iZ,$$

where $Z$ is either a constant times the identity operator $\mathbf{1}$ or another operator. Let

$$\sigma_\Xi^2 = E[\Xi^2] - E[\Xi]^2 \tag{17}$$

denote the mean-square deviation of the outcomes of a measurement of $\Xi$. Similarly, define

$$\sigma_\Upsilon^2 = E[\Upsilon^2] - E[\Upsilon]^2. \tag{18}$$

When the system is in the state $|\psi\rangle$ before the measurement,

$$\sigma_\Xi^2 = \langle\psi|\Xi^2|\psi\rangle - (\langle\psi|\Xi|\psi\rangle)^2$$

and

$$\sigma_\Upsilon^2 = \langle\psi|\Upsilon^2|\psi\rangle - (\langle\psi|\Upsilon|\psi\rangle)^2.$$

By using the Schwarz inequality, it can be shown [26] that the product $\sigma_\Xi\sigma_\Upsilon$ of the standard derivations satisfies the inequality

$$\sigma_\Xi\sigma_\Upsilon \geq |\langle\psi|Z|\psi\rangle|/2 \tag{19}$$

for all state vectors $|\psi\rangle$. Equation (19) is called the Heisenberg uncertainty relation.

This principle can be illustrated by an example. The two operators $P$ and $Q$ satisfy the commutation relation,

$$[Q, P] = QP - PQ = i\hbar,$$

where $\hbar = h/2\pi$ is Planck's constant. The corresponding observables are the coordinate $q$ and momentum $p$, respectively, of a particle with one degree of freedom. The same commutation relation holds for the operators corresponding to the charge and current in a lossless LC circuit. From (19),

$$\sigma_Q \sigma_P \geq \hbar/2. \tag{20}$$

In order to interpret this relation, one must think of a large ensemble of $N$ independent systems, all of them in the same state $|\psi\rangle$. On some systems $Q$ is measured, on others $P$. The outcomes will be random variables, differing from one system to another, but when $N \gg 1$, the average values will be near their mean values and the mean-square deviations near $\sigma_Q^2$ and $\sigma_P^2$, respectively. Just what average values and mean-square deviations $\sigma_Q^2$, $\sigma_P^2$ are obtained depends on the state $|\psi\rangle$ in which the systems were originally prepared. The uncertainty principle (20) asserts that no state $|\psi\rangle$ can the product of the standard deviations $\sigma_Q\sigma_P$ be less than $\frac{1}{2}\hbar$.

*Density Operators*

Given an ensemble of independent systems, all in the same state $|\psi\rangle$, measurement of an observable such as $\Xi$ on each will in general produce a random collection of results, the probability of obtaining the value of $\xi_n$ being $|\langle\xi_n|\psi\rangle|^2$, $n=1, 2, \cdots$. This randomness is strictly a quantum phenomenon. The kind of randomness met in classical physics must also somehow be incorporated into the framework of quantum mechanics, so that we can treat problems involving noise or random signals. The means of doing so is provided by the density operator $\rho$ [27], [28].

Let a large number of systems of the same kind be prepared, each in one of a set of orthonormal states $|\phi_n\rangle$, and let the fraction of systems in state $|\phi_n\rangle$ be $P_n$, $n=1, 2, \cdots$, with

$$\langle\phi_m|\phi_n\rangle = \delta_{mn} \tag{21}$$

$$\sum_{n=1}^{\infty} P_n = 1. \tag{22}$$

If now we measure the observable $\Xi$, the probability of obtaining the value $\xi_k$ will be

$$\Pr(\xi_k) = \sum_{n=1}^{\infty} P_n|\langle\xi_k|\phi_n\rangle|^2 = \langle\xi_k|\rho|\xi_k\rangle. \tag{23}$$

In this expression, the operator $\rho$ defined by

$$\rho = \sum_{n=1}^{\infty} P_n|\phi_n\rangle\langle\phi_n| \tag{24}$$

is called the *density operator*. Since $\rho$ is a linear operator, it can also be thought of as a square matrix. The expected value of the outcome of our measurement of $\Xi$ is

$$E(\Xi) = \sum_{k=1}^{\infty} \xi_k \Pr(\xi_k) = \sum_{k=1}^{\infty} \xi_k\langle\xi_k|\rho|\xi_k\rangle = \sum_{k=1}^{\infty} \langle\xi_k|\rho\Xi|\xi_k\rangle = \mathrm{Tr}(\rho\Xi), \tag{25}$$

where Tr stands for the trace of a matrix, the sum of its diagonal elements.

Clearly, the density operator $\rho$ is Hermitian. It has a complete set of orthonormal eigenvectors $|\phi_n\rangle$ corresponding to nonnegative eigenvalues $P_n$ and $\mathrm{Tr}\,\rho = 1$. Moreover, any Hermitian operator with nonnegative eigenvalues and trace 1 may be considered as a density operator that describes an ensemble of quantum-mechanical systems.

A density operator $\rho$ also has the property $\mathrm{Tr}\,\rho^2 \leq 1$, with equality if and only if one of the prior probabilities $P_n$ equals 1 and all the rest 0. When this is so, the density operator is a projection operator, $\rho = |\phi_n\rangle\langle\phi_n|$, and the ensemble is a collection of systems all in the same state $|\phi_n\rangle$. When $\rho$ is a projection operator we say that it represents a system in a *pure* state; otherwise, with $\mathrm{Tr}\, b^2 < 1$, it represents a *mixed* state.

*Time Dependence*

Thus far, we have not shown how a quantum-mechanical system behaves dynamically. To discuss the manner in which the state of a system changes with time, let us denote the state vector at time $t$ by $|\psi(t)\rangle$. It is clear from the discussions on quantum-mechanical measurements that the state vector changes irreversibly in an unpredictable way when the system interacts with a measuring device. But when a closed quantum-mechanical system is not perturbed by any measurement, its state vector $|\psi(t)\rangle$ at time $t$ obeys a linear differential equation of the first order in time [29]

$$i\hbar \frac{\partial}{\partial t}|\psi(t)\rangle = H|\psi(t)\rangle, \tag{26}$$

where $H$ is an operator called the Hamiltonian of the system. We shall be concerned solely with conservative systems. The Hamiltonian of a conservative system does not contain time explicitly; (26) can be solved to obtain

$$|\psi(t)\rangle = \exp\left[-i\frac{H}{\hbar}(t - t_0)\right]|\psi(t_0)\rangle, \tag{27}$$

which relates the state vector $|\psi(t)\rangle$ at time $t$ to that at an earlier time $t_0$.

The Hamiltonian $H$ is the operator corresponding to the energy of the system. For many systems $H$ can be obtained from the classical expression for the energy in terms of coordinates and momenta, these being simply replaced by their quantum-mechanical operators and properly symmetrized. Thus, for a simple harmonic oscillator of mass $m$ and frequency $\omega$, the Hamiltonian operator is

$$H = (2m)^{-1}(P^2 + \omega^2 Q^2) \tag{28}$$

in terms of the operators $P$ and $Q$ for its momentum and its coordinate. The operator

$$\exp\left[-i\frac{H}{\hbar}(t-t_0)\right]$$

executes a unitary transformation on the state vectors $|\psi\rangle$, as in (27). Under this transformation the lengths of the kets $|\psi\rangle$ and the angles between them in the Hilbert space do not change. This representation of the time dependence of a system as a rigid rotation of its state vectors is called the "Schrödinger picture." In the Schrödinger picture, operators not depending explicitly on the time are taken as constants.

We shall use a different, but physically equivalent, representation of the time dependence of quantum-mechanical systems, which is called the "Heisenberg picture" [30]. The state vector in the Heisenberg picture is independent of time. At time $t$, an observable $\Xi(t)$ is related to the operator $\Xi$ in the Schrödinger picture by

$$\Xi(t) = \exp\left[i\frac{H}{\hbar}(t-t_0)\right]\Xi\exp\left[-i\frac{H}{\hbar}(t-t_0)\right]\cdot \quad (29)$$

From this transformation and (26), the equation of motion for the observable $\Xi$ in the Heisenberg picture is

$$i\hbar\frac{d\Xi(t)}{dt} = [\Xi(t), H] + i\hbar\frac{\partial\Xi(t)}{\partial t}\cdot \quad (30)$$

The Hamiltonian $H$ equals the Hamiltonian in the Schrödinger picture, since the system is conservative.

If a system is in a statistical mixture of states represented by a density operator $\rho$, $\rho$ is independent of time in the Heisenberg picture. The expectation value of a measurement of an observable $\Xi(t)$ at time $t$ will be

$$E_t[\Xi] = \mathrm{Tr}\,[\rho\Xi(t)].$$

It is easy to see that this expectation value equals $\mathrm{Tr}\,[\Xi\rho(t)]$, where

$$\rho(t) = \exp\left[-\frac{i}{\hbar}H(t-t_0)\right]\rho\exp\left[\frac{i}{\hbar}H(t-t_0)\right]$$

and $\Xi$ are the operators at time $t$ in the Schrödinger picture.

### *Ideal Measurement of Incompatible Observables*

The class of exact measurements of compatible observables discussed above does not include those measurements yielding approximate values of several incompatible observables. As an example of devices that make such approximate measurements on the received field, we mention a high-gain laser amplifier followed by a classical receiver. The field at the output of such an amplifier can be treated as a classical field with precisely measurable amplitude and phase. Therefore, the amplifier performs simultaneous approximate measurements of the amplitude and phase of its input field [31]. The additive Gaussian noise injected by the amplifier accounts for the inevitable error in the measurement imposed by the uncertainty principle.

We shall briefly consider a definition [32] for ideal measurements to include such approximate measurements of incompatible observables. Let $\boldsymbol{x}_n$ denote the set of numbers that are the observed values of the measured observables. An *ideal measurement* means one in which each possible outcome $\boldsymbol{x}_n$ is associated with a state vector $|\boldsymbol{x}_n\rangle$ such that the probability for obtaining $\boldsymbol{x}_n$ is

$$P(\boldsymbol{x}_n) = w|\langle \boldsymbol{x}_n|\psi\rangle|^2 \quad (31)$$

when the system is in the state $|\psi\rangle$ prior to the measurement and $w$ is a normalization constant. Moreover, the state of the system after the measurement depends only on the measurement result, and not at all on its initial state before the measurement. Thus subsequent measurements cannot yield additional information about that initial state.

The normalized state vector $|\boldsymbol{x}_n\rangle$ is called a measurement state vector. Since some result must be obtained from any measurement, the set of measurement state vectors must satisfy a completeness relation of the form

$$\sum_n w|\boldsymbol{x}_n\rangle\langle\boldsymbol{x}_n| = \mathbf{1}. \quad (32)$$

Any ideal measurement, therefore, is characterized by a complete set of measurement state vectors.

Exact measurements of compatible observables are ideal by the previously mentioned criterion. They are characterized by complete sets of orthonormal measurement state vectors that are the simultaneous eigenvectors of the measured observables. In such cases the relation (31) is satisfied with the normalization constant $w$ equal to 1, and (32) is simply the completeness relation in (4). The measurement of field amplitude and phase as made by an ideal high-gain amplifier is also ideal. In this case, the measurement state vectors are the coherent state vectors defined in (50), and the appropriate completeness relation is given by (52). These measurement state vectors are not orthogonal.

Sets of nonorthogonal vectors that satisfy a completeness relation such as (32) are called overcomplete sets. Ideal measurements yielding approximate values of several incompatible observables can be characterized by overcomplete sets of measurement state vectors. It is probably true that for every such measurement, in principle, there is an equivalent exact measurement characterized by an orthonormal set of measurement state vectors. Many conveniently realizable measuring processes correspond, however, to overcomplete sets of measurement state vectors, while realization of the equivalent exact measurements might prove difficult.

A fairly general way of implementing ideal measurement of incompatible observables is to combine the system to be measured with an auxiliary system whose initial state is known. The two systems may be allowed to interact for a length of time. An exact measurement of a complete set of compatible observables for the expanded system is then made. As an example of this prescription, consider the observables $Q$ and $P$ for a simple harmonic oscillator. We may combine this system with an auxiliary system comprising a similar but independent oscillator in its ground state, whose corresponding observables are $Q'$ and $P'$. The observables $Q-Q'$ and $P+P'$ of the expanded system are compatible, and their simultaneous exact measurement yields approximate values of $Q$ and $P$. Further analysis [33] shows that this prescription indeed yields an ideal measurement of $Q$ and $P$.

## III. Quantum-Mechanical Description of Communication Systems

A typical communication system is shown in Fig. 1. In every signaling interval of duration $T$, the input $m$ of the system is either one of $M$ messages generated by a digital data source or a set of parameters carrying analog data. A signal field, whose characteristics depend on the input message, is generated by the transmitter and is sent through the channel to the receiver. During each signaling interval, the receiver makes an estimate $\hat{m}$ of the transmitted message. Our objective is to design the receiver so that $\hat{m}$ minimizes a given cost function used to measure the fidelity of this estimate. Examples of commonly used cost functions are the probability of error, Pr $[\hat{m} \neq m]$, for digital messages, and the mean-square error, $E[|\hat{m}-m|^2]$, for analog data.

For simplicity, input messages in different signaling intervals are assumed to be statistically independent. Furthermore, discussion will be restricted to systems in which the channel is memoryless and no coding schemes are employed. In these systems, the receiver makes independent estimates of input messages in successive signaling intervals on the basis of the electromagnetic field observed during each of these intervals. Therefore, we need discuss only the problem of making an optimum estimate of a single message. The signal field representing such a message is a time-limited one with nonzero instantaneous power only in a time interval of duration $T$. Without loss of generality, we let this interval be $(0, T)$.

The receiver admits the incident field through an area normal to the direction of the transmitter. In an ordinary receiver, this area corresponds to the effective area of the antenna, which in practice must be limited to a finite size. This area will be called the receiving aperture.

Since at any time the instantaneous power associated with a time-limited signal is nonzero only in a finite region in space and the noise fields at different points in space are statistically independent, the receiver can be idealized as a large lossless box or cavity with perfectly conducting walls. During the time interval $(0, T)$, the incident field is admitted into the cavity, initially empty, through the receiving aperture. At the end of this interval, the aperture is closed, and measurements are made by the receiver on the field inside the cavity, which is called the received field.

The received field can be represented as a superposition of normal modes of the cavity. Each mode behaves like a harmonic oscillator with frequency $\omega_k$; the frequencies $\omega_k$ depend on the shape of the cavity. To be more specific, the classical waveform $\boldsymbol{\mathcal{E}}(\boldsymbol{r}, t)$ of the received electric field can be expanded in terms of standing-wave normal-mode functions $\boldsymbol{u}_k(\boldsymbol{r})$ of an appropriately chosen cavity of volume $V$,

$$\boldsymbol{\mathcal{E}}(\boldsymbol{r}, t) = -\varepsilon_0^{-1/2} \sum_k p_k(t)\boldsymbol{u}_k(\boldsymbol{r}), \tag{33}$$

where the dielectric constant $\varepsilon_0$ is used here for normalization. As a result of boundary conditions at the walls of the

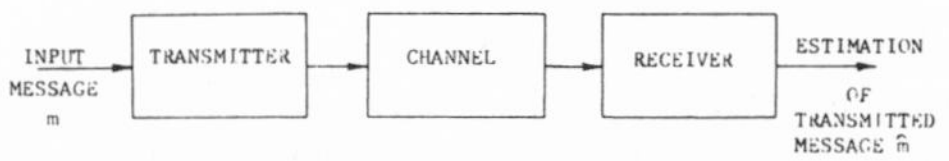


Fig. 1. Quantum-mechanical model of communication systems.

cavity, the functions $\boldsymbol{u}_k(\boldsymbol{r})$ are orthonormal,

$$\int_{\text{cavity}} \boldsymbol{u}_k(\boldsymbol{r})\boldsymbol{u}_n(\boldsymbol{r})d^3\boldsymbol{r} = \delta_{kn}. \tag{34}$$

Inside the cavity, $\boldsymbol{u}_k(\boldsymbol{r})$ is a solution of the Helmholtz equation

$$\nabla^2\boldsymbol{u}_k(\boldsymbol{r}) + (\omega_k^2/c^2)\boldsymbol{u}_k(\boldsymbol{r}) = 0 \tag{35}$$

for all $k$, where $c$ is the velocity of light in a vacuum. The oscillation frequencies $\omega_k$ of the normal modes are determined by (34) and (35).

As a consequence of Maxwell's field equations, the functions $q_k(t)$ defined by

$$p_k(t) = dq_k(t)/dt, \tag{36}$$

in association with the mode amplitudes $p_k(t)$ in (33), satisfy the equation of motion

$$\frac{d^2}{dt^2} q_k(t) + \omega_k^2 q_k(t) = 0. \tag{37}$$

Therefore, we may associate each mode of the field with a harmonic oscillator of frequency $\omega_k$. Furthermore, it can be shown from Maxwell's field equations and from (33)–(35) that the total energy $H$ contained in the received field is the sum of the energies of the uncoupled harmonic oscillators [34],

$$H = \sum_k (p_k^2 + \omega_k^2 q_k^2)/2. \tag{38}$$

It is often preferable to represent the received field in terms of plane traveling waves rather than standing waves. A particular set of mode functions suitable for our purpose is the set of plane traveling-wave mode functions of a cubical cavity of volume $V$. That is,

$$\boldsymbol{u}_k(\boldsymbol{r}) = V^{-1/2}\boldsymbol{e}_k \exp(i\boldsymbol{k}\cdot\boldsymbol{r}), \tag{39}$$

where $\boldsymbol{e}_k$ is a unit polarization vector perpendicular to the propagation vector $\boldsymbol{k}$, and $|\boldsymbol{k}|^2 = \omega_k^2/c^2$, for all $k$. The complex amplitude $\alpha_k(t)$ of each plane traveling-wave mode is related to the real variables $p_k(t)$ and $q_k(t)$ by

$$\alpha_k(t) = (2\hbar\omega_k)^{1/2}\left[\omega_k q_k(t) + ip_k(t)\right]. \tag{40}$$

Hence the equations of motion for $\alpha_k(t)$ are

$$\frac{d}{dt}\alpha_k(t) = -i\omega_k\alpha_k(t),$$

having solutions

$$\alpha_k(t) = \alpha_k \exp\left[-i\omega_k t\right]. \tag{41}$$

In terms of these complex amplitudes, the energy of each normal mode is

$$H_k = \hbar\omega_k|\alpha_k|^2. \tag{42}$$

*Quantization of the Radiation Field*

The quantum theory of radiation [35] also treats each mode of the field as a harmonic oscillator. The "coordinates" $q_k(t)$ and "momenta" $p_k(t)$ are replaced by their corresponding quantum-mechanical operators $Q_k(t)$ and $P_k(t)$, which obey the commutation rule

$$[Q_k(t), P_n(t)] = Q_k(t)P_n(t) - P_n(t)Q_k(t) = i\hbar\delta_{kn} \quad (43)$$

for all $k$ and $n$. The complex amplitudes $\alpha_k$ in (41) are replaced by operators $a_k$ that are related to the operators $Q_k(t)$ and $P_k(t)$ by

$$a_k \exp[-i\omega_k t] = (2\hbar\omega_k)^{1/2}[\omega_k Q_k(t) + iP_k(t)]. \quad (44)$$

It follows from the commutation rules (43) that the commutation relations between the operators $a_k$ and their Hermitian adjoints $a_k^+$ are

$$[a_k, a_n^+] = \delta_{kn}\mathbf{1} \qquad \text{for all } n \text{ and } k.$$

In terms of these operators, the electric field operator is

$$\boldsymbol{E}(\boldsymbol{r}, t) = i\sum_k (\hbar\omega_k/2\varepsilon_0 V)^{1/2}\boldsymbol{e}_k\{a_k \exp[-i(\omega_k t - \boldsymbol{k}\cdot\boldsymbol{r})] - a_k^+ \exp[+i(\omega_k t - \boldsymbol{k}\cdot\boldsymbol{r})]\}. \quad (45)$$

The Hamiltonian of the field becomes

$$H = \sum_k H_k,$$

where

$$H_k = \hbar\omega_k(a_k a_k^+ + a_k^+ a_k) = \hbar\omega_k(a_k^+ a_k + \tfrac{1}{2}). \quad (46)$$

For reasons that will appear immediately, the operator $a_k^+ a_k$ is called the *number operator* of the $k$th mode. In texts on quantum mechanics, it is shown that the eigenvalues of the operators $a_k^+ a_k$ are the positive integers and zero [36]. We denote the eigenvectors by the corresponding eigenvalues

$$a_k^+ a_k|n_k\rangle = n_k|n_k\rangle. \quad (47)$$

Hence by (46), the eigenvalues $E_k$ of the energy in the $k$th mode are

$$E_k = \hbar\omega_k(n_k + \tfrac{1}{2}).$$

When the mode is in the state $|n_k\rangle$, it is customary to say that it contains $n_k$ photons, each of which carries an energy of $\hbar\omega_k$. The ground state $|0\rangle$ possesses a *zero-point fluctuation energy* $\frac{1}{2}\hbar\omega_k$.

When the operator $a_k$ acts to the right on an eigenvector $|n_k\rangle$ of the number operator $a_k^+ a_k$, it converts the eigenvector $|n_k\rangle$ to $|n_k - 1\rangle$,

$$a_k|n_k\rangle = n_k^{1/2}|n_k - 1\rangle, \quad (48)$$

thereby reducing the number of photons of the mode by one. For this reason, $a_k$ is called the *annihilation operator* of the $k$th mode. Its Hermitian adjoint $a_k^+$ raises the number of photons by one and is called the *creation operator*,

$$a_k^+|n_k\rangle = (n_k + 1)^{1/2}|n_k + 1\rangle. \quad (49)$$

When the $k$th mode of the field is in a state described by a state vector $|\alpha_k\rangle$, that is, a right eigenvector of the annihilation operator $a_k$,

$$a_k|\alpha_k\rangle = \alpha_k|\alpha_k\rangle, \quad (50)$$

where $\alpha_k = \alpha_{kx} + i\alpha_{ky}$ is a complex eigenvalue, the mode is said to be in a coherent state [37]. Alternatively, we say that the mode contains a coherent signal. The coherent state vector $|\alpha_k\rangle$ can be expressed in terms of the eigenvectors $|n_k\rangle$ of the number operator $a_k^+ a_k$ [38]

$$|\alpha_k\rangle = \exp[-|\alpha_k|^2/2] \sum_{n_k=0}^{\infty} (n_k!)^{-1/2}\alpha_k^{n_k}|n_k\rangle, \quad (51)$$

which are normalized so that $\langle\alpha_k|\alpha_k\rangle = 1$. Moreover, they are complete in the sense that

$$\int |\alpha_k\rangle\langle\alpha_k| d^2\alpha_k/\pi = \mathbf{1}, \quad (52)$$

where $d^2\alpha_k = d\alpha_{kx} d\alpha_{ky}$ is the element of integration in the complex plane, over the entirety of which the integration is performed. The coherent state vectors $|\alpha_k\rangle$ and $|\beta_k\rangle$, however, are not orthogonal. Their inner product is

$$\langle\alpha_k|\beta_k\rangle = \exp[\alpha_k^*\beta_k - |\alpha_k|^2/2 - |\beta_k|^2/2]. \quad (53)$$

The entire field is in a coherent state $|\{\alpha_k\}\rangle$ when all of its normal modes are in coherent states. The state vector $|\{\alpha_k\}\rangle$ is simultaneously a right eigenvector of all the annihilation operators $a_k$.

$$a_k|\{\alpha_k\}\rangle = \alpha_k|\{\alpha_k\}\rangle. \quad (54)$$

It can be taken to be the direct product of the state vectors for the individual modes

$$|\{\alpha_k\}\rangle = |\alpha_1, \alpha_2, \cdots, \alpha_k, \cdots\rangle = \prod_k |\alpha_k\rangle.$$

The vector space spanned by the vectors $|\{\alpha_k\}\rangle$ is the direct product space of those spanned by the vectors $|\alpha_k\rangle$.

It has been shown [39] that an antenna having a known current distribution and suffering no unpredictable reaction from the surrounding field will produce an electromagnetic field that is in a coherent state. When the field is in the coherent state $|\{\alpha_k\}\rangle$, the classical waveform of the electric field can be obtained from (45) and (54) as the expected value of the operator $\boldsymbol{E}(\boldsymbol{r}, t)$,

$$\mathcal{E}(\boldsymbol{r}, t) = \langle\{\alpha_k\}|\boldsymbol{E}(\boldsymbol{r}, t)|\{\alpha_k\}\rangle = 2\,\mathrm{Im}\left[\sum_k (\hbar\omega_k/2\varepsilon_0 V)^{1/2}\alpha_k \exp[-i(\omega_k t - \boldsymbol{k}\cdot\boldsymbol{r})]\right]. \quad (55)$$

An extensive calculus involving coherent-state vectors has been developed by Glauber [40], [41]. In particular, it has been shown that a large class of density operators, including those met in communication theory, can be expanded in terms of them,

$$\rho = \int P(\{\alpha_k\}) \prod_{k=1}^{\infty} |\alpha_k\rangle\langle\alpha_k| d^2\alpha_k, \quad (56)$$

where the function $P(\{\alpha_k\})$ is called the weight function. This expansion is called the $P$ representation of the density operator $\rho$. The weight function $P(\{\alpha_k\})$ has many of the properties of a classical probability density function, but it is not always positive. In particular,

$$\int P(\{\alpha_k\}) \prod_{k=1}^{\infty} d^2\alpha_k = 1$$

follows from Tr $\rho = 1$. The expected value of an operator $\Xi$ is given by

$$E[\Xi] = \text{Tr}[\rho\Xi] = \int P(\{\alpha_k\})\langle\{\alpha_k\}|\Xi|\{\alpha_k\}\rangle \prod_{k=1}^{\infty} d^2\alpha_k$$

when the state of the field is specified by the density operator $\rho$ in (56).

*Representation of Noise*

For the moment, let us suppose that the field inside the cavity consists of thermal radiation alone. When this random field is in thermal equilibrium at an absolute temperature $\mathscr{T}$, the density operator $\rho_k$ describing the state of the $k$th normal mode in the $P$ representation is

$$\rho_k = \int \exp[-|\alpha|^2/\mathscr{N}_k]|\alpha\rangle\langle\alpha|d^2\alpha/\pi\mathscr{N}_k, \quad (57)$$

where

$$\mathscr{N}_k = \text{Tr}[\rho_k a_k^+ a_k] = \{\exp(\hbar\omega_k/K\mathscr{T}) - 1\}^{-1} \quad (58)$$

is the average number of photons in the $k$th mode with frequency $\omega_k$ [42]. $K = 1.38 \times 10^{-23}$ J/deg is Boltzmann's constant. From (51), it follows that $\rho_k$ can be expanded in terms of the eigenvectors $|n_k\rangle$ of the number operator $a_k^+ a_k$,

$$\rho_k = \sum_{n_k=0}^{\infty} (1 - v_k)v_k^{n_k}|n_k\rangle\langle n_k|,$$
$$v_k = \mathscr{N}_k/(\mathscr{N}_k + 1) = \exp(-\hbar\omega_k/K\mathscr{T}). \quad (59)$$

In the classical limit, $K\mathscr{T} \gg \hbar\omega_k$, the weight function

$$P(\alpha_k) = (\pi\mathscr{N}_k)^{-1}\exp[-|\alpha_k|^2/\mathscr{N}_k]$$
$$= (\pi\mathscr{N}_k)^{-1}\exp[-(\alpha_{kx}^2 + \alpha_{ky}^2)/\mathscr{N}_k]$$

yields the joint probability density function of the real part $\alpha_{kx}$ and the imaginary part $\alpha_{ky}$ of the complex amplitude $\alpha_k$ of the mode [43]. Since $\mathscr{N}_k$ in (58) becomes approximately equal to $K\mathscr{T}/\hbar\omega_k$, it follows from (42) that the average energy of this mode equals $K\mathscr{T}$ independently of its frequency. In classical communication theory, this type of noise is called the additive white Gaussian noise with spectral density.

When a normal mode of the received field contains both thermal noise and a coherent signal that alone is represented by the coherent state vector $|\mu_k\rangle$, the center of the Gaussian weight function in the $P$ representation is simply shifted from the origin by a phasor $\mu_k$. The density operator $\rho_k$ becomes

$$\rho_k = (\pi\mathscr{N}_k)^{-1}\int \exp[-|\alpha - \mu_k|^2/\mathscr{N}_k]|\alpha\rangle\langle\alpha|d^2\alpha. \quad (60)$$

In the representation of the operator $\rho_k$ as a matrix in terms of the basis specified by the eigenvectors $|n_k\rangle$ of the number operator $a_k^+ a_k$, the matrix elements are [44]

$$\langle n|\rho_k|m\rangle = (1 - v_k)(n!/m!)^{1/2}v_k^m(\mu_k^*/\mathscr{N}_k)^{m-n}$$
$$\cdot \exp[-(1 - v_k)|\mu_k|^2]$$
$$\cdot L_n^{m-n}[-(1 - v_k)^2|\mu_k|^2/v_k], \quad m \geq n$$
$$\langle n|\rho_k|m\rangle = \langle m|\rho_k|n\rangle^*, \quad m < n$$
$$v_k = \mathscr{N}_k/(\mathscr{N}_k + 1), \quad (61)$$

where $L_n^{m-n}(x)$ is the associated Laguerre polynomial.

The density operator $\rho$ for the entire received field when it contains only thermal radiation in equilibrium is given by the direct product

$$\rho = \pi^{-\nu}\prod_k \int \exp[-|\alpha_k|^2/\mathscr{N}_k]|\alpha_k\rangle\langle\alpha_k|d^2\alpha_k/\mathscr{N}_k, \quad (62)$$

where $\nu$ is the number of modes. The operator $\rho$ is defined in the linear vector space that is the direct product of the linear vector spaces spanned by the coherent state vectors of the individual modes. When a coherent signal is present in the cavity with Gaussian thermal noise, the density operator in the $P$ representation is

$$\rho = \int \cdots \int P(\{\alpha_k\})\prod_k |\alpha_k\rangle\langle\alpha_k|d^2\alpha_k,$$
$$P(\{\alpha_k\}) = \pi^{-\nu}|\det \boldsymbol{\phi}|^{-1}$$
$$\cdot \exp\left[-\sum_m\sum_n(\alpha_m^* - \mu_m^*)(\boldsymbol{\phi}^{-1})_{mn}(\alpha_n - \mu_n)\right], \quad (63)$$

where $\mu_m$ is the complex amplitude of the coherent signal in mode $m$. Here $\boldsymbol{\phi}$ is the mode correlation matrix, whose elements are

$$\phi_{nm} = \text{Tr}[\rho a_m^+ a_n] - \text{Tr}[\rho a_m^+]\,\text{Tr}[\rho a_n]. \quad (64)$$

When the modes are statistically independent, the mode correlation matrix $\boldsymbol{\phi}$ is diagonal,

$$\phi_{mk} = \mathscr{N}_k\delta_{mk}, \quad (65)$$

where $\mathscr{N}_k$ is the average number of thermal photons in mode $k$ and is given in terms of the frequency $\omega_k$ by (58) when the modes are in thermal equilibrium.

At this point, let us note that $P$ representation of a density operator $\rho$ is not unique. Instead of the coherent states $|\{\alpha_k\}\rangle$, $\rho$ can be expressed in the $P$ representation in terms of the right eigenvectors of a set of operators $b_j$, where

$$b_j = \sum_{k=1}^{\infty} V_{jk}a_k, \quad (66)$$

and the coefficients $V_{jk}$ are elements of unitary matrix $\boldsymbol{V}$. That is,

$$\sum_{k=1}^{\infty} V_{jk}V_{kn}^+ = \sum_{k=1}^{\infty} V_{jk}V_{nk}^* = \delta_{jk}. \quad (67)$$

An easy algebraic manipulation shows that the operators $b_j$ and their Hermitian adjoints $b_j^+$ satisfy the same commutation relations as the operators $a_k$ and $a_k^+$. Hence, $b_j$ and $b_j^+$ can be regarded as the annihilation and creation operators, respectively, of a set of new modes. The right eigenvectors $|\{\beta_k\}\rangle$ of the operators $b_k$

$$b_k|\{\beta_k\}\rangle = \beta_k|\{\beta_k\}\rangle$$

are coherent-state vectors spanning the same vector space as spanned by the vectors $|\{\alpha_k\}\rangle$. When the density operator $\rho$ is expressed in terms of $|\{\beta_k\}\rangle$ in the $P$ representation

$$\rho = \int P'(\{\beta_k\})|\{\beta_k\}\rangle\langle\{\beta_k\}| \prod_{k=1}^{\infty} d^2\beta_k, \tag{68}$$

the new weight function $P'(\{\beta_k\})$ can be obtained by substituting the relation

$$\alpha_k = \sum_{j=1}^{\infty} \beta_j V_{jk}^+ \tag{69}$$

into the weight function $P(\{\alpha_k\})$.

If the unitary matrix $V$ is such that the matrix $V\phi^{-1}V^+$ is diagonal, the density operator $\rho$ in (63), when expressed in terms of eigenvectors of the operators $b_j$ given by (66), is

$$\rho = \pi^{-\nu}\int \exp\left[-\sum_{k=1}^{\infty} |\beta_k - \mu_k'|^2/\mathcal{N}_k'\right] \cdot|\{\beta_k\}\rangle\langle\{\beta_k\}| \prod_k d^2\beta_k/\mathcal{N}_k', \tag{70}$$

where $\mathcal{N}_k'$ is the $k$th diagonal element of the matrix $V\phi^{-1}V^+$, and

$$\mu_k' = \sum_{m=1}^{\infty} V_{km}\mu_m. \tag{71}$$

Therefore, for any particular coherent signal in Gaussian thermal noise, a set of normal modes can be chosen, by appropriately choosing the shape of the receiver cavity, to represent the received field so that the individual modes are uncorrelated.

When the frequency range of the signal is so small that for all $k$ for which $\mu_k \neq 0$,

$$\mathcal{N}_k \approx \mathcal{N}, \tag{72}$$

then $\mathcal{N}_k' = \mathcal{N}$ in (70) can also be taken to be the average number of thermal photons in the new normal mode $k$. The density operator $\rho$ can be expressed in terms of coherent states $|\{\gamma_k\}\rangle$ that are the right eigenvectors of the annihilation operators $g_j$,

$$\rho = (\pi\mathcal{N})^{-\nu}\int \exp\left[-\left\{|\gamma_1 - \mu|^2 + \sum_{k\neq 1} |\gamma_k|^2\right\}\Big/\mathcal{N}\right] \cdot\prod_k |\{\gamma_k\}\rangle\langle\{\gamma_k\}|d^2\gamma_k. \tag{73}$$

In this expression,

$$g_j = \sum_{m=1}^{\infty} V_{jm}b_m, \qquad \gamma_j = \sum_{m=1}^{\infty} V_{jm}\beta_m,$$

where the matrix elements $V_{1m}$ are chosen to be

$$V_{1m} = \mu_m'/|\mu|, \qquad |\mu|^2 = \sum_{m=1}^{\infty} |\mu_m'|^2. \tag{74}$$

The other rows of the matrix $V$ are chosen so that $V$ is unitary. We see that only the mode with annihilation operator $g_1 = \sum_m \mu_m' b_m/|\mu|$ contains a coherent signal [18], [45]. Hence without loss of generality, we often need to consider only one properly chosen normal mode of the received field.

*Quantum-Mechanical Receiver*

In an ideal receiver, the signal field accompanied by chaotic thermal noise is admitted through the receiving aperture into a lossless cavity during the signaling interval (0, *T*). At the end of this interval, the aperture is closed, and measurements are made by the receiver on the received field whose quantum-mechanical description has just been presented.

Let us assume that the measurement made by the receiver is ideal. Again, an ideal measurement is one in which the state of the field after the measurement does not depend on that before the measurement. It follows that the probability distribution of the outcome of any subsequent measurement does not depend on the transmitted input message. That is, any measurement made after an ideal measurement yields no information relevant to the optimum estimation of the transmitted message [46].

It will become apparent that the optimum performance of the system is independent of the time (after the receiving aperture is closed) at which the observation is made. The choice of the observables measured by the optimum receiver does depend, however, on the time of the observation.

The ideal receiver discussed thus far might seem to be much too remote from an ordinary receiver to be relevant to a real optical communication system. A real optical receiver takes in light from the signal source, along with thermal radiation, through an aperture of fixed size, and processes this light by lenses, photodetectors, and possibly coherent heterodying light generated by a local laser. The data upon which it bases its decisions are the values of observables of the electromagnetic field at the aperture during the interval (0, *T*). The field in the cavity of our ideal receiver is a linear functional of this aperture field. The optimum performance derived for the ideal receiver really sets a limit to the performance of any optical receiver processing the same aperture field.

When the signal radiation occupies a narrow band of frequencies and arrives from a narrow cone of directions, and when the background radiation is distributed broadly in frequency and angle, the quantum detection theory developed for the field in the ideal receiver can be applied to the aperture field itself. The important entities in that theory are the annihilation and creation operators for the mode fields and the Hilbert space spanned by their eigenvectors. Operators having the same properties can be defined for the aperture field by representing the field as a superposition of spatio-temporal modes. Just as the mode functions for the cavity field are orthonormal with respect to integration over the three dimensions of the cavity, these spatio-temporal modes are orthonormal for integration over the aperture and the observation interval (0, *T*). The eigenvectors of the associated annihilation and creation operators span a Hilbert space of state vectors to which the concepts and techniques just outlined can be applied [47], [48].

## IV. Quantum Detection Theory

When the data source in Fig. 1 is digital, the input $m$ to the transmitter in the signaling interval $(0, T)$ is one of $M$ message denoted by $m_1, m_2, \cdots, m_M$. When the transmitted message is $m_j$, the electromagnetic field in the receiver cavity is in the statistical mixture of states specified by the density operator $\rho_j$. Therefore, in the time interval $(0, T)$, the state of the received field is specified by one of $M$ density operators $\rho_1, \rho_2, \cdots, \rho_M$.

The output $\hat{m}$ of the system is also one of $M$ messages, and is the estimate of the input message $m$. That is, the receiver decides in the time interval $(0, T)$ among the $M$ hypotheses $H_1, H_2, \cdots, H_M$, of which the hypothesis $H_j$ is that the message $m_j$ is transmitted. The receiver is designed so that the probability of error

$$P_e = \Pr[\hat{m} \neq m] \tag{75}$$

is minimum.

Let $X = (X_1, X_2, \cdots, X_L)$ denote the $L$-tuple of Hermitian operators corresponding to those observables chosen to be measured by the receiver. When these operators commute, a simultaneous measurement of the corresponding observables yields an $L$-tuple $x_n = (x_{1n}, x_{2n}, \cdots, x_{Ln})$ of parameters, where $x_{jn}$ is an eigenvalue of the operator $X_j; j = 1, 2, \cdots, L$. For simplicity, we assume that the eigenspectra of the operators $X_j$ and $\rho_j$ are discrete. That this assumption imposes no real restriction has been pointed out in Section II.

Let $|x_n\rangle$ denote the simultaneous eigenvector of the commuting operators $X_1, X_2, \cdots, X_L$ corresponding to the eigenvalue $x_n$. From (23), the conditional probability that the outcome of the measurement of $X$ yields $x_n$, given that the message $m_j$ is transmitted, is

$$P(x_n|m_j) = \langle x_n|\rho_j|x_n\rangle. \tag{76}$$

Let $\zeta_j$ be the prior probability of the message $m_j$, and $p_{jn}$ be the probability that the receiver chooses the hypothesis $H_j$ when the outcome of the measurement is $x_n$

$$\sum_{j=1}^{M} p_{jn} = 1. \tag{77}$$

The probability of error in (75) is

$$P_e = 1 - \sum_n \sum_{j=1}^{M} \zeta_j p_{jn} \langle x_n|\rho_j|x_n\rangle. \tag{78}$$

The manner in which the optimum receiver processes the data obtained in the measurement is the same as that determined by the principles of classical detection theory [49]. Specifically, the receiver chooses the hypothesis $H_j$ to minimize $P_e$, when the observed value of $X$ is $x_n$, if the conditional probability

$$P(m_j|x_n) = \zeta_j P(x_n|m_j) / \sum_{i=1}^{M} \zeta_i P(x_n|m_i)$$

is maximum. In other words, the probability $p_{jn}$ is 1 for all $j$ such that

$$\zeta_j \langle x_n|\rho_j|x_n\rangle \geq \zeta_i \langle x_n|\rho_i|x_n\rangle, \quad \text{all } i \neq j, \tag{79}$$

and all other $p_{in}$ equal zero. This rule becomes ambiguous when the equality sign in (79) holds for some $i$. The ambiguity can be resolved, however, and the resultant minimum value of $P_e$ is not affected by the way in which this ambiguity is resolved.

Let us define the operators $\Pi_j$ as

$$\Pi_j = \sum_n p_{jn} |x_n\rangle\langle x_n|; \qquad j = 1, 2, \cdots, M. \tag{80}$$

Since the probabilities $p_{jn}$ are either one or zero, the operators $\Pi_j$ are projection operators; therefore, they obey the defining equation (14). Moreover, it follows from (80), and that $p_{in}p_{jn}$ equals zero when $i \neq j$, that

$$\Pi_i \Pi_j = \Pi_i \delta_{ij} \tag{81}$$

and

$$\sum_{j=1}^{M} \Pi_j = \mathbf{1}. \tag{82}$$

In terms of the projection operators $\Pi_j$, the probability of error $P_e$ in (78) becomes

$$P_e = 1 - \sum_{j=1}^{M} \zeta_j \operatorname{Tr}[\rho_j \Pi_j]. \tag{83}$$

Therefore, the problem of finding the best receiver structure becomes that of finding the projection operators $\Pi_j$ that satisfy the constraints (81) and (82) and minimize $P_e$.

It has been shown [50], [51] that a necessary condition for the set of projection operators $\Pi_j$ satisfying constraints (81) and (82) to minimize $P_e$ in (83) is

$$\sum_{j=1}^{M} \zeta_j \Pi_j \rho_j = \sum_{j=1}^{M} \zeta_j \rho_j \Pi_j. \tag{84}$$

This equation, together with the conditions

$$\left\{ \sum_{i=1}^{M} \zeta_i \Pi_i \rho_i - \zeta_j \rho_j \right\} \begin{array}{l} \text{are positive semidefinite} \\ \text{for all } j = 1, 2, \cdots, M, \end{array} \tag{85}$$

provides a sufficient condition for the set of projection operators $\Pi_j$ to be an optimum solution.

When the projection operators $\Pi_j$ have a complete set of eigenvectors in common, they can be taken as observables of the field, and the receiver measures them simultaneously. Hypothesis $H_j$ is chosen when the observed value of $\Pi_j$ is equal to 1. Because of (82), an optimum receiver in a binary communication system is specified simply by one projection operator $\Pi$.[1]

When the receiver is allowed to make ideal measurements of incompatible observables in the sense discussed in Section II, the structure of the receiver is specified by the over-

[1] A note of caution is advisable here. While it is true that all hypotheses relating to the values of compatible observables are evaluated based on the outcomes of measurements of projection operators such as $\Pi_j$, it is not obvious that all projection operators can be measured physically. Equivalently, while all observables correspond to Hermitian operators, it is not clear that all Hermitian operators with complete sets of eigenvectors correspond to observables that in principle are measurable. This problem, of obvious practical importance, is beyond the scope of this paper, and we do in fact assume that any Hermitian operator that has a complete set of eigenvectors is an observable.

complete set of measurement state vectors $\{|x_n\rangle\}$, when the outcomes of the measurements are $x_n$. Since with $\{|x_n\rangle\}$ given, the probabilities $p_{jn}$ are determined by the rule (79), the problem of finding the optimum receiver structure is that of finding the overcomplete set $\{|x_n\rangle\}$ to minimize

$$P_e = 1 - w \sum_n \max_{1 \leq j \leq M} \zeta_j \langle x_n|\rho\,|x_n\rangle. \tag{86}$$

Very little is known about the solution of this minimization problem. When only orthonormal sets of measurement state vectors are allowed as solutions, this problem is equivalent to finding the operators $\Pi_j$, subject to constraints (81) and (82) to minimize $P_e$ in (83). In general, the two maximization problems are not equivalent [52].

To find optimum receivers in many communication systems of practical interest, there is no need to consider ideal measurements of incompatible observables. It can be shown from the completeness (32) of $\{|x_n\rangle\}$ that in all binary communication systems and in those $M$-ary systems in which the density operators $\rho_j$ commute, optimum receivers measure observables corresponding to Hermitian commuting operators [53].

*Binary Detection*

This part discusses binary communication systems in which the input message in the time interval $(0, T)$ is either the digit "1" or the digit "0." A digit 1 is represented by the presence of a signal pulse of duration $T$; a digit 0 is represented by the absence of the pulse. Therefore, in the time interval $(0, T)$ the ideal receiver chooses between two hypotheses: $(H_0)$ "the field in the cavity is due only to thermal radiation," and $(H_1)$ "the field contains besides thermal radiation a signal of some specified form." The best receiver is one that enables the choice between the two hypotheses to be made with minimum probability of error.

Hypothesis $H_1$ represents a proposition that is either true or false. We have seen that such propositions are decided by measuring a projection operator $\Pi$. The outcome of the measurement is one of the two eigenvalues of $\Pi$, 0 or 1. If 1, hypothesis $H_1$ is adopted; if 0, $H_0$. The question remains, however, which of all the projection operators $\Pi$ that exist for the received field is best. It is answered in the same way as classical detection theory: the operator for which the average probability of error is minimum [15], [18], [54].

Under hypothesis $H_0$ the normal modes of the receiver are excited only by random noise; they are in a mixture of states described by a density operator $\rho_0$, such as the one exhibited in (62). Under hypothesis $H_1$ the normal modes are in some other mixture of states described by a density operator $\rho_1$ such as the one in (63). Let $\zeta$ be the prior probability of hypothesis $H_0$. The average probability $P_e$ of error in (83) can be rewritten

$$\begin{aligned} P_e &= \zeta \operatorname{Tr}[\rho_0\Pi] + (1-\zeta)[1 - \operatorname{Tr}[\rho_1\Pi]] \\ &= (1-\zeta)\{1 - \operatorname{Tr}[(\rho_1 - \Lambda_0\rho_0)\Pi]\}, \quad \Lambda_0 = \zeta/(1-\zeta). \end{aligned} \tag{87}$$

This quantity is to be minimized by properly choosing the projection operator $\Pi$. The minimizing operator we call the *detection operator*. We have put $P_e$ in (87) in such a form that the problem of maximizing

$$\operatorname{Tr}[(\rho_1 - \Lambda_0\rho_0)\Pi]$$

is clearly equivalent.

Let $\eta_k$ be the eigenvalues, and $|\eta_k\rangle$ the associated eigenvectors of the operator $\rho_1 - \Lambda_0\rho_0$.

$$(\rho_1 - \Lambda_0\rho_0)|\eta_k\rangle = \eta_k|\eta_k\rangle. \tag{88}$$

Then

$$\begin{aligned} \operatorname{Tr}[(\rho_1 - \Lambda_0\rho_0)\Pi] &= \sum_k \langle\eta_k|(\rho_1 - \Lambda_0\rho_0)\Pi|\eta_k\rangle \\ &= \sum_k \eta_k\langle\eta_k|\Pi|\eta_k\rangle. \end{aligned} \tag{89}$$

This quantity is maximum for that projection operator for which $\langle\eta_k|\Pi|\eta_k\rangle = 1$ when $\eta_k \geq 0$, and $\langle\eta_k|\Pi|\eta_k\rangle = 0$ when $\eta_k < 0$, and the projection operator that fulfills the requirement is

$$\Pi = \sum_k U(\eta_k)|\eta_k\rangle\langle\eta_k|, \tag{90}$$

where $U(x)$ is the unit step function. The average probability of error is then

$$P_e = (1-\zeta)\left[1 - \sum_k \eta_k U(\eta_k)\right]. \tag{91}$$

Prescription of the optimum receiver is simplest when the density operators $\rho_0$ and $\rho_1$ commute. The vectors $|\eta_k\rangle$ are then identical with the eigenvectors $|\phi_k\rangle$ common to both $\rho_0$ and $\rho_1$, which can now be written

$$\rho_j = \sum_k P_k^{(j)}|\phi_k\rangle\langle\phi_k|, \qquad j = 0, 1,$$
$$\sum_k P_k^{(j)} = 1. \tag{92}$$

In fact, the eigenvalues $\eta_k$ of $\rho_1 - \Lambda_0\rho_0$ are

$$\eta_k = P_k^{(1)} - \Lambda_0 P_k^{(0)}. \tag{93}$$

If the system is in such a state $|\phi_k\rangle$ that $\eta_k > 0$, or equivalently,

$$P_k^{(1)}/P_k^{(0)} > \Lambda_0,$$

hypothesis $H_1$ is chosen; otherwise $H_0$ is adopted. This is just the classical likelihood-ratio test.

Suppose, for instance, that the signal has the same statistical properties as thermal noise, placing an average number $N_s$ of photons into a single mode of the receiver and none into any of the others. Only that mode needs to be observed, and we assume that under hypothesis $H_0$ it contains thermal noise with an average number $\mathcal{N}$ of photons. The density operators under the two hypotheses then, by (59), are

$$\rho_i = (1 - v_i)\sum_{m=0}^{\infty} v_i^m|m\rangle\langle m|, \qquad i = 0, 1, \tag{94}$$

where

$$v_0 = \mathcal{N}/(\mathcal{N}+1), \quad v_1 = (\mathcal{N}+N_s)/(\mathcal{N}+N_s+1). \tag{95}$$

These density operators commute, and since both commute with the number operator $a^+a$, it suffices for optimum detection to count the number $m$ of photons in the mode. The likelihood ratio is

$$P_m^{(1)}/P_m^{(0)} = \left(\frac{1 - v_1}{1 - v_0}\right)(v_1/v_0)^m, \qquad (96)$$

and it is decided that a signal is present whenever this ratio exceeds $\Lambda_0 = \zeta/(1-\zeta)$; that is, when

$$m > \left[\ln \Lambda_0 - \ln\left(\frac{1 - v_1}{1 - v_0}\right)\right] \Big/ \ln (v_1/v_0) = M.$$

The probability of error is then

$$P_e = \zeta v_0^{[M]+1} + (1 - \zeta)(1 - v_1^{[M]+1}), \qquad (97)$$

where $[M]$ is the greatest integer in the decision level $M$.

*Choice Between Pure States:* When the density operators $\rho_0$ and $\rho_1$ do not commute, it is necessary to solve the eigenvalue equation (88) before the structure of the optimum receiver can be specified and its performance assessed. This is generally very difficult. In a special case that can be solved exactly, the received field is in one pure state $|\psi_0\rangle$ under hypothesis $H_0$ and in another, $|\psi_1\rangle$, under $H_1$. The density operators are

$$\rho_0 = |\psi_0\rangle\langle\psi_0|, \qquad \rho_1 = |\psi_1\rangle\langle\psi_1|. \qquad (98)$$

Unless $|\psi_0\rangle$ and $|\psi_1\rangle$ happen to be orthogonal, $\rho_0$ and $\rho_1$ do not commute. An example is the detection of a coherent signal in the absence of any thermal radiation. The eigenvectors $|\eta_i\rangle$ are now linear combinations of $|\psi_0\rangle$ and $|\psi_1\rangle$,

$$|\eta_i\rangle = a_{i0}|\psi_0\rangle + a_{i1}|\psi_1\rangle, \qquad i = 1, 2. \qquad (99)$$

Only two eigenvalues differ from zero, and they are found by substituting (99) in (88) and setting the determinant of the coefficients in the resulting pair of simultaneous equations equal to zero. The minimum average probability of error is found to be [16], [55]

$$\begin{aligned} P_e &= (1 - \zeta)[\tfrac{1}{2}(1 + \Lambda_0) - \mathscr{P}] \\ \mathscr{P} &= \{[\tfrac{1}{2}(1 - \Lambda_0)]^2 + \Lambda_0 \mathscr{Q}\}^{1/2} \\ \mathscr{Q} &= 1 - |\langle\psi_0|\psi_1\rangle|^2. \end{aligned} \qquad (100)$$

In the detection of a coherent signal occupying a single mode in the absence of thermal noise, the states $|\psi_0\rangle$ and $|\psi_1\rangle$ are the coherent states $|0\rangle$ and $|\mu\rangle$, respectively, where $|\mu|^2 = N_s$ is the average number of signal photons. Then in (100), by (53),

$$\mathscr{Q} = 1 - |\langle 0|\mu\rangle|^2 = 1 - \exp(-N_s). \qquad (101)$$

The error probability $P_e$ is plotted in Fig. 2 against the signal-to-noise ratio

$$D = [4N_s/(2\mathscr{N} + 1)]^{1/2} \qquad (102)$$

as the curve marked $\mathscr{N} = 0$; the prior probabilities were taken as $\zeta = 1 - \zeta = 1/2$, and $\Lambda_0 = 1$. This signal-to-noise ratio $D$ goes into the classical signal-to-noise ratio $[N_s\hbar\omega/K\mathscr{T}]^{1/2}$, in the limit $\hbar\omega \ll K\mathscr{T}$.

*Detection of a Coherent Signal in Thermal Noise:* When the mode excited by a coherent signal also contains thermal noise of absolute temperature $\mathscr{T}$, the density operators $\rho_0$

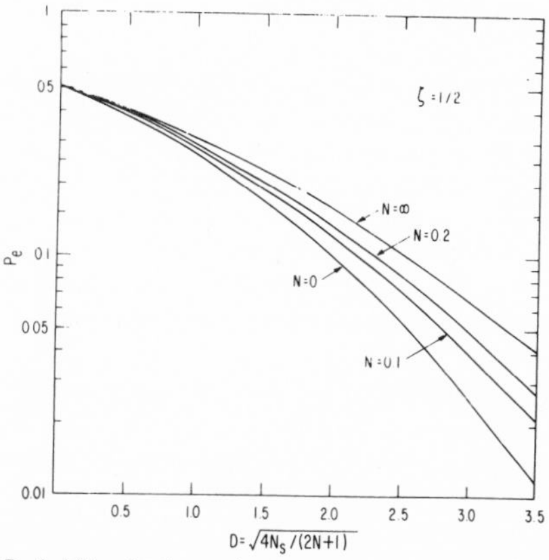


Fig. 2. Probability $P_e$ of error in detection of known signal with prior probability $\zeta = 1/2$. $D$ = signal-to-noise ratio $= [4N_s/(2\mathscr{N}+1)]^{1/2}$, $N_s$ = average number of signal photons, and $\mathscr{N}$ = average number of thermal photons.

and $\rho_1$ take the forms in (57) and (60), respectively. An exact solution of the eigenvalue equation (88) with these density operators has not been obtained. It is possible to solve it approximately by using the matrix representation of $\rho_1$ in (61) and diagonalizing a truncated version of the infinite matrix by means of a digital computer. Fig. 2 gives the error probabilities so obtained; the largest matrix found necessary used the first fifteen rows and columns of the infinite matrix $\langle n|(\rho_1 - \Lambda_0\rho_0)|m\rangle$.

When the average number $\mathscr{N}$ of thermal photons is very large, the classical limit is approached. The classical detector of a signal of known phase in thermal noise corresponds in this model to measuring the component of the operator $a$ along the phase of the signal. If, without loss of generality, we take the phase arg $\mu$ as zero, the classical detector measures the operator $Q$ and compares it with a decision level. The probability density functions of the outcome $q$ under hypotheses $H_0$ and $H_1$, respectively, are [56]

$$P_0(q) = \langle\alpha|\rho_0|\alpha\rangle = (2\pi\sigma^2)^{-1/2} \exp[-q^2/2\sigma^2]$$

and

$$P_1(q) = \langle\alpha|\rho_1|\alpha\rangle = (2\pi\sigma^2)^{-1/2} \exp[-\{q - (2\hbar/\omega)^{1/2}\mu\}^2/2\sigma^2],$$

where $\mu$ now is real and $\sigma^2 = \hbar(\mathscr{N} + \frac{1}{2})/\omega$.

The decision level $q_0$ with which $q$ is compared is determined from the likelihood-ratio formula,

$$P_1(q_0)/P_0(q_0) = \Lambda_0. \qquad (103)$$

It is not hard to show that the probability of error by using this classical detector is

$$P_e = \zeta \operatorname{erfc}(\tfrac{1}{2}D + D^{-1}\ln\Lambda_0) + (1 - \zeta)\operatorname{erfc}(\tfrac{1}{2}D - D^{-1}\ln\Lambda_0), \qquad (104)$$

where $D$ is given by (101) and

$$\operatorname{erfc} x = (2\pi)^{-1/2}\int_x^\infty \exp(-t^2/2)\,dt \qquad (105)$$

is the error-function integral. For $\zeta = \frac{1}{2}$, the error probability is simply

$$P_e = \operatorname{erfc}(\tfrac{1}{2}D), \tag{106}$$

which has been plotted against $D$ in Fig. 2 as the curve marked $\mathcal{N} = \infty$. This classical detector can be used at any value of $\mathcal{N}$ but it suffers a higher probability of error than the optimum detector. The difference between the two detectors vanishes rapidly once the average number $\mathcal{N}$ of thermal photons in the mode becomes of the order of 1.

If the signal occupies many modes of the received field, the problem appears much more complicated. If it is a narrow-band signal, however, all of the modes excited by the signal will have nearly the same average number $\mathcal{N}$ of thermal photons. It is then possible to combine the amplitudes of those modes linearly in such a way that the resulting field amplitude contains the entire signal, in effect creating a new mode matched to the signal, as discussed in Section III. By means of other linear combinations, a new set of modes orthogonal to the matched mode and containing no signal excitation is formed. The problem is then reduced to detection of the signal in a single mode and the results just derived apply [57].

If the absolute phase $\phi$ of the signal is unknown, as will happen if no attempt is made to maintain phase coherence between transmitter and receiver, the density operator $\rho_1$ must be averaged with respect to this phase. In the least favorable situation, the phase is a random variable uniformly distributed from 0 to $2\pi$.

The elements of the matrix $\langle n|\rho_1|m\rangle$ specifying $\rho_1$ in the number representation are given in (61). When we average with respect to $\phi$ over $(0, 2\pi)$, all of the off-diagonal elements will be zero. The average density operator $\langle\rho_1\rangle$ then, like $\rho_0$, is diagonal in the number representation

$$\langle\rho_1\rangle = \sum_{k=0}^{\infty} P_k^{(1)}|k\rangle\langle k|, \tag{107}$$

with

$$P_k^{(1)} = (1-v)v^k \exp\left[-(1-v)N_s\right]L_n\left[-(1-v)^2N_s/v\right],$$
$$N_s = |\mu|^2, \tag{108}$$

where $L_n(x)$ is the ordinary Laguerre polynomial.

The optimum receiver, therefore, simply counts the number of photons in the matched mode and compares it with a decision level determined by the likelihood-ratio formula (103). The average error probability can be computed from (108) [58]. Curves calculated for $\zeta = (1-\zeta) = \frac{1}{2}$ by digital computer are given in Figs. 3 and 4. In the limit $\mathcal{N} = \infty$ the error probability coincides with that of the classical detector of a signal of random phase.

*M-ary Detection*

In general, there may exist no solution to the problem of finding projection operators $\Pi_j$, satisfying the constraints (81) and (82), to minimize the probability of error $P_e$ in (83). Here our attention will be confined to the special case in which the density operators $\rho_j$ commute. For this case, the projection operators $\Pi_j$, which satisfy the sufficient conditions given by (84) and (85), can be written

$$\Pi_j = \sum_n p_{jn}|\phi_n\rangle\langle\phi_n|, \tag{109}$$

where $|\phi_n\rangle$ are the simultaneous eigenvectors of the density operators $\rho_j$, $j = 1, 2, \cdots, M$. Let $p_n^{(j)}$ denote the eigenvalue of the density operator $\rho_j$ corresponding to the eigenvector $|\phi_n\rangle$. For any $j = 1, 2, \cdots, M$, and $n = 1, 2, \cdots$, the probability $p_{jn}$ in (109) equals one if $\zeta_j p_n^{(j)} \geq \zeta_i p_n^{(i)}$ for all $i \neq j$, and equals zero otherwise.

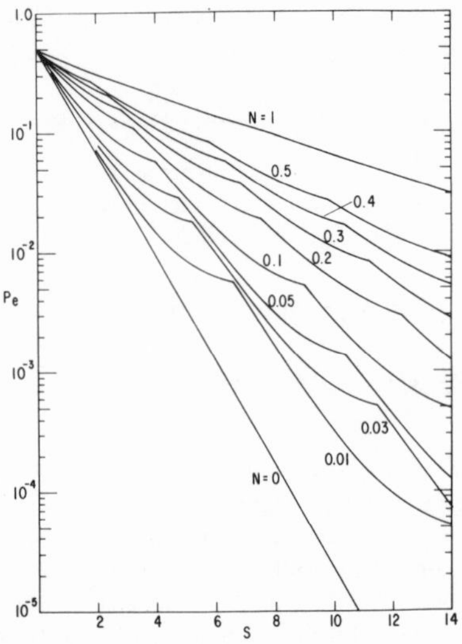


Fig. 3. Average probability $P_e$ of error versus average number $S$ of signal photons for ideal quantum receiver of a coherent signal of random phase.

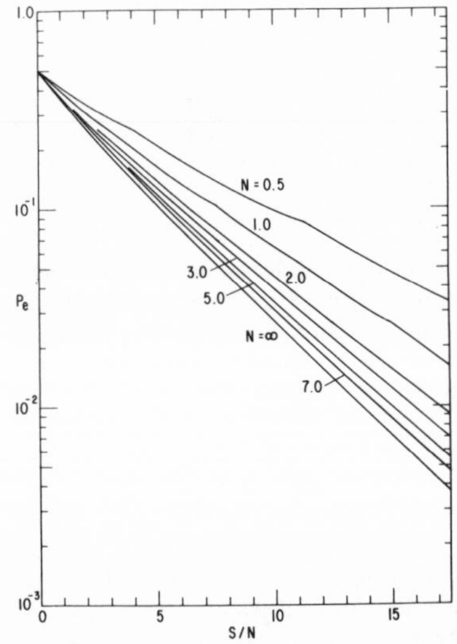


Fig. 4. Average probability $P_e$ of error versus signal-to-noise ratio $S/N$ for ideal quantum receiver of a coherent signal of random phase.

For simplicity, we assume that the $M$ messages $m_1$, $_2, \cdots, m_M$, occur with equal prior probabilities. Therefore, e information rate $R$, in nats per second, of the communi- tion system is

$$R = [\ln M]/T. \tag{110}$$

*Detection of Orthogonal Signals with Known Amplitudes t Random Phases:* Let us envision an $M$-ary communica- on system in which each transmitted message is repre- nted by a signal pulse of duration $T$ with known classical nplitude, but with an unknown absolute phase. Let $z$ note the direction of signal propagation. When the signal ld is not modulated spatially and is linearly polarized, its assical waveform at the receiver can be described by the nction

$$2Rl[S(t)\exp\{i\omega_0(z/c - t) + i\phi\}],$$

here $S(t)$ is one of a set of complex time functions $\{S_j(t)\}$ pending on the transmitted message. The absolute phase of the signal is taken to be a random variable uniformly stributed over the interval $(0, 2\pi)$. In particular, let us sume that the functions $S_j(t)$ are essentially narrow-band 9] orthogonal time functions over any signaling interval,

$$\int_0^T S_j(t)S_i^*(t)dt = E^2\delta_{ij}; \qquad i, j = 1, 2, \cdots, M. \tag{111}$$

To describe this signal set quantum-mechanically, we gard the received field to be a superposition of plane aveling-wave modes with normal mode functions $^{-12}\exp[-i\omega_k z/c]$. When the transmitted message is $m_j$, e received field would be in one of the coherent states $_k|\mu_{jk}e^{i\phi}\rangle$ in the absence of thermal radiation. The complex nplitudes $\mu_{jk}$ of the individual modes are known and are lated to the waveforms $S_j(t)$ by

$$(t) = \sum_n (\hbar\omega_n/2\varepsilon_0 V)^{1/2} i\mu_{jn}\exp[i(\omega_n - \omega_0)(z/c - t)],$$

$$j = 1, 2, \cdots, M.$$

most practical systems, the width of the frequency range interest is small compared with the carrier frequency $\omega_0$; erefore, we may assume that for all $n$ for which $\mu_{jn} \neq 0$,

$$\omega_n \approx \omega. \tag{112}$$

nce the complex functions $S_j(t)$ are orthogonal, the com- ex amplitudes $\mu_{jn}$ satisfy the condition

$$\sum_n \mu_{jn}\mu_{kn}^* = |\mu_j|^2\delta_{jk}; \qquad j, k = 1, 2, \cdots, M. \tag{113}$$

In the presence of an additive thermal-noise field, the ceived field is the mixed state specified by the density erator

$$\rho_j = \int_0^{2\pi}\frac{d\phi}{2\pi}\int\prod_k \exp[-|\alpha_k - \mu_{jk}e^{i\phi}|^2/\mathcal{N}_k]$$
$$\cdot|\alpha_k\rangle\langle\alpha_k|d^2\alpha_k/\pi\mathcal{N}_k \tag{114}$$

hen the input message is $m_j$. Since by (112), the average mbers $\mathcal{N}_k$ of thermal photons in different modes are approximately equal, $\mathcal{N}_k \approx \mathcal{N}$, the density operators $\rho_j$ are commutative [60]. For the reception of these $M$ signals, the optimum receiver measures simultaneously the projection operators $\Pi_j$ in (109). Equivalently, it measures the numbers of photons in the $M$ modes associated with normal-mode functions $S_j(t)/E^2$ and with annihilation operators

$$b_j = \sum_n \mu_{jn}a_n/|\mu_j|,$$

where [61]

$$|\mu_j|^2 = \sum_n |\mu_{jn}|^2.$$

When the outcome is $\boldsymbol{n} = (n_1, n_2, \cdots, n_M)$, hypothesis $H_j$, "the transmitted message is $m_j$," is chosen if the conditional probability $P(\boldsymbol{n}|m_j)$ is the largest among all $j$. For $M$ signals with disjoint frequency spectra, as in a frequency-position modulation system, the optimum receiver can be implemented as shown in Fig. 5. The function of the mode transformation filter is similar to that of an optical matched filter [62]. The optimum receiver for a set of pulse-position modulated signals is simply a direct detection system.

To compute the performance of this system, we shall assume for simplicity that

$$|\mu_j|^2 = pT. \tag{115}$$

Since $|\mu_j|^2$ is the average number of photons in the signal field when $m_j$ is transmitted, $p$ is the average number of signal photons arriving at the receiver per unit time, which by (115) is independent of the transmitted message. In this case, the probability of error $P_e$ can be bounded [63] as

$$K_2\exp[-TCE(R)] \le P_e \le K_1\exp[-TCE(R)], \tag{116}$$

where the coefficients $K_1$ and $K_2$ are not exponential functions of $T$. The information rate $R$ is given by (110), $C$ is the channel capacity,[2] and the exponential factor $E(R)$ is the system reliability function.

The channel capacity $C$ is found to be

$$C = p\ln(1 + 1/\mathcal{N}); \qquad \mathcal{N}_k \approx \mathcal{N}$$
$$= \frac{P}{2\eta_z}\ln(1 + 2\eta_z/\eta_0), \tag{117}$$

where $P = p\hbar\omega$ is the average received signal power, $\eta_z = \frac{1}{2}\hbar\omega$ is the so-called zero-point fluctuation energy, and $\eta_0 = \mathcal{N}\hbar\omega$ is the average thermal energy in each mode of the received field. In the classical limit $\mathcal{N} \gg 1$, the channel capacity $C$ is approximately equal to $C_c = P/\eta_0$, the capacity of the classical additive white Gaussian channel with no bandwidth constraints [64] and with noise spectral density $\eta_0 \approx K\mathcal{T}$.

For rates $R$ in the range $0 \le R \le R_c$, where $R_c$ is given by

$$R_c/C = \mathcal{N}(1 + \mathcal{N})/(1 + 2\mathcal{N})^2, \tag{118}$$

[2] The channel capacity is the maximum rate at which the error probability $P_e$ can be made arbitrarily small when constrained in signal power. Operation at a rate higher than capacity condemns the system to a high probability of error, regardless of the choice of signals and receiver.

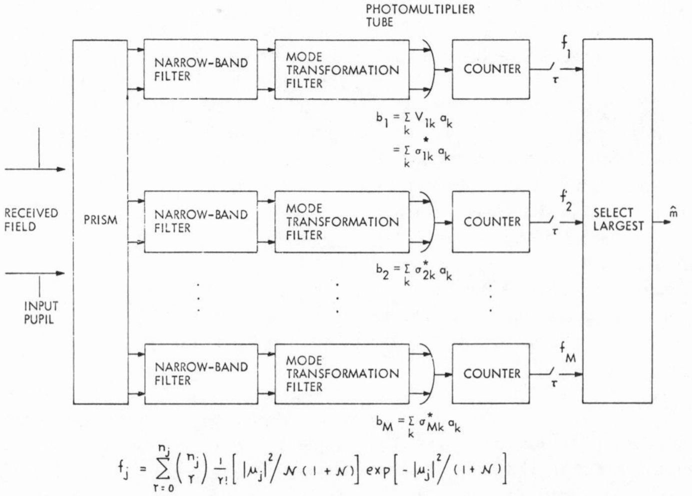


Fig. 5. Quantum-mechanical optimum receiver for narrow-band orthogonal signals with known classical amplitudes but random phases.

the system reliability function $E(R)$ is bounded from below by

$$E(R) \geq \left[(1 + 2\mathcal{N}) \ln (1 + 1/\mathcal{N})\right]^{-1} - R/C. \quad (119)$$

For rates $R$ in the range $R_c \leq R \leq C$, the reliability function $E(R)$ is given by

$$E(R) = \{\mathcal{N} \ln (1 + 1/\mathcal{N})\}^{-1} \left\{ \frac{1 + 2\mathcal{N}R/C - [1 + 4R\mathcal{N}(1 + \mathcal{N})/C]^{1/2}}{1 - [1 + 4R\mathcal{N}(1 + \mathcal{N})/C]^{1/2}} - \frac{\mathcal{N}R}{C} \ln \left\{ \frac{1 + 2\mathcal{N}(1 + \mathcal{N})R/C + [1 + 4R\mathcal{N}(1 + \mathcal{N})/C]^{1/2}}{2R(1 + \mathcal{N})^2/C} \right\} \right\}. \quad (120)$$

The general behavior of the system reliability function for several different values of $\mathcal{N}$ is shown in Fig. 6. In contrast to the corresponding classical additive white Gaussian channel, $E(R)$ depends not only on $R/C$ but also on the average noise level $\mathcal{N}$.

When $\mathcal{N} = 0$, the channel capacity $C$ in (117) becomes infinite while $E(R)$ approaches zero. The probability of error becomes

$$P_e \approx \exp[-Tp]. \quad (121)$$

The fact that $P_e$ is independent of the number $M$ of messages when $\mathcal{N}$ equals zero implies that an arbitrarily small probability of error can be achieved at an arbitrarily large information rate for a finite number $p$ of photons per second in the signal field. Since signals are orthogonal, however, the average power in the signal field grows linearly with the number of input messages when $p$ is being held constant. Hence the small probability of error is accomplished only by an accompanied increase in the power of the transmitted signal. It is more meaningful to derive the expressions of the channel capacity and the system reliability function under the assumption that the average power in the signal, $\sum_n |\mu_{jn}(\hbar\omega_k)^{1/2}|^2/T$, is held constant independently of th transmitted message. Unfortunately, analytic results can not be obtained in this case. It has been shown [65] heu ristically, by use of the uncertainty principle, that, with n bandwidth constraints, the channel capacity has an uppe limit $\mathcal{B}(P/\hbar)^{1/2}$, where $P$ is the average signal power, and $\mathcal{B}$ is a number that approximately equals 2.

*Detection of Orthogonal Signals in a Rayleigh Fadin Channel:* We now consider a communication system i which the received field in the presence of thermal radiatio is in the completely incoherent mixture of states describe by the density operator

$$\rho_j = [\det \phi_j]^{-1} \int \cdots \int \exp\left[ -\sum_m \sum_n \alpha_m^* (\phi_j)_{mn}^{-I} \alpha_n \right] \cdot \prod_m |\alpha_m\rangle\langle\alpha_m| d^2\alpha_m/\pi^{\nu M}, \quad (122)$$

when the transmitted message is $m_j$. In this expression, $\phi$ is the mode correlation matrix whose elements are

$$[\phi_j]_{nm} = \text{Tr}\,[\rho_j a_m^+ a_n] = [\phi_j^{(t)}]_{nm} + \mathcal{N}\delta_{mn}, \quad (123)$$

where $\mathcal{N}$ is the average number of thermal photons i each normal mode. $[\phi_j^{(t)}]_{mn}$ are elements of the mode cor relation matrix in the absence of the thermal radiation When the signals have orthogonal classical waveforms a the receiver, the mode correlation matrices $\phi_j$ commute and therefore the density operators $\rho_j$ commute. The com

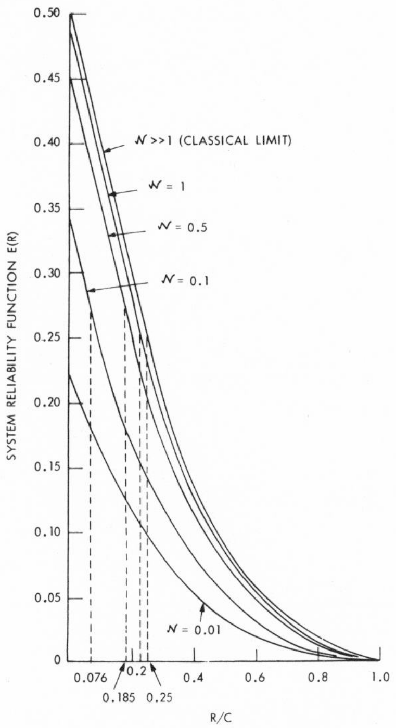


Fig. 6. System reliability function for orthogonal coherent signals.

nutativity of the matrices $\phi_j$ implies the existence of unitary ransformation $V$ such that the matrices

$$R_j = V^{+}\phi_j V, \qquad j = 1, 2, \cdots, M, \tag{124}$$

re diagonal. When the elements of $\phi_j$ are given by (123), he $k$th diagonal element of the matrix $R_j$ can be written

$$[R_j]_{kk} = \mathcal{N} + s_{jk}; \qquad j = 1, 2, \cdots, M. \tag{125}$$

The system just described can serve as a quantum-nechanical model of a diversity transmission system in vhich signals are transmitted over a Rayleigh fading chan-el. When a signal pulse with classical waveform $S_j(t) \cos \omega_0 t$ transmitted through such a channel, the classical wave-orm of the received signal is $xS_j(t) \cos (\omega_0 t + \phi)$, where $x$ nd $\phi$ are sample functions of random processes such that t any time $t$ and any point $\boldsymbol{r}$, $x(\boldsymbol{r}, t)$ and $\phi(\boldsymbol{r}, t)$ are Rayleigh-istributed and uniformly distributed random variables, espectively. (For simplicity, we suppose that in a given ignaling interval and over the receiving aperture, they can e considered as constant random variables.) It has been hown [66], [67] that the probability of error in the recep-on of orthogonal signals transmitted over a Rayleigh fad-ng channel can be reduced by making several transmissions or each input message. These transmissions are spaced in me, space, or frequency so that fadings experienced by dif-erent transmissions are statistically independent. Such a ystem is called a diversity transmission system. The density perators $\rho_j$ in (122) describe, quantum-mechanically, the received field in a diversity transmission system in which each input message is represented by several narrow-band signals with orthogonal classical waveforms [68]. In (125), $s_{jk}$ is the average number of signal photons received at the end of the $k$th diversity path when the message $m_j$ is transmitted. Let $\nu$ denote the number of diversity transmissions; for each $j$, $s_{jk} \neq 0$ only for $\nu$ of the possible values of the subscript $k$.

Without loss of generality, we confine our discussion to frequency-diversity systems in which frequency-position modulation is used; the frequency spectra of the signals are disjoint. The optimum receiver for the reception of these signals measures simultaneously the observables corresponding to operators $b_n^{+} b_n$, where $b_n = \sum_k V_{nk} a_k$; $V_{nk}$ are the elements of the matrix $V$ in (124). The operators $a_k$ are the annihilation operators in terms of whose right eigenvectors $\rho_j$ is expressed in (122). Again, hypotheses are chosen by using the decision rule (79).

The performance of such a system has been evaluated when the number of signal photons $s_{jk}$ is equal [69]

$$s_{jk} \equiv s \tag{126}$$

for $j = 1, 2, \cdots, M$ and all $k$ for which $s_{jk} \neq 0$. For the narrow-band signals considered here, (126) also implies that the signal energies in the $\nu$ diversity paths are equal, as in an equal-strength diversity system. For this special case, the structure of the optimum receiver simplifies to that shown in Fig. 7.

Just as in the case of known signals in thermal noise, the bounds of the probability of error $P_e$ can be expressed as in (116). The quantity $C$ given by (117) is the capacity of the system in which signals are in coherent states. The average number $p$ of signal photons per second equals $S/T$ in this case, where

$$S = \nu s \tag{127}$$

is the total number of photons transmitted through $\nu$ diversity paths. The system reliability function $E(R)$ is the solution of the maximization problem,

$$E(R) = \max_{0 \le \delta \le 1} \{e(\delta, s) - \delta R/C\}$$

$$e(\delta, s) = \left\{(1 + \delta) \ln \left\{1 + (\mathcal{N} + s) \cdot \left[1 - \left(\frac{\mathcal{N}}{1 + \mathcal{N}} \; \frac{1 + \mathcal{N} + s}{s + \mathcal{N}}\right)^{\delta/(1+\delta)}\right]\right\} - \delta \ln [1 + s/(1 + \mathcal{N})]\right\} s \ln (1 + 1/\mathcal{N}). \tag{128}$$

As in the case of coherent signals, the reliability function depends not only on the signal-to-noise ratio $s/\mathcal{N}$, but also on the average noise level $\mathcal{N}$ and the number of diversity paths $\nu$. The optimum reliability function $E^{o}(R)$ is obtained by maximizing the function $E(R)$ in (128) with respect to $\nu$, or alternatively, with respect to $s$. Let $s^{o}$ denote the value

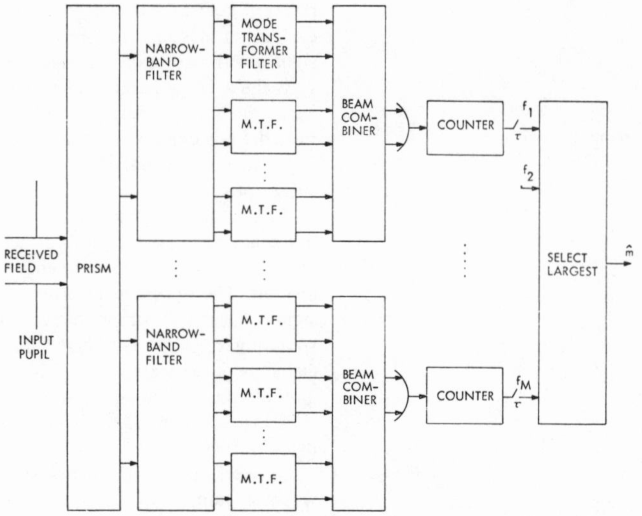


Fig. 7. Optimum receiver for equal-strength orthogonal signals in a Rayleigh fading channel.

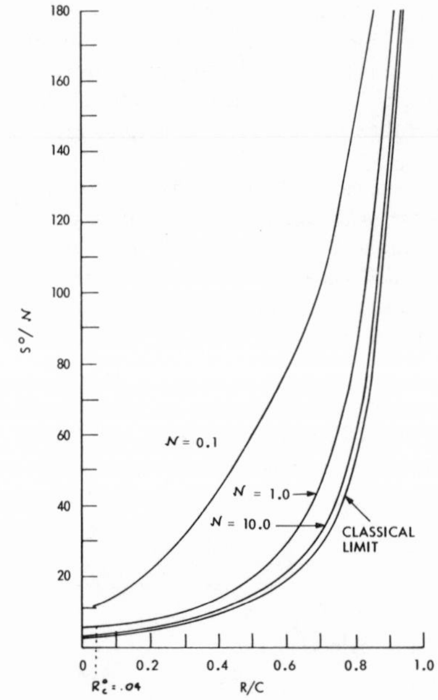


Fig. 8. Optimum number $s^o$ of signal photons per diversity path/average number $\mathcal{N}$ of thermal noise photons versus $R/C$. (Classical limit taken from [67].)

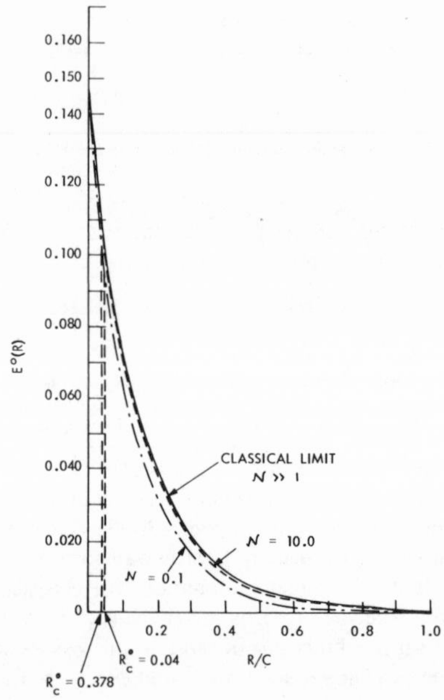


Fig. 9. Optimum system reliability function for equal-strength orthogonal signals in a Rayleigh fading channel. (Classical limit taken from [67].)

of $s$ that maximizes the function $e(\delta, s)$; then

$$E^o(R) = \max_{0 \le \delta \le 1} \{e(\delta, s^o) - \delta R/C\} \tag{129}$$

if the value of $s^o$ does not exceed $S$. When $s^o$ is larger than $S$, we have

$$E^o(R) = \max_{0 \le \delta \le 1} \{e(\delta, S) - \delta R/C\}. \tag{130}$$

This maximization problem has been solved numerically. The results are shown in Fig. 8, where the optimum average number $s^o$ of signal photons per diversity path is plotted as a function of $R/C$ for $\mathcal{N} = 0.1$ and $\mathcal{N} = 10$. Also shown in Fig. 8 is the value of $s^o$ in the classical limit [70]. The values of $s^o/\mathcal{N}$ for rates $R$ less than $R_c^o$ are independent of $R/C$, but they are functions of the average noise level $\mathcal{N}$. If the effective noise in the system is taken to be $(\mathcal{N} + \frac{1}{2})$, the ptimum ratio $s^o/(\mathcal{N}+\frac{1}{2})$ is roughly 3 for $R \le R_c^o$ independent f the value of $\mathcal{N}$.

For rates greater than $R_c^o$, the value of $s^o$ increases rapidly ith $R/C$. That is, for a fixed value of $S$, the optimum num- er of equal-strength diversity paths decreases at informa- ion rates higher than $R_c^o$. From Fig. 8, it is clear that for ncreasing $R/C$, $s^o$ increases without bound. Hence, when the verage number of transmitted photons is fixed at $S$, a point here the value of $s^o$ is equal to $S$ will eventually be reached. hat is, the optimum value of $v$ is equal to one. The rate at hich $S=s^o$ is called the threshold rate for the given value f $S$.

Let us assume for the moment that for any given value of $/C$, $S$ is large so that $S/s^o$ is larger than one. In this limiting ase, the optimum value of $E^o(R)$ as a fraction of $R/C$ is iven by (130). The general behavior of $E^o(R)$ at rates above ne threshold is given by Fig. 9 for different thermal noise vels. The reliability function for the optimum classical ding channel is also shown for comparison.

## V. Quantum Estimation Theory

The communication systems treated thus far transmit in- rmation digitally by encoding it into symbols from an lphabet of two or more elements; the receiver is designed ) make decisions among two or more corresponding hy- otheses. It is also possible to transmit information on a ontinuous basis, by encoding it into the amplitude of the gnal (pulse-amplitude modulation), into its carrier fre- uency (pulse-frequency modulation), or into its epoch ulse-time modulation). The receiver is then confronted ith a task not of decision but of estimation. The informa- on to be extracted appears as a set of *parameters* $=(\theta_1, \theta_2, \cdots, \theta_M)$ of the received field.

In studying classical communication systems, we assume at the receiving aperture field can be sampled in as much etail as we wish in order to generate a set $\boldsymbol{x}=(x_1, x_2, \cdots, x_n)$ f data having a known joint probability density function $(\boldsymbol{x}, \boldsymbol{\theta})$, which depends on the information-bearing param- ters $\boldsymbol{\theta}$. Estimation theory is applied to determine an esti- ator $\hat{\boldsymbol{\theta}}(\boldsymbol{x})$ of the parameters that minimizes some cost func- on $C(\hat{\boldsymbol{\theta}}, \boldsymbol{\theta})$ that measures the cost to the experimenter of ssigning a set of estimates $\hat{\boldsymbol{\theta}}$ to the parameters when their ue values are $\boldsymbol{\theta}$. Examples of commonly used cost func- ons are the mean-square error and the absolute error [71]. or the purpose of finding the best estimator, it is usually ecessary to provide a prior joint probability density func- on $z(\boldsymbol{\theta})$ of the parameters, which represents the distribution f relative frequencies with which $\boldsymbol{\theta}$ will appear in certain nges of values in the communication system envisioned. n example of the prescriptions derived from estimation eory is the maximum-likelihood estimator, which assigns the estimate of a parameter $\theta$ that value for which $P(x, \theta)$ maximum, with the prior probability density function $z(\theta)$ ssumed as very broad.

When the communication system is described quantum- echanically, the received field is described by a density perator $\rho(\boldsymbol{\theta})$, which is a function of the unknown param- ters $\boldsymbol{\theta}$. If the receiver measures observables corresponding to commuting Hermitian operators $\boldsymbol{X}=(X_1, X_2, \cdots, X_L)$, the joint conditional probability density function of the out- comes $\boldsymbol{x}=(x_1, x_2, \cdots, x_L)$ is given by

$$P(\boldsymbol{x}|\boldsymbol{\theta}) = \langle \boldsymbol{x}|\rho(\boldsymbol{\theta})|\boldsymbol{x}\rangle. \tag{131}$$

Again, $|\boldsymbol{x}\rangle$ are the simultaneous eigenvectors of the oper- ators $\boldsymbol{X}$ corresponding to the eigenvalues $\boldsymbol{x}$. It follows that the joint probability density function of the parameters $\boldsymbol{\theta}$ and the observed data $\boldsymbol{x}$ is just

$$P(\boldsymbol{x}, \boldsymbol{\theta}) = z(\boldsymbol{\theta})\langle \boldsymbol{x}|\rho(\boldsymbol{\theta})|\boldsymbol{x}\rangle. \tag{132}$$

The optimum estimation function $\hat{\boldsymbol{\theta}}(\boldsymbol{x})$, which assigns the data $\boldsymbol{x}$ to an estimate $\hat{\boldsymbol{\theta}}$ of the parameters, can be determined from classical estimation theory. Our problem is, therefore, that of finding the operators $\boldsymbol{X}$ whose orthonormal set of eigenvectors $\{|\boldsymbol{x}\rangle\}$ is such that the average cost

$$\bar{C} = \iint z(\boldsymbol{\theta})C(\hat{\boldsymbol{\theta}}(x), \boldsymbol{\theta})\langle \boldsymbol{x}|\rho(\boldsymbol{\theta})|\boldsymbol{x}\rangle \, d\boldsymbol{\theta} d\boldsymbol{x} \tag{133}$$

is minimum.

Alternatively, "the values of the parameters $\boldsymbol{\theta}$ lie between $\boldsymbol{\theta}'$ and $\boldsymbol{\theta}'+\Delta\boldsymbol{\theta}$" is a proposition of the kind described in Section II [72]. If the range of possible values of $\boldsymbol{\theta}$ is broken up into contiguous but nonoverlapping intervals $\Delta\boldsymbol{\theta}$, and if the entire array of corresponding propositions is tested, one of them must be declared true and the rest false. The result is an estimate of $\boldsymbol{\theta}$ within an uncertainty $\Delta\boldsymbol{\theta}$ that in principle can be made as small as desired. When the observables mea- sured by the receiver correspond to commuting Hermitian operators, each such proposition is associated with a pro- jection operator, which we denote by $\Delta E(\boldsymbol{\theta}')$ for the range $(\boldsymbol{\theta}', \boldsymbol{\theta}'+\Delta\boldsymbol{\theta}')$. These projection operators commute and add up to the identity operator

$$\sum_{\boldsymbol{\theta}'} E(\boldsymbol{\theta}') = 1. \tag{134}$$

Passing to the limit $\Delta\boldsymbol{\theta}'\to 0$, we speak of a *resolution of the identity* $dE(\boldsymbol{\theta}')$, with

$$\int dE(\boldsymbol{\theta}') = 1, \tag{135}$$

and this resolution is in effect an estimator of the param- eters $\boldsymbol{\theta}$.

Since $\boldsymbol{\theta}$ is the true value of the parameters, the prob- ability that the estimates lie between $\boldsymbol{\theta}'$ and $\boldsymbol{\theta}'+d\boldsymbol{\theta}'$ is $\mathrm{Tr}\,[\rho(\boldsymbol{\theta})dE(\boldsymbol{\theta}')]$, and the average cost is therefore [73]

$$\bar{C} = \iint z(\boldsymbol{\theta})C(\hat{\boldsymbol{\theta}}, \boldsymbol{\theta})\,\mathrm{Tr}\left[\rho(\boldsymbol{\theta})dE(\boldsymbol{\theta}')\right] d\boldsymbol{\theta}. \tag{136}$$

This average cost $\bar{C}$ is to be minimized by choosing the resolution of the identity $dE(\boldsymbol{\theta}')$ over the entire range of possible values of $\boldsymbol{\theta}'$.

When the receiver makes an ideal measurement of in- compatible observables as discussed in Section II, its struc- ture is specified by a complete set of measurement state vectors $\{|\boldsymbol{x}\rangle\}$, when the outcome of the measurement is $\boldsymbol{x}$. For a given set of measurement state vectors $\{|\boldsymbol{x}\rangle\}$, the manner in which the receiver assigns to the data $\boldsymbol{x}$ an estimate $\hat{\boldsymbol{\theta}}(\boldsymbol{x})$ is prescribed by classical estimation theory. Our problem is to find the set of measurement state vectors $\{|\boldsymbol{x}\rangle\}$ to minimize the average cost function in (133). Since very little is known about the solution to this problem, we shall not be concerned with it hereafter.

In the following discussion, the cost function with which we shall be solely concerned is the mean-square error of the estimate

$$\varepsilon = \sum_{i=1}^{M} E[(\hat{\theta}_i - \theta_i)^2]. \tag{137}$$

The specification of the measured compatible observables $\boldsymbol{X}$ and the estimate functions $\hat{\theta}_i(\boldsymbol{x})$ can be combined in the specification of quantum-mechanical estimators $\hat{\boldsymbol{\Theta}} = (\hat{\Theta}_1, \hat{\Theta}_2, \cdots, \hat{\Theta}_M)$ of the parameters $\theta_1, \theta_2, \cdots, \theta_M$, where

$$\hat{\Theta}_i = \int \theta_i(\boldsymbol{x})|\boldsymbol{x}\rangle\langle\boldsymbol{x}|\,d\boldsymbol{x} = \int \theta_i'\,dE(\boldsymbol{\theta}'). \tag{138}$$

These operators are Hermitian and commutative, $|\boldsymbol{x}\rangle$ being the simultaneous eigenvectors of $\boldsymbol{X}$. A measurement of $\hat{\Theta}_i$ yields an estimate $\hat{\theta}_i$ of $\theta_i$. The mean-square error $\varepsilon$ in (137) becomes

$$\varepsilon(\boldsymbol{\Theta}) = \sum_{i=1}^{M} \int z(\boldsymbol{\theta})\,\mathrm{Tr}\left[\rho(\boldsymbol{\theta})(\hat{\Theta}_i - \theta_i\mathbf{1})^2\right] d\boldsymbol{\theta} \tag{139}$$

when $\boldsymbol{\theta}$ is a set of random parameters with prior probability density function $z(\boldsymbol{\theta})$. When $\boldsymbol{\theta}$ is a set of unknown parameters whose prior probability density functions are unknown, estimators are sought which have small or zero bias and at the same time have a small mean-square error over a broad range of true values of the parameters. The bias of an estimator $\hat{\Theta}_i$ of a parameter $\theta_i$ is

$$\langle\hat{\theta}_i\rangle - \theta_i = \mathrm{Tr}\left[\hat{\Theta}_i\rho(\boldsymbol{\theta})\right] - \theta_i. \tag{140}$$

The mean-square error is

$$\varepsilon_i = \mathrm{Tr}\left[\rho(\boldsymbol{\theta})(\hat{\Theta}_i - \langle\hat{\theta}_i\rangle\mathbf{1})^2\right]. \tag{141}$$

The problem of finding commuting Hermitian quantum-mechanical estimators $\hat{\Theta}_i$ to minimize the mean-square error $\varepsilon(\boldsymbol{\Theta})$ has not been solved for density operators $\rho(\boldsymbol{\theta})$ that do not commute for different values of the parameters $\boldsymbol{\theta}$. When the density operators commute, they possess a common set of orthonormal eigenvectors, $|\phi_n\rangle$. In other words,

$$\rho(\boldsymbol{\theta}) = \sum_n P_n(\boldsymbol{\theta})|\phi_n\rangle\langle\phi_n|.$$

The quantum-mechanical estimators $\hat{\Theta}_1, \hat{\Theta}_2, \cdots, \hat{\Theta}_M$ that minimize the mean-square error in (139) and (141) can be written

$$\hat{\Theta}_i = \sum_n \hat{\theta}_i(n)|\phi_n\rangle\langle\phi_n|. \quad (14$$

Here $\hat{\theta}_i(n)$ is just the conditional mean

$$\hat{\theta}_i(n) = \int \theta_i z(\boldsymbol{\theta})P_n(\boldsymbol{\theta})\,d\boldsymbol{\theta} \Big/ \left\{\int z(\boldsymbol{\theta}')P_n(\boldsymbol{\theta}')\,d\boldsymbol{\theta}'\right\} \quad (14$$

when the parameters are random variables.

Suppose that we wish to estimate the signal strengths c different modes of the received field described by a densit operator

$$\rho(\boldsymbol{\theta}) = \pi^{-\nu}\int \prod_{k=1}^{\nu} \exp\left[-|\alpha_k|^2/(\mathcal{N}+s_k)\right]|\alpha_k\rangle\langle\alpha_k|\,d^2\alpha_k/(\mathcal{N}+s_k$$

The parameters $\boldsymbol{\theta}$ are identified with the average numbe $s_k$ of signal photons in the different modes. As discussed i Section IV, $s_k$ can be considered as the signal strength in th $k$th transmission through a Rayleigh fading channel in diversity system. Since for all values of $s_k$, the eigenvecto of $\rho(\boldsymbol{\theta})$ are $|n_1, n_2, \cdots, n_\nu\rangle$, the simultaneous eigenvectors c the number operators $a_k^+ a_k$, it suffices to measure th operators $a_k^+ a_k$. The outcome $\boldsymbol{n} = (n_1, n_2, \cdots, n_\nu)$ of thi measurement is a sufficient statistic [74] whose joint prob ability is

$$P(\boldsymbol{n}; \{s_k\}) = \prod_{j=1}^{\nu} (1 - v_j)v_j^{\,n_j},$$
$$v_j = (\mathcal{N} + s_k)/(1 + \mathcal{N} + s_k). \quad (14$$

In this equation, $\mathcal{N}$ is the average number of noise photon The outcome of a measurement of the operator $a_k^+ a_k$ is a unbiased estimate of the sum $\mathcal{N} + s_k$. By subtracting th known value of $\mathcal{N}$, an unbiased estimate of $s_k$ is obtaine which happens to have the smallest possible mean-squar error.

It has been shown [75] that the quantum-merchanic estimator $\hat{\Theta}$ of a single random parameter $\theta$ with a pri probability density function $z(\theta)$ that minimizes the mea square error satisfies the operator equation

$$\Gamma\hat{\Theta} + \hat{\Theta}\Gamma = 2\eta \quad (14$$

when the operator

$$\Gamma = \int z(\theta)\rho(\theta)d\theta \quad (14$$

is positive definite, and $\eta = \int \theta\rho(\theta)z(\theta)\,d\theta$. Moreover, th optimum estimator $\hat{\Theta}$ is uniquely given by

$$\hat{\Theta} = 2\int_0^\infty e^{-\Gamma\alpha}\eta e^{\Gamma\alpha}\,d\alpha. \quad (14$$

This result can be used to find the optimum quantum mechanical mean-square-error estimate of the compl plane-wave envelope $m(t)$ in double-sideband modulati [76]. Since $m(t)$ can be represented by its Karhunen–Loè expansion

$$m(t) = \sum_k m_k s_k(t), \quad (14$$

e problem of waveform estimation is reduced to the timation of the random parameters $m_k$. When the band- idth of $m(t)$ is very small compared with the carrier fre- uency $\omega$, the density operator $\rho(\{m_k\})$ describing the state the received fields is

$$\{m_k\}) \doteq \int \exp\left[-\sum_k |\beta_k - (2\varepsilon_0 V/\hbar\omega)^{1/2} m_k|^2/\mathcal{N}\right] \cdot \prod_k |\beta_k\rangle\langle\beta_k| d^2\beta_k/\pi\mathcal{N},$$

here the vectors $|\beta_k\rangle$ are right eigenvectors of the annihila- on operators $b_k$ associated with the modes with normal- ode functions $s_k(t)$. When the prior joint probability nsity function of the parameters $m_k$ is

$$P(\{m_k\}) = \prod_k (2\pi\lambda_k)^{-1/2} \exp\left[-m_k^2/2\lambda_k\right],$$

e minimum mean-square-error estimator $\hat{\Theta}_k$ of $m_k$ can found from (147),

$$\hat{\Theta}_k = (b_k^+ + b_k)\lambda_k/2x(\tfrac{1}{2}\mathcal{N} + \lambda_k x^{-2} + \tfrac{1}{4})$$
$$x = (\hbar\omega/2\varepsilon V)^{1/2}.$$

he mean-square error associated with the optimum esti- ator $\hat{\Theta}_k$ is

$$\varepsilon_k = \boldsymbol{E}[(\hat{\Theta}_k - m_k)^2] = \lambda_k(\mathcal{N} + \tfrac{1}{2})/(2\lambda_k x^{-2} + \mathcal{N} + \tfrac{1}{2})$$

hich is the same as the classical estimation error in white oise, whose spectral density is $(\mathcal{N} + \frac{1}{2})\hbar\omega$ [77].

*uantum-Mechanical Cramér–Rao Inequality*

*Single Unknown Parameter:* Although the best estimator a parameter $\theta$, given the density operator $\rho(\theta)$, has not en found in general, a lower bound can be set to the ean-square error attainable by any estimator. It is the antum-mechanical counterpart of the Cramér–Rao in- uality of classical statistics [78], [79].

Let $\hat{\Theta}$ be an operator whose measurement yields an esti- ate $\hat{\theta}$ of the parameter $\theta$. The expected value of the estimate when the true value of the parameter is $\theta$, is

$$\boldsymbol{E}[\hat{\theta}] = \mathrm{Tr}\left[\rho(\theta)\hat{\Theta}\right] = \langle\hat{\theta}\rangle, \tag{149}$$

d the mean-square error is

$$\varepsilon = \boldsymbol{E}[(\hat{\theta} - \langle\hat{\theta}\rangle)^2] = \mathrm{Tr}\left[\rho(\theta)(\hat{\Theta} - \langle\hat{\theta}\rangle)^2\right]. \tag{150}$$

$\langle\hat{\theta}\rangle = \theta$, the estimate is said to be unbiased.

According to the quantum-mechanical form of the ramér–Rao inequality, $\varepsilon$ cannot be smaller than [17], [80]

$$\varepsilon \geq [\partial\langle\hat{\theta}\rangle/\partial\theta]^2/[\mathrm{Tr}\,[\rho L^2]] \tag{151}$$

ere $L$ is the symmetrized logarithmic derivative of $\rho\langle\theta\rangle$ th respect to $\theta$, defined by

$$\frac{\partial\rho(\theta)}{\partial\theta} = \frac{1}{2}(\rho L + L\rho). \tag{152}$$

rthermore, the lower bound can be attained if and only the symmetrized logarithmic derivative $L$ has the form

$$L = k(\theta)(\hat{\Theta} - \theta), \tag{153}$$

where $k(\theta)$ is a function only of the true value $\theta$ of the parameter. The estimate $\hat{\theta}$ is then unbiased, for by (149) and (150), $k(\theta)(\langle\hat{\theta}\rangle - \theta) = \mathrm{Tr}\,(\rho L) = \mathrm{Tr}\,[\partial\rho(\theta)/\partial\theta] = \partial[\mathrm{Tr}\,\rho(\theta)]/\partial\theta = 0$, since $\mathrm{Tr}\,\rho(\theta) = 1$ independently of $\theta$, whereupon $\langle\hat{\theta}\rangle = \theta$. The first factor $(\partial\langle\theta\rangle/\partial\theta)^2$ in (151) then equals one, and we find that the mean-square error attains the minimum possible value

$$\varepsilon_{\min} = |k(\theta)|^{-1}. \tag{154}$$

An example in which the lower bound is attained is the estimate of the amplitude $A$ of a coherent signal in a single mode, corresponding to the state $|A\mu\rangle$, where $\mu$ is a known complex number, $|\mu| = 1$. Here $A^2 = N_s$ is the average number of signal photons in the mode. The noise is of the thermal variety, and the density operator $\rho(A)$ takes the form

$$\rho(A) = (\pi\mathcal{N})^{-1}\int \exp\left[-|\alpha - A\mu|^2/\mathcal{N}\right]|\alpha\rangle\langle\alpha|\,d^2\alpha, \tag{155}$$

where $\mathcal{N}$ is the average number of thermal photons per mode. The symmetrized logarithmic derivative $L$ can be shown to be

$$L = 4(\mathscr{A} - A)/(2\mathcal{N} + 1), \tag{156}$$

with

$$\mathscr{A} = \tfrac{1}{2}(\mu a^+ + \mu^* a) \tag{157}$$

an unbiased estimator of the amplitude $A$ in terms of the annihilation and creation operators of the mode. The mini- mum mean-square error of this estimate, by (153) and (154), is

$$\varepsilon_{\min} = \tfrac{1}{4}(2\mathcal{N} + 1),$$

and the relative mean-square error is

$$\varepsilon_{\min}/A^2 = (2\mathcal{N} + 1)/4N_s = D^{-2}, \tag{158}$$

where $D$ is the signal-to-noise ratio defined in (101) for de- tection of a coherent signal in thermal noise. The estimating operator $\mathscr{A}$ is proportional to the quasi-classical detection statistic described in Section IV [81].

*Single Random Parameter:* Let $\hat{\Theta}$ be the quantum- mechanical estimator of a random parameter $\theta$ with a prior probability density function $z(\theta)$. The quantum-mechanical form of the Cramér–Rao inequality is [82]

$$\varepsilon = \int z(\theta)\,\mathrm{Tr}\left[(\Theta - \theta\mathbf{1})^2\rho(\theta)\right]d\theta$$
$$\geq Rl\left\{\int z(\theta)\,\mathrm{Tr}\left[\rho(\theta)\left[L(\theta) + \frac{d}{d\theta}\ln z(\theta)\right]^2\right]d\theta\right\},$$

where $L(\theta)$ is defined in (152). Equality holds if and only if

$$\hat{\Theta} - \theta\mathbf{1} = k\left[\frac{d}{d\theta}\ln p(\theta) + L(\theta)\right]$$

for some constant $k$.

## References


[1] D. Middleton, *An Introduction to Statistical Communication Theory*. New York: McGraw-Hill, 1960.

[2] J. C. Hancock and P. A. Wintz, *Signal Detection Theory*. New York: McGraw-Hill, 1966.

[3] C. W. Helstrom, *Statistical Theory of Signal Detection*, 2nd ed. Oxford: Pergamon, 1968.

[4] H. L. Van Trees, *Detection, Estimation and Modulation Theory*, vol. 1. New York: Wiley, 1968.

[5] W. B. Davenport, Jr., and W. L. Root, *An Introduction to the Theory of Random Signals and Noise*. New York: McGraw-Hill, 1958, pp. 185–189.

[6] C. W. Helstrom, *op. cit.*, pp. 56–65.

[7] T. E. Stern, "Some quantum effects in information channels," *IEEE Trans. Inform. Theory*, vol. IT-6, pp. 435–440, September 1960.

[8] ——, "Information rates in photon channels and photon amplifiers," *1960 IRE Int. Conv. Rec.*, pt. 4, pp. 182–188.

[9] J. P. Gordon, "Quantum effects in communications systems," *Proc. IRE*, vol. 50, pp. 1898–1908, September 1962.

[10] T. Hagfors, "Information capacity and quantum effects in propagation circuits," M.I.T. Lincoln Lab., Cambridge, Mass., Tech. Rep. 344, January 24, 1964.

[11] C. Y. She, "Quantum electrodynamics of a communication channel," *IEEE Trans. Inform. Theory*, vol. IT-14, pp. 32–37, January 1968.

[12] H. Takahasi, *Advances in Communication Systems*, vol. 1, A. V. Balakrishnan, Ed. New York: Academic Press, 1965, p. 227.

[13] G. Fillmore and G. Lachs, "Information rates for photocount detection systems," *IEEE Trans. Inform. Theory*, vol. IT-15, pp. 465–468, July 1969.

[14] C. W. Helstrom, "Quantum limitations on the detection of coherent and incoherent signals," *IEEE Trans. Inform. Theory*, vol. IT-11, pp. 482–490, October 1965.

[15] ——, "Detection theory and quantum mechanics," *Inform. Contr.*, vol. 10, pp. 254–291, March 1968.

[16] ——, "Detection theory and quantum mechanics (II)," *Inform. Contr.*, vol. 13, pp. 156–171, August 1968.

[17] ——, "The minimum variance of estimates in quantum signal detection," *IEEE Trans. Inform. Theory*, vol. IT-14, pp. 234–242, March 1968.

[18] ——, "Fundamental limitations on the detectability of electromagnetic signals," *Int. J. Theor. Phys.*, vol. 1, pp. 37–50, May 1968.

[19] P. A. M. Dirac, *Quantum Mechanics*, 3rd ed. London: Oxford University Press, 1947.

[20] W. H. Louisell, *Radiation and Noise in Quantum Electronics*. New York: McGraw-Hill, 1964, ch. 1, pp. 1–68.

[21] P. A. M. Dirac, *op. cit.*, sec. 5, pp. 14–18.

[22] P. R. Halmos, *Finite-Dimensional Vector Space*. Princeton, N. J.: Van Nostrand, 1958, sec. 7, pp. 10–11.

[23] P. A. M. Dirac, *op. cit.*, ch. 3, pp. 53–83.

[24] *Ibid.*, sec. 12, pp. 45–48.

[25] *Ibid.*, sec. 13, pp. 49–52.

[26] W. H. Louisell, *op. cit.*, ch. 1, pp. 47–53; P. A. M. Dirac, *op. cit.*, ch. 4, pp. 84–107.

[27] U. Fano, "Description of states in quantum mechanics by density matrix and operator techniques," *Rev. Mod. Phys.*, vol. 29, pp. 74–93, January 1957.

[28] W. H. Louisell, *op. cit.*, ch. 6, pp. 220–252.

[29] P. A. M. Dirac, *op. cit.*, sec. 27, pp. 108–111; W. H. Louisell, *op. cit.*, sec. 1.14 and 1.15, pp. 53–56.

[30] *Ibid.*, sec. 28, pp. 111–118; *ibid.*, sec. 1.16, pp. 57–61.

[31] R. Serber and C. H. Townes, "Limits in electromagnetic amplifications due to complementarity," in *Quantum Electronics*, C. H. Townes, Ed. New York: Columbia University Press, 1960, pp. 233–255.

[32] J. P. Gordon and W. H. Louisell, "Simultaneous measurements of noncommuting observables," in *Physics of Quantum Electronics*, P. L. Kelley, B. Lax, and P. E. Tannenwald, Eds. New York: McGraw-Hill, 1966, pp. 833–840.

[33] S. D. Personick, "Efficient analog communication over quantum channels," M.I.T. Res. Lab. Electron., Cambridge, Mass., Tech. Rep. 477, sec. 4.

[34] W. H. Louisell, *op. cit.*, sec. 4.4, pp. 148–156.

[35] *Ibid.*, ch. 4, pp. 138–174.

[36] P. A. M. Dirac, *op. cit.*, sec. 34, pp. 136–139; W. H. Louisell, *op. cit.*, pp. 71–85.

[37] R. J. Glauber, "Coherent and incoherent states of the radiation field," *Phys. Rev.*, vol. 131, pp. 2766–2788, September 15, 1963.

[38] *Ibid.*, p. 2769, eq. (3.7).

[39] *Ibid.*, sec. 9, pp. 2781–2784.

[40] R. J. Glauber, *Quantum Optics and Electronics*, Lecture Notes a Les Houches 1964 Session of the Summer School of Theoretica Physics, University of Grenoble, France.

[41] R. J. Glauber, *Phys. Rev.*, vol. 131, p. 2771, eq. (3.32).

[42] W. H. Louisell, *op. cit.*, sec. 6.6, pp. 228–233.

[43] R. J. Glauber, *Phys. Rev.*, vol. 131, sec. 8, pp. 2779–2781.

[44] Equation (61) was obtained by applying Kummer's transformatio to a form derived by R. Yoshitani (UCLA thesis, unpublished).

[45] J. W. S. Liu, "Reliability of quantum-mechanical communicatio systems," M.I.T. Res. Lab. Electron., Cambridge, Mass., Tech. Re 468, December 31, 1968, App. A, pp. 78–81. Also, *IEEE Tran. Inform. Theory*, vol. IT-16, pp. 319–329, May 1970.

[46] J. M. Wozencraft and I. M. Jacobs, *Principles of Communicatio Engineering*. New York: Wiley, 1965, pp. 220–222.

[47] A. S. Kuriksha, "Optimum reception of quantized signals," *Radi Eng. Electron. Phys.* (USSR), vol. 13, pp. 1567–1575, October 196

[48] C. W. Helstrom, "Modal decomposition of aperture fields in detec tion and estimation of incoherent objects," *J. Opt. Soc. Am.*, vo 60, pp. 521–530, April 1970.

[49] J. M. Wozencraft and I. M. Jacobs, *op. cit.*, pp. 212–214.

[50] H. P. H. Yuen, "Theory of quantum signal detection," M.I.T. Re Lab. Electron., Cambridge, Mass., Quart. Progr. Rep. 96, January 1 1970, pp. 154–157.

[51] H. P. H. Yuen and M. Lax, "Theory of quantum signal detection, submitted as a short paper to be presented at the Symp. on Inform Theory, 1970.

[52] H. P. H. Yuen, private communications, 1969.

[53] J. W. S. Liu, *op. cit.*, pp. 17–20.

[54] C. W. Helstrom, "Quantum detection and estimation theory, *J. Statist. Phys.*, vol. 1, no. 2, pp. 231–252, 1969.

[55] P. A. Bakut and S. S. Shchurov, "Optimum reception of a quantu signal," *Prob. Peredach. Inform.*, vol. 4, no. 1, pp. 77–82, 1968 (i Russian).

[56] R. J. Glauber, *Phys. Rev.*, vol. 131, p. 2771, eq. (3.29).

[57] C. W. Helstrom, *Int. J. Theor. Phys.*, vol. 1, sec. 5, pp. 47–50.

[58] ——, "Performance of an ideal quantum receiver of a coherent sign of random phase," *IEEE Trans. Aerosp. Electron. Syst.*, vol. AES- pp. 562–564, May 1969.

[59] H. L. Landau and H. O. Pollak, "Prolate spheroidal wave function Fourier analysis and uncertainty—III: The dimension of the spac and essentially time- and band-limited signals," *Bell Syst. Tech. J* vol. 41, pp. 1295–1336, July 1962.

[60] J. W. S. Liu, *op. cit.*, App. F, pp. 96–98.

[61] *Ibid.*, pp. 37–43.

[62] *Ibid.*, App. G, pp. 99–102.

[63] *Ibid.*, pp. 31–37; 91–95.

[64] J. M. Wozencraft and I. M. Jacobs, *op. cit.*, p. 342, eq. (5.95b).

[65] J. P. Gordon, "Information capacity of communications chann in the presence of quantum effects," in *Advances in Quantum Ele tronics*, J. K. Singer, Ed. New York: Columbia University Pres 1961, pp. 509–519.

[66] J. M. Wozencraft and I. M. Jacobs, *op. cit.*, sec. 7.4, pp. 527–550.

[67] R. S. Kennedy, *Performance Limitations of Fading Dispersive Cha nels*. New York: Wiley, 1969, pp. 109–141.

[68] J. W. S. Liu, *op. cit.*, pp. 49–55.

[69] *Ibid.*, pp. 55–75.

[70] R. S. Kennedy, *op. cit.*, p. 123.

[71] C. W. Helstrom, *Statistical Theory of Signal Detection*, *op. cit.*, ch. pp. 249–289; H. L. Van Trees, *op. cit.*, vol. 1, sec. 2.4, pp. 52–86.

[72] J. von Neumann, *Mathematical Foundations of Quantum Mechanic* transl. by R. T. Beyer. Princeton, N. J.: Princeton University Pres 1955, ch. 3, sec. 1, pp. 196–200.

[73] C. W. Helstrom, *Inform. Contr.*, vol. 10, *op. cit.*, p. 265.

[74] ——, *Statistical Theory of Signal Detection*, *op. cit.*, p. 260.

[75] S. D. Personick, *op. cit.*, sec. 2.2.1.

[76] *Ibid.*, pp. 71–75.

[77] H. L. Van Trees, *op. cit.*, pp. 423–433.

[78] C. R. Rao, "Information and the accuracy attainable in the estim tion of statistical parameters," *Bull. Calcutta Math. Soc.*, vol. 3 pp. 81–91, 1945.

[79] H. Cramér, *Mathematical Methods of Statistics*. Princeton, N. J Princeton University Press, 1946, pp. 473 ff.

[80] C. W. Helstrom, "Minimum mean-squared error of estimates quantum statistics," *Phys. Lett.*, vol. 25A, pp. 101–102, July 31, 196 in (2) of this paper, $\mathrm{Tr}(\rho L)^2$ should read $\mathrm{Tr}(\rho L^2)$.

[81] ——, *Inform. Contr.*, vol. 13, sec. 11, pp. 166–169.

[82] S. D. Personick, *op. cit.*, sec. 2.2.2.

Part II

# OPTICAL COMMUNICATION THEORY WITH POISSON PROCESS MODELS

# Editor's Comments on Papers 9 Through 14

9 **REIFFEN and SHERMAN**
*An Optimum Demodulator for Poisson Processes: Photon Source Detectors*

10 **BAR-DAVID**
*Communication under the Poisson Regime*

11 **GAGLIARDI and KARP**
*M-ary Poisson Detection and Optical Communications*

12 **KARP and CLARK**
*Photon Counting: A Problem in Classical Noise Theory*

13 **SNYDER**
*Filtering and Detection for Doubly Stochastic Poisson Processes*

14 **HOVERSTEN et al**
*Direct-Detection Optical Communication Receivers*

It is fortunate that quantum effects can be accounted for in a considerably simpler way that, while less general, seems able to encompass effectively the required analysis of the majority of practical optical communication-system problems *provided* the receiver structure is specified up to the point where the received optical field irradiates the detector. Under appropriate conditions [1] the detector output current is a point process with Poisson process occurrence times whose intensity, or rate, function $\lambda(t)$ is determined by the classical field: $\lambda(t) = \eta P(t)/h\nu$, where $P(t) = \int\int_A |E(r,t)|^2 dt$ is the received power density $|E(r, t)|^2$ integrated over the receiving aperture $A$, and $E$ is the voltage of the optical field. If $E$ is random for other classical reasons—e.g., random channel loss—then the points are those of a Poisson process conditioned on any such randomness held fixed.

This result can be derived from the more fundamental quantum mechanics along the following lines [2, 3]. For the majority of detectors the "photoelectric effect" describes the interaction of the optical field and the material of the detector: this is the ionization of an atom, creating, e.g., a "free" electron in a phototube or an electron-hole pair in a semiconductor by the absorption of a photon. Starting with a Hamiltonian description, the distribution of the number of such ionization transitions from "initial" to "final" quantum states is calculated—Fermi's famous "golden rule"—from which the Poisson process results easily. Though certain approximations have been made, this theory gives the correct quantum description of absorption and stimulated and spontaneous emission first derived by Einstein.

I shall here call this the "semiclassical quantum theory," though this term is variously employed. It has been very widely used by physicists as the basic model for statistical inference; thus there was a considerable body of knowledge available for direct application to optical communication systems. For example, photon count distributions were (and are) studied to "classify" optical sources by their spectral characteristics. The communication theory viewpoint would eventually result in much more sophisticated models and methods of statistical inference, in part required by the much more varied class of sources under consideration.

Ignoring all other possible sources of randomness, except the "dark current" that has Poisson process occurrence times, one has, e.g., the following simple model appropriate to $M$-ary communication: if the $m$th signal $S_m(t)$ is transmitted, the received Poisson point process has intensity $[\lambda_m(t) + \lambda_n]$, $m = 1, \ldots, M$, where $\lambda_m(t) \equiv \eta \int_A |E_m(r, t)|^2 \, dr$, $E_m(r, t) = F(r)S_m(t)$, and $\lambda_n$ accounts for the dark current. This was a popular model in the sixties; $S_m(t)$ was either constant, or piecewise constant, and photon counting was performed over each constant interval. Since such counts are independent random variables (the Poisson process is an independent increment process), likelihood ratio tests and hence optimal receiver processor structures are readily formulated though performance calculation can be more involved.

In 1963 B. Rieffen and H. Sherman showed that a sufficient statistic for the binary case was

$$\phi \equiv \sum_i n_i \ln\left(\frac{\lambda_i^{(1)} + \lambda_n}{\lambda_i^{(2)} + \lambda_n}\right)$$

where $n_i$ is the photon count over the $i$th interval (Paper 9). They calculated the mean and variance of $\phi$ and defined a certain signal-to-noise ratio that is proportional to

$$\sum_i [\lambda_i^{(1)} - \lambda_i^{(2)}]^2$$

Under such an optimality criterion, in the detector-noise-limited case ($\lambda_i^{(m)} << \lambda_n$) with an average energy restraint, it is shown that on–off modulation is optimal and that the "on" pulse should be as narrow as possible.

Helstrom uses a similar model [4] except that he considers optical fields piecewise constant spatially rather than temporally. Again the detector-limited ("threshold") case is more tractable: under it, detection and resolution of "point" sources are analyzed with extended discussion of the calculation of the appropriate classical diffraction theory.

Paper 10, "Communication under the Poisson Regime" by Isreal Bar-David, was a very timely discourse. Its major contribution was the derivation of the likelihood ratio for continuously varying intensity functions, a result easily derived formally from the Reiffen and Sherman form for the piecewise continuous case (and similarly from Helstrom's paper), and the result was noted *en passe* long before by Grenander [5, p. 224] in his remarkable thesis. Also presented was a very useful expectation for products of an identical function of the occurrence times, a realization of the maximum likelihood receiver, a Gram–Charlier series for the detection statistic, and a discussion of parameter estimation.

"*M*-ary Poisson Detection and Optical Communication" by Robert Gagliardi and Sherman Karp continues the development of the theory of the design of good signal sets for *M*-ary communication over "Poisson channels," specifically under the "hard" criterion of probability of error. Given a signalling time of $T$ s, each signal is transmitted as an *M*-tuple of possible constant intensities over $M$ equal subintervals of width $\Delta T \equiv T/M$. In two special cases, (1) $M = 2$ and "symmetric" intensity sets and (2) device-noise limited case, they show, under an energy restraint, that the "pulsed intensity set" is optimal, each signal encoded into one maximal energy pulse in a unique time slot.

Other sources of randomness in the received field, such as thermal background noise, had to be addressed for realistic analysis of optical communication systems. The important case of the distribution of photon counts $N_T$ over the interval $(0, T)$ when a fixed signal is received along with thermal noise was comprehensively reviewed and studied by Sherman Karp and John Clark (Paper 12). They note that the characteristic function $\phi$ of the count distribution is simply $\exp \lambda_t u$, $u \equiv \exp i\,v - 1$, for fixed $\lambda \equiv (\eta/h\nu)\int_0^T |E(t)|^2\,dt$; the characteristic function is found by averaging $\phi$ over the distribution of $\lambda$. As $E(t)$ is a Gaussian random process, use of its Karhunen–Loeve expansion reduces the calculation to essentially $E\{\exp c\chi^2\}$, $\chi$ normal, which is easily done. The overall characteristic function is then a product; hence the count distribution will be a multiple convolution. They show that, for narrow band thermal noise, $N_T$ is the sum of independent Laguerre random variables; for any such variate having zero signal component, the well-known Bose–Einstein distribution obtains.

For zero signal and white Gaussian noise of spectral amplitude $\eta_0$ and bandwidth $2B$, when $2BT << 1$, $N_T$ is approximately a Bose–Einstein random variable; when $2BT >> 1$ and $\eta\eta_0 h\nu << 1$—large time—bandwidth product and on average less than one photoelectron produced in time $T$ — $N_T$ is approximately Poisson, as it is in the signal-only case.

In the signal-plus-white-noise case, the Laguerre-type distribution is given; a simplification for $2BT << 1$ is noted as is its approach to Poisson when $2BT >> 1$ and $\eta\eta_0/h\nu << 1$: in this case the Poisson process's intensity function is indeed representable as $\lambda_s + \lambda_n$, where $\lambda_s \equiv (1/T)\int\int_{T\times A} E(r, t)\, dt\, dr(\eta/h\nu)$ and $\lambda_n \equiv 2B\eta_0\eta/h\nu$.

Karp and Clark go on to consider random waveform estimation with bandlimited, white Gaussian background noise by using counters in each interval of 1/2*B* s. They give a likelihood ratio and consider maximum likelihood estimators. For example, they find a reasonable estimation structure for Gaussian waveforms and small average noise count per degree of freedom.

The need to consider more general point process models to account for random modulations, random channel effects such as turbulence, and other random detector effects such as avalanche gain and thermal noise led to the consideration of more abstract and complex models for the detection and estimation process. One such model, employing a "doubly stochastic Poisson process," is the subject of Paper 13, by Donald Snyder. Recall again the log-likelihood ratio $\ell(t)$ given by Bar-David for reception of a sample function of a Poisson process received over the interval $[0, t]$,

$$\ell(t) = \ell_0 - \int_0^t \lambda(s)\, ds + \sum_{i=1}^{m} \ln\left(1 + \frac{\lambda(ti)}{\lambda_n}\right)$$

the log of the ratio of the probabilities of observing the set of counts $\{t_1, \ldots, t_M\}$ under the assumption that the intensity function is either $\lambda(t) + \lambda_n$ or $\lambda_n$. If $\{N_t,\ t \geq 0\}$ is the "counting process," which takes unit jumps at the distinct times $\{t_i\}$, one can write formally

$$\ell(t) = \ell_0 - \int_0^t \lambda(s)\, ds + \int_0^t \ln\left(1 + \frac{\lambda(s)}{\lambda_n}\right) dN_s \qquad (1)$$

in fact the integral can be well defined imposing certain conditions on the counting process, as stated in Snyder's paper. When other random effects, such as those listed above, are present, one can be led to model the intensity function with the form $\lambda[t, x(t)]$ where $x(t)$ is a vector-valued random process. Now the counting process is termed, not surprisingly, a "doubly stochastic Poisson counting process." A "brute force" approach to finding the likelihood ratio would be to average the likelihood ratio exp $\ell(t)$ over the distributions of $\{x(t)\}$: generally this is not feasible analytically—through it can be, as we have already seen in Karp and Clark's paper.

The situation is similar to the problem of finding the likelihood ratio for a random signal received in white, Gaussian noise: a brute force averaging of the well-known likelihood ratio for a known signal in white, Gaussian noise is rarely fruitful and instead a more sophisticated approach, employing certain assumptions about the nature of the random signal and well exposited by Kailath and others, leads to the elegant result that the likelihood ratio has the form appropriate to the known signal case except, in place of the known signal, its minimum mean-square error, realizable estimate appears.

Here a surprisingly similar result holds: if $\{x_t\}$ is a vector Markov process (and certain other technical conditions hold), the likelihood ratio for the doubly stochastic Poisson process is Eq. (1) except that $\lambda(t)$ is replaced by $\hat{\lambda}(t)$, its minimum mean-square error, realizable estimate. Its derivation also utilizes a special case of a generalized Ito rule. In principle, the recursive calculation of the conditional expectation is possible using the conditional characteristic function for $x_t$ that is given by stochastic differential Eq. (8) of the paper. However, the calculation is "generally analytically intractable so that numerical techniques will be required"; such techniques are discussed in the paper. The case when $x_t$ is the solution of a stochastic differential equation is of special interest. In particular, a certain linearization can greatly reduce the complexity. The paper concludes with an explicit optical communication application and a discussion of simulation results.

The realistic modeling of detectors can require other and more complex random processes. For example, an avalanche photodiode detector produces a random, "large" number—"mark"—of photoelectrons. While the emission times may be those of a Poisson process, the random, cardinal number "jump" leads to a so-called marked point process [6, Ch. 3]. If the marks are identically distributed and mutually independent among themselves and of the underlying Poisson point process, one has a "compound Poisson process"; the sample function density required for statistical inference is given in Snyder [6, Ch. 3]. Of course, one may wish to use a model of the point process that is also doubly stochastic: such models are also discussed in Snyder [6, Ch. 7], where the author points out that spatial dependence can be handled with such a model. The sample-function density and posterior statistics required for statistical inference are given there.

A still further generalization is needed, e.g., to account for the unavoidable thermal noise present in a detector. Such a model is discussed in Paper 14, "Direct-detection Optical Communication Receivers" by Estil Hoversten, Donald Snyder, R. O. Harger, and Koji Kurimoto. The structures of optimal detectors for randomly filtered, doubly stochastic Poisson processes received along with additive white Gaussian noise is studied, and representations are found, in recursive form, for the posterior statistics of the vector-valued Markov process $N_t$. Again the results are generally too complex for direct analytic solution: thus approximate structures are derived for several optical communication applications.

## REFERENCES


1. Mandel, L. "Fluctuations of Photon Beams; the Distribution of Photo-electrons." *Phys. Soc. Proc.* **74**:233–243 (Sept. 1959).
2. Yariv, A. *Quantum Electronics*. New York: John Wiley & Sons, 1967.
3. Marcuse, D. *Engineering Quantum Electrodynamics*. New York: Harcourt, Brace & World, 1970.
4. Helstrom, C. W. "The Detection and Resolution of Optical Signals." *IEEE Trans. Inf. Theory* **IT-10**:275–287 (Oct. 1964).
5. Grenander, U. "Stochastic Processes and Statistical Inference." *Ark. Math.* **1**:195–277 (April 1950).
6. Snyder, D. L. *Random Point Processes*. New York: John Wiley & Sons, 1975.

# 9



Reprinted from *IEEE Proc.* **51**(10):1316–1320 (1963)

# An Optimum Demodulator for Poisson Processes: Photon Source Detectors*

B. REIFFEN† AND H. SHERMAN†, SENIOR MEMBER, IEEE

***Summary***—**The optimum demodulator for time-varying Poisson processes is derived from consideration of the likelihood ratio. In the case of high background level radiation, it has been found that the optimum signal processing is cross-correlation. Under an average energy constraint and conditions of high background radiation, an optimum binary signaling method is "on-off" modulation. For both binary signaling and radar purposes, the "on" waveform should be a narrow pulse in order to maximize the "signal-to-noise" ratio.**

## I. Introduction

CURRENT INTEREST in optical devices for purposes of communication and radar suggests that we consider the optimum detector to be placed at the output of a photon-electron converter, its physical realization and the statistics of the detector output.

In our model we assume that the average power output of the photon source is modulated with a deterministic waveform $\lambda(t)$. Incident upon the photon converter will be photons from the photon source (attenuated by $1/R^2$ spreading with or without scattering from a target) plus photons from background radiation. This background radiation will usually have bandwidth much greater than that of the source whose bandwidth is taken as $W$. Thus to reduce the effect of background radiation, it is reasonable to introduce an optical filter in front of the photon converter.[1]

We assume that the photon-electron converter is a photon counter with quantum efficiency $\eta \leq 1$. In other words, an incident photon is converted to a single photoelectron with probability $\eta$.

In what follows, we shall be talking about numbers of photons counted in a given time interval. The uncertainty principle imposes a constraint on the minimum time interval that we may consider. We start with a statement of the uncertainty principle in the form

$$(\Delta E)(\Delta t) \geq h/4\pi, \tag{1}$$

where $\Delta E$ is the uncertainty in the energy received in time $\Delta t$ and $h$ is Planck's constant. Since, for a single photon,

$$\Delta E = hW, \tag{2}$$

* Received June 10, 1963; revised manuscript received July 25, 1963.

† Lincoln Laboratory, Massachusetts Institute of Technology, Cambridge, Mass.; operated with support from the U. S. National Aeronautics and Space Administration.

[1] This filter should be viewed as a window which passes photons with energy in a given band and rejects photons whose energy falls outside this band. We do not consider here the deliberate shaping of the pass band of the optical filter for the most favorable reception of the modulation.

we obtain

$$\Delta t \geq \frac{1}{4\pi W} \cdot \tag{3}$$

For large numbers of photons, $\Delta t$ can be smaller than the right-hand side of (3). In this paper, however, we are concerned with small photon counts. Thus we take $1/4\pi W$ as the lower limit of time resolvability.

In order to obtain the desired results, the probability distribution of photon arrivals must be known. For $\lambda(t)$, a constant, the work of Purcell[2] and Mandel[3] shows that first-order photo-electrons (one photon giving rise to one photo-electron) will occur with time-varying Poisson statistics, with the time variation a random process related to the spectral shape of the source.[4] It is shown that in time $\Delta t$, the variance in the number of photo-electrons $n$ is

$$\overline{n^2} - (\bar{n})^2 = \bar{n}[1 + \epsilon] \tag{4}$$

where

$$\epsilon \approx \frac{\bar{n}}{W\Delta t}, \tag{5}$$

and it has been assumed that

$$\Delta t \gg \frac{1}{W} \cdot \tag{6}$$

Note that (6) implies that $\Delta t$ is larger than that required by the uncertainty principle (3). As $\epsilon \rightarrow 0$, (4) reduces to the standard result for the nontime-varying Poisson distribution.

In this analysis we *assume* that in the interval $\Delta t$ the photo-electrons occur with nontime-varying Poisson statistics. We may expect this to be a reasonable model of the physical situation if the ratio of $\bar{n}/\Delta t$ (average rate of photo-electrons) to $W$ (bandwidth of the photon source) is very much less than unity.[5]

The problem we now address is the optimum processing of the photo-electron counts in successive intervals of duration $\Delta t$. The processing has the purpose of deciding which of two waveforms were used to modulate the photon source. The likelihood ratio $\Lambda$ will be formed corresponding to a particular sequence of photo-electron counts. It will be shown that $\Lambda$ is uniquely defined by the output of a linear digital filter whose input is the sequence of photo-electron counts. Thus applying the photo-electron count to the filter represents optimum demodulation.

It should be recognized that the problem addressed here is not that of determining the capacity (in the information theoretic sense) of a photon channel.[6] In this analysis we have *a priori* knowledge of a finite set of time-limited modulation waveforms. This contrasts with the capacity problem where the time and the number of alternatives are both permitted to become infinite.

[2] E. M. Purcell, "The question of correlation between photons in coherent light rays," *Nature*, vol. 178, no. 4548, pp. 1449–1450; December, 1956.

[3] L. Mandel, "Fluctuation of photon beams and their correlations," *Proc. Physical Society*, vol. 72, 1 pt. 6, pp. 1037–1048; July–December, 1958.

[4] This does not necessarily imply that the probability distribution of the number of photo-electrons in time $\Delta t$ is Poisson. (*Caveat emptor!*)

[5] The assumption of nontime-varying Poisson statistics is frequently made; *e.g.*, see Yariv and Gordon, "The laser," PROC. IEEE, vol. 51, pp. 4–29; January, 1963.

## II. Formulation of the Likelihood Ratio

In the time interval $(0, T)$, consider the times $t_i$, where

$$0 = t_0 < t_1 \cdots < t_{N-1} < t_N = T, \tag{7}$$

and

$$t_i - t_{i-1} = \Delta t, \qquad i = 1, 2, \cdots, N. \tag{8}$$

Suppose that the modulation waveform $\lambda(t)$ is a staircase function of the form

$$\lambda(t) = \lambda_i, \; t_{i-1} < t \leq t_i; \qquad i = 1, 2, \cdots, N. \tag{9}$$

In the time interval $t_{i-1} < t \leq t_i$, the probability that $n_i$ photo-electrons occur is

$$P(n_i) = \frac{[\eta(\lambda_i + \lambda_0)\Delta t]^{n_i}}{n_i!} e^{-\eta(\lambda_i+\lambda_0)\Delta t}. \tag{10}$$

Since the photon arrivals in the various intervals are statistically independent, the joint probability of arrivals is

$$P(n) = \prod_{i=1}^{N} \frac{[\eta(\lambda_i + \lambda_0)\Delta t]^{n_i}}{n_i!} e^{-\eta(\lambda_i+\lambda_0)\Delta t}, \tag{11}$$

where $\lambda_0$ is the average rate of photon arrival due to background radiation, and

$$n = (n_1, n_2, \cdots, n_N). \tag{12}$$

Suppose the vector $n$ might have resulted from one of two modulation functions, $\lambda^{(1)}(t)$ or $\lambda^{(2)}(t)$.

In this case

$$\frac{P[n \mid \lambda^{(1)}(t)]}{P[n \mid \lambda^{(2)}(t)]} = \prod_{i=1}^{N} \left[\frac{\lambda_i^{(1)} + \lambda_0}{\lambda_i^{(2)} + \lambda_0}\right]^{n_i} e^{\eta\Delta t(\lambda_i^{(2)} - \lambda_i^{(1)})}. \tag{13}$$

The likelihood ratio $\Lambda$ is the natural logarithm of (13), *i.e.*,

$$\Lambda = \eta \sum_i [\lambda_i^{(2)} - \lambda_i^{(1)}]\Delta t + \sum_i n_i \ln \frac{\lambda_i^{(1)} + \lambda_0}{\lambda_i^{(2)} + \lambda_0} \cdot \tag{14}$$

[6] J. P. Gordon, "Quantum effects in communication systems," PROC. IRE, vol. 50, pp. 1898–1908; September, 1962.

The first summation in (14) is independent of $n$. Thus for any decision that is to be made on the basis of the received signal it is sufficient to form the quantity

$$\phi = \sum_i n_i \ln \left[ \frac{\lambda_i^{(1)} + \lambda_0}{\lambda_i^{(2)} + \lambda_0} \right]. \tag{15}$$

In the foregoing it should be noted that in order to satisfy the uncertainty principle the time interval $\Delta t$ must be large compared to $1/W$ (3). Roughly speaking, the same condition (6) is necessary for (4) and (5) to be valid. These latter equations, under the described conditions, are compatible with the assumed Poisson statistics.

$\phi$ is a random variable whose statistics are dependent on whether the modulation is $\lambda^{(1)}(t)$ or $\lambda^{(2)}(t)$. Let $m_k$ and $\sigma_k^2 (k=1, 2)$ be, respectively, the mean and variance of $\phi$ when the modulation is $\lambda^{(k)}(t)$. These quantities are easily found to be

$$m_k = \eta \Delta t \sum_i [\lambda_0 + \lambda_i^{(k)}] \ln \left[ \frac{\lambda_i^{(1)} + \lambda_0}{\lambda_i^{(2)} + \lambda_0} \right] \tag{16}$$

and

$$\sigma_k^2 = \eta \Delta t \sum_i [\lambda_0 + \lambda_i^{(k)}] \ln^2 \left[ \frac{\lambda_i^{(1)} + \lambda_0}{\lambda_i^{(2)} + \lambda_0} \right]. \tag{17}$$

If the background level is high; *i.e.*, if for $k=1, 2$

$$\frac{\lambda_i^{(k)}}{\lambda_0} \ll 1, \qquad i = 1, 2, \cdots, N, \tag{18}$$

an extension can be made in the results. Using the approximation

$$\ln (1 + x) = x \tag{19}$$

valid for $|x| \ll 1$, we obtain

$$m_1 - m_2 = \frac{\eta \Delta t}{\lambda_0} \sum_i [\lambda_i^{(1)} - \lambda_i^{(2)}]^2 \tag{20}$$

and

$$\sigma_1^2 = \sigma_2^2 = \frac{\eta \Delta t}{\lambda_0} \sum_i [\lambda_i^{(1)} - \lambda_i^{(2)}]^2 = \sigma^2 \tag{21}$$

The output "signal-to-noise" ratio is defined naturally as

$$\frac{S}{N} = \frac{(m_1 - m_2)^2}{\sigma^2}, \tag{22}$$

for the conditions of (18), (22) becomes

$$\frac{S}{N} = \frac{\eta \Delta t}{\lambda_0} \sum [\lambda_i^{(1)} - \lambda_i^{(2)}]^2. \tag{23}$$

Note that high background level (18) does not necessarily imply small output signal-to-noise ratio.

## III. Application to Communication

### A. *M-ary Formulation*

For binary signaling with modulation waveforms $\lambda^{(1)}(t)$ and $\lambda^{(2)}(t)$, the form of (15) for $\phi$ suggests that it be written in the form

$$\phi = \phi^{(1)} - \phi^{(2)}, \tag{24}$$

where

$$\phi^{(k)} = \sum_i n_i \ln [\lambda_0 + \lambda_i^{(k)}], \qquad k = 1, 2. \tag{25}$$

Trivially, this generalizes to the case of $M$-ary signaling, where the index $k$ assumes the values $k=1, 2 \cdots, M$. The decision on which one of the $M$ waveforms was sent can be made using the quantities $\phi^{(1)}, \phi^{(2)}, \cdots, \phi^{(M)}$. Thus the received signal should be processed in $M$ parallel channels as shown in Fig. 1. The decision scheme is straightforward and is not shown.

Each of the parallel processors may take either of the equivalent forms shown in Fig. 2. Fig. 2(a) shows a digital correlator; Fig. 2(b) shows a digital filter. In both cases the output of the processor following the $N$th input sample is $\phi^{(k)}$.

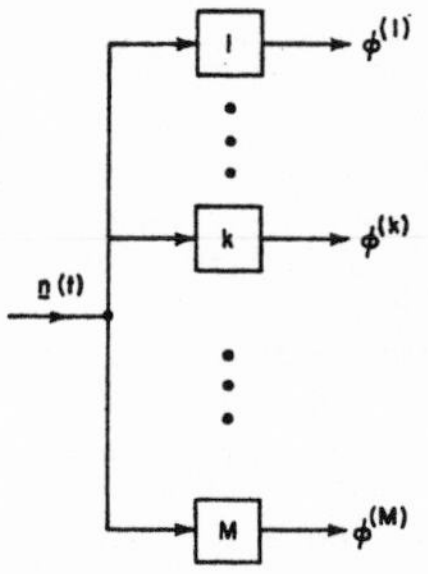


Fig. 1—Processing for $M$-ary communication.

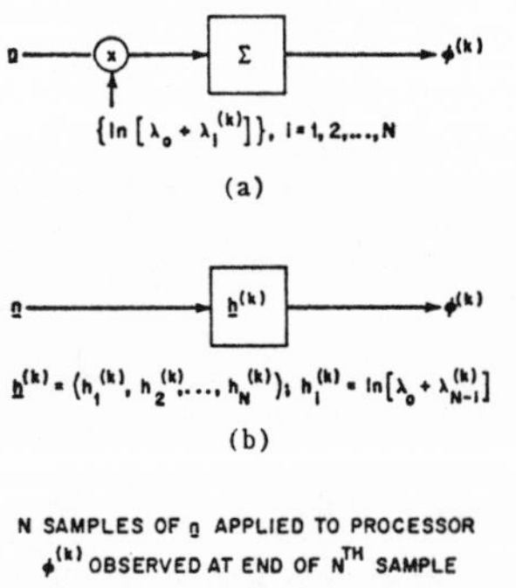


Fig 2—Alternate forms of the $k$th processor (a) Digital correlation processing. (b) Digital filter processing.

### *B. High Background Radiation Case*

If the background level is high; *i.e.*, if for all $k$,

$$\frac{\lambda_i^{(k)}}{\lambda_0} \ll 1, \qquad i = 1, 2, \cdots, N, \tag{26}$$

a significant simplification can be made in the results. Using the approximation of (19), (25) simplifies to

$$\phi^{(k)} = \ln \lambda_0 \sum_i n_i + \frac{1}{\lambda_0} \sum_i n_i \lambda_i^{(k)}. \tag{27}$$

For a given $\mathbf{n}$, the first summation in (27) is independent of $\lambda_i^{(k)}$. Thus for optimum detection it is sufficient to form the $M$ quantities

$$\theta^{(k)} = \sum_i n_i \lambda_i^{(k)}, \qquad k = 1, 2, \cdots, M. \tag{28}$$

The optimum processing still takes the form of Fig. 1 (with the outputs $\theta^{(k)}$ rather than $\phi^{(k)}$. However, the $k$th processor is now digitally correlating $\mathbf{n}$ with $\lambda_1^{(k)}$, or alternately, passing $\mathbf{n}$ through a digital filter with impulsive response $h_i^{(k)} = \lambda_{N-i}^{(k)}$. In other words, the digital filter is matched to $\lambda_i^{(k)}$.

### *C. Waveform Selection*

For binary signaling under conditions of high background radiation, optimum modulation waveforms may be specified. The following conditions are imposed:

$$\lambda_i^{(k)} \geq 0, \qquad k = 1, 2 \tag{29}$$

$$\frac{\Delta t}{2} \sum_i [\lambda_i^{(1)} + \lambda_i^{(2)}] = E. \tag{30}$$

Eq. (29) recognizes the fact that the photon source is intensity modulated. Eq. (30) is an average energy constraint on the photon source where it is assumed that the two waveforms are equally likely.

For any $i$ where $\lambda_i^{(1)} + \lambda_i^{(2)} > 0$, one of the two, say $\lambda_i^{(1)}$, is larger than (or at least equal to) the other. Thus

$$|\lambda_i^{(1)} - \lambda_i^{(2)}|^2 = [\lambda_i^{(1)}]^2 \left[1 - \frac{\lambda_i^{(2)}}{\lambda_i^{(1)}}\right]^2 \leq [\lambda_i^{(1)}]^2. \tag{31}$$

In (31) equality holds if, and only if, $\lambda_i^{(2)} = 0$. Thus we conclude that in order to maximize the signal-to-noise ratio as given in (23) under the constraints of (29) and (30) if one of the $\lambda_i^{(k)}$ is nonzero, the other must be zero. Accordingly, we can maximize $S/N$ under the constraints by setting one of the modulation waveforms equal to zero.

The other modulation waveform, which we now call $\lambda(t)$, should be a narrow pulse. This can be seen by the following argument:

$$\Delta t \sum_{i=1}^{N} \lambda_i^2 \leq \Delta t \left[\sum_{i=1}^{N} \lambda_i\right]^2, \tag{32}$$

where the inequality in (32) follows from the fact that $\lambda_i \geq 0$. Equality in (32) holds if, and only if, all but one of the samples $\lambda_i$ is zero. The right-hand side of (32) is a constant, set by the constraint of (30). We conclude that the modulation waveform $\lambda(t)$ should be a pulse with width $\Delta t$.

This result is valid only if several assumptions, implicit in the discussion, are not violated. Practical considerations may compromise certain of these assumptions. In particular:

1) We have assumed $(\lambda_i/\lambda_0) \ll 1$. Narrowing the pulse under a fixed energy constraint may violate this assumption if $\Delta t$ is too small.
2) We have assumed that $\lambda_0$ is a constant. This is valid only if the optical filter preceding the photon counter has a bandwidth wide enough to pass the modulation pulse of duration $\Delta t$.
3) The photon counter is assumed to be able to resolve individual photons. The finite response time of a practical device will set a lower limit on $\Delta t$.

If $\lambda(t)$ is a pulse of amplitude $\lambda$ and duration $\Delta t$, we obtain from (23)

$$\frac{S}{N} = \frac{\eta \Delta t \lambda^2}{\lambda_0} = \frac{\lambda}{\lambda_0} \eta \lambda \Delta t, \qquad \frac{\lambda}{\lambda_0} \ll 1. \tag{33}$$

A condition of high $S/N$ and high background can result if

$$1 \ll \eta \lambda \Delta t \ll \lambda_0 \Delta t. \tag{34}$$

## IV. Application to Radar

### *A. Radar Signal Detection*

In this case there are two hypotheses:

1) Signal present, in which case $\lambda^{(1)}(t) = \lambda(t)$.
2) Signal absent, in which case $\lambda^{(2)}(t) = 0$.

The likelihood ratio can be formed from the quantity $\phi$ defined in (15). The quantity $\phi$ can be considered as the output of a digital filter as shown in Fig. 3.

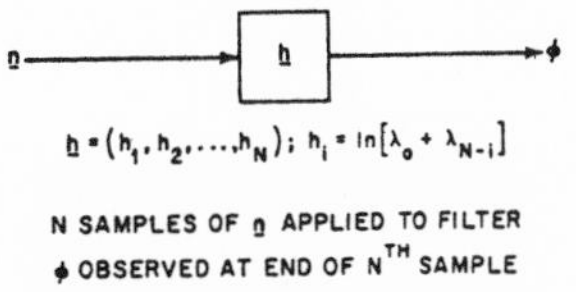


Fig. 3—Processing for radar detection.

For high background levels (*i.e.*, the conditions of (26)), the remarks of Sections III, B and III, C apply, namely,

1) $h$ in Fig. 3 reduces to filter matched to the modulation $\lambda(t)$; *i.e.*, $h_i = \lambda_{N-i}$.

2) The signal-to-noise ratio of the filter output $\phi$ is

$$\frac{S}{N} = \frac{\eta \Delta t}{\lambda_0} \sum_i \lambda_i^2. \tag{35}$$

3) Subject to the energy constraint

$$\Delta t \sum_i \lambda_i = 2E. \tag{36}$$

$S/N$ is maximized when $\lambda(t)$ is a short pulse. The qualifications following (32) pertain.

*B. Radar Range (Delay) Estimation*

In this case there are a continuum of hypotheses; namely, that a time limited modulation $\lambda(t)$ is delayed by time $\tau$, where $0 \leq \tau \leq \tau_{max}$. Clearly a time resolution finer than that implied by the uncertainty principle is impossible. Thus it is sufficient to quantize time and perform digital processing. The interval $(0, \tau_{max})$ is divided into a number, say $k$, of smaller intervals of length $\Delta t$ where $k = \tau_{max}/\Delta t$.

The matched filter of Fig. 3 is sufficient for delay estimation but with the processing indicated in Fig. 4. The maximum likelihood estimate of delay is that $i$ for which $\phi_{N+i}$ is maximum. Other estimates of delay (minimum variance, etc.) can be formed from the sample values of $\phi$.

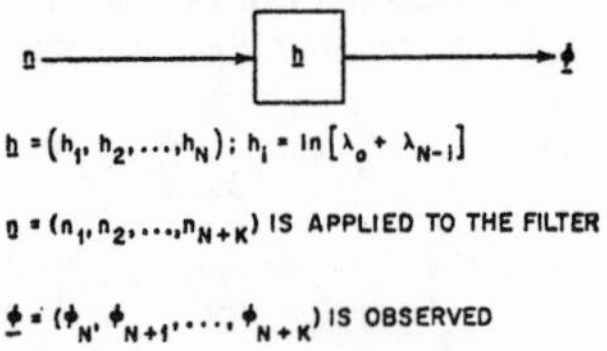


Fig. 4—Processing for delay estimation.

ACKNOWLEDGMENT

The authors acknowledge helpful discussions with Dr. M. Macrakis.

# 10



Reprinted from *IEEE Trans. Inf. Theory* **IT-15**(1):31–37 (1969)

# Communication under the Poisson Regime

ISRAEL BAR-DAVID, MEMBER, IEEE

***Abstract*—By "Poisson regime" we mean a model in which intelligence is communicated by random discrete occurrences in time that obey Poisson statistics of arbitrarily time-varying mean, as for example when modulated electromagnetic radiation and background radiation at optical frequencies is incoherently detected by photon-sensitive surfaces.**

**The problems of optimal detection of signals of arbitrary shape and of the estimation of signal amplitude and delay are treated under a maximum-likelihood criterion. Detection probabilities, delay estimation errors, and the probability of "noise threshold" in delay estimation, are derived. Some results are basically different from those of parallel problems treating known signals in Gaussian noise.**

**The treatment is based on a representation of nonstationary Poisson processes in which the observables are the instants of the occurrences rather than their numbers in given intervals of time.**

## I. Introduction

In this paper the following mathematical model is analyzed. During a given time interval $(-T, +T)$, a realization of a Poisson point process of time-varying expectation $\lambda(t)$ is observed. The realization consists in general of randomly distributed points $t_j$, $|t_j| \leq T$, $j = 1, 2, \cdots, M$, with $M$ itself a random variable. Two different, though related, cases are considered. The first is a decision problem. It is assumed that $\lambda(t)$ can assume one of two possible a priori known functional forms, $\lambda_0(t)$ and $\lambda_1(t)$ corresponding, repectively, to the different hypotheses $H_0$ and $H_1$. It is required to decide between the two hypotheses on the basis of the observed points, $t_j$. The second case is an estimation problem. It is assumed that the expectation $\lambda(t : \alpha)$ depends on an additional parameter $\alpha$, the functional form of $\lambda(t : \alpha)$ being known in both $t$ and $\alpha$. It is required to estimate the parameter $\alpha$, again, on the basis of the observed points.

Both problems are solved in principle for arbitrary expectation functions $\lambda$, under a maximum-likelihood criterion. Expressions for the probability of correct decision and for the variance of the time-delay estimate are derived. The possibility of gross errors in the delay estimate is described by the probability of "threshold," and an upper-bounding expression for it is derived.

The solution is based on a representation of Poisson processes of time-varying expectation in which the observables are the instants of the occurrences $t_j$, rather than the number of occurrences in any specified interval. The $M$-dimensional joint probability density function of the $t_j$, derived in the next section, enables the description of the likelihood function in terms of these observables.

In optical communication systems, in which incident radiation is intercepted by means of photon-sensitive devices, the emission of the photoelectrons corresponds to the point process in the model introduced above. It has been shown [1] that if the transmitted beam is generated by a single-mode laser, the beam fluctuations, and hence the photoelectron count, obey Poisson statistics. Furthermore, the expectation of the count varies as the signal that modulates the laser beam, when noise is absent, and as the signal plus the noise average when noise is also present. The noise is due mainly to detector dark current and background radiation, which are also thought to obey Poisson statistics. Thermal (Gaussian) noise is usually negligible, in particular when high-gain photomultiplier tubes are used as detectors.

It should, however, be realized that if the transmitted beam is due to several interacting laser modes or, in extreme cases, to incoherent sources, the probability distribution of the photoelectron count is an average over Poisson distributions [1] and is not necessarily Poisson itself. In such cases, the model introduced previously only approximates the physical situation. Another limitation of the model is that it assumes accurate observation of the instants of electron emissions. Actually, slight variations (of the order of $10^{-11}$ seconds) exist in the outputs of some devices, notably of high-gain photomultiplier tubes. An attempt is presently being made to account for such variations in a more elaborate model.

Previous treatments [2], [3], [4] of the photon communication problem were restricted to cases in which the transmitted signal energy is piecewise constant. Imposing such a restriction enables the use of a number of photoelectrons in the subintervals of constant $\lambda$ as the observables of the process. A serious drawback in such a treatment is that delay can be estimated only up to the length of the subintervals. The representation of the Poisson processes in terms of the instants of arrival introduced in this paper enables the treatment of arbitrary signals. Some of the results of this paper, pertaining to the decision problem, can, however, also be obtained by proper interpretation of the previous results in the limit of vanishing lengths of the constant-$\lambda$ subintervals. This point is further discussed in Section III.

## II. A Representation of Poisson Processes

### *Probability Density Functions*

Given a Poisson process with time-varying expectation $\lambda(t) \geq 0$, the probability $P[k, (a, b)]$ that the number of occurrences in the time interval $(a, b)$ equals the integer $k$ is [5]

$$P[k, (a, b)] = \left\{\exp\left[-\int_a^b \lambda(t)\, dt\right]\right\}\cdot\left[\int_a^b \lambda(t)\, dt\right]^k/k!\,. \tag{1}$$

Manuscript received February 9, 1968; revised August 9, 1968.
The author is with the Scientific Department, Israel Ministry of Defense, Haifa, Israel.

A complete description of the process over an interval $(-T, +T)$, using (1), is obtained only by considering all possible partitions, $-T = a_0 < a_1 \cdots < a_K = T$ and observing the number of occurrences in each of intervals $(a_i, a_{i+1})$, $i = 0, 1, \cdots, K-1$. To cover all possibilities, $K$ would have to become infinitely large. An alternative representation, which seems to be natural for this process, uses the instants $t_j$ of the occurrences as the observables. One obvious advantage is that there are only a finite number of such instants.

One recalls that for the derivation of (1), the following axioms are postulated.

1) The probability of one occurrence in an infinitesimal interval $\Delta t$, $P[1, \Delta t]$, is given by

$$P[1, \Delta t] = \lambda(t)\, \Delta t, \qquad \Delta t \to 0. \tag{2}$$

2) The probability of more than one occurrence in $\Delta t$ is zero for $\Delta t \to 0$.
3) The number of occurrences in any interval is independent of those in all other disjoint intervals.

In particular, for $k = 0$, (1) reduces to

$$P[0, (a, b)] = \exp\left[-\int_a^b \lambda(t)\, dt\right]. \tag{3}$$

Consider now a possible realization of the process, as in Fig. 1. Denote by $\{t_M\}$ the set of $M$ numbers $-T \le t_1 < t_2 < \cdots < T_M \le T$. The $M$-dimensional joint probability density function $p\{t_M\}$ of such a realization can be calculated by first allowing infinitesimal intervals of width $\pm \Delta t_j/2$ about $t_j$, $j = 1, 2, \cdots, M$. The probability that one and only one point would fall within each one of these intervals and none outside them is $p\{t_M\}\, \Delta t_1\, \Delta t_2 \cdots \Delta t_M$ and is given by (2) and condition (3). Thus,

$$\begin{aligned} p\{t_M\}\, \Delta t_1\, \Delta t_2 \cdots \Delta t_M &= P[0, (-T, t_1 - \tfrac{1}{2}\Delta t_1)] \\ &\cdot \lambda(t_1)\, \Delta t_1 \cdot P[0, (t_1 + \tfrac{1}{2}\Delta t_1, t_2 - \tfrac{1}{2}\Delta t_2)] \cdots \\ &\cdot \lambda(t_M)\, \Delta t_M\, P[0, (t_M + \tfrac{1}{2}\Delta t_M, T)]. \end{aligned}$$

Using (3) in the limit of $\Delta t_j \to 0$, for all $j$, one obtains, for $M \ge 1$,

$$p\{t_M\} = e^{-Q} \prod_{j=1}^{M} \lambda(t_j), \qquad -T \le t_1 < t_2 \cdots < t_M \le T, \tag{4}$$

where $Q$ is given by

$$Q = \int_{-T}^{T} \lambda(t)\, dt. \tag{5}$$

If $M = 0$, $\{t_M\}$ is empty, i.e., no occurrence is observed, and by (3),

$$P[0, (-T, T)] = e^{-Q}. \tag{6}$$

Thus, for $M = 0$, if $p\{t_M\}$ is interpreted as the probability of no occurrence and $\prod_{j=1}^{M} \lambda(t_j)$ is interpreted as 1, then (4) holds for all $M$ and provides a complete statistical description of the Poisson process in the interval $(-T, +T)$.

It should be pointed out that $p\{t_M\}$ is *not* a conditional

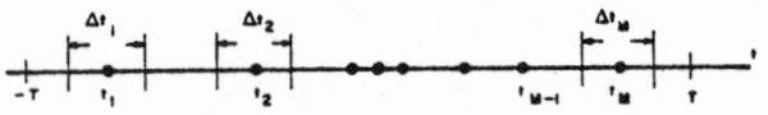

Fig. 1. A sample realization of a point process.

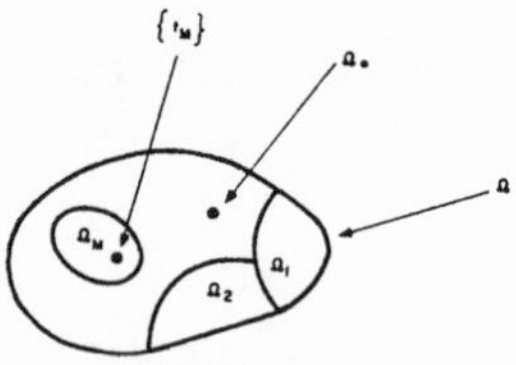

Fig. 2. The sample space of events.

density function since $M$ itself is a random variable.[1] The sample space of events is illustrated in Fig. 2, where $\Omega_M$ denotes the set of all possible sets $\{t_M\}$, $\Omega_0$ the event of no occurrence in $(-T, +T)$ and $\Omega$ the sure event, i.e., the event that any number of points occured at any instants in the interval $(-T, T)$. In particular, if the process is stationary and $\lambda(t) = \bar{k}$ is the constant mean, then all sample sequences of $M$ occurrences within the interval $(-T, +T)$, are equally likely, with a joint probability *density* given by

$$p\{t_M\} = (\bar{k})^M \exp(-2\bar{k}T). \tag{7}$$

*Expectation of Product Functions*

Of interest in what follows are expectations of product functions $f_\pi(\{t_M\})$, which are defined here by means of a function $f(t)$, as follows.

$$\begin{aligned} f_\pi(\{t_M\}) &= \prod_{j=1}^{M} f(t_j), \qquad j = 1, 2, \cdots, M, \quad M \ge 1 \\ &= 1, \qquad M = 0. \end{aligned} \tag{8}$$

Symbolically,

$$\begin{aligned} E[f_\pi] &= \int_\Omega p\{t_M\} \prod_{j=1}^{M} f(t_j) \\ &= \sum_{M=0}^{\infty} \int_{\Omega_M} p\{t_M\} \prod_{j=1}^{M} f(t_j) \triangleq \sum_{0}^{\infty} E_M(f_\pi). \end{aligned}$$

Using (4), the $M$th summand becomes

$$E_M[f_\pi] = \int_{-T}^{T} \int_{t_1}^{T} \cdots \int_{t_{M-1}}^{T} dt_1\, dt_2 \cdots dt_M \cdot p\{t_M\} \prod_{j=1}^{M} f(t_j) \tag{9}$$

$$= e^{-Q} \int_{-T}^{T} \int_{t_1}^{T} \cdots \int_{t_{M-1}}^{T} dt_1\, dt_2 \cdots dt_M \prod_{j=1}^{M} g(t_j), \tag{10}$$

where $g(t)$ is defined by

$$g(t) = f(t)\lambda(t).$$

[1] The conditional density function appears in (14).

The $M$-fold integral is over a region that is $(1/M!)$ of the hypercube $-T < t_i < T$, all $j$. By permuting the indices another integral of equal value over a similar, albeit different, region is obtained. By adding the $M!$ similarly obtained integrals one obtains

$$e^{-Q} \int_{-T}^{T} \int_{-T}^{T} \cdots \int_{-T}^{T} dt_1\, dt_2 \cdots dt_M \prod_{j=1}^{M} g(t_j) = e^{-Q} G^M(T)$$

where

$$G(T) = \int_{-T}^{T} g(t)\, dt. \tag{11}$$

Thus,[2]

$$E_M[f_r] = \frac{e^{-Q} G^M(T)}{M!}. \tag{12}$$

Finally,

$$E[f_r] = e^{-Q} \sum_0^\infty \frac{G^M(T)}{M!} = e^{-Q+G(T)}. \tag{13}$$

In particular, if $f(t) = 1$, then $E_M[1]$ = probability of $\Omega_M$, i.e., the probability of exactly $M$ occurrences in the interval $(-T, +T)$. Indeed, from (11), $G(T) = Q$ and (12) reduces to (1), providing an alternative derivation of the latter. Also the expectation in (13) becomes the probability of the sure event and equals 1.

*Conditional Probabilities*

The event $[\{t_M\}, M]$, i.e., that a given sequence $\{t_M\}$ occurs simultaneously with a total of $M$ occurrences in the interval $(-T, T)$, is evidently included in the event $\Omega_M$. Therefore the joint density function $p_J[\{t_M\}, M]$ equals

$$p_J[\{t_M\}, M] = p\{t_M\},$$

Also, evidently, the conditional probability of $\Omega_M$ given $\{t_M\}$ is

$$\Pr[M \mid \{t_M\}] = 1.$$

On the other hand, the conditional density function $p_c$, is the ratio of (4) and (12), with $G(T) = Q$:

$$p_c[\{t_M\} \mid M] = Q^{-M} M! \prod_{j=1}^{M} \lambda(t_j). \tag{14}$$

In the particular case that $\lambda(t) = \bar{k}$

$$p_c[\{t_M\} \mid M] = (2\bar{k}T)^{-M} M!\, \bar{k}^M = (2T)^{-M} M! \tag{15}$$

is uniform overall $\Omega_M$.

## III. The Decision Problem[3]

*Decision Functions*

Let $\{t_M\}$ be, as before, the representation of the observed sample, assumed to be a realization of either of two Poisson processes. Under hypothesis $H_k$ the mean is $\lambda_k(t)$, its integral is $Q_k$, and the probability law is $p_k\{t_M\}$, $k = 0, 1$.

Basing the decision between the two hypotheses on comparison of the likelihood ratio $L = p_1\{t_M\}/p_0\{t_M\}$ with a threshold $\gamma_L$, one has from (4),

$$L = e^{-(Q_1 - Q_0)} \prod_{j=1}^{M} \frac{\lambda_1(t_j)}{\lambda_0(t_j)} \gtrless \gamma_L. \tag{16}$$

It is assumed that the ratio $\lambda_1(t)/\lambda_0(t)$ is a finite number for all $t$.

It is assumed temporarily that during the interval of interest neither process has zero mean. The singular cases of zero-valued means are considered in a later section. The logarithm being a monotone function, the above is equivalent to

$$G \triangleq \log L + (Q_1 - Q_0)$$
$$= \sum_{j=1}^{M} \log \frac{\lambda_1(t_j)}{\lambda_0(t_j)} \gtrless \gamma_G \triangleq \log \gamma_L + (Q_1 - Q_0). \tag{17}$$

In particular, if costs and a priori probabilities are equal, $\gamma_L = 1$, and $\gamma_G = (Q_1 - Q_0)$. The implementation of the decision function $G$ is as follows: The time function

$$v(t) = \log \frac{\lambda_1(t)}{\lambda_0(t)}, \tag{18}$$

which is defined because by definition $\lambda_k(t)$ are nonnegative and by assumption nonzero, is generated locally and fed into a sampler that is operated at the instants $t_j$, as in Fig. 3(a). In a noncoherent optical communication channel, $t_j$ is the time when an electron is emitted at a photocathode. If the electrical pulse caused by such an emission is sufficiently narrow, i.e., if the band of the output circuit of the photomultiplier tube (PMT) is much wider than that of $v(t)$, then each electron causes an output signal that approximates a Dirac impulse. Then the above is equivalent to a correlation between the "received signal,"

$$r(t) = \sum_{j=1}^{M} \delta(t - t_j)$$

and $v(t)$, and it can be implemented either as a correlation receiver or as a time-invariant filter with impulse response $h(t) = v(T - t)$, Fig. 3(b). The particular case of communicating binary data over such a link can correspond to

$H_0$ : noise alone $\rightarrow \lambda_0(t) = \bar{n}$, where $\bar{n}$ is the average of noise (background) photons,

$H_1$ : signal plus noise $\rightarrow \lambda_1(t) = \bar{n} + s(t)$, where $s(t)$ is the shape of the envelope of the transmitted light pulse.

Then

$$v(t) = \log\left(\frac{n + s(t)}{\bar{n}}\right) = \log\left(1 + \frac{s(t)}{\bar{n}}\right). \tag{19}$$

For small SNR

$$v(t) \simeq \frac{s(t)}{\bar{n}}, \tag{20}$$

[2] This simplified proof has been suggested by the Editor. A different proof is given in [11].

[3] For a discussion of the philosophy of decision methods see [6].

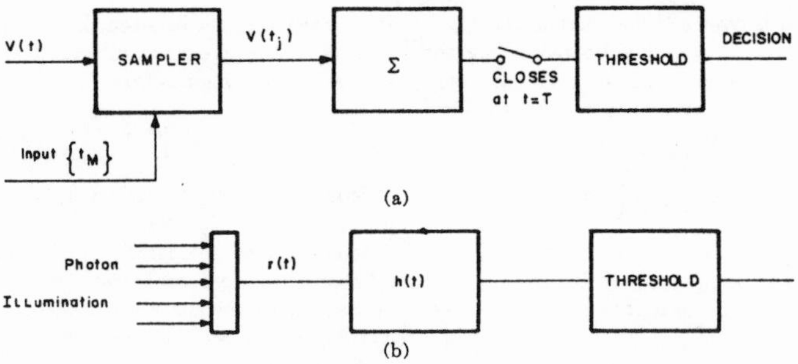


Fig. 3. Maximum-likelihood receiver: (a) correlation type, (b) matched-filter type.

which indicates a matched-filter receiver. For large SNR, however, logarithmic weighting is required. If $\lambda_1(t)$ and $\lambda_0(t)$ are both piecewise constant in $(-T, T)$, then there can be found subintervals $(t_k, t_{k+1})$ $k = 1, 2, \cdots, K$ such that both $\lambda_i(t)$ are constant within them, say $\lambda_{ik}$. Then the decision function $G$ of (17) reduces to

$$\sum_{j=1}^{M} \log \frac{\lambda_1(t_j)}{\lambda_0(t_j)} = \sum_{k=1}^{K} n_k \log \frac{\lambda_{1k}}{\lambda_{0k}} \tag{21}$$

where $n_k$ is the number of occurrences in the $k$th such interval, indicating that the set of $n_k$ is a sufficient statistic and observation of the set $\{t_M\}$ is not required. Equation (21) has been previously derived [2], by considering at the outset the piecewise constant case. On the basis of this result a processing scheme was suggested that first counts the number of occurrences $n_k$ in each subinterval and then performs the digital convolutions of (21). The generally valid schemes of Fig. 3, which require no counting, evidently cover such situations as well.

On the other hand the result (17), of this paper could be obtained from (2) by the following argument. Assume that $K \to \infty$, in such a way that the width of each subinterval $(t_k, t_{k+1}) \to 0$. Then, by axiom 2) of Section II, $n_k$ is either 0 or 1, and those $t_k$ that correspond to $n_k = 1$ denote the instants of occurrences, hence the set $\{t_M\}$. Then the test statistic (21) becomes

$$\sum_{k:n_k=1} \log \frac{\lambda_1(t_k)}{\lambda_0(t_k)} = \sum_{j=1}^{M} \log \frac{\lambda_1(t_j)}{\lambda_0(t_j)}, \qquad j = 1, 2, \cdots, M, \tag{22}$$

where the set $\{t_M\} = \{t_1, t_2, \cdots, t_i, \cdots, t_M\}$ denotes the infinitesimal intervals at which $n_k = 1$, as before. An analogous derivation has been used by Helstrom [8] for a spatial optical signal.

*Decision Probabilities*

These can be calculated by deriving a Gram–Charlier series [7] for the distribution of the test statistic $G$. The cummulants $\chi_i$ of the distribution of $G$, which appear in this series, are given by

$$\chi_i = \int_{-T}^{T} \lambda_k(t) \log (\lambda_1(t)/\lambda_0(t))^i \, dt, \tag{23}$$

where the index $k = 0, 1$ denotes the two hypotheses. This result is obtained from the characteristic function $H_G(ix)$ of $G$,

$$H_G(ix) = E[\exp (ixG)] = E\left\{\prod_{j=1}^{M} \exp \{ix \log [\lambda_1(t_j)/\lambda_0(t_j)]\}\right\}, \tag{24}$$

which, upon using (13), reduces to

$$H_G(ix) = \exp\left\{-Q_k + \int_{-T}^{T} \lambda_k(t)[\lambda_1(t)/\lambda_0(t)]^{ix} \, dt\right\}. \tag{25}$$

The influence of the third-order term in the Gram–Charlier series, in a typical case where $\lambda_1(t) = e^2\lambda_0(t)$, is seen from the corresponding correction term in the probability of correct decision, $P_D = 1 - 0.274 - 0.010 + \cdots$, [11].

*Singular Cases*

If either $\lambda_1(t)$, or $\lambda_0(t)$, is zero over any finite subinterval, the test statistic can be modified so as to be itself zero over each such subinterval:

$$G_{\text{mod}}(t) = 0, \quad t \text{ such that } \lambda_0(t) \text{ or } \lambda_1(t) = 0$$
$$= G(t), \quad \text{otherwise.}$$

If no occurence is recorded during these subintervals, $G_{\text{mod}}$ serves perfectly. If, however, an occurrence is recorded during the subinterval in which either $\lambda_k$ vanishes, evidently the alternative hypothesis holds with probability 1. The probability of such an event can be easily calculated.

## IV. Signal Parameter Estimation

Let the time-varying mean value of the process depend on a parameter $\alpha$ as follows.

$$\lambda(t : \alpha) = s(t, \alpha) + \lambda_n, \tag{26}$$

where the signal part $s(t, \alpha)$ is a known function of both $t$ and $\alpha$ and $\lambda_n$ is a constant, representing the average noise power. Let $\{t_M\}$ be the set of the observables, as before, and $Q(\alpha) = \int_{-T}^{T} \lambda(t : \alpha) \, dt$. Then the likelihood function is

$$p\{t_M\} = e^{-Q(\alpha)} \prod_{j=1}^{M} [s(t_j, \alpha) + \lambda_n]. \tag{27}$$

The maximum-likelihood estimate $\hat{\alpha}$ is that value of $\alpha$ that maximizes the above expression or, equivalently, that yields

$$\max_{\alpha} \left[ \sum_{i=1}^{M} \log (s(t_i, \alpha) + \lambda_n) - Q(\alpha) \right]. \tag{28}$$

A search procedure is in general required for the estimate $\hat{\alpha}$.

Assuming that $s(t, \alpha)$ is piecewise differentiable and denoting the derivative with respect to $\alpha$ by an upper dot, one obtains the following for $\hat{\alpha}$:

$$\sum_{i=1}^{M} \frac{\dot{s}(t_i, \alpha)}{\lambda_n + s(t_i, \alpha)} = \dot{Q}(\alpha). \tag{29}$$

A simple example is that of transmission of the parameter by amplitude modulation: $s(t, \alpha) = \alpha\lambda_0(t)$, with $\int_{-T}^{T} \lambda_0(t)\, dt = 1$. Then

$$\sum_{i=1}^{M} \frac{\lambda_0(t_i)}{\hat{\alpha}\lambda_0(t_i) + \lambda_n} = 1, \tag{30}$$

which is an algebraic equation of power $M$. An approximate solution is obtained by assuming high SNR,

$$\hat{\alpha} \simeq M - \frac{1}{M} \sum_{1}^{M} \frac{\lambda_n}{\lambda_0(t_i)}. \tag{31}$$

The above is exact if $\lambda_0(t)$ is constant within $(-T, T)$. Then also $\hat{\alpha} = M - \lambda_n/\lambda_0$, so that the number $M$ alone is a sufficient statistic for estimation of the parameter.

*Pulse Position Modulation—Estimation of Delay*

This case is of considerable interest in a noncoherent communication link as well as in distance measurements. The parameter $\alpha$ is delay time $\tau$, and the signal can be written $s(t - \tau)$. Assuming that the signal duration $(\tau - D, \tau + D)$ is very short compared with the interval of a priori incertitude, and neglecting end effects (i.e., values of $\tau$ near $T$), $\dot{Q}(\tau) = 0$. Then the logarithm of the likelihood function (27), here denoted by $F(\tau)$, becomes

$$F(\tau) = \sum_{i} \log [s(t_i - \tau) + \lambda_n] \tag{32}$$

The search for $\hat{\tau}$ that yields a maximum of $F(\tau)$ can be mechanized by constructing the time function

$$v(t) = \log (s(t) + \lambda_n), \tag{33}$$

or the time function

$$q(t) = \dot{s}(t)/(\lambda_n + s(t)) \tag{34}$$

and passing impulses through a filter matched to either $v(t)$ or $q(t)$ at the instants $t_i$ of the occurrences (as in Fig. 3). The instants at which the outputs pass, respectively, through a maximum or a zero yield, in principle, the estimate $\hat{\tau}$. Several maxima or zero crossings, respectively, of the outputs of the filters may, however, be due to the noise process, yielding ambiguities in location of the estimate. One has to pick, therefore, the maximum, or the zero crossing, that appears in the neighborhood of the "strongest" reception, i.e., where the occurrences are densest. An erroneous decision as to this neighborhood causes an error which is very large compared with the error involved in locating the maximum, or the zero crossing, in its correct neighborhood. The probability $P_t$ of such an erroneous decision has been called the "threshold" probability [9], [10]. It is shown in the Appendix that $P_t$ for the assumed Poisson regime, is bounded above by the following expression

$$P_t \leq \frac{T}{2D} \left( \frac{2Q_n}{Q_D + Q_n} \right)^{1/2} \cdot \exp \{ -(Q_D + Q_n) + 2(2Q_n(Q_D + Q_n))^{1/2} \} \tag{35}$$

where

$$Q_n = 2D\lambda_n \quad \text{and} \quad Q_D = \int_{-D}^{D} s(t)\, dt$$

are, respectively, the expectations of the number of occurrences due to noise and to signal within the interval $(-D, +D)$ of signal duration. The bound increases linearly with the number of signal "bins" $T/D$ and decreases nearly exponentially with $Q_D$, with considerable similarity to the parallel case of known signal in Gaussian noise [9], [10]. As a numerical example, if $Q_D = 20$, $Q_n = 1$ and $T = 1000\, D$, then $P_t < 0.02$. For a tighter bound the double sum in (59) in the Appendix must be evaluated.

Assuming, now, that the maximum that has been selected *is* in the correct neighborhood, the variance of the estimator $\hat{\tau}$ can be approximated in terms of the first two derivatives of $F(\tau)$, calculated at the true value of the delay, $\tau_0$. This method of calculation has been used in similar problems [6, ch. VIII], [8], [9]. Thus, if $F(\tau)$ is twice differentiable about $\tau_0$, then $\dot{F}(\tau)$ can be expressed as

$$\dot{F}(\tau) = \dot{F}(\tau_0) + (\tau - \tau_0)\ddot{F}(\tau_0) + \cdots. \tag{36}$$

By the definition of $\hat{\tau}$,

$$0 = \dot{F}(\hat{\tau}) = \dot{F}(\tau_0) + (\hat{\tau} - \tau_0)\ddot{F}(\tau_0) + \cdots,$$

from which it follows that, provided $F''(\tau_0)$ does not vanish,[4]

$$\epsilon_\tau \triangleq \hat{\tau} - \tau_0 \doteq -\frac{\dot{F}(\tau_0)}{\ddot{F}(\tau_0)}.$$

It will be shown below that the mean of the numerator is zero; then letting $\dot{F}(\tau_0) = f_n$ and $\ddot{F}(\tau_0) = f_d + m_d$, where $m_d$ is the mean of $\ddot{F}(\tau_0)$, and assuming that $f_d \ll m_d$ with high probability, one can write

$$\epsilon_\tau = -\frac{f_n}{m_d + f_d} \doteq -\frac{f_n}{m_d}\left(1 - \frac{f_d}{m_d}\right), \tag{38}$$

whence it follows that

$$\overline{\epsilon_\tau^2} \doteq \frac{\overline{f_n^2}}{m_d^2} - 2\frac{\overline{f_n^2 f_d}}{m_d^3} + \frac{\overline{f_n^2 f_d^2}}{m_d^4}.$$

[4] Owing to the nature of $F(\tau)$, (32), this requirement excludes strictly flat-topped signals from the analysis. This is discussed in more detail in [11].

By the above assumption, $m_d^2 \gg \overline{f_d^2}$, so that the last two terms are negligible and

$$\overline{\epsilon_\tau^2} \doteq \frac{\overline{f_n^2}}{m_d^2}. \tag{40}$$

The characteristic functions of $\dot{F}(\tau_0)$ and $\ddot{F}(\tau_0)$ are, respectively,

$$E\left[\exp\left\{ix \sum_{i=1}^{M} \frac{\dot{s}(t_i - \tau_0)}{s(t_i - \tau_0) + \lambda_n}\right\}\right];$$

$$E\left[\exp\left\{ix \sum_{i=1}^{M} \frac{d}{d\tau} \frac{s(t_i - \tau_0)}{s(t_i - \tau_0) + \lambda_n}\right\}\right],$$

and can be evaluated using (13). Differentiating twice the results of the evaluations, the following expressions are obtained for the moments:

$$m_n = \int_{-T}^{T} \dot{s}(t)\, dt,$$

$$\overline{f_n^2} = m_d = -\int_{-T}^{T} (s(t) + \lambda_n) \frac{d}{dt}\left[\frac{\dot{s}(t)}{s(t) + \lambda_n}\right] dt,$$

$$\overline{f_d^2} = \int_{-T}^{T} (s(t) + \lambda_n)\left(\frac{d}{dt}\left[\frac{\dot{s}(t)}{s(t) + \lambda_n}\right]\right)^2 dt. \tag{41}$$

(Having set $\tau_0 = 0$ does not involve any loss in generality if end effects are neglected.) Evidently $m_n = 0$ and $\overline{f_d^2}/m_d^2$ goes to zero, as $s(t)$ increases, justifying the approximations. Finally from (40) and (41), one obtains

$$\overline{\epsilon_\tau^2} \doteq \frac{1}{m_d} = \left[\int_{-T}^{T} \frac{[\dot{s}(t)]^2}{s(t) + \lambda_n} dt\right]^{-1}, \tag{42}$$

where it has been assumed that pulse-type signals are used for which $s(\pm T) = \dot{s}(\pm T) = 0$.

According to the basic requirement that $\lambda(t) > 0$, one can set $s(t) = Qa^2(t)$, where $Q > 0$ denotes the total energy in the signal, if the normalizing constraint $\int_{-T}^{T} a^2(t)\, dt = 1$ is added. Then,

$$\overline{\epsilon_\tau^2} \doteq \left[4Q \int_{-T}^{T} (\dot{a}(t))^2 \frac{Qa^2(t)}{\lambda_n + Qa^2(t)} dt\right]^{-1} \tag{43}$$

For sufficiently large $Q$, the fractional term in the integral is close to 1 whenever $a(t)$ is nonzero. Then the integral is recognized as the square of the effective bandwidth of $a(t)$, usually denoted by $W_a$. Thus,

$$\overline{\epsilon_\tau^2} \doteq \tfrac{1}{4} Q^{-1} W_a^{-2} \tag{44}$$

which resembles somewhat the familiar result in the estimation problem involving a known signal in Gaussian noise, except that here $Q$ is the total energy in the signal, and not the SNR, indicating that the error has a finite nonzero value even in the case of vanishing noise. This behavior is due, of course, to the random nature of the signal process. In optical communication terminology such a situation is referred to as being *photon-limited.*

The problem of signal design is, nevertheless, the same as in the classical case; the square of any *real* large bandwidth signal $a(t)$ that would be used to amplitude-modulate an RF carrier can be used to modulate the energy of the laser beam. Phase-modulating (complex) $a(t)$ are of course excluded by the requirement that $s(t)$ be positive, reflecting the lack of sensitivity of photon detectors to the phase of the radiation.

Whenever peak-power constraints exist, the tendency to increase the effective bandwidth by using amplitude modulation alone leads by necessity to a signal made up of a sequence of nonoverlaping pulses. A sequence of $K$ identical pulses has the same effective bandwidth, but $K$ times the energy, of each elementary pulse. From (44), the improvement in $\overline{\epsilon^2}$ is, then, linear in $K$. Ostensibly, the same improvement results from averaging $K$ independent measurements, such as could be obtained by checking the $K$ maxima of the output of a filter "matched" (as prescribed by (34)) to one of the elementary pulses. The loss in using such a suboptimal processing scheme is apparent, first in the increase in the threshold probability, (35), which is nearly exponential in the total energy involved in any single measurement, and second in the increase in the error due to neglected terms in (43).

As a last point of interest, if a bell-shaped signal is used, e.g., $s(t) = Q(2\pi D^2)^{-1/2} \exp(-1/2\, t^2/D^2)$, then, for large $Q$, (29) yields $\hat{\tau} \doteq (1/M) \sum_1^M t_i$, i.e., the estimate of the delay is at the center of gravity of the observed times of emission. In this particular case, it can be shown by direct calculation [11], that (44) holds down to low values of signal energy.

## V. Conclusion

By using the instant-of-occurrence representation of Poisson processes, expressions for optimal decision and estimation procedures and their performance have been obtained. Unlike the cases of known signals in Gaussian noise, in which the performance of the system depends only on certain functionals of the transmitted wave form, e.g., total energy, equivalent bandwidth, etc., in the Poisson cases signal shape also influences the detectability. Even in the ideal noiseless situation the random nature of the received signal restricts the variance of the delay estimate to a finite value that depends on the expected number of occurrences, i.e., on signal energy. Such a result was to be expected considering that what has been modeled is a photon in which the quantum nature of the radiation sets a bound on the accuracy of delay measurement. The results on the probability of threshold have a strong similarity to the classical case.

## Appendix

### The Noise Threshold

The noise threshold, as defined in Section IV, is reached whenever another interval of length $2D$, disjoint from the interval in which the true delay is located, is chosen in order to estimate the delay within its limits. This happens whenever there is an interval of length $2D$ in $(-T, +T)$ such that it includes more points than does the correct interval. The probability $P_t$ ($t$ stands for threshold) of such an event is overbounded by

$$P_e \leq \sum_{k=0}^{\infty} P_1(k)P_2(k)$$

where $P_1(k) \equiv \Pr$ [$k$ points in the proper interval] and $P_2(k) \equiv \Pr$ [there is an interval of length $2D$ in the domain $(-T, +T)$ in which the number of points due to noise alone is larger than $k$]. This expression is an upper bound since the event of which $P_2(k)$ is the probability includes also the possibility that the number is larger than $k$ within the proper interval of width $2D$. This bound is, however, very tight since if there is a threshold problem at all, $T \gg D$. By (1),

$$P_1(k) = \exp(-Q_p)\, Q_p^k/k!, \quad Q_p \triangleq Q_D + Q_n, \; Q_n = 2D\lambda_n.$$

To calculate $P_2(k)$, assume first that in the interval $(-T, T)$ there are exactly $M$ points due to the noise of uniform mean $\lambda_n$. The probability of such an event is

$$P[M, (-T, T)] = \exp(-Q_N)\, Q_N^M/M!; \quad Q_N \triangleq Q_n T/D$$

The probability that exactly 2 points out of these $M$ be within $2D$ of each other somewhere in $(-T, T)$ is trivially overbounded by $(2D/T)$, if $M = 2$, and by $(2D/T)\binom{M}{2}$ if $M \geq 2$ and the probability that $m$ points out of $M$ be so close is by induction overbounded by $(2D/T)^{m-1}\binom{M}{m}$. Lifting the condition of a total of $M$ points yields

$$\Pr[m \text{ points within } (-D, D) \text{ somewhere in } (-T, T)]$$

$$\leq \sum_{M=m}^{\infty} e^{-Q_N} \frac{Q_N^M}{M!} \left(\frac{2D}{T}\right)^{m-1} \frac{M!}{(M-m)!\, m!}$$

$$= e^{-Q_N} \left(\frac{2D}{T}\right)^{m-1} \frac{Q_N^m}{m!} \sum_{M=m}^{\infty} \frac{Q_N^{M-m}}{(M-m)!} = \left(\frac{2D}{T}\right)^{m-1} \frac{Q_N^m}{m!}$$

$$= \frac{T}{2D} \frac{2^m Q_n^m}{m!}.$$

$P_2(k)$ is overbounded by summing this result over all $m$ larger than $k$,

$$P_2(k) < \frac{T}{2D} \sum_{k+1}^{\infty} \frac{(2Q_n)^m}{m!} \tag{58}$$

and therefore

$$P_e \leq \frac{T}{2D} [\exp(-Q_p)] \sum_{k=0}^{\infty} \frac{Q_p^k}{k!} \sum_{k+1}^{\infty} \frac{(2Q_n)^m}{m!}. \tag{59}$$

Using a Chernov-type upper bound,

$$P_e \leq \frac{T}{2D} e^{-Q_p} \sum_{k=0}^{\infty} \frac{Q_p^k}{k!} \sum_{0}^{\infty} \frac{(2Q_n)^m}{m!} c^{m-(k+1)}, \qquad c \geq 1$$

$$= \frac{T}{2D} e^{-Q_p} \frac{1}{c} e^{2cQ_n + Q_D/c}.$$

Minimizing the exponent over all possible values of $c \geq 1$, one has $c = (Q_p/2Q_n)^{1/2}$ from where (35) follows. This value of $c$ is larger than 1 whenever $Q_D > Q_n$.

ACKNOWLEDGMENT

The author is pleased to acknowledge interesting discussions on photon receivers with I. Ziskind.

REFERENCES

[1] L. Mandel and E. Wolf, "Coherence properties of optical fields," *Rev. Mod. Phys.*, vol. 37, pp. 231–287, April 1965. L. Mandel, "Phenomenological theory of laser beam fluctuations and beam mixing," *Phys. Re.*, vol. 138, pp. B753–B762, May 1965.
[2] B. Reiffen and H. Sherman, "An optimum demodulator for Poisson processes: Photon source detectors," *Proc. IEEE*, vol. 51, pp. 1316–1320, October 1963.
[3] K. Abend, "Optimum photon detection," *IEEE Trans. Information Theory (Correspondence)*, vol. IT-12, pp. 64–65, January 1966.
[4] T. F. Curran and M. Ross, "Optimum detection thresholds in optical communications," *Proc. IEEE (Correspondence)*, vol. 53, pp. 1770–1771, November 1965.
[5] A. Papoulis, *Probability, Random Variables, and Stochastic Processes*. New York: McGraw-Hill, 1965, p. 74.
[6] C. W. Helstrom, *Statistical Theory of Signal Detection*. London: Pergamon, 1960, ch. 3.
[7] *Ibid.*, p. 177.
[8] C. W. Helstrom, "The detection and resolution of optical signals," *IEEE Trans. Information Theory*, vol. IT-10, pp. 275–287, October 1964.
[9] P. M. Woodward, *Probability and Information Theory with Applications to Radar*. London: Pergamon, 1957, chs. 5 and 6.
[10] J. M. Wozencraft and I. M. Jacobs, *Principles of Communications Engineering*. New York: Wiley, 1965, ch. 8.
[11] I. Bar-David, "Communication under Poissonian regime," Sci. Dept., Ministry of Defence, Israel, Rept. 40/07-526, January 1968.

# 11



Reprinted from *IEEE Trans. Commun. Technol.* **COM-17**(2):208–216 (1969)

# $M$-ary Poisson Detection and Optical Communications

ROBERT M. GAGLIARDI, MEMBER, IEEE, AND SHERMAN KARP, MEMBER, IEEE

REFERENCE: Gagliardi, R. M., and *Karp, S.: $M$-ARY POISSON DETECTION AND OPTICAL COMMUNICATIONS, University of Southern California, Los Angeles, Calif. 90007, and NASA Electronics Research Center, Cambridge, Mass. 02138. *Formerly with the University of Southern California. Rec'd 2/19/68; revised 9/3/68 and 12/20/68. Paper 69TP6-COM, approved by the IEEE Communication Theory Committee for publication without oral presentation. IEEE TRANS. ON COMMUNICATION TECHNOLOGY, 17-2, April 1969, pp. 208–216.

ABSTRACT: This paper presents an investigation of the problem of maximum likelihood detection of one of $M$ Poisson processes in a background of additive Poisson noise. When the observables correspond to counts of emitted photoelectrons, the problem models a discrete version of a coherent $M$-ary optical communication system using photon counters in the presence of background radiation. Consideration is given to an average distance and a detection probability criterion. The advantages of an $M$-ary pulsed intensity set (Poisson intensities wholly concentrated in a single counting interval) are demonstrated. The performance of such intensity sets is exhibited in terms of error probabilities, pulse widths, signal-to-noise ratio, and channel capacity. Behavior as a function of number $M$ of intensities is also discussed. By appropriate conversion these results may be used for determining power requirements in an optical pulse position modulation system.

## I. Introduction

THE APPLICATION of detection theory to optical communications has been a subject of increasing interest. Since the output of a photodetecting surface is often modeled as sequences of electron "counts," and since optical photoelectrons have been generally accepted as obeying Poisson statistics, the analysis problem is basically one of signal detection involving Poisson processes. The problem was first formulated in this context by Reiffen and Sherman [1], and further contributions were made by Abend [2], Kailath [3], and Helstrom [4]. In this paper we investigate the general problem of $M$-ary detection based upon observations of events described by a time discrete Poisson process. Though the formulation of the problem is of a general nature, the principal application is to optical communications, and the practical limits of such a system will govern the mathematical assumptions imposed. Consideration is given to the divergence criterion for detection and to a criterion of maximization of probability of detection, both readily accepted as suitable design objectives. The intensity set yielding optimal performance on the basis of special cases of these criteria is shown to be a special type of orthogonal intensity set, composed of $M$ disjoint intensities wholly concentrated in a counting interval. Previously, the superiority of this type of signal set in binary detection had been shown by Abend [2] using a signal-to-noise ratio criterion, and by Kailath [3] using a distance criterion. This paper represents an extension of these results to $M$-ary Poisson detection.

The formulation of the problem follows that of Reiffen and Sherman [1]. The occurrence of events over an observed interval $\Delta T$ is said to obey a Poisson process if the probability of exactly $k$ (an integer) events occurring is given by

$$P(k) = \frac{(n\Delta T)^k}{k!} e^{-n\Delta T}. \tag{1}$$

The parameter $n$ is the average rate of occurrence and is called the intensity of the process. The average number of events occurring is then $n\Delta T$ and is often called the level of the process. If the events occur over a sequence of intervals $\Delta T$ in which the intensity may vary from one interval to the next, but is constant over each interval, we have a discrete time-varying Poisson process. In photodetection, each event corresponds to the emission of an electron, which occurs upon arrival of a photon, each photon having a fixed energy. The level is therefore proportional to the average energy received per interval, while the intensity $n$ is proportional to the average power (see Section V). Thus, constraints upon level and intensity in Poisson processes are equivalent to energy and power constraints on the incident radiation.

In optical pulse-code modulation (PCM) communications information is transmitted, as shown in Fig. 1(a), by sending an optical signal intensity modulated with one of a set of possible intensities. The modulated signal is corrupted by background radiation of fixed intensity during reception, resulting in a process whose intensity is the sum of both intensities. The output of the photodetecting surface at the receiver is then a time-varying Poisson process of electron counts having the received intensity. In an $M$-ary system, the transmitter selects one of a set of $M$ intensities for the optical process. The receiver, after photodetection, counts the number of electrons in each of $M$ intervals $\Delta T$ seconds long and attempts to maximum likelihood detect which of $M$ intensities is controlling the observed process. We shall assume $\Delta T$ is suitably shorter than the inverse bandwidth of the intensities so that the intensity remains approximately constant over $\Delta T$. In addition, we assume that the counting interval is exactly known at the receiver by a perfect synchronization link. Thus, the above system can be modeled by the block diagram in Fig. 1(b). The input signal corresponds to a discrete Poisson process, while the interference appears as additive Poisson noise. (Recall that the sum of independent Poisson processes is itself a Poisson process having an intensity equal to the sum of the intensities.) The model

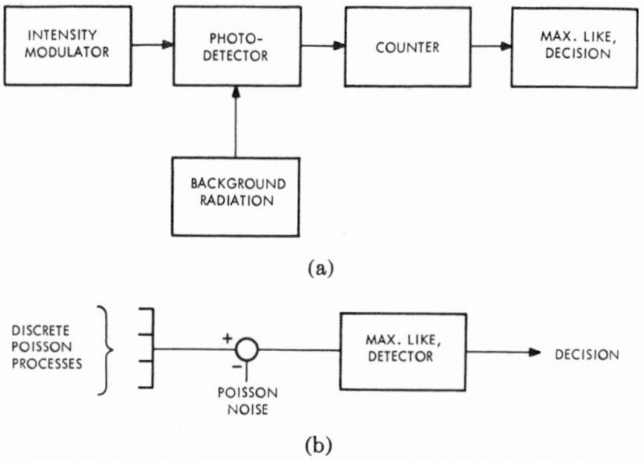


Fig. 1. A PCM optical communications receiver and its equivalent model

is idealized since other sources of interference, such as thermal noise and dark currents, are neglected. With this model the $M$-ary Poisson detection problem can be formulated as follows. Let a sequence of events obeying a discrete Poisson process occur over a sequence of $M$ disjoint intervals $\Delta T$, where $M\Delta T = T$, and the count over each interval is independent of all others. Let the observed process be controlled by one of $M$ possible[1] intensity vectors $\boldsymbol{n}_q + \boldsymbol{n}_0$ for $q = 1,2,\cdots,M$, where

$$\begin{aligned} \boldsymbol{n}_q &= \{n_{q1}, n_{q2}, \cdots, n_{qM}\} \\ \boldsymbol{n}_0 &= \{n_0, n_0, n_0, \cdots, n_0\} \end{aligned} \tag{2}$$

for $n_{qi}, n_0 \geq 0$. The nonnegative $n_{qi}$ is thus the intensity of $\boldsymbol{n}_q$ during the $i$th interval. Under a fixed energy constraint for each signal, we require

$$\sum_{i=1}^{M} n_{qi}\Delta T = N, \quad \text{for all } q. \tag{3}$$

The intensity vector $\boldsymbol{n}_0$ represents background noise of constant intensity superimposed upon the desired intensity. Let the corresponding number of events occurring in the $i$th interval be $k_i$. The problem then is to determine which of the possible intensity vectors $\boldsymbol{n}_q$ is controlling the received Poisson process by observing the sequence of independent counts $\boldsymbol{k} = \{k_1, k_2, k_3, \cdots, k_M\}$. Under a maximum likelihood detection criterion and a priori equilikely intensities, it is well known [1] that the optimal test is to form the likelihood functions

$$\Lambda_q(\boldsymbol{k}) = \sum_{i=1}^{M} \alpha_{qi} k_i \tag{4}$$

where

$$\alpha_{qi} = \log\left[\left(1 + \frac{n_{qi}}{n_0}\right)\right] \tag{5}$$

[1] In the statement of the problem, we assume $M$ signals over $M$ counting intervals. Subsequent discussion with the divergence criterion disproves the need for more than $M$ intervals. The problem of designing $M$ signals over fewer than $M$ intervals is not considered here.

and select $\boldsymbol{n}_q+\boldsymbol{n}_0$ as the true intensity if no other likelihood function exceeds $\Lambda_q(\boldsymbol{k})$. If a likelihood draw occurs (more than one $\Lambda_q(\boldsymbol{k})$ is maximum), it is known that any randomized choice among the maxima can be used. In the following, we shall use a purely random selection in the case of likelihood draws. Equation (4) can be interpreted as a cross correlation of $\boldsymbol{k}$ with the $\alpha_{qi}$, an operation readily performed by a digital cross correlator [1].

## II. Divergence of Detection Test

The divergence between two intensities $\boldsymbol{n}_j$ and $\boldsymbol{n}_q$ of the above test is defined as

$$D_{jq} = E_{k/j}(\Lambda_{jq}) - E_{k/q}(\Lambda_{jq}) \tag{6}$$

where

$$\Lambda_{jq} = \Lambda_j(\boldsymbol{k}) - \Lambda_q(\boldsymbol{k})$$

and $E_{k/j}(\Lambda)$ is the conditional average of $\Lambda$ with respect to $\boldsymbol{k}$ given the intensity $\boldsymbol{n}_j$. Abend [2] has shown that for $M=2$ (binary detection) and the condition $\boldsymbol{n}_2=0$, the divergence, normalized by the variance of $\Lambda$, is maximized by a "pulsed" type of intensity, where the level of the process is wholly concentrated in a single counting interval. Kailath [3] has extended this result by showing that, under a total energy constraint, other suitable forms of "distance" are maximized by similar pulsed intensities. We extend these notions here to the $M$-ary case and the equal energy constraint of (3).

The average divergence of an $M$-ary intensity set $\{\boldsymbol{n}_q\}$ will be defined as

$$\overline{D} = \frac{1}{M^2} \sum_j \sum_q D_{jq}. \tag{7}$$

Since $E_{k/j}(k_i) = (n_{ji}+n_0)\Delta T$, the average divergence becomes

$$\begin{aligned}\overline{D} &= \frac{\Delta T}{M^2} \sum_j \sum_q \sum_i (n_{ji} - n_{qi}) \left\{ \log\left[1 + \frac{n_{ji}}{n_0}\right] - \log\left[1 + \frac{n_{qi}}{n_0}\right]\right\} \\ &= \frac{2\Delta T}{M^2} \sum_i \left[ M \sum_j n_{ji} \log\left(1 + \frac{n_{ji}\Delta T}{K}\right) - \sum_{j \neq q} \sum n_{ji} \log\left(1 + \frac{n_{qi}\Delta T}{K}\right)\right] \end{aligned} \tag{8}$$

where $K = n_0 \Delta T$. The nonnegativeness of the $n_{ji}$ and $n_0$ allows us to write

$$\begin{aligned}\overline{D} &\leq \frac{2\Delta T}{M} \sum_i \sum_j n_{ji} \log\left(1 + \frac{n_{ji}\Delta T}{K}\right) \\ &\leq \frac{2}{M}\left[\max_{i,j} \log\left(1 + \frac{n_{ji}\Delta T}{K}\right)\right] \sum_j \sum_i n_{ji}\Delta T \\ &\leq 2N \log\left(1 + \frac{N}{K}\right)\end{aligned} \tag{9}$$

as an upper bound under the constraint of (3). However the first equality holds if the second term in (8) is zero requiring $n_{ji}$, for $j \neq q$, to be zero for all $i$ at which $n_{qi}$ is nonzero. That is, the intensities must be mutually disjoint. The second and third equalities in (9) hold if $n_{ji}=N$ for one $i$ and $n_{ji}=0$ for all other $i$. Thus, the upper bound for $\overline{D}$ occurs if the intensities of the set are disjoint and wholly concentrated in a single counting interval. This is satisfied with the set

$$\boldsymbol{n}_q = \left\{\frac{N}{\Delta T}\delta_{iq}\right\}, \qquad q = 1,2,\cdots,M \tag{10}$$

where $\delta_{iq}$ is the Kronecker delta. The above represents an $M$-ary pulsed intensity set with each intensity occupying one of $M$ intervals. It is significant that any disjoint intensity set, no matter how many intervals are used, yields the bound of the first inequality of (9), but only the pulsed intensity set of (10) yields the second bound. Thus, of all disjoint intensity sets, only the pulsed set maximizes $\overline{D}$, which immediately implies that only $M$ intervals are required for maximization with $M$ intensities. Last, it may be noted that with an average energy constraint over all intensities,

$$\frac{1}{M} \sum_j \sum_i n_{ji}\Delta T = N \tag{11}$$

instead of (3), we have $n_{ji} \leq MN/\Delta T$, and (9) becomes

$$\overline{D} \leq 2N \log\left(1 + \frac{MN}{K}\right) \tag{12}$$

which exceeds that previously derived. Furthermore, the upper bound in (12) occurs when $M-1$ intensities are zero everywhere, and one intensity is a pulsed intensity having value $MN/\Delta T$. In binary communications, for example, this means that an ON–OFF binary signal is superior to pulse position ($M=2$) signaling using the same average energy.

## III. Detection Probability

The optimality of the $M$-ary pulsed intensity set has been shown, based on a divergence criterion. In this section we show that in certain cases this superiority also extends over a criterion based on maximization of the detection probability. We first require an expression for the detection probability for a general intensity set $\{\boldsymbol{n}_q\}$. Usually this is obtained by first writing the conditional probability density of $\Lambda_q(\boldsymbol{k})$, then integrating over regions of correct decisioning. However, $\Lambda_q(\boldsymbol{k})$ in (4) is a weighted sum of independent Poisson variates which in general is not a Poisson variable. Rather, the true density involves an $M$-fold convolution of modified Poisson densities, yielding a result that is difficult to integrate. We shall instead use an alternative expression for the detection probability, derived in the Appendix, having the form

$$P_D = \frac{e^{-N}}{M} \sum_{R^M} \max_q \{\Psi(q,j)\} \tag{13}$$

where $N$ is the intensity energy constraint of (3), $R^M$ the space of all $M$-dimensional vectors $j$ having nonnegative integer components, and

$$\Psi(q,j) = \prod_{i=1}^{M} \frac{[(n_{q_i} + n_0)\Delta T]^{j_i}}{j_i!} e^{-Mn_0\Delta T}. \tag{14}$$

The derivation of (13) follows an analogous procedure used in Gaussian channels (see [5]), but is somewhat complicated by the fact that likelihood draws occur with nonzero probability.

We would like to determine the intensity set $\{n_q\}$ for which $P_D$ is maximum. This has been obtained for two particular cases of interest.

*Case I: $M=2$ and Symmetric Intensity Sets*

Let $M=2$ and consider the set of all possible symmetric intensity sets; i.e., if $n_1 = \{a,b\}$, then $n_2=\{b,a\}$. For this case it is easy to show that for any intensity set of this type, the vectors $j$ for which $\Psi(1,j) \gtreqless \Psi(2,j)$ when $a>b$, is simply the set $j=\{j_1,j_2\}$, such that $j_1 \gtreqless j_2$. Using the constraint of (3) and letting $n_1=\{a,N-a\}$ and $n_2=\{N-a,a\}$, for $N/2<a\leq N$, the detection probability is

$$P_D = \frac{e^{-(N+K)}}{2}\left\{\sum_{j_1=0}^{\infty}\sum_{j_2=0}^{j_1-1} \frac{(a+K)^{j_1}}{j_1!}\cdot\frac{(N-a+K)^{j_2}}{j_2!} + \sum_{j_1=0}^{\infty}\sum_{j_2=j_1}^{\infty} \frac{(N-a+K)^{j_1}}{j_1!}\cdot\frac{(a+K)^{j_2}}{j_2!}\right\} \tag{15}$$

where again $K=n_0\Delta T$. Differentiating with respect to $a$ yields

$$\frac{\partial P_D}{\partial a} = \frac{e^{-(N+K)}}{2}\left\{\sum_{j_1=0}^{\infty}\sum_{j_2=0}^{j_1-1} \frac{A^{j_1-1}}{(j_1-1)!}\cdot\frac{B^{j_2}}{j_2!} - \frac{A^{j_1}}{j_1!}\cdot\frac{B^{j_2-1}}{(j_2-1)!} + \sum_{j_1=0}^{\infty}\sum_{j_2=j_1}^{\infty}\frac{B^{j_1}}{j_1!}\cdot\frac{A^{j_2-1}}{(j_2-1)!} - \frac{A^{j_2}}{j_2!}\cdot\frac{B^{j_1-1}}{(j_1-1)!}\right\}$$
$$= \frac{e^{-(N+K)}}{2}\left\{1 + \sum_{j_1=1}^{\infty}\sum_{j_2=j_1-1}^{j_1} \frac{A^{j_1}B^{j_2} + B^{j_1}A^{j_2}}{j_1!j_2!}\right\}$$

where $A=(a+K)$ and $B=(N-a+K)$. Since $A$ and $B$ are positive, the above substantiates $P_D$ as a monotone increasing function of $a$. Therefore $P_D$ is maximized with $a$ having its maximum value $a=N$ corresponding to the pulsed intensity set of (10) with $M=2$.

*Case II: Any $M$, $N/K\to 0$*

The limit above implies a high background noise level situation. We observe here that

$$P_D = \frac{e^{-N}}{M}\sum_{R^M}\max_q \Psi(q,j)$$
$$= \frac{e^{-N}}{M}\sum_{R^M} C \max_q\left\{\exp\left[\sum_{i=1}^{M} j_i \ln\left(1+\frac{n_{q_i}\Delta T}{K}\right)\right]\right\}$$
$$\xrightarrow[N/K\to 0]{} \frac{e^{-N}}{M}\sum_{R^M} C \max_q\left\{\exp\sum_{i=1}^{M}\frac{j_i n_{q_i}\Delta T}{K}\right\} \tag{16}$$

where

$$C = e^{-MK}\prod_i (1/j_i!)$$

and the limit follows since $n_{q_i}\Delta T/K \leq N/K \to 0$.

Now, with the constraint of (3),

$$\sum_i \frac{j_i n_{q_i}\Delta T}{K} \leq j_{\max}\frac{N}{K} \tag{17}$$

where $j_{\max} = \max_i\{j_i\}$. Thus

$$P_D \leq \frac{e^{-N}}{M}\sum_{R^M} C \exp\left\{j_{\max}\frac{N}{K}\right\}, \quad \frac{N}{K}\to 0.$$

The upper bound occurs when

$$\max_q\left\{\exp\sum_{i=1}^{M}\frac{j_i n_{q_i}\Delta T}{K}\right\} = \exp\left\{j_{\max}\frac{N}{K}\right\} \tag{18}$$

which clearly is true for the pulsed intensity set of (10), signifying asymptotic optimality for any $M$.

To determine optimal intensity sets (either global or local) in the general case, using (13), still remains a difficult task. It has been conjectured by many (e.g., see [1] and [3]) that the pulsed intensity set is in fact the optimal set, but to the authors' knowledge a rigorous proof has not been shown.

## IV. Error Probabilities with Pulsed Intensity Sets

In this section we investigate the performance of the pulsed intensity set in $M$-ary detection by evaluating the error probability $P_E=1-P_D$. This can be obtained by using (13), but the computation can be more conveniently handled by noting that for the pulsed intensity set of (10) $\{\Lambda_q\}$ of (4) constitutes a set of independent Poisson random variables. The variables $\Lambda_q$ have level $(N+K)$ if the $q$th intensity is sent, and have level $K$ otherwise ($K=n_0\Delta T$). Recall that if the $q$th intensity is sent, a correct decision will be made with probability $1/(r+1)$ if $\Lambda_q$ equals $r$ other $\Lambda$'s, and exceeds the remaining $M-1-r$. Therefore, upon considering all possibilities, the conditional detection probability is

$$P_{D/q} = \frac{e^{-(N+MK)}}{M} + \sum_{r=0}^{M-1}\sum_{x=1}^{\infty}\left[\frac{(N+K)^x}{x!}e^{-(N+K)}\right] \cdot\left[\sum_{t=0}^{x-1}\frac{K^t}{t!}e^{-K}\right]^{M-1-r}\left[\frac{K^x}{x!}e^{-K}\right]^r \cdot\left[\frac{(M-1)!}{r!(M-1-r)!(r+1)}\right]. \tag{19}$$

The right side is independent of $q$ and thus represents the average detection probability. By applying the identity

$$\sum_{r=0}^{M-1}\frac{(M-1)!}{(r+1)!(M-1-r)!}A^{M-1-r}B^r = \frac{A^{M-1}}{M(B/A)}\left[\left(1+\frac{B}{A}\right)^M - 1\right]$$

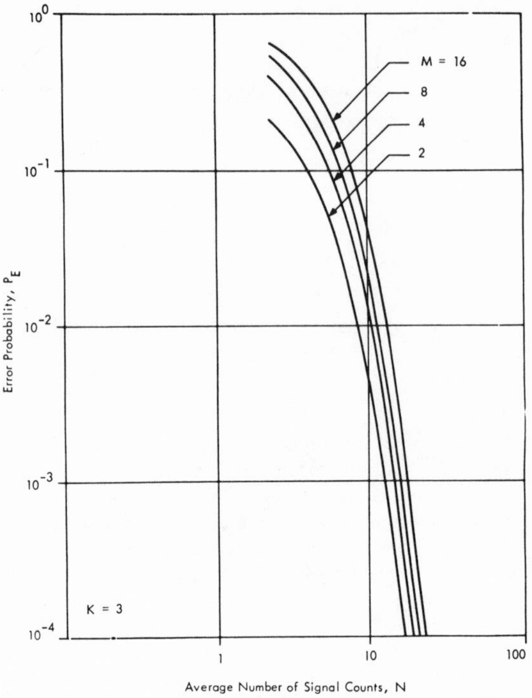


Fig. 2. Error probability versus normalized signal energy $N$ for $M$-ary communications and $K=3$.

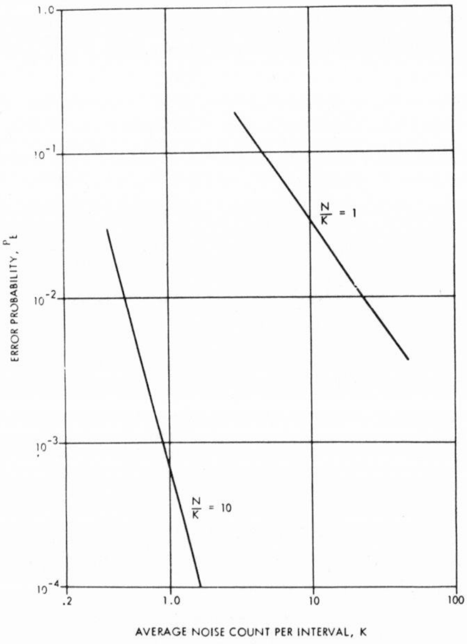


Fig. 3. Error probability versus normalized noise energy $K$. $N$ = normalized signal energy.

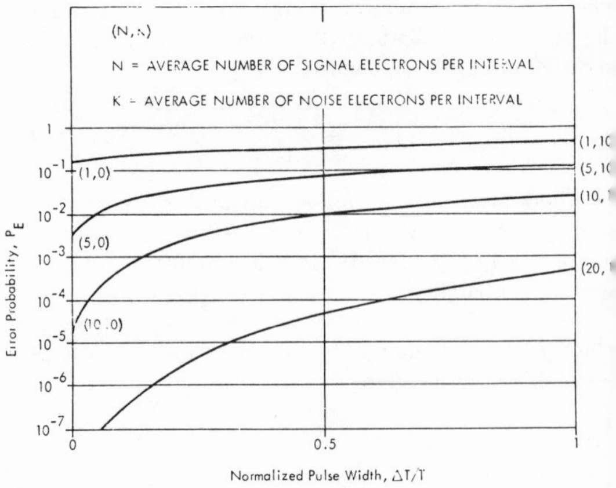


Fig. 4. Error probability versus normalized pulse width wit $M=2$ and various operating conditions.

we can rewrite the error probability as

$$P_E(N,K,M) = 1 - P_D$$

$$= 1 - \frac{e^{-(N+MK)}}{M} - \sum_{x=1}^{\infty} \left[ \frac{(N+K)^x e^{-(N+K)}}{x!} \right.$$

$$\cdot \left[ \sum_{t=0}^{x-1} \frac{K^t e^{-K}}{t!} \right]^{M-1} \frac{1}{Ma} \left[ (1+a)^M - 1 \right] \quad (2($$

where

$$a = \frac{K^x}{x! \left[ \sum_{t=0}^{x-1} \frac{K^t}{t!} \right]}.$$

The parameter $P_E(N,K,M)$ has been digitally compute for various values of $N$, $K$, and $M$. An exemplary plc is shown in Fig. 2 in which $P_E(N,3,M)$ has bee plotted for various $M$ as a function of $N$.

It is important to note that $P_E$ depends on both th normalized signal energy $N$ and the normalized nois energy $K$ in the counting interval, and not simply c their ratio. This fact is emphasized in Fig. 3 in whic $P_E(N,K,2)$ is plotted as a function of $K$ for 2 fixed ratic $N/K$. This dependence on both signal and noise energi distinguishes the Poisson detection problem from th analogous coherent Gaussian channel problem. Note th the interfering noise energy $K$ depends only upon th background energy in the interval $\Delta T$, which is the widt of the transmitted intensity pulse. The prime advantag of optical systems is precisely their ability to remove th effect of background noise by making $\Delta T$ small, and ha been emphasized in previous reportings [6], [7]. This fa can be illustrated graphically, using (20), by considerin a binary Poisson channel ($M=2$) sending information a

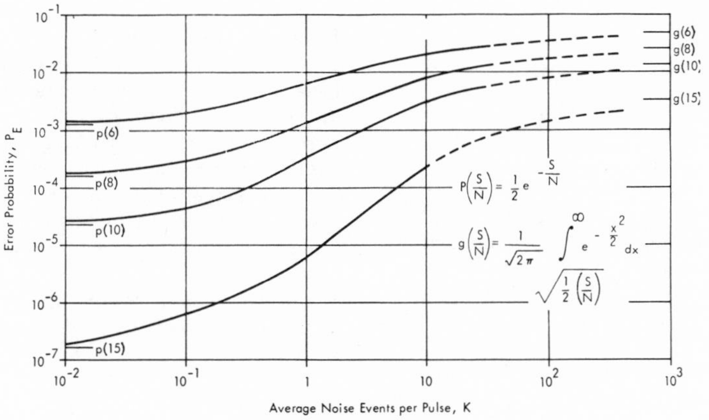


Fig. 5. Error probability versus normalized noise energy $K$ for fixed values of $S/N = N^2/N + K$. $M = 2$.

rate $1/T$ bit/s. The effect of the parameter $\Delta T$ is ıdicated by plotting $P_E(N, n_0T\Delta T/T, 2)$ as a function f $\Delta T/T$, for fixed energy $N$ and background noise nergy per bit interval $n_0T$. This is shown in Fig. 4. The esults indicate the continuous improvement obtained by ecreasing the "duty cycle" $\Delta T/T$, the ultimate limit orresponding to $\Delta T = 0$. The improvement, of course, is ıade at the expense of information bandwidth and peak ower (both inversely proportional to $\Delta T$). Surprisingly, ıe improvement is quite small at low values of $N$, and ıe increase in bandwidth may not be worth the decrease btained in error probability.

A quantity of particular interest to communication ıgineers is the detected signal-to-noise ratio. This is ften defined [8] as the ratio of the square of the average ectron count with no noise to the variance of the count hen noise is present. For Poisson counting statistics ith pulsed intensities, this becomes $S/N = N^2/N + K$. he behavior of $P_E$ of (20) as a function of $K$ for fixed $/N$ is illustrated in Fig. 5 for a binary system. The esults again indicate the ambiguity in using $S/N$ as a esign criterion. The asymptotes show the wide funconal variation of $P_E$ as $K$ increases from zero.

As illustrated in Fig. 2, the error probabilities increase $M$ increases. However, the use of a single set of curves compare various $M$-ary systems is misleading. An $M$-y system with $\Delta T$-second counting intervals transmits $g_2$ $M$ bits of information in $M\Delta T$ seconds. It therefore mmunicates at a rate

$$R = \frac{\log_2 M}{M\Delta T} \quad \text{bit/s.} \tag{21}$$

the transmission rate is normalized for each $M$, $\Delta T$ ust be readjusted to maintain a fixed rate $R = R_0$. The fective noise level per counting interval is then

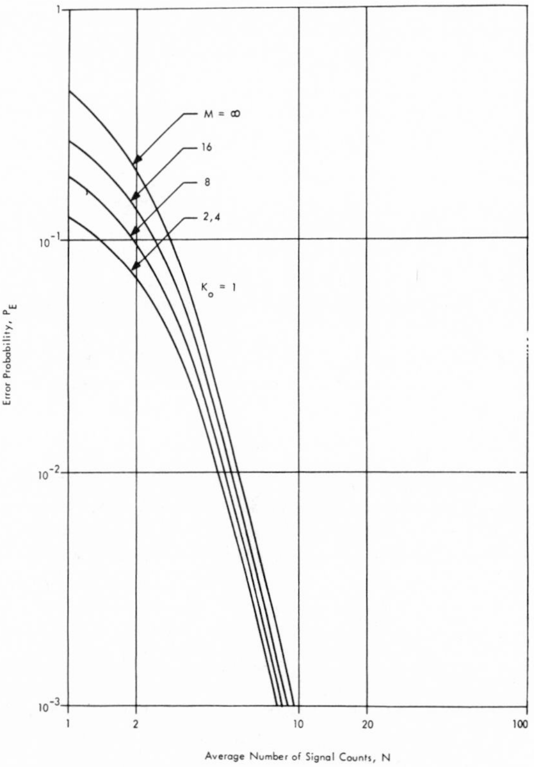


Fig. 6. Error probability versus normalized signal energy $N$, each $M$ adjusted for fixed information rate $R_0$. $K_0$ = normalized noise energy per interval $1/2R_0$.

$$
\begin{aligned}
n_0\Delta T &= n_0 \frac{\log_2 M}{MR_0} \\
&= \left(\frac{n_0}{2R_0}\right)\frac{2\log_2 M}{M} \qquad (22)\\
&= 2K_0 \frac{\log_2 M}{M}
\end{aligned}
$$

where $K_0$ is the noise energy in an interval $1/2R_0$. Thus, for a comparison of different $M$-ary systems, each with fixed information rates, one should compare the parameter $P_E(N, 2K_0(\log M)/M, M)$ for each $N$. If this adjustment is made using (20), the curves of Fig. 6 are generated, with $K_0 = 1$.

The curve corresponding to $M = \infty$ is also shown, and is determined by taking the limit of $P_E(N, 2K_0(\log M)/M, M)$ as $M \to \infty$. This can be obtained by replacing $K$ in (20) by $K' = 2K_0(\log M)/M$ and noting

$$\lim_{M\to\infty} e^{-(N+MK')} \to 0$$

$$\lim_{M\to\infty}\left[\sum_{t=0}^{x-1}\frac{(K')^t}{t!}e^{-K'}\right]^{M-1}\left[\frac{(1+a)^M-1}{Ma}\right] \to \begin{cases}0, & x = 1\\ 1, & x > 1.\end{cases}$$

Using the above we then have

$$
\begin{aligned}
\lim_{M\to\infty} P_E\left(N, 2K_0\frac{\log M}{M}, M\right) &\to 1 - \sum_{x=2}^{\infty}\frac{(N)^x e^{-N}}{x!}\\
&= 1 - (1 - Ne^{-N} - e^{-N})\\
&= (1+N)e^{-N} \qquad (23)
\end{aligned}
$$

which is plotted as $M = \infty$ in Fig. 6. It is noteworthy that (23) is precisely the probability of an event count of zero or one occurring in a noiseless counting interval of signal energy $N$. This has the following interpretation. As $M \to \infty$, the number of intervals becomes infinite, but the normalized noise energy per interval $K' = 2K_0(\log M)/M$ approaches zero. The probability that more than one event will occur in any one of $M-1$ independent nonsignaling intervals having noise energy $K'$ is given by

$$1 - [(1+K')e^{-K'}]^{M-1}$$

This approaches zero as $M \to \infty$, indicating that counts of zero or one will occur in every such interval with probability one. Furthermore, there will be an infinite number of intervals with a zero count and with a one count. Therefore, as $M \to \infty$, an error will occur (with probability approaching one) whenever the signaling interval has a count of zero or one, and an error will never occur when the latter interval has a count greater than one. Hence we have (23).

It is also interesting to note in Fig. 6 that the best system operation, in terms of minimal error probability, does not always correspond to $M \to \infty$. In fact, it can be shown that best $M$ operation depends strongly on the amount of background noise $K_0$. For example, if $K_0 \approx 0$, it is easy to show, using (20), that for $M$ finite, $P_E(N, K', M) \approx (M-1)e^{-N}/M$, which is monotonically decreasing with $M$ and always less than the $M = \infty$ value of (23). Thus, with negligible background noise, system operation improves with decreasing $M$, and is best for $M = 2$. Physically, this means the noise reduction advantag due to decreasing $\Delta T$ as $M$ increases does not offset th increasing errors due to the larger numbers of likelihoo draws that will occur. (Recall a random choice is mad in the event of draws.) For large amounts of backgroun noise, however, the converse is true, and $M = \infty$ doe yield minimal error probability.

It should be emphasized that a fixed energy constrain was imposed on the signal intensity, and therefore th time average power $P_0 = N/T = NR/\log M$ actuall approaches zero as $M \to \infty$. If the average power lev of the source has been fixed at some level $P_0$, $N$ mus be replaced by $P_0 \log M/R$ in the previous equation and we find $P_E \to 0$ is $M \to \infty$ for any $P_0 > 0$. This resul may be compared to a similar result for an additiv Gaussian channel [9] in which zero error probabilit occurred only if $P_0$ satisfied a condition dependent o the rate $R$.

The $P_E$ results above are useful for determining th channel capacity (maximum information rate) of an $M$-ary pulsed intensity set. Assume a transmitter sends on of an $M$ pulsed intensities every $T$ seconds, with eac pulse having width $\Delta T = T/M$. If the transmitter oper ates at a fixed rate $R_0$, then again $T = (\log M)/R_0$ a given by (21). The channel can now be represented as symmetric channel in which each of the $M$ equally likel intensities is converted to itself with probability $1 - P_E$ and is converted to any of the other intensities with equa probability $P_E/(M-1)$. The channel capacity for th type of system is known to be

$$C = \frac{\log M + P_E \log (P_E/(M-1)) + (1-P_E)\log(1-P_E)}{\log M/R_0} \qquad (2\cdot)$$

where $P_E = P_E(N, n_0 \log M/MR_0, M)$. We shall aga consider the signal intensity energy $N$, the backgroun noise power $n_0$, and the rate $R_0$ to be held fixed. Then, a $M \to \infty$, $P_E$ approaches the limit in (23), while the cha nel capacity has the limit

$$C \to [1 - (1+N)e^{-N}]R_0 \qquad (2\cdot)$$

for $N$ finite. The above indicates that information transf can be forced to approach any desired rate with a fini signal energy by using an increasingly larger number intensities and adjusting $R_0$ at the transmitter. Howeve each level is transmitted with a nonzero error probabilit and the information bandwidth and peak power becom infinite. Again introduction of a transmitter power co straint, instead of an energy constraint, will yield oper tion at a capacity $R_0$ with a zero error probability a $M \to \infty$.

## V. Summary and Application of Results

In this paper we have investigated $M$-ary Poiss detection, defined as the maximum likelihood detecti of one of a set of $M$ discrete Poisson processes in t presence of an additive discrete Poisson noise proces 'he model represents a discrete version of an optical ommunication system in which the observables are ounts of photoelectrons, the signals are intensity modu- ated continuous-wave optical sources, and the noise is ackground radiation received within the optical band- idth. The photoelectron count can then be modeled as time varying Poisson process whose average rate is roportional to the sum of the intensities of the modu- ted source and the background radiation. In practical peration, the intensity of the optical source is a con- nuous process, but the analysis can be put on a discrete asis by partitioning the signaling intervals into sub- tervals over which the intensity is taken to be con- tant. The above Poisson model is examined, and the dvantages of a pulsed type of intensity set are demon- trated. The latter corresponds to an optical system sing pulse position modulation in which information is ransmitted by a burst or pulse of optical energy located one of a set of pulse positions. The performance of such system, in terms of pulse width and numbers of pulse ositions, is presented here. The results of this paper asically represent theoretical limits which an optical nk can approach, since the deleterious effects of re- eiver (thermal) noise have been neglected. This latter ssumption becomes valid, for example, when photo- ultipliers are used in detection, and the background diation collected at the receiver is the predominant urce of noise.

The analyses and performance results are in terms of $N$ and $K$, the average electron counts due to signal and oise, respectively. However, these results can be easily onverted to average power requirements by using the lations

$$N = \eta P_s M / hfB$$

$$K = \eta P_n / hfB$$

here $P_s$ and $P_n$ are the average signal and background oise power, $h = 6.62 \times 10^{-34}$ J·s, $\eta$ is the photodetector ficiency (including photomultiplication), $f$ is the optical equency of the continuous-wave source, and $B = 1/\Delta T$. he average power $P_s$ and $P_n$ can be further converted to ansmitted power by introducing space losses and re- iver optics (e.g., see [10, chs. 1 and 2]). Exact syn- ronization has been assumed here between transmitter d receiver at all times. Besides receiver thermal noise, e analysis has excluded the effects of photomultiplier atistics, saturation, and dark currents. We also have sumed constant intensity background radiation which plies a wide-band optical filter. This assumption stricts the minimum value of $\Delta T$ to approximately $0^{-10}$–$10^{-12}$ second.

## APPENDIX

In this Appendix we derive (13) of the report. The erage probability of correctly determining the true tensity in $M$-ary transmission is

$$P_D = \frac{1}{M} \sum_{q=1}^{M} P(D|q) \tag{26}$$

where $P(D|q)$ is the probability of correct detection, given that $\boldsymbol{n}_q + \boldsymbol{n}_0$ is the true intensity. Now the conditional probability of the occurrence of an observed vector $\boldsymbol{k} = \boldsymbol{j} = \{j_1, j_2, j_3, \cdots, j_M\}$, given $\boldsymbol{n}_q + \boldsymbol{n}_0$, is

$$P(k = j | q) = \prod_{i=1}^{M} \frac{[(n_{q_i} + n_0)\Delta T]^{j_i}}{j_i!} e^{-(Mn_0)\Delta T} e^{-N}$$
$$\triangleq \Psi(q,j)\, e^{-N} \tag{27}$$

where $N$ is the energy constraint given in (3). The conditional detection probability $P(D|q)$ is then obtained by summing over the set of all $j$, such that a correct decision is made. A correct decision will occur when the $q$th intensity is used, if $\Lambda_q$ is selected as being the largest. If no other $\Lambda_t$ exceeds $\Lambda_q$, but $r$ of the $\Lambda_t$ equal $\Lambda_q$, the receiver will be correct with a probability of $1/(r+1)$, assuming a purely random selection is made when likelihood equalities occur. Now $j$ is an $M$ dimensional vector with nonnegative integer components, and we shall denote the space of all such vectors as $R^M$. The conditional detection probability $P(D|q)$ can therefore be written by summing over all $j \in R^M$ leading to a correct decision. Thus,

$$P(D|q) = \sum_{r=0}^{M-1} \frac{1}{r+1} \sum_{J_{q_r}} \Psi(q,j)\, e^{-N} \tag{28}$$

where $J_{q_r}$ is the set of $j \in R^M$ such that no other $\Lambda_t$ exceeds $\Lambda_q$, and $r$ other $\Lambda_t$ equal $\Lambda_q$. If we let $I_q$ denote the $r$ dimensional index set corresponding to these $r$ $\Lambda_t$, we can for simplicity denote $J_{q_r}$ symbolically as

$$J_{q_r} = \{j \subset R^M\colon\ \Lambda_q = \max_k \Lambda_k = \Lambda_t,\ t \subset I_q\}. \tag{29}$$

Substituting (28) into (26) yields a general expression for the detection probability:

$$P_D = \frac{e^{-N}}{M} \sum_{q=1}^{M} \sum_{r=0}^{M-1} \sum_{J_{q_r}} \frac{1}{r+1} \Psi(q,j). \tag{30}$$

Now by examining carefully the set $J_{q_r}$ we can simplify the above. Making use of the monotonicity of the exponential function, we can write:

$$\begin{aligned} J_{q_r} &= \{j \subset R^M\colon\ \exp(\Lambda_q) = \exp(\max_k \Lambda_k) \\ &= \exp \Lambda_t,\ t \subset I_q\} \\ &= \Big\{j \subset R^M\colon\ \prod_{i=1}^{M} [(n_{q_i} + n_0)\Delta T]^{j_i} \\ &= \max_k \prod_{i=1}^{M} [(n_{k_i} + n_0)\Delta T]^{j_i} \\ &= \prod_{i=1}^{M} [(n_{t_i} + n_0)\Delta T]^{j_i},\ \ t \subset I_q\Big\} \\ &\doteq \{j \subset R^M\colon\ \Psi(q,j) = \max_k \Psi(k,j) \\ &= \Psi(t,j),\ t \subset I_q\}. \end{aligned} \tag{31}$$

Thus $J_{q_r}$ can be alternatively defined as the set of $j$ for which $(\Psi q,j)$ is one of $r+1$ maximum $\Psi(k,j)$ functions. This means every $j$ in $J_{q_r}$ also belongs to $r$ other sets $J_{t_r}$, $t \subset I_q$, or correspondingly, a point $j$ in $J_{t_r}$, $t \subset I_q$, exists such that $\Psi(t,j) = \Psi(q,j)$. Note that the set of subspaces $\{J_{q_r}\}$ are disjoint for different $r$, but not for different $q$. With these facts consider the summation

$$\sum_{q=1}^{M} \sum_{J_{q_r}} \frac{\Psi(q,j)}{r+1} \tag{32}$$

for fixed $r$. For any term of the sum, say $\Psi(q_0,j_0)/(r+1)$, there exist $r$ other terms having the same value, one for each point $j_0$ of $J_{t_r}$, $t \subset I_{q_0}$. The total contribution to the sum above from this set of $r+1$ terms is then

$$\begin{aligned}(r+1)\left[\frac{\Psi(q_0,j_0)}{r+1}\right] &= \Psi(q_0,j_0) \\ &= \max_q \Psi(q,j_0)\end{aligned} \tag{33}$$

the last equation following since $j_0 \in J_{q_0 r}$. Thus, overlapping points in the summation of (32) contribute a total amount given by (33). It therefore follows that

$$\sum_{q=1}^{M} \sum_{J_{q_r}} \frac{\Psi(q,j)}{r+1} = \sum_{\bigcup_q J_{q_r}} \max_q \Psi(q,j) \tag{34}$$

where $\bigcup_q J_{q_r}$ is the union over $q$ of the subsets $\{J_{q_r}\}$. Inverting the order of summation in (30) and using (34) allows us to rewrite

$$\begin{aligned}P_D &= \frac{e^{-N}}{M} \sum_{r=0}^{M-1} \sum_{\bigcup_q J_{q_r}} \max_q \Psi(q,j) \\ &= \frac{e^{-N}}{M} \sum_{R^M} \max_q \Psi(q,j)\end{aligned} \tag{35}$$

where we have employed the fact that the $\bigcup_q J_{q_r}$ are disjoint subspaces, and the sum over all $r$ spans the whole space $R^M$. Equation (35) is the same as (13).

## References


[1] B. Reiffen and H. Sherman, "On optimum demodulator for Poisson processes: photon source detectors," *Proc. IEEE*, vol. 51, pp. 1316–1320, October 1963.

[2] K. Abend, "Optimum photon detection," *IEEE Trans. Information Theory (Correspondence)*, vol. IT-12, pp. 64–6 January 1966.

[3] T. Kailath, "The divergence and Bhattacharyya distance measures in signal selection," *IEEE Trans. Communication Technology*, vol. COM-15, pp. 52–60, February 1967.

[4] C. W. Helstrom, "The detection and resolution of optic signals," *IEEE Trans. Information Theory*, vol. IT-1 pp. 275–287, October 1964.

[5] A. Viterbi, *Principles of Coherent Communication*. New York: McGraw-Hill, 1966, p. 234.

[6] M. Ross, "Pulse interval modulation laser communications," presented at the Eastcon Convention, Washington D. C., October 1967.

[7] S. Karp and R. Gagliardi, "A low duty cycle optical communication system," presented at the Eastcon Convention Washington, D. C., October 1967.

[8] W. Pratt, "Binary detection in an optical polarization modulation communication channel," *IEEE Trans. Communication Technology (Concise Papers)*, vol. COM-1 pp. 664–665, October 1966.

[9] A. Viterbi [5], p. 226.

[10] M. Ross, *Laser Receivers*. New York: Wiley, 1966.

# 12



Reprinted from *IEEE Trans. Inf. Theory* **IT-16**(6):672–680 (1970)

# Photon Counting: A Problem in Classical Noise Theory

SHERMAN KARP, MEMBER, IEEE, AND JOHN R. CLARK, STUDENT MEMBER, IEEE

*Abstract*—In this paper we formulate the general problem of determining the photoelectron "counting" distribution resulting from an electromagnetic field impinging on a quantum detector. Although the detector model used was derived quantum mechanically, our treatment is wholly classical and includes all results known to date. This combination is commonly referred to as the semiclassical approach. The emphasis, however, lies in directing the problem towards optical communication.

The electromagnetic field is assumed to be the sum of a deterministic signal and a zero-mean narrow-band Gaussian random process, and is expanded in a Karhunen–Loève series of orthogonal functions. Several examples are given. It is shown that all the results obtainable can be written explicitly in terms of the noise covariance function. Particular attention is given to the case of a signal plus white Gaussian noise, both of which are band-limited to $\pm B$ Hz. Since the result is a fundamental one, to add some physical insight, we show four methods by which it can be obtained. Various limiting forms of this distribution are derived, including the necessary conditions for those commonly accepted. The likelihood functional is established and is shown to be the product of Laguerre polynomials. For the problem of continuous estimation, the Fisher information kernel is derived and an important limiting form is obtained. The maximum a posteriori (MAP) and maximum-likelihood (ML) estimation equations are also derived. In the latter case the results are also functions of Laguerre polynomials.

Manuscript received January 26, 1970; revised April 10, 1970.
S. Karp is with NASA Electronics Research Center, Cambridge, Mass. 02139.
J. R. Clark was with NASA Electronics Research Center, Cambridge, Mass. He is presently with the Research Laboratory of Electronics, Massachusetts Institute of Technology, Cambridge, Mass. 02139.

## Introduction

SINCE the advent of the laser, a problem of growing importance in optical communications and coherence theory has been the determination of the output statistics of a quantum detector excited by a narrow-band Gaussian source. In optical communications, knowledge of these statistics is necessary for the application of the techniques of optimum detection and estimation theory. In the physical theory of coherence, these statistics are a means by which the light incident on the detector can be studied. In both cases a useful statistic, which is relatively easy to evaluate, is the probability $p_{N_t}(k)$ of detecting $k$ events, or "counts," in the time interval $(0, t]$. In an idealized detector the conditional probability of $k$ counts in $(0, t]$, given the incident radiation, can be shown to obey a Poisson law, with the time-averaged intensity of the field as rate parameter.

Although this idealized detector model is based on the quantum theory of photodetection, statistics such as $p_{N_t}(k)$ can be correctly calculated, if desired, by using only classical tools, provided the proper quantum model has been postulated. This is the essence of the so-called "semiclassical" approach, which we shall use in this report [1]. The value of this approach lies not so much in its freedom from quantum-mechanical subtleties as in the ease with which it allows meaningful physical interpretations to be made and comparisons to be drawn. We shall therefore not dwell on the physical considerations leading to the derivation of the Poisson model, since it is generally accepted as an adequate probabilistic description of an ideal quantum detector localized at a point in space [2]. The physics underlying this model and others is discussed at length in the literature on quantum detectors.

The problem of determining the counting distribution $p_{N_t}(k)$ has been approached by a number of authors, within the framework of laser intensity fluctuation studies [3]–[8]. It is intimately connected with the classic noise-theory problem of finding the statistics of the time-averaged square of a real process. Random functionals of this type have been treated in considerable generality for Gaussian processes; we list only a few of the more important works in [9]–[15].

Here, we present a general method for finding $p_{N_t}(k)$ when the light incident on the detector is a deterministic signal plus a narrow-band Gaussian process. Our results are shown to encompass as special cases several previously known results. The method is a generalization of Mandel's [5] in which we allow the incident field to have a nonzero mean, and $p_{N_t}(k)$ is expressed in terms of the cumulants of the time-averaged intensity. Several specific examples are worked out in detail, which are in agreement with known results when such results exist. Considerable attention is given to the important case in which the radiation is a deterministic signal in band-limited white Gaussian noise. For this example, we show how the results can be applied to some problems of interest in optical communications.

## Derivation of the Counting Distribution

First, we consider the Poisson model for the ideal quantum detector. Given a counting statistic $N_t$ at time $t$, conditioned on a function $[a(\tau); 0 < \tau \leq t]$, such that it obeys a Poisson law,

$$\Pr\{N_t = k \mid [a(\tau); 0 < \tau \leq t]\} = \{[m(t)]^k/k!\}e^{-m(t)} \quad (1)$$

$$m(t) = \alpha \int_0^t |a(\tau)|^2 \, d\tau \quad (2)$$

we want to know the probability $\Pr\{N_t = k\}$ when $a(\tau)$ is the complex envelope of a narrow-band Gaussian process. Here $\alpha = \eta/h\nu$, where $\eta$ is the quantum efficiency, $h$ is Planck's constant, and $\nu$ is the frequency. With $m_t$ the random value assumed by $m(t')$ at time $t' = t$, it is clear from (1) that the probability of $k$ counts in $(0, t]$ is given formally by

$$p_{N_t}(k) = (1/k!)E\{e^{-m_t}m_t^k\} \quad (3)$$

where the expectation is taken over the random variable $m_t$.

We shall take $a(\tau)$ to be the complex envelope of a real, not necessarily stationary, Gaussian process $\alpha(\tau)$,

$$\alpha(\tau) = \mathrm{Re}\,[a(\tau)e^{j2\pi f_0 \tau}], \quad (4)$$

which is assumed to be narrow-band about some very high frequency $f_0$. We shall also assume that the covariance function of $a(\tau)$ is real. With these assumptions we can show that the real and imaginary parts of $a(\tau)$ are independent and have the same covariance function. In addition we assume that $a(\tau)$ can be written

$$a(\tau) = s(\tau) + n(\tau) \quad (5)$$

where $s(\tau)$ is a deterministic signal and $n(\tau)$ is a zero-mean Gaussian random process.

Instead of evaluating (3) directly for $p_{N_t}(k)$, we shall find the characteristic function of $N_t$:

$$M_{N_t}(jv) = E\{M_{N_t|m_t}(jv)\} \quad (6)$$

$$= E\{e^{m_t(e^{jv}-1)}\}. \quad (7)$$

Then $p_{N_t}(k)$ can be found either by direct inversion of $M_{N_t}(jv)$, or from one of the following formulas:

$$p_{N_t}(k) = [(-1)^k/k!](\partial^k/\partial\xi^k)M_{N_t}[\ln(1-\xi)]_{\xi=1} \quad (8)$$

$$p_{N_t}(k) = (1/k!)\sum_{n=0}^{\infty}[(-1)^n/n!]\mu_{k+n}. \quad (9)$$

$\mu_i$ is the $i$th moment of $m_t$; in terms of $M_{N_t}(jv)$,

$$\mu_i = (\partial^i/\partial\xi^i)M_{N_t}[\ln(1+\xi)]_{\xi=0}. \quad (10)$$

Equation (8) is the equivalent of differentiating the probability generating function of $N_t$, and (9) is the result of expanding the exponential in (3) in a power series.

We see from (7) that $M_{N_t}(jv)$ is simply the moment generating function of $m_t$,

$$M_{m_t}(u) = E\{e^{m_t u}\} \quad (11)$$

'aluated at $u = e^{iv} - 1$; thus, we can confine our ;tention to the random variable $m_t$.

It is convenient to expand $a(\tau)$ in a Karhunen–Loéve ries on $[0, t]$ [16]:

$$a(\tau) = \sum_{i=1}^{\infty} a_i \phi_i(\tau) = \sum_i (s_i + n_i)\phi_i(\tau). \tag{12}$$

he equality, of course, is in the sense of "limit-in-the-ean." The coefficients are given by

$$n_i = (n, \phi_i) \tag{13}$$

$$s_i = (s, \phi_i) \tag{14}$$

here

$$(x, y) = \int_0^t x(\tau)y^*(\tau)\, d\tau \tag{15}$$

d the $\{\phi_i\}$ are eigenfunctions of the integral equation

$$\lambda_i \phi_i(u) = K_n \phi_i = \int_0^t K_n(u, v)\phi_i(v)\, dv. \tag{16}$$

ere $K_n(u, v) = E\{n(u)n^*(v)\}$ is the covariance kernel of e noise. The $\{\phi_i\}$ are normalized so that $(\phi_i, \phi_j) = \delta_{ij}$. It is clear from the orthonormality of the eigenfunctions at $m_t$ can be written

$$m_t = \alpha \sum_i |a_i|^2 = \alpha \sum_i |s_i + n_i|^2. \tag{17}$$

otice that $m_t$ is the energy in the process at time $t$. nce $n(\tau)$ is a zero-mean Gaussian random process, e $\{n_i\}$ are Gaussian random variables, with $E(n_i) = 0$ d $E(n_i n_j^*) = \lambda_i \delta_{ij}$. This orthogonality depends critically on choosing the basis to satisfy (16) uniquely. If, wever, there is no noise ($n(\tau) = 0$), $a(t) = s(\tau)$ can be panded in any complete orthonormal set $\{\psi_i\}$ on $[0, t]$, d (16) is irrelevant. For this case, with $c_i = (a, \psi_i)$, (1) n be written

$$\Pr\{N_t = k \mid [a(\tau); 0 < \tau \le t]\} = (k!)^{-1}\left[\sum_i \alpha |c_i|^2\right]^k \exp\left[-\sum_i \alpha |c_i|^2\right]. \tag{18}$$

ch coordinate axis in the space contributes an indepennt Poisson variate $N_{ti}$,

$$\{N_{ti} = k_i \mid [a(\tau); 0 < \tau \le t]\} = \Pr\{N_{ti} = k_i \mid c_i\} = [\alpha |c_i|^2]^{k_i} e^{-\alpha |c_i|^2}/k_i! \tag{19}$$

ere $N_t = \sum_i N_{ti}$ and $k = \sum_i k_i$ [17]. This is clearly lependent of the particular basis chosen; only the $\{c_i\}$ ange. Each axis always contributes an independent isson variate. In addition, since $\sum_i |c_i|^2$ is the energy $a(\tau)$ in $[0, t]$, the conditional density of $N_t$ is independent the functional form of $a(\tau)$. If we choose $\{\psi_i\}$ to be the usoidal set on $[0, t]$, then $|c_i|^2$ represents the energy $a(\tau)$ at the frequency of $\psi_i$. If $a(\tau) = \psi_j(\tau)$ for some $j$, n $k = k_j$ and (18) reduces to (19) with $i = j$.

For the more general case of nonzero noise, we observe that only one particular orthonormal set can be used as a basis for expanding $a(\tau)$, if we desire each axis in the space to contribute an independent variate to $N_t$. That basis, of course, must satisfy $K_n\phi = \lambda\phi$, (16). (The only exception is white Gaussian noise, for which (16) is satisfied by any complete orthonormal set; then each axis in the space contributes an independent, identically distributed random variable.)

For narrow-band Gaussian noise, we now show that the contribution from each axis is an independent Laguerre-distributed variate and, consequently, that $N_t$ can always be represented as the sum of independent Laguerre random variables.

The real and imaginary parts of $n_i = (n, \phi_i)$ are independent, each with variance $\lambda_i/2$, thus, ([18] p. 196),

$$p_{|a_i|}(A) = \begin{cases} \dfrac{2A}{\lambda_i} \exp\left[-\dfrac{|s_i|^2 + A^2}{\lambda_i}\right] \cdot I_0\left(2\dfrac{|s_i|}{\lambda_i} A\right) & A \ge 0 \\ 0 & \text{elsewhere} \end{cases} \tag{20}$$

the so-called Ricean density, where $I_0$ is the zero-order modified Bessel function of the first kind. It follows that $|a_i|^2$ has the density function

$$p_{|a_i|^2}(A) = \begin{cases} \dfrac{1}{\lambda_i} \exp\left[-\dfrac{|s_i|^2 + A}{\lambda_i}\right] \cdot I_0\left(2\dfrac{|s_i|}{\lambda_i} A^{1/2}\right) & A \ge 0 \\ 0 & \text{elsewhere.} \end{cases} \tag{21}$$

Since the $\{a_i\}$ are independent, it follows that the $\{|a_i|^2\}$ are also independent. Thus, from (11) and (17) we see that

$$M_{m_t}(u) = \prod_i E\{e^{\alpha |a_i|^2 u}\}. \tag{22}$$

Now, with $x$ a real Gaussian variate, $E\{e^{x^2 u}\}$ is given by ([19] p. 396)

$$E\{e^{x^2 u}\} = \frac{\exp\left[(E^2(x)u)/[1 - 2\,\mathrm{var}\,(x)u]\right]}{[1 - 2\,\mathrm{var}\,(x)u]^{1/2}}, \quad \left(\mathrm{Re}\, u < \frac{1}{2\,\mathrm{var}\,(x)}\right). \tag{23}$$

Thus,

$$M_{m_t}(u) = \prod_i \frac{1}{1 - \alpha\lambda_i u} \exp\left[\frac{\alpha |s_i|^2 u}{1 - \alpha\lambda_i u}\right], \quad \left[\mathrm{Re}\, u < \frac{1}{\alpha \max_i \lambda_i}\right] \tag{24}$$

and

$$M_{N_t}(jv) = \prod_i \left\{\frac{1}{1 - \alpha\lambda_i(e^{jv} - 1)} \cdot \exp\left[\frac{\alpha |s_i|^2 (e^{jv} - 1)}{1 - \alpha\lambda_i(e^{jv} - 1)}\right]\right\}. \tag{25}$$

The quantity within the brackets is the characteristic function of a Laguerre random variable for which the probability distribution is [20]

$$p_{N_{t,i}}(k_i) = \frac{[\alpha\lambda_i]^{k_i}}{(1+\alpha\lambda_i)^{1+k_i}} \cdot \exp\left[-\frac{\alpha\,|s_i|^2}{1+\alpha\lambda_i}\right] L_{k_i}\left(-\frac{|s_i|^2}{\lambda_i(1+\alpha\lambda_i)}\right). \qquad (26)$$

$L_k$ is the zero-order Laguerre polynomial ([21] eq. 8.97). Thus, we see that $N_t$ can be represented as the sum $\sum N_{ti}$ of Laguerre variates, as asserted. If the noise is Gaussian, there always exists an operation that acts on (18), producing another independent coordinate system of orthogonal axes [(25) and (26)].

If $s_i = 0$ for some $i$,

$$p_{N_{t,i}}(k_i) = \frac{[\alpha\lambda_i]^{k_i}}{(1+\alpha\lambda_i)^{1+k_i}}. \qquad (27)$$

Hence any coordinate $\phi_i$ for which $s_i = 0$ contributes a Bose-Einstein random variable to $N_t$.

Proceeding formally, we note that $p_{N_t}(k)$ is just the infinite convolution of the $\{p_{N_{t,i}}(k_i)\}$ for all $i$. As this is usually difficult to evaluate explicitly by using (26), we shall concentrate our attention on (24) instead.

We mention in passing that if the noise $n(\tau)$ is not Gaussian, the interpretation in the preceding three paragraphs can not be used; i.e., there does not exist an orthonormal basis in which $a(\tau)$ can be expanded such that $N_t$ can be represented as the sum of independent variates.

$M_{m_t}(u)$, (24), can be cast into a completely equivalent form that does not explicitly involve the eigenvalues $\{\lambda_i\}$ [9], [22]. The identities that make this possible are [23]

$$\sum_i \lambda_i^k = \operatorname{Tr} K_n^{(k)} = \int_0^t K_n^{(k)}(t', t')\,dt' \qquad (28)$$

and

$$\sum_i |s_i|^2 \lambda_i^k = (s, K_n^{(k)} s) \qquad (29)$$

where

$$K_n^{(k)}(u, v) = \int_0^t K_n^{(k-1)}(u, \xi) K_n(\xi, v)\,d\xi \qquad (30)$$

$$K_n^{(1)} = K_n \qquad (31)$$

$$K_n^{(0)} \equiv \text{identity operator}. \qquad (32)$$

By expanding $\log(1 - \alpha\lambda_i u)$ and $(1 - \alpha\lambda_i u)^{-1}$ in power series, and using (28) and (29), we get the immediate result

$$M_{m_t}(u) = \exp\left[\sum_{k=1}^{\infty} \frac{\kappa_k}{k!} u^k\right], \qquad \left(\operatorname{Re} u < \frac{1}{\alpha \max_i (\lambda_i)}\right) \qquad (33)$$

and $\{\kappa_i\}$, the cumulants of $m_t$, are

$$\kappa_i = [(i-1)!\operatorname{Tr} K_n^{(i)} + i!(s, K_n^{(i-1)} s)]\alpha^i. \qquad (34)$$

For the case, $s(\tau) \equiv 0$, a number of authors ha obtained expressions equivalent to (24) or (33) [3], [ [7], [9]. Related results have also been obtained for re rather than complex, $a(\tau)$ [9]-[12], [14], [15].

The form of the noise will often dictate which of t two formulas, (24) or (33), will be the more convenient practice. The integral equation (16) is difficult to sol and even when the eigenvalues are available, (24) mig not simplify significantly. On the other hand, as Slepi [11] has pointed out, the iterated kernels [(30)] are usua difficult to evaluate beyond the first few orders; howev they are often all that is needed for a good approximati

We can now find $p_{N_t}(k)$ by using one of the formul (8) or (9). It turns out that (9) can be evaluated alm trivially with the help of the moment generating functi $M_{m_t}(u)$. Since the moments $\{\mu_i\}$ and the cumulants { are related, we need not evaluate (10) directly. We instead the formula [24]

$$\mu_k = \sum_{i=1}^{k} \frac{1}{i!} \sum_{\substack{\sum_{j=1}^{i} k_j = k \\ k_j \ge 1}} \frac{k!}{k_1! \cdots k_i!} \kappa_{k_1}\kappa_{k_2} \cdots \kappa_{k_i}. \qquad (\text{}$$

Along with (34) and (35), (9) gives an exact expressi for $p_{N_t}(k)$, the desired counting distribution, in terms the covariance $K_n$ and the signal $s$.

The fundamental quantities here are the cumula $\{\kappa_i\}$, in terms of which a number of the statistical char teristics of $N_t$ can be expressed. Some of the more i portant relations are derived in the Appendix. Using (2 (29), (34), and (86), we find the mean and variance of to be

$$E(N_t) = \sum_i \alpha\lambda_i + \alpha(s, s) = \alpha \operatorname{Tr} K_n + \alpha(s, s) \qquad (\text{}$$

$$\operatorname{var}(N_t) = \sum_i \alpha\lambda_i + \alpha(s, s) + \sum_i [\alpha\lambda_i]^2 + 2\sum_i [\alpha\lambda_i]\alpha\,|s_i|^2 = \alpha \operatorname{Tr} K_n + \alpha(s, s) + \alpha^2 \operatorname{Tr} K_n^{(2)} + 2\alpha^2(s, K_n s). \qquad (\text{}$$

Notice that the only quantities involved in (36) and ( are the noise covariance, the signal, and the time $t$.

It should be emphasized that our method of find $p_{N_t}(k)$ through the characteristic function is not alw the easiest path to the desired answer. Indeed, for cert noise sources the most direct route to $p_{N_t}(k)$ might be direct evaluation of $p_{m_t}(M)$, the density function of and use of (3). Whichever method is to be used is b decided when the precise form of $K_n$ has been ascertain

## Examples and Applications

It can be seen that the mathematical form of $p_{N_t}(k$ considerably more complicated than that of $M_{N_t}(jv)$— a surprising situation in nonlinear noise problems. In m applications of interest, one expects that $p_{N_t}(k)$ will ich easier to find by evaluating $M_{N_t}(jv)$ first, rather an by going directly to (9), (34), and (35). In the amples to follow, this is certainly the case.

*oise Only—* ($s(\tau) \equiv 0$)

*Integrated White Noise—* $K_n(u, v) = \rho^2 \min(u, v)$: though this example appears to be only of academic lue, it is illustrative of a particularly simple means of taining $p_{N_t}(k)$. It is well known that the eigenvalues (16) are ([19], p. 196)

$$\lambda_i = [4\rho^2 t^2/\pi^2(2i - 1)^2] \qquad i = 1, 2, 3, \cdots. \tag{38}$$

serting this in (24) and using a tabulated product rule, get ([21] eq. 1.4313)

$$M_{m_t}(u) = \sec(\rho t \sqrt{\alpha u}). \tag{39}$$

e coefficients in the Taylor series expansion of (39) are moments $\{\mu_i\}$ of $m_t$; since ([21], eq. 1.4119)

$$\sec x = \sum_{k=0}^{\infty} [|E_{2k}|/(2k)!]x^{2k}, \qquad (x^2 < \pi^2/4) \tag{40}$$

have

$$\mu_k = [k!/(2k)!]|E_{2k}|(\alpha\rho^2 t^2)^k \tag{41}$$

d the $\{E_i\}$ are the Euler numbers. Equation (9) now es $p_{N_t}(k)$ directly:

$$(k) = \sum_{n=0}^{\infty} \frac{(-1)^n}{(2k + 2n)!} \binom{k+n}{n} |E_{2k+2n}| (\alpha\rho^2 t^2)^{k+n}. \tag{42}$$

Because of the simple form of $M_{m_t}(u)$, we can find the unting distribution without first having to compute the mulants $\{\kappa_i\}$. The mean and variance of the counts work t to be

$$E(N_t) = (\alpha/2)\rho^2 t^2 \tag{43}$$

$$\text{var}(N_t) = (\alpha/2)\rho^2 t^2 + (\alpha^2/6)\rho^4 t^4. \tag{44}$$

*First-Order Markov Noise—* $K_n(u, v) = P \exp - \beta|u - v|$: uation (24) becomes

$$M_{m_t}(u) = \prod_i [1/(1 - \alpha\lambda_i u)] \tag{45}$$

h $\lambda_i$ a solution of a transcendental equation [9]. uation (45) has been evaluated by an indirect technique ] and is given by

$$_t(u) = e^{\beta t}\left\{\cosh\left[\beta t\left(1 - \frac{2P\alpha}{\beta}u\right)\right] + \frac{1 - (P\alpha/\beta)u}{1 - (2P\alpha/\beta)u}\sinh\left[\beta t\left(1 - \frac{2P\alpha}{\beta}u\right)\right]\right\}^{-1}. \tag{46}$$

This does not easily yield a useful expression for $p_{N_t}(k)$; wever, using the Leibnitz differentiation rule, Bédard [3] s obtained recurrence relations for the counting distri- tion and its factorial moments. For certain limiting es, approximate counting distributions have been ained [7].

The mean and variance of $N_t$ are easily found to be

$$E(N_t) = \alpha P t \tag{47}$$

$$\text{var}(N_t) = \alpha P t + [(\alpha P)^2/2\beta^2][2\beta t + e^{-2\beta t} - 1]. \tag{48}$$

*Band-limited White Gaussian Noise:* Let $n(\tau)$ be a white Gaussian process, band-limited to $\pm B$ Hz, with two-sided spectral height $N_0$. Taking the first $2Bt + 1$ eigenvalues of (16) to be the same ($N_0$), and the rest to be zero ([19], p. 193), (24) becomes

$$M_{m_t}(u) = [1/(1 - \alpha N_0 u)]^{2Bt+1}, \tag{49}$$

that is,

$$M_{N_t}(jv) = [1 - \alpha N_0(e^{jv} - 1)]^{(-2Bt+1)}. \tag{50}$$

This can be recognized as the characteristic function of the negative binomial distribution [17]

$$p_{N_t}(k) = \binom{2Bt + k}{k}\left(\frac{1}{1 + \alpha N_0}\right)^{2Bt+1}\left(\frac{\alpha N_0}{1 + \alpha N_0}\right)^k. \tag{51}$$

If $2Bt \ll 1 (t \ll 1/2B)$, only one eigenvalue of (16) is significant, and (50) reduces to

$$M_{N_t}(jv) = [1 - \alpha N_0(e^{jv} - 1)]^{-1}. \tag{52}$$

In other words, the counting distribution is Bose–Einstein:

$$p_{N_t}(k) = [1/(1 + \alpha N_0)][\alpha N_0/(1 + \alpha N_0)]^k \tag{53}$$

in agreement with (27). For $2Bt \gg 1$, and $\alpha N_0 \ll 1$, it can easily be shown that $p_{N_t}(k)$ approaches a Poisson distribution. (*Note:* This limiting form can also be shown to be true for first-order Markov noise, (46), when $\beta t \gg 1$ and $\beta \gg 4P\alpha$.) On the other hand, for a nonzero signal and no noise, $p_{N_t}(k)$ is also Poisson, as we have seen. This behavior, in the case of band-limited white Gaussian noise, is due to the complete "smoothing out" of the intensity fluctuations, while in the signal-only case, it is due to the deterministic nature of the signal.

*Signal Plus Noise*

Now we remove the restriction that $s(\tau)$ be zero. Assume that $n(\tau)$ is band-limited white Gaussian noise, as above. In addition, assume that $s(\tau)$ is band-limited to $\pm B'$ Hz, $B' \leq B$. Equation (25) applies with $\lambda_i = N_0$, and $p_{N_t}(k)$ is just the $(2Bt + 1)$-fold convolution of the Laguerre density (26) with itself. Omitting the details, we note that the result is ([21], eq. 8.9771)

$$p_{N_t}(k) = \frac{(\alpha N_0)^k}{(1 + \alpha N_0)^{k+2Bt+1}} \cdot \exp\left[-\frac{\alpha(s, s)}{1 + \alpha N_0}\right] L_k^{2Bt}\left[\frac{-(s, s)}{N_0(1 + \alpha N_0)}\right] \tag{54}$$

where $L_k^{2Bt}$ is the $2Bt$-order Laguerre polynomial. The mean and variance of $N_t$ are found to be

$$E(N_t) = (2Bt + 1)\alpha N_0 + \alpha(s, s) \tag{55}$$

$$\text{var}(N_t) = (2Bt + 1)(1 + \alpha N_0)\alpha N_0 + (1 + 2\alpha N_0)\alpha(s, s). \tag{56}$$

Equation (54) could have been found by evaluating $p_{m_t}(M)$ first, and using (3)—the alternative approach suggested earlier. For this example, $p_{m_t}(M)$ turns out to be a "noncentral chi-square" density (i.e., the density of the sum of $2Bt + 1$ independent Ricean variates):

$$p_{m_t}(M) = \begin{cases} \dfrac{1}{N_0\alpha}\left[\dfrac{M}{(s, s)\alpha}\right]^{Bt} \exp\left[-\dfrac{M + (s, s)\alpha}{\alpha N_0}\right] \\ \cdot I_{2Bt}\left(\dfrac{2(s, s)^{1/2}}{\alpha^{1/2}N_0} M^{1/2}\right) \cdot \quad M > 0 \\ 0 \qquad \text{elsewhere} \end{cases} \tag{57}$$

$p_{N_t}(k)$, (54), results when the expression

$$\int_0^\infty \frac{1}{k!} M^k e^{-M} p_{m_t}(M)\, dM \tag{58}$$

is evaluated.

For $2Bt \ll 1$, (54) reduces to (26); for $2Bt \gg 1$, however, $p_{N_t}(k)$ approaches a Poisson distribution when $\alpha N_0$ is small. This is clear from the following discussion.

Let $\alpha N_0 \ll 1$ and $2Bt \gg 1$; then, assymptotically,

$$\left(\frac{1}{1 + \alpha N_0}\right)^{2Bt+1} \sim e^{-2Bt\alpha N_0} \tag{59}$$

$$\frac{\alpha(s, s)}{1 + \alpha N_0} \sim \alpha(s, s) \tag{60}$$

$$\frac{\alpha N_0}{1 + \alpha N_0} \sim \alpha N_0 \tag{61}$$

$$L_k^{2Bt}\left[-\frac{(s, s)}{N_0(1 + \alpha N_0)}\right] \sim \frac{1}{k!}\left(2Bt + \frac{(s, s)}{N_0}\right)^k. \tag{62}$$

These equations, together with (54), yield

$$p_{N_t}(k) \sim \frac{[\alpha(s, s) + 2Bt\alpha N_0]^k}{k!} \cdot \exp -[\alpha(s, s) + 2Bt\alpha N_0]. \tag{63}$$

Thus for small $\alpha N_0$ and large $2Bt$, the counting distribution is Poisson, with the rate parameter the sum of a signal intensity and an independent noise intensity. Expressing this in another way, we note that $N_t$ is the sum of two independent Poisson variates, one associated with the signal (intensity $(1/t)(s, s)\alpha$) and one associated with the noise (intensity $2BN_0\alpha$).

Our results for band-limited Gaussian noise are well known in the field of coherence theory [1], [2], [5], [6], [8], [20], [25]; in optical communications, however, they are just beginning to find application [26]–[28]. In earlier papers the asymptotic form (63) was used, with heuristic justification [29], [30].

## Estimation for Continuous Waveforms

For band-limited white Gaussian noise, simple detection and estimation problems can be solved with relative ease because of the independence of noise samples taken at the Nyquist rate. Assume that the interval $[0, t]$ is broken into $2Bt$ equal subintervals, each of length $1/2B$ second. Then the probability of $k_i$ detector counts in the subinterval is given by

$$\frac{(\alpha N_0)^{k_i}}{(1 + \alpha N_0)^{1+k_i}} \exp\left[-\frac{\alpha |s_i|^2}{1 + \alpha N_0}\right] L_{k_i}\left[-\frac{|s_i|^2}{N_0(1 + \alpha N_0)}\right]$$

where $|s_i|^2 = |s(i/2B)|^2/2B$. Moreover, the counts different subintervals are independent, because the n samples are independent. Thus the joint probability $p_N$ of the counts in each subinterval is simply the proc of probabilities [(64)]:

$$p_N(k) = \prod_{i=1}^{2Bt} \frac{(\alpha N_0)^{k_i}}{(1 + \alpha N_0)^{1+k_i}} \cdot \exp\left[-\frac{\alpha |s_i|^2}{1 + \alpha N_0}\right] L_{k_i}\left[-\frac{|s_i|^2}{N_0(1 + \alpha N_0)}\right]$$

with

- $\boldsymbol{N}$ vector of $2Bt$ counting observables
- $\boldsymbol{k}$ $(k_1, k_2, \cdots, k_{2Bt})$.

It is important to note that for this representation tc valid when the signal waveform is band-limited to $\pm B$ it is essential that the subintervals be of length preci $1/2B$ second.

Equation (65) suggests that we define the likelih function $\Lambda(\boldsymbol{k} \mid \boldsymbol{s})$ to be

$$\Lambda(\boldsymbol{k} \mid \boldsymbol{s}) = \prod_{i=1}^{2Bt} \exp\left[-\frac{\alpha |s_i|^2}{1 + \alpha N_0}\right] L_{k_i}\left[-\frac{|s_i|^2}{N_0(1 + \alpha N_0)}\right]$$

It is now straightforward to set up decision structures the multiple-hypothesis detection problem. This has b done elsewhere for a number of signaling schemes [27 we shall restrict our attention to the estimation prob

We start with the assumption that $s$ is a transforma $s[\tau, x(\tau)]$ of some function $x(\tau)$ that we wish to estim $x$ can be a modulation, a set of parameters, or a si number. As is well known, a necessary condition $\hat{x}_{MAP}(\tau)$ to be the maximum a posteriori (MAP) estim of $x(\tau)$, $0 < \tau \leq t$, is

$$\nabla_x[\ln \Lambda + \ln p_{x(\tau)}[X(\tau)]]_{x=\hat{x}_{MAP}} = 0$$

where $\nabla_x$ is the gradient operator with respect to $x(\tau)$, $p_{x(\tau)}[X(\tau)]$ is the a priori probability density function $x(\tau)$. In the absence of prior information, of course, reduces to the maximum-likelihood (ML) equation,

$$\nabla_x \ln \Lambda|_{x=\hat{x}_{ML}} = 0.$$

With some manipulation, $\nabla_x \ln \Lambda$ works out to be

$$\nabla_x \ln \Lambda = \frac{2\alpha}{1 + \alpha N_0} \sum_{i=1}^{2Bt} c(k_i, s_i) \operatorname{Re}\left[s_i^* \frac{\partial s_i}{\partial x(\tau)}\right] \qquad 0 < \tau \leq t$$

where

$$_i, s_i) = \frac{1}{\alpha N_0} \frac{L^1_{k_i-1}\{-(|s_i|^2)/[N_0(1+\alpha N_0)]\}}{L_{k_i}\{-(|s_i|^2)/[N_0(1+\alpha N_0)]\}} - 1. \quad (70)$$

e problem is now simplified if we consider $x$ as a of parameters (say, $M$ of them). Then, with $x =$ $, x_2, \cdots, x_M)$, (69) reduces to the set of $M$ expressions:

$$\ln \Lambda = \frac{2\alpha}{1+\alpha N_0} \sum_{i=1}^{2Bt} c(k_i, s_i) \operatorname{Re}\left[s_i^* \frac{\partial s_i}{\partial x_k}\right]$$

$$k = 1, 2, \cdots, M. \quad (71)$$

rther simplification is possible if $s$ is a memoryless pping; thus, with $x_i = x(i/2B)$, (69) becomes

$$\ln \Lambda = \frac{2\alpha}{1+\alpha N_0} c(k_i, s_i) \operatorname{Re}\left[s_i^* \frac{\partial s_i}{\partial x_i}\right]$$

$$i = 1, 2, \cdots, 2Bt. \quad (72)$$

general, it appears that a search procedure is necessary find $\hat{x}_{MAP}$ or $\hat{x}_{ML}$.

If we now assume that the a priori density $p_{x(\tau)}[x(\tau)]$ is ussian, then (67) reduces to

$$\hat{x}(\tau) = \frac{2\alpha}{(1+\alpha N_0)} \sum_{i=1}^{2Bt} \left\{\frac{(1/\alpha N_0) L^1_{k_i-1}\{-(|s_i|^2)/[N_0(1+\alpha N_0)]\}}{L_{k_i}\{-(|s_i|^2)/[N_0(1+\alpha N_0)]\}} - 1\right\} \operatorname{Re}\left[s_i^* \frac{\partial s_i}{\partial x(\tau)}\right]\Bigg|_{x(\tau)=\hat{x}(\tau)} \qquad (0 < \tau \le t) \quad (73)$$

ich, as we can see from Fig. 1, has very limited use. wever, by making one more assumption, namely, that average noise count per degree of freedom is small:

$$\alpha N_0 \ll \min[\alpha |s_i|^2, 1] \quad (74)$$

3) reduces to

$$) \cong \sum_{i=1}^{2Bt} [k_i - \alpha |s_i|^2] \frac{\partial}{\partial x(\tau)} \ln |s_i|^2 \Bigg|_{x=\hat{x}(\tau)} \qquad 0 < \tau \le t \quad (75)$$

d is shown in Fig. 2.

Notice that the optimum MAP estimate is performed on intensity of the process. That is, $k_i$ is first compared $\alpha|s_i|^2$, the expected count of the received process. Since is the envelope of the process, it can be written as $^{s_i|}$, and $(\partial/\partial\hat{x}) \ln |s_i|$ serves the same function as $\partial\hat{x})s(t, x)$ in the MAP equations for Gaussian systems 9] p. 432).

If the intensity of the process is constant, such as FM, phase information can be obtained since $(\partial/\partial x) \ln |s_i| = 0$, king $\hat{x} = 0$. To obtain phase information from an FM a PM signal, optimal heterodyne detection must be ployed. That is, the signal from a local oscillator is gned and mixed with the received signal over the surface the detector. Then,

$$s_i = E_1 e^{j\omega_1 t + \phi(t)} + E_{L_0} e^{j\omega_2 t}$$

ere $E_1$ and $E_{L_0}$ are the two electric field strengths, and

$$^2 = |E_1|^2 + |E_{L_0}|^2 + \{E_1 E^*_{L_0} e^{[j(\omega_1-\omega_2)t+\phi]} + E_1^* E_{L_0} e^{-[j(\omega_1-\omega_2)t+\phi]}\}. \quad (76)$$

suming narrow-band signals, we have

$$|s_i|^2 \simeq |E_1|^2 + |E_{L_0}|^2 + 2E_1 E_{L_0} \cos[(\omega_1 - \omega_2)t + \phi(t)]. \quad (77)$$

By making the local oscillator signal large $|E_{L_0}| \gg |E_1|$,

$$|s_i|^2 \simeq |E_{L_0}|^2 \left\{1 + \frac{2E_1}{E_{L_0}} \cos[(\omega_1 - \omega_2)t + \phi(t)]\right\} \quad (78)$$

and

$$\ln |s_i| = \tfrac{1}{2} \ln |s_i|^2 \simeq \ln |E_{L_0}| + \frac{E_1}{E_{L_0}} \cos[(\omega_1 - \omega_2)t + \phi(t)].$$

Hence,

$$\frac{\partial}{\partial x(\tau)} \ln |s_i| \simeq -\frac{E_1}{E_{L_0}} \frac{\partial \phi}{\partial x(\tau)} \sin[(\omega_1 - \omega_2)t + \phi(t)]. \quad (79)$$

We see, then, that the optimum detector is similar, in this case, to a phase-lock loop. It can also be shown by using (26) and [18] and [26] that if we consider the random variable $k_i$ as a shot-noise process and pass it through a narrow-band filter with bandwidth $2\omega$ tuned to $(\omega_1 - \omega_2)$, the density will approach a Gaussian density with mean $2\alpha E_1 E_{L_0} \cos[(\omega_1 - \omega_2)t + \phi(t)]$ and variance $\alpha|E_{L_0}|2W$.

Using the notion of an *information kernel*, we can lower-bound the mean-square error of *any* estimator resulting from (66), without specifying the form of the estimator ([19] p. 80). Defining

$$J_D = E\left[\frac{\partial \ln \Lambda}{\partial x(u)} \frac{\partial \ln \Lambda}{\partial x(v)}\right] \quad (80)$$

$$J_P = E\left[\frac{\partial \ln p_{x(\tau)}[X(\tau)]}{\partial x(u)} \frac{\partial \ln p_{x(\tau)}[X(\tau)]}{\partial x(v)}\right] \quad (81)$$

$$J_T = J_D + J_P = \text{information kernel} \quad (82)$$

we can show that

$$\int_0^t [x(\tau) - \hat{x}(\tau)]^2 \, d\tau \ge \operatorname{Tr} J_T^{-1}. \quad (83)$$

The expectation in (80) and (81) is over the random function $x$. Combining (69) and (80), we have

$$J_D = E\left\{\frac{4\alpha^2}{(1+\alpha N_0)^2} \sum_{i=1}^{2Bt} \sum_{j=1}^{2Bt} c(k_i, s_i) \cdot c(k_j, s_j) \operatorname{Re}\left[s_i^* \frac{\partial s_i}{\partial x(u)}\right] \operatorname{Re}\left[s_j^* \frac{\partial s_j}{\partial x(v)}\right]\right\}. \quad (84)$$

To evaluate this further, the transformation $s$ must be specified.

## Conclusions

We have presented general results for the photoelectron counting distributions arising from the quantum detection of a narrow-band Gaussian process. The semiclassical approach has led to probability distributions that could

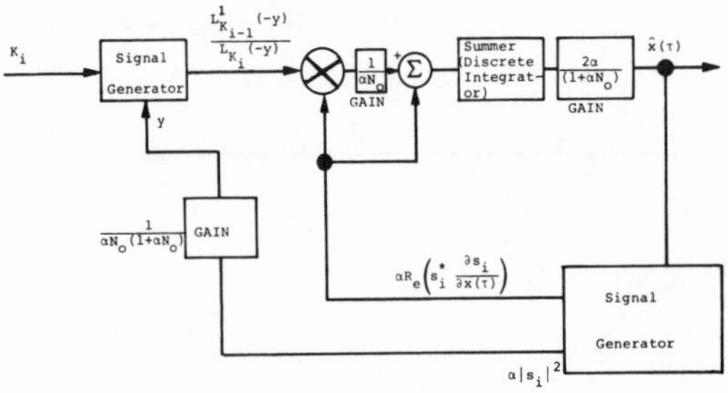


Fig. 1. Schematic of (73).

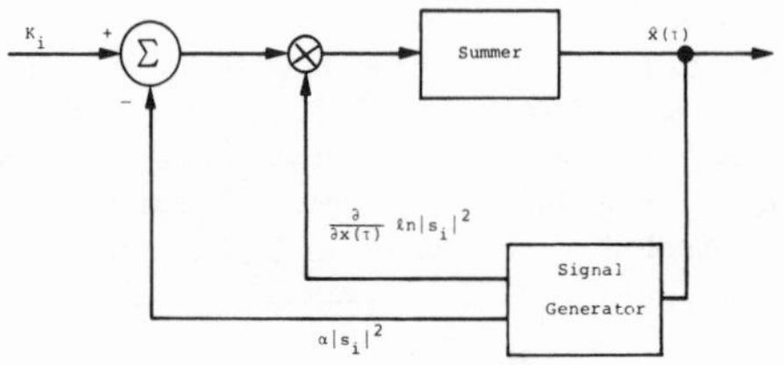


Fig. 2. Schematic of (75).

be written explicitly in terms of the covariance function of the Gaussian radiation. Four different, but equivalent, methods for evaluating the counting distribution have been presented, the last of which is valid only for white noise. These could be descriptively titled, "the eigenvalue approach," "the iterated kernel approach," "the compound Poisson approach," and "the time-sampling approach." The third method is the one in which (3) is evaluated directly. Of the four methods, the third and fourth ones lend the most physical insight, although the third method is seldom tractable, computationally. The eigenvalue approach will probably find the most use in problems of practical importance.

Several examples have been given, with special emphasis on the important case of a deterministic signal in white Gaussian noise. Some limiting forms have been derived, and rigorous justification has been given for the often-made assumption of a Poisson signal in Poisson noise. Finally, the likelihood functional has been defined, and formal answers have been found for the continuous MAP and ML estimation problems, including a simple approximation for low noise, and an expression for the minimum mean-square error of any estimator.

It should be emphasized that from a communications viewpoint, the detector senses variations in the signal modulus only; all carrier phase information is lost. This does not mean, however, that our results are applicable only to direct (or "energy") detectors. Heterodyne detection can be accomplished simply by illuminating the detector with a local oscillator field; the squared modulus then contains the *difference* frequency term and the phase information from both the local oscillator and the received field.

## Appendix

Here we mention a few of the more important statistic quantities associated with the counting distributio $p_{N_t}(k)$. First we note that the factorial moments $\{\tilde{\mu}_{[i]}\}$ the counting distribution are *equal* to the momen $\{\mu_i\}$ of $m_t$. (The tilde ($\sim$) will be used to distinguis moments, etc., of the counting distribution, from corr sponding quantities associated with $m_t$.) This is clear fro

$$\begin{aligned}\tilde{\mu}_{[n]} &= \sum_{k=n}^{\infty} k(k-1)\cdots(k-n+1)p_{N_t}(k)\\ &= (-1)^n \frac{\partial^n}{\partial \xi^n} M_{N_t}[\ln(1-\xi)]\Big|_{\xi=0}\\ &= (-1)^n \frac{\partial^n}{\partial \xi^n} M_{m_t}(-\xi)\Big|_{\xi=0}\\ &= \mu_n.\end{aligned}$$ (8

Also, the cumulants of the counting distribution a connected with the cumulants of $m_t$ by

$$\tilde{\kappa}_n = \sum_{i=1}^{n} A(n, i)\frac{\kappa_i}{i!}$$ (8

where

$$A(n, i) = \sum_{k=1}^{i} \binom{i}{k}(-1)^{i-k}k^n.$$ (8

Equation (86) is a consequence of differentiating t logarithm of

$$\begin{aligned}M_{N_t}(jv) &= M_{m_t}(e^{jv} - 1)\\ &= \exp \sum_{k=1}^{\infty} \frac{\kappa_k}{k!}(e^{jv} - 1)^k.\end{aligned}$$ (8

Similarly, it can be shown that

$$\tilde{\mu}_n = \sum_{i=1}^{n} A(n, i)\frac{\mu_i}{i!}.$$ (8

Further, the moments $\{\tilde{\mu}_i\}$ of $N_t$ are related to the cum lants $\{\tilde{\kappa}_i\}$ of $N_t$ by (35).

With the help of these formulas and known identiti [24], an exhaustive set of relations can be found for t moments, factorial moments, cumulants, and factor cumulants of $N_t$ and $m_t$. We shall not, however, reprodu these relations here.

## References

[1] L. Mandel and E. Wolf, "Letter to the editor," *Proc. Ph Soc. J. Phys.*, ser. 2, vol. 1A, pp. 625–627, 1968.
[2] R. J. Glauber, *Optical Coherence and Photon Statistics: Quant Optics and Electronics*, C. de Witt *et al.*, Eds. New Yo Gordon and Breach, 1965, pp. 65–185.
[3] G. Bédard, "Photon counting statistics of Gaussian ligh *Phys. Rev.*, vol. 151, pp. 1038–1039, November 25, 1966
[4] E. Jakeman and E. R. Pike, "The intensity-fluctuation tribution of Gaussian light," *Proc. Phys. Soc. J. Phys.*, ser. vol. 1A, pp. 128–138, 1968.
[5] L. Mandel, *Fluctuations of Light Beams, Progress in Opt II*, E. Wolf, Ed. New York: Wiley, 1963, pp. 181–248
[6] R. J. Glauber, *Photon Counting and Field Correlations: Phy*

*of Quantum Electronics*, P. L. Kelly *et al.*, Eds. New York: McGraw-Hill, 1965, pp. 788–811.

] C. W. Helstrom, "The distribution of photoelectric counts from partially polarized Gaussian light," *Proc. Phys. Soc.*, vol. 83, pp. 777–782, 1964.

] J. Peřina, "Determination of the statistical properties of light from photoelectric measurements," *Czech J. Phys.*, vol. B17, p. 1086, 1967.

] D. Middleton, *Introduction to Statistical Communication Theory.* New York: McGraw-Hill, 1960.

] R. C. Emerson, "First probability densities for receivers with square-law detectors," *J. Appl. Phys.*, vol. 24, p. 1168, 1953.

] D. Slepian, "Fluctuations of random noise power," *Bell Sys. Tech. J.*, vol. 37, pp. 163–184, 1958.

] M. Kac and A. J. F. Siegert, "On the theory of noise in radio receivers with square-law detectors," *J. Appl. Phys.*, vol. 18, p. 383, 1947.

] D. A. Darling and A. J. F. Siegert, "A systematic approach to a class of problems in the theory of noise and other random phenomena: Pt. I," *IRE Trans. Information Theory*, vol. IT-3, pp. 32–36, March 1957.

] A. J. F. Siegert, "A systematic approach to a class of problems in the theory of noise and other random phenomena: Pt. II—Examples," *IRE Trans. Information Theory*, vol. IT-3, pp. 38–43, March 1957.

] M. Ohta and T. Koizumi, "Intensity fluctuation of stationary random noise containing an arbitrary signal wave," *Proc. IEEE* (Letters), vol. 57, pp. 1231–1232, June 1969.

] W. Davenport and W. L. Root, *Introduction to Random Signals and Noise.* New York: McGraw-Hill, 1958.

] E. Parzen, *Stochastic Processes.* San Francisco, Calif.: Holden-Day, 1962.

[18] A. Papoulis, *Probability, Random Variables, and Stochastic Processes.* New York: McGraw-Hill, 1965.

[19] H. L. Van Trees, *Detection, Estimation, and Modulation Theory, Part I.* New York: Wiley, 1968.

[20] G. Lachs, "Theoretical aspects of mixtures of thermal and coherent radiation," *Phys. Rev.*, vol. 138, pp. B1012–B1016, 1965.

[21] I. S. Gradshteyn and I. M. Ryzhik, *Table of Integrals Series and Products.* New York: Academic Press, 1965.

[22] R. Deutsch, *Nonlinear Transformations of Random Processes.* Englewood Cliffs, N. J.: Prentice-Hall, 1962.

[23] R. Courant and D. Hilbert, *Methods of Mathematical Physics*, vol. 1. New York: Interscience, 1953.

[24] M. G. Kendall and A. Stuart, *The Advanced Theory of Statistics*, vol. 1. London: Griffin, 1963.

[25] J. R. Klauder and E. C. G. Sudarshan, *Fundamentals of Quantum Optics.* New York: Benjamin, 1968.

[26] S. Karp, "A statistical model for radiation with applications to optical communications," Ph.D. dissertation, Dept. of Elec. Engrg., University of Southern California, Los Angeles, 1967.

[27] J. W. S. Liu, "Reliability of quantum-mechanical communication systems," M.I.T. Research Lab. of Electron., Cambridge, Mass., Tech. Rept. 468, December 31, 1968.

[28] G. L. Fillmore and G. Lachs, "Information rates for photocount detection systems," *IEEE Trans. Information Theory*, vol. IT-15, pp. 465–468, July 1969.

[29] B. Reiffen and H. Sherman, "An optimum demodulator for Poisson processes: Photon source detectors," *Proc. IEEE*, vol. 51, pp. 1316–1320, October 1963.

[30] R. M. Gagliardi and S. Karp, "*M*-ary Poisson detection and optical communications," *IEEE Trans. Communications Technology*, vol. COM-17, pp. 208–216, April 1969.

# 13



Reprinted from *IEEE Trans. Inf. Theory* **IT-18**(1):91–102 (1972)

# Filtering and Detection for Doubly Stochastic Poisson Processes

DONALD L. SNYDER, MEMBER, IEEE

***Abstract*—Equations are derived that describe the time evolution of the posterior statistics of a general Markov process that modulates the intensity function of an observed inhomogeneous Poisson counting process. The basic equation is a stochastic differential equation for the conditional characteristic function of the Markov process.**

**A separation theorem is established for the detection of a Poisson process having a stochastic intensity function. Specifically, it is shown that the causal minimum-mean-square-error estimate of the stochastic intensity is incorporated in the optimum Reiffen–Sherman detector in the same way as if it were known.**

**Specialized results are obtained when a set of random variables modulate the intensity. These include equations for maximum *a posteriori* probability estimates of the variables and some accuracy equations based on the Cramér–Rao inequality.**

**Procedures for approximating exact estimates of the Markov process are given. A comparison by simulation of exact and approximate estimates indicates that the approximations suggested can work well even under low count rate conditions.**

## I. Introduction

THE GENERAL mathematical model we formulate in Section II is motivated by the following procedure used in medical diagnosis and research. A quantity of a radioactive labeled substance (such as oxygen, carbon dioxide, water, and hemoglobin) is introduced into an organ (such as the lung and brain) and the radioactive emissions are then monitored externally with a particle counting device [1]–[4]. The observed-particle emission rate is generally time dependent because it decreases with time as the labeled substance is removed from the organ by natural processes such as blood circulation.

At least to a first approximation, it appears reasonable to model the counter registrations as an inhomogeneous Poisson counting process with an intensity $\lambda_t(\boldsymbol{x})$ counts per second, where $\boldsymbol{x}$ represents a set of parameters describing the state of the organ. A commonly assumed form for $\lambda_t(\boldsymbol{x})$ is simply a sum of a few decaying exponentials in which the coefficients and decay constants are the elements of $\boldsymbol{x}$, but other forms have also been suggested [4], [5]. The diagnostic problem is that of estimating the parameters $\boldsymbol{x}$ from the observed counter registrations and then using these estimates with any additional clinical information that may be available to judge whether the organ is normal or abnormal. A frequently used procedure for estimating the parameters is to least-squares curve fit an assumed form for $\lambda_t(\boldsymbol{x})$ to a histogram of the counting rate. Moreover, it is often desired to estimate some funct say $\boldsymbol{h}_t(\boldsymbol{x})$, of the parameters. Some examples are: $\boldsymbol{h}_t(\boldsymbol{x})$ = as before; $\boldsymbol{h}_t(\boldsymbol{x}) = \lambda_t(\boldsymbol{x})$, the intensity; and $\boldsymbol{h}_t(\boldsymbol{x}) = \lambda_0$ $\int_0^\infty \lambda_\sigma(\boldsymbol{x})\, d\sigma$, a function used as a measure of blood [6]. In what follows, we shall offer an alternative to procedure of curve fitting to count histograms for form these estimates.

In the general mathematical model formulated bel we allow the parameters to vary stochastically with t as a vector Markov process; the case of constant parame described above is then a special, but important, subc of the model. While the applicability of the more gen model to medical problems is presently unclear, th exist such applications, one being to optical communi tions in which photon counters are used as detectors. intensity of the photon counting process varies stochastic due to two sources, one of which is message modulation the incident optical field and the other is fading of optical field introduced by turbulence and scattering in optical link [7], [8].

## II. Model Formulation and Problem Statement

### *A. Model Formulation*

Let $\{N_t, t \geq t_0\}$ be a doubly stochastic Poisson count process with a stochastic intensity function $\{\lambda_t, t \geq$ These processes were first introduced by Cox [9] and la described by Cox and Lewis [10, ch. 7]. By a dou stochastic Poisson process, we mean that $N_{t_0} = 0$ a $\{N_t, t \geq t_0\}$ is an integer-valued process with independ increments given the intensity $\{\lambda_t, t \geq t_0\}$, and a.s. $t > s \geq t_0$

$$\Pr[N_t - N_s = n \mid \lambda_\sigma, s < \sigma \leq t] = (n!)^{-1} \left( \int_s^t \lambda_\sigma \, d\sigma \right)^n \exp\left( -\int_s^t \lambda_\sigma \, d\sigma \right).$$

We assume that the following limits, which describe incremental properties of $N_t$, exist a.s.:

i) $\lim_{\Delta t \to 0} (\Delta t)^{-1} \cdot \{1 - \Pr(\Delta N_t = 0 \mid \lambda_\sigma, t < \sigma \leq t + \Delta t)\} =$

ii) $\lim_{\Delta t \to 0} (\Delta t)^{-1} \Pr(\Delta N_t = 1 \mid \lambda_\sigma, t < \sigma \leq t + \Delta t) =$

iii) $\lim_{\Delta t \to 0} \Pr(\Delta N_t = m \mid \lambda_\sigma, t < \sigma \leq t + \Delta t) = 0, \quad m >$

where $\Delta N_t = N_{t+\Delta t} - N_t$. Thus, for $\Delta t$ sufficiently sma

Manuscript received March 27, 1970; revised December 28, 1970. This work was supported by the Division of Research Resources, National Institutes of Health, under Research Grant RR 00396.

The author is with the Department of Electrical Engineering and the Biomedical Computer Laboratory, Washington University, St. Louis, Mo. 63110.

$$[\Delta N_t = i \mid \lambda_\sigma, t < \sigma \leq t + \Delta t] = (1 - \lambda_t \, \Delta t)\, \delta_{0i} + \lambda_t \, \Delta t \, \delta_{1i} + o(\Delta t), \quad (2)$$

ıere

$$\lim_{\Delta t \to 0} (\Delta t)^{-1} o(\Delta t) = 0$$

d where $\delta_{ij}$ is the Kronecker delta function.

Certain statistics of a doubly stochastic Poisson process e given by Cox and Lewis [10, ch. 7] and Bartlett [11, 325]. A useful relation can be given for the characteristic nctional of the process $\{N_t, t \geq t_0\}$ in terms of the aracteristic functional of the process $\{m_t, t \geq t_0\}$, where $= \int_{t_0}^{t} \lambda_\sigma \, d\sigma = E[N_t \mid \lambda_\sigma, t_0 < \sigma \leq t]$. Let $\phi_y(v) =$ $[\exp (j \int_{t_0}^{t} v_\sigma \, dy_\sigma)]$ denote the characteristic functional r a process $\{y_t, t \geq t_0\}$. Then $\phi_N(v) = \phi_m[j\{1 -$ p$(jv)\}]$. This relation is useful for investigating the obability density function, $r$th correlations $E[\prod_{j=1}^{r} N_{t_j}]$, d other statistics of $\{N_t, t \geq t_0\}$ when $\phi_m$ is known. amples are given by Cox and Lewis [10, p. 183] and rtlett [11, p. 325]. Karp and Clark [12] and Clark and oversten [13] have investigated the first-order statistics $\{N_t, t \geq t_0\}$ for the special, but important case in tical communications when $\lambda_t = |a_t|^2$, where $\{a_t, t \geq t_0\}$ a Gaussian process. Additional references on this case e given by Karp and Clark.

We shall assume in what follows that $\lambda_t = \lambda_t(x_t)$ for $\geq t_0$ is a positive function of an $n$-vector Markov process $, t \geq t_0\}$. For the following discussion of these processes, refer to the work of Frost [14, p. 37]. Let $c_t(v)$ be the aracteristic function for $x_t$ at time $t$,

$$c_t(v) = E\{\exp [j\langle v, x_t \rangle]\}, \quad (3)$$

ere $\langle \cdot , \cdot \rangle$ denotes vector inner (dot) product. Assume that

$$(\Delta t)^{-1} |E\{(\exp [j\langle v, \Delta x_t \rangle] - 1) \mid x_t\}| \leq g(v; t, x_t) \quad \text{a.s.}$$

ere $\Delta x_t = x_{t+\Delta t} - x_t$ and $E[|g|] < \infty$; and

$$p \lim_{\Delta t \to 0} (\Delta t)^{-1} E\{(\exp [j\langle v, \Delta x_t \rangle] - 1) \mid x_t\} \triangleq \psi_t(v \mid x_t)$$

ists.

The function $\psi_t(v \mid x_t)$ in b) is the characteristic form of differential generator for $x_t$. From these assumptions, an be shown that the time evolution of the unconditional aracteristic function for $x_t$ is described by

$$(\partial/\partial t) c_t(v) = E\{\exp [j\langle v, x_t \rangle] \psi_t(v \mid x_t)\}$$

$$c_{t_0}(v) = E\{\exp [j\langle v, x_{t_0} \rangle]\}. \quad (4)$$

e proof is straightforward; because we need a similar oof later, we include it here. Still following Frost (also Bartlett [11, p. 87]), we have the proof:

$$\begin{aligned} c_{t+\Delta t}(v) &= E\{\exp [j\langle v, x_{t+\Delta t} \rangle]\} \\ &= E\{\exp [j\langle v, x_t \rangle] \exp [j\langle v, \Delta x_t \rangle]\} \\ &= E\{\exp [j\langle v, x_t \rangle] E\{\exp [j\langle v, \Delta x_t \rangle] \mid x_t\}\}, \end{aligned}$$

ere the last equality follows from the definition of conditional expectation. Thus,

$$\begin{aligned} (\Delta t)^{-1} \Delta c_t(v) &= (\Delta t)^{-1} [c_{t+\Delta t}(v) - c_t(v)] \\ &= E\{\exp [j\langle v, x_t \rangle] (\Delta t)^{-1} \\ &\quad \cdot E\{(\exp [j\langle v, \Delta x_t \rangle] - 1) \mid x_t\}\}. \end{aligned}$$

Taking the limit as $\Delta t \to 0$ results in the desired expression. The interchange of limit and expectation is justified by assumption a) and Lebesgue's bounded convergence theorem [15, p. 110].

It is of interest to consider the case when $\{x_t, t \geq t_0\}$ has a well-defined representation as the solution to a stochastic differential equation of the form

$$dx_t = f_t(x_t)\, dt + G_t(x_t)\, d\chi_t$$

$$x_{t_0} = x_0, \quad (5)$$

where $\{\chi_t, t \geq t_0\}$ is a martingale with independent infinitely divisible increments. Three examples of the type of modulation process $\{x_t, t \geq t_0\}$ included are as follows.

1) Let $f_t(x_t) = \mathbf{0}$ and $G_t(x_t) = \mathbf{0}$. Then $x_t = x_0$ is simply a collection of *random variables* for all $t \geq t_0$. It is easily seen that $\psi_t(v \mid x_t) = 0$ in this case. Substitution of this expression into (4) and then inverse Fourier transforming shows the obvious fact that $p_t(x_t) = p(x_0)$, the probability density for $x_0$, for all $t \geq t_0$.

2) Let $\chi_t$ be a standardized vector Wiener process. Then for appropriate restrictions on $f_t$ and $G_t$, $x_t$ is a Markov diffusion process. If $f_t$ is linear in $x_t$ and $G_t$ does not depend on $x_t$, then $x_t$ is a Gauss–Markov diffusion process. The characteristic form for the differential generator of $x_t$ in this case is given by

$$\psi_t(v \mid x_t) = j\langle v, f_t(x_t) \rangle - \tfrac{1}{2}\langle v, G_t(x_t) G_t'(x_t) v \rangle. \quad (6)$$

Substitution of this expression into (4) and then inverse Fourier transforming results in the forward Kolmogorov Fokker–Planck equation for the probability density $p_t(x_t)$ of $x_t$.

3) Let $\chi_t = \tilde{\chi}_t - E(\tilde{\chi}_t)$, where $\tilde{\chi}_t$ is an $m$-vector of independent Poisson counting processes with intensities $\mu_1, \mu_2, \cdots, \mu_m$ and assume $G_t$ is not a function of $x_t$. Then for appropriate restrictions on $f_t$, $x_t$ is a "Poisson driven" Markov process [16]. The characteristic form for the differential generator of $x_t$ in this case is given by

$$\psi_t(v \mid x_t) = j\langle v, f_t(x_t) \rangle + \sum_{i=1}^{m} \mu_i (\exp [j\langle v, G_t e_i \rangle] - 1),$$

where $e_i$ is an $m$-vector with a 1 in row $i$ and 0's elsewhere. Substitution of this expression into (4) and then inverse Fourier transforming results in the following equation for the probability density $p_t(x_t)$ of $x_t$:

$$(\partial/\partial t) p_t(x_t) = -\langle \partial/\partial x_t, f_t(x_t) p_t(x_t) \rangle + \sum_{i=1}^{m} \mu_i [p_t(x_t - G_t e_i) - p_t(x_t)],$$

where $\partial/\partial x_t$ denotes the gradient operator.

## B. Problem Statement

We consider the problem of causally estimating $\boldsymbol{h}_t = \boldsymbol{h}_t(\boldsymbol{x}_t)$, a given vector-valued function of $t$ and $\boldsymbol{x}_t$, from observations of the counting process on the interval $(t_0,t]$. Let $N_{t_0,t} = \{N_\sigma, t_0 < \sigma \leq t\}$ be the record of the observed counting process. Then the solution to this estimation problem depends on knowing the posterior density $p_t(\boldsymbol{x}_t \mid N_{t_0,t})$ of $\boldsymbol{x}_t$. For instance, the minimum-mean-square error (MMSE) and maximum *a posteriori* probability (MAP) estimates of $\boldsymbol{h}_t$ can be determined when this density is known. We therefore concentrate on the basic problem of describing the time evolution of $p_t(\boldsymbol{x}_t \mid N_{t_0,t})$ as additional observations are accumulated.

## III. The Evolution of the Posterior Statistics

Let $c_{t|t_0}(\boldsymbol{v} \mid N_{t_0,t})$ be the characteristic function for $\boldsymbol{x}_t$ given $N_{t_0,t}$,

$$c_{t|t_0}(\boldsymbol{v} \mid N_{t_0,t}) = E\{\exp[j\langle \boldsymbol{v},\boldsymbol{x}_t\rangle] \mid N_{t_0,t}\}. \tag{7}$$

Assume that

a) $(\Delta t)^{-1}|E\{(\exp[j\langle \boldsymbol{v},\Delta\boldsymbol{x}_t\rangle] - 1) \mid N_{t_0,t},\boldsymbol{x}_t\}| \leq g(\boldsymbol{v};t,N_{t_0,t},\boldsymbol{x}_t)$,

where $E[|g|] < \infty$; and

b) $p \lim_{\Delta t \to 0} (\Delta t)^{-1}E\{(\exp[j\langle \boldsymbol{v},\Delta\boldsymbol{x}_t\rangle] - 1) \mid N_{t_0,t},\boldsymbol{x}_t\} = \psi_t(\boldsymbol{v} \mid N_{t_0,t},\boldsymbol{x}_t)$

exists.

It then follows that the time evolution of the conditional characteristic function for $\boldsymbol{x}_t$ is described by the stochastic differential equation:

$$\begin{aligned} dc_{t|t_0}(\boldsymbol{v} \mid N_{t_0,t}) &= E\{\exp[j\langle \boldsymbol{v},\boldsymbol{x}_t\rangle]\psi_t(\boldsymbol{v}|N_{t_0,t},\boldsymbol{x}_t)|N_{t_0,t}\}\, dt \\ &\quad + E\{\exp[j\langle \boldsymbol{v},\boldsymbol{x}_t\rangle](\lambda_t(\boldsymbol{x}_t) - \hat{\lambda}_t) \mid N_{t_0,t}\} \\ &\quad \cdot \hat{\lambda}_t^{-1}(dN_t - \hat{\lambda}_t\, dt) \\ c_{t_0|t_0}(\boldsymbol{v} \mid N_{t_0,t_0}) &= E\{\exp[j\langle \boldsymbol{v},\boldsymbol{x}_{t_0}\rangle]\}, \end{aligned} \tag{8}$$

where $\hat{\lambda}_t \triangleq E[\lambda_t(\boldsymbol{x}_t) \mid N_{t_0,t}]$ is the causal MMSE estimate of the intensity $\lambda_t(\boldsymbol{x}_t)$ given $N_{t_0,t}$.

Before proving (8), let us interpret it briefly in terms of previous results. Suppose $\{\boldsymbol{x}_t, t \geq t_0\}$ is a solution to the stochastic differential equation in (5) and that $\{\boldsymbol{\chi}_t, t \geq t_0\}$ is a standard vector Wiener process that is independent of the past of the counting process $N_t$. It then follows that

$$\psi_t(\boldsymbol{v} \mid N_{t_0,t},\boldsymbol{x}_t) = j\langle \boldsymbol{v},\boldsymbol{f}_t(\boldsymbol{x}_t)\rangle - \tfrac{1}{2}\langle \boldsymbol{v},\boldsymbol{G}_t(\boldsymbol{x}_t)\boldsymbol{G}_t'(\boldsymbol{x}_t)\boldsymbol{v}\rangle.$$

Using this expression in (8) and inverse Fourier transforming then results in the following stochastic differential equation for the posterior probability density of $\boldsymbol{x}_t$:

$$\begin{aligned} dp_t(\boldsymbol{x}_t \mid N_{t_0,t}) &= L[p_t(\boldsymbol{x}_t \mid N_{t_0,t})]\, dt \\ &\quad + p_t(\boldsymbol{x}_t \mid N_{t_0,t})\{\lambda_t(\boldsymbol{x}_t) - \hat{\lambda}_t\} \\ &\quad \cdot \hat{\lambda}_t^{-1}\{dN_t - \hat{\lambda}_t\, dt\} \\ p_{t_0}(\boldsymbol{x}_{t_0} \mid N_{t_0,t_0}) &= p(\boldsymbol{x}_0), \end{aligned} \tag{9}$$

where $L[\cdot]$ is the forward Kolmogorov differential operator for the diffusion process $\boldsymbol{x}_t$. It is by now well known tha rather than the counting process $N_t$, the observations $\lambda_t(\boldsymbol{x}_t)$ were of the additive form $dy_t = \lambda_t(\boldsymbol{x}_t)\, dt + \epsilon$ where $w_t$ is an independent Wiener process with param $W$, then the last term on the right in (9) is $p_t(\boldsymbol{x}_t \mid y_{t_0}$ $\{\lambda_t(\boldsymbol{x}_t) - \hat{\lambda}_t\}W^{-1}\{dy_t - \hat{\lambda}_t\, dt\}$. The similarity betw the two expressions is striking in view of the nonaddi way in which $\lambda_t(\boldsymbol{x}_t)$ enters the statistics of $N_t$.

*Proof of (8)*: Let $B_{t_0}{}^s$ be the minimal $\sigma$-field induced $N_{t_0,s} = \{N_\alpha, t_0 < \alpha \leq s\}$. The conditional characteri function of $\boldsymbol{x}_s$ given $B_{t_0}{}^t$ is then

$$c_{s|t_0}(\boldsymbol{v} \mid B_{t_0}{}^s) = E[\exp(j\langle \boldsymbol{v},\boldsymbol{x}_t\rangle) \mid B_{t_0}{}^s].$$

Partition the interval $(t_0, t + \Delta t]$ into $(t_0,t]$ and $t + \Delta t]$, and let $B_{t_0}{}^t \otimes B(\Delta N_t)$ denote the minimal $\sigma$-fi induced by $N_{t_0,t}$ and the increment $\Delta N_t = N_{t+\Delta t} - N_t$.

Now examine the characteristic function for $\boldsymbol{x}_{t+\Delta t}$ gi $B_{t_0}^{t+\Delta t}$, which is given by

$$\begin{aligned} c_{t+\Delta t|t_0}(\boldsymbol{v} \mid B_{t_0}^{t+\Delta t}) &= E[\exp(j\langle \boldsymbol{v},\boldsymbol{x}_t\rangle)\exp(j\langle \boldsymbol{v},\Delta\boldsymbol{x}_t\rangle) \mid B_{t_0}^{t+\Delta t}] \\ &= \int_{R^{2n}} \exp(j\langle \boldsymbol{v},\boldsymbol{X}\rangle)\exp(j\langle \boldsymbol{v},\boldsymbol{Y}\rangle)\, d^{2n}P(\boldsymbol{X},\boldsymbol{Y} \mid B_{t_0}^{t+} \end{aligned}$$

where $\Delta\boldsymbol{x}_t = \boldsymbol{x}_{t+\Delta t} - \boldsymbol{x}_t$ and $P(\boldsymbol{X},\boldsymbol{Y} \mid B_{t_0}^{t+\Delta t})$ is the jc conditional probability distribution function of $\boldsymbol{x}_t$ $\Delta\boldsymbol{x}_t$ given $B_{t_0}^{t+\Delta t}$.

To evaluate $c_{t+\Delta t|t_0}$, let us define

$$\begin{aligned} c^{\Delta}_{t+\Delta t|t_0}[\boldsymbol{v} \mid B_{t_0}{}^t \otimes B(\Delta N_t)] &= \int_{R^{2n}} \exp(j\langle \boldsymbol{v},\boldsymbol{X}\rangle) \\ &\quad \cdot \exp(j\langle \boldsymbol{v},\boldsymbol{Y}\rangle)\, d^{2n}P[\boldsymbol{X},\boldsymbol{Y} \mid B_{t_0}{}^t \otimes B(\Delta N \end{aligned}$$

Then

$$c^{\Delta}_{t+\Delta t|t_0} \xrightarrow{\text{a.s.}} c_{t+\Delta t|t_0} \text{ as } t \to t + \Delta t$$

because $B_{t_0}{}^t \otimes B(\Delta N_t) \uparrow B_{t_0}^{t+\Delta t}$ and, consequently,

$$P(\boldsymbol{X},\boldsymbol{Y} \mid B_{t_0}{}^t \otimes B(\Delta N_t)) \xrightarrow{\text{a.s.}} P(\boldsymbol{X},\boldsymbol{Y} \mid B_{t_0}^{t+\Delta t}) \quad \text{as } t \to t +$$

by the martingale convergence theorem (Feller [17, p. 23 We evaluate $c^{\Delta}_{t+\Delta t|t_0}$ for fixed $\Delta N_t$; namely, for $\Delta N_t =$ $\Delta N_t = 1$, and $\Delta N_t = m$ where $m > 1$. For $\Delta N_t = 0$, have

$$\begin{aligned} c^{\Delta}_{t+\Delta t|t_0}(\boldsymbol{v} \mid B_{t_0}{}^t \otimes B(0)) &= \int_{R^{2n}} \exp(j\langle \boldsymbol{v},\boldsymbol{X}\rangle) \\ &\quad \cdot \exp(j\langle \boldsymbol{v},\boldsymbol{Y}\rangle)\, d^{2n}P(\boldsymbol{X},\boldsymbol{Y} \mid B_{t_0}{}^t \otimes B \end{aligned}$$

The finite difference

$$\begin{aligned} &\delta^{2n}P(\boldsymbol{X},\boldsymbol{Y} \mid B_{t_0}{}^t \otimes B(0)) \\ &= \Pr[\boldsymbol{x}_t \in (\boldsymbol{X} - \delta\boldsymbol{X},\boldsymbol{X}], \Delta\boldsymbol{x}_t \in (\boldsymbol{Y} - \Delta\boldsymbol{Y},\boldsymbol{Y}] \mid B_{t_0}{}^t \otimes B \end{aligned}$$

n be evaluated as

$$\cdot P(X,Y \mid B_{t_0}' \otimes B(0)) =$$

$$\text{Pr}\,[\Delta N_t = 0 \mid x_t \in (X - \delta X, X], \Delta x_t \in (Y - \delta Y, Y], B_{t_0}'] \times \delta^{2n} P(X,Y \mid B_{t_0}')/\text{Pr}\,[\Delta N_t = 0 \mid B_{t_0}'],$$

here as $\delta X \to \mathbf{0}$ and $\delta Y \to \mathbf{0}$

$$[\Delta N_t = 0 \mid x_t \in (X - \delta X, X], \Delta x_t \in (Y - \delta Y, Y], B_{t_0}'] = 1 - \lambda_t(X)\,\Delta t + o(\Delta t)$$

d where

$$[\Delta N_t = 0 \mid B_{t_0}'] = E\{\text{Pr}\,[\Delta N_t = 0 \mid x_t, B_{t_0}'] \mid B_{t_0}'\} = 1 - \hat{\lambda}_t\,\Delta t + o(\Delta t),$$

here $\hat{\lambda}_t = E[\lambda_t(x_t) \mid B_{t_0}']$. Putting these results together, obtain

$$_{+\Delta t|t_0}[v \mid B_{t_0}' \otimes B(0)] = E\{\exp(j\langle v,x_t\rangle)\exp(j\langle v,\Delta x_t\rangle)[1 - \lambda_t(x_t)\,\Delta t] \mid B_{t_0}'\} \cdot (1 - \hat{\lambda}_t\,\Delta t)^{-1} + o(\Delta t)$$
$$= E\{\exp(j\langle v,x_t\rangle)\exp(j\langle v,\Delta x_t\rangle) \cdot [1 - \lambda_t(x_t)\Delta t + \hat{\lambda}_t\,\Delta t] \mid B_{t_0}'\} + o(\Delta t).$$

milarly, by using the same procedure, we obtain

$$_{+\Delta t|t_0}[v \mid B_{t_0}' \otimes B(1)] = E[\exp(j\langle v,x_t\rangle)\exp(j\langle v,\Delta x_t\rangle)\lambda_t(x_t) \mid B_{t_0}']\hat{\lambda}_t^{-1} + o(\Delta t)$$

d

$$c^{\Delta}_{t+\Delta t|t_0}[v \mid B_{t_0}' \otimes B(m)] = o(\Delta t), \qquad m > 1.$$

follows that for $\Delta N_t$ variable, we have

$$_{+\Delta t|t_0}[v \mid B_{t_0}' \otimes B(\Delta N_t)] = E[\exp(j\langle v,x_t\rangle)\exp(j\langle v,\Delta x_t\rangle) \cdot [1 - \lambda_t(x_t)\,\Delta t + \hat{\lambda}_t\,\Delta t] \mid B_{t_0}']\delta_{0,\Delta N_t}$$
$$+ E[\exp(j\langle v,x_t\rangle)\exp(j\langle v,\Delta x_t\rangle)\lambda_t(x_t) \mid B_{t_0}'] \cdot \hat{\lambda}_t^{-1}\,\delta_{1,\Delta N_t} + o(\Delta t).$$

ecause

$$\delta_{0,\Delta N_t} \xrightarrow{\text{a.s.}} 1 - \Delta N_t \qquad \text{and} \qquad \delta_{1,\Delta N_t} \xrightarrow{\text{a.s.}} \Delta N_t \qquad \text{as } t \to t + \Delta t,$$

e can write

$$_{+\Delta t|t_0}[v \mid B_{t_0}' \otimes B(\Delta N_t)] = E[\exp(j\langle v,x_t\rangle)\exp(j\langle v,\Delta x_t\rangle) \mid B_{t_0}']$$
$$+ E[\exp(j\langle v,x_t\rangle)\exp(j\langle v,\Delta x_t\rangle)[\lambda_t(x_t) - \hat{\lambda}_t] \mid B_{t_0}'] \cdot \hat{\lambda}_t^{-1}(\Delta N_t - \hat{\lambda}_t\,\Delta t) + o(\Delta t).$$

y subtracting the characteristic function for $x_t$ given $B_{t_0}'$, we establish the desired theorem as follows:

$$dc_{t|t_0}(v \mid B_{t_0}')$$
$$= \lim_{\Delta t \to 0} [c_{t+\Delta t|t_0}(v \mid B_{t_0}^{t+\Delta t}) - c_{t|t_0}(v \mid B_{t_0}')]$$
$$= \lim_{\Delta t \to 0} [c^{\Delta}_{t+\Delta t|t_0}(v \mid B_{t_0}' \otimes B(\Delta N_t) - c_{t|t_0}(v \mid B_{t_0}')]$$
$$= E[\exp(j\langle v,x_t\rangle)\psi_t(v \mid B_{t_0}', x_t) \mid B_{t_0}']\,dt$$
$$+ E\{\exp(j\langle v,x_t\rangle)[\lambda_t(x_t) - \hat{\lambda}_t] \mid B_{t_0}'\}\hat{\lambda}_t^{-1}(dN_t - \hat{\lambda}_t\,dt),$$

where the interchange of limit and expectation for the first term in the last equality is justified by assumption a) and the bounded convergence theorem.

Equation (8) is our basic result. The procedure for implementing an estimate of some specified function $h_t(x_t)$ of $x_t$ is clearly very complicated in general. First it is necessary to solve (8) for $c_{t|t_0}(v \mid N_{t_0,t})$; then this characteristic function must be inverse Fourier transformed to determine $p_t(x_t \mid N_{t_0,t})$, and finally the estimate must be determined from this probability density. These steps are generally analytically intractable, so that numerical techniques will be required as discussed in Sections V and VI.

## IV. Application to Detection

The detection model we consider in this section is motivated by an optical communication or radar system in which the optimum detector is placed at the output of an ideal photon-electron converter. The model is a generalization of the one first considered by Reiffen and Sherman [18], and we assume a familiarity with their formulation and results.

The generalization we include is to allow the intensity $\lambda_t$ to be stochastic rather than deterministic as assumed by Reiffen and Sherman. The motivation is to account in the model for stochastic effects introduced in the optical channel between the photon source and the photon converter. These arise, for instance, from atmospheric turbulence, target scintillation, and the use of an incoherent modulation.

Our results are similar in spirit to those obtained by Duncan [19] and Kailath [20] for the optimum detection of stochastic signals in additive white Gaussian noise. They obtained the interesting and fundamental result that the causal MMSE estimate of the stochastic signal should be incorporated in the optimum detector in exactly the same way as if the signal were known. The result we obtain is that the causal MMSE estimate of the intensity function of the Poisson process should be incorporated in the optimal detector in exactly the same way as if the function itself were known. This is surprising in view of the nonadditive way the intensity function affects the statistics of the Poisson process. The fact that the estimate is causal is important because it means that the detector can be updated continuously in time as the Poisson process is observed.

In this section, we shall use (8) to derive an equation for the log-likelihood ratio, which defines the optimum detector.

### A. Model Formulation and Problem Statement for Detection

Let $\{N_t, t \geq t_0\}$ be a doubly stochastic Poisson process with either a known positive constant intensity $\lambda_0$ or a time-varying stochastic intensity $\lambda_0 + \lambda_t$. $\lambda_0$ represents the rate of arrival of photons from background radiation and $\{\lambda_t, t \geq t_0\}$ represents the stochastic rate of arrival of photons from the source. Thus we can write the intensity of $N_t$ as $\lambda_0 + \alpha\lambda_t$, where $\alpha$ is a discrete random variable that is 1 or 0. Let the prior probabilities of $\alpha$ be $P_1 = \Pr[\alpha = 1]$ and $P_0 = 1 - P_1 = \Pr[\alpha = 0]$. We assume as before that $\lambda_t = \lambda_t(\boldsymbol{x}_t)$ is a positive function of a general vector Markov process $\{\boldsymbol{x}_t, t \geq t_0\}$.

The problem we wish to consider is that of defining the optimum detector for deciding whether the random variable $\alpha$ is 0 or 1 given a record $N_{t_0,t} = \{N_\sigma, t_0 < \sigma \leq t\}$ of the Poisson counting process having an intensity $\lambda_0 + \alpha\lambda_t(\boldsymbol{x}_t)$.

### B. The Optimum Detector

Let $l_t$ be the log-likelihood ratio defined by $l_t = \ln[p/(1-p)]$, where for notational convenience we define

$$p \triangleq \Pr(\alpha = 1 \mid N_{t_0,t})$$

as the posterior probability that $\alpha = 1$. It is well known that the optimum detector first computes $l_t$ from the observations and then compares the computed value to a preset decision level that depends on the criterion of performance, costs, etc. The result we wish to establish is that $l_t$ is given for $t \geq t_0$ by

$$l_t = l_{t_0} - \int_{t_0}^{t} \hat{\lambda}_\sigma \, d\sigma + \int_{t_0}^{t} \ln[\lambda_0^{-1}(\lambda_0 + \hat{\lambda}_\sigma)] \, dN_\sigma, \quad (10)$$

where $l_{t_0}$ depends on the prior probabilities of $\alpha$ according to $l_{t_0} = \ln(P_1/P_0)$. In this equation, $\hat{\lambda}_t$ is a causal functional of the observed data defined by $E[\lambda_t \mid N_{t_0,t}, \alpha = 1]$. Thus, if $\alpha = 1$, the functional $\hat{\lambda}_t$ is the MMSE estimate of $\lambda_t$ given the record $N_{t_0,t}$. However, if $\alpha = 0$, $\hat{\lambda}_t$ does not have an interpretation as an estimate.

The interpretation of (10) in terms of previous results is interesting. If (10) is compared to the log-likelihood ratio obtained by Reiffen and Sherman [18, eq. (14)], it is seen that $\hat{\lambda}_t$ simply replaces their known intensity function. This interpretation has practical implications because it suggests a structure for suboptimal detectors when $\hat{\lambda}_t$ is unknown or too complicated for practical realization. Namely, there is still a strong motivation to incorporate a suboptimal estimate directly in the Reiffen–Sherman detector.

The log-likelihood ratio for other detection problems that may be of interest can be obtained from (10) using the chain rule for likelihood ratios, as discussed by Kailath [20]. For instance, the optimum detector for the following two problems can be obtained easily this way:

i) $\lambda_t^{(0)}(\boldsymbol{x}_t) + \lambda_0$ versus $\lambda_t^{(1)}(\boldsymbol{x}_t) + \lambda_0$

and

ii) $s_t + \lambda_t(\boldsymbol{x}_t) + \lambda_0$ versus $\lambda_t(\boldsymbol{x}_t) + \lambda_0$,

where $s_t$ is a known intensity function. The first probler that of deciding which of two stochastic intensities is pres in $\{N_t, t \geq t_0\}$. The second problem is that of detecti a known signal in a stochastic background radiation.

We use the result in (8) for the derivation of (10). T intensity of $\{N_t, t \geq t_0\}$ is $\lambda_0 + \alpha\lambda_t(\boldsymbol{x}_t)$, where $\alpha$ is discrete random variable, 0 or 1, and $\boldsymbol{x}_t$ is a vector-valu Markov process. As the collection $(\alpha,\boldsymbol{x}_t)$ is also a vect valued Markov process, the general results in (8) can used to describe the time evolution of the statistics $(\alpha,\boldsymbol{x}_t)$ given $N_{t_0,t}$. Let the conditional characteristic functi for $(\alpha,\boldsymbol{x}_t)$ be defined by

$$c_t(u,\boldsymbol{v} \mid N_{t_0,t}) = E\{\exp(ju\alpha)\exp[j\langle \boldsymbol{v},\boldsymbol{x}_t\rangle] \mid N_{t_0,t}\}.$$

Then from (8) $c_t$ satisfies the stochastic differential equati

$$\begin{aligned} dc_t(u,\boldsymbol{v} \mid N_{t_0,t}) &= E\{\exp(ju\alpha)\exp[j\langle \boldsymbol{v},\boldsymbol{x}_t\rangle]\psi(u,\boldsymbol{v} \mid N_{t_0,t},\alpha,\boldsymbol{x}_t) \mid N_{t_0,t}\} \\ &\quad + E\{\exp(ju\alpha)\exp[j\langle \boldsymbol{v},\boldsymbol{x}_t\rangle](\lambda_0 + \lambda_t(\boldsymbol{x}_t) \\ &\quad - e_t) \mid N_{t_0,t}\} e_t^{-1}(dN_t - e_t\,dt), \end{aligned} \quad (11)$$

where $e_t$ is the estimate defined by

$$e_t = E[\lambda_0 + \alpha\lambda_t(\boldsymbol{x}_t) \mid N_{t_0,t}]$$

and where $\psi_t$ is defined by

$$\begin{aligned} \psi_t(u,\boldsymbol{v} \mid N_{t_0,t},\alpha,\boldsymbol{x}_t) &= p \lim_{\Delta t \to 0} (\Delta t)^{-1} \\ &\quad \cdot E\{(\exp(ju\,\Delta\alpha)\exp[j\langle \boldsymbol{v},\Delta\boldsymbol{x}_t\rangle] - 1) \mid N_{t_0,t},\alpha,\boldsymbol{x} \end{aligned}$$

Let $\hat{\lambda}_t = E[\lambda_t \mid N_{t_0,t}, \alpha = 1]$. Then, since $\alpha$ is 1 or 0, follows that $e_t = \lambda_0 + p\hat{\lambda}_t$. Noting that $\Delta\alpha = 0$ a setting $\boldsymbol{v} = \boldsymbol{0}$ in (11), we obtain

$$\begin{aligned} dc_t(u,\boldsymbol{0} \mid N_{t_0,t}) &= E\{\exp(ju\alpha)(\alpha\lambda_t - p\hat{\lambda}_t) \mid N_{t_0,t}\}(\lambda_0 + p\hat{\lambda}_t)^{-1} \\ &\quad \cdot (dN_t - (\lambda_0 + p\hat{\lambda}_t)\,d \\ &= \exp(ju)\{p(1-p)\hat{\lambda}_t(\lambda_0 + p\hat{\lambda}_t)^{-1}(dN_t - (\lambda_0 + p\hat{\lambda}_t)\,dt \\ &\quad - \{(1-p)p\hat{\lambda}_t(\lambda_0 + p\hat{\lambda}_t)^{-1}(dN_t - (\lambda_0 + p\hat{\lambda}_t)\,dt)\}. \end{aligned}$$

Upon inverse Fourier transforming, it follows that satisfies the following stochastic differential equation:

$$dp = -p(1-p)\hat{\lambda}_t\,dt + p(1-p)\hat{\lambda}_t(\lambda_0 + p\hat{\lambda}_t)^{-1}\,dN_t. \quad (1$$

The log-likelihood ratio is defined by $l_t = \ln[p/(1-p)]$. Consequently, to establish (10), we need a stochast differential rule relating the differential of $p$ to the differenti of a function $l_t = l_t(p)$ of $p$. Such a rule is given formally the following lemma.

*Lemma:* Let $\zeta_t$ satisfy $d\zeta_t = \alpha_t\,dt + \beta_t\,dN_t$, where is the jump process defined above. Let $\phi = \phi(\zeta)$ be ntinuously differentiable scalar function of $\zeta$ with rivative $\phi_\zeta = d\phi/d\zeta$. Then

$$d\phi(\zeta_t) = \phi_\zeta(\zeta_t)\alpha_t\, dt + [\phi(\zeta_t + \beta_t) - \phi(\zeta_t)]\, dN_t. \tag{13}$$

*Proof:* This is a special case of the generalized Ito fferential rule established by Kunita and Watanabe 1, theorem 5.1]. The following argument motivates the sult. For $\Delta t$ sufficiently small, $\Delta\zeta_t = \alpha_t\,\Delta t$ or $\Delta\zeta_t =$ $\Delta t + \beta_t$ because $\Delta N_t$ is 0 or 1. Thus, $\Delta\phi(\zeta_t) = \phi(\zeta_{t+\Delta t}) -$ $\zeta_t)$ can be written as

$$\phi(\zeta_t) = [\phi(\zeta_t + \alpha_t\,\Delta t) - \phi(\zeta_t)](1 - \Delta N_t) + [\phi(\zeta_t + \alpha_t\,\Delta t + \beta_t) - \phi(\zeta_t)]\,\Delta N_t + o(\Delta t).$$

bserve that $\phi(\zeta_t + \alpha_t\,\Delta t) - \phi(\zeta_t) \rightarrow \phi_\zeta(\zeta_t)\alpha_t\,\Delta t + o(\Delta t)$ ad

$$(\zeta_t + \alpha_t\,\Delta t + \beta_t) - \phi(\zeta_t) \rightarrow \phi(\zeta_t + \beta_t) - \phi(\zeta_t) + 0(\Delta t) \qquad \text{as } \Delta t \rightarrow 0.$$

onsequently, for $\Delta t$ sufficiently small

$$\phi(\zeta_t) = \phi_\zeta(\zeta_t)\alpha_t\,\Delta t(1 - \Delta N_t) + [\phi(\zeta_t + \beta_t) - \phi(\zeta_t)]\,\Delta N_t + o(\Delta t).$$

aking the limit as $\Delta t \rightarrow 0$ results in (13).

Now make the following identifications in the lemma: $= p$, $\alpha_t = -p(1-p)\hat{\lambda}_t$, $\beta_t = p(1-p)\hat{\lambda}_t(\lambda_0 + p\hat{\lambda}_t)^{-1}$, d $\phi_t = l_t = \ln[p/(1-p)]$. It is easy to verify that (13) en becomes

$$dl_t = -\hat{\lambda}_t\, dt + \ln[\lambda_0^{-1}(\lambda_0 + \hat{\lambda}_t)]\, dN_t.$$

ith the obvious initial condition $l_{t_0} = \ln[P_1/(1 - P_1)]$, is stochastic differential equation implies (10), which was be established.

## V. Constant Parameters

An important special case of the model obtains when $= \boldsymbol{x}$ for $t \geq t_0$, where $\boldsymbol{x}$ is a vector of random variables. e wish to indicate briefly some results that apply for this tuation. Let $p_0(\boldsymbol{x})$ be the prior probability density for $\boldsymbol{x}$ d $p_t(\boldsymbol{x} \mid N_{t_0,t})$ the posterior density given $\{N_\sigma, t_0 < \sigma \leq t\}$. hen (9) becomes

$$p_t(\boldsymbol{x} \mid N_{t_0,t}) = p_t(\boldsymbol{x} \mid N_{t_0,t})\{\lambda_t(\boldsymbol{x}) - \hat{\lambda}_t\}\hat{\lambda}_t^{-1}\{dN_t - \hat{\lambda}_t\, dt\}$$

$$_0(\boldsymbol{x} \mid N_{t_0,t_0}) = p_0(\boldsymbol{x}), \tag{14}$$

here $\hat{\lambda}_t = E[\lambda_t(\boldsymbol{x}) \mid N_{t_0,t}]$ in the causal MMSE estimate $\lambda_t(\boldsymbol{x})$ given $\{N_\sigma, t_0 < \sigma \leq t\}$. This equation is a non-near integral-differential equation for the posterior ensity because $\hat{\lambda}_t$ requires an integration with respect to $(\boldsymbol{x} \mid N_{t_0,t})$. In the following paragraphs, we discuss some oplications of this equation.

### . *Numerical Solutions*

Equation (14) is analytically intractible for most intensity nctions $\lambda_t(\boldsymbol{x})$ so that numerical solutions are required. However, the equation is well suited for this because of its recursive form. We have been exploring the technique of replacing (14) by a finite difference equation, which is then used as a numerical algorithm for updating the posterior density as data arrives. Desired estimates are obtained by numerical integration with respect to the generated density. Some preliminary simulation results are given in Figs. 1 and 2. Note that no approximations are being made here beyond those required for digital computations.

The results in Fig. 1 were obtained by assuming that $\lambda_t(x) = x$, where $x$ had a uniform prior probability density between 1.0 and 2.0. The value of $x$ used in the simulation was selected at random with a random number generator. The numerically generated time evolution for $p_t(x \mid N_{t_0,t})$ is shown as well as for the MMSE estimate of $\lambda_t(x) = x$. The results shown are typical of those obtained with other randomly selected values for $x$.

The results in Fig. 2 were obtained by assuming that $\lambda_t(x) = 100 \exp(-xt)$ for $t > 0$, where $x$ had a uniform prior probability density between 0.5 and 1.0. As before, the value of $x$ used in the simulation was selected at random with a random number generator. The numerically generated time evolution for $p_t(x \mid N_{t_0,t})$ is shown as well as for $\hat{\lambda}_t$ and $\hat{x}_t$. The results shown are typical of those obtained with other randomly selected values for $x$.

A simulation for the parameterized intensity $\lambda_t(\boldsymbol{x}) =$ $x_1 \exp(-x_2 t)$ for $t > 0$ has also been performed and the results are similar.

### B. *Estimation of a Constant Intensity*

For the homogeneous process with $\lambda_t(x) = x$, a scalar random variable, the solution to (14) is

$$p_t(x \mid N_{t_0,t}) = x^{N_t} \exp(-xt)p_0(x) \cdot \left[\int_0^\infty \xi^{N_t} \exp(-\xi t)p_0(\xi)\, d\xi\right]^{-1}.$$

This can be verified using the differential rule in (13) and may also be derived directly because $N_t$ is a sufficient statistic for the homogeneous process. Our simulation results in Fig. 2 are in good agreement with this analytic expression.

### C. *MAP Estimates* [22]

MAP estimate of $\boldsymbol{x}$ is the value of $\boldsymbol{x}$ that maximizes $l_t(\boldsymbol{x}) = \ln p_t(\boldsymbol{x} \mid N_{t_0,t})$. Using (14) and (13) it follows that

$$l_t(\boldsymbol{x}) = \ln p_0(\boldsymbol{x}) - \int_{t_0}^t (\lambda_\sigma(\boldsymbol{x}) - \hat{\lambda}_\sigma)\, d\sigma + \int_{t_0}^t \ln(\lambda_\sigma(\boldsymbol{x})/\hat{\lambda}_\sigma)\, dN_\sigma.$$

Let $\partial/\partial\boldsymbol{x}$ denote the gradient operator. Then the MAP estimate of $\boldsymbol{x}$ satisfies

$$\boldsymbol{0} = \frac{\partial}{\partial \boldsymbol{x}}\left\{\ln p_0(\boldsymbol{x}) - \int_{t_0}^t \lambda_\sigma(\boldsymbol{x})\, d\sigma + \int_{t_0}^t \ln \lambda_\sigma(\boldsymbol{x})\, dN_\sigma\right\}.$$

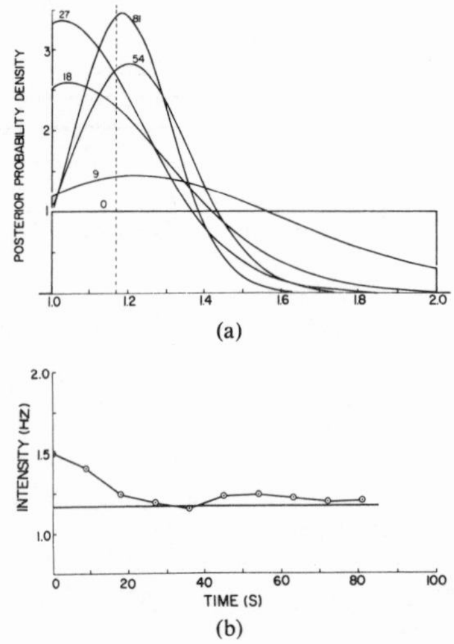


Fig. 1. (a) Time evolution for the posterior probability density function of $x$ when $\lambda_t(x) = x$. The true value of $x$ generated at random, uniformly between 1.0 and 2.0, is indicated by the dashed line at $x = 1.170$. The density is shown for $t = 0, 9, 18, 27, 54,$ and 81 s. All densities are zero outside the interval [1,2]. (b) Time evolution for the MMSE estimate of $\lambda_t(x) = x$. The solid curve is the true value of $\lambda_t(x) = 1.170$, and the data points are the MMSE estimates of this value taken at 9.0 s intervals.

### *D. Parameter Estimation Accuracy* [22]

Let $\boldsymbol{\Sigma}_t = E[(\boldsymbol{x} - \hat{\boldsymbol{x}}_t)(\boldsymbol{x} - \hat{\boldsymbol{x}}_t)^T]$ be the error covariance matrix associated with an estimate $\hat{\boldsymbol{x}}_t$ of $\boldsymbol{x}$ given the record $N_{t_0,t}$. Then, under appropriate regularity conditions, $\boldsymbol{\Sigma}_t \geq \boldsymbol{J}_t^{-1}$ where $\boldsymbol{J}_t$ is the information matrix given by $E\,[\partial l_t(\boldsymbol{x})/\partial \boldsymbol{x})(\partial l_t(\boldsymbol{x})/\partial \boldsymbol{x})^T]$. It can be shown using the above expression for $l_t(\boldsymbol{x})$ that the $(i,j)$ element of $\boldsymbol{J}_t$ is given by

$$J_{ij} = -E\left[\frac{\partial^2 \ln p_0(\boldsymbol{x})}{\partial x_i\, \partial x_j}\right] + E\left[\int_{t_0}^{t} \frac{\partial^2 \lambda_\sigma(\boldsymbol{x})}{\partial x_i\, \partial x_j}\, d\sigma\right] - E\left[\int_{t_0}^{t} \lambda_\sigma(\boldsymbol{x})\, \frac{\partial^2 \ln \lambda_\sigma(\boldsymbol{x})}{\partial x_i\, \partial x_j}\, d\sigma\right],$$

where $E(\cdot)$ indicates integration with respect to $p_0(\boldsymbol{x})$.

## VI. Approximate Filtering

Let the modulation process $\boldsymbol{x}_t$ satisfy the stochastic equation

$$d\boldsymbol{x}_t = \boldsymbol{f}_t(\boldsymbol{x}_t)\, dt + \boldsymbol{G}_t\, d\boldsymbol{\chi}_t,\ \boldsymbol{x}_{t_0} = \boldsymbol{x}_0, \tag{15}$$

where $\{\boldsymbol{\chi}_t, t \geq t_0\}$ is a standardized vector Wiener process. Then $p_t(\boldsymbol{x}_t \mid N_{t_0,t})$ satisfies (9). We have described how (9) can be used to define a numerical algorithm for determining $p_t(\boldsymbol{x}_t \mid N_{t_0,t})$, $\hat{\lambda}_t$, and $\hat{\boldsymbol{x}}_t = E[\boldsymbol{x}_t \mid N_{t_0,t}]$ computationally. However, at each stage of the numerical solution, the integration to determine $\hat{\lambda}_t$ must be performed. Consequently, the computation time can become excessive if the dimension of $\boldsymbol{x}_t$ is more than one or two. Moreover, the array for storing the updated versions of $p_t(\boldsymbol{x}_t \mid N_{t_0,t})$ can become so large that a small computer cannot be used. For these reasons, we are led to consider approximate techniques for generating estimates of $\boldsymbol{x}_t$. The approxima tions we suggest here closely parallel those in Snyde [23, ch. 4]. The quasi-optimum estimates that result ar *ad hoc* so their usefulness must be examined in individu applications.

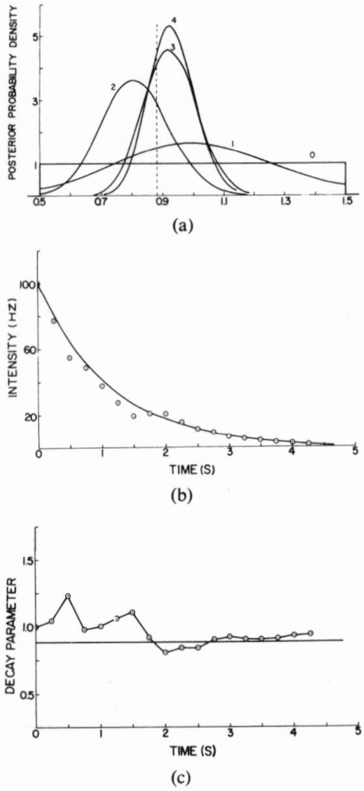


Fig. 2. (a) Time evolution for the posterior probability density of when $\lambda_t(x) = 100 \exp(-xt)$. The true value of $x$ generated random, uniformly between 0.5 and 1.5, equals 0.8822. The posteri density is shown for $t = 0, 1, 2, 3,$ and 4 s. All densities are ze outside the interval [0.5,1.5]. (b) Time evolution for the MMS estimate for $\lambda_t(x) = 100 \exp[-xt]$. The solid curve is the true val of $\lambda_t(x) = 100 \exp[-0.8822t]$, and the data points are the MMS estimates of this curve taken at 0.25 s intervals. (c) Time evolutic for the MMSE estimate of $x$. The solid curve is the true paramet value of 0.8822 and the data points are the MMSE estimates of th value at 0.25 s intervals.

### *A. Derivation for Quasi-Optimum Estimation*

Let

$$\hat{\boldsymbol{x}}_t = E[\boldsymbol{x}_t \mid N_{t_0,t}] = \int_{R^n} \xi p_t(\xi \mid N_{t_0,t}) \prod^{n} d\xi_i \quad (1$$

be the causal MMSE estimate of $\boldsymbol{x}_t$ given the record $N_{t_0}$ An equation for $\hat{\boldsymbol{x}}_t$ can be derived by multiplying (9) b $\boldsymbol{x}_t$ and then integrating according to (16). The result is

$$d\hat{\boldsymbol{x}}_t = E[\boldsymbol{f}_t(\boldsymbol{x}_t) \mid N_{t_0,t}]\, dt + E[(\boldsymbol{x}_t - \hat{\boldsymbol{x}}_t)\lambda_t(\boldsymbol{x}_t) \mid N_{t_0,t}]\hat{\lambda}_t^{-1}\, [dN_t - \hat{\lambda}_t\, dt]$$

$$\hat{\boldsymbol{x}}_{t_0} = E(\boldsymbol{x}_0) \quad (1$$

We next assume that $f_t(x_t)$ and $\lambda_t(x_t)$ have Taylor series out the estimate $\hat{x}_t$ as

$$x_t) = f_t(\hat{x}_t) + [\partial f_t(\hat{x}_t)/\partial \hat{x}_t]^T(x_t - \hat{x}_t) + \tfrac{1}{2}\sum_{i,j}(x_i - \hat{x}_i)(x_j - \hat{x}_j)\,\partial^2 f_t(\hat{x}_t)/\partial \hat{x}_i\,\partial \hat{x}_j + \cdots \quad (18)$$

d

$$x_t) = \lambda_t(\hat{x}_t) + [\partial \lambda_t(\hat{x}_t)/\partial \hat{x}_t]^T(x_t - \hat{x}_t) + \tfrac{1}{2}\sum_{i,j}(x_i - \hat{x}_i)(x_j - \hat{x}_j)\,\partial^2 \lambda_t(\hat{x}_t)/\partial \hat{x}_i\,\partial \hat{x}_j + \cdots, \quad (19)$$

here $\partial v/\partial x$ denotes the Jacobian matrix associated with e vector $v = v(x)$; the ($i$-row, $j$-column) element of $/\partial x$ is $\partial v_j/\partial x_i$.

Upon substituting these expansions into (17), we obtain

$$\hat{x}_t = f_t(\hat{x}_t)\,dt + \tfrac{1}{2}\sum_{i,j}\sigma_{ij}\,\partial^2 f_t(\hat{x}_t)/\partial \hat{x}_i\,\partial \hat{x}_j\,dt + \Sigma_t[\partial \lambda_t(\hat{x}_t)/\partial \hat{x}_t]\hat{\lambda}_t^{-1}[dN_t - \hat{\lambda}_t\,dt] + o(x - \hat{x}_t) \quad (20)$$

which

$$\Sigma_t = (\sigma_{ij}) = E[(x_t - \hat{x}_t)(x_t - \hat{x}_t)^T \mid N_{t_0,t}]$$

the conditional error covariance matrix in estimating , and $o(x_t - \hat{x}_t)$ denotes terms of order three or more in e error.

Note that no approximations have been introduced up this point; $\hat{x}_t$ is the exact causal MMSE estimate of $x_t$ ven $N_{t_0,t}$. We now introduce the following approximations.

i) Disregard all the higher than second-order error terms ontained in $o(x_t - \hat{x}_t)$.

ii) Replace $\hat{\lambda}_t$ by $\lambda_t(\hat{x}_t)$; it is seen from (19) that this ubstitution implies disregarding second-order error terms.

These approximations are *ad hoc* and must be verified or specific functions $f_t$ and $\lambda_t$, but they appear reasonable it is assumed that the error $x_t - \hat{x}_t$ is sufficiently small.

Thus, we are led to define the quasi-optimum estimate $_t^*$ by

$$dx_t^* = f_t(x_t^*)\,dt + \tfrac{1}{2}\sum_{i,j}\sigma_{i,j}^*\,\partial^2 f_t(x_t^*)/\partial x_i^*\,\partial x_j^*\,dt + \Sigma_t^*[\partial \lambda_t(x_t^*)/\partial x_t^*]\lambda_t^{-1}(x_t^*)[dN_t - \lambda_t(x_t^*)\,dt]$$

$$x_{t_0}^* = E[x_0], \quad (21)$$

here $\Sigma_t^* = (\sigma_{ij}^*)$ is an approximation to the error ovariance matrix $\Sigma_t$ as described below. The advantages f (21) compared to the exact equations are i) no integrations re required; and ii), a storage array for $p_t(x_t \mid N_{t_0,t})$ is ot required—the number of data points to be stored for he updating of $x_t^*$ and $\Sigma_t^*$ is $n(n+3)/2$. It is convenient or later use to rewrite (21) in the form

$$x_t^* = f_t(x_t^*)\,dt + \tfrac{1}{2}\sum_{i,j}\sigma_{ij}^*\,\partial^2 f_t(x_t^*)/\partial x_i^*\,\partial x_j^*\,dt - \Sigma_t^*[\partial \lambda_t(x_t^*)/\partial x_t^*]\,dt + \Sigma_t^*[\partial \ln \lambda_t(x_t^*)/\partial x_t^*]\,dN_t$$

$$x_{t_0}^* = E[x_0]. \quad (22)$$

We next derive an equation for the conditional error covariance matrix

$$\Sigma_t = (\sigma_{ij}) = E[\varepsilon_t\varepsilon_t^T \mid N_{t_0,t}]$$

where $\varepsilon_t = x_t - \hat{x}_t$ is the error at time $t$. Note first that

$$\varepsilon_t\varepsilon_t^T = \varepsilon_{t+dt}\varepsilon_{t+dt}^T + \varepsilon_{t+dt}\,d\hat{x}_t^T + dx_t\varepsilon_{t+dt}^T + d\hat{x}_t\,d\hat{x}_t^T. \quad (23)$$

Multiply (9) for $p_t(x_t \mid N_{t_0,t})$ by $\varepsilon_t\varepsilon_t^T$ and integrate using (23) to obtain

$$d\Sigma_t + d\hat{x}_t\,d\hat{x}_t^T = E[f_t(x_t)\varepsilon_t^T + \varepsilon_t f_t^T(x_t) + G_tG_t^T]\,dt + E\{\varepsilon_t\varepsilon_t^T[\lambda_t(x_t) - \hat{\lambda}_t] \mid N_{t_0,t}\}\hat{\lambda}_t^{-1} \cdot [dN_t - \hat{\lambda}_t\,dt]$$

$$\Sigma_{t_0} = \operatorname{cov}(x_0). \quad (24)$$

For each of the expressions on the right in (24), we retain only the leading terms that result when the series (18) and (19) are substituted for $f_t(x_t)$ and $\lambda_t(x_t)$ and the following approximations are made.

i) $\hat{\lambda}_t$ is replaced by $\lambda_t(\hat{x}_t)$, as before.

ii) $\hat{x}_t$ is replaced by $x_t^*$.

iii) Fourth-order moments of the error are factored in products of second-order moments in the way Gaussian moments factor.

These approximations lead us to define $\Sigma_t^*$ by

$$d\Sigma_t^* + dx_t^*\,dx_t^{*T} = [\partial f_t(x_t^*)/\partial x_t^*]^T\Sigma_t^*\,dt + \Sigma_t^*[\partial f_t(x_t^*)/\partial x_t^*]\,dt + G_tG_t^T\,dt + \Sigma_t^*[\partial^2\lambda_t(x_t^*)/\partial x_t^{*2}]\Sigma_t^*\lambda_t^{-1}(x_t^*) \cdot [dN_t - \lambda_t(x_t^*)\,dt], \quad (25)$$

where we use the notation $\partial^2 v/\partial x^2 = \partial\,[\partial v/\partial x]/\partial x$ for a vector $v = v(x)$. From (22) it is seen that to terms of order $dt$,

$$dx_t^*\,dx_t^{*T} = \Sigma_t^*[\partial \ln \lambda_t(x_t^*)/\partial x_t^*][\partial \ln \lambda_t(x_t^*)/\partial x_t^*]^T\Sigma_t^*\,dN_t.$$

Using this in (25) along with the observation that

$$\partial^2 \ln \lambda_t(x_t^*)/\partial x_t^{*2} = -[\partial \ln \lambda_t(x_t^*)/\partial x_t^*][\partial \ln \lambda_t(x_t^*)/\partial x_t^*]^T + [\partial^2\lambda_t(x_t^*)/\partial x_t^{*2}]\lambda_t^{-1}(x_t^*),$$

we obtain the final equation defining $\Sigma_t^*$ as

$$d\Sigma_t^* = [\partial f_t(x_t^*)/\partial x_t^*]^T\Sigma_t^*\,dt + \Sigma_t^*[\partial f_t(x_t^*)/\partial x_t^*]\,dt + G_tG_t^T\,dt - \Sigma_t^*[\partial^2\lambda_t(x_t^*)/\partial x_t^{*2}]\Sigma_t^*\,dt + \Sigma_t^*[\partial^2 \ln \lambda_t(x_t^*)/\partial x_t^{*2}]\Sigma_t^*\,dN_t$$

$$\Sigma_{t_0}^* = \operatorname{cov}(x_0). \quad (26)$$

We take (22) and (26) as our definitions for the quasi-optimum estimate of the state $x_t$ given the data record $N_{t_0,t}$. As mentioned previously, the utility of this definition depends on the form of $f_t(x_t)$ and $\lambda_t(x_t)$ and must be investigated in individual cases. The definition appears reasonable when the estimation error is small.

In the following two sections, we first specialize the approximation equations (22) and (26) for three intensity functions. Then we present some preliminary simulation results for these same functions. The results indicate the potential usefulness of the approximations introduced.

*B. Applications*

1) Let $\lambda_t(x) = A \exp(-xt)$, $t \geq 0$, where $A$ is a known positive constant and $x$ is a positive random variable with known mean $\bar{x}_0$ and variance $\sigma_0^2$. In this case (22) and (26) become

$$dx_t^* = At\Sigma_t^* \exp(-x_t^* t)\, dt - t\Sigma_t^*\, dN_t, \qquad x_0^* = \bar{x}_0 \tag{27}$$

$$d\Sigma_t^* = -At^2\Sigma_t^* \exp(-x_t^* t)\, dt, \qquad \Sigma_0^* = \sigma_0^2. \tag{28}$$

2) Let $\lambda_t(x_1,x_2) = x_1 \exp(-x_2 t)$, $t \geq 0$, where $x_1$ and $x_2$ are uncorrelated positive random variables with known means $\bar{x}_1$ and $\bar{x}_2$ and variances $\sigma_1^2$ and $\sigma_2^2$. In this case, (22) and (26) become

$$\begin{aligned} d\boldsymbol{x}_t^* &= -\Sigma_t^*[1 \;\; -tx_1^*]^T \exp(-x_2^* t)\, dt \\ &\quad + \Sigma_t^*[x_1^{*-1} \;\; -t]^T\, dN_t, \qquad \boldsymbol{x}_0^* = [\bar{x}_1 \bar{x}_2]^T \end{aligned} \tag{29}$$

$$\begin{aligned} d\Sigma_t^* &= -\Sigma_t^* \begin{bmatrix} 0 & -t \\ -t & t^2 x_1^* \end{bmatrix} \Sigma_t^* \exp(-x_2^* t)\, dt \\ &\quad - \Sigma_t^* \begin{bmatrix} x_1^{*-2} & 0 \\ 0 & 0 \end{bmatrix} \Sigma_t^*\, dN_t, \qquad \Sigma_0^* = \begin{bmatrix} \sigma_0^2 & 0 \\ 0 & \sigma_1^2 \end{bmatrix}. \end{aligned} \tag{30}$$

3) Let $\lambda_t(\boldsymbol{x}_t) = A[1 + m\cos(\omega_0 t + \theta_t)]$, $t \geq t_0$, be a phase-modulated intensity function, where $A$ $(A > 0)$ and $m$ $(0 < m < 1)$ and known constants and where $\theta_t$ is a Gaussian diffusion defined by $\theta_t = \boldsymbol{h}_t^T \boldsymbol{x}_t$, where $\boldsymbol{x}_t$ is defined by (15) when $\boldsymbol{f}_t(\boldsymbol{x}_t) = \boldsymbol{F}_t \boldsymbol{x}_t$ and $\boldsymbol{x}_0$ is normal, $p_0(\boldsymbol{x}_0) = N(\boldsymbol{0}, \boldsymbol{\Lambda}_0)$. This is a generalization of an intensity mentioned by Helstrom [25] in connection with optical communications. The simplest nonstationary example results when $\boldsymbol{F}_t = 0$, $\boldsymbol{G}_t$ = constant, and $\boldsymbol{h}_t = 1$, in which case $\theta_t$ is a Wiener process; our results may then be viewed as establishing a coherent phase reference when an unstable oscillator modulates the intensity [23]. A frequency-modulated intensity including preemphasis, would be treated in the same manner as this example and is, in fact, contained in it as a special case [23, ch. 5].

For this intensity, (21) becomes

$$\begin{aligned} d\boldsymbol{x}_t^* &= \boldsymbol{F}_t \boldsymbol{x}_t^*\, dt - m\sin(\omega_0 t + \theta_t^*) \\ &\quad \cdot [1 + m\cos(\omega_0 t + \theta_t^*)]^{-1} \Sigma_t^* \boldsymbol{h}_t \\ &\quad \cdot \{dN_t - A[1 + m\cos(\omega_0 t + \theta_t^*)]\, dt\} \\ \boldsymbol{x}_{t_0}^* &= \boldsymbol{0}, \end{aligned} \tag{31}$$

where $\theta_t^* = \boldsymbol{h}_t^T \boldsymbol{x}_t^*$.

The following equation for $\Sigma_t^*$ can be obtained specializing (26) for the phase-modulated intensity

$$\begin{aligned} d\Sigma_t^* &= \boldsymbol{F}_t^T \Sigma_t^*\, dt + \Sigma_t^* \boldsymbol{F}_t\, dt + \boldsymbol{G}_t \boldsymbol{G}_t^T\, dt \\ &\quad + Am\cos(\omega_0 t + \theta_t^*) \Sigma_t^* \boldsymbol{h}_t \boldsymbol{h}_t^T \Sigma_t^*\, dt \\ &\quad - m[m + \cos(\omega_0 t + \theta_t^*)] \\ &\quad \cdot [1 + m\cos(\omega_0 t + \theta_t^*)]^{-2} \Sigma_t^* \boldsymbol{h}_t \boldsymbol{h}_t^T \Sigma_t^*\, dN_t \\ \Sigma_{t_0}^* &= \boldsymbol{\Lambda}_0. \end{aligned} \quad (\text{:}$$

Equations (31) and (32) define the approximate estim $\theta_t^*$ of the phase. However, if $\omega_0$ is sufficiently large, a ditional approximations that appear reasonable can made. These result in estimation equations having t distinct advantage that the approximate covariance equati is uncoupled from both the approximate state estimate a the data process $N_t$; the equation is a Riccati equati of the type occurring commonly in Kalman–Bucy filterir Furthermore, the estimation equations suggest the use o form of tanlock loop [24] operating on the impulse proc $\dot{N}_t$ to estimate $\theta_t$.

We assume in what follows that the elements of $\boldsymbol{G}_t$, $\boldsymbol{h}_t$, $\boldsymbol{x}_t$, $\boldsymbol{x}_t^*$, and $\Sigma_t^*$ are slowly varying compared $\sin(\omega_0 t + \theta_t^*)$ and $\cos(\omega_0 t + \theta_t^*)$. Then for $\omega_0$ suf ciently large, it appears reasonable to neglect the su tractive term $A[1 + m\cos(\omega_0 t + \theta_t^*)]$ in (31) becau of the implied time integration of the product of the slow varying function $Am\Sigma_t^* \boldsymbol{h}_t$ and $\sin(\omega_0 t + \theta_t^*)$.

Define the zero-mean jump process $\{\tilde{N}_t, t \geq t_0\}$ by

$$\tilde{N}_t = N_t - \int_{t_0}^{t} A[1 + m\cos(\omega_0 \sigma + \theta_\sigma)]\, d\sigma.$$

Then (32) can be written as

$$\begin{aligned} d\Sigma_t^* &= \boldsymbol{F}_t^T \Sigma_t^*\, dt + \Sigma_t^* \boldsymbol{F}_t\, dt + \boldsymbol{G}_t \boldsymbol{G}_t^T\, dt \\ &\quad - Am^2[1 - \cos^2(\omega_0 t + \theta_t^*)] \\ &\quad \cdot [1 + m\cos(\omega_0 t + \theta_t^*)]^{-1} \Sigma_t^* \boldsymbol{h}_t \boldsymbol{h}_t^T \Sigma_t^*\, dt \\ &\quad - m[m + \cos(\omega_0 t + \theta_t^*)] \\ &\quad \cdot [1 + m\cos(\omega_0 t + \theta_t^*)]^{-2} \Sigma_t^* \boldsymbol{h}_t \boldsymbol{h}_t^T \Sigma_t^* \\ &\quad \cdot \{d\tilde{N}_t + A[\cos(\omega_0 t + \theta_t) - \cos(\omega_0 t + \theta_t^*)]\, dt\} \end{aligned} \quad (3$$

We first examine the fourth term on the right side in (33 The function

$$f(\phi) = (1 - \cos^2\phi)(1 + m\cos\phi)^{-1}$$

is an even periodic function of $\phi$. Consequently, $f$ has Fourier cosine series of the form

$$f(\phi) = a_0 + a_1\cos\phi + a_2\cos 2\phi + \cdots,$$

where it can be verified that $a_0$ is given by

$$a_0 = [1 - (1 - m^2)^{1/2}]m^{-2}.$$

we let $\phi = \omega_0 t + \theta_t^*$ and substitute this series into the urth term, then it appears reasonable to neglect all the rmonic components involving $\cos(n\omega_0 t + n\theta_t^*)$, $n \geq 1$, d retain only $a_0$ because of the implied time integration. We shall arbitrarily drop the last term on the right side in 3). The motivation for doing so is as follows. $\tilde{N}_t$ is on the erage zero and $d\tilde{N}_t$ is a future increment of an independent crement process. A Taylor series about $\theta_t^*$ shows that the fference $\cos(\omega_0 t + \theta_t) - \cos(\omega_0 t + \theta_t^*)$ is of the order $\theta_t - \theta_t^*$. Consequently, the contribution of this differ- ce in the last term is, on the average, of the order of the th moment of the error, which we have neglected.

The result of these approximations is the following pair of uations for the approximate estimate of the phase $\theta_t^*$:

$$dx_t^* = F_t x_t^* \, dt - m \sin(\omega_0 t + \theta_t^*) \cdot [1 + m \cos(\omega_0 t + \theta_t^*)]^{-1} \Sigma_t^* h_t \, dN_t$$

$$x_{t_0}^* = 0 \tag{34}$$

1d

$$d\Sigma_t^* = F_t^T \Sigma_t^* \, dt + \Sigma_t^* F_t \, dt + G_t G_t^T \, dt - A[1 - (1 - m^2)^{1/2}] \Sigma_t^* h_t h_t^T \Sigma_t^* \, dt$$

$$\Sigma_{t_0}^* = \Lambda_0, \tag{35}$$

here $\theta_t^* = h_t^T x_t^*$. Equation (34) suggests the use of a rm of tanlock loop to estimate $\theta_t$, and (35) is a Riccati quation.

*. Simulation Results*

1) The simulation results presented in Figs. 3 and 4 ere obtained for the intensity $\lambda_t(x) = A \exp(-xt)$ escribed in Section VI-B1). The value $A = 100$ was used nd the prior pdf for $x$ was taken to be uniform on the nterval (0.5,1.5); thus, $\bar{x}_0 = 1.0$ and $\sigma_0^2 = \frac{1}{12}$. The xact and approximate estimates for $x$ and for $\lambda_t(x)$ are hown in Figs. 3 and 4, respectively, for three parameter alues. The exact estimate was generated using the procedure escribed in Section V and is indicated by a circle. The pproximate estimate is indicated by a star.

2) The simulation results presented in Figs. 5 and 6 were btained for the intensity $\lambda_t(x_1,x_2) = x_1 \exp(-x_2 t)$ des- ribed in Section VI-B2). Both $x_1$ and $x_2$ were assumed to ave a uniform prior pdf on the intervals (90,110) and 0.5,1.5), respectively; thus $\bar{x}_{10} = 100$, $\bar{x}_{20} = 1.0$, $\sigma_{10}^2 = \frac{100}{3}$, and $\sigma_{20}^2 = \frac{1}{12}$. The exact and approximate estimates or $x_1$, $x_2$, and $\lambda_t(x_1,x_2)$ are shown in Figs. 5 and 6. The xact estimates were generated using the procedure des- ribed in Section V and is indicated by a circle. The ap- roximate estimate is indicated by a star.

3) The simulation results presented in Fig. 7 were obtained or the intensity $\lambda_t(\theta) = A[1 + m \cos(\omega_0 t + \theta)]$ des- ribed in Section VI-C3) for the special case of a constant hase parameter $\theta$, $-\pi \leq \theta \leq \pi$. This occurs when $F_t = 0$, $G_t = 0$, and $p_0(\theta)$ is uniform on the interval $-\pi,\pi)$. For the simulation, it was assumed that $A = 500$, $n = 0.75$, and $\omega_0 = 2\pi(100)$. The count rate was such that bout five counts per cycle of the modulation occurred.

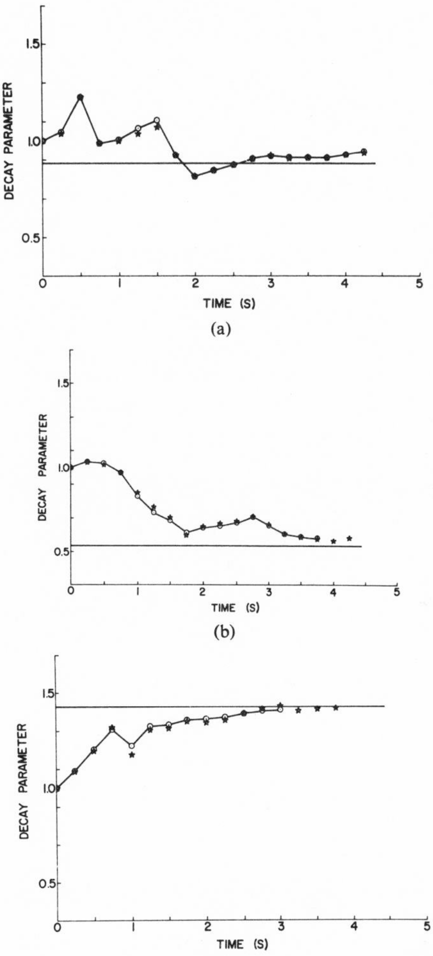


(c)

Fig. 3. Simulation record for the exact (circle) and approximate (star) estimates for the decay parameter $x$ of the intensity $\lambda_t(x) = 100 \exp(-xt)$, where $x$ is uniformly distributed on [0.5,1.5]. The values for $x$ are 0.8822, 0.538, and 1.429 in (a), (b), and (c), respectively. At $t = 4.25$ s, the total number of counts is 100 and 144 in (a) and (b), respectively. At $t = 3.00$ s, the total number of counts is 59 in (c).

The simulation time 0.7 s corresponds to 70 cycles of the modulation.

The results presented in Fig. 8 were obtained for the phase-modulated intensity $\lambda_t(\theta_t) = A[1 + m \cos(\omega_0 t + \theta_t)]$, where $\theta_t$ was a Wiener process with parameter $1/\tau_c$. The parameter $\tau_c$ may be interpreted as the coherence time of an unstable oscillator; it is the time at which 1 rad rms of phase drift is accumulated. This occurs when $F_t = 0$, $G_t = \tau_c^{-1/2}$, and $p_0(\theta) = \delta(\theta)$ in Section VI-B3). For the simulation, it was assumed that $A = 500$, $m = 0.75$, $\omega_0 = 2\pi(100)$, and $\tau_c = 0.1$.

The estimate of the constant phase and Wiener process were generated using (34) and (35) and is indicated by a star.

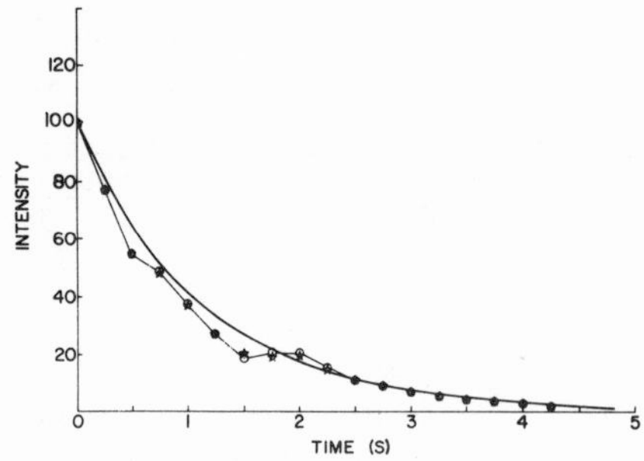


(a)

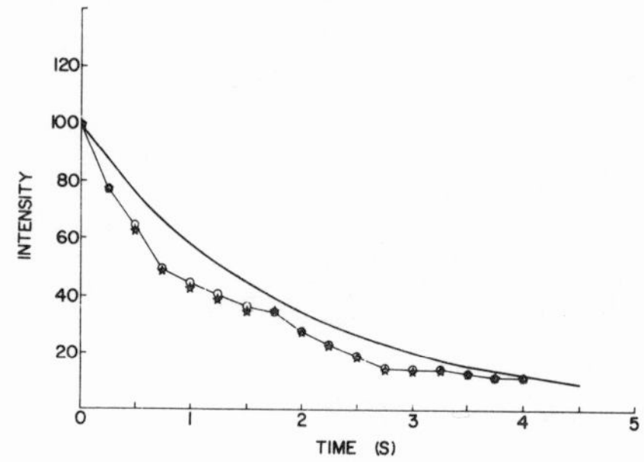


(b)

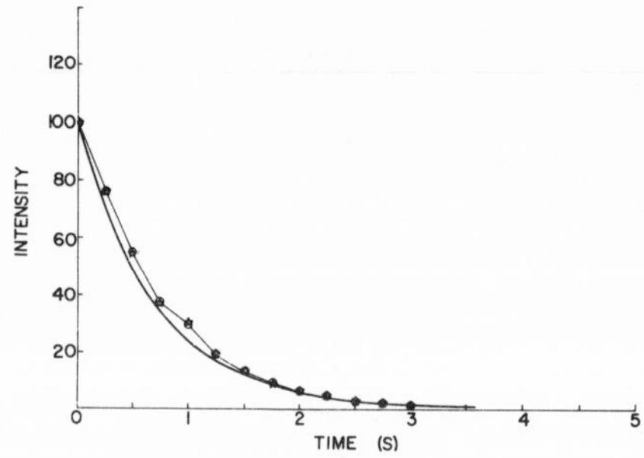


(c)

Fig. 4. Simulation record for the exact (circle) and approximate (star) estimates for the intensity $\lambda_t(x) = 100 \exp(-xt)$. Parameter values are identical to those of Fig. 3.

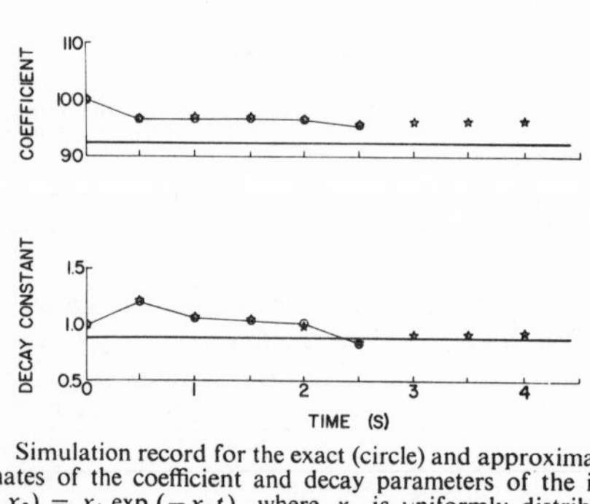


Fig. 5. Simulation record for the exact (circle) and approximate (star) estimates of the coefficient and decay parameters of the intensity $\lambda_t(x_1,x_2) = x_1 \exp(-x_2 t)$, where $x_1$ is uniformly distributed on [90,100] and $x_2$ is uniformly distributed on [0.5,1.5]. The values for $x_1$ and $x_2$ are 92.19 and 0.8822, respectively. At $t = 4.00$ s, the total number of counts is 94.

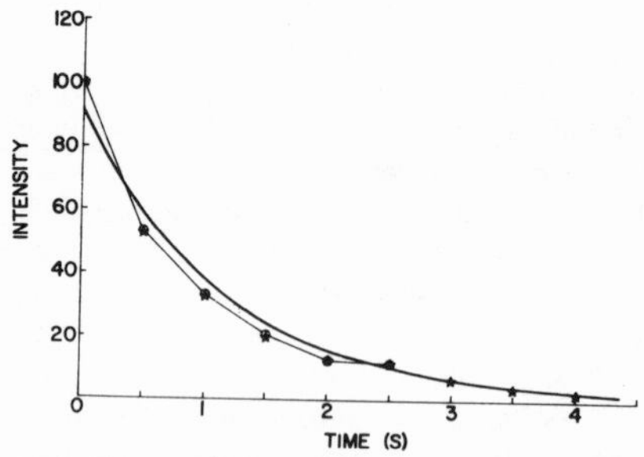


Fig. 6. Simulation record for the exact (circle) and approximate (sta estimate for the intensity $\lambda_t(x_1,x_2) = x_1 \exp(-x_2 t)$. Paramet values are identical to those of Fig. 5.

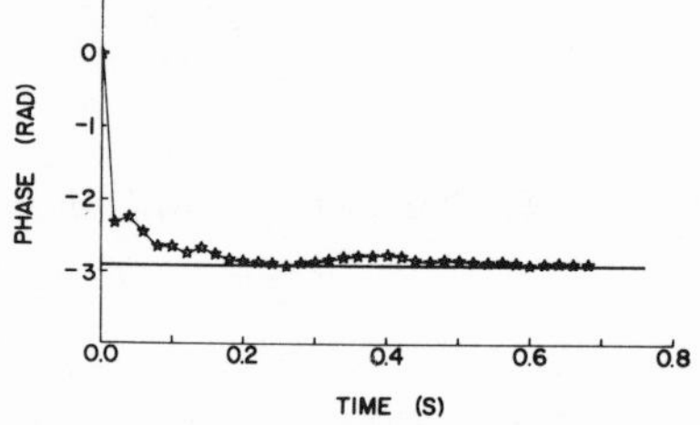


Fig. 7. Simulation record for the approximate (star) estimate of for the intensity $\lambda_t(\theta) = A(1 + m \cos(\omega_0 t + \theta))$, where $A = 50$ $m = 0.75$, $\omega_0 = 100\,(2\pi)$, and $\theta$ is uniformly distributed on $(-\pi,\pi$ The value of $\theta$ is $-2.905$ rad. The total number of counts at $t = 0.6$ is 267.

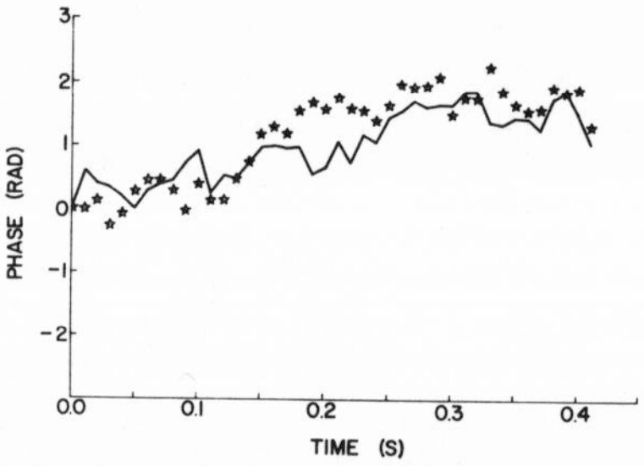


Fig. 8. Simulation record for the approximate estimate (star) of for the intensity $\lambda_t(\theta_t) = A(1 + m \cos(\omega_0 t + \theta_t))$, where $A = 50$ $m = 0.75$, $\omega_0 = 100(2\pi)$, and $\theta_t$ is a Wiener process with coherenc time parameter $\tau_c = 0.1$. The total number of counts at $t = 0.4$ 211.

## VII. Conclusion

The approximate estimates introduced in Section V represent only one procedure for reducing the infinit dimensionality of the exact estimates associated with th results in Section III to a manageable form. Their usefulnes for particular applications must be compared to alternative that may be suggested by the particular functions involved For the intensity functions chosen for simulation, the exac and approximate estimates introduced here appear t agree remarkably well considering the low count rate involved.

## Acknowledgment

The author would like to thank Prof. E. Hoversten and J. Clark of the Massachusetts Institute of Technology, Cambridge, for carefully reading the manuscript and making valuable suggestions. He would also like to thank the anonymous reviewers for their helpful comments.

## References

[1] J. B. West and C. T. Dollery, "Distribution of blood flow and ventilation perfusion ratio in the lung, measured with radioactive $CO_2$," *J. Appl. Physiol.*, vol. 15, 1960, pp. 405–410.
[2] J. B. West, C. T. Dollery, and P. Hugh-Jones, "The use of radioactive carbon-dioxide to measure regional blood flow in the lungs of patients with pulmonary disease," *J. Clin. Invest.*, vol. 40, Jan. 1961, pp. 1–12.
[3] M. M. Ter-Pogossian, J. O. Eichling, D. O. Davis, and M. J. Welch, "The measure in vivo of regional cerebral oxygen utilization by means of oxyhemoglobin labeled with radioactive oxygen-15," *J. Clin. Invest.*, vol. 49, 1970, pp. 381–391.
[4] C. W. Sheppard, *Basic Principles of the Tracer Method*. New York: Wiley, 1962.
[5] J. A. Jacquez, "Tracer kinetics," in *Principles of Nuclear Medicine*, H. N. Wagner, Jr., Ed. Philadelphia: Saunders, 1968, pp. 44–74.
[6] P. Meier and K. L. Zierler, "On the theory of the indicator-dilution method for measurement of blood flow and volume," *J. Appl. Physiol.*, vol. 12, June 1954, pp. 731–744.
[7] *Optical Space Communication*, Proc. M.I.T.–NASA workshop, Williams College, Williamstown, Mass., NASA-SP-217, Aug. 4–17, 1968.
[8] E. V. Hoversten, R. O. Harger, and S. J. Halme, "Communication theory for the turbulent atmosphere," *Proc. IEEE*, vol. 58, Oct. 1970, pp. 1626–1650.
[9] D. R. Cox, "Some statistical methods connected with series of events," *J. Res. Statist. Soc. B.*, vol. 17, 1955, pp. 129–164.
[10] D. R. Cox and P. A. W. Lewis, *The Statistical Analysis of Series of Events*. London: Methuen, 1966.
[11] M. S. Bartlett, *Stochastic Processes*. Cambridge: Cambridge Univ. Press, 1966.
[12] S. Karp and J. R. Clark, "Photon counting: A problem in classical noise theory," *IEEE Trans. Inform. Theory*, vol. IT-16, Nov. 1970, pp. 672–680.
[13] J. R. Clark and E. Hoversten, "Poisson process as a statistical model for photodetectors excited by Gaussian light," Res. Lab. Electron., M.I.T., Cambridge, Quart. Prog. Rep. 98, July 1970, pp. 95–101.
[14] P. A. Frost, "Nonlinear estimation in continuous time systems," Syst. Theory Lab., Stanford Univ., Stanford, Calif., Tech. Rep. 6304-4, May 1968.
[15] P. R. Halmos, *Measure Theory*. New York: Van Nostrand, 1950.
[16] H. J. Kushner, *Stochastic Stability and Control*. New York: Academic Press, 1967, p. 18.
[17] W. Feller, *An Introduction to Probability Theory and Its Applications*, vol. 2. New York: Wiley, 1966.
[18] B. Reiffen and H. Sherman, "An optimum demodulator for Poisson processes: Photon source detectors," *Proc. IEEE*, vol. 51, Oct. 1963, pp. 1316–1320.
[19] T. E. Duncan, "Evaluation of likelihood functions," *Inform. Contr.*, vol. 13, July 1968, pp. 62–74.
[20] T. Kailath, "A general likelihood-ratio formula for random signals in Gaussian noise," *IEEE Trans. Inform. Theory*, vol. IT-15, May 1969, pp. 350–361.
[21] H. Kunita and S. Watanabe, "On square-integrable martingales," *Nagoya Math. J.*, vol. 30, Aug. 1967, pp. 209–245.
[22] H. L. Van Trees, *Detection, Estimation and Modulation Theory, Part I*. New York: Wiley, 1968.
[23] D. L. Snyder, *The State-Variable Approach to Continuous Estimation, With Applications to Analog Communication Theory*. Cambridge, Mass.: M.I.T. Press, 1969.
[24] L. M. Robinson, "Tanlock: A phase-lock loop of extended tracking capability," in *Proc. Nat. Winter Conf. Military Electronics*, 1962.
[25] C. W. Helstrom, "Estimation of the modulation frequency of a light beam," in *Optical Space Communication*, Proc. M.I.T.–NASA workshop, Williams College, Williamstown, Mass., NASA SP-217, Aug. 1968, pp. 121–123.

# 14



Reprinted from *IEEE Trans. Commun.* **COM-22**(1):17–27 (1974)

# Direct-Detection Optical Communication Receivers

ESTIL V. HOVERSTEN, MEMBER, IEEE, DONALD L. SNYDER, MEMBER, IEEE, ROBERT O. HARGER, MEMBER, IEEE, AND KOJI KURIMOTO, MEMBER, IEEE

***Abstract*–A model that is sufficiently general to describe the predominant statistical characteristics of the output of many real optical detectors is formulated. This model is used to study the optimum receiver processing for direct-detection optical communication systems. In particular, the structures of detectors and estimators for randomly filtered doubly stochastic Poisson processes observed in additive white Gaussian noise are considered. Representations for the posterior statistics of a vector-valued Markov process that modulates the intensity of the doubly stochastic Poisson process are obtained. Quasi-optimum estimators and detectors are specified in general terms and specialized for several important applications. These include a demodulator for subcarrier angle modulation, a detector structure for binary signaling with known intensities, and a detector structure for binary signaling in the turbulent atmosphere.**

## I. INTRODUCTION

MANY optical communication systems use direct-detection techniques. In the usual form of such systems, the optical field at the receiving aperture is first preprocessed by linear temporal and spatial filtering, e.g., passed through an optical system that contains an interference filter and field stop to reduce the effects of background radiation. An optical detector then makes an energy measurement on this preprocessed field. This paper is concerned with the subsequent processing that should be performed on the detector output to estimate the transmitted signal, if analog modulation is employed, or to make decisions, if the communication system is transmitting digital information.

Thus, our first objective in this paper is to formulate a statistical model that describes the various dominant effects associated with a broad class of real optical detectors. The model, which accounts for random gains, finite bandwidths, dark current, and additive thermal noise, includes photomultipliers, avalanche photodiodes, and ordinary photodiodes that employ photovoltaic effects. The model is not sufficiently general to accommodate detectors that employ photoconductive effects. The reason for this is explained in Appendix A, where an extended model that includes nonlinear effects is developed.

Our second objective in the paper is to use this model to examine the optimum receiver processing of the detector output for a broad class of detection and estimation problems. The processing results, which are obtained in Sections IV and V, are applicable to any situation in which the optical modulation can be described by the state-space model discussed in Section III. Our third objective is to apply these general results to some important optical communication problems. This is done in Section VII, after first developing some quasi-optimum estimator structures in Section VI.

In the next section, we describe the characteristics of real optical detectors to motivate their statistical models, which are developed in Section III.

## II. OPTICAL DETECTORS

All of the physical phenomena currently used to convert optical signals into electrical signals involve energy measurement. This is true whether the detectors are photoemissive, photovoltaic, or photoconductive. Thus, for example, in a photoemitter a quantum of optical energy is absorbed by an atom and an electron is emitted from the photoemissive surface.

A quantum mechanically correct description of the output of such detectors can be given in terms of the classical field incident on them. The output of an ideal detector is conditionally an inhomogeneous Poisson process [1], [2]. A reasonable statistical model that includes the effects of the most important deviations of real detectors from the ideal is given by [3], [4]

$$i(t) = \sum_{n=1}^{N(t)} h(t, \tau_n; g_n) + i_D(t) + i_T(t) \tag{1}$$

where

$$P[N(t) = k \mid \mu(\sigma),\ 0 \leqslant \sigma \leqslant t] = \frac{\left[\int_0^t \mu(\tau)\, d\tau\right]^k}{k!} \cdot \exp\left[-\int_0^t \mu(\tau)\, d\tau\right], \tag{2}$$

Paper approved by the Associate Editor for Communication Theory of the IEEE Communications Society for publication after presentation at the 1972 International Conference on Communications, Philadelphia, Pa., and at the Tenth Annual Allerton Conference on Circuit and System Theory, 1972. Manuscript received February 17, 1973; revised June 25, 1973. This work was supported in part by the National Aeronautics and Space Administration under Grants NGL-22-009-013 and NGR-21-002-237, in part by the National Institutes of Health, Division of Resources, under Grant RR00396, and in part by the National Science Foundation under Grants GK-32239 and GK-14920.

E. V. Hoversten was with the Department of Electrical Engineering and the Research Laboratory of Electronics, Massachusetts Institute of Technology, Cambridge, Mass. 02139. He is now with the Defense Communications Agency, Washington, D.C. 20305.

D. L. Snyder is with the Department of Electrical Engineering and the Biomedical Computer Laboratory, Washington University, St. Louis, Mo. 63130.

R. O. Harger is with the Department of Electrical Engineering, University of Maryland, College Park, Md. 20742.

K. Kurimoto was with the Department of Electrical Engineering, University of Maryland, College Park, Md. 20742. He is now with Toyo Kogyo and Company, Ltd., Hiroshima, Japan.

$$\mu(t) = \frac{\eta}{2h\nu} \int_{\alpha_d} |U_d(t, \vec{r})|^2 \, d\vec{r}, \tag{3}$$

and the $\tau_n$ are the photoelectron emission times. Here the detector output is $i(t)$, the classical field incident upon it is $u_d(t, \vec{r})$ and this field is assumed to be optically narrowband, $\mu(t)$ is the intensity function of the underlying counting process $N(t)$, $\eta$ is the quantum efficiency of the detector, $U_d(t, \vec{r})$ is the complex envelope of $u_d(t, \vec{r})$, $h\nu$ is the energy in a photon, and $a_d$ is the active area of the detector. Thus $\mu(t)$ is the instantaneous average rate of photoelectron emissions. $P[N(t) = k \mid \mu(\sigma), 0 \leqslant \sigma \leqslant t]$ in (2) is the probability that $k$ photoelectrons are emitted in the time interval $[0, t)$ given that the detector field is $\{u_d(\sigma, \vec{\rho}); 0 \leqslant \sigma \leqslant t, \vec{\rho} \in a_d\}$. The random time-varying impulse response $h(t, \tau; g)$ depends on the type of detector; it models the finite bandwidth of real detectors and the statistical variations in the detector response from photoelectron to photoelectron. These statistical variations are assumed to be mutually independent and independent of the other statistical processes. For an ideal detector with a nonrandom gain $G$,

$$h(t, \tau; g) = G\delta(t - \tau). \tag{4}$$

For a photomultiplier or avalanche photodiode,

$$h(t, \tau; g) = gh(t - \tau), \tag{5}$$

where $g$ reflects the random gain and $h(\cdot)$ the finite bandwidth. For an ordinary photodiode that employs the photovoltaic effect, (5) applies with $g = 1$ with probability one, and for a photodiode employing the photoconductive effect

$$h(t, \tau; g) = h\left(\frac{t - \tau}{g}\right) \tag{6}$$

where $g$ is an exponentially distributed random variable modeling random recombination time.

The current $i_D(t)$ models the detector dark current; that is, the detector output in the absence of an optical input signal. This current can usually be thought of as the output of a random time-varying filter driven by a homogeneous Poisson process, that is, a Poisson process with constant intensity function $\mu_D$.

The current $i_T(t)$ is a wide-band noise of thermal origin associated with any internal detector resistances, the load resistor, and the front-end noise of any following electronics. It is reasonably modeled as a white Gaussian random process with zero mean and bilateral spectral density $2kT/R_e$; here, $k$ is Boltzmann's constant, $T$ is the temperature, and $R_e$ is the effective resistance. This thermal noise will be especially significant for detectors that do not have internal gain.

We plan to investigate filtering and detection problems for which $i(t)$ is the observation process. For this purpose, we impose the following state-space structure on the problem.

## III. The State-Space Model

We now develop mathematical models for the physical detector effects described in the previous section. First we model the random intensity $\mu(t)$ of the counting process $N(t)$; this is a state-variable model that accounts for information signals that modulate the optical carrier, random channel effects, and background radiation. Then we model the first two terms of (1). We use a state-variable model for the photoelectron response function $h(t, \tau : g)$ and for the response function associated with $i_D(t)$; for simplicity, we assume these response functions to be the same. Finally, we represent the detector output in terms of these state-variable models.

### A. State Description for $\mu(t)$

Let $\{N(t), t \geqslant 0\}$ be a doubly stochastic Poisson counting process (DSPP) with a stochastic intensity function $\{\mu(t); t \geqslant 0\}$. As in [5], we assume that

$$\mu(t) = \lambda(t, x_\lambda(t)), \tag{7}$$

where $\{x_\lambda(t); t \geqslant 0\}$ is an $n_\lambda$-dimensional vector Markov process. The following specializations of the model are of interest in practice.

*1) Known signal in fixed background:* Here $\mu(t) = \lambda_s(t) + \lambda_0$, where $\lambda_0$ is a known constant modeling the dark current and background radiation, and $\lambda_s(t)$ is the count rate due to a known signal field. Natural background radiation is reasonably modeled as a constant intensity when the number of temporal and spatial modes passed by the preprocessing filters is large [4], [6]. In this special case, useful in the detection context, $n_\lambda = 0$; that is, the process $x_\lambda(t)$ is not present.

*2) Random signal in fixed background:* Here $\mu(t) = \lambda_s(t, x_\lambda(t)) + \lambda_0$, where $\lambda_0$ is as before. In this case $x_\lambda(t)$ models information signals that modulate $\lambda_s$, random channel effects such as those caused by atmospheric turbulence, or a combination of these. We assume that these can be described as Markov processes.

*3) Known or random signal in random background:* Here $\mu(t) = \lambda(t, x_\lambda(t))$, where

$$\lambda(t, x_\lambda(t)) = \|s(t, x_{\lambda s}(t)) + s_{lo}(t) + n(t, x_{\lambda n}(t))\|^2 + \lambda_0,$$

in which $x_\lambda' \triangleq [x_{\lambda s}' \, x_{\lambda n}']$ and $s$, $s_{lo}$, and $n$ are vectors having dimension equal to twice the number of spatial modes $L$ of the field on the detector surface. The first $L$ components of these vectors are the real parts of the mode amplitudes and the remaining $L$ components are the imaginary parts. The vector $s_{lo}(t)$ is included to represent a possible local oscillator signal. The magnitude of this signal is arbitrary; for hetrodyne detection, the magnitude would be chosen in practice to be large relative to $s$ and $n$, and for direct detection it is zero. The noise vector $n$ models the random background radiation and can often be assumed to be a Gauss-Markov process with independent components, as the background is usually taken to be a Gaussian random field [7]. Here $\lambda_0$ models the detector dark current.

### B. State Description for h

We use a DSPP-driven Markov process model for the first two terms on the right in (1). This holds if $h$ has a state-space realization. It is assumed for simplicity that the response function associated with $i_D(t)$ is $h$; this restriction can easily be removed. The linear model for $h$ that we formulate here is generalized in Appendix A to include possible nonlinear detector effects.

Let $\{x_h(t); t \geq 0\}$ denote the $n_h$-dimensional state vector of $h$, and assume this satisfies the linear state equation

$$dx_h(t) = A(t)\, x_h(t)\, dt + b(t)\, d\alpha(t) \tag{8}$$

where

$$\alpha(t) \triangleq \int_0^t \int_{-\infty}^{\infty} GM(dt, dG), \tag{9}$$

in which $M$ is a DSPP on the two-dimensional space representing time greater than zero and possible detector gains. Here, $\{\alpha(t); t \geq 0\}$ is a compound DSPP; that is, $\alpha$ is a jump process with independent identically distributed jump random variables $g$ and jump times that occur according to the DSPP $\{N(t); t \geq 0\}$ described previously. The interpretation of $M$ is that:

1) $N(t) = \int_0^t \int_{R^1} M(dt, dG)$, where $\{N(t); t \geq 0\}$ is the DSPP in (1).

2) $E[M(dt, dG) \mid \mu(\sigma); \alpha > 0] = \mu(t)\, p_g(G)\, dt\, dG$, where $\mu(t)$ is given in (7) and $p_g(G)$ is the probability density function of the gain variable $g$. Thus, the product $\mu(t)\, p_g(G)$ is the stochastic intensity of the two-dimensional DSPP $M$.

3) $\int_{t_1}^{t_2} \int_A M(dt, dG)$ is the random number of photoelectrons emitted in the interval $[t_1, t_2)$ for which the associated realizations of the random gain $g$ have values in the subset $A$ of possible gain values.

4) $M$ can alternatively be viewed as a marked point process; i.e., a point process in time with a one-dimensional vector variable associated with each occurrence time. The occurrence times represent photoelectron emission times, and the mark variable is associated with the random filter and accounts for a random gain associated with each photoelectron.

Let $\{z(t); t \geq 0\}$ denote the output of the filter $h$; here, $z(t)$ represents the first two terms on the right in (1). We assume that this output can be expressed as a linear transformation of the state $x_h$, according to the relation

$$z(t) = c'(t)\, x_h(t). \tag{10}$$

The filter impulse response $h(t, \tau : g)$ can be expressed in terms of the matrices $A$, $b$, and $c$ of the linear state equations (8) and (10) as

$$h(t, \tau : g) = gc'(t)\, \Phi(t, \tau)\, b(\tau) \tag{11}$$

where $\Phi$ is the state transition matrix [8] associated with $A$. Perhaps the simplest example occurs when $n_\lambda = 1$ and $A$, $b$, and $c$ are scaler constants independent of time. In this case, the filter is time invariant and has the exponential response function

$$h(t, \tau : g) = \begin{cases} gcb \exp\,[-A(t-\tau)], & t \geq 0 \\ 0, & t < 0. \end{cases} \tag{12}$$

The detector model developed here includes all the physical effects for the real detectors described in Section II except for the time scaling required for (6). Thus, photoconductive detectors are not included in our model. Some further remarks about this issue are given in Appendix A.

### *C. Observation Equation*

Let $\{y_t; t \geq 0\}$ be the observation process, where

$$dy(t) = \zeta(t)\, dt + e(t)\, dN(t) + R^{1/2}(t)\, d\eta(t), \tag{13}$$

where: 1) $\zeta(t) = \rho(t, x(t))$ in which $x' = [x'_\lambda\, x'_h]$ and $\rho$ is a known function of $t$ and $x$; 2) $\{N(t); t \geq 0\}$ is the DSPP of (1); and 3) $\{\eta(t); t \geq 0\}$ is a standardized Wiener process that is statistically independent of $N$ and $x$.

Special cases of (13) have been studied previously. If in (13) we set $\zeta(t) = 0$, $e(t) = 1$, and $R(t) = 0$, then the observation process model is the DSPP model studied in [5]. If, in this case, $e(t)$ is nonzero and continuous and $R(t) \neq 0$, then the results in [5] still apply after preprocessing that separates $N$ from $\eta$; such separation is always possible because $\eta$ is almost surely sample function continuous. Alternatively, if we set $e(t) = 0$ and make $\zeta(t)$ a function of $x_\lambda$ only, then the observation process model is the additive white Gaussian noise model in [9]. Fisher and Stear [10] examine (13) for the special case when $n_\lambda = 0$. Here, we study the case when $e(t) = 0$ and $\zeta(t)$ equals $z(t)$ of (10) so that $\zeta(t)$ is a linear function of $x_h$ only. It is perhaps worth noting that $x_h(t)$ is statistically coupled to $x_\lambda(t)$; consequently, $\zeta(t)$ does carry information about $x(t)$ even though it is only directly a function of $x_h(t)$. Various aspects of this case have been examined independently in [11] and [12]. In Appendix A we study the situation where this linearity constraint is removed. Note that in (13) with $e(t) = 0$, we formally identify $i(t)$ and $i_T(t)$ with $y(t)$ and $R^{1/2}(t)\, \dot{\eta}(t)$, respectively.

Fig. 1 summarizes the state-space model that will be used to investigate filtering and detection problems in the subsequent sections.

## IV. Estimation Problem

We consider the problem of causally estimating a given vector-valued function, say $\beta(t, x(t))$, of $t$ and $x(t)$, where $x'(t) = [x'_\lambda(t)\, x'_h(t)]$, from an observation $\{y(\sigma); 0 \leq \sigma < t\}$. For instance, $\beta$ could be the intensity $\lambda$, the state $x_\lambda$, or an information signal $s(t, x_\lambda(t))$. The solution to this estimation problem can be given in terms of the posterior density $p_{x(t)}(X, t \mid y(\sigma); 0 \leq \sigma < t)$. For instance, the minimum mean-square error (MMSE) and maximum *a posteriori* probability (MAP) estimates of $\beta$ can be determined when this density is known. Therefore, we concentrate on the basic problem of describing the time evolution of $p_{x(t)}(X; t \mid \mathcal{Y}_t)$ as additional observations are accumulated; here, we define $\mathcal{Y}_t = \{y(\sigma); 0 \leq \sigma < t\}$.

Let $c(v, t \mid \mathcal{Y}_t)$ be the conditional characteristic function for $x(t)$ given $\mathcal{Y}_t$,

$$c(v, t \mid \mathcal{Y}_t) = E\{\exp\,[j\langle v, x(t)\rangle] \mid \mathcal{Y}_t\} \tag{14}$$

where $\langle v, x\rangle$ denotes the inner or dot product of the vectors $v$ and $x$.

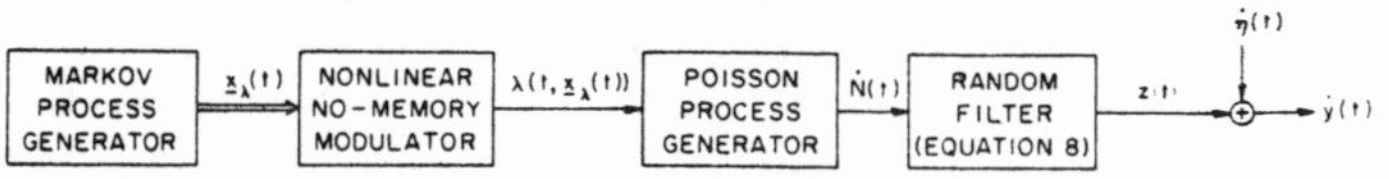


Fig. 1. State-space model.

As shown in Appendix B the time evolution of the conditional characteristic function for $x(t)$ is described by the stochastic differential equation

$$\begin{aligned} dc(v, t \mid \mathcal{Y}_t) = E\{\Psi(v, t \mid \mathcal{Y}_t, x(t)) \exp [j\langle v, x(t)\rangle] \mid \mathcal{Y}_t\}\, dt \\ + E\{\exp [j\langle v, x(t)\rangle]\ [z(t) - \hat{z}(t)]\} \\ \cdot R^{-1}(t)\ [dy(t) - \hat{z}(t)\, dt] \end{aligned} \quad (15)$$

where

$$\hat{z}(t) = E[z(t) \mid \mathcal{Y}_t] = c'(t)\, E[x_h(t) \mid \mathcal{Y}_t] = c'(t)\, \hat{x}_h(t)$$

is the MMSE estimate of $z(t)$ given the data $\mathcal{Y}_t$ and $\Psi(v, t \mid \mathcal{Y}_t, x(t))$ is defined by

$$\begin{aligned} \Psi(v, t \mid \mathcal{Y}_t, x(t)) = \Psi_\lambda(v_1 \mid x_\lambda(t)) + j\langle v_2, A(t)\, x_h(t)\rangle \\ + \lambda(t, x_\lambda(t))\, E_g\{\exp [j\langle v_2, gb(t)\rangle] - 1\} \end{aligned} \quad (16)$$

where $\Psi_\lambda$ is the differential generator for the Markov process $x_\lambda(t)$, as defined in (57) and where the remaining two terms on the right in (16) can be interpreted as the conditional differential generator for $x_h(t)$ given $x_\lambda(t)$. In (16), $v_1$ and $V_2$ are partitions of $v$ having the same dimensions as the $x_\lambda$ and $x_h$ partitions of $x$. Inverse Fourier transformation of (15) yields an equation for the time evolution of the conditional probability density $p_{x(t)}(X, t \mid \mathcal{Y}_t)$ for $x(t)$ given $\mathcal{Y}_t$, the observed data up to time $t$. Thus (15) describes the time evolution of the posterior statistics of the state $x$, and in principle provides the solution to the estimation problem. In fact, it can be the point of departure for the development of various approximate estimators; this idea is developed in Section VI below.

## V. Detection Problem

Here we consider the problem of deciding which of $M$ hypotheses $H_1, \cdots, H_M$ governs the statistics of an observed path $\{y(t); 0 \leqslant t \leqslant T\}$ where, on $H_i$,

$$dy(t) = z_i(t)\, dt + R^{1/2}(t)\, d\eta(t) \quad (17)$$

for $i = 1, 2, \cdots, M$ and $0 \leqslant t \leqslant T$. Here each $\{z_i(t); 0 \leqslant t \leqslant T\}$ has the general structure described above for $\{z(t); 0 \leqslant t \leqslant T\}$. In the usual situation, a particular $z_i$ occurs due to the modulation of the intensity $\{\mu(t); 0 \leqslant t \leqslant T\}$ by one of a set of $M$ waveforms. The solution to this decision problem involving random signals in white Gaussian noise has been given in general terms by Duncan [13] and Kailath [14]. $M$ sufficient statistics for implementing the decision are

$$\ln \Lambda_i = \int_0^T R^{-1}(t)\, \hat{z}_i(t)\, dy(t) - \frac{1}{2} \int_0^T R^{-1}(t)\, \hat{z}_i^2(t)\, dt \quad (18)$$

for $i = 1, 2, \cdots, M$ where $\hat{z}_i(t)$ is a function of the observed data defined by $\hat{z}_i(t) = E[z_i(t) \mid \mathcal{Y}_t, H_i]$; thus, $\hat{z}_i(t)$ is the causal MMSE estimate of $z_i(t)$ when $H_i$ holds and is, therefore, determined in principle by the estimation results of Section IV.

The first integral in (18) is an Ito stochastic integral requiring special care for its evaluation. An analog evaluation is discussed by Kailath [14, sec. V. 3]. For digital evaluation using a discrete approximating sum, it is necessary to interpret $dy(t)$ in the integral as a forward difference $y(t + \Delta t) - y(t)$ relative to the integrand evaluated at time $t$ [15].

## VI. Quasi-Optimum Estimator Structures

Our objective in this section is to derive estimator structures that can be realized in practice for causally estimating the state $x(t)$ or some specified function $\beta(t, x(t))$ of the state in terms of the past observations $\mathcal{Y}_t$. The estimators we obtain approximate the MMSE estimator, and they are nearly optimal when the estimation error is sufficiently small. The procedure we use for accomplishing this has been used several times previously [5], [9], [16] for other models. The characteristic function representation of Section IV will be used to get an equation for the conditional probability density of $x(t)$ given $\mathcal{Y}_t$, and from this, a representation for the MMSE estimator for $x(t)$ will be derived. As typically occurs with nonlinear estimation problems, this equation cannot be solved explicitly for the optimal estimator, and approximations are required. We use a truncated Taylor series approximation with the Gaussian assumption for factorization of moments of the estimation error. In the next section we will consider the application of the approximate estimator equations to problems of estimation and hypothesis testing in optical communications.

### A. State Model for $x_\lambda(t)$

To be explicit, we assume that $\{x_\lambda(t); t \geqslant 0\}$ is a Markov diffusion satisfying the stochastic differential equation

$$dx_\lambda(t) = f(t, x_\lambda(t))\, dt + Q(t)\, dw(t) \quad (19)$$

where $\{w(t); t \geqslant 0\}$ is a standard Wiener process that is independent of the observation noise $\{\eta(t); t \geqslant 0\}$ and whose future is independent of the past of the marked DSPP $M$. For this case, the differential generator $\Psi_\lambda$ for $x_\lambda$ in (16) becomes

$$\Psi_\lambda(v_1, t \mid x_\lambda(t)) = j\langle v_1, f(t, x_\lambda(t))\rangle - \tfrac{1}{2}\langle v_1, Q(t)\, Q'(t)\, v_1\rangle. \quad (20)$$

This function completely characterizes the transitional statistics of $x_\lambda(t)$ [15].

The choice of $x_\lambda(t)$ as a Markov diffusion includes as a special case time-independent random variables, nonstationary Gauss-Markov processes, and stationary Gaussian processes with rational power-density spectra. Consequently, by selecting the particular Markov diffusion and the intensity function $\lambda(t, x_\lambda(t))$, many physical phenomena encountered in optical communications can be accommodated by our model. Several examples are treated explicitly in Section VII.

### B. The Exact Estimator Equations

A representation for the posterior probability density $p_{x(t)}(X, t \mid \mathcal{Y}_t)$ for $x(t)$ in the above simplified state model can be obtained by inverse Fourier transforming (15). Denoting this density by $p(X)$ for brevity, we obtain after some manipulations that

$$dp(X) = -\left\langle \partial(\cdot)/\partial X, \begin{bmatrix} f(t, X_\lambda) \\ A(t) X_h \end{bmatrix} p(X) \right\rangle dt + \frac{1}{2}\sum_{i=1}^{n_\lambda}\sum_{j=1}^{n_\lambda} [Q(t)Q'(t)]_{ij}\,\partial^2 p(X)/\partial X_{\lambda i}\,\partial X_{\lambda j}\,dt + \left[\lambda(t, X_\lambda) E_g\left\{p\left(X - \begin{bmatrix} 0 \\ gb(t)\end{bmatrix}\right) - p(X)\right\}\right] dt + p(X)\,[z(t) - \hat{z}(t)]\,R^{-1}(t)\,[dy(t) - \hat{z}(t)\,dt], \quad (21)$$

where $\partial(\cdot)/\partial X$ denotes the gradient operator, $\hat{z}(t) = E[z(t) \mid \mathcal{Y}_t]$ is the causal MMSE estimate of $z$, and $X_\lambda$ and $X_h$ are partitions of $X$ corresponding to the $x_\lambda(t)$ and $x_h(t)$ partitions of $x(t)$.

The representation for $p(X) = p_{x(t)}(X, t \mid \mathcal{Y}_t)$ in (21) is a nonlinear differential difference integral equation for the posterior density of $x(t)$. In general, it is impossible to solve it for an explicit expression for $p(X)$. However, the equation does form the point of departure for developing reasonable suboptimal estimators of the state $x(t)$ and functions of the state $\beta(t, x(t))$; for the latter, we use as an approximation that the quasi-optimal MMSE estimate of $\beta(t, x(t))$ is $\beta^*(t) = \beta(t, x^*(t))$, where $x^*(t)$ is a quasi-optimal MMSE estimate of $x(t)$. Thus, in our approximation scheme, the basic issue is specifying a reasonable suboptimal estimate for the state $x(t)$. Our procedure for doing this is first to use (21) to get an equation for the optimal MMSE estimate $\hat{x}(t) = E[x(t) \mid \mathcal{Y}_t]$. By multiplying (21) by $X$ and integrating, there results

$$d\hat{x}(t) = \begin{bmatrix} \hat{f}(t) \\ A(t)\,\hat{x}_h(t) \end{bmatrix} dt + \begin{bmatrix} 0 \\ E_g\{gb(t)\} \end{bmatrix} \hat{\lambda}(t)\,dt + \widehat{(x(t) - \hat{x}(t))\,[z(t) - \hat{z}(t)]}\,R^{-1}(t)\,[dy(t) - \hat{z}(t)\,dt] \quad (22)$$

where the caret "^" denotes integration with respect to $p(X)$ and, therefore, causal MMSE estimation.

### C. The Approximate Estimator Equations

We now follow a procedure used several times elsewhere [5], [9], [16] for obtaining from (22) an equation for an approximation $x^*(t)$ to $\hat{x}(t)$. In this procedure, the nonlinear functions $f$ and $\lambda$ of $x(t)$ are expanded in a Taylor series about the estimate $\hat{x}(t)$. The Gaussian moment factorization property is used on the error moments that result, and the series is truncated at the "most significant" terms on the assumption that the error moments are sufficiently small. The result of these manipulations is the following pair of coupled equations for the quasi-optimum MMSE estimate $x^*(t)$ and for the matrix $\Sigma^*(t)$, which is an approximation to the conditional error covariance matrix:

$$dx^*(t) = \begin{bmatrix} f(t, x_\lambda^*(t)) \\ A(t)\,x_h^*(t) \end{bmatrix} dt + \left[\frac{1}{2}\sum_{i=1}^{n_\lambda}\sum_{j=1}^{n_\lambda} \sigma^*_{\lambda_{ij}}(t)\,\partial^2 f(t, x_\lambda^*(t))/\partial x^*_{\lambda_i}\,\partial x^*_{\lambda_j}\right] dt + \begin{bmatrix} 0 \\ E_g\{gb(t)\}\end{bmatrix}\left[\lambda(t, x_\lambda^*(t)) + \frac{1}{2}\operatorname{tr}\left\{H_{x^*}[\lambda(t, x_\lambda^*(t)]\,\Sigma^*(t)\right\}\right] dt + \Sigma^*(t)\begin{bmatrix} 0 \\ c(t)\end{bmatrix} R^{-1}(t)\,[dy(t) - c'(t)\,x_h^*(t)\,dt] \quad (23)$$

where $H_{x^*}[\lambda(t, x_\lambda^*(t))]$ is the $(n_\lambda + n_h) \times (n_\lambda + n_h)$ Hessian matrix of second derivatives $\partial^2\lambda(t, x_\lambda^*(t))/\partial x_i^*\,\partial x_j^*$ of $\lambda(t, x_\lambda^*(t))$ with respect to all components of $x^*(t)$, and where $\sigma^*_{\lambda_{ij}}(t)$ is the $(i, j)$ element of the matrix $[I_{n_\lambda}\ \mathbf{0}]\,\Sigma^*(t) \times [I_{n_\lambda}\ \mathbf{0}]'$ in which $I_n$ denotes the $n \times n$ identity matrix. The operator tr $\{\cdot\}$ denotes the trace of the enclosed matrix. The matrix $\Sigma^*(t)$ satisfies

$$d\Sigma^*(t) = \left\{\partial\begin{bmatrix} f(t, x_\lambda^*(t)) \\ A(t)x_h^*(t)\end{bmatrix}\Big/\partial x^*\right\}' \Sigma^*(t)\,dt + \Sigma^*(t)\left\{\partial\begin{bmatrix} f(t, x_\lambda^*(t)) \\ A(t)x_h^*(t)\end{bmatrix}\Big/\partial x^*\right\} dt + \begin{bmatrix} Q(t) \\ 0\end{bmatrix}\begin{bmatrix} Q(t) \\ 0\end{bmatrix}' + \begin{bmatrix} 0 \\ E_g\{gb(t)\}\end{bmatrix} \cdot [\partial\lambda(t, x_\lambda^*(t))/\partial x^*]'\,\Sigma^*(t)\,dt + \Sigma^*(t)\,[\partial\lambda(t, x_\lambda^*(t))/\partial x^*]\begin{bmatrix} 0 \\ E_g\{gb(t)\}\end{bmatrix}' dt + E_g\left\{\begin{bmatrix} 0 \\ gb(t)\end{bmatrix}\begin{bmatrix} 0 \\ gb(t)\end{bmatrix}'\right\}\left[\lambda(t, x_\lambda^*(t)) + \frac{1}{2}\operatorname{tr}\left\{H_{x^*}[\lambda(t, x_\lambda^*(t))]\,\Sigma^*(t)\right\}\right] dt - \Sigma^*(t)\begin{bmatrix} 0 \\ c(t)\end{bmatrix} R^{-1}(t)\begin{bmatrix} 0 \\ c(t)\end{bmatrix}' \Sigma^*(t)\,dt \quad (24)$$

where $\partial v(x^*(t))/\partial x^*$ denotes the Jacobian matrix of first derivatives of the vector function $v(x^*(t))$; here, the $(i, j)$ element of $\partial v(x^*(t))/\partial x^*$ is $\partial v_i(x^*(t))/\partial x_j^*$. The initial conditions for (23) and (24) are the initial mean and covariance for $x(t)$; that is,

$$x^*(0) = E[x(0)] \tag{25}$$

and

$$\sum^*(0) = E\{[x(0) - x^*(0)]\ [x(0) - x^*(0)]'\}. \tag{26}$$

Equations (23) and (24) will be generalized in Appendix A to a nonlinear detector model. These equations are written here in a form to facilitate this generalization.

Equations (23) and (24) define the quasi-optimum MMSE estimator for $x(t)$ in terms of $\mathcal{Y}_t$. The use of these equations in estimation and hypothesis-testing problems in optical communication is pursued in the next section.

## VII. Detection and Estimation Structures

In this section we will examine several applications. These include the determination of a demodulator structure for angle modulation on a subcarrier, the detector structure for binary hypothesis testing with known signals, and the detector structure for binary signaling in the turbulent atmospheric channel.

### A. *Subcarrier Angle Modulation*

A common technique for transmitting information at optical frequencies is to use intensity modulation of a subcarrier. For this example, we confine our attention to a free-space channel so that the complex envelope of the received-signal field satisfies

$$|U_s(t, \vec{r})|^2 = \frac{I}{2}\{1 + A(t)\cos[\omega t + \phi(t)]\} \tag{27}$$

where $|A(t)| \leqslant 1$, and $A(t)$ and $\phi(t)$ are, respectively, amplitude and angle modulation signals, and $I/4$ is the signal irradiance at the detector when $A(t) = 0$. In this example, we will confine our attention to angle modulation, for which $A(t) = \alpha$, and the random signal in fixed background model described in Section III-A, i.e., $\mu(t) = \lambda_s(t, \phi(t)) + \lambda_0$. Thus, using (3), the signal component of the detector intensity function $\mu(t)$ is

$$\lambda_s(t, \phi(t)) = \Lambda\{1 + \alpha\cos[\omega t + \phi(t)]\} \tag{28}$$

where $\Lambda = \eta a_d I/4h\nu$.

For the purpose of illustration, we assume that the information process $\{\phi(t);\ t \geqslant 0\}$ has the linear, finite-dimensional state representation

$$\phi(t) = \xi'(t)\, x_\lambda(t) \tag{29}$$

where $\{x_\lambda(t), t \geqslant 0\}$ is a Gauss-Markov process satisfying the following linear specialization of (19):

$$dx_\lambda(t) = F(t)\, x_\lambda(t)\, dt + Q(t)\, dw(t). \tag{30}$$

The initial condition $x_\lambda(0)$ is a zero-mean Gaussian random variable with covariance $\Sigma_\lambda(0)$. This model contains all the common forms of angle modulation including phase, frequency, and preemphasized frequency modulation [9].

For this angle modulation model, (23) becomes

$$\begin{aligned} dx^*(t) = {} & \begin{bmatrix} F(t) & 0 \\ 0 & A(t) \end{bmatrix} x^*(t)\, dt \\ & + \bar{g}\begin{bmatrix} 0 \\ b(t) \end{bmatrix} \{\Lambda[1 + \alpha\cos(\omega t + [\xi'(t)\ 0']\, x^*(t)] + \lambda_0\}\, dt \\ & - (\Lambda\alpha\bar{g}/2)\begin{bmatrix} 0 \\ b(t) \end{bmatrix} \begin{bmatrix} \xi(t) \\ 0 \end{bmatrix}' \sum^*(t) \begin{bmatrix} \xi(t) \\ 0 \end{bmatrix} \\ & \cdot \cos(\omega t + [\xi'(t)\ 0']\ x^*(t))\, dt \\ & + \sum^*(t)\begin{bmatrix} 0 \\ c(t) \end{bmatrix} R^{-1}(t)\, [dy(t) - [0'\, c'(t)]\ x^*(t)\, dt]. \end{aligned} \tag{31}$$

Similarly, for this angle modulation model, (24) becomes

$$\begin{aligned} d\sum^*(t)/dt = {} & \begin{bmatrix} F(t) & 0 \\ 0 & A(t) \end{bmatrix}' \sum^*(t) + \sum^*(t) \begin{bmatrix} F(t) & 0 \\ 0 & A(t) \end{bmatrix} \\ & + \begin{bmatrix} Q(t) \\ 0 \end{bmatrix} \begin{bmatrix} Q(t) \\ 0 \end{bmatrix}' - \left\{ \begin{bmatrix} 0 \\ b(t) \end{bmatrix} \begin{bmatrix} \xi(t) \\ 0 \end{bmatrix}' \sum^*(t) \right. \\ & \left. + \sum^*(t) \begin{bmatrix} \xi(t) \\ 0 \end{bmatrix} \begin{bmatrix} 0 \\ b(t) \end{bmatrix}' \right\} \Lambda\alpha\bar{g} \\ & \cdot \sin(\omega t + [\xi'(t)\ 0']\ x^*(t)) + \overline{g^2} \begin{bmatrix} 0 \\ b(t) \end{bmatrix} \begin{bmatrix} 0 \\ b(t) \end{bmatrix}' \\ & \cdot \left[ (\Lambda + \lambda_0) + \Lambda\alpha \left( 1 - \frac{1}{2} \begin{bmatrix} \xi(t) \\ 0 \end{bmatrix}' \sum^*(t) \begin{bmatrix} \xi(t) \\ 0 \end{bmatrix} \right) \right. \\ & \left. \cdot \cos(\omega t + [\xi'(t)\ 0']\ x^*(t)) \right] \\ & - \sum^*(t) \begin{bmatrix} 0 \\ c(t) \end{bmatrix} R^{-1}(t) \begin{bmatrix} 0 \\ c(t) \end{bmatrix}' \sum^*(t). \end{aligned} \tag{32}$$

A block-diagram realization for $x^*(t)$ and $\phi^*(t) = [\xi'(t)\ 0']\ x^*(t)$ is shown in Fig. 2. A similar diagram showing the details of generating $\Sigma^*(t)$ can be obtained from (32); we note that $\Sigma^*(t)$ is not directly coupled to the observation $y(t)$, but it is coupled to $x^*(t)$ and, therefore, cannot be precomputed, as would be the case with the Kalman-Bucy filter. For the estimator shown in Fig. 2, the high-frequency simplifications for $\Sigma^*(t)$ used in [9] do not appear justified because the detector filter must pass the subcarrier modulation frequency $\omega$. The estimator admits the following interpretation: 1) if the intensity $\lambda(t, x_\lambda(t))$ of the photoelectron emission process was known and not random, then the portion of the estimator enclosed in the dashed lines is the linear MMSE estimator of the state $x_\lambda(t)$ of the detector filter, i.e., it is an appropriate Kalman-Bucy filter taking into consideration the fact that the random drive for $x_\lambda(t)$ is not zero mean; 2) however, the intensity is not known because of the information process $\phi(t)$, and the purpose of that portion of the estimator exterior to the dashed lines is to form an estimate of the unknown in-

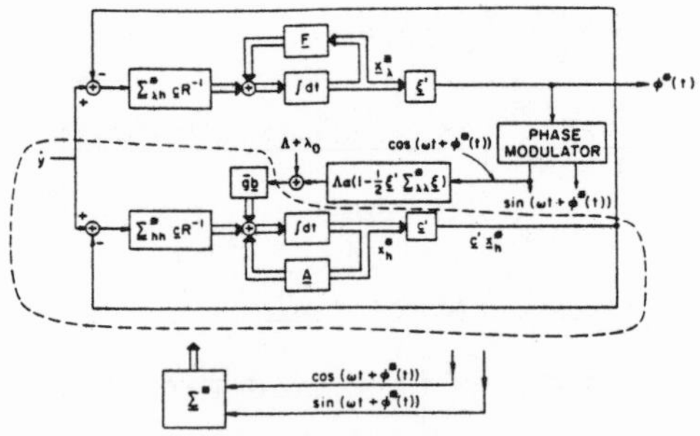


Fig. 2. Receiver for subcarrier angle modulation. (The subscripts on $\Sigma^*$ denote the appropriate partitions.)

tensity; 3) this intensity estimate is introduced, with a weighting $(1 - \frac{1}{2}\xi' \Sigma^*_{\lambda\lambda} \xi)$ depending on the error in the estimate, in the same way as if it were the known intensity.

### *B. Binary Detection of Known Signals*

Here we consider the problem of binary hypothesis testing for optical communication through the free-space channel. For this channel the intensity model corresponding to a known signal plus fixed background (see Section III-A) is often appropriate. Thus we choose the intensity functions $\mu_i(t)$ of the photoelectron emission processes under the two hypotheses, $H_0$ and $H_1$, as

$$H_1:\ \mu_1(t) = \lambda_1(t, x_\lambda(t)) = \lambda_s(t) + \lambda_0, \qquad t \in [0, T]$$
$$H_0:\ \mu_0(t) = \lambda_2(t, x_\lambda(t)) = \lambda_0, \qquad t \in [0, T]. \quad (33)$$

Here $[0, T]$ is the detection interval and $n_\lambda = 0$.

The optimum detector processing for $M$-ary detection problems, and hence the above binary problem, was considered in Section V. The processing indicated by (18) requires the use of the causal MMSE estimates $E[z_i(t) | \mathcal{Y}_t, H_i]$ for each hypothesis of (33). As we have indicated in Section VI, these MMSE estimators appear to be impossible to implement exactly. Thus, it is necessary to use a suboptimal detector structure. A reasonable suboptimal detector appears to be that obtained by using the quasi-optimal estimators of Section VI in the estimator-correlator detector structure of Section V in exactly the same way as if they were the optimal estimators. Such a procedure has been suggested by Kailath [14], and we shall use it here.

The quasi-optimum estimates required for this suboptimum detector are obtained by specializing (23) and (24) for each hypothesis. The result under $H_0$ is

$$dx_h^*(t) = [A(t)\, x_h^*(t) + \bar{g}\, b(t)\, \lambda_0]\, dt + \Sigma_{hh}^*(t)\, c(t)\, R^{-1}(t)\, [dy(t) - c'(t)\, x_h^*(t)\, dt]$$

$$d\Sigma_{hh}^*(t)/dt = A'(t)\, \Sigma_{hh}^*(t) + \Sigma_{hh}^*(t)\, A(t) + \overline{g^2}\, b(t)\, b'(t)\, \lambda_0 - \Sigma_{hh}^*(t)\, c(t)\, R^{-1}(t)\, c'(t)\, \Sigma_{hh}^*(t). \quad (34)$$

The result under $H_1$ is obtained by replacing $\lambda_0$ by $(\lambda_s(t) + \lambda_0)$ in (34). These equations specify the linear MMSE causal estimator, i.e., the Kalman-Bucy filter, for a filtered Poisson process observed in independent additive white Gaussian noise. Note that these filters appropriately account for the nonzero mean of the excitation through the terms that depend on $\lambda_0$ or $\lambda_s(t) + \lambda_0$.

The suboptimal detector for this problem is shown in Fig. 3. Note that the threshold constant $\gamma$ depends only on the *a priori* probabilities of the hypotheses and the performance criterion chosen.

### *C. Binary Detection for Fading Channels*

While the model we have developed is general enough to include arbitrary time fading, as long as it is state representable, we here confine our attention to flat-flat fading channels. This model is often suitable for digital communication over the turbulent atmospheric channel [7]. Our model for this situation is

$$H_1:\ \mu_1(t) = \lambda_1(t, x_\lambda(t)) = x_\lambda\, \lambda_s(t) + \lambda_0, \qquad t \in [0, T]$$
$$H_0:\ \mu_0(t) = \lambda_0(t, x_\lambda(t)) = \lambda_0, \qquad t \in [0, T]. \quad (35)$$

Again $[0, T]$ is the detection interval. Here $n_\lambda = 1$, and the state equation for $x_\lambda$ is simply $dx_\lambda(t) = 0$. The quasi-optimum estimator equations required under $H_0$ for the suboptimum detector described in Section VII-B are given by (34). Under $H_1$, the required equations are

$$dx_\lambda^*(t) = \Sigma_{\lambda h}^*(t)\, c(t)\, R^{-1}(t)\, [dy(t) - c'(t)\, x_h^*(t)\, dt] \quad (36)$$

$$dx_h^*(t) = A(t)\, x_h^*(t)\, dt + \bar{g} b(t)\, [x_\lambda^*(t)\, \lambda_s(t) + \lambda_0]\, dt + \Sigma_{hh}^*(t)\, c(t)\, R^{-1}(t)\, [dy(t) - c'(t)\, x_h^*(t)\, dt] \quad (37)$$

where $\Sigma_{\lambda h}^*$ and $\Sigma_{hh}^*$ are the appropriate partitions of $\Sigma^*$ corresponding to $x_\lambda$ and $x_h$, and $\Sigma^*$ satisfies

$$d\Sigma^*(t)/dt = \begin{bmatrix} 0 & 0 \\ 0 & A(t) \end{bmatrix}' \Sigma^*(t) + \Sigma^*(t) \begin{bmatrix} 0 & 0 \\ 0 & A(t) \end{bmatrix} + \bar{g}\lambda_s(t) \left\{ \begin{bmatrix} 0 & 0 \\ b(t) & 0 \end{bmatrix} \Sigma^*(t) + \Sigma^*(t) \begin{bmatrix} 0 & 0 \\ b(t) & 0 \end{bmatrix}' \right\} + \overline{g^2} \begin{bmatrix} 0 & 0 \\ 0 & b(t)\, b'(t) \end{bmatrix} [x_\lambda^*(t)\, \lambda_s(t) + \lambda_0] - \Sigma^*(t) \begin{bmatrix} 0 \\ c(t) \end{bmatrix} R^{-1}(t) \begin{bmatrix} 0 \\ c(t) \end{bmatrix}' \Sigma^*(t). \quad (38)$$

Equation (37) has an interesting interpretation: 1) if the channel gain $x_\lambda$ was known and not random, then $x_\lambda^*(t)$ in (37) would simply be $x_\lambda$, and the situation becomes that of Section VII-B; 2) however, $x_\lambda$ is not known, and its quasi-optimum MMSE estimate as specified by (36) is used instead. A block diagram realization for the suboptimum detector is shown in Fig. 4.

For a time-invariant filter, i.e., $A$, $b$, and $c$ are time invariant, and $\lambda_s(t)$ a constant $\lambda_s$, it is reasonable to expect the estimator

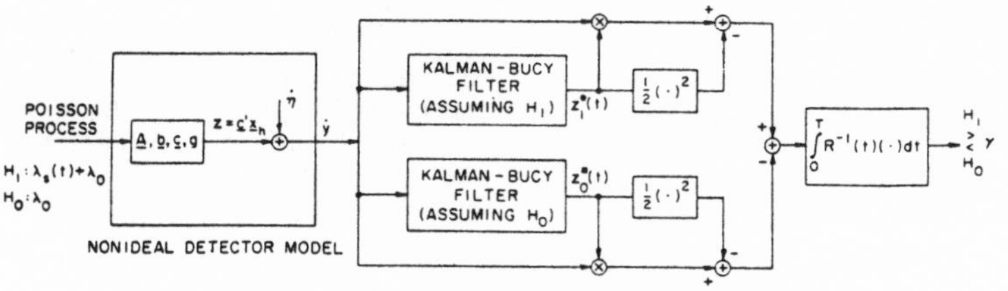


Fig. 3. Detector structure for known signals.

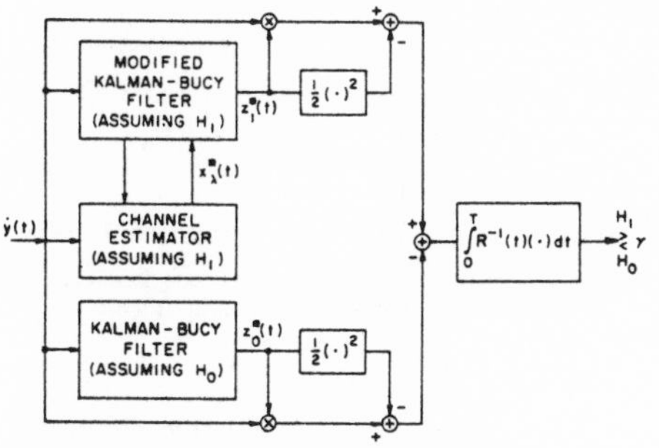


Fig. 4. Detector structure for fading channel.

to approach steady state. In this case $d\Sigma^*(t)/dt = 0$ and (36)–(38) become

$$dx^*_\lambda(t) = 0 \tag{39}$$

$$dx^*_h(t) = Ax^*_h(t)\,dt + \bar{g}b\,[x^*_\lambda(\infty)\,\lambda_s + \lambda_0]\,dt + \Sigma^*_{hh}(\infty)\,cR^{-1}\,[dy(t) - c'x^*_h(t)\,dt] \tag{40}$$

$$0 = A'\Sigma^*_{hh}(\infty) + \Sigma^*_{hh}(\infty)A + \overline{g^2}\;bb'\,[x^*_\lambda(\infty)\lambda_s + \lambda_0] - \Sigma^*_{hh}(\infty)\,cR^{-1}\,c'\,\Sigma^*_{hh}(\infty) \tag{41}$$

where the remaining partitions of $\Sigma^*(\infty)$ are zero. We note that even with these simplifications, there is not a significant reduction in complexity because $x^*_\lambda(\infty)$ is not known *a priori*. In general, (36)–(38) would have to be implemented to generate $x^*_\lambda(\infty)$. With a further loss in optimality, $x^*_\lambda(\infty)$ could be replaced with an arbitrarily chosen constant, e.g., $\overline{x_\lambda}$; this would allow precomputation from (41) of the gain $\Sigma^*_{hh}(\infty)$ in (40) and greatly simplify the implementation at an unknown cost in performance.

## Conclusions

We have formulated a model for the detector output in an optical direct-detection receiver. The model not only describes the interaction of an ideal detector with the received electromagnetic field in a quantum-mechanically correct way, but also includes the effects of thermal noise associated with the detector and subsequent processing. It also includes real detector effects, such as random gain and finite bandwidth. Estimation and detection problems associated with this model have been formulated and general representations for the solutions have been obtained. The general estimation representations have been used to identify quasi-optimal estimator structures. These results have been applied to several optical communication applications. While the receiver structures thus obtained are probably too complex to justify being implemented in routine practice, they do form the basis with engineering judgement for choosing other suboptimal but practical structures that can be implemented economically.

## Appendix A

### Generalization to a Nonlinear Model

In this appendix, we introduce a nonlinear generalization of the linear model specified in Section III. We have found that the basic estimation results for this more general model can be established with essentially no increase in the fundamental complexity of the derivations. Thus, in Appendix B, we give a derivation for the differential equation of the conditional characteristic function of the state in our nonlinear model. Equation (15) follows directly from this by specialization to the linear model.

In our generalization, we first replace the linear state equation (8) by the following nonlinear equation:

$$dx_h(t) = a(t, x_h(t), \mathfrak{M}_t)\,dt + \int_{R^m} b(t, x_h(t), G)\,M(dt, dG). \tag{42}$$

In this equation, we have allowed the first term on the right in (8) to become a nonlinear function of $x_h(t)$ and a quantity $\mathfrak{M}_t$ to be defined below. The function $gb(t)$ associated with the second term on the right in (8) is here replaced by a nonlinear function of $x_h(t)$ and of an $m$-dimensional vector random variable $g$. The process $M$ is a DSPP on the $(m + 1)$-dimensional space corresponding to time greater than zero and the values $g$ can assume. The interpretation of $M$ is the same as that indicated for equation (8) but with the obvious generalizations required for the $m$-dimensional mark variable $g$.

In (42), we let $\mathfrak{M}_t$ denote the past of $M$ up to time $t$. This past includes the occurrence time and mark for each point of the marked-point process on $[0, t)$. By the notation $a(t, x_h(t), \mathfrak{M}_t)$, we mean that $a$ can depend on the entire past of $M$ and, hence, models a very general class of random filters.

In our generalization, we also allow the filter output to be a nonlinear function of the state $x_h(t)$ defined in (42). Thus, in the observation equation (13) we now assume that $\zeta(t)$ has the form $\rho(t, x_h(t))$ where $\rho$ is a known and possibly nonlinear function of $t$ and $x_h(t)$. As before, we set $e(t) = 0$.

As an example, let $m = 1$ and suppose $n_h = 1$, $a(t, x_h(t), \mathfrak{M}_t) = -g^{-1}_{N(t)}x_h(t)$, and $b(t, x_h(t), G) = 1$, where $g_{N(t)}$ is the mark variable on the $N(t)$th point; i.e., $g_{N(t)}$ is the most recently occurring mark random variable. In this case $\{x_h(t); t > 0\}$ has the sample function structure indicated in Fig. 5. Between each event time, $x_h(t)$ decays exponentially with a

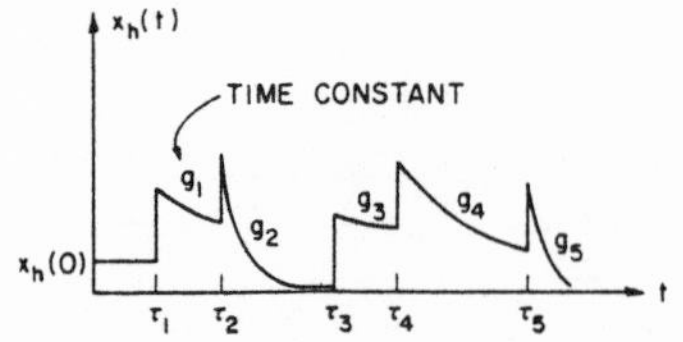


Fig. 5. Sample function for $\{x_h(t);\, t > 0\}$. Between each event time $x_h(t)$ decays exponentially with the time constant indicated and all jumps are of unit amplitude. Note that $x_h(t)$ is not a superposition of exponentials with different decay rates.

time constant equal to the mark of the preceding event. Note that $x_h(t)$ is not a superposition of exponentials with different decay rates. In general, the dependence of $a$ on $\mathfrak{M}_t$ is seen to result in structural changes in the filter, but this does not result in superposition of individual effects for each event. A two-dimensional mark vector $g$ would be required if each exponential also had a random amplitude in addition to the random decay constant.

Even with the generality afforded in the above model, we cannot accommodate photoconductive detectors with time-scaled response functions in the form of (6). The reason is that (42) cannot be specialized to a superposition of randomly time-scaled responses. Thus, it does not appear to us that (6) can be accommodated with any finite-dimensional Markov model.

For technical reasons evident in the proof of Appendix B, we need to assume that the nonlinear functions introduced here are sufficiently well behaved that, for some function $r$ such that $E[|r|] < \infty$, there holds

$$(\Delta t)^{-1} |E\{(\exp[j\langle v, \Delta x(t)\rangle] - 1) | \mathcal{Y}_t, x(t)\}| \leq r(v, t; \mathcal{Y}_t, x(t)). \tag{43}$$

We further need to assume that the limit of

$$(\Delta t)^{-1} E\{(\exp[j\langle v, \Delta x(t)\rangle] - 1) | \mathcal{Y}_t, x(t)\}$$

exists in probability as $\Delta t$ tends to zero. We denote this limit by $\Psi(v, t | \mathcal{Y}_t, x(t))$; that is,

$$\Psi(v, t | \mathcal{Y}_t, x(t)) \triangleq \lim_{\Delta t \downarrow 0} (\Delta t)^{-1} E\{(\exp[j\langle v, \Delta x(t)\rangle] - 1 | \mathcal{Y}_t, x(t))\}. \tag{44}$$

A differential equation for the conditional characteristic function of $x(t)$ given $\mathcal{Y}_t$ is derived in Appendix B. This equation can be used to derive estimator structures for the nonlinear generalization in exactly the same way we have used (15) in Sections VI and VII. Here, we shall only indicate the appropriate changes that occur in the differential equations for the posterior probability density of $x$, the MMSE state estimate $\hat{x}$, and the approximate estimator equations under the assumption that $a(t, x_h(t), \mathfrak{M}_t) = a(t, x_h(t))$ and $b(t, x_h(t), g) = b(t, g)$. In (21) and (22), the following replacements are required:

1) replace $A(t)\, x_h(t)$ by $a(t, x_h(t))$;
2) replace $g b(t)$ by $b(t, g)$;
3) replace $E_g(\cdot)$ by $Eg(\cdot)$;
4) replace $z(t)$ by $\rho(t, x_h(t))$; and
5) replace $A(t)\, \hat{x}(t)$ by $\hat{a}(t) \triangleq E[a(t, x_h(t)) | \mathcal{Y}_t]$.

In (23) and (24), the following replacements are required in addition to 2 and 3:

6) replace $A(t)\, x_h^*(t)$ by $a(t, x_h^*(t))$;
7) replace $\left[\begin{smallmatrix} 0 \\ c(t) \end{smallmatrix}\right]$ by $\partial \rho(t, x_h^*(t))/\partial x^*$; and
8) replace $c'(t) x_h^*(t)$ by $\rho(t, x_h^*(t))$.

Moreover, the term

$$\frac{1}{2} \sum_{i=1}^{n_h} \sum_{j=1}^{n_h} \sigma_{h_{ij}}^*(t)\, \partial^2 a(t, x_h^*(t))/\partial x_{h_i}^*\, \partial x_{h_j}^*\, dt$$

must be added to the right side of (23), and the term

$$\left[\Sigma^*(t)\, H_{x^*}[\rho(t, x^*(t))]\, \Sigma^*(t)\right] R^{-1}(t) \cdot [dy(t) - \rho(t, x^*(t))\, dt]$$

must be added to the right side of (24), where $\sigma_{h_{ij}}^*(t)$ is the $(i, j)$-element of the matrix $[0\, I_{n_h}]\, \Sigma^*(t)\, [0\, I_{n_h}]'$.

## Appendix B

### Derivation of Characteristic Function Equation

Corresponding to an incremental increase in time from $t$ to $t + \Delta t$, the conditional characteristic function of (14) changes to

$$c(v, t + \Delta t | \mathcal{Y}_{t+\Delta t}) = E\{\exp[j\langle v, x(t)\rangle] \cdot \exp[j\langle v, \Delta x(t)\rangle] | \mathcal{Y}_{t+\Delta t}\}$$

in which $\Delta x(t) = x(t + \Delta t) - x(t)$ and $x(t)$ is the vector obtained by adjoining $x_\lambda(t)$ to $x_h(t)$, where $x_h(t)$ satisfies (42). The expectation can be written in terms of the joint conditional probability distribution function $P_{x(t), \Delta x(t)}(X, Y | \mathcal{Y}_t, \Delta y(t))$ for $x(t)$ and $\Delta x(t)$ given $\mathcal{Y}_{t+\Delta t} = \{\mathcal{Y}_t, \Delta y(t)\}$ according to

$$c(v, t + \Delta t | \mathcal{Y}_{t+\Delta t}) = \int \cdots \int \exp[j\langle v, X\rangle] \cdot \exp[j\langle v, Y\rangle]\, d^{2n} P_{x(t), \Delta x(t)}(X, Y | \mathcal{Y}_t, \Delta y(t)). \tag{45}$$

Let us now examine the finite difference

$$\delta^{2n} P_{x(t), \Delta x(t)}(X, Y | \mathcal{Y}_t, \Delta y_t = Z) \triangleq P(x(t) \in [X, X + \delta X),\ \Delta x(t) \in [Y, Y + \delta Y] | \mathcal{Y}_t, \Delta y(t) = Z)$$

for eventual use in (45). Using Bayes' rule and (13), we obtain

$$\delta^{2n} P_{x(t), \Delta x(t)}(X, Y | \mathcal{Y}_t, \Delta y(t) = Z) = \frac{\exp[-(Z - \rho(t, X_h)\Delta t)^2/2R(t)\Delta t]\, \delta^{2n} P_{x(t), \Delta x(t)}(X, Y | \mathcal{Y}_t)}{E\{\exp[-(Z - \rho(t, x_h(t))\Delta t)^2/2R(t)\Delta t] | \mathcal{Y}_t\}}. \tag{46}$$

Upon letting $|\delta x| \to 0$ and $|\delta Y| \to 0$, we thus have from (45) that

$$c(v, t + \Delta t | \mathcal{Y}_t, \Delta y(t)) = \frac{E\{\exp[j\langle v, x(t)\rangle]\, \exp[j\langle v, \Delta x(t)\rangle]\, \exp[-(\Delta y(t) - \rho(t, x_h(t))\Delta t)^2/2R(t)\Delta t] | \mathcal{Y}_t\}}{E\{\exp[-(\Delta y(t) - \rho(t, x_h(t))\Delta t)^2/2R(t)\Delta t | \mathcal{Y}_t\}} \tag{47}$$

where the expectation in the numerator is over $x(t)$ and $\Delta x(t)$ with $\mathcal{Y}_t$ given, and that in the denominator is over $x(t)$ with $\mathcal{Y}_t$ given. Thus

$$c(v, t + \Delta t | \mathcal{Y}_t, \Delta y(t)) = E\left\{\exp[j\langle v, x(t)\rangle]\, \exp[j\langle v, \Delta x(t)\rangle] \times \frac{\exp[R^{-1}(t)\rho(t, x_h(t))\Delta y(t) - \frac{1}{2}R^{-1}(t)\rho^2(t, x_h(t))\Delta t]}{E\{\exp[R^{-1}(t)\rho(t, x_h(t))\Delta y(t) - \frac{1}{2}R^{-1}(t)\rho^2(t, x_h(t))\Delta t] | \mathcal{Y}_t\}} \,\middle|\, \mathcal{Y}_t\right\}. \tag{48}$$

We next expand this expression in a Taylor series about $\Delta y(t) = 0$ and $\Delta t = 0$, keep terms to order $\Delta t$, and use the incremental properties of Wiener processes [17] to replace $(\Delta y(t))^2$ by $R(t)\,\Delta t$. The result after some manipulations is

$$c(v, t+\Delta t \mid \mathcal{Y}_t, \Delta y_t) = E\{\exp[j\langle v, x(t)\rangle] \exp[j\langle v, \Delta x(t)\rangle] \times (1 + [\rho(t, x_h(t)) - \hat{\rho}(t)] R^{-1}(t)[\Delta y(t) - \hat{\rho}(t)\Delta t]) \mid \mathcal{Y}_t\} \quad (49)$$

where $\hat{\rho}(t) \triangleq E[\rho(t, x_h(t)) \mid \mathcal{Y}_t]$ is the MMSE estimate of $\rho$ given $\mathcal{Y}_t$. Thus, by subtracting $c(v, t \mid \mathcal{Y}_t)$ from both sides, we obtain

$$\Delta c(v, t \mid \mathcal{Y}_t) \triangleq c(v, t+\Delta t \mid \mathcal{Y}_{t+\Delta t}) - c(v, t \mid \mathcal{Y}_t)$$

$$= E\left[\exp(j\langle v, x(t)\rangle) E\left(\frac{\exp[j\langle v, \Delta x(t)\rangle] - 1}{\Delta t} \Bigg| \mathcal{Y}_t, x(t)\right) \Bigg| \mathcal{Y}_t\right] \Delta t$$

$$+ E\{\exp[j\langle v, x(t)\rangle] \exp[j\langle v, \Delta x(t)\rangle] \times [\rho(t, x_h(t)) - \hat{\rho}(t)] \mid \mathcal{Y}_t\} R^{-1}(t)[\Delta y(t) - \hat{\rho}(t)\Delta t] \quad (50)$$

where we have used iterated expectation in writing the first term on the right. We now take the limit as $\Delta t \to 0$, use (43) and Lebseque's bounded convergence theorem to interchange this limit with expectation, and the definition of $\psi$ in (44) to obtain the desired result:

$$dc(v, t \mid \mathcal{Y}_t) = E\{\psi(v, t \mid \mathcal{Y}_t, x(t)) \exp[j\langle v, x(t)\rangle] \mid \mathcal{Y}_t\}\, dt + E\{\exp[j\langle v, x(t)\rangle] [\rho(t, x_h(t)) - \hat{\rho}(t)] \mid \mathcal{Y}_t\} \times R^{-1}(t)[dy(t) - \hat{\rho}(t)\,dt]. \quad (51)$$

Equation (51) is a representation for the conditional characteristic function for $x(t)$ given the observed data $\mathcal{Y}_t$ up to time $t$. Representations of this type for the additive-white-Gaussian-noise observation model have been given before [18] when $x(t)$ is a Markov process, which is not the case here. Similar representations have been given for doubly stochastic Poisson process observations [5]. The interpretation and use of (51) is exactly the same as with these alternative situations.

We next evaluate the differential generator $\psi$ appearing in (51).

*Evaluation of $\psi$*

By using iterated expectations, we obtain

$$\psi(v, t \mid \mathcal{Y}_t, x(t)) \triangleq \lim_{\Delta t \to 0} (\Delta t)^{-1} E[(\exp[j\langle v, \Delta x(t)\rangle] - 1) \mid \mathcal{Y}_t, x(t)] = \lim_{\Delta t \to 0} (\Delta t)^{-1} E\{E[(\exp[j\langle v, \Delta x(t)\rangle] - 1) \mid \mathcal{Y}_t, x(t), \mathfrak{M}_t] \mid \mathcal{Y}_t, x(t)\}. \quad (52)$$

The inner expectation can be written as

$$E[(\exp[j\langle v, \Delta x(t)\rangle] - 1) \mid \mathcal{Y}_t, x(t), \mathfrak{M}_t]$$
$$= E\{\exp[j\langle v_1, \Delta x_\lambda(t)\rangle] E(\exp[j\langle v_2, \Delta x_h(t)\rangle] \mid \Delta x_\lambda(t), \mathcal{Y}_t, x(t), \mathfrak{M}_t) - 1 \mid \mathcal{Y}_t, x(t), \mathfrak{M}_t\}. \quad (53)$$

The term

$$E(\exp[j\langle v_2, \Delta x_h(t)\rangle] \mid \Delta x_\lambda(t), \mathcal{Y}_t, x(t), \mathfrak{M}_t)$$

can be written to order $\Delta t$ as

$$E\{\exp[j\langle v_2, \Delta x_h(t)\rangle] \mid \Delta x_\lambda(t), \mathcal{Y}_t, x(t), \mathfrak{M}_t, \Delta N(t) = 0\} \times \Pr[\Delta N(t) = 0 \mid \Delta x_\lambda(t), \mathcal{Y}_t, x(t), \mathfrak{M}_t]$$
$$+ E\{\exp[j\langle v_2, \Delta x_h(t)\rangle] \mid \Delta x_\lambda(t), \mathcal{Y}_t, x(t), \mathfrak{M}_t, \Delta N(t) = 1\} \times \Pr[\Delta N(t) = 1 \mid \Delta x_\lambda(t), \mathcal{Y}_t, x(t), \mathfrak{M}_t].$$

This expression can be evaluated using (42) and (7), and the result incorporated into (53) yields

$$E[(\exp[j\langle v, \Delta x(t)\rangle] - 1) \mid \mathcal{Y}_t, x(t), \mathfrak{M}_t]$$
$$= E\Bigg\{\exp[j\langle v_1, \Delta x_\lambda(t)\rangle] \Bigg(\exp[j\langle v_2, a(t, x_h(t), \mathfrak{M}_t)\rangle \Delta t] \times (1 - \lambda(t, x_\lambda(t))\Delta t) + \int_{R^m} \exp[j\langle v_2, a(t, x_h(t), \mathfrak{M}_t)\rangle \Delta t + j\langle v_2, b(t, x_h(t), G)\rangle] p_g(G)\, dG_1 \cdots dG_m\, \lambda(t, x_\lambda(t))\Delta t\Bigg) - 1 \mid \mathcal{Y}_t, x(t), \mathfrak{M}_t\Bigg\}. \quad (54)$$

By expanding (54) in a Taylor series about $\Delta t = 0$ and keeping terms to order $\Delta t$, we obtain

$$(\Delta t)^{-1} E[(\exp[j\langle v, \Delta x(t)\rangle] - 1) \mid \mathcal{Y}_t, x(t), \mathfrak{M}_t]$$
$$= E\left\{\frac{\exp[j\langle v_1, \Delta x_\lambda(t)\rangle] - 1}{\Delta t} \Bigg| \mathcal{Y}_t, x(t), \mathfrak{M}_t\right\}$$
$$+ E\Bigg\{\exp[j\langle v_1, \Delta x_\lambda(t)\rangle] \Big(j\langle v_2, a(t, x_h(t), \mathfrak{M}_t)\rangle + \lambda(t, x_\lambda(t)) \int_{R^m} (\exp[j\langle v_2, b(t, x_h(t), G)\rangle] - 1) \times p_g(G)\, dG_1 \cdots dG_m\Big) \mid \mathcal{Y}_t, x(t), \mathfrak{M}_t\Bigg\}. \quad (55)$$

Dividing (55) by $\Delta t$ and taking the limit as $\Delta t$ approaches zero, then yields

$$\lim_{\Delta t \downarrow 0} (\Delta t)^{-1} E[(\exp[j\langle v, \Delta x(t)\rangle] - 1) \mid \mathcal{Y}_t, x(t), \mathfrak{M}_t]$$
$$= \psi_\lambda(v_1, t \mid x_\lambda(t)) + j\langle v_2, a(t, x_h(t), \mathfrak{M}_t)\rangle + \lambda(t, x_\lambda(t)) E_g\{(\exp[j\langle v_2, b(t, x_h(t), g)\rangle] - 1)\} \quad (56)$$

where

$$\psi_\lambda(v_1, t \mid x_\lambda(t)) \triangleq \lim_{\Delta t \to 0} (\Delta t)^{-1} \times E\{(\exp[j\langle v_1, \Delta x_\lambda(t)\rangle] - 1) \mid x_\lambda(t)\} \quad (57)$$

is the differential generator for the Markov process $\{x_\lambda(t); t \geqslant 0\}$; we have used the fact that the future of $x_\lambda(\tau)$ for $\tau > t$ is independent of $\mathcal{Y}_t$, $x_h(t)$, and $\mathfrak{M}_t$ given $x_\lambda(t)$.

By interchanging the limit with the outer expectation in (52) on the basis of (43) and using (56), we have the desired result that

$$\psi(v, t \mid \mathcal{Y}_t, x(t)) = \psi_\lambda(v_1, t \mid x_\lambda(t)) + j\langle v_2, \hat{a}(t, x_h(t))\rangle + \lambda(t, x_h(t)) \times E_g\{(\exp[j\langle v_2, b(t, x_h(t), g)\rangle] - 1)\} \quad (58)$$

where

$$\hat{a}(t, x_h(t)) \triangleq E\{a(t, x_h(t), \mathfrak{M}_t) \mid \mathcal{Y}_t, x(t)\} \quad (59)$$

is the MMSE estimate of $a$ given $\mathcal{Y}_t$ and $x(t)$.

## References

[1] S. Karp, E. L. O'Neill, and R. M. Gagliardi, "Communication theory for the free-space optical channel," *Proc. IEEE*, vol. 58, pp. 1611–1626, Oct. 1970.

[2] P. L. Kelley and W. H. Kleiner, "Theory of electromagnetic field measurement and photoelectron counting," *Phys. Rev.*, vol. 136, pp. 316–334, Oct. 19, 1964.

[3] R. S. Kennedy and S. Karp, Ed., *Proc. MIT-NASA Workshop Optical Space Communication* (August 1968), NASA SP-217. Washington, D.C.: U.S. Government Printing Office, 1969, pp. 12–14.
[4] E. V. Hoversten, "Optical communication theory," in *Laser Handbook*, F. T. Arecchi and E. O. Schulz-DuBois, Ed. Amsterdam, The Netherlands: North-Holland, 1972, pp. 1805–1862.
[5] D. L. Snyder, "Filtering and detection for doubly stochastic Poisson processes," *IEEE Trans. Inform. Theory*, vol. IT-18, pp. 91–102, Jan. 1972.
[6] J. R. Clark and E. V. Hoversten, "The Poisson process as a statistical model for photodetectors excited by Gaussian light," Res. Lab. of Electronics, Massachusetts Inst. Technol., Cambridge, Quarterly Progress Rep. 98, pp. 95–101, July 1970.
[7] E. V. Hoversten, R. O. Harger, and S. J. Halme, "Communication theory for the turbulent atmosphere," *Proc. IEEE*, vol. 58, pp. 1626–1650, Oct. 1970.
[8] R. Brockett, *Finite Dimensional Linear Systems*. New York: Wiley, 1970.
[9] D. L. Snyder, *The State-Variable Approach to Continuous Estimation, With Applications to Analog Communication Theory*. Cambridge, Mass.: MIT Press, 1969.
[10] J. R. Fisher and E. B. Stear, "Optimal nonlinear filtering for independent increment processes–Part I," *IEEE Trans. Inform. Theory*, vol. IT-13, pp. 558–568, Oct. 1967.
——, "Optimal nonlinear filtering for independent increment processes–Part II," *IEEE Trans. Inform. Theory*, vol. IT-13, pp. 568–578, Oct. 1967.
[11] E. V. Hoversten and D. L. Snyder, "Receiver processing for direct-detection optical communication system," *Proc. IEEE 1972 Int. Conf. Communications*, Philadelphia, Pa., June 1972, pp. 4-21-4-24.
[12] K. Kurimoto, "Optimum filtering and detection for doubly stochastic shot noise processes in white Gaussian noise," Ph.D. dissertation, Dep. Elec. Eng., Univ. of Maryland, College Park, May 1972.
[13] T. E. Duncan, "Evaluation of likelihood functions," *Inform. Contr.*, vol. 13, pp. 62–74, July 1968.
[14] T. Kailath, "A general likelihood-ratio formula for random signals in Gaussian noise," *IEEE Trans. Inform. Theory*, vol. IT-15, pp. 350–361, May 1969.
[15] A. V. Skorokhod, *Studies in the Theory of Random Processes*. Reading, Mass.: Addison-Wesley, 1965, ch. 2.
[16] A. H. Jazwinski, *Stochastic Processes and Filtering Theory*. New York: Academic, 1970.
[17] E. Wong, *Stochastic Processes in Information and Dynamical Systems*. New York: McGraw-Hill, 1971, pp. 53–54.
[18] P. A. Frost and T. Kailath, "An innovations approach to least-squares estimation–Part III: Nonlinear estimation in white Gaussian noise," *IEEE Trans. Automat. Contr.*, vol. AC-16, pp. 217–226, June 1971 [see eq. (49)].

# Part III

# OPTICAL CHANNELS

# Editor's Comments on Papers 15 and 16

**15 HOVERSTEN, HARGER, and HALME**
*Communication Theory for the Turbulent Atmosphere*

**16A PERSONICK**
*Receiver Design for Digital Fiber Optic Communication Systems, I*

**16B PERSONICK**
*Receiver Design for Digital Fiber Optic Communication Systems, II*

An obvious channel for an optical communication syetem is the atmosphere because it is "free" and multiple users have little likelihood of mutual interference if they utilize the spatial coherence of the laser beam. There are obvious frequent degradations, however, due to particles (rain, fog, aerosols, etc.) and, even in clear-air, turbulence-induced index of refraction variations, all of which place limitations on the reliable use of this channel. It was concluded early on that for common carrier traffic, the atmosphere channel would not be satisfactory; in the 1960s attention turned to guided systems—e.g., a considerable effort was devoted to rather complex lenslike guiding systems only to be abandoned when the optical fiber's loss was dramatically reduced at the beginning of the 1970s.

Nevertheless, the atmosphere remained a promising channel, e.g., for short-distance, cheap, quick set-up channels and satellite-ground channels. Also, the possibility existed that communication theory ideas could alleviate at least partially atmospheric degradations, especially in the clear-air, turbulent channel.

The immediate problem from the communication theory point of view was, of course, channel characterization. In the early 1960s the so-called Rytov approximation, as expounded in Tatarski [1] and Cernov [2], for example, was one of the few viable propagation theories that held promise of describing the optical field beyond the few tens of meters of transmission distance where the (single) Born approximation holds; it found application to the analysis of performance of specific optical systems. [The Born approximation typically predicts Gaussian fields for very short distances (a few tens of meters) and such field distributions seem reasonable for very long distances (perhaps thousands of meters); the Rytov model typically predicts lognormal fields.] Generally, these analyses were classical analyses, ignoring quantum effects but accounting for background noise. Typical was Fried's analysis [3] of a heterodyne receiver with an SNR criterion using the Rytov propagation model. Fried demonstrated the existence of an optimum size aperture, which is not surprising when background noise is important, since such a receiver can add the received field only coherently and therefore should be primarily restricted to processing one "coherence area."

To those with appropriate communications background, it was relatively clear that additional incoherent processing should be helpful against background noise. One way was simply to incoherently sum outputs from a number of spatially disjunct heterodyne receivers; still better would be to incoherently sum *all possible* such coherent integrations over a given aperture. This last operation can be realized elegantly by an optical receiver and shown to be strictly optimal for Gaussian fields [4]—its exact probability of error performance was given—and, in limiting cases, for the lognormal fields given by the Rytov theory [5]. In the former case the optimum aperture weighting for a heterodyne receiver was given and its performance was calculated exactly: the optimum receiver had dramatically better performance when the receiving aperture was as large as a few coherence areas.

Experience with diversity communications indicated a route of analysis taken by Kennedy and Hoversten [6]. The received field was divided a priori into disjunct areas to be processed separately; with an idealized assumption about the received field's phase covariance function, there resulted an equal-strength, independent $M$-diversity path problem with lognormal distributions. Optimum diversity receiver structures were given and it was shown that if the amount of diversity could be controlled, the minimum energy-to-noise ratio per bit for which the probability of error vanished was independent of the turbulence and just that of the channel without turbulence.

By the end of the sixties, difficulties with the Rytov model became apparent and the still-continuing search for better channel-propagation models was renewed while the incorporation of quantum effects into this communication channel began. The semiclassical analysis required specification of the field processing—which the classical analysis could suggest—prior to photodetection. The full quantum description quickly led to difficult analysis.

The status of this work on optimal structures and their performance was reviewed by Estil Hoversten, R. O. Harger and Seppo Halme in "Communication Theory for the Turbulent Atmosphere" (Paper 15). The authors discuss the modeling and representation of the received fields at length, including modal expansions and their quantizations; they assume a filtered Poisson process for the semiclassical analysis. Digital communication systems are discussed at length; e.g., the optimum quantum receiver for lognormal signal fields is given. A general important conclusion—in fact, a triumph for communication theory—is that optimal, albeit complicated, spatial and temporal processing can dramatically reduce or eliminate performance degradation due to atmospheric turbulence (the paper includes a quite complete summary). Estimation problems are also discussed, primarily using classical models, although the authors indicate how quantum effects can be included if specific quantum measurements are used.

Hoversten (7) gives a masterly summary of optimum optical communication systems and their performance, as known in 1972, for the free-space, turbulent, and scatter channels, emphasizing quantum and spatial effects.

There is now no doubt that optical communications will utilize optical fibers in an important way: the research and development effort in industry is already very large, "off-the-shelf" systems are becoming available, and reviews—such as Miller, Marcatili, and Li [8], Gloge [9], and Barnoski [10]—have appeared. Of course, the special nature of the fiber channel has reoriented and focused much optical communication systems research and development, both in devices and theory. For example, the avalanche photodiode is especially appealing and is used in a direct detection receiver; semiconductor lasers and even (incoherent) light emitting diodes are useful with these multimode fibers.

Because of the quantum noise, good design results in a different receiver configuration than is common at lower frequencies, and it significantly improves system performance. This is the general subject of Papers 16A and 16B, "Receiver Design for Digital Fiber Optic Communication Systems, I, II" by Stewart Personick. The design optimization is studied under a signal-to-noise ratio criterion for tractability of analysis and the receiver requires integral equalization. Personick shows that despite the intrinsic nonlinear nature of the direct detector, under certain conditions the equalization may be performed at baseband with an attendant, tolerable decrease in system performance.

An interesting comparison of approaches to error rate calculation is given in Personick et al. [11]: work of this type is now appearing rapidly.

## REFERENCES


1. Tatarksi, V. I. *Wave Propagation in a Turbulent Medium*, transl. by R. A. Silverman. New York: McGraw-Hill, 1961.
2. Cernov, L. A. *Wave Propagation in a Random Medium*, transl. by R. A. Silverman. New York: Dover, 1960.
3. Fried, D. L. "Optical Heterodyne Detection of an Atmospherically Distorted Signal Wave Front." *IEEE Proc.* **55**:57–67 (Jan. 1967).
4. Harger, R. O. "Maximum Likelihood and Optimized Coherent Heterodyne Receivers for Strongly Scattered Gaussian Fields." *Optica Acta* **16**:745–760 (Dec. 1969).
5. Harger, R. O. "On Processing Optical Images Propagated Through the Atmosphere." *IEEE Trans. Aerosp. Electron. Syst.* **AES-3**:819–828 (Sept. 1967).
6. Kennedy, R. S., and E. V. Hoversten. "On the Atmosphere as an Optical Communication Channel." *IEEE Trans. Inf. Theory* **IT-14**:716–725 (Sept. 1968).
7. Hoversten, E. V. "Optical Communication Theory," in *Laser Handbook*, edited by F. T. Arecchi and E. O. Schulz-Du Bois. Amsterdam: North-Holland, 1972.
8. Miller, S. E., E. A. J. Marcatili, and T. Li. "Research Toward Optical-Fiber Transmission Systems, Part I: The Transmission Medium; Part II: Devices and System Considerations." *IEEE Proc.* **61**:1703–1781 (Dec. 1973).
9. Gloge, D., ed. *Optical Fiber Technology*. New York: IEEE Press, 1976.
10. Barnoski, M. K., ed. *Fundamentals of Optical Fiber Communications*. New York: Academic Press, 1976.
11. Personick, S. D., P. Balaban, J. H. Bobsin, and P. R. Kumar. "A Detailed Comparison of Four Approaches to the Calculation of Error Rates of Optical Fiber System Receivers." to appear in *IEEE Trans. Commun.* May, 1977.

# 15



Reprinted from *IEEE Proc.* **58**(10):1626–1650 (1970)

# Communication Theory for the Turbulent Atmosphere

E. V. HOVERSTEN, MEMBER, IEEE, R. O. HARGER, MEMBER, IEEE, AND S. J. HALME

*Abstract*—This paper is concerned with an examination of how statistical communication theory can be used to combat the effects of atmospheric turbulence in optical communication systems. The objective is to provide a framework to be used in discussing and relating the analytical results presently available in the literature as well as some new, or at least not widely known, results and in motivating and guiding future work.

Both digital communication and parameter and waveform estimation are considered, with the greater emphasis on the former. As necessary mathematical preliminaries, the relevant statistical channel model, the problems of spatial representation, quantum field models, and the output statistics of optical detectors are considered. For digital-communication systems, the structure and performance of optimum quantum receivers and of structured receivers, e.g., di and heterodyne-detection receivers with either a single detector detector array, are discussed and related. The simplifying approxi tions and assumptions required to obtain these results are emphasi Estimation theory is considered primarily from a classical (nonq tum) viewpoint. The quadratic functional structure of the proces that result from certain approximations to the likelihood functi are emphasized. Cramer–Rao bounds on the estimation performa are considered and applied to several examples.

Manuscript received July 16, 1970. The research of E. V. Hoversten was supported by the National Aeronautics and Space Administration under Grant NGL 22-009-013. The research of R. O. Harger was supported by the National Aeronautics and Space Administration under Grant NGR 21-002-0237 and by the National Science Foundation under Grant GK-14920.

E. V. Hoversten is with the Department of Electrical Engineering and the Research Laboratory of Electronics, Massachusetts Institute of Technology, Cambridge, Mass.

R. O. Harger is with the Department of Electrical Engineering, University of Maryland, College Park, Md.

S. J. Halme is with the Department of Electrical Engineering and Radio Laboratory, Technical University of Helsinki, Otaniemi, Finland.

## I. Introduction

THIS PAPER is concerned with the structure and formance of optimum and near-optimum opt communication systems for the clear turbulent mospheric channel. The channel effects of interest here caused by random variations of the optical refractive in in time and space along the propagation path. These ref tive index changes are due to small temperature variati in the atmosphere which, in turn, are caused by turbu mixing of various thermal layers. Although the typ temperature variations are on the order of 1° K, the res ing refractive index variations of a few parts in a mil cause extensive effects on optical radiation propaga through the turbulent atmosphere [1]. These effects, w considered in detail elsewhere in this issue, include -space fading of the received field, distortion of the ived phase front, and spreading of the transmitted n [2]–[4].

or simplicity, the term atmospheric turbulence will be l here to refer to the random refractive index variations. emphasized that haze, smog, fog, clouds and other ospheric conditions characterized by concentrations of osols causing scattering effects are not considered except gross attenuation of the signal power.

he objective of this paper is to provide a tutorial exami- on of how statistical communication theory ideas can sed to combat the effects of atmospheric turbulence, to probe and review some of the recent research on the lamental capabilities and limitations of the turbulent osphere as a communication channel at infrared and cal frequencies. The paper will consider digital, param- estimation, and analog communication systems. ory will be emphasized and the space allocated to the ous topics will be roughly equivalent to their current of development. It should be emphasized that in many s only fragmentary results are available and hence the tment here is far from complete; also, some topics have omitted altogether because of the breadth of the sub- and the necessary limitation on space. For the most part, nagnitudes of the turbulent effects [2] and the practical iderations associated with building turbulent-channel munication systems [5] are left for discussion else- re in this issue.

## II. Models and Representations

is necessary to formulate an appropriate statistical nel model before statistical communication theory can pplied. For our purposes the modeling problem can be rated into three parts.

rst, an appropriate statistical model of the classical received at the output of the turbulent channel will be idered. This model must reflect the relevant propaga- features discussed elsewhere [2].

hether the detection or estimation problem is ap- ched from a structured or quantum viewpoint (see the wing) it is necessary to represent the received field over etection interval and aperture by a countable set of ob- ables, i.e., a countable set of random variables. In gen- this will correspond to the decomposition of the re- d field into appropriate orthogonal time-space modes. s several types of representations that will be useful in following discussion will be considered.

t optical frequencies quantum effects, which are not ortant at lower frequencies, must be considered. These ts can be considered by quantizing the radiation field describing the output statistics of the physical devices e used to measure the fields. The former is the more amental point of view and is necessary for the applica- of the ideas of quantum detection and estimation ry. The latter is perhaps the more useful when consider- the design and performance of structured receivers. , as preparation for the material to follow, we will con- both approaches in this section.

### A. Statistical Channel Model

The statistical description of the received electromagnetic field is considered here. For simplicity, assume that the transmitted field is linearly polarized, and that the relevant background noise field has statistically independent polarizations. These assumptions permit the use of a scalar model because the depolarization effects of atmospheric turbulence are negligible [2], [6], [7]. Fig. 1 defines the various scalar fields of interest. Here $u_i(t, \boldsymbol{r}_i)$ is the transmitted field reflecting the transmitting antenna properties, $u_0(t, \boldsymbol{r}_0)$ is the signal portion of the received field, $u_b(t, \boldsymbol{r}_0)$ is the relevant polarization component of the background noise field, and $u_r(t, \boldsymbol{r}_0)$ is the total received field. For convenience, all the fields are assumed to be so normalized that the impedance of the medium can be taken to be unity, i.e., the fields considered here are the actual fields divided by the square root of the propagation medium impedance, approximately 377 ohms. The vectors $\boldsymbol{r}_i$ and $\boldsymbol{r}_0$ are two dimensional and define points in the input and output planes, respectively; for simplicity, these planes are assumed to be parallel and separated by the propagation distance $L$.

The model and analysis are simplified by introducing the complex envelopes of the fields. The complex envelope $U(t, \boldsymbol{r})$ is related to the corresponding field by the definition

$$u(t, \boldsymbol{r}) = \mathrm{Re}\left[U(t, \boldsymbol{r})e^{j2\pi\nu t}\right] \tag{1}$$

where Re indicates the real part of the quantity in brackets and $\nu$ is the optical carrier frequency. If it is assumed that time-varying spatial modulation is not employed, then

$$U_i(t, \boldsymbol{r}_i) = S(t)U(\boldsymbol{r}_i) \tag{2}$$

and the complex envelope of the output field can be written

$$U_0(t, \boldsymbol{r}_0) = S\left(t - \frac{L}{c}\right)\int d\boldsymbol{r}_i U(\boldsymbol{r}_i)h(t, \boldsymbol{r}_0, \boldsymbol{r}_i : L)/2 \tag{3}$$

where $U(\boldsymbol{r}_i)$ represents the complex transmitting aperture illumination function (i.e., the antenna properties of the transmitter), $S(t)$ accounts for the temporal modulation of the transmitted signal, $L/c$ accounts for the propagation delay, and $h(t, \boldsymbol{r}_0, \boldsymbol{r}_i : L)$ is the complex low-pass envelope of the random time-varying spatial impulse response that represents the turbulent channel effects. This equation, which exploits the linearity of the scalar wave equation, emphasizes that the statistical description of the output field depends in general on the spatial properties of the transmitted field. This description also exploits the fact that the turbulent channel has a very large coherence bandwidth (typically the multipath is less than a picosecond) by assuming that the signal bandwidth is small relative to the channel coherence bandwidth [2], [8].

A more convenient form of the relationship between the channel's input and output fields is

$$U_0(t, \boldsymbol{r}_0) = ZS\left(t - \frac{L}{c}\right)z(t, \boldsymbol{r}_0 : L) \tag{4a}$$

$$= ZS\left(t - \frac{L}{c}\right)\exp \gamma(t, \boldsymbol{r}_0) \tag{4b}$$

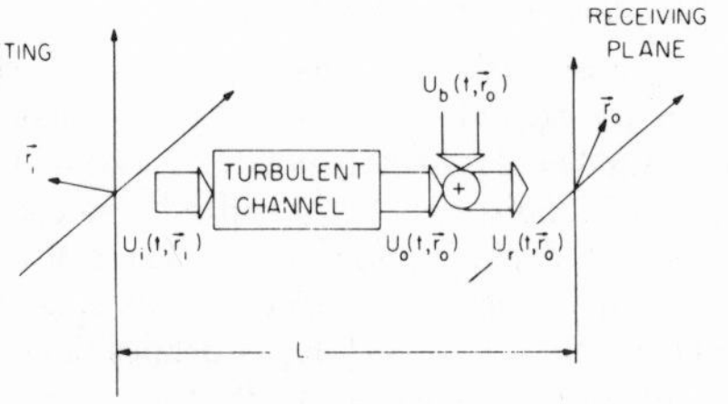


Fig. 1. Schematic model defining the scalar fields of interest in the turbulent-channel communication problem. $u_b(t, r_0)$ is the additive background noise field and $u_0(t, r_0)$ is the signal portion of the received field.

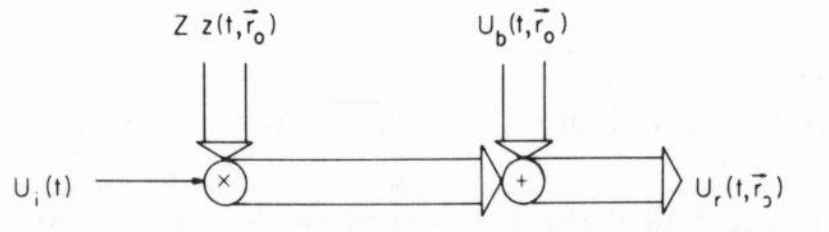

Fig. 2. Statistical model of the turbulent atmospheric channel. Z normalization constant that includes the channel attenuation $z(t, r)$ is a lognormal random process accounting for the fading pr ties of the channel. $U_b(t, r)$ represents the additive background ation.

where $Zz(t, r_0 : L)$ is a random process representing the turbulent effects. These relationships emphasize that the channel effects can be treated as a multiplicative disturbance under the assumption that the signaling bandwidth is small relative to the channel coherence bandwidth. The expression of (4b) is convenient because it is normally reasonable to assume that $z(t, r_0 : L)$ is a complex lognormal process, i.e., that $\gamma(t, r_0)$ is a complex Gaussian process of the form [2]

$$\gamma(t, r_0) = \chi(t, r_0) + j\phi(t, r_0). \tag{5}$$

Thus the output process is completely specified by the means and covariance functions (including the cross covariance) of $\chi$ and $\phi$ which have been considered elsewhere [2], [3].

As noted, the spatial properties of these processes depend in part on the spatial properties of the transmitted field. However, if the field over the receiving aperture is a plane wave in the absence of turbulence (as is often true for the problems of interest and as will be assumed here), the receiving aperture field in the presence of turbulence can be assumed to be spatially homogeneous and isotropic. For this case the normalization constant $Z$ is so chosen that $\overline{|z(t, r_0 : L)|^2} = 1$. Further it will be assumed that $\chi$ and $\phi$ are stationary in time, and often, for simplicity, that they are independent. This latter assumption is not well justified physically [2], [9].

At this point, the detailed mean and time-space covariance functions of $\chi$ and $\phi$ are not important, but it is useful to have parameters to describe grossly the scale of the temporal and spatial variations. Note that for $Z$ chosen as above, $\bar{\chi} = -\sigma_\chi^2$, where $\sigma_\chi^2$ is the variance of $\chi$; also there is no loss in generality for communication problems in choosing $\bar{\phi} = 0$. The amplitude and phase coherence times will be denoted by the parameters $T_\chi$ and $T_\phi$; their minimum $T_c$, the channel coherence time, is often of the order of one ms or more for the atmospheric channel [2]. The scale of the spatial variations is such that they are often important for typical receiving apertures. Consequently it is useful to define the amplitude and phase coherence areas $\mathscr{A}_{c\chi}$ and $\mathscr{A}_{c\phi}$. In the case of the amplitude variations, $\mathscr{A}_{c\chi}$ essentially corresponds to an area with a diameter equal to the spatial correlation distance; for the phase variations the diameter of the coherence area is determined by the separation at which the mean-square phase difference is $(\pi \text{ rad})^2$.

The resulting channel model, neglecting propagatior lay, is shown in Fig. 2. Here $U_b(t, r_0)$ represents the com envelope of the relevant polarization component of background radiation. This complex noise envelor normally assumed to be a zero-mean complex Gaus random process with independent components that are tionary in time and homogeneous in space [10], Further it is assumed that the noise over a 2 $\pi$ stera field of view is white in time and space with the covari function

$$K_{U_b}(r_1, r_2, t_1, t_2) = N_0\delta(r_1 - r_2)\delta(t_1 - t_2)$$

where $N_0 = 2\lambda^2 N_b$, $\lambda$ is the optical wavelength and $N$ the radiance of the relevant polarization component o background, which is discussed elsewhere [12]. This reasonable approximation to the actual covariance func as long as the dimensions of any apertures used are l relative to optical wavelengths.

In summary, the turbulent atmospheric channel is c acterized by fading in time and space with logno amplitude and Gaussian phase processes; the time va tions are slow. The background radiation is additive, si independent, and can normally be modeled as tempo and spatially white.

*B. Field Representations*

We now consider various orthogonal representation the field in the receiver aperture $\mathscr{A}_r$ during the decisio terval $T$, $[0, T]$, which permit this field to be represente a countable set of random variables. The additive sig independent background radiation is essentially white hence, can be represented in terms of any complete s eigenfunctions. It is possible, then, to concentrate or representation of the received signal field $U_0(t, r_0)$.

The representations of interest have the form

$$U_0(t, r) = \sum_j U_j f_j(t, r); \qquad r \in \mathscr{A}_r, t \in [0, T]$$

$$U_j = \int_T \int_{\mathscr{A}_r} U_0(t, r) f_j^*(t, r) dt dr$$

where the functions $\{f_j(t, r)\}$ are orthonormal and, satisfy

$$\int_T \int_{\mathscr{A}_r} f_i(t, r) f_j^*(t, r) dt dr = \delta_{ij}$$

where $\delta_{ij}$ is the Kronecker delta.

The random variables $\{U_j\}$ have the covariance

$$K_{ij} = \overline{[U_i - \bar{U}_i][U_j - \bar{U}_j]^*}$$
$$= \int_T \int_T \int_{\mathscr{A}_r} \int_{\mathscr{A}_r} K_{U_0}(t_1, t_2, \boldsymbol{r}_1, \boldsymbol{r}_2) f_i^*(t_1, \boldsymbol{r}_1) f_j(t_2, \boldsymbol{r}_2) \cdot dt_1 dt_2 d\boldsymbol{r}_1 d\boldsymbol{r}_2 \quad (8)$$

ere $K_{U_0}(t_1, t_2, \boldsymbol{r}_1, \boldsymbol{r}_2)$ is the covariance function of $U_0(t, \boldsymbol{r})$. e coefficient covariance matrix is diagonal if, and only if, expansion functions $f_j(t, \boldsymbol{r})$ satisfy the integral equation

$$\alpha_j f_j(t_1, \boldsymbol{r}_1) = \int_T \int_{\mathscr{A}_r} K_{U_0}(t_1, t_2, \boldsymbol{r}_1, \boldsymbol{r}_2) f_j(t_2, \boldsymbol{r}_2) dt_2 d\boldsymbol{r}_2; \quad t_1 \in T, \boldsymbol{r}_1 \in \mathscr{A}_r \quad (9)$$

nonnegative constants $\{\alpha_j\}$. If the $f_j$'s satisfy (9), the expansion is a time-space Karhunen–Loeve expansion; this is rticularly advantageous when $U_0$ is a Gaussian process 3].

If the actual coefficients are required in the receiver processing, the Karhunen–Loeve representation has the disvantage of requiring knowledge of the exact covariance nction and often makes the physical generation of the efficients complicated. Also, for the lognormal field of erest here it is difficult to specify the statistics of the cocients. At the present time little is known about these tistics in the general case.

Let us now consider two expansions in which the coefient generation process is very physical. These will, in neral, involve some approximation, with the coefficients ually correlated. For simplicity in discussing these reprentations assume that the covariance function of $U_0(t, \boldsymbol{r})$ tors into time and spatial components as

$$K_{U_0}(t_1, t_2, \boldsymbol{r}_1, \boldsymbol{r}_2) = K_1(t_1, t_2) K_2(\boldsymbol{r}_1, \boldsymbol{r}_2) \quad (10)$$

that the temporal and spatial representation questions n be separated. In what follows we concentrate on the atial representation problem and assume that an approiate set of orthonormal time functions, $\{g_i(t)\}$, is used to present the temporal behavior. If the detection interval $T$ small relative to the turbulent channel coherence time, en (10) is valid and

$$K_1(t_1, t_2) = |Z|^2 S(t_1) S^*(t_2). \quad (11)$$

this case the choice of the $\{g_i(t)\}$ is straightforward [14].

A particularly important representation is the sampling pansion. Here we assume that the square integrable field spatially homogeneous so that $K_2(\boldsymbol{r}_1, \boldsymbol{r}_2) = K_2(\boldsymbol{r}_1 - \boldsymbol{r}_2)$ and, rther, that the Fourier transform of $K_2$, $\mathscr{S}_2(\boldsymbol{\kappa})$, has comct support, i.e.,

$$\mathscr{S}_2(\boldsymbol{\kappa}) = 0 \qquad |\kappa_x| \geq \kappa_1, \qquad |\kappa_y| \geq \kappa_2 \quad (12a)$$

ere a rectangular coordinate system is assumed and $=(\kappa_x, \kappa_y)$ is a wavenumber. Then for an infinite aperture

$$U_0(\boldsymbol{r}) = \underset{\substack{N \to \infty \\ M \to \infty}}{\text{l.i.m.}} \sum_{n=-N}^{N} \sum_{m=-M}^{M} \frac{U_0\left(\frac{n\pi}{\kappa_1}, \frac{m\pi}{\kappa_2}\right)}{\sqrt{\kappa_1 \kappa_2/\pi}} f_{nm}(x, y) \quad (12b)$$

where the orthonormal expansion functions are

$$f_{nm}(x, y) = \frac{\sqrt{\kappa_1 \kappa_2}}{\pi} \frac{\sin(\kappa_1 x - n\pi)}{\kappa_1 x - n\pi} \frac{\sin(\kappa_2 y - m\pi)}{\kappa_2 y - m\pi}. \quad (12c)$$

Strictly speaking the sampling representation is not applicable for a finite aperture because the wavenumber spectrum no longer has compact support and only a finite number of samples are available [15]; also the expansion functions are no longer orthogonal over the aperture. However, the representation error can be made negligible by the use of a sufficiently fine sampling grid, i.e., large enough values of $\kappa_1$ and $\kappa_2$ in (12b) and (12c).

A more exact representation for finite apertures corresponds to sampling in wavenumber space. This representation is the Fourier series

$$U_0(\boldsymbol{r}) = \underset{N,M \to \infty}{\text{l.i.m.}} \sum_{n=-N}^{N} \sum_{m=-M}^{M} U_{nm} e^{j\boldsymbol{\kappa}_{nm} \cdot \boldsymbol{r}} \quad (13a)$$

where

$$U_{nm} = \frac{1}{\sqrt{\mathscr{A}_r}} \int_{\mathscr{A}_r} U_0(\boldsymbol{r}) e^{-j\boldsymbol{\kappa}_{nm} \cdot \boldsymbol{r}} d\boldsymbol{r} \quad (13b)$$

and

$$\boldsymbol{\kappa}_{nm} = \left(\frac{2\pi n}{a}, \frac{2\pi m}{b}\right) \quad (13c)$$

for an aperture contained in a rectangle of length $a$ and width $b$. The representation can be interpreted as a decomposition of the field into a countable set of plane waves with $U_{nm}$ as the complex plane-wave amplitudes. It can further be viewed as spatial sampling in the focal plane of an ideal thin lens (except for a known phase distortion) and this is probably the technique that would be used to generate the coefficients when required. It should be noted that in the limit of apertures very large relative to the spatial correlation of the field, the wavenumber sampling representation approaches the Karhunen–Loeve representation.

The statistical properties of the coefficients of these orthonormal expansions are, of course, very important in the design of receivers and the evaluation of their performance. For the sampling representation, the coefficients correspond to samples of the received field. If one considers the signal field only, the coefficients are correlated complex lognormal variables and it is easy to form an arbitrary joint density or evaluate an arbitrary joint moment [15]. The addition of the noise field, however, greatly complicates the problem.

The problem for the Karhunen–Loeve and wavenumber sampling representations is even more severe. Here it is very difficult to evaluate other than second-order moments. The statistics of the individual samples, even in the absence of the background noise field, are difficult to establish.

Recent work has established some results for the wavenumber sampling representation. To illustrate these results, consider the coefficient $U_{00}$. For an aperture that is very small relative to the spatial correlation distance, $U_{00}$ is a complex lognormal variable because it is essentially a field sample. As the aperture increases and approaches the phase coherence radius, the random wavefront tilt becomes important and $|U_{00}|$ is no longer a lognormal random variable [15]. As the aperture gets still larger, it is possible to use a central limit theorem to argue that $U_{00}$ converges in distribution to a complex Gaussian random variable with independent real and imaginary parts (Rayleigh amplitude and uniform phase) [15], [16]. In fact, it can be shown that all the $U_{nm}$ are asymptotically complex Gaussian random variables for large enough apertures; this has been confirmed experimentally [15]. Further, it can be shown that the $U_{nm}$ are essentially uncorrelated for large enough apertures [15]. However, it is not consistent to assume that the coefficients are jointly Gaussian random variables as this would imply a Gaussian input field; thus, their joint density is not known at this time.

For any of the expansions of the received field into time and space modes the expansion coefficients are the sum of a coefficient due to the signal part of the field and a coefficient associated with the background noise. The coefficients associated with the noise modes are complex Gaussian random variables with zero means and variances which are approximately $N_0 = 2N_b\lambda^2$. This is roughly the power spectral density in watts per hertz of the background noise collected by a diffraction-limited antenna. It should further be noted, using the values of $N_b$ corresponding to naturally occurring background radiation, that the average number of noise photons per mode, $\langle n \rangle = 2N_b\lambda^2/h\nu$, is very much less than one. Here $h$ is Planck's constant and $h\nu$ is the energy per photon. At visible frequencies $\langle n \rangle$ is approximately $10^{-6}$ and at 10 $\mu$ it is on the order of $10^{-2}$; this fact will be exploited later in the discussion of direct-detection systems.

### C. *Quantum Field Models and Physical Detectors*

This section considers ways of including the quantum effects that are so important in detection and estimation problems at optical frequencies. Quantum detection and estimation theory is concerned with the choice of measurement(s) to be made on the received field to optimize a desired performance criterion. In the theory the allowed measurements correspond to a class of operators; ideally, although not the case for most of the present work, the class should be so chosen to include all measurements consistent with the laws of physics. We here consider quantum detection and estimation theory for the turbulent channel; more general results are available elsewhere [17]. Specifically, we consider the case where the field can be described by a single linear polarization component, where all the significant components of the plane-wave decomposition of the field over the receiving aperture (see (13)) have propagation vectors approximately normal to the receiving aperture, the field is narrow band about a frequency $\nu$, and the field is time limited to the time interval $T$, $[0, T]$.

The usual artifice for obtaining a state description of the field is to think of enclosing the observed field within a sufficient large lossless volume $V$; the volume is so chosen that it includes the receiving aperture and the entire sig interval $T$. Normally, one is concerned with simultane measurements on the field within the measurement reg and thus time can be considered fixed in the field repres tation; the performance associated with these simultane quantum measurements can sometimes be achieved physical measurements made over a time interval at a fi aperture plane [18]. The scalar field within the measurem region can be written in terms of the generalized Fou series

$$u(t, \mathbf{r}) = \sum_l \sqrt{\frac{h\nu}{2}} \left[C_l \Phi_l(t, \mathbf{r}) e^{-j2\pi\nu t} + C_l^* \Phi_l^*(t, \mathbf{r}) e^{j2\pi\nu t}\right] \quad (1$$

where the $\Phi_l(t, \mathbf{r})$ are mode functions which satisfy Maxw equations and appropriate boundary conditions with

$$\int_V \Phi_l(t, \mathbf{r}) \Phi_k^*(t, \mathbf{r}) d\mathbf{r} = \delta_{lk}. \quad (1$$

If we think of the measurement region $V$ as the volume hind the actual receiving aperture assumed to be opene time $t=0$ and closed at $t=T$, then, for fields satisfying conditions just specified, the mode functions $\Phi_l(t, \mathbf{r})$ ca related to the time-space representation discussed in previous section, i.e.,

$$\Phi_l(t, \mathbf{r}) = \int_0^T \int_{\mathscr{A}_r} f_l(\xi, \boldsymbol{\rho}) G(t, \xi, \mathbf{r}, \boldsymbol{\rho}) \, d\xi \, d\boldsymbol{\rho} \quad (1$$

where $G(t, \xi, \mathbf{r}, \boldsymbol{\rho})$ is a normalized Green's function and

$$\int_T \int_{\mathscr{A}_r} G(t, \xi_1, \mathbf{r}, \boldsymbol{\rho}_1) G^*(t, \xi_2, \mathbf{r}, \boldsymbol{\rho}_2) \, d\mathbf{r} \, dt = \delta(\xi_1 - \xi_2)\delta(\boldsymbol{\rho}_1 - \boldsymbol{\rho}_2). \quad (1$$

Here the $\{f_l(\xi, \boldsymbol{\rho})\}$ are any of the expansion functions cussed in Section II-B.

In terms of the preceding representation, the f can be pictured as a set of independent harmonic oscilla excited by the received field. These oscillators are r quantized. The result is the $u$-field operator formed replacing $C_l$ with the annihilation operator $a_l$, and $C_l^*$ v the creation operator $a_l^+$, the adjoint of $a_l$. Thus the $u$- operator is

$$u(t, \mathbf{r}) = \sum_{l=1}^{\infty} \sqrt{\frac{h\nu}{2}} \left[a_l \Phi_l(t, \mathbf{r}) e^{-j2\pi\nu t} + a_l^+ \Phi^*(t, \mathbf{r}) e^{j2\pi\nu t}\right] \quad (1$$

where the operators $a_l$ and $a_l^+$ obey the commutation r

$$[a_l, a_k^+] = a_l a_k^+ - a_k^+ a_l = \delta_{lk} \quad (1$$

$$[a_l, a_k] = [a_l^+, a_k^+] = 0, \qquad \text{for all } l \text{ and } k \quad (1$$

and the bracket symbolizes the commutator operation fined in (16b). The Hamiltonian, or energy, operator of field can be shown to have the form

$$H = \sum_l \left[a_l^+ a_l + \tfrac{1}{2}\right] h\nu \quad ($$

where it has been assumed that for every mode conside

photon energy is $h\nu$. The operator $N_l = a_l^+ a_l$ is called number operator; its eigenvalues are the nonnegative gers. It describes the quantized allowed energy levels.

he field is said to be in a coherent state when the state or $|\{\alpha_l\}\rangle$ is the direct product

$$\prod_{l=1}^{\infty} |\alpha_l\rangle = |\alpha_1, \alpha_2, \cdots, \alpha_l, \cdots\rangle = |\{\alpha_l\}\rangle \tag{18}$$

he mode annihilation operator eigenstates [19]. A non-dom classical source radiating into a vacuum will lead uch a state. Here $|\alpha_l\rangle$ is a right eigenvector of the opera- $a_l$, i.e.,

$$a_l|\alpha_l\rangle = \alpha_l|\alpha_l\rangle \tag{19}$$

the complex number $\alpha_l$ is the corresponding right eigen-e. The set of coherent state vectors $|\{\alpha_l\}\rangle$ form a com-e set and thus any state vector of the field and any linear rator can be expanded in terms of the coherent state tors $|\{\alpha_l\}\rangle$ [19]. The $|\alpha_l\rangle$ are not orthogonal. They are ted to the orthogonal eigenstates $|n_l\rangle$ of the number rator by [19]

$$|\alpha_l\rangle = \exp\left[-\tfrac{1}{2}|\alpha_l|^2\right] \sum_{n_l} \frac{\alpha_l^{n_l}}{[n_l!]^{1/2}} |n_l\rangle \tag{20}$$

re the $n_l$ are the eigenvalues of $N_l$.

Vhen the radiation propagates through a slowly chang-random medium, the field at the receiving aperture can nodeled by saying that it is driven by a classical source se modes have amplitudes and phases only known istically. This situation is usually described as a mixture ure coherent states specified by a density operator $\rho$ se eigenvalues are nonnegative. $\rho$ is so chosen that the e, tr $(\rho)$, equals one, and the trace, tr $(\rho X)$, equals the ex-ted outcome when the observable (Hermitian operator) responding to the operator $X$ is measured. Usually $\rho$ be expressed in terms of the coherent state vectors to n the $P$-representation

$$\rho = \int p(\{\alpha_l\}) |\{\alpha_l\}\rangle\langle\{\alpha_l\}| \prod_{l=1}^{\infty} d\alpha_l \tag{21}$$

re $p(\{\alpha_l\})$ is called the weight function. The weight func- may be thought of as a probability density for our pur-es (in general, it can be negative). Note that the integra- is over both the real and imaginary parts of $\alpha_l$. In cases terest here the density operator is a function of the signal smitted.

he actual fields of interest are the sum of signal and kground noise fields. To specify the background noise assume that the weight function in its $P$-representation the form

$$p_b(\{\alpha_l\}) = \prod_l \frac{1}{\pi\langle n\rangle} \exp\left(-\frac{|\alpha_l|^2}{\langle n\rangle}\right) \tag{22}$$

ependent of the choice of normal mode functions. Here $= 2N_b\lambda^2/h\nu$ is the average number of photons per noise de and the noise modes are uncorrelated [20]. The weight function for the total received field is the convolution of the weight functions of the signal and noise fields.

The correspondence between the classical and quantum field descriptions is that $\mathrm{tr}\,(\rho u) = \overline{u_r(t, \mathbf{r})}$ where $\rho$ is the density operator of the received field and $u$ is the field operator of (16).

Often the set of dynamical variables that are to be measured correspond to a set of linear operators $X_1, X_2, \cdots, X_k$ that are Hermitian and commutative. The possible out-comes of a single measurement $X$ are the eigenvalues $x_i$ of the operator $X$. After the measurement, the field is left in the eigenstate corresponding to $x_i$, $|x_i\rangle$. Given that the field is in the mixture of states specified by the density operator $\rho$ before the measurement, the conditional prob-ability of the outcome $x_i$ is

$$\Pr(x_i|\rho) = \langle x_i|\rho|x_i\rangle. \tag{23}$$

As an example consider measuring the number of pho-tons in the $l$th mode. This corresponds to the operator $N_l = a_l^+ a_l$ having the eigenstates $|n_{li}\rangle$ and corresponding eigenvalues $n_l = i$, $i = 0, 1, \cdots$. If, as is true in some cases of interest, the field density operator is diagonal in the number representation, i.e.,

$$\rho = \sum_{n_l=0}^{\infty} \cdots \sum r(\{n_l\}) \prod_l |n_l\rangle\langle n_l|, \tag{24a}$$

then

$$\Pr(n_l) = \langle n_l|\rho|n_l\rangle = r(n_l). \tag{24b}$$

The assumption that $X_1, X_2, \cdots, X_k$ are commutative means that there exists a complete set of orthogonal states that are simultaneous eigenstates of these $k$ operators. Then the simultaneous measurement of these observables results in the ordered $k$-tuple $\mathbf{x}_k = (x_{1i_1}, x_{2i_2}, \cdots, x_{ki_k})$ whose conditional probability is

$$\Pr(\mathbf{x}_k|\rho) = \langle \mathbf{x}_k|\rho|\mathbf{x}_k\rangle \tag{25}$$

where $|\mathbf{x}_k\rangle$ is the single associated eigenstate [20].

Sometimes it is convenient to consider measurements that do not correspond to commutative Hermitian operators. An example is a measurement of the complex envelope of the $l$th mode of the field corresponding to the non-Her-mitian operator $a_l$; this can be considered the simultaneous measurement of the real and imaginary parts of $a_l$ which do not commute. In general, ideal noisy measurements of oper-ators, even if noncommuting, can still be characterized by a complete set of states $\{|\mathbf{x}_k\rangle\}$; these $|\mathbf{x}_k\rangle$ are no longer in gen-eral orthogonal [17], [21]. An ideal measurement is one in which the final state of the measured system depends on the outcome of the measurement and not on the system state prior to the measurement. The measurements are noisy if the operators do not commute; this is just the uncertainty principle. Again, even in the more general case when the field is in a state specified by the density operator $\rho$, the probability that the outcome of a measurement associated with the complete set $\{|\mathbf{x}_k\rangle\}$ is $\mathbf{x}_k$ is given by (25).

It should be noted that if the spectra of the operators are

not discrete, the only modifications required are to replace sums with integrals and probability distributions with density functions.

The material just considered is necessary to optimize over the possible measurements that a receiver may perform. A second way to account for the quantum effects is to specify the type of measurements to be made by the receiver and then introduce a quantum-mechanically correct description of the noise associated with these measurements. This less general procedure, called the structured approach, has the merits of simplicity, may provide insight into the realization of the optimum measurements previously considered, and permits the study of receiving structures that are intuitive and/or very reasonable to build, e.g., heterodyning and direct-detection receivers (see Section III). The key to a correct statistical description in this case is a quantum-mechanically correct description of the output of the physical detector used, given the classical field incident upon it. The output of such a general physical detector at optical frequencies is conditionally a filtered inhomogeneous Poisson process [3], [22].

We now make explicit the mathematical detector models that will be used in what follows. Assume that the detector output is $y(t)$ and that the classical field incident upon it is $u_d(t, \boldsymbol{r})$. Then

$$y(t) = \sum_{i=1}^{N(t)} \mathfrak{h}(t, \tau_i) \tag{26a}$$

where

$$P(N(t) = k) = \frac{\left[\int_0^t \mu(\tau)d\tau\right]^k}{k!} \exp\left[-\int_0^t \mu(\tau)d\tau\right] \tag{26b}$$

$$\mu(t) = \frac{\eta}{h\nu}\int_{\mathscr{A}_d} |U_d(t, \boldsymbol{\rho})|^2 d\boldsymbol{\rho} \tag{26c}$$

and the $\tau_i$ are the Poisson event times. The impulse response $\mathfrak{h}(t, \tau)$ depends on the detector, $\eta$ is the quantum efficiency of the detector, and $U_d(t, \boldsymbol{\rho})$ is the complex envelope of $u_d(t, \boldsymbol{\rho})$.[1] For simplicity in what follows it will be assumed that the detector is either an ideal photon counter with

$$\mathfrak{h}(t, \tau) = \delta(t - \tau) \tag{27a}$$

or that it acts as a time-invariant filter such that

$$\mathfrak{h}(t, \tau) = \mathfrak{h}(t - \tau). \tag{27b}$$

For simplicity the detector dark current has been omitted in the preceding description; it is easily included in the following analysis. The thermal noise associated with any subsequent electronic processing is also omitted; this seems necessary for tractability in the direct-detection case, but it can easily be included in the heterodyne case (see Section III-A).

[1] In the most general case the impulse response is also random to account for such phenomena as a variable detector gain [3].

## III. Digital Communication Systems

### A. Introduction

It is assumed in this section that the complex envelope the transmitted signal field is one of the set of $M$ comp waveforms $S_i(t)$, $i = 1, \cdots, M$, corresponding to the messages $m_i$, $i = 1, \cdots, M$. We are concerned with the desi and performance of receivers that make decisions ab which of the $M$ messages was transmitted; the decision w be denoted $\hat{m}$. The performance criterion in all cases $P[\varepsilon]$, the average probability (over the set of messag that $\hat{m}$ does not equal the transmitted message.

The receiver structures that minimize $P[\varepsilon]$ for a giv waveform set $\{S_i\}$, the bounds on the values of $P[\varepsilon]$ tl result for particular receivers and waveform sets, and waveform sets that are optimum or near optimum in sense of minimizing $P[\varepsilon]$ will be examined for turbul channels characterized by the model of Section II-A. most of what follows it will be assumed that the signal wa forms $S_i(t)$ are time-limited to an interval $T$, $[0, T]$, a that $T$ is short relative to the coherence time of the chann thus

$$U_r(t, \boldsymbol{r}) = Zz(\boldsymbol{r})S_i(t) + U_b(t, \boldsymbol{r}). \quad (\!\!$$

For convenience the $\{S_i(t)\}$ are assumed to have unit ene and (Section II-B) $\overline{|z(\boldsymbol{r})|^2} = 1$; $|Z|^2$ is thus the received-sig energy per unit area.

Intersymbol interference between any two message tra missions is negligible due to the extremely small multipa and it is assumed that there is no coding on successive tra missions. It is further assumed that the receiver does n exploit the statistical dependence of the channel fading fr signal baud to signal baud; exploiting this dependence c improve the performance. Thus, the receiver makes in pendent decisions on each successive message transmissi The performance is characterized by the so called "sin shot" error probability, i.e., the probability of error for t transmission of a single message.

Receiver design will be approached from both the op mum quantum detection and structured receiver vie points. In both of these approaches the receiver perfor measurements on the incident field and makes the minim $P[\varepsilon]$ decision $\hat{m} = m_i$, where $m_i$ is the message wh a posteriori probability, i.e., the conditional probabil that $m_i$ was transmitted given the data (measurement o comes), is the largest. An equivalent decision rule is to $\hat{m}$ equal to the $m_i$ that maximizes the product of the con tional probability of the data (given $m_i$) and the a pri probability that $m_i$ was transmitted.

In the optimum quantum detection case there is first optimization over the measurement to be performed the receiver and the decision is based on the outcome this measurement. The density operator that describes state of the received field depends on the message tra mitted; it also reflects the statistical features of the chan model (Section II-A). The received field is expanded modes (see (15a)) and, with the previous assumptions,

$f_i(t, \boldsymbol{r})\}$ factor into the product of a time-dependent and a ɔace-dependent part, i.e., (10) and (11) apply. The sampling epresentation will be used to specify the aperture spatial odes (spatial part of $f_i(t, \boldsymbol{r})$) because it is the only repre-ntation for which the coefficient statistics are sufficiently ell understood to permit specification of the weight func-ons of the density operators. Attention will be confined to ne case where the received signals are orthogonal, i.e., dif-erent $S_i(t)$ excite no common temporal modes at the re-eiver, and even further restricted to the case where the ensity operators, $\rho_i$, corresponding to the various trans-nitted signals $S_i(t)$ commute, i.e., $\rho_i\rho_j = \rho_j\rho_i$ for all $j = 1, \cdots, M$. This latter restriction corresponds to the nly circumstance under which quantum detection results or an $M$-ary alphabet are available [20]. When the density perators commute, there exists a complete orthogonal set f states that are simultaneous eigenstates of all $M$ density perators [20]. In this case an optimum set of simultaneous neasurements is the set of commuting Hermitian operators observables) whose eigenstates are the states common to ne density operators. Under the assumption of equally robable messages the receiver sets $\hat{m}$ equal to the $m_i$ that aximizes the conditional probability of the resulting mea-urement eigenvector, given $\rho_i$ (see (25)).

In the structured approach the quantum measurement specified and the resulting quantum noise must be appro-riately accounted for in the statistical description of the ata available for decision making. General structures of e form shown in Fig. 3 are considered. As indicated in the gure, $D$ signals, represented by the components of the ctor $\boldsymbol{y}(t)$, are available to be processed. It is assumed that e receiver contains an array of $D$ photodetectors and that ch component of $\boldsymbol{y}(t)$ is the output of one of these detec-rs; thus, from the discussion of photodetectors in Section -C, each component of $\boldsymbol{y}(t)$ is an inhomogeneous filtered oisson process when conditioned on the detected field $(t, \boldsymbol{r})$.

The model allows for linear time-space processing on the ceived field $u_r(t, \boldsymbol{r})$, which is described in Section II-A, efore the energy detection operation; the additive field $(t, \boldsymbol{r})$ accounts for the possibility that this processing is oisy, or that the receiver introduces a local oscillator field. he field processing may, for example, be some combination time filtering with an optical bandpass filter, spatial filter-g with some optical system and preamplification with an ptical preamplifier. In particular, such processing might used to decompose the field into various spatial modes.

For a structured receiver, the receiver design problem duces to specifying the linear field processing, including e additive field $u_h(t, \boldsymbol{r})$, and then determining the process-g on the output vector $\boldsymbol{y}(t)$ which will generate the posteriori probabilities (or their equivalents) for the $M$ ssible messages. This, of course, requires a statistical de-ription of $\boldsymbol{y}(t)$ given $m_i$, $1 \le i \le M$, and an appropriate presentation for this vector process over the decision terval, $T$. Ideally there would then be an optimization er the linear processing, or at least over parameters asso-ciated with a particular type of processing, to minimize the resulting $P[\varepsilon]$.

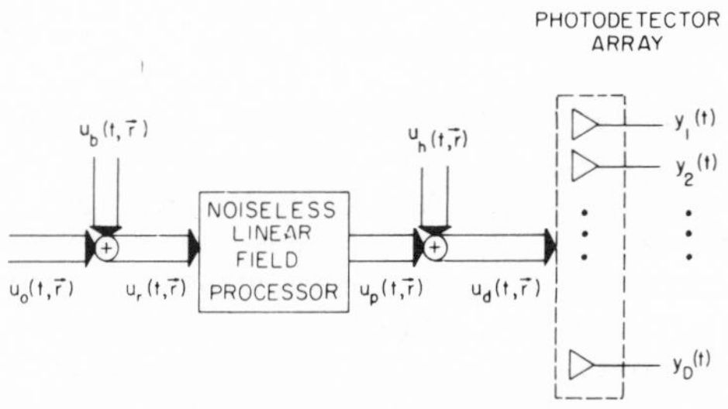


Fig. 3. General model for structured optical receivers.

The two most common structured receivers are the heterodyne and direct-detection receivers. In the heterodyne receiver the field $u_h(t, \boldsymbol{r})$ is a purposely introduced local oscillator field with the complex envelope

$$U_h(t, \boldsymbol{r}) = U_h(\boldsymbol{r}) \exp\left[j2\pi f_h t\right]. \tag{29}$$

This field, whose magnitude is assumed to be much larger than that of $u_p(t, \boldsymbol{r})$ (see Fig. 3), can also be introduced ahead of the linear field processing, but this introduces no fundamental change because the processing is known and linear. The detectors are assumed to have impulse responses of the form of (27b). In this case the complex envelopes of the normalized and filtered detector outputs, conditioned on knowledge of $U_p(t, \boldsymbol{r})$, can be modeled as

$$Y_i(t) = \frac{\displaystyle\int_{\mathscr{A}_i} U_p(t, \boldsymbol{r}) U_h^*(\boldsymbol{r}) d\boldsymbol{r}}{\left[\displaystyle\int_{\mathscr{A}_i} |U_h(\boldsymbol{r})|^2 d\boldsymbol{r}\right]^{1/2}} + W_i(t) \tag{30}$$

where $\mathscr{A}_i$ is the area of the $i$th detector, and where the normalization involves division by

$$2(\eta/h\nu) \int \mathfrak{h}(\tau) d\tau \left[\int_{\mathscr{A}_i} |U_h(\boldsymbol{r})|^2 d\boldsymbol{r}\right]^{1/2}.$$

The additive signal-independent noise processes $W_i(t)$ are independent zero-mean complex Gaussian random processes whose real and imaginary parts are independent with identical correlation functions [23]. The actual output process is at bandpass about the IF $f_h$, i.e.,

$$y_i(t) = \operatorname{Re}\left[Y_i(t) \exp\left[j2\pi f_h t\right]\right]. \tag{31}$$

It has been assumed that the detector bandwidth is sufficiently large to pass the signal portion of $y_i(t)$ without distortion. In this case the real noise processes $w_i(t)$ can be treated as white within the signal bandwidth of interest with a two-sided spectral density of

$$S_w(f) = \frac{h\nu}{4\eta}, \tag{32a}$$

i.e., the real and imaginary parts of $W_i(t)$ each have a two-sided spectrum of $h\nu/2\eta$ and the complex noise spectrum is

$$S_W(f) = \frac{h\nu}{\eta}. \tag{32b}$$

Further, the natural background noise contribution to the output is negligible with respect to $w_i(t)$ assuming the linear field processing does not involve amplification. This is true because the heterodyning operation extracts a single spatial mode (plane-wave component) of the filtered background noise field, [24], and hence the resulting complex noise process has a spectral density $N_{0b} = 2N_b\lambda^2$ which, for a natural background, is small relative to $h\nu/\eta$ at the frequencies of interest (see Section II-B).

Thus, for a natural background, the detector outputs are adequately modeled by (30) with $U_p(t, \boldsymbol{r})$ replaced by $U_{p0}(t, \boldsymbol{r})$, the signal portion of the filtered field. Also, it should be noted that any white Gaussian noise associated with preamplifiers or other processing on the detector outputs is easily accounted for by including it with the $w_i(t)$ and increasing $S_w(f)$. For a heterodyne receiver the detection problem for the turbulent channel reduces to that of making decisions when the received signal consists of one or more fading signal-dependent waveforms in additive, signal-independent, Gaussian noise, and all the well-known analysis techniques for this class of channel become applicable. The situation is, however, still complicated because of the statistics associated with $U_0(t, \boldsymbol{r})$.

For direct-detection receivers, the field $u_h(t, \boldsymbol{r})$ is normally set equal to zero. As indicated earlier, the vector process $\boldsymbol{y}(t)$ is now conditionally a set of independent filtered Poisson processes with rate parameters that depend upon the intensity of the field at the detectors, i.e.,

$$\mu_i(t) = \frac{\eta}{h\nu}\int_{\mathscr{A}_i} |U_d(t, \boldsymbol{r})|^2 d\boldsymbol{r}. \tag{33}$$

Here it is assumed that the detector is adequately modeled by the impulse response of (27a). Optimum processing requires knowledge of the statistics that result from averaging over both the filtered Gaussian background noise and the filtered form of the multiplicative process that models the turbulent channel. Often the processes that result from averaging over the Gaussian background noise can be adequately treated, conditioned on knowledge of the signal portion of the filtered field, $U_{p0}(t, \boldsymbol{r})$, as independent inhomogeneous Poisson processes with rate parameters

$$\mu_i(t) = \frac{\eta}{h\nu}\int_{\mathscr{A}_i} |U_{p0}(t, \boldsymbol{r})|^2 d\boldsymbol{r} + \frac{\eta}{h\nu}\int_{\mathscr{A}_i} \overline{|U_{pb}(t, \boldsymbol{r})|^2} d\boldsymbol{r} \tag{34}$$

where $\overline{|U_{pb}(t, \boldsymbol{r})|^2}$ is proportional to the average intensity of the filtered background noise [25], [26]. It is assumed that the noise field at each detector is uncorrelated. The adequacy of the Poisson model depends strongly on the average number of noise counts per mode being small; the adequacy of rate parameters with the form indicated in (34) also depends on the ratio of the average signal and noise count rates [26]. For a Poisson random variable all the cumulants are equal; in particular the mean and variance are equ Assuming equal energy noise modes, the following con tions must hold to assure that the mean is approximat equal to the variance and that both are approximately giv by (34):

$$2\eta M_n\langle n\rangle = 2\eta M_n 2N_b\lambda^2/h\nu \ll 1 \quad (3$$

and

$$2(\eta M_n\langle n\rangle)^2 \ll 2\eta M_n\langle n\rangle$$

$$\left[\frac{\text{average signal count rate}}{\text{average noise count rate}}\right] \ll 1 \quad (3$$

where $M_n$ is the number of noise spatial modes per sig spatial mode. These inequalities are indicative of the mc general conditions considered in [26].

In the discussion of direct-detection receivers that f lows it will be assumed that (34) is valid. This is one of t few situations for which any results are presently availal and also seems to include many cases of practical intere Another case for which results are available is when t detector impulse response is given by (27b), the noise cou rate is very large relative to the signal count rate, and t product of the noise count rate and the time constant the detector impulse response is large relative to one. this case the detector output can again be modeled as signal term plus additive signal-independent noise. As t is similar to the heterodyning case we will not consider it detail.

In the following sections the emphasis will be on orthc onal signals. Thus an appropriate field representation o the detection interval can be obtained by using the expa sion functions

$$f_{lij}(t, \boldsymbol{r}) = S_l(t) f_{ij}(\boldsymbol{r}) \qquad 1 \le l \le M, \boldsymbol{r} \in \mathscr{A}_r \quad ($$

where $f_{ij}(\boldsymbol{r})|_{\boldsymbol{r}=(x,y)}$ is defined in (12c). As indicated earl the $\{S_l(t)\}$ are assumed to have unit energy over the decis interval $T$; the set is completed by choosing additio orthogonal time functions which are also orthogonal to $S_l(t)$, $1 \le l \le M$. For convenience we designate the result field coefficients as

$$U_l(\boldsymbol{r}_{ij}) \triangleq \int_0^T \int_{\mathscr{A}_r} U_r(t, \boldsymbol{r}) S_l^*(t) f_{ij}^*(\boldsymbol{r}) d\boldsymbol{r}\, dt$$

$$= \frac{\pi}{\sqrt{\kappa_1 \kappa_2}}[Zz(\boldsymbol{r}_{ij})] + U_{bl}(\boldsymbol{r}_{ij}) \quad ($$

where the latter equality results from (28). It is assumed t the spatial spectrum of the noise is band-limited by a spa filter so that (12a) is satisfied for wavenumbers $\kappa_1 = \kappa_2 =$ for some $\kappa_0$ large enough that all the significant compone of the signal's spatial spectrum are included. Assum that the filter passes uniformly all spatial frequencies l than $\kappa_0$, the $U_{bl}(\boldsymbol{r}_{ij})$ are independent zero-mean comp Gaussian random variables with the variance $N_0$ ( Sections II-A and II-B). For convenience we design

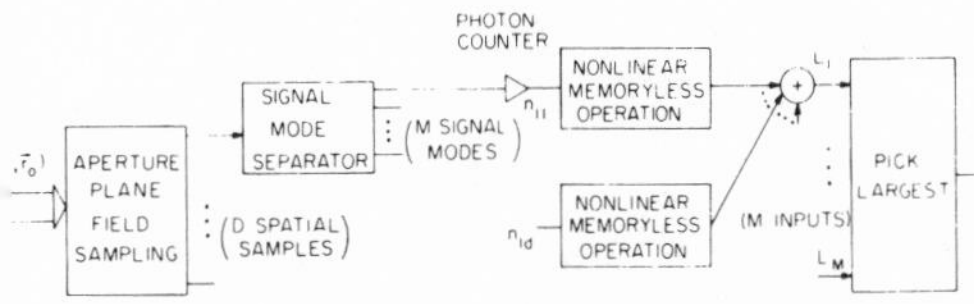


. 4. Optimum quantum receiver for lognormal signal fields under the assumption that the received field can be represented by independent spatial samples.

$\kappa_0)^2$ as $\mathscr{A}_s$, the sampling area. The joint density of the $(r_{ij})$, $r_{ij} \in \mathscr{A}_r$, is

$$U^l|m_i) = \left(\frac{1}{\pi N_0}\right)^D$$

$$\cdot \prod_{d=1}^{D} \exp\left\{-\frac{|U_l(r_d) - \sqrt{\mathscr{A}_s} Zz(r_d)\delta_{li}|^2}{N_0}\right\} \quad (38)$$

ere, for convenience, the single index $d$, $1 \le d \le D$, is used represent the sample position, $U^l = (U_l(r_1), \cdots, U_l(r_D))$, d the average is over the $\{z(r_d)\}$ which are not in general dependent.

*Receiver Structures*

*1) Optimum Quantum Receivers:* If message $m_l$ is transtted, the received field is assumed to be in a statistical xture of coherent states described by the density operator for which the $P$-representation is

$$\rho_l = \int \cdots \int \prod_{j=1}^{M} \left[ p(\{\alpha_{dj}\}|m_l) \prod_{d=1}^{D} |\alpha_{dj}\rangle \langle \alpha_{dj}| d\alpha_{dj} \right] \quad (39)$$

ere $p(\{\alpha_{dj}\}|m_l)$ can be obtained from (38) by using the ation $U_j(r_d) = \alpha_{dj}\sqrt{h\nu}$. This $P$-representation cannot in neral be transformed so that it depends only on the abute values of the $\alpha_{dj}$ and hence the $\rho_l$, $1 \le l \le M$, are not gonal in the number representation. Further, it is not own in what other representation they might be diagonal. us, the general optimum quantum receiver is not known.

If it is assumed that the spatial samples are independent d further that the Gaussian phase of $z(r_d)$ is independent its amplitude and has a sufficiently large variance to be ated as a uniform variable, then the $\rho_l$ are diagonal in the mber representation and the optimum quantum receiver unts photons [15]. In this case

$$U^l|m_l) = \prod_{d=1}^{D} \left(\frac{1}{\pi N_0}\right)$$

$$\cdot \exp -\left\{\frac{|U_l(r_d)|^2 + |\zeta_d|^2}{N_0}\right\} I_0\left(\frac{2|U_l(r_d)||\zeta_d|}{N_0}\right) \quad (40a)$$

ere

$$\zeta_d = \sqrt{\mathscr{A}_s} Zz(r_d) \quad (40b)$$

d the average is over $|\zeta_d|$ which has a lognormal density. The form of $\rho_l$ in the number representation is now easily obtained. See (4.3.20) of [15]. This result can be used in (25) to find Pr $(\{n_{ld}\}|m_l)$ where $n_{ld}$ is the number of counts associated with coefficient $U_l(r_d)$. It is convenient to divide this conditional probability by the same expression with the signal set equal to zero, i.e., to use a dummy (noise-only) hypothesis, and then to take the logarithm of the ratio. The resulting likelihood function is

$$L_l = \sum_{d=1}^{D} \ln \int_0^\infty \exp\left[-\frac{v^2 S}{N+1}\right]$$

$$\cdot L_{n_{ld}}\left(-\frac{v^2 S}{N(N+1)}\right) p(v)\, dv \quad (41a)$$

where $p(v)$ is the lognormal density

$$p(v) = [2\pi\sigma_\chi^2 v^2]^{-1/2} \exp[-(\ln v + \sigma_\chi^2)^2/2\sigma_\chi^2] \quad (41b)$$

with log amplitude variance $\sigma_\chi^2$,

$$N = N_0/h\nu = \langle n \rangle \quad (41c)$$

$$S = \frac{\mathscr{A}_s |Z|^2}{h\nu} \quad (41d)$$

and $L_n(\cdot)$ is a zero-order Laguerre polynomial. Here $S$ and $N$, the average number of signal and noise counts, are assumed to be the same for each sample because of the spatial homogeneity of the field. The integral in (41a) is an expectation over the lognormal fading variable associated with each sample. The receiver should set $\hat{m} = m_l$ if $L_l \ge L_i$ for all $i$ not equal to $l$.

The resulting receiver structure is shown in Fig. 4. The receiver does no spatial processing, other than treating the spatial samples separately, because of the independence assumption. The optimum quantum measurement is photon counting; the counts are weighted nonlinearly by a curve whose exact form depends strongly on the lognormal standard deviation. The weighted counts are added to form the likelihood functions.

If there is no background noise ($N = 0$), it is sufficient to detect just one photon in the proper signal mode in order to secure a correct decision. In this case the nonlinear weighting can be omitted and all the spatial samples can be combined at the input to the signal mode separator, i.e., it is not necessary to have $D$ parallel processors.

*2) Heterodyne Receivers:* When discussing heterodyne receivers, it is convenient to consider separately receivers that use a single detector and those that involve an array of detectors. In both cases the linear processing before the detection operation will involve both spatial and temporal filtering to limit the background noise. Because of the spatial filtering inherent in the heterodyning operation and the subsequent temporal processing of the detector outputs, the performance is relatively independent of this predetection processing. This processing may also scale the input field to permit the use of smaller detectors; for convenience in the following we assume operation in the aperture plane.

The complex envelope of a detector output after heterodyning, assuming the preprocessing does not distort the signal field and that (28) applies, is reasonably modeled as (see (30))

$$Y(t) = ZS(t)\frac{\int_{\mathscr{A}} z(\mathbf{r})U_h^*(\mathbf{r})\,d\mathbf{r}}{\left[\int_{\mathscr{A}} |U_h(\mathbf{r})|^2 d\mathbf{r}\right]^{1/2}} + W(t) \qquad (42)$$

where $W(t)$ is complex white Gaussian noise of spectral height $h\nu/\eta + N_{0b}$. As noted earlier the background contribution $N_{0b}$ can usually be ignored relative to $h\nu/\eta$ for natural background and this is the case that will be considered in the following. If $N_{0b}$ were large relative to $h\nu/n$, a classical approach to receiver design ignoring the quantum noise associated with the measurement would be appropriate; however, in this case the preprocessor spatial filtering of the noise is significant. The optimum spatial filtering has been considered for this case [27]–[29]. See also Section IV.

*a) Single detector:* For the assumptions discussed, the optimum processing after detection corresponds to that for a fading signal in independent additive white Gaussian noise. The form of the receiver depends on the density associated with the phase of the fading random variable

$$X = \frac{\int_{\mathscr{A}_r} z(\mathbf{r})U_h^*(\mathbf{r})\,d\mathbf{r}}{\left[\int_{\mathscr{A}_r} |U_h(\mathbf{r})|^2 d\mathbf{r}\right]^{1/2}}. \qquad (43)$$

For equal energy signals, the receiver can be realized as a set of bandpass matched filters followed by envelope detectors if the phase of $X$ can be assumed uniform; the filters are matched to the transmitted signals $S_i(t)$ [30]. If $X$ does not have a uniform phase, the receiver processing is modified to contain a phase-coherent component [14, Sec. 4.4.1]. For signals of unequal energy the receiver processing must account for an averaging operation over the fading statistics of $X$ and the processing becomes more complicated [31].

*b) Detector arrays:* Single-detector heterodyning systems will give good performance only as long as the receiving aperture is smaller than the phase-coherence area of $z(\mathbf{r})$. The efficient use of larger apertures requires detector arrays so that the spatial diversity of the signal field is effectively used.

Assume that there is a separate heterodyne detector for each spatial sample taken in the aperture. Further, assume that each detector output is correlated against the set of transmitted signals to form the set of independent random vectors, $\{\mathbf{U}^l\}$, $l=1, 2, \cdots, M$. These vectors have the density of (38) where $N_0$ is now $h\nu/\eta$ (assumed large relative to the background noise contribution). The heterodyne and correlation operations thus yield the coefficients of a sampling representation for the field except that the additive noise includes the shot noise of the local oscillator. In actual practice, of course, the field samples would be obtained by

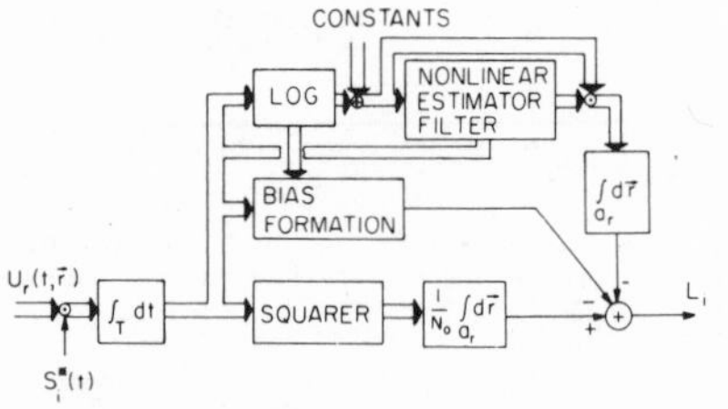


Fig. 5. Optimum processing for a heterodyne (or classical) turbulen atmosphere receiver when $\mathscr{A}_s|Z|^2/N_0 \gg 1$, the weak noise case. Tl structure shown is repeated for each $S_i(t)$, $1 \le i \le M$. The spatial sampl are indicated as a continuum for convenience and are not assumed to be independent. (Similar to Fig. 19 of [15].)

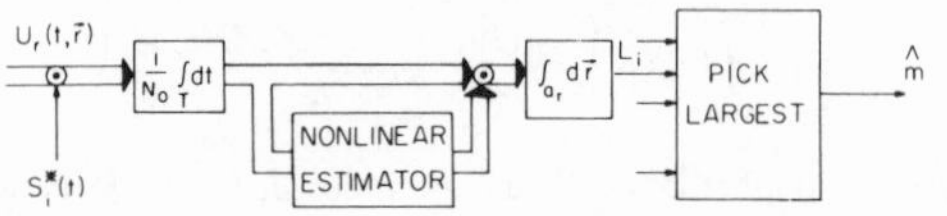


Fig. 6. Optimum processing for a heterodyne (or classical) turbulen atmosphere receiver when $\mathscr{A}_s|Z|^2/N_0 \ll 1$, the strong noise cas The structure that generates the decision statistic $L_i$ is repeated f each $S_i(t)$, $1 \le i \le M$. The spatial samples are indicated as a continuu for convenience and are not assumed to be independent.

using a field $U_h(\mathbf{r})$ localized to the sampling point rath than requiring it to have the form of (12c). For convenienc we designate $U_l(\mathbf{r}_d)$ as $U_{ld}$ and $z(\mathbf{r}_d)$ as $z_d$. The condition mean of $U_{ld}$ is $\zeta_d = \sqrt{\mathscr{A}_s}\, Zz_d$ when message $l$ is transmitte

Assuming equally probable signals, the optimum pos detection processing sets $\hat{m}$ equal to the $m_i$ that maximiz $p(\mathbf{U}^1, \mathbf{U}^2, \cdots, \mathbf{U}^M|m_i)$ or, equivalently, using a dumn (noise-only) hypothesis, to the $m_i$ that maximizes the likel hood ratio $L$, which is the logarithm of the ratio $p(\mathbf{U}^1, \mathbf{U}^2, \cdots, \mathbf{U}^M|m_i)$ and $p(\mathbf{U}^1, \mathbf{U}^2, \cdots, \mathbf{U}^M|\text{noise only})$ For orthogonal signals the form of $L_i$ is

$$L_i = \ln \frac{p(\mathbf{U}^i|m_i)}{p(\mathbf{U}^i|\text{noise only})} \triangleq \ln \frac{p_1(\mathbf{U}^i)}{p_0(\mathbf{U}^i)}. \qquad (4$$

In the general case of dependent signal field samples th likelihood function has been studied for various values the sample signal-to-noise ratio, $\mathscr{A}_s|Z|^2/N_0$ [15]. F $\mathscr{A}_s|Z|^2/N_0 \gg 1$, the weak-noise case, useful results can b obtained for $p_1(\mathbf{U}^l)$ by writing it as an average over th noise rather than the fading. The receiver processing to for $L_i$ is shown schematically in Fig. 5. See [15] for details. I this figure, the samples are indicated as a spatial continuu for convenience; the indicated bias constants depend on th fading statistics and the signal energy. The processing co sists of three parts. The first evaluates the total receiv energy at the outputs of the $i$th signal correlators. Th second part involves an estimator-correlator operation o the logarithm of the field samples under hypothesis $i$. Th estimator filter (a matrix filter) depends on $\mathbf{U}^l$ and hen is nonlinear; its function is to de-emphasize samples th tend to be dominated by noise because of severe fading an to properly weight the spatial frequencies contained in th

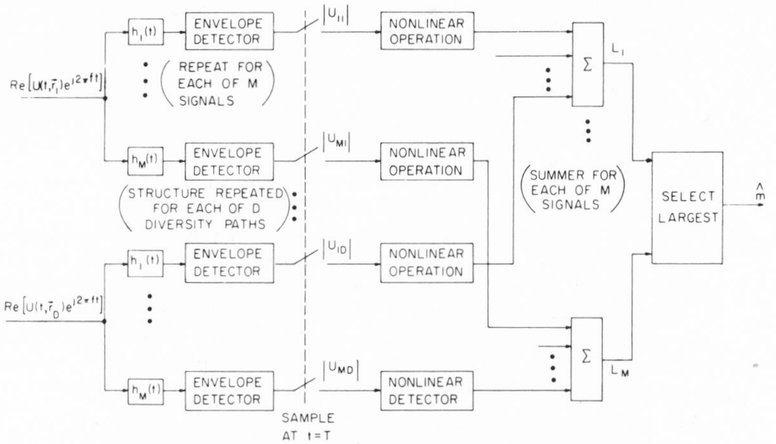


Fig. 7. Min–max phase receiver for heterodyne detection under the assumption of independent spatial samples. The matched filters are $h_i(t) = \mathrm{Re}\,[S_i^*(T-t)\exp[-j2\pi ft]$. (After Fig. 3 of [11].)

fading signal field. The third part corresponds to a signal-dependent bias which again helps to discriminate against samples dominated by noise because of the fading.

For $\mathscr{A}_s|Z|^2/N_0 \ll 1$, the strong-noise case, $p_1(\boldsymbol{U}^l)$ can be evaluated by using a series expansion for the exponential of (38) (factor out $\exp -[|U_l(\boldsymbol{r}_d)|^2/N_0]$ before expanding). This leads to the processing shown in Fig. 6 where again the spatial samples are indicated as a continuum. The form of the optimum nonlinear estimating filter is discussed in [15].

If the spatial samples are assumed independent more can be said about the receiver structure. In this case the sampling representation along with the homogeneous field assumption leads to a $D$-fold equal strength diversity model for the channel, and it is convenient to associate each sample with a coherence area, $\mathscr{A}_c$. Under the lognormal assumption, the samples are independent if the $\{\chi_d\}$ are uncorrelated and the $\{\phi_d\}$ are uncorrelated (see (5)). The correlation distances for $\chi$ and $\phi$ are, in general, quite different [2]. At the expense of performing the sampling over an area larger than the effective aperture area of $D\mathscr{A}_c$, where $\mathscr{A}_c$ is the phase coherence area $\mathscr{A}_{c\phi}$ (see Section II-A), the sample amplitude independence should be easily attainable, even then, however, the assumption of phase independence is probably not warranted [32]. Not exploiting the residual phase dependence leads to a slightly suboptimum receiver. However, the importance of this model lies in the simplicity of the resulting analysis and the insight that it provides.

Under the assumption of independent samples, the optimum receiver structure for $M$ equiprobable equal-energy signals depends on the variance of $\phi_d$ and, in general, a quadrature channel matched filter is required for each diversity path. Under the assumptions of an extremely large phase variance ($\phi_d$ considered modulo $2\pi$ is essentially a uniform random variable) and independence between $\chi_d$ and $\phi_d$, the processing required on each diversity path simplifies to a matched-filter envelope-detector receiver followed by an appropriate nonlinearity [11]. The resulting receiver structure, which is min–max with respect to phase, is shown in Fig. 7. It implements the decision rule of choosing the signal that maximizes the likelihood function

$$L_i = \sum_{d=1}^{D} \ln \int_0^\infty dv p(v) I_0(2v\sqrt{\mathscr{A}_c}|ZU_{id}|/N_0)\exp(-v^2\alpha_p) \quad (45a)$$

where $v = |z_d|$ and

$$\alpha_p = \frac{\mathscr{A}_c|Z|^2}{N_0}. \quad (45b)$$

Here $p(v)$ is the lognormal density of (41b), $I_0(\cdot)$ is the zero-order modified Bessel function of the first kind, and $\alpha_p$ is the average received energy-to-noise ratio per diversity path.

It is convenient to give the integral in (45a) a name; thus we introduce the "frustration" function $\mathrm{Fr}(\cdot, \cdot; \cdot)$ defined as

$$\mathrm{Fr}(\alpha, \beta; \sigma) = \int_0^\infty dv I_0(2\beta\sqrt{\alpha}\, v)\exp[-\alpha v^2]p(v). \quad (46)$$

The behavior of this function and its logarithm has been studied [31], [33]. As

$$L_i = \sum_{d=1}^{D} \ln \mathrm{Fr}(\alpha_p, |U_{id}|/\sqrt{N_0}; \sigma), \quad (47)$$

$\ln \mathrm{Fr}(\cdot, \cdot; \cdot)$ is the required nonlinear operation that the receiver must perform. This nonlinear function depending on both the energy-to-noise ratio per diversity path and the variance of $\ln|z_d|$, $\sigma_\chi^2$ is often reasonably approximated as a biased square-law device [31].

*3) Direct-Detection Receivers:* In this section structured receivers that make energy measurements are considered. Again it is convenient to consider separately receivers that use a single detector and those that employ a detector array; however, this time the array receivers will be considered first. The linear field processing indicated in Fig. 3 is assumed to consist of temporal and spatial filtering which limits the background noise while passing essentially all of the signal field energy; the processing may also scale the size of the receiving aperture. As with heterodyne detection we assume that the detection operation occurs in the (perhaps scaled) receiving aperture, so that the signal field statistics are well defined. Receivers that perform the detection operation in the focal plane of receiving aperture collecting optics will be discussed in the summary of this section. Attention will also be confined to the case where the field is represented by independent spatial samples and where (34) is valid, i.e., the detector output is a conditional inhomogeneous Poisson process after averaging over the background noise. Almost all of the presently available results are based on these assumptions.

*a) Detector arrays:* We assume that each detector output depends on an independent sample of the processed field $u_p(t, \mathbf{r})$. We further assume that the effective sampling area is the amplitude coherence area $\mathscr{A}_{c\chi}$, i.e., each sample represents an integral of the field over an area $\mathscr{A}_{c\chi}$ of the aperture plane. The detector array has $D$ elements. For equiprobable signals the optimum receiver sets $\hat{m}$ equal to the $m_i$ that maximizes the likelihood function

$$L_i = \sum_{d=1}^{D} \ln p(\mathbf{t}_d, n_d | m_i) \tag{48}$$

where $\mathbf{t}_d$ is the vector of event times for the $d$th detector output counting process. The vector $\mathbf{t}_d$ has $n_d$ components, where $n_d$ is the number of events that occur within the detection interval $T$. Using the previous assumptions and (28) and (34), $p(\mathbf{t}_d, n_d | m_i)$ is the average over $|z_d|^2$ of the joint event time density of an inhomogeneous Poisson process; the intensity function, conditioned on message $m_i$ and lognormal multiplier $z_d$, is

$$\mu_d(t|m_i, z_d) = \beta\mathscr{A}_{c\chi}\left[|z_d|^2|ZS_i(t)|^2 + I_b\right] \tag{49a}$$

where

$$\beta = \frac{\eta}{h\nu} \tag{49b}$$

$$I_b = \overline{|U_{pb}(t, \mathbf{r})|^2}. \tag{49c}$$

For simplicity it is assumed that $I_b$ is the same for each detector and that the preprocessing does not change the signal.

The important receiver operation for $D = 1$ and a fixed $z_d$ corresponds to a weighted counting [34]–[36]. For $z_d$ a lognormal random variable, $L_i$ can be approximated as

$$\begin{aligned} L_i = \sum_{d=1}^{D} \Bigg\{ & \sum_{j=1}^{n_d} \ln \mu_d(t_j|m_i, \tilde{z}_{di}) - \beta\mathscr{A}_{c\chi}|Z|^2|\tilde{z}_{di}|^2 \\ & - \frac{(\ln|\tilde{z}_{di}|^2 + 2\sigma^2)^2}{8\sigma^2} \\ & - \frac{1}{2}\ln\left[\sum_{j=1}^{n_d}\left(\frac{|Ze^{-\sigma^2}S_i(t_j)|^2}{|Ze^{-\sigma^2}S_i(t_j)|^2 + I_b}\right)^2 \right. \\ & \left. + \frac{1 - 2\sigma^2 - \ln|\tilde{z}_{di}|^2}{4\sigma^2}\right]\Bigg\} \end{aligned} \tag{50a}$$

where $|\tilde{z}_{di}|^2$ is the solution to

$$-\beta\mathscr{A}_{c\chi}|Z|^2|\tilde{z}_{di}|^2 + \sum_{j=1}^{n_d} \frac{|ZS_i(t_j)|^2|\tilde{z}_{di}|^2}{|ZS_i(t_j)|^2|\tilde{z}_{di}|^2 + I_b} - \frac{(\ln|\tilde{z}_{di}|^2 + 2\sigma^2)}{4\sigma^2} = 0. \tag{50b}$$

Here $\sigma_\chi^2$ is written as $\sigma^2$ for convenience, and $I_b$ is given by (49c). This likelihood function was first derived in [37] using the technique of subdividing the decision interval into subintervals over which the signal intensity was essentially constant and using the resulting set of subinterval counts as the data. To form the likelihood function, the counting statistics must be averaged over the lognormal statistics of $|z_d|^2$; the expectation was performed approximately using saddle-point integration [38].

In the receiver specified by (50), the first two terms correspond to the optimum processing for a direct-detection receiver structure when, conditioned on $m_i$ being the transmitted message, the signal field incident on each detector is known and has the value $\tilde{z}_{di}ZS_i(t)$. This processing corresponds to weighted counting and the subtraction of an energy bias term which is data dependent because of $|\tilde{z}_{di}|$. If the parameter $|\tilde{z}_{di}|^2$ defined by (50b) is assumed to have the form exp $2\tilde{\chi}_{di}$, the $2\tilde{\chi}_{di}$ specifies the modal point used in the saddle-point integration. Further if message $m_i$ was actually transmitted, then $\tilde{\chi}_{di}$ is a maximum a posteriori probability estimate of ln $|z_d|$ where $z_d$ is the lognormal variable that describes the fading on the $d$th diversity path. The remaining nonlinear terms are apparently bias terms that tend to discriminate against choices corresponding to $|\tilde{z}_{di}|^2$'s abnormally large or small. It is important to note that the receiver specified by (50) can only be realized with delay. The resulting receiver structure is shown in Fig. 8.

*b) Single detector:* We now consider direct-detection receiver structures in which all the received signal energy is incident on a single detector; such a receiver is called an aperture-integration receiver or "photon bucket." (The receiver might actually have several photodetectors, e.g., when binary orthogonal polarization modulation is used the preprocessing changes the polarization modulation into a spatial modulation and two detectors are needed.) If the receiving aperture area is less than or equal to $\mathscr{A}_{c\chi}$, then the optimum processing of the detector output is approximately specified by (50) with $D = 1$ and $\mathscr{A}_{c\chi}$ equal to $\mathscr{A}_d$, the detection area. As the receiving aperture area increases beyond $\mathscr{A}_{c\chi}$, the detector output is again assumed to be an inhomogeneous Poisson process, but its conditional rate parameter is now

$$\mu(t|m_i, z) = \beta\mathscr{A}_d\left[|z|^2|ZS_i(t)|^2 + I_b\right] \tag{51a}$$

where $\mathscr{A}_d$ is the total detection area and the random variable $z$ is defined as

$$|z|^2 \triangleq \frac{1}{\mathscr{A}_d}\int_{\mathscr{A}_d} |z(\mathbf{r})|^2\, d\mathbf{r}. \tag{51b}$$

The statistics of $|z|^2$, which are needed to specify the receiver processing, have been studied [39], [15], [16]. Based on

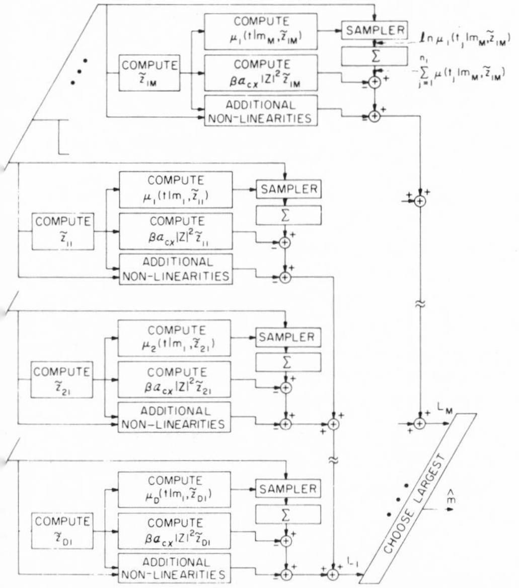


ʒ. 8. Approximate processing for a direct-detection turbulent-atmosphere receiver under the assumption of independent spatial samples. The $\tilde{z}_{di}$ are estimates of the fading variables. (Similar to Fig. 2.3 of [37].)

ese studies it is reasonable to assume that, for $\mathscr{A}_d$ large ative to $\mathscr{A}_{c\chi}$, $|z|^2$, and hence $|z|$, are well approximated lognormal random variables. Thus $|z| = \exp x$, where $x$ is Gaussian random variable with mean $\Delta$ and variance $\Sigma^2$; ıce $\overline{|z|^2} = 1$, $\Delta = -\Sigma^2$. Further $\Sigma^2$ is approximately

$$\Sigma^2 = [\ln[(D-1) + \exp(4\sigma_\chi^2)] - \ln D]/4 \qquad (52)$$

ıere $D$ is the number of amplitude coherence areas con- ined in $\mathscr{A}_d$. Note that the variance of $|z|^2$ is $1/D$ times the riance of $|z_d|^2$; this is an example of the decrease in fading riance due to aperture averaging of the turbulence [2].

With the assumption that $|z|$ is a lognormal random riable, the techniques used for detector arrays can be plied to determine the optimum processing. The resulting elihood functions are

$$= \sum_{j=1}^{n} \ln \mu(t_j|m_i, \tilde{z}_i) - \beta \mathscr{A}_d |Z|^2 |\tilde{z}_i|^2 - \frac{(\ln|\tilde{z}_i|^2 + 2\Sigma^2)^2}{8\Sigma^2}$$
$$- \frac{1}{2} \ln \left[ \sum_{j=1}^{n} \left( \frac{|Ze^{-\Sigma^2} S_i(t_j)|^2}{|Ze^{-\Sigma^2} S_i(t_j)|^2 + I_b} \right)^2 + \frac{1 + 2\Sigma^2 - \ln|\tilde{z}_i|^2}{4\Sigma^2} \right] \qquad (53a)$$

ıere

$$\beta \mathscr{A}_d |Z|^2 |\tilde{z}_i|^2 + \sum_{j=1}^{n} \frac{|ZS_i(t_j)|^2 |\tilde{z}_i|^2}{|ZS_i(t_j)|^2 |\tilde{z}_i|^2 + I_b} - \frac{(\ln|\tilde{z}_i|^2 + 2\Sigma^2)}{4\Sigma^2} = 0. \qquad (53b)$$

ie $t_j$ are the count occurrence times and $n$ is the total num- r of counts during the decision interval.

Just as in the case of the separate coherence area processor, the single detector, or aperture-integration processor, involves a term that corresponds to weighted counting, a term that corresponds to an energy bias term, and two nonlinear terms that discriminate against $|\tilde{z}_i|^2$ values with logarithms that are too large or small relative to the mean of $\ln|z|^2$. All the terms depend on $|\tilde{z}_i|^2 = e^{2\tilde{\chi}_i}$, where $2\tilde{\chi}_i$ is the modal value for the saddle-point integration and, if $m_i$ is the transmitted message, $\tilde{\chi}_i$ is the maximum a posteriori estimate of $x = \ln|z|$. Thus, for the correct message, $|\tilde{z}|^2$ can be viewed as an estimate of the fading.

*4) Summary:* In this section the processing performed by optimum quantum and structured receivers has been considered. Attention has been confined exclusively to the structures that result when aperture plane sampling representations are used; this was done in part to limit the scope of the presentation, but primarily because the resulting sample statistics are better understood. All the results discussed in detail are for the idealistic assumption of independent spatial samples; the insight that can be gained from these answers tends to compensate for the relatively crude model.

In the independent spatial sample model the optimum quantum receiver counts photons; this does not seem to be the case for dependent samples except perhaps when the noise is large relative to the signal, at which point the optimum "gauss-in-gauss" receiver is conjectured to be nearly optimum [15]. The counts undergo a nonlinear weighting and the resulting likelihood function is given by (41a). It is instructive to compare this likelihood function, which is for orthogonal signals (no common modes), with the corresponding likelihood function for heterodyne receivers, (45a). It can easily be shown that if $S$ and $N$ of (41a) increase while their ratio remains fixed as would be the case for heterodyne detection, then (41a) approaches (45a). In both the quantum and heterodyne receivers the processing is associated with the coefficients $\{U_i(\boldsymbol{r}_d)\}$; in the heterodyne case these coefficients are easily generated from the detected signal, but in the quantum case (see (37)) the time processing required is at optical frequencies and may, in general, be difficult to implement.

It is not easy to compare the optimum quantum and direct-detection receivers. The direct-detection receiver processing involves, in general, a weighted counting operation, even before the average over the turbulence; further, the counts are not directly associated with the sample coefficients $\{U_i(\boldsymbol{r}_d)\}$ as the measurements generally involve some modes that contain no signal energy. While the direct-detection array processing receiver can be expected to provide poorer performance than the optimum quantum receiver, it will often be easier to implement. For a general signal set, the aperture-integration direct-detection receiver is, of course, the easiest of all the receivers to build.

Situations for which the postdetection processing of the direct-detection receivers can be simplified are of interest. For any signal set such that $|S_i(t)|^2$ is independent of $i$ for all $t \in T$, the optimum aperture-integration direct-detection processing is just photon counting. Binary orthogonal polarization modulation and frequency shift keying are examples of such signal sets. Surprisingly, the aperture-integration receiver processing of (53) does not reduce to unweighted photon counting for equal energy PPM (pulse-position modulation) signals. The relevant data for this signal set are the numbers of detected photons during each possible pulse position; however, the fact that the fading estimate $\tilde{z}_i$ retains its $i$ dependence means that additional processing is required on these counts. For PPM signals, the separate area processing receiver also uses the numbers of detected photons during pulse intervals as the data but again does some nonlinear processing before adding up the counts from the various spatial modes.

If a focal plane sampling representation had been used, the receivers would have had different forms. If one assumes independent Gaussian samples (an assumption which cannot be rigorously justified), the optimum quantum receiver is known; just as for the independent lognormal sample case, the optimum measurements on each spatial sample are the modal photon counts of the modes that correspond to the possible signals [15]. Thus the processing is still described by Fig. 4 except the nonlinear memoryless operation applied to the counts before summing over the spatial samples differs from that used for lognormal samples. Similarly, for independent focal plane samples and heterodyne detection, the min–max receiver processing would differ from that shown in Fig. 8 only in that the nonlinear operation on each subchannel would be changed; if the sample amplitudes are Rayleigh, the nonlinear operation is squaring [32]. Similar results could easily be obtained for direct-detection array receivers.

### C. Receiver Performance

As previously indicated, the average "single shot" message error probability, $P[\varepsilon]$, will be used to characterize the receiver performance. Further it will be assumed that the decision intervals are short relative to the channel coherence time, i.e., (28) applies. For simplicity in considering the effect of turbulence upon the performance, most of the emphasis will be on the performance that is achieved by equiprobable equal-energy $M$-ary signal sets whose complex envelopes are orthogonal at the receiver.

While some numerical error probability results will be considered, typically the $P(\varepsilon)$ for orthogonal signals will be specified in terms of upper and lower bounds of the form

$$B_1 2^{-KE} \leq P[\varepsilon] \leq B_2 2^{-KE} \qquad \text{(54a)}$$

where $K = \log_2 M$ is the number of bits per message, $E$ is the system reliability function, and $B_1$ and $B_2$ are, at most, slowly changing algebraic functions of $K$ and the other system parameters. $E$ has the form

$$E = \max_{0 \leq \delta \leq 1} \left[ \frac{\xi E_0(\delta)}{\ln 2} - \delta \right] \qquad \text{(54b)}$$

where $\delta$ is an optimization parameter, $\xi$ is the energy-to-noise ratio per information bit, and the function $E_0(\delta)$ is a function that depends on the receiver structure, the turbulence, and signal and noise parameters. If $\delta$ is set equal to one, the upper bound corresponds to a union bound on $P(\varepsilon)$; the bound of (27) is, in general, tighter than a union bound when $\xi$ is less than a certain value, $\xi_{\text{crit}}$.

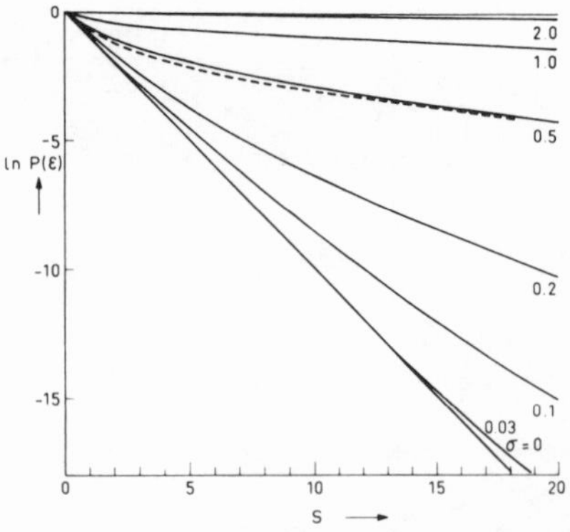


Fig. 9. Error exponent for the optimum quantum receiver in the absen of background radiation. Orthogonal signals are assumed: ln $[1/P($ $= -D \ln \text{Fr}(S, 0; \sigma)$ and $D = 1$. The dashed curve is for a Gaussian fiel Also error exponent for heterodyne receiver with binary orthogon signals and no spatial diversity ($D = 1$) when replace $S$ by $\mathscr{A}_r|Z|^2/N$ (After Fig. 26 of [15].)

*1) Optimum Quantum Receiver:* For the case where th received field representing the transmitted message $m$ $1 \leq i \leq M$, is in a state specified by the density operator $\rho$ and $\rho_i$, $1 \leq i \leq M$, commute, the probability of error asso ciated with any measurement operator $X$ (or set of commu ing measurement operators, $X_k$) is lower bounded by [2

$$P[\varepsilon] \geq 1 - \frac{1}{M} \sum_k \left( \max_{1 \leq i \leq M} r_{ik} \right) \qquad (5$$

where $r_{ik}$ is an eigenvalue of $\rho_i$, and $\rho_i$ can be expanded terms of common eigenstates

$$\rho_i = \sum_k r_{ik} |r_k\rangle \langle r_k|, \qquad 1 \leq i \leq M. \qquad (5$$

This lower bound is achieved by the receiver that impl ments the linear measurement operator $X$ whose set eigenstates coincides with the set $\{|r_k\rangle\}$ (or a set of operato whose simultaneous eigenstates are $|r_k\rangle$) [20].

For the lognormal channel model and independe spatial samples, the simultaneous measurements achievin the minimum probability of error correspond to mod photon counting (see Section III-B1). In this case

$$E_0(\delta) = -\frac{(1+\delta)}{\alpha} \sum_{d=1}^{D} \ln \left[ \sum_{n_{ld}} \left( \int_0^\infty e^{-v^2 S/(N+1)} \cdot L_{n_{ld}}(-S/[N(N+1)]) p(v) dv \right)^{1/1+\delta} \frac{1}{N+1} \left( \frac{N}{N+1} \right)^{n_{ld}} \right], \quad (5$$

where $\alpha = \mathscr{A}_r |Z|^2 / N_0$, and the remaining notation is define by (41) and the text following [15]. Thus performan bounds can be obtained by substituting this result into (5 with $\xi = \alpha/K$. At the present time this is the most gener optimum quantum receiver performance result availab under the assumption of a lognormal fading model.

Under the assumption of no background noise more co plete performance results are available. In this situati (see Section III-B1) an error occurs only when all the nu bers $n_{ld}$, $1 \leq d \leq D$, are zero when signal $l$ is sent. For i ependent lognormal spatial samples the error probability ecomes

$$P(\varepsilon) = [\mathrm{Fr}\,(S, 0; \sigma_\chi)]^D \qquad (58)$$

where Fr $(\cdot, \cdot; \cdot)$ is defined by (46) and $D$ is the number of ndependent samples. This $P(\varepsilon)$ is plotted in Fig. 9 for $D=1$.

2) *Heterodyne Receivers:* The phase-front distortions are nore important than the amplitude scintillations in determining the structure of optimum heterodyne receivers. The scintillations, however, play an important role in determining the receiver performance. We again make the ame assumptions as in Section III-B2. While it has not been nathematically proven, it is a reasonable conjecture that rthogonal signals yield essentially optimum performance.

*a) Single detector:* If the heterodyne receiver contains a ingle detector and the receiving aperture is so small that the hase is essentially constant across it, the receiver output is a ognormal signal plus independent white Gaussian noise. The error performance of such a system for binary orthogonal signals has been studied by several authors [31], [33], 40], [41]. An upper bound on $P(\varepsilon)$ for binary orthogonal ignals is

$$P(\varepsilon) \le \mathrm{Fr}\,(\alpha, 0; \sigma_\chi) \qquad (59)$$

where $\alpha = \mathscr{A}_r|Z|^2/N_0$ and $N_0 \approx h\nu/\eta$ for $h\nu \gg 2N_b\lambda^2$ [31]. This $P[\varepsilon]$ is shown in Fig. 9 when $S$ is replaced by $\alpha$. Thus it is eadily seen that more average signal power is required to naintain a given level of performance as the variance of the og amplitude $\sigma_\chi^2$ increases. The performance of $M$-ary orthogonal signals in this situation can be obtained as a special case of the results to be discussed in the next section.

As the receiver aperture increases, signal variations due o the spatial fading, especially the phase variations, of the eceived field start to become important. Under the assumption of a uniform local oscillator field, experimental and heoretical studies of this effect show that the average signal power saturates as the receiver aperture increases, and that or any aperture size, it will not exceed that associated with an aperture of diameter $r_0$ [42]–[46]. The parameter $r_0$ is approximately the diameter of the phase coherence area $\mathscr{A}_{c\phi}$ defined in Section II-A and depends approximately on he 6/5 power of the optical wavelength [2], [42]. The curve of average signal power versus diameter has a knee at $r_0$ and s approximately 3 dB below the saturated value for an actual receiving diameter of $r_0$. Further, the theoretical esults available indicate that the performance is actually degraded as the aperture diameter approaches and exceeds $r_0$. In particular the signal variance increases rapidly with aperture size beyond $r_0$ [47]. The calculation of $P(\varepsilon)$ for this situation is complicated by the fact that the model of lognormal signal fluctuations is probably no longer adequate when the aperture size approaches $r_0$ [15]; however, the signal variance calculations tend to indicate that the receiving aperture should be limited to approximately $r_0/2$ [47].

If an attempt is made to match the local oscillator field to the average spatial characteristics of the received signal field,

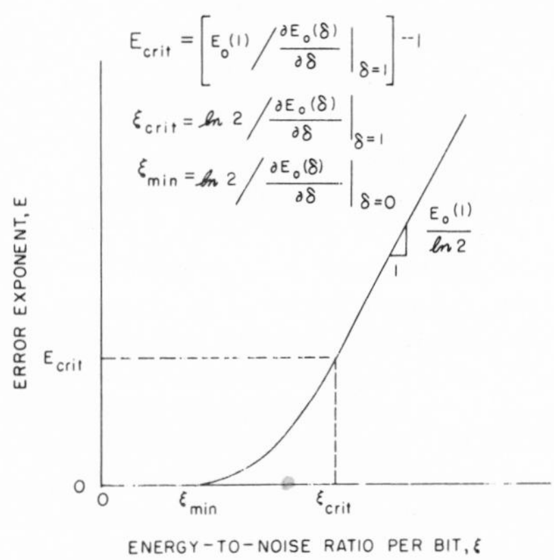


Fig. 10. Reliability curve.

the performance can be somewhat, although not dramatically, improved; the local oscillator field is now spatially varying and the technique is equivalent to antenna beam shaping [48].

*b) Detector array:* Heterodyning arrays can properly use the spatial diversity inherent in the received field and hence, can offer greatly improved performance over that available with a single detector. In particular they need not exhibit a saturation effect with respect to receiver aperture. For lognormal fading statistics the only complete performance results are those for the independent spatial sample model. For the min–max phase receiver of Fig. 7 and $M$ orthogonal equiprobable equal-energy signals

$$E_0(\delta) = -\frac{1+\delta}{\alpha_p}\ln\left\{\int_0^\infty e^{-y}[\mathrm{Fr}\,(\alpha_p, y; \sigma)]^{1/(1+\delta)}dy\right\} \qquad (60)$$

where $\alpha_p = \mathscr{A}_c|Z|^2/N_0$ (45b) and Fr $(\cdot, \cdot; \cdot)$ is defined by (46) [11]. Here $B_2$ can be taken as one and $B_1$ is a complicated function of $\alpha_p$, $\xi$, and $K$, and is in general much less than one.

The system reliability $E$, whose general form is shown in Fig. 10, is a monotone function of $\xi$. Although numerical evaluation is required, in general, it is possible to deduce certain important conclusions without actually performing the evaluation. The first is that $KE$ increases at least linearly with $D$ for fixed values of $\alpha_p$ and $K$; thus the error exponent increases at least linearly with increasing receiver aperture. Second, performance is a function of $\alpha_p$ and hence diversity control is desirable. For any fixed nonzero $\sigma_\chi$ there is an optimum finite value of $\alpha_p$ which tends to zero as $\sigma_\chi$ increases. Spatial diversity is not completely controllable, but it can be influenced by varying the transmitter power or antenna gain; temporal diversity can also be used.

The minimum $\xi$ value at which reliable communication is possible for the system being considered is [32]

$$\xi_{\min} = \frac{\ln 2}{\int q(x)\ln[q(x)\exp \alpha_p x]} \qquad (61a)$$

where

$$q(x) = e^{-\alpha_p x}\,\mathrm{Fr}\,(\alpha_p, \sqrt{\alpha_p x}\,; \sigma_\chi). \tag{61b}$$

If $\alpha_p$ can be adjusted to its optimum value, then $\xi_{\min}$ is ln 2 for all $\sigma_\chi$. In this case the minimum usable energy-to-noise ratio per information bit is independent of the severity of the turbulence and equal to that of an equivalent nonfading additive white Gaussian noise channel.

For $\xi > \xi_{\min}$, the value of $E$ depends on $\sigma_\chi$ whether $\alpha_p$ is optimized or not. The case of large $\xi(\delta = 1)$ has been studied numerically [11]. The performance is completely characterized by $E_0(1)$ in this case, which corresponds to the familiar union bound, i.e.,

$$P(\varepsilon) \leq M \exp -\alpha E_0(1). \tag{62}$$

$E_0(1)$ is plotted in Fig. 11 for various values of $\sigma_\chi^2$ and the performance degradation caused by the turbulence is apparent. Note that, while there is an optimum value of $\alpha_p$, the performance is relatively insensitive to $\alpha_p$ over a range; however, too much diversity can greatly degrade the performance. A $\sigma_\chi^2$ value of 0.25 gives a performance comparable to that for a Rayleigh fading channel.

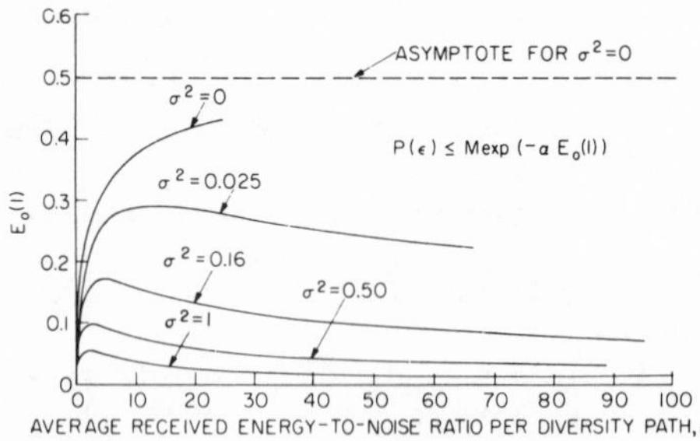


Fig. 11. Dependence of the error exponent on $\alpha_p$ and $\sigma^2$ for large energy-to-noise ratio per information bit, $\xi > \xi_{\text{crit}}$. The receiver of Fig. 7 and $M$ orthogonal signals are assumed. (After Fig. 7 of [11].)

3) *Direct-Detection Receivers:* The performance, as well as the structure, of direct-detection receivers is primarily determined by the time-space envelope scintillations of the received field. At the present time complete analytical performance results for turbulent-channel direct-detection receivers are not available. Almost all of the results available assume that the photodetector acts as an ideal photon counter, thus neglecting the random impulse response associated with most physical detectors and any additive signal-independent noise associated with either the photodetector or the following circuitry (dark current is often treated as an equivalent background noise). Further, the available results usually assume the validity of (34), i.e., that the detector output is a conditional inhomogeneous Poisson process after averaging over the background noise.

While there are relatively few results for the turbulent channel, it seems reasonable that some of the general results from the free-space channel extrapolate to this case. Thus, the performance should, in general, depend strongly on the amount of background noise passed by the temporal and spatial filters preceding the photodetector. In particular, the performance should depend on the signal-to-noise intensity ratio during the decision interval and thus should be dependent on the shape of the signal envelope. In particular, assuming decision intervals that are short relative to the channel coherence time, pulse signals that concentrate their energy in a subinterval with high peak power should normally offer better performance than signals with the same energy but lower peak power spread over the whole decision interval. This is true because the pulse signals enhance the receiver's ability to discriminate against the fixed background radiation by permitting the use of time gating, i.e., counting only during subintervals of the basic decision interval which reduces the background count.

Most of the performance results available are for counting receivers which do not weight the counts; the optimality of such receivers depends on the particular signal set (see Section III-B3). Signal sets that provide optimum $P[\varepsilon]$ performance are not yet known; signal sets that correspond to orthogonal received fields will be emphasized here for simplicity and because they offer good performance. It should be noted that for a direct-detection receiver, preprocessing in the receiver must be used to convert the signal format to energy or spatial variations if it is not already in that form. For example, a Wollaston prism can be used to spatially separate two orthogonal polarizations; polarization modulation is attractive for binary signaling. A particularly attractive $M$-ary signal set, both for receiver simplicity and performance, is pulse-position modulation.

*a) Single detector:* The performance of aperture-integration receivers has been considered by several authors [32], [37], [40], [49]. These authors, if they consider receivers larger than a single amplitude coherence area, assume that the fading variable $z$ associated with the spatially integrated signal intensity (see (51b)) is a lognormal random variable.

Reference [49] contains numerical results for the probability of error versus the variance of $x = \ln|z|$ for a counting receiver with binary orthogonal signals and no background or detector noise. This work, which assumes orthogonal circularly polarized signals, should agree with the no-noise results considered for the optimum quantum receiver (see (58)) to the extent that the spatially integrated fading variable, $z$, has a lognormal density. In [40], the conditional error probability for PPM signals is bounded, but the final average over the fading variable is not carried out. Bucknam [37] attempts to upper and lower bound the one-shot error performance of an optimum receiver for arbitrary $M$-ary orthogonal signals by considering the performances of the receiver which is optimum in the absence of fading and the receiver with a perfect estimate of the fading variable. The final average over the fading variable was again generally neglected.

Bounds of the type in (54a) have been established for the direct-detection performance of counting receivers (no weighting) with equiprobable equal-energy $M$-ary orthogonal signals [32]. (Counting receivers without weighting are optimum for binary polarization modulation and frequency shift-keyed signals (see Section III-B).) Unfortunately, the bounds do not yet have an explicit form because they involve a difficult average over the lognormal fading variable. These bounds, which are obtained by using Chernov bounding techniques and by exploiting the fact that the average number of noise counts per mode due to background radiation is small (see Section II-B), have an exponent of the form in (54b), where

$$\xi = \frac{\overline{n_s}}{K} \tag{63a}$$

and

$$E_0(\delta) = \frac{1+\delta}{\mu} - \frac{1}{\mu n_n} \ln \overline{\left[ \exp\left\{ n_n(1+\delta)\left(1+\frac{n_s}{n_n}\right)^{1/1+\delta}\left(1-\frac{\Upsilon}{1+\Upsilon}\right) - (1-\langle n\rangle)n_s \right\} \right]} \tag{63b}$$

with

$$\Upsilon = \langle n\rangle\left[1-\left(1+\frac{n_s}{n_n}\right)^{1/1+\delta}\right]. \tag{63c}$$

Here $n_s$, the conditional average number of detected signal photons, is $\beta\mathscr{A}_d|Z|^2|z|^2$ where $|z|^2$ is defined by (51b), and $n_n$ is the corresponding average number of detected noise photons. The overbars in (63a) and (63b) indicate averages with respect to the lognormal random variable $|z|^2$. Further, $\mu = \overline{n_s}/n_n$ is a kind of average signal-to-noise ratio and $\langle n\rangle$ is the average number of noise counts per mode (assumed uniform for simplicity). Note that $\xi$ can again be thought of as an energy-to-noise spectral density ratio per bit if the noise level is taken as $h\nu/\eta$.

The preceding expression can be simplified by neglecting $\Upsilon$ and $\langle n\rangle$ relative to one. Because $\langle n\rangle$ is small this is reasonable as long as $n_s/n_n$ is not too large. It is interesting to examine the bound exponent for very large receiving apertures where the aperture averaging is sufficient that the received signal energy is very near its average value (see Section III-B3b). In this case $|z|$ is the sum of a large number of independent random variables and a law of large numbers result can be employed to replace $n_s$ with $\overline{n_s}$; while the aperture required to justify this substitution may be too large to be realistic, this case does establish the performance in the no-turbulence limit.

It is easy to see that the nonturbulent performance, as for a free-space channel, depends strongly on the value of $\mu$. For small $\mu$, the performance is dominated by the background noise and $E_0(\delta)$ becomes

$$E_0(\delta) = \frac{\mu}{2}\,\frac{\delta}{1+\delta} \tag{64a}$$

which yields

$$\begin{aligned} E &= 0, && \xi < \frac{2\ln 2}{\mu} \\ E &= \left[\sqrt{\frac{\xi\mu}{2\ln 2}} - 1\right]^2, && \frac{2\ln 2}{\mu} \le \xi \le \frac{8\ln 2}{\mu} \\ E &= \frac{\mu\xi}{4\ln 2} - 1, && \frac{8\ln 2}{\mu} \le \xi. \end{aligned} \tag{64b}$$

For $\mu$ very large, the so-called quantum limited case, the performance is dominated by the quantum nature of the radiation and

$$E_0(\delta) \approx 1 \tag{65a}$$

and

$$E = \frac{\xi}{\ln 2}. \tag{65b}$$

The last result is true for all $\xi$ satisfying the $\mu$ condition and hence all $\xi$ in the limit of no noise. The type of dependence on $\mu$ discussed previously can be expected even when the fading cannot be neglected. Of course, the performance will be further degraded by the fading.

*b) Detector arrays:* Relatively little work has been done on the performance of optimum direct-direction array receivers. These receivers should provide better performance than receivers using a single detector and aperture integration because the processing can minimize the weight given to those portions of the receiving aperture which have strong fades and are hence relatively more dominated by noise. Bucknam has tried to study the relative performance of array and aperture-integration receivers by considering upper bounds to the performance of the array and single-detector counting receivers which would be optimum in the absence of fading and which would be optimum if perfect estimates of the fading were available [37]. He shows, under the assumption of nonzero noise, that the array receiver will always yield better performance in the perfect-estimation case. Also the array and aperture-integration receivers designed for the nonfading case yield the same performance when there is fading. Thus the nonlinear processing associated with optimum turbulent receivers is necessary if the array receiver is to offer superior performance.

As yet, the magnitude of the performance enhancement to be expected with array receivers is not known. It seems reasonable to expect that the gains will only be large when the fading is severe, the number of amplitude coherence areas in the receiving aperture is not too large, and the background noise is significant, i.e., $\mu$ is not large.

4) *Summary:* The results discussed show that for digital signaling, proper processing can negate or minimize most of the performance degradation due to the turbulence. This is illustrated, for example, by the capacity result for array heterodyne receivers. The turbulence has, however, increased the complexity of the processing required to achieve optimum performance. The results emphasize the optimality of parallel spatial processing with nonlinear diversity combining to combat the spatial incoherence and lognormal fading.

The results discussed are in the form of bounds. While these bounds do not usually provide extremely sharp numerical estimates of $P[\varepsilon]$, they have great utility in establishing accurate estimates of the system parameters required to provide a given level of performance. Thus they can be used to study the interrelationships between the various system parameters and to estimate the complexity required to achieve a given level of performance.

The performance results presently available are far from complete. The mathematical model used to obtain most of the results discussed assumes independent spatial samples. This assumption, which is motivated by the analytical difficulty of dealing with dependent non-Gaussian variables (sum of lognormal and Gaussian), tends to lead to optimistic results because of the extra diversity. It is expected, however, that the predictions can be achieved in actual systems with small changes in the values of the system parameters.

A quantitative comparison between the performance of the optimum quantum receiver and the structured receivers is not available; numerical results for $E_0(\delta)$ are not available in the quantum case. The heterodyne results, which correspond to those for a classical field measurement receiver except for the modified $N_0$ value, emphasize the importance of properly using the spatial diversity. Proper processing removes the coherence area limit on performance; the resulting situation is similar to that for a Rayleigh diversity channel except the optimum energy-to-noise ratio per diversity path depends on the $\sigma_\chi^2$ value. The performance is sometimes better and sometimes worse than that of the comparable Rayleigh channel; for $\sigma_\chi^2=0.25$ the Rayleigh and lognormal performance is very similar [15], [33].

The direct-detection performance, which depends largely on the amplitude scintillations, is not so sensitive to the spatial processing as the heterodyne performance. While an array receiver will give better performance than an aperture-integration receiver, the gain is not expected to be very great in many situations, i.e., the aperture-integration receiver uses the spatial diversity in a reasonably optimum manner. The direct-detection results show the importance of background noise and of the preprocessing used to minimize it. For fixed preprocessing, signal selection to provide operation in the shot-noise limited regime, if possible, is important. If the preprocessing can be optimized, then signal selection is not as important.

Both the unspecified direct-detection preprocessing and the characteristics of real physical detectors, which have been in part suppressed in the analysis, make a direct practical comparison of the performance of heterodyne and direct-detection receivers difficult. If a detector with sufficient gain to suppress the importance of the preamplifier noise exists at the wavelength of interest, then direct detection, with reasonable preprocessing, is simpler and probably will provide better performance than heterodyning. On the other hand, if the detector does not have gain, heterodyning which minimizes the importance of the background and preamplifier noise may be preferable in spite of its complexity.

The performance improvement achievable using various adaptive techniques has not been considered in detail. One of the simplest and most completely analyzed adaptive receivers is a single-detector phase-front-tracking heterod receiver. By following the linear tilt of the received ph front, the effective phase-coherence diameter can be creased by a factor of roughly three, and the signal-to-nc ratio can be increased by 10 dB [50], [51]. Most of the ot adaptive techniques, while very promising, are not yet cc pletely analyzed; they will be discussed in Section V.

## IV. Estimation Theory

### A. *Introduction*

In this section, the methods of statistical inference wil used to study the accuracy limitations imposed by tur lence on the estimation of parameters or waveforms. statistical information required to study the form and p formance of estimation structures is given by the app priate likelihood functional, $l(\{U_j\};\boldsymbol{\theta})$, essentially the ra of the probabilities of appropriate field measurements der the hypotheses $H_1$ and $H_0$ [14], [52]–[54]. Hypoth $H_1$ is that the received field is signal plus noise while $H$ the noise-only hypothesis; the signal depends on the para eters $\boldsymbol{\theta}$ (or waveform $\theta(t)$) to be estimated. As the notat indicates, the likelihood functional depends on the para eters to be estimated. As in the detection case, the statis of the field measurements $\{U_j\}$ depend on the quant measurement performed; to emphasize the turbul effects, classical field measurements will be used for mos this section.

An estimate of the parameter $\theta$ will be denoted $\hat{\theta}(\{U_j\}$ $\overline{\hat{\theta}}=\theta$ the estimate is said to be unbiased. The Cramer–R inequality [14], [52]–[54] gives a lower bound—deno CRLB here—for the variance of the error for any unbias estimate:

$$\overline{(\theta-\hat{\theta})^2} \geq \left[\overline{-\frac{\partial^2}{\partial\theta^2}\ln l(\{U_j\};\theta)}\right]^{-1}.$$

An unbiased estimate $\check{\theta}$ that achieves the bound is term "efficient"; if such an estimate exists, then it is also "maximum likelihood estimate" MLE, denoted as $\tilde{\theta}$ a defined as the value of $\theta$ that maximizes $l(\{U_j\};\theta)$.

If a finite number of parameters $\boldsymbol{\theta}=(\theta_1,\cdots,\theta_N)$ are to jointly estimated, the joint performance of unbiased e mates can be lower bounded in terms of the matrix $C$ wh elements are $c_{ij}\equiv-\overline{\{\partial^2 \ln l(\{U_j\};\boldsymbol{\theta})/\partial\theta_i\partial\theta_j\}}$, $i,j=1,\cdots,$ The inverse matrix $\Lambda\equiv C^{-1}$, with elements $\lambda_{ij}$ $\overline{(\theta_i-\hat{\theta}_i)(\theta_j-\hat{\theta}_j)}$, is then the covariance matrix of the err for efficient unbiased estimates $\check{\boldsymbol{\theta}}=(\check{\theta}_1,\cdots,\check{\theta}_N)$. The ext sion of the MLE procedure to the vector case is obvio replace $\theta$ and $\tilde{\theta}$ by $\boldsymbol{\theta}$ and $\tilde{\boldsymbol{\theta}}$. The previous results are g eralized to the case where $\boldsymbol{\theta}$ is a random vector with a kno joint probability density function $p(\boldsymbol{\theta})$ by replacing $l(\{U_j\}$ with $l(\{U_j\}|\boldsymbol{\theta})\,p(\boldsymbol{\theta})$.

An application that includes all of these generalization waveform estimation [14], [55]. Waveform estimation c be related to joint parameter estimation (normally with infinite number of parameters) by using an orthonormal expansion for the waveform, i.e.,

$$\theta(t) = \theta_t = \sum \theta_n f_n(t),\ t \in [0, T],$$

where $\{f_n(t)\}$ is an orthonormal set. (If $\theta_t$ is a sample function of a Gaussian random process with covariance function $R_\theta$, then it is natural to use the Karhunen–Loeve expansion [14], [56].) The estimates $\{\hat{\theta}_n\}$ of the $\{\theta_n\}$ give an estimate $\hat{\theta}_t$ of $\theta_t$. If the mean square error is defined as

$$\text{mse} = \overline{\int_0^T |\theta_t - \hat{\theta}_t|^2 dt} \tag{67a}$$

then

$$\text{mse} = \lim_{N\to\infty} \sum_{n=1}^{N} \overline{(\theta_n - \hat{\theta}_n)^2}. \tag{67b}$$

This limit has been underbounded for Gaussian processes [14], [57].

To account for quantum effects $\hat{\theta}$ is represented by an operator denoted $\hat{A}$. An estimate $\hat{\theta}$ is then the outcome of a measurement, an eigenvalue of the operator $\hat{A}$. The optimum quantum estimation problem is concerned with choosing $\hat{A}$ such that the peformance, in terms of an appropriate criterion, is optimized. The received field is again described by a density operator $\rho$ which now depends on the unknown parameter $\theta$. The $k$th moment of the estimate is, of course, $\overline{\hat{\theta}^k} = \text{Tr}\,(\rho\hat{A}^k)$.

The CRLB has been extended to the quantum case [58], but there are few results for turbulent channels as modeled here; Rayleigh fading channels have been discussed [18]. As in Section III, one can consider structured receivers; then the quantum measurement is specified and the usual statistical inference methods may be used. We shall use this approach later.

For the estimation problems discussed here, the complex envelope of the transmitted field for coherent sources is $U_i(t, \boldsymbol{r}) = S(t, \theta_t)U(\boldsymbol{r})$. For example, $S(t, \theta_t) = \exp(i\theta_t)$ models phase modulation.

### B. *Likelihood Functionals*

Propagation models for the turbulent channel were discussed in Section II. For covenience we will use the following model: if $U_0(t, \boldsymbol{r}) = F(t, \boldsymbol{r})$ is the received field in the absence of turbulence, then $ZF(t, \boldsymbol{r})z(\boldsymbol{r})$ is the received random field in the presence of turbulence. The field $F$ is related to the source field $U_i$ by

$$F(t, \boldsymbol{r}) = \int_S G(\boldsymbol{r}, \boldsymbol{r}')U_i(t, \boldsymbol{r}')d\boldsymbol{r}' \tag{68}$$

where $S$ is the source surface and $G(\boldsymbol{r}, \boldsymbol{r}')$ the free-space Green's function [59]. If the source is in the far field, $F$ is essentially the spatial Fourier transform of $U_i$. This model agrees with that of (4a) when $F$ is spatially constant over $\mathscr{A}_r$.

Usually we have in mind the form $\exp[\chi(\boldsymbol{r}) + i\phi(\boldsymbol{r})]$ for $z(\boldsymbol{r})$ (see Section II-A), but some of the results cited later do not depend on this. We will see that some useful approximate estimators can be obtained using only second-order statistics, a considerable simplification.

*1) Classical Field Measurement:* In the absence of quantum effects (i.e., classical field measurements are assumed) and with $z(\boldsymbol{r})$ fixed, the problem reduces to that of receiving a signal, known except for parameters, in additive, white Gaussian noise. The resulting conditional likelihood functional is [54]

$$l(\{U_j\}|z) = \exp\left\{\frac{2}{N_0}\text{Re}\int_T\int_{\mathscr{A}_r} U_r^*(t, \boldsymbol{r})ZF(t, \boldsymbol{r})z(\boldsymbol{r})dt\,d\boldsymbol{r} - \frac{|Z|^2}{N_0}\int_T\int_{\mathscr{A}_r} |F(t, \boldsymbol{r})z(\boldsymbol{r})|^2 dt\,d\boldsymbol{r}. \tag{69}$$

If $l(\{U_j\}|z)$ is now averaged over the statistics of $z(\boldsymbol{r})$ we will have the desired likelihood functional. Two approximate calculations will be discussed.

First, suppose that the exponent is a Gaussian random variable. This could be argued if $z$ and $|z|^2$ fluctuate many times over $\mathscr{A}_r$, for then the integral would presumably be summing many independent random variables and a crude appeal to a central limit theorem could be made. This assumption is reasonable for the first term of the exponent (see Section II-B) but more dubious for the second term (see Section III-B3b). The result is still somewhat involved [28], [60], but, if $\sigma_\phi^2 \gg 1$, then the approximate likelihood functional [28] is

$$\ln l(\{U_j\}) = L_1 + \frac{|Z|^2}{N_0^2} Q(\{U_j\}) \tag{70}$$

where

$$Q(\{U_j\}) \equiv \int_T\int_{\mathscr{A}_r} U_r^*(t, \boldsymbol{r})F(t, \boldsymbol{r})dt\,d\boldsymbol{r} \int_T\int_{\mathscr{A}_r} U_r(t', \boldsymbol{r}') \cdot F^*(t', \boldsymbol{r}')q(\boldsymbol{r} - \boldsymbol{r}')dt'd\boldsymbol{r}'. \tag{71}$$

Here $q(\boldsymbol{r} - \boldsymbol{r}')$ is the covariance function of $z(\boldsymbol{r})$, and $L_1$ is a form involving first and second moments of the received signal energy.

Second, just as in Section III-B2b, suppose that $|Z|^2/2N_0$ is so small that we may approximate the exponential form of $l(\{U_j\}|z)$ by the first three terms of its Taylor series. Also assume that the received phase of the signal is not known (even in the absence of turbulence) and, in fact, is a random variable uniformly distributed over $(0, 2\pi)$. Then we find the threshold form is

$$\ln l(\{U_j\}) \approx L_2 + \frac{|Z|^2}{N_0^2} Q(\{U_j\}) \tag{72}$$

where $q(\boldsymbol{r} - \boldsymbol{r}')$ in (71) is now the correlation function of $z(\boldsymbol{r})$ and $L_2$ is again a form involving first and second moments of the received energy.

The similarity of these forms, along with their remarkably easy physical realization to be discussed, and their optimality for Gaussian signal fields [29], lends weight to using a structure of this quadratic functional form to make suboptimal estimates.

*2) Quantum Mechanical Measurement:* The weight function for the density operator $\rho_0$ when only thermal background noise is present, is in the *P*-representation, given by (19); when thermal noise plus narrow-band coherent signal is present, the weight function is $(\pi\langle n\rangle)^{-1} \exp(-|\alpha_k-\mu_k|^2/\langle n\rangle)$, where $\mu_k$ is the coherent signal's mode amplitude, normalized by $\sqrt{h\nu}$. We take a structured approach and make measurements represented by the real and imaginary parts of the non-Hermitian annihilation operators $\{a_k\}$ [61]. As pointed out in Section II (see also [21]), there is a distribution defined on the space of outcomes $\{\alpha_k\}$; it can be shown that the real and imaginary parts of $\alpha_k$ are independent Gaussian random variables with variance $\sigma^2 \equiv (\langle n\rangle+1)/2$. See, for example, [18]. The mean of $\alpha_k$ is zero under $H_0$ and $\mu_k$ under $H_1$.

The likelihood functional is therefore, for fixed $z(\boldsymbol{r})$,

$$l(\{\alpha_k\}|z) = \exp\left\{\sum_k \frac{2\,\mathrm{Re}\,(\alpha_k\mu_k^*) - |\mu_k|^2}{\sigma^2}\right\}. \tag{73}$$

To average this conditional likelihood functional over the distribution of $z$, it is possible to use either of the approximations made in the classical case. In the threshold case, we have

$$l(\{\alpha_k\}) \approx L_4 + \sigma^{-4} \sum_{k,k'} \mu_k\mu_{k'}^*\overline{(\mu_k^*\mu_{k'})} \tag{74}$$

where $L_4$ involves, just as in the classical case, the sum of the average energy and the average squared energy. The overbar indicates an expectation operation with respect to $Z$. Using the definition of $\mu_k$ as a modal amplitude, one can write $l(\{\alpha_k\})$ in the same form as (72) except that $N_0$ is replaced by $\sigma^2 h\nu$. Therefore the classical results in this section carry over to this quantum measurement case if $N_0$ is replaced by $\sigma^2 h\nu$.

### C. Estimation of Source Parameters

*1) Physical Realization:* The kernel $q$ in the quadratic functional $Q(\{U_j\})$ of (70) and (72) depends only on spatial variables. Thus the realization of $Q$ may be viewed as a time processing followed by a spatial processing. This is inconvenient in practice. Temporal processing at light frequencies is less advanced presently than at lower frequencies while spatial processing of light is fairly well developed.

Defining the temporally processed data to be

$$Y(\boldsymbol{r}) \equiv \begin{cases} \int_T U_r(t,\boldsymbol{r})F^*(t,\boldsymbol{r})dt, & \boldsymbol{r}\in\mathscr{A}_r, \\ 0, & \boldsymbol{r}\notin\mathscr{A}_r, \end{cases} \tag{75}$$

we may write

$$Q(\{U_j\}) = \frac{1}{4\pi^2}\int |\tilde{Y}(\omega)|^2\tilde{q}(\omega)d\omega \tag{76}$$

where we have used Parseval's identity and where the tilde denotes a (two-dimensional) Fourier transform.

This form for $Q(\{U_j\})$ suggests [28], [29], [60] an optical realization because a lens can be used to perform the

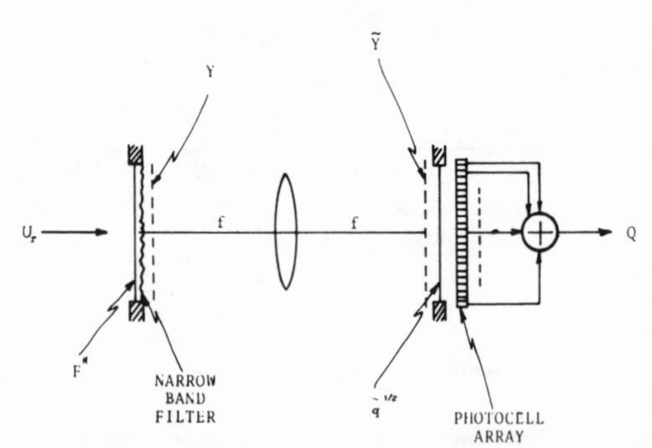


Fig. 12. Optical system realization of the quadratic functional define by the approximate likelihood functionals of (70) and (72). Note th $F(t, \boldsymbol{r})$ depends on the parameters or waveform to be estimated. T tilde denotes a two-dimensional Fourier transform.

Fourier transformation [62]–[64]. Approximating the inte gration over $T$ with a narrow-band filter, the appropriat structure is shown in Fig. 12. Since angle-of-arrival vari ations correspond to position variations in the back foca plane of the lens, we have a physical interpretation for $\tilde{q}$; is an optimum angle-of-arrival (or "field") weighting func tion.

Another interesting interpretation [28] of $Q(\{U_j\})$ is a a "mixed integrator" defined as the functional

$$\int_{\mathscr{A}_r}\left|\int_{\mathscr{A}_r} Y(\boldsymbol{r}')\Delta(\boldsymbol{r}-\boldsymbol{r}')d\boldsymbol{r}'\right|^2 d\boldsymbol{r}.$$

It can be shown [28] that a quadratic functional $Q$ is a mixe integrator (with real weighting function $\Delta$) if and only if $Q$ positive semi-definite; then $|\tilde{\Delta}|^2 = \tilde{q}$. Since the $q$ of (71) is covariance function, $Q$ is positive semi-definite. If $\tilde{\Delta}$ assumed to be real, $\Delta$ has roughly the spatial extent of the coherence area. Thus, as in the detection case, the processing may be interpreted as coherent over a fiel coherence area and then incoherent between coherenc areas.

*2) Cramer–Rao Lower Bounds:* The calculation of th CRLB using (70) or (72) is simplified if the received energ is invariant to changes in the unknown parameter $\theta$ Then the elements of the matrix $C$ are

$$c_{ij} = \frac{-(2\varepsilon/N_0)^2}{\|F\|^4}\int_T\int_{\mathscr{A}_r}\int_T\int_{\mathscr{A}_r} F^*(t,\boldsymbol{r})F(t',\boldsymbol{r}') \cdot\left[\frac{\partial^2}{\partial\alpha_i\partial\alpha_j}F(t,\boldsymbol{r})F^*(t',\boldsymbol{r}')\right]w(\boldsymbol{r}-\boldsymbol{r}')dtd\boldsymbol{r}dt'd\boldsymbol{r}' \quad (7$$

where

$$\|F\|^2 \equiv \int_T\int_{\mathscr{A}_r}|F(t,\boldsymbol{r})|^2\, dtd\boldsymbol{r},$$

[2] It is important to realize that the error bounds obtained using t approximate likelihood functions may not be bounds for the actual es mation problem. However, they provide useful approximations th identify the important performance parameters.

the expected received signal energy

$$\varepsilon = |Z|^2 ||F||^2/2,$$

$R_z(\boldsymbol{r})$ is the correlation function of $z$, and $w(\boldsymbol{r}-\boldsymbol{r}') \simeq q(\boldsymbol{r}-\boldsymbol{r}')R_z(\boldsymbol{r}-\boldsymbol{r}')$.

For example, suppose $F(\boldsymbol{r}) = \exp(ik\theta_1 x)$ where $\theta_1$ is the unknown angle-of-arrival of a signal wavefront and $k = 2\pi/\lambda$. Then var $(\theta_1 - \hat{\theta}_1) \geq c_{11}^{-1}$, where

$$c_{11} = \left(\frac{2\varepsilon}{N_0}\right)^2 \frac{k^2}{\mathscr{A}_r^2} \int_{\mathscr{A}_r}\int_{\mathscr{A}_r} (x - x')^2 w(\boldsymbol{r} - \boldsymbol{r}') d\boldsymbol{r} d\boldsymbol{r}'. \quad (78)$$

If we assume $z = \exp(\chi + i\phi)$ and consider the threshold case where $q(\boldsymbol{r}) = R_z(\boldsymbol{r})$, then $w(\boldsymbol{r}) \approx \exp\{-2\sigma_\phi^2 + 2R_\phi(\boldsymbol{r})\}$. In this approximation the amplitude fluctuations have been neglected since the phase variance is usually larger and the phase fluctuations more rapid than the log amplitude fluctuations [2]. If the bandwidth of the phase process is $\Omega_\phi$, an instructive approximation is $w(\boldsymbol{r}) \approx \exp(-\sigma_\phi^2 \Omega_\phi^2 |\boldsymbol{r}|^2/2)$. Assuming the correlation distance $\mathscr{W}_\phi = (\sigma_\phi \Omega_\phi)^{-1}$ of $\exp(i\phi)$ is short relative to $\mathscr{W}$, where $\mathscr{A}_r$ is a square of side $\mathscr{W}$, then

$$c_{11} \approx \left(\frac{2\varepsilon}{N_0}\right)^2 \frac{\mathscr{W}}{6} \left(\frac{\mathscr{W}_\phi}{\mathscr{W}}\right)^3. \quad (79)$$

The expected received signal energy is $\varepsilon = |Z|^2 T \mathscr{W}^2/2$ in this case. From (78) it is easily verified that as $\mathscr{W}_\phi \to \infty$, $c_{11} \to (2\varepsilon/N_0)^2 \mathscr{W}/6$, so the ratio $\mathscr{W}_\phi/\mathscr{W}$ clearly indicates the cost of the turbulence-induced phase fluctuations.

For this example the MLE of $\theta_1$, as indicated by (76), corresponds to that focal plane position at which a maximum occurs, at an appropriate instant of time.

As another example, suppose $F(t, \boldsymbol{r}) = \exp(i\theta_2 t)$ where $\alpha_2$ is an unknown Doppler frequency. Then var $(\theta_2 - \hat{\theta}_2) \geq c_{22}^{-1}$, where

$$c_{22} = \left(\frac{2\varepsilon}{N_0}\right)^2 \cdot \frac{T^2}{6} \cdot \frac{1}{\mathscr{A}_r^2} \int_{\mathscr{A}_r}\int_{\mathscr{A}_r} w(\boldsymbol{r}_1 - \boldsymbol{r}_2) d\boldsymbol{r}_1 d\boldsymbol{r}_2. \quad (80)$$

With $w(\boldsymbol{r}) = \exp(-\sigma_\phi^2 \Omega_\phi^2 |\boldsymbol{r}|^2/2)$, then

$$c_{22} \approx \left(\frac{2\varepsilon}{N_0}\right)^2 \frac{T^2}{6} \cdot \frac{1}{2\pi} \left(\frac{\mathscr{W}_\phi}{\mathscr{W}}\right)^2. \quad (81)$$

In the threshold case, it is easily verified that $c_{22} \to (2\varepsilon/N_0)^2 T^2/6$ as $\mathscr{W}_\phi \to \infty$, so the ratio $\mathscr{W}_\phi/\mathscr{W}$ again clearly indicates the degradation due to the phase fluctuations.

Comparing the results of these two examples, it is apparent that the random phase fluctuations more seriously affect the estimate of a spatially linear phase than the estimate of a temporally linear phase. This might be expected because we assumed only spatial phase fluctuations.

It is easily seen that an efficient estimate of position or Doppler frequency, or any other phase parameter, is uncorrelated with $\theta_3 = (2\varepsilon/N_0)^2$. This is significant because $|Z|^2$ is often unknown. More generally, for $w$ real, as in the threshold case, and for parameters whose variations do not affect the received energy, the efficient estimate of any parameter affecting only the phase of $F$ and any parameter affecting only the amplitude of $F$ are uncorrelated.

### D. Waveform Estimation

We now extend the parameter estimation theory to waveform estimation. For illustration, assume that the classically measurable received signal waveform has no spatial variation over $\mathscr{A}_r$ aside from that due to turbulence and that the modulation is phase modulation. These are the results presently available.

As in classical estimation theory [52], one can obtain a necessary condition, called the likelihood equation, for a maximum likelihood waveform estimate. If the phase modulation $\theta_t$ is a real, zero-mean, Gaussian random process, then assuming the threshold case and using (72), the likelihood equation for the estimate $\tilde{\theta}_t$ is

$$\tilde{\theta}_t = \frac{|Z|^2}{N_0^2} \cdot 2\,\mathrm{Re}\left\{ i \int_T \int_{\mathscr{A}_r} U_r^*(t', \boldsymbol{r}') e^{i\tilde{\theta}_{t'}} R_\theta(t - t') \cdot \int_T \int_{\mathscr{A}_r} U_r(t'', \boldsymbol{r}'') e^{-i\tilde{\theta}_{t''}} R_z(\boldsymbol{r}' - \boldsymbol{r}'') dt' d\boldsymbol{r}' dt'' d\boldsymbol{r}'' \right\}. \quad (82)$$

While this equation does not have a simple solution, it can be used to suggest potentially useful demodulator structures.

To study the mean square estimation error, we assume that $\theta_t$ is approximately represented by $N$ coefficients and find the matrix elements of $C$, using the likelihood functional of (72). For this threshold case the matrix elements are

$$c_{nk} \equiv -\overline{E\left\{\frac{\partial^2}{\partial\theta_n \partial\theta_k}\left[\ln l(\{U_i\}|\boldsymbol{\theta}) - \frac{1}{2}\sum \frac{\theta_n^2}{\sigma_n^2}\right]\right\}}$$

$$= \frac{\delta_{nk}}{\sigma_n^2} + \left(\frac{2\varepsilon}{N_0}\right)^2 ¢_1 ¢_{nk} \quad (83a)$$

where

$$¢_1 \equiv \mathscr{A}_r^{-2} \int_{\mathscr{A}_r}\int_{\mathscr{A}_r} |w(\boldsymbol{r} - \boldsymbol{r}')|^2 d\boldsymbol{r} d\boldsymbol{r}' \quad (83b)$$

$$¢_{nk} \equiv 2T^{-2}\left(T\delta_{nk} - \int_T f_n(t)dt \cdot \int_T f_k(t')dt'\right) \quad (83c)$$

and $\delta_{nk}$ is the Kronecker delta.

Using (67), we see the mse, in this finite coefficient approximation, is lower bounded by Tr $(\Lambda)$, $\Lambda = C^{-1}$. If $C$ is diagonal, then Tr $(\Lambda)$ is just the sum of the reciprocals of the diagonal elements of $C$. If $\Omega_\theta$ is the bandwidth (reasonably defined) of $\theta_t$ and $\Omega_\theta T \gg 1$, the $\{f_n(t)\}$ converge weakly to $\{\exp(in2\pi t)/\sqrt{T}\}$, the characteristic values are approximately $\sigma_n^2 \approx S_\theta(n2\pi/T)$, and $C$ is indeed approximately diagonal [65]. Here $S_\theta(\omega)$ is the power spectral density of $\theta_t$. Thus for $\Omega_\theta T \gg 1$,

$$\mathrm{Tr}(\Lambda) \approx \sigma_0^2 + \sum_{n \neq 0}^{N} \left(\frac{1}{\sigma_n^2} + ¢\right)^{-1} \quad (84a)$$

where

$$\not{C}' = (2\varepsilon/N_0)^2 2\not{C}_1/T. \tag{84b}$$

To make the interpretation of this answer still easier, assume $T$ sufficiently large that $S_\theta$ does not change appreciably over the frequency interval $2\pi/T$. Then, letting $N \to \infty$,

$$\begin{aligned} \text{mse} &\geq \lim_{N\to\infty} \operatorname{Tr}(\Lambda) \\ &\approx \sigma_0^2 + \frac{T}{\pi}\int_{2\pi/T}^{\infty} \frac{S_\theta(\omega)d\omega}{1 + \not{C}' S_\theta(\omega)} \end{aligned} \tag{85}$$

where it is assumed that the limit exists. The turbulence affects the mse through $\not{C}'$, which depends on the average received signal energy and the spatial correlation properties of the received field (see (84b)). For example, a decrease in the coherence area, which decreases $\not{C}'$, increases the value of the lower bound and presumably the mse.

### E. Summary

We have outlined some methods of calculating bounds on estimation accuracy and of finding useful measuring structures for coherent sources used with the turbulent atmosphere channel. Although the multiplicative nature of the turbulence effects and the nonlinear nature of the processors prevent simple interpretation, one can say roughly that the turbulence more seriously affects the accuracy of spatial-parameter estimates than temporal-parameter estimates. The use of various channel models and approximations lead to quadratic processors which are appealing even though they are usually suboptimal. They efficiently use the available aperture and their spatial processing is naturally accomplished by a basically simple optical system. The need to perform the time processing before the spatial processing complicates the practical realization, but obvious suboptimum structures worthy of study are suggested.

## V. Conclusions and Comments

This paper has dealt with the analysis of the turbulent atmosphere as an optical-communication channel. In particular, it has been primarily concerned with the discussion of those available results relevant to the establishment of the fundamental capabilities and limitations of this channel for the communication of information. Thus, while many important practical considerations have been neglected, in part for analytical simplicity, care has been taken to use a mathematical channel model that reflects the important features of the turbulent atmospheric channel.

The optical-frequency communication analysis of the turbulent atmosphere has several unique aspects, at least as contrasted to microwave fading channels. These are the importance of the spatial incoherence of the received field, the lognormal fading statistics, and the importance of quantum effects. The analysis is mathematically complex and results, in general, can only be obtained by making a number of simplifications and approximations. However, the results that have been obtained lead to some important general conclusions about the forms of optimum processors and their performance. The spatial incoherence implies array processing, the lognormal amplitude statistics imply nonlinear (nonsquare-law) diversity combining, and the phase incoherence implies energy detection. The available results indicate that the loss in performance from that available with a nonfading channel can usually be made small at the cost of complexity in the receiver processing. Thus it is reasonable to conclude that the turbulent atmosphere is a useful and reliable communication medium when the signals and receivers are properly designed.

An important practical question that needs to receive more attention is realizable performance with less complex suboptimal processing. Thus, for example, the relative performance of an aperture-integration direct-detection receiver and an array direct-detection (or preferably the optimum quantum mechanical) receiver is an important question. While the answer to this question is not yet known, it seems clear that aperture-integration direct-detection receivers, with *appropriate* preprocessing, are attractive from both the performance and simplicity viewpoints, when heterodyning is not required to combat detector noise.

While there are a number of theoretical results available for the turbulent channel, there is still a lot of useful work to be done. At the present time the spatial aspect of the problem is typically handled in a rather crude manner; most of the results assume independent spatial samples. This is due to the difficulty, as discussed, in establishing the coefficient statistics associated with various representations and to the difficulty in dealing with dependent non-Gaussian random variables. A new approach to the problem of representing random fields may be required. The quantum aspect of the problem should also receive more attention. Many of the present results are classical (or heterodyne) and the only true quantum results are for independent spatial samples. Work is needed both on the full quantum problem and on the performance and processing of direct-detection systems. Work is also needed to evaluate the effects of more realistic detector models, including the effects of preamplifier noise, variable detector gain, and finite bandwidth. As previously indicated, the performance of various suboptimal receiver structures should be assessed, ideally with very realistic detector models. In the same vein, work is needed on understanding the physical implications of some of the theoretical approximations and simplifications and on ways of implementing, at least approximately, some of the required time–space field processing.

At the present time detection theory is more advanced than estimation or analog modulation theory. A partial list of the work to be done in the estimation area would include obtaining the CRLB and MLE performance for specific applications [66], studying the effects of various combinations of temporal- and spatial-source incoherence [67], obtaining optimum quantum parameter estimation results onsidering other representations and approximations to ikelihood functionals, and studying the optimum quantum eceivers for analog modulation.

Many important topics have not been included. The missions are due to both space considerations and, in some ases, the lack of available results. Among the topics mitted are coding, adaptive techniques, and active and assive imaging systems. The various adaptive techniques, vhich exploit the slowness of the channel time variations, eem to offer real promise for improving the turbulent hannel performance. In some cases they may permit the ame level of performance with a less complex system. he basic idea is to estimate the "state" of the channel, in vhole or in part, and then to use this information in the ommunication process. The most studied systems using his technique are the wavefront tracking receivers menioned in Section III-C4. A more sophisticated version of uch a system is a measurement receiver that tries to estinate the fading process and to use this estimate in the reeiver processing. The same idea can be applied to the transnitter, where the channel-state knowledge can be used to ary either the antenna pattern (spatial modulation) or the ommunication rate. Of course, in this latter case, there nust be a probe available to supply the channel-state inormation. The results can be quite dramatic. The use of daptive spatial modulation can, for example, yield diffracion-limited apodization performance on an earth-to-space ath [68]. These adaptive systems, which are an important opic of current research, are mentioned in another paper in his issue [5] and have been discussed in more detail elsevhere [3]. Reference [3] also discusses transmitted reference ystems.

While the important problem of imaging ("completely") bjects viewed through turbulence, using either coherent r incoherent light, has not been discussed, one approach to his problem was skirted when we discussed analog comnunication. Imaging can be considered as the estimation f a spatial rather than a temporal function. Moldon [69] has aken this approach and considered the problem of estimatng the amplitude and phase of the Fourier transform of the bject. Among his results, which did not account for uantum effects but did include the effects of additive deector noise, are a set of CLRB's for various approximaions and an interesting discussion of the conditions under vhich previously known structures are near optimum. ther work on imaging includes that of Harris [70] using ng-time-averaged data and restoration by linear filtering. lueller and Reynolds [71] did similar work using a timeveraged modulation transfer function. Linear minimumariance estimation has been considered by Harger [72]. here has also been considerable work done on holographic naging through turbulence [73]–[75] prompted at least in art of some early work of Leith and Uptanieks [76]. The eports of a summer study [77] and a seminar [78] provide a seful survey of this so-called "image-restoration" area vith many references.

ACKNOWLEDGMENT

The authors acknowledge with thanks the assistance of J. R. Clark, B. K. Levitt, and R. S. Orr who carefully read the manuscript.

REFERENCES

[1] V. I. Tatarski, *Wave Propagation in a Turbulent Medium*, transl. by R. A. Silverman. New York: McGraw-Hill, 1961.
[2] R. S. Lawrence and J. W. Strohbehn, "A survey of clear-air propagation effects relevant to optical communications," this issue, pp. 1523–1545.
[3] S. Karp and R. S. Kennedy, Eds., "NASA-M.I.T. Summer Study on Optical Space Communication," NASA SP-217, 1969.
[4] J. R. Meyer-Arendt and C. B. Emmanuel, "Optical scintillation: a survey of the literature," Natl. Bur. Stand., Washington, D. C., Tech. Note 225, April 5, 1965.
[5] J. R. Kerr, P. J. Titterton, A. R. Kraemer, and C. R. Cooke, "Atmospheric optical communication systems," this issue, pp. 1691–1709.
[6] A. A. M. Saleh, "An investigation of laser wave depolarization due to atmospheric transmission," *IEEE J. Quantum Electron.*, vol. QE-3, pp. 540–543, November 1967.
[7] J. W. Strohbehn and S. F. Clifford, "Polarization and angle-of-arrival fluctuations for a plane wave propagated through a turbulent medium," *IEEE Trans. Antennas Propagat.*, vol. AP-15, pp. 416–421, May 1967.
[8] E. Brookner, "Atmospheric propagation and communication channel model for laser wavelengths," *IEEE Trans. Commun. Technol.*, vol. COM-18, pp. 396–416, August 1970.
[9] J. W. Strohbehn, "Line-of-sight wave propagation through the turbulent atmosphere," *Proc. IEEE*, vol. 56, pp. 1301–1318, August 1968.
[10] E. V. Hoversten, "The atmosphere as an optical communication channel," *1967 IEEE Internatl. Conv. Rec.*, pt. 11, vol. 15, pp. 137–145.
[11] R. S. Kennedy and E. V. Hoversten, "On the atmosphere as an optical communication channel," *IEEE Trans. Inform. Theory*, vol. IT-14, pp. 716–725, September 1968.
[12] N. S. Kopeika and J. Bordogna, "Background noise in optical communication systems," this issue, pp. 1571–1577.
[13] H. L. Van Trees, *Detection, Estimation, and Modulation Theory*, vol. 3. New York: Wiley, to be published in 1970.
[14] ——, *Detection, Estimation, and Modulation Theory*, vol. 1. New York: Wiley, 1968.
[15] S. J. Halme, "Efficient optical communications in a turbulent atmosphere," M.I.T. Res. Lab. Electron., Cambridge, Mass., Tech. Rept. 474, April 1970.
[16] B. K. Levitt, "Detector statistics for optical communication through the turbulent atmosphere," to be published by M.I.T. Res. Lab. Electron., Cambridge, Mass., Quart. Prog. Rep. 99, October 1970.
[17] C. W. Helstrom, J. W. S. Liu, and J. P. Gorden, "Quantum-mechanical communication theory," this issue, pp. 1578–1598.
[18] S. D. Personick, "Efficient analog communication over quantum channels," Sc.D. dissertation, Dept. of Elec. Engrg., M.I.T., Cambridge, Mass., January 1970.
[19] R. J. Glauber, "Optical coherence and photon statistics," in *Quantum Optics and Electronics*, C. de Witt *et al.* Eds. New York: Gordon and Breach, pp. 65–185, 1965.
[20] J. W. S. Liu, "Reliability of quantum-mechanical communication systems," M.I.T. Res. Lab. Electron., Cambridge, Mass., Tech. Rept. 468, December 1968.
[21] J. P. Gordon and W. H. Louisell, "Simultaneous measurements of noncommuting observables," in *Physics of Quantum Electronics*, P. L. Kelley, B. Lax, and P. E. Tannenwald, Eds. New York: McGraw-Hill, pp. 833–840, 1966.
[22] S. Karp, E. L. O'Neill, and R. M. Gagliardi, "Communication theory for the free space optical channel," this issue, pp. 1611–1626.
[23] C. W. Helstrom, "Detectability of coherent optical signals in a heterodyne receiver," *J. Opt. Soc. Am.*, vol. 57, pp. 353–361, March 1967.
[24] A. E. Siegman, "The antenna properties of optical microwave receivers," *Appl. Opt.*, vol. 5, pp. 1588–1594, October 1966.
[25] S. Karp and J. R. Clark, "Photon counting: a problem in classical

noise theory," to be published in *IEEE Trans. Inform. Theory*, November, 1970; also, NASA Tech. Rep. TR R-334.

[26] J. R. Clark and E. V. Hoversten, "The poisson process as a statistical model for photodetectors excited by Gaussian light," to be published by M.I.T. Res. Lab. Electron., Cambridge, Mass., Quart. Prog. Rep. 98, July 1970.

[27] S. J. Halme, "Efficient optical communication through a turbulent atmosphere," M.I.T. Res. Lab. Electron., Cambridge, Mass., Quart. Prog. Rept. 91, pp. 191–201, October 1968.

[28] R. O. Harger, "On processing optical images propagated through the atmosphere," *IEEE Trans. Aerosp. Electron. Syst.*, vol. AES-3, pp. 819–828, September 1967.

[29] ——, "Maximum likelihood and optimized coherent heterodyne receivers for strongly scattered Gaussian fields," *Opt. Acta*, vol. 16, pp. 745–760, December 1969.

[30] J. M. Wozencraft and I. M. Jacobs, *Principles of Communication Engineering*. New York: Wiley, 1965, ch. 7.

[31] S. J. Halme, "On optimum reception through a turbulent atmosphere," M.I.T. Res. Lab. Electron., Cambridge, Mass., Quart. Prog. Rept. 88, pp. 247–254, January 1968.

[32] E. V. Hoversten and R. S. Kennedy, "Efficient optical communication within the earth's atmosphere," *Opto-Electronics Signal Processing Techniques*, AGARD Conf. Proc. 50, February 1970.

[33] S. J. Halme, B. K. Levitt, and R. S. Orr, "Bounds and approximations for some integral expressions involving lognormal statistics," M.I.T. Res. Lab. Electron., Cambridge, Mass., Quart. Prog. Rep. 93, pp. 163–175, April 1969.

[34] J. W. Goodman, "Optimum processing of photoelectron counts," *IEEE J. Quantum Electron.*, vol. QE-1, pp. 80–81, July 1965.

[35] B. Reiffen and H. Sherman, "An optimum demodulator for Poisson processes: photon source detectors," *Proc. IEEE*, vol. 51, pp. 1316–1320, October 1963.

[36] I. Bar-David, "Communication under the Poisson regime," *IEEE Trans. Inform. Theory*, vol. IT-15, pp. 31–37, January 1969.

[37] J. N. Bucknam, "Direct detection of optical signals in the presence of atmospheric turbulence," M.S. thesis, Dept. of Elec. Engrg., M.I.T., Cambridge, Mass., June 1969.

[38] A. Papoulis, *The Fourier Integral and Its Applications*. New York: McGraw-Hill, pp. 302–307, 1962.

[39] R. L. Mitchell, "Permanence of the lognormal distribution," *J. Opt. Soc.. Am.*, vol. 58, pp. 1267–1272, September 1968.

[40] D. A. Ohori, "Detection of signals in the turbulent atmospheric optical channel," M.S. thesis, Dept. of Elec. Engrg., M.I.T., Cambridge, Mass., February 1968.

[41] D. L. Fried and R. A. Schmeltzer, "The effect of atmospheric scintillation on an optical data channel-laser radar and binary communications," *Appl. Opt.*, vol. 6, pp. 1729–1738, October 1967.

[42] D. L. Fried, "Optical heterodyne detection of an atmospherically distorted signal wave front," *Proc. IEEE*, vol. 55, pp. 57–67, January 1967.

[43] I. Goldstein, P. A. Miles, and A. Chabot, "Heterodyne measurements of laser-beam scintillation in the atmosphere," *J. Opt. Soc. Am.*, vol. 57, pp. 787–797, June 1967.

[44] R. F. Lucy, K. Lang, C. J. Peters, and K. Duval, "Optical superheterodyne receiver," *Appl. Opt.*, vol. 6, pp. 1333–1342, August 1967.

[45] S. Gardner, "Some effects of atmospheric turbulence on optical heterodyne communications," *1964 IEEE Conv. Rec.*, pt. 6, pp. 337–342.

[46] R. D. Rosner, "Heterodyne detection of an optical signal after one-way propagation on an Atmospheric path," *Proc. IEEE*, (Lett.) vol. 56, pp. 126–128, January 1968.

[47] D. L. Fried, "Atmospheric modulation noise in an optical heterodyne receiver," *IEEE J. Quantum Electron.*, vol. QE-3, pp. 213–221, June 1967.

[48] J. P. Moreland, "Optical heterodyne detection of a randomly distorted signal beam," Ph.D. dissertation, Ohio State University, Columbus, Ohio, 1969.

[49] W. N. Peters and R. J. Arguello, "Fading and polarization noise of a PCM/PL system," *IEEE J. Quantum Electron.*, vol. QE-3, pp. 532–539, November 1967.

[50] D. L. Fried, "Statistics of a geometric representation of wavefront distortion," *J. Opt. Soc. Am.*, vol. 55, pp. 1427–1435, November 1965.

[51] G. R. Heidbreder and R. L. Mitchell, "Effects of a turbulent mediur on the power pattern of a wavefront-tracking circular aperture," *J. Opt. Soc. Am.*, vol. 56, pp. 1677–1684, December 1966.

[52] H. Cramer, *Mathematical Methods of Statistics*. Princeton, N. J. Princeton University Press, 1946.

[53] U. Grenander, "Stochastic Processes and Statistical Inference," *Ark. Mat.*, band 1, no. 17, pp. 195–277, 1950.

[54] C. W. Helstrom, *Statistical Theory of Signal Detection*, 2nd ed New York: Pergamon, 1969.

[55] D. C. Youla, "The use of the method of maximum likelihood in estimating continuous-modulated intelligence which has been cor rupted by noise," *IRE Trans. Inform. Theory*, vol. IT-3, pp. 90–105 March 1954.

[56] W. B. Davenport and W. C. Root, *An Introduction to Random Signals and Noise*. New York: McGraw-Hill, 1958, ch. 6.

[57] H. L. Van Trees, "Bounds on the accuracy attainable in the estimation of continuous random processes," *IEEE Trans. Inform. Theory* vol. IT-12, pp. 298–304, July 1966.

[58] C. W. Helstrom, "The minimum variance of estimates in quantum signal detection," *IEEE Trans. Inform. Theory*, vol. IT-14, pp. 234–242, March 1968.

[59] M. Born and E. Wolf, *Principles of Optics.*, 3rd ed. New York Pergamon, 1965.

[60] R. O. Harger, "On processing signals with multiplicative and additive errors," in "Restoration of Atmospherically Degraded Images," Rept. of Nat. Acad. Sci.-Nat. Res. Counc. Woods Hole Summer Study, 1966.

[61] C. W. Helstrom, "Quantum limitations on the detection of coherent and incoherent signals," *IEEE Trans. Inform. Theory*, vol. IT-11 pp. 482–490, October 1965.

[62] L. J. Cutrona, E. N. Leith, C. J. Palermo, and L. J. Porcello, "Optical data processing and filtering systems," *IRE Trans. Inform. Theory* vol. IT-6, pp. 386–400, June 1960.

[63] A. Vander Lugt, "Signal detection by complex spatial filtering," *IEEE Trans. Inform. Theory*, vol. IT-10, pp. 139–145, April 1964.

[64] J. W. Goodman, *Introduction to Fourier Optics*. New York McGraw-Hill, 1968.

[65] U. Grenander and G. Szego, *Toeplitz Forms and Their Applications* Berkeley, Calif.: University of California Press, 1958.

[66] R. O. Harger, "On processing optical images propagated through the atmosphere from objects with unknown motion parameters," in "Evaluation of Motion Degraded Images," NASA SP-193, 1969.

[67] C. W. Helstrom, "Detection and resolution of incoherent objects seen through a turbulent medium," *J. Opt. Soc. Am.*, vol. 59, pp 331–341, March 1969.

[68] J. H. Shapiro, "Optimal spatial modulation for reciprocal channels," M.I.T. Res. Lab. Electron., Cambridge, Mass., Tech. Rep. 476, April 1970.

[69] J. C. Moldon, "Imaging of objects viewed through a turbulent atmosphere," M.I.T. Res. Lab. Electron., Cambridge, Mass., Tech. Rep. 469, March 1969.

[70] J. L. Harris, "Image evaluation and restoration," *J. Opt. Soc. Am.*, vol. 56, pp. 569–574, May 1966.

[71] P. F. Mueller and G. O. Reynolds, "Image restoration by removal of random media degradations," *J. Opt. Soc. Am.*, vol. 57, pp. 1338–1344, November 1967.

[72] R. O. Harger, "Linear minimum variance estimation with complex phase errors," *IEEE Trans. Aerosp. Electron. Syst.*, vol. AES-3, pp. 681–687, July 1967.

[73] H. Kogelink and K. S. Pennington, "Holographic imaging through a random medium," *J. Opt. Soc. Am.*, vol. 58, pp. 273–274, February 1968.

[74] J. W. Goodman, W. H. Huntley, Jr., D. W. Jackson, and M. Lehmann, "Wavefront-reconstruction imaging through random media," *Appl. Phys. Lett.*, vol. 8, pp. 311–313, June 1966.

[75] J. D. Gaskill, "Atmospheric degradation of holographic images," *J. Opt. Soc. Am.*, vol. 59, pp. 308–318, March 1969.

[76] E. N. Leith and J. Uptanieks, "Holographic imagery through diffusing media," *J. Opt. Soc. Am.*, vol. 56, p. 523, 1966.

[77] "Restoration of Atmospherically Degraded Images," 3 Vols., Nat. Acad. Sci. Woods Hole Summer Study, July 1966.

[78] "Evaluation of Motion Degraded Images," Nat. Aeronaut. and Space Admin. Seminar, Dec. 1968, NASA SP-193, 1969.

# 16A



Reprinted from *Bell Syst. Tech. J.* **52**(6):843–874 (1973)

# Receiver Design for Digital Fiber Optic Communication Systems, I

By S. D. PERSONICK

(Manuscript received January 15, 1973)

*This paper is concerned with a systematic approach to the design of the "linear channel" of a repeater for a digital fiber optic communication system. In particular, it is concerned with how one properly chooses the front-end preamplifier and biasing circuitry for the photodetector; and how the required power to achieve a desired error rate varies with the bit rate, the received optical pulse shape, and the desired baseband-equalized output pulse shape.*

*It is shown that a proper front-end design incorporates a high-impedance preamplifier which tends to integrate the detector output. This must be followed by proper equalization in the later stages of the linear channel. The baseband signal-to-noise ratio is calculated as a function of the preamplifier parameters. Such a design provides significant reduction in the required optical power and/or required avalanche gain when compared to a design which does not integrate initially.*

*It is shown that, when the received optical pulses overlap and when the optical channel is behaving linearly in power,*[1] *baseband equalization can be used to separate the pulses with a practical but significant increase in required optical power. This required power penalty is calculated as a function of the input and equalized pulse shapes.*

## I. INTRODUCTION

The purpose of this paper is to provide insight into a systematic approach to designing the "linear channel" of a repeater for a digital fiber optic communication system.

In particular, we are interested in how one properly chooses the biasing circuitry for the photodetector; and how the required power to achieve a desired error rate varies with the bit rate, the received optical pulse shape, and desired baseband output pulse shape.

Throughout this paper, performance will be measured in terms of signal-to-noise ratios. Efforts to calculate exact error rates and bounds to error rates are difficult to carry out, and, in the past, the results of such efforts have shown little deviation (for practical design purposes) from calculations of error rates using the signal-to-noise ratio (Gaussian approximation) approach. (See Refs. 2 through 5 and Appendix A.)

## II. INPUT–OUTPUT RELATIONSHIPS FOR AN AVALANCHE DETECTOR

An avalanche photodiode is the device of interest in fiber applications for converting optical power into current for amplification and equalization, ultimately to produce a baseband voltage for regeneration.

In order to appreciate its performance in practical optical systems, we have to characterize the avalanche photodiode from three points of view: the physical viewpoint, the circuit viewpoint, and the statistical viewpoint.

When we study the device from the physical viewpoint, we ask how does it operate, how do we develop circuit and statistical models of its operation, and what are the limitations of the models.

From the circuit viewpoint, we investigate how to design a piece of equipment in which the device will perform some function.

From the statistical viewpoint, we investigate the probabilistic behavior of the device to allow us to quantify its performance in a circuit.

### 2.1 *The Physical Viewpoint*

The avalanche photodiode is a semiconductor device which is normally operated in a backbiased manner–producing a region within the device where there is a high field (see Fig. 1). Due to thermal agitation and/or the presence of incident optical power, pairs of holes and electrons can be generated at various points within the diode. These carriers drift toward opposite ends of the device under the influence of the applied field. When a carrier passes through the high-field region, it may gain sufficient energy to generate one or more new pairs of holes and electrons through collision ionization. These new pairs can in turn generate additional pairs by the same mechanism. Carriers accumulate at opposite ends of the diode, thereby reducing the potential across the device until they are removed by the biasing and other circuitry in parallel with the diode (see Fig. 2). The chances that a carrier will generate a new pair when passing through the high-field region depends upon the type of carrier (hole or electron), the material out of which the diode is constructed, and the voltage across the device. To the extent that carriers do not accumulate to significantly modulate the

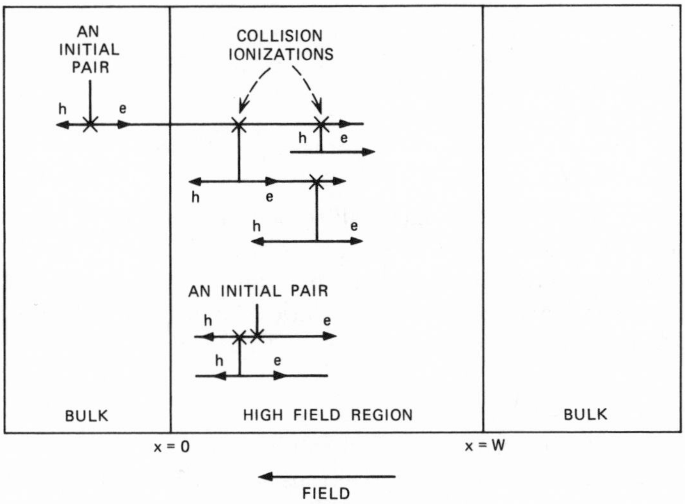


Fig. 1—Avalanche detector.

voltage across the device, it can be assumed that all ionizing collisions are statistically independent. This assumption also requires that the mean time between ionizing collisions be large compared to the time it takes for a carrier in the high-field region to randomize its momentum.

2.2 *The Circuit Viewpoint*

From the discussion above, and of course more detailed investigations,[3,6–8] it has been concluded that a reasonable small-signal model of an avalanche photodiode with a biasing circuit shown in Fig. 2 is the equivalent circuit of Fig. 3. In Fig. 3, $C_d$ is the junction capacitance of the diode† across which voltage accumulates when charges produced within the device separate under the influence of the bias field. The current generator $i(t)$ represents the production of charges (holes and electrons) by optical and thermal generation and collision ionization in the diode high-field region. In order to use the photodiode efficiently,

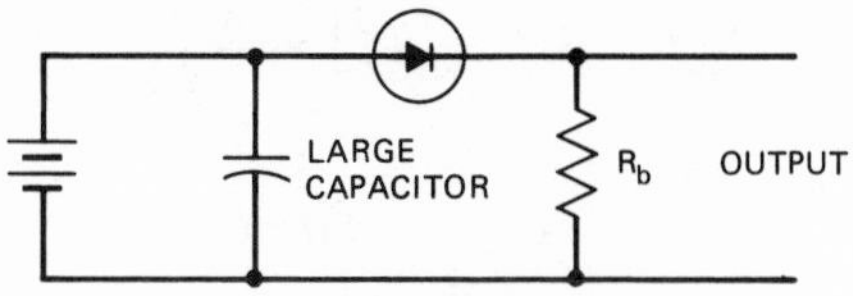


Fig. 2—Detector biasing circuit.

† Not to be confused with the large power supply bypass capacitor of Fig. 2.

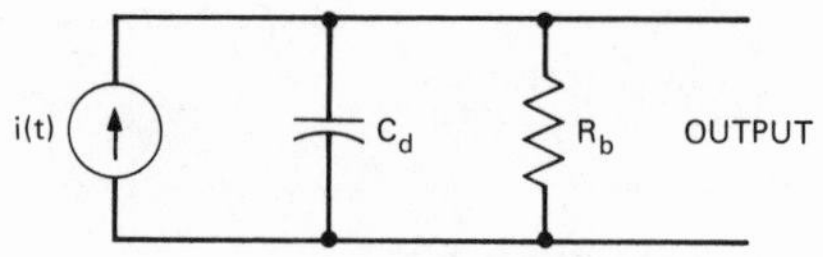


Fig. 3—Equivalent circuit of biased detector.

we must design a circuit which will respond to the current $i(t)$ with as little distortion and added noise as possible.

In order to derive information from the circuit responding to $i(t)$, we must understand the statistical relationship between $i(t)$ (the equivalent current generator) and the incident optical power $p(t)$.

### 2.3 *The Statistical Viewpoint*

In Fig. 3, the current source $i(t)$ can be considered to be a sequence of impulses corresponding to electrons generated within the photodiode due to optical or thermal excitation or collision ionization. We shall now specify, in a statistical way, how many electrons are produced and when they are produced.

From various physical studies,[3,7,9] it has been concluded that for cases of current interest the electron production process can be modeled as shown in Fig. 4.

Let the optical power falling upon the photon counter be $p(t)$.† In response to this power and due to thermal effects, the photon counter of Fig. 4 produces electrons at average rate $\lambda(t)$ per second where

$$\lambda(t) = [(\eta/\hbar\Omega)p(t)] + \lambda_0, \tag{1}$$

where

$$\eta = \text{photon counter quantum efficiency}$$
$$\hbar\Omega = \text{energy of a photon}$$
$$\lambda_0 = \text{dark current "counts" per second.}$$

$\lambda(t)$ is only the average rate at which electrons are produced. In any interval $T$ seconds long, the probability that exactly $N$ counts are produced is given by

$$P[N, (t_0, t_0 + T)] = \frac{\Lambda^N e^{-\Lambda}}{N!},$$

where

$$\Lambda = \int_{t_0}^{t_0+T} \lambda(t)dt. \tag{2}$$

† The reader is cautioned not to confuse $p(t)$, the optical power, with the probability densities (e.g., $P[N, \{t_k\}]$) in this paper.

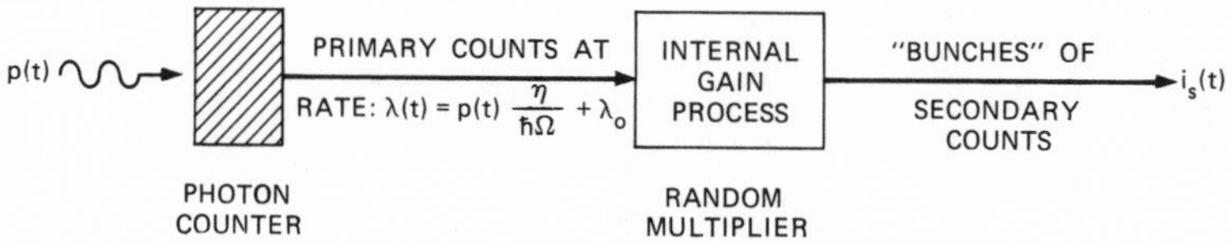


Fig. 4—Model of $i_s(t)$ generation process.

Given $p(t)$, the number of electrons produced in any interval is statistically independent of the number produced in any other disjoint interval.

A process of impulse (electron) production satisfying (2) and the above independent increments condition is said to be a "Poisson impulse process" with arrival rate $\lambda(t)$.[10]

A useful equivalent description of the above process follows.

If $T$ is an interval, the probability that exactly $N$ electrons will be produced at the (approximate) times $t_1 \pm \frac{1}{2}\Delta$, $t_2 \pm \frac{1}{2}\Delta$, $\cdots$ $t_N \pm \frac{1}{2}\Delta$ where the widths $\Delta$ are very small is

$$P[N, \{t_k\}] = \{e^{-\Lambda} \prod_1^N [\lambda(t_k)\Delta]/N!\} + o(\Delta), \tag{3}$$

where $\Lambda$ is defined in (2) and $o(\Delta)$ is a term such that

$$\lim_{\Delta \to 0} \frac{o(\Delta)}{\Delta} = 0.$$

It is *important* to note that in (3) the times $\{t_k\}$ are *not* in order, that is, in (3) it is *not* necessarily true that $t_1 < t_2$, etc.

Each of the "primary" impulses (electrons) produced by the photon counter enters a random multiplier where, corresponding to collision ionization, it is replaced by $g$ contiguous "secondary" impulses (electrons). The number $g$ is governed by the statistics of the internal gain mechanism of the photodiode. Each primary impulse (electron) is "multiplied" in this manner by a value $g$ which is statistically independent of the value $g$ assigned to other primaries.

Thus the current leaving the photodiode consists of "bunches" of electrons, the number of electrons in the bunch being a random quantity having statistics to be described below. For applications of interest here, it will be assumed that all electrons in a bunch exit the photodiode at the time when the primary is produced. This implies that the duration of the photodiode response to a single primary hole-electron pair is very short compared to the response times of circuitry to be used with the photodiode.

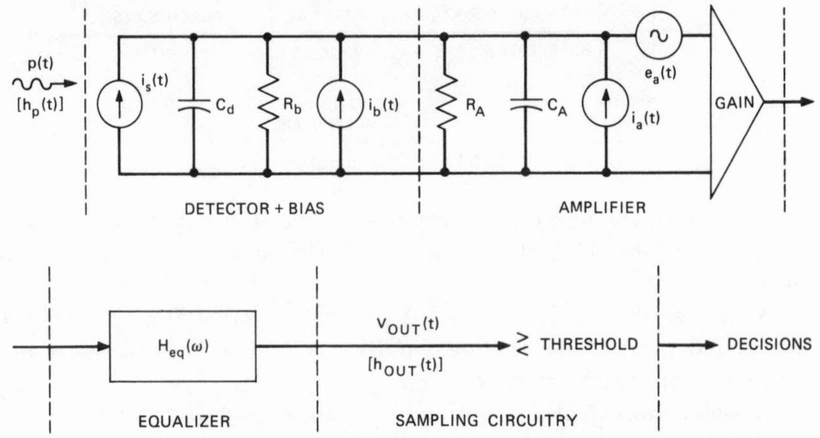


Fig. 5—Receiver.

Different avalanche photodiodes have different statistics governing the number of electrons in a bunch, i.e., the gain. For applications below, we will only need to know the mean gain $\langle g \rangle$ and the mean square gain $\langle g^2 \rangle$. For a large class of avalanche photodiodes of interest, it has been found that[3,7]

$$\langle g^2 \rangle \cong \langle g \rangle^{2+x}, \tag{4}$$

where $\langle g \rangle$ is determined by the applied bias voltage and $x$, a number usually between 0 and 1, depends upon the materials out of which the diode is constructed. For germanium photodiodes, $x \cong 1$; for well-designed silicon photodiodes, $x \approx 0.5$.

## III. AN OPTICAL RECEIVER

Figure 5 shows a fairly typical receiver, in schematic form, consisting of an avalanche photodiode, an amplifier, and an equalizer.

The amplifier is modeled as an ideal high-gain infinite-impedance amplifier with an equivalent shunt capacitance and resistance at the input and with two noise sources referred to the input. For the purposes of this paper, the noise sources will be assumed to be white, Gaussian, and uncorrelated. Extensions to other amplifier models will be straightforward when the techniques of this paper are understood.†

It is assumed that the amplifier gain is sufficiently high so that noises introduced by the equalizer are negligible.

† With this model, the noise sources of the amplifier do not change when the input and output load circuitry changes.

The power falling upon the detector will be assumed to be of the form of a digital pulse stream

$$p(t) = \sum_{-\infty}^{\infty} b_k h_p(t - kT), \tag{5}$$

where $b_k$ takes on one of two values for each integer value of $k$, $T$ = the pulse spacing, $h_p(t - kT)$ = pulse shape and is positive for all $t$. We shall assume $\int_{-\infty}^{\infty} h_p(t - kT)dt = 1$, therefore $b_k$ is the energy in pulse $k$. The assumption that the received power will be in the form (5) appears reasonable for intensity modulation and fiber systems of interest.[1]

From (1) we have the average detector output current $\langle i_s(t) \rangle$ given by

$$\langle i_s(t) \rangle = \frac{\eta \langle g \rangle e p(t)}{\hbar \Omega} + \langle g \rangle e \lambda_0,$$

where

$\langle g \rangle$ = average detector internal gain

$e$ = electron charge

$\lambda_0$ = dark current electrons per second

$\frac{\eta}{\hbar\Omega} p(t)$ = average optical primary electrons per second.

Therefore, the average voltage (neglecting dc components) at the equalizer output is

$$\langle v_{\text{out}}(t) \rangle = \frac{A \eta \langle g \rangle e p(t)}{\hbar \Omega} * h_{\text{fe}}(t) * h_{\text{eq}}(t), \tag{6}$$

where "*" indicates convolution and $A$ is an arbitrary constant.

$$h_{\text{fe}}(t) = F \left\{ \frac{1}{\dfrac{1}{R_T} + j\omega(C_d + C_A)} \right\}$$

= amplifier input circuit current impulse response,

$$R_T = \left[ \frac{1}{R_b} + \frac{1}{R_A} \right]^{-1} = \text{total detector parallel load resistance,}$$

and $h_{\text{eq}}(t)$ = equalizer impulse response.

Clearly, $\langle v_{\text{out}}(t) \rangle$ is of the form

$$\langle v_{\text{out}}(t) \rangle = \sum_{-\infty}^{\infty} b_k h_{\text{out}}(t - kT) \tag{7}$$

and $v_{out}(t)$ is of the form

$$v_{out}(t) = \sum_{-\infty}^{\infty} b_k h_{out}(t - kT) + n(t),$$

where $n(t)$ represents *deviations* (or noises) of $v_{out}(t)$ from its average.

The fundamental task ahead is to pick $R_b$ (the bias circuit resistor) and $h_{eq}(t)$ so that a system which samples $v_{out}(t)$ at the times $\{kT\}$ can make decisions as to which value $b_k$ has assumed (by comparing the sample to a threshold) with minimum chance of error.

## IV. CALCULATING SIGNAL–TO–NOISE RATIO IN TERMS OF THE EQUALIZED PULSE SHAPE

Having defined the receiver and its statistics in the above sections, we can now calculate the variance of $n(t)$, the noise portion of the output $v_{out}(t)$ of the system of Fig. 5, defined as follows:

$$N = \langle (n(t))^2 \rangle = \langle v_{out}^2(t) \rangle - \langle v_{out}(t) \rangle^2. \tag{8}$$

The noise, $N$, of (8) above depends upon the coefficients $\{b_k\}$ defined in (5) and upon the time $t$.

We shall first of all restrict consideration to the set of times $t = \{kT\}$ when a decision as to the values $\{b_k\}$ will be made by sampling $v_{out}(t)$. We shall next assume that the equalized pulses satisfy

$$\begin{aligned} h_{out}(0) &= 1 \\ h_{out}(t) &= 0 \qquad \text{for} \qquad t = kT, \qquad k \neq 0. \end{aligned} \tag{9}$$

That is, we shall assume that the equalized pulse stream has no intersymbol interference at the sampling times $kT$.† Therefore,

$$v_{out}(kT) = b_k + n(kT). \tag{10}$$

In eq. (10) the noise, $n(t)$, still depends upon all the $\{b_k\}$ and the time $t$. This is a property which distinguishes fiber optic systems from many other systems where the noise is signal-independent and stationary (not time-dependent). Consider, without loss of generality, the output, $v(t)$, at $t = 0$. We define the worst-case noise, $NW(b_0)$, for each of the two possible values of $b_0$ as follows:

$$NW(b_0) = \max_{\{b_k\}, k \neq 0} [\langle v_{out}^2(0) \rangle - \langle v_{out}(0) \rangle^2], \tag{11}$$

where in (11) the maximization is over all possible sets $\{b_k\}$ for $k \neq 0$, and where $b_0$ can take on either of two values as previously stated. The

† The limitations imposed by this assumption are discussed in Section VII.

quantity $NW(b_0)$ shows, for the two possible values of $b_0$, what the noise for the worst combination of the other symbols is.

We shall next calculate $\langle v_{\text{out}}^2(t)\rangle - \langle v_{\text{out}}(t)\rangle^2$ as a function of the set $\{b_k\}$.

Examine Fig. 5. We shall define the two-sided spectral density of the amplifier-current noise source $i_a(t)$ as $S_I$ and the two-sided spectral height of the amplifier-voltage noise source $e_a(t)$ as $S_E$. The two-sided spectral density of the Johnson-current noise source $i_b(t)$ associated with $R_b$ is $2\text{k}\theta/R_b$, where k is Boltzmann's constant and $\theta$ is the absolute temperature.

We can write the output noise as follows:

$$v_{\text{out}}(t) - \langle v_{\text{out}}(t)\rangle = n_S(t) + n_R(t) + n_I(t) + n_E(t), \tag{12}$$

where

- $n_S(t)$ is the output noise due to the random multiplied Poisson process nature of the current $i_s(t)$ produced by the detector,
- $n_R(t)$ is the output noise due to the Johnson noise current source of the resistor $R_b$,
- $n_I(t)$ is the output noise due to the amplifier input current noise source $i_a(t)$, and
- $n_E(t)$ is the output noise due to the amplifier input voltage noise source $e_a(t)$.

We have

$$\begin{aligned}
&\langle v_{\text{out}}^2(t)\rangle - \langle v_{\text{out}}(t)\rangle^2 \\
&\quad = \langle (v_{\text{out}}(t) - \langle v_{\text{out}}(t)\rangle)^2\rangle \\
&\quad = \langle n_S^2(t)\rangle + \langle n_R^2(t)\rangle + \langle n_I^2(t)\rangle + \langle n_E^2(t)\rangle \\
&\quad = \langle n_S^2(t)\rangle + (2\text{k}\theta/R_b)\frac{1}{2\pi}\int_{-\infty}^{\infty}\left|H_{\text{eq}}(\omega)\frac{1}{\dfrac{1}{R_b}+\dfrac{1}{R_A}+j\omega(C_d+C_A)}\right|^2 d\omega \\
&\qquad + (S_I)\frac{1}{2\pi}\int_{-\infty}^{\infty}\left|H_{\text{eq}}(\omega)\frac{1}{\dfrac{1}{R_b}+\dfrac{1}{R_A}+j\omega(C_d+C_A)}\right|^2 d\omega \\
&\qquad + (S_E)\frac{1}{2\pi}\int_{-\infty}^{\infty}|H_{\text{eq}}(\omega)|^2 d\omega.
\end{aligned} \tag{13}$$

In (13), the last three terms were evaluated using the well-known formula for the average-squared output of a filter driven by white noise. We must now calculate the "shot noise" term $\langle n_S^2(t)\rangle$.

Recall that $i_s(t)$ consists of impulses of random charge corresponding to "bunches" of electrons with a random number $g$ per bunch, this number being independent from bunch to bunch.

Consider a finite interval of duration $L$. Let $g_k$ be the number of electrons in bunch $k$ in the interval; where the bunches are labeled *not* in order of time but at random. Let $t_k$ be the arrival time of bunch $k$. Let $h_I(t)$ be the response of the $RC$ circuit, amplifier, equalizer combination to a current impulse from $i_s(t)$. Then the output $v_{\text{out}}(t)$ *just due to the current* $i_s(t)$ *in the interval* $L$ is

$$v_{\text{out}}^L(t) = \sum_1^N eg_k h_I(t - t_k), \tag{14}$$

where $N$ is the number of bunches.

Recall that the probability density of $N$ bunches at the times $\{t_k\}$ is

$$p[N, \{t_k\}] = \frac{e^{-\Lambda} \prod_1^N \lambda(t_k)}{N!}, \tag{15}$$

where

$$\lambda(t) = p(t) \frac{\eta}{\hbar\Omega} + \lambda_0.$$

Thus combining (14) and (15) and leaving out some tedious algebra we obtain[10]

$$\langle v_{\text{out}}^L(t) \rangle = \int_{\text{interval } L} e\langle g \rangle (p(t')\eta/\hbar\Omega + \lambda_0) h_I(t - t')dt'. \tag{16}$$

In a similar manner, we obtain

$$\langle (v_{\text{out}}^L(t))^2 \rangle - \langle v_{\text{out}}^L(t) \rangle^2 = \int_{\text{interval } L} e^2 \langle g^2 \rangle \left( p(t') \frac{\eta}{\hbar\Omega} + \lambda_0 \right) h_I^2(t - t')dt,$$

where $\langle g \rangle$ is the mean internal gain of the detector and $\langle g^2 \rangle$ is the mean-squared internal gain.

We therefore obtain, letting $L \to \infty$, the result

$$\begin{aligned} \langle n_S^2(t) \rangle &= \lim_{L \to \infty} [\langle [v_{\text{out}}^L(t)]^2 \rangle - \langle v_{\text{out}}^L(t) \rangle^2] \\ &= \int_{-\infty}^{\infty} e^2 \langle g^2 \rangle \left\{ [\sum b_k h_p(t' - kT)] \frac{\eta}{\hbar\Omega} + \lambda_0 \right\} h_I^2(t - t')dt'. \end{aligned} \tag{17}$$

Further,

$$H_I(\omega) = F\{h_I(t - t')\} = H_{\text{eq}}(\omega) \frac{1}{\frac{1}{R_b} + \frac{1}{R_A} + j\omega(C_d + C_A)}. \tag{18}$$

Thus we have the remaining term in (13) in terms of the input optical pulse, the equalizer response, and the $RC$ circuit at the amplifier input.

Converting everything to the frequency domain and recalling that we have normalized the equalized output pulse $h_{\text{out}}(t)$ to unity at $t = 0$, we obtain

$$NW(b_0) \underset{\{b_k, k \neq 0\}}{\overset{=}{\max}} \Bigg[ \left(\frac{1}{2\pi}\right)^2 \int_{-\infty}^{\infty} \frac{\langle g^2 \rangle}{\langle g \rangle^2} \frac{\hbar\Omega}{\eta} H_p(\omega) \left( \sum_{-\infty}^{\infty} b_k e^{j\omega kT} \right)$$

$$\times \left( \frac{H_{\text{out}}(\omega)}{H_p(\omega)} * \frac{H_{\text{out}}(\omega)}{H_p(\omega)} \right) d\omega$$

$$+ \frac{(\hbar\Omega/\eta)^2}{2\pi \langle g \rangle^2 e^2} \left( \frac{2\text{k}\theta}{R_b} + S_I + e^2 \langle g^2 \rangle \lambda_0 \right) \int_{-\infty}^{\infty} \left| \frac{H_{\text{out}}(\omega)}{H_p(\omega)} \right|^2 d\omega$$

$$+ \frac{(\hbar\Omega/\eta)^2}{2\pi \langle g \rangle^2 e^2} S_E \int_{-\infty}^{\infty} \left| \frac{H_{\text{out}}(\omega) \left( \frac{1}{R_b} + \frac{1}{R_A} + j\omega(C_d + C_A) \right)}{H_p(\omega)} \right|^2 d\omega \Bigg], \quad (19)$$

where

$H_p(\omega) = F\{h_p(t)\}$ = input power pulse transform,
$H_{\text{out}}(\omega) = F\{h_{\text{out}}(t)\}$ = output pulse transform,
"$*$" = convolution,
$b_0$ = coefficient multiplying zeroth input pulse,

and

$$\frac{1}{2\pi} \int_{-\infty}^{\infty} H_{\text{out}}(\omega) d\omega = 1. \quad (20)$$

In principle, we wish to minimize $NW(b_0)$ by choosing $R_b$ and $H_{\text{eq}}(\omega)$ for the worst-case combination of symbols $\{b_k\}$, subject to the zero intersymbol interference condition on the ouput pulse stream $v_{\text{out}}(t)$ [recognizing that we have normalized $h_{\text{out}}(t)$ and $H_{\text{out}}(\omega)$ as given in (9) and (20) above].

### 4.1 *Comments*

(*i*) One observation, which follows regardless of the choice of $H_{\text{out}}(\omega)$, is that the noise is always made smaller when $R_b$ is increased. Therefore, subject to practical constraints and for a fixed amplifier and a fixed desired output pulse shape (which is determined by the equalizer and $R_b$), it is always best to make $R_b$, the bias circuit resistor, as large as possible.

(*ii*) It is also clear, from (17) and the fact that the input pulse $h_p(t)$ is positive for all $t$, that the worst-case noise occurs when all the $b_k$ (except $b_0$) assume the larger of the two possible values. Recall that we are interested in the noise for both values of $b_0$.

(*iii*) Furthermore, for a given $S_E$ and $S_I$ and a given output pulse shape, it is desirable that the amplifier input resistance be as large as possible and that the amplifier shunt capacitance be as small as possible.

(*iv*) It is desirable that the diode shunt capacitance be as small as possible.

## V. CHOOSING THE EQUALIZED PULSE SHAPE

In principle, using (19) and given $H_p(\omega)$, $\langle g \rangle$, $\langle g^2 \rangle$, $S_I$, $S_E$, $R_b$, $R_A$, $C_d$, and $C_A$ one can find the equalized pulse shape $H_{\text{out}}(\omega)$ for each value of $b_0$ that minimizes the worst-case noise.

In practice, other considerations in addition to the noise are also of interest. In particular, it is important not only that the intersymbol interference be low at the nominal decision times $kT$, but that it be sufficiently small at times offset from $\{kT\}$ to allow for timing errors in the sampling process.

Therefore, rather than seeking the equalized pulse shape that minimizes the noise, we shall consider various equalized pulse shapes to see how the noise trades off against eye width.

Before proceeding, it is helpful to perform some normalizations upon (19) to reduce the number of parameters.

Make the following definitions:

$$R_T = \left(\frac{1}{R_b} + \frac{1}{R_A}\right)^{-1} = \text{total detector parallel load resistance,} \qquad (21)$$

$C_T = C_d + C_A =$ total detector parallel load capacitance,
$b_{\max} =$ larger value of $b_k$, $b_{\min} =$ smaller value of $b_k$,

$$H'_p(\omega) = H_p\left(\frac{2\pi\omega}{T}\right),$$

$$H'_{\text{out}}(\omega) = \frac{1}{T} H_{\text{out}}\left(\frac{2\pi\omega}{T}\right).$$

In this normalization, the functions $H'_p(\omega)$ and $H'_{\text{out}}(\omega)$ depend only upon the *shapes* of $H_p(\omega)$ and $H_{\text{out}}(\omega)$, not upon the time slot width $T$. The previous normalizing conditions on $H_p(\omega)$ and $H_{\text{out}}(\omega)$ imply conditions on $H'_p(\omega)$ and $H'_{\text{out}}(\omega)$

$$H_p(0) = 1 \Rightarrow H'_p(0) = 1 \qquad (22)$$

which implies

$$\int_{-\infty}^{\infty} h_p(t)dt = 1.$$

Also,

$$h_{\text{out}}(0) = 1 \Rightarrow \frac{1}{2\pi}\int_{-\infty}^{\infty} H_{\text{out}}(\omega)d\omega = 1 \Rightarrow \int_{-\infty}^{\infty} H'_{\text{out}}(f)df = 1.$$

With the above normalizations, (19) becomes

SHOT NOISES

$$NW(b_0) = \left(\frac{\hbar\Omega}{\eta}\right)^2 \left\{ \frac{\langle g^2\rangle}{\langle g\rangle^2}\frac{\eta}{\hbar\Omega}\left[b_0 I_1 + b_{\max}\left[\Sigma_1 - I_1\right]\right]\right.$$

SHOT NOISE

$$+ \frac{T}{(\langle g\rangle e)^2}\left[S_I + \frac{2k\theta}{R_b} + \langle g^2\rangle e^2 \lambda_d + \frac{S_E}{R_T^2}\right] I_2$$

THERMAL NOISES

$$\left. + \frac{(2\pi C_T)^2 S_E I_3}{T(\langle g\rangle e)^2}\right\}, \tag{23}$$

where

$$I_1 = \int_{-\infty}^{\infty} H'_p(f)\left[\frac{H'_{\text{out}}(f)}{H'_p(f)} * \frac{H'_{\text{out}}(f)}{H'_p(f)}\right] df$$

$$\Sigma_1 = \sum_{k=-\infty}^{\infty} H'_p(k)\left[\frac{H'_{\text{out}}(k)}{H'_p(k)} * \frac{H'_{\text{out}}(k)}{H'_p(k)}\right]$$

$$I_2 = \int_{-\infty}^{\infty}\left|\frac{H'_{\text{out}}(f)}{H'_p(f)}\right|^2 df$$

$$I_3 = \int_{-\infty}^{\infty}\left|\frac{H'_{\text{out}}(f)}{H'_p(f)}\right|^2 f^2 df.$$

In (23), the first shot-noise term is due to the pulse in the time slot under decision, the second term being shot noises from the other pulses which are assumed to be all "on." From this normalized form of (19), we see that for a fixed input pulse *shape* and a fixed output pulse *shape* and with fixed $R_b$, $R_A$, $C_T$, $S_E$, and $S_I$, the noise decreases as the bit rate, $1/T$, increases (a consequence of the square-law detection) until the term involving $I_3$ dominates. After that, the noise increases with increasing bit rate (due to the shunt capacitance $C_T$).

$$h_p(t) = \frac{1}{\alpha T} \text{ FOR } \frac{-\alpha T}{2} < t < \frac{\alpha T}{2}, 0 \text{ OTHERWISE}$$

$$h_p(t) = \frac{1}{\sqrt{2\pi}\alpha T} \text{ EXP} \left\{ -t^2/[2(\alpha T)^2] \right\}$$

$$h_p(t) = \frac{1}{\alpha T} \text{ EXP} \left\{ -t/[\alpha T] \right\}$$

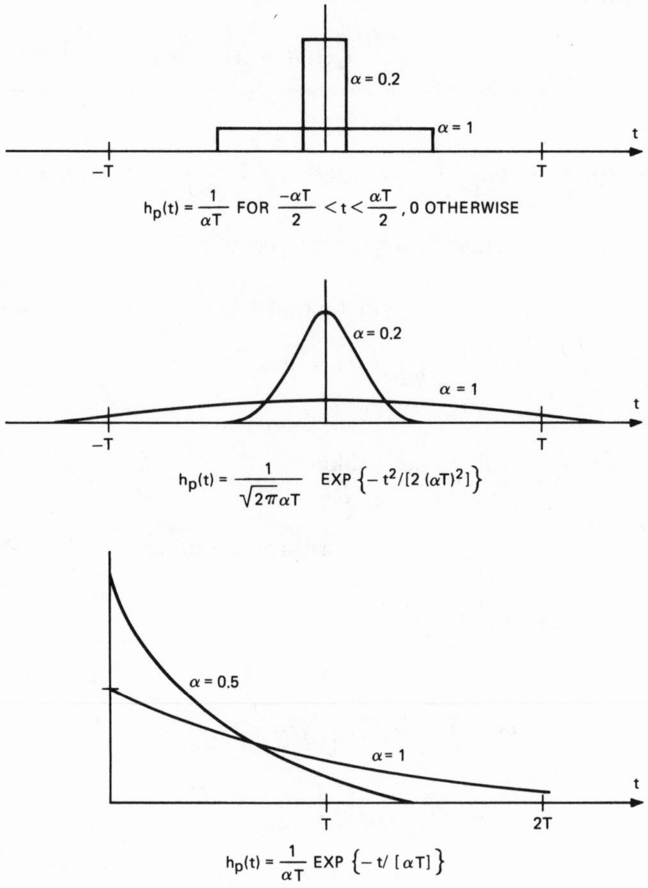

Fig. 6a—Input pulse families.

*Example of Normalization:*

Suppose the input optical pulse is a rectangular pulse of unit area having width equal to one-half a time slot $T$; then

$$H_p(\omega) = \int_{-\frac{1}{4}T}^{\frac{1}{4}T} \frac{2}{T} e^{i\omega t} dt$$

$$= \frac{1}{i\omega} \left( \frac{2}{T} \right) (e^{i\omega t/4} - e^{-i\omega T/4})$$

$$= \sin \frac{(\omega T/4)}{\omega T/4}. \tag{24}$$

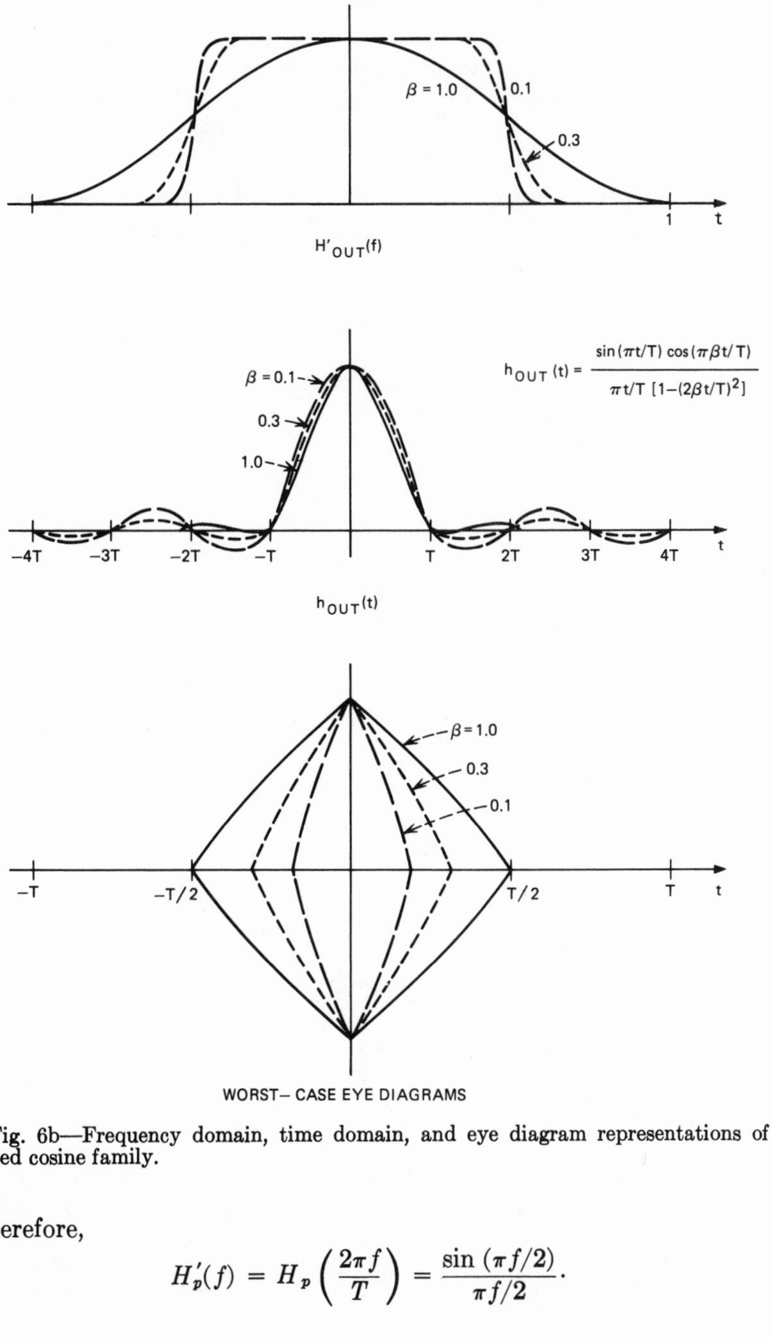


Fig. 6b—Frequency domain, time domain, and eye diagram representations of raised cosine family.

Therefore,

$$H_p'(f) = H_p\left(\frac{2\pi f}{T}\right) = \frac{\sin (\pi f/2)}{\pi f/2}.$$

As expected, the normalized pulse spectrum $H_p'(f)$ is independent of the time slot width $T$ and merely reflects the fact that the pulse $h_p(t)$ is a rectangular pulse with width equal to half a time slot.

In order to obtain the noise for various input and output (equalized) pulse shapes, one needs to calculate the three integrals $I_1$, $I_2$, and $I_3$ and the sum $\sum_1$.

Consider the following three families of input pulse shapes (see Fig. 6a) and single family of output pulse shapes (see Fig. 6b).

(*i*) Rectangular input pulses:

$$h_p(t) = \frac{1}{\alpha T}, \qquad -\frac{\alpha T}{2} < t < \frac{\alpha T}{2}, \qquad 0 \text{ otherwise} \tag{25}$$

$$H_p'(f) = \frac{\sin(\alpha\pi f)}{\alpha\pi f}.$$

(*ii*) Gaussian input pulses:

$$h_p(t) = \frac{1}{\sqrt{2\pi}\alpha T} e^{-[t^2/2(\alpha T)^2]}$$

$$H_p'(f) = e^{-(2\pi\alpha f)^2/2}.$$

(*iii*) Exponential input pulses:

$$h_p(t) = \frac{1}{\alpha T} e^{-t/\alpha T}$$

$$H_p'(f) = \frac{1}{1 + j2\pi\alpha f}.$$

(*iv*) "Raised cosine" output pulses:

$$h_{\text{out}}(t) = \left[\sin\left(\frac{\pi t}{T}\right)\cos\left(\frac{\pi\beta t}{T}\right)\right]\left[\frac{\pi t}{T}\left(1 - \left(\frac{2\beta t}{T}\right)^2\right)\right]^{-1}$$

$$H_{\text{out}}'(f) = 1, \qquad \text{for} \qquad 0 < |f| < \frac{(1-\beta)}{2}$$

$$= \frac{1}{2}\left[1 - \sin\left(\frac{\pi f}{\beta} - \frac{\pi}{2\beta}\right)\right], \qquad \text{for } \frac{1-\beta}{2} < |f| < \frac{1+\beta}{2}$$

$$= 0 \text{ otherwise.}$$

(Time, frequency, and eye diagram representations of the raised cosine family are shown as a function of $\beta$ in Fig. 6b.[11])

In Figs. 7 through 18 calculations of $I_1$, $I_2$, $I_3$, and $I_4$ are given graphically for each input pulse family as a function of $\alpha$ and $\beta$.

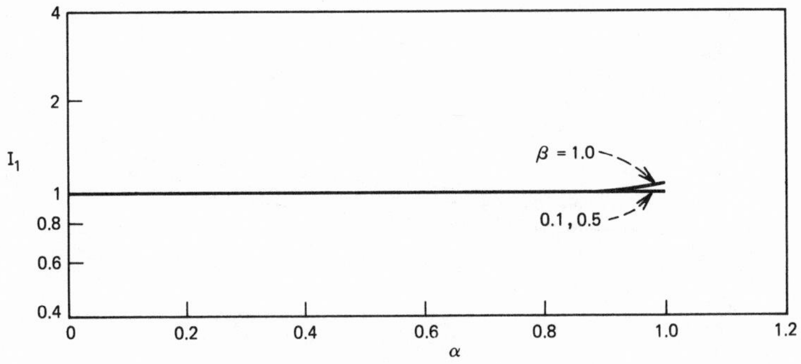


Fig. 7—Rectangular family $I_1$ vs $\alpha$ and $\beta$.

### 5.1 *Comments on the Numerical Results*

For the rectangular input pulses with widths between 0.1 and 1 time slot, $I_1$, $\sum_1$, $I_2$, and $I_3$ vary very little. Thus, if one expects to receive rectangular optical pulses which are fixed in energy, the required energy per pulse is insensitive to the pulse width for widths up to 1 time slot.

The curves for Gaussian-shaped input pulses imply very strong sensitivity of required energy per pulse to pulse width. This is a consequence of the rapid falloff of the spectrum of a Gaussian pulse with frequency. It is suspected that, although for certain fiber systems the received pulses may appear approximately Gaussian in the time domain, the frequency spectrum will not suffer such a rapid falloff. The results for the exponential-shaped input pulses seem much more realistic.

For exponential-shaped optical pulses we notice, from Figs. 15 and 16, that the shot noise coefficients $I_1$ and $\sum_1$ are sensitive to the optical

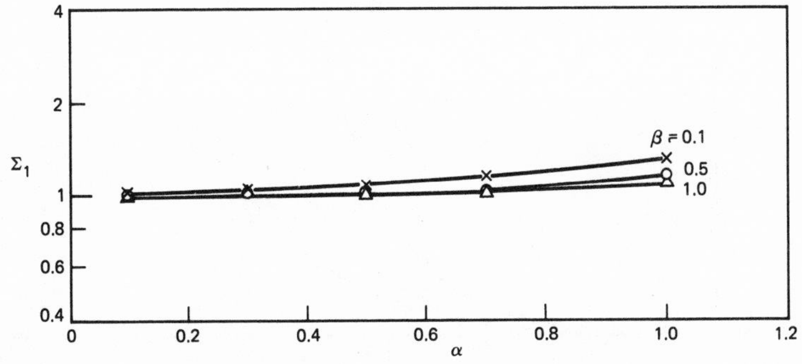


Fig. 8—Rectangular family $\Sigma_1$ vs $\alpha$ and $\beta$.

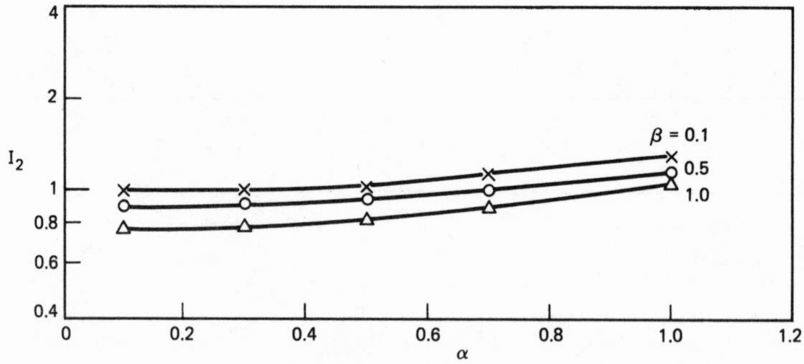


Fig. 9—Rectangular family $I_2$ vs $\alpha$ and $\beta$.

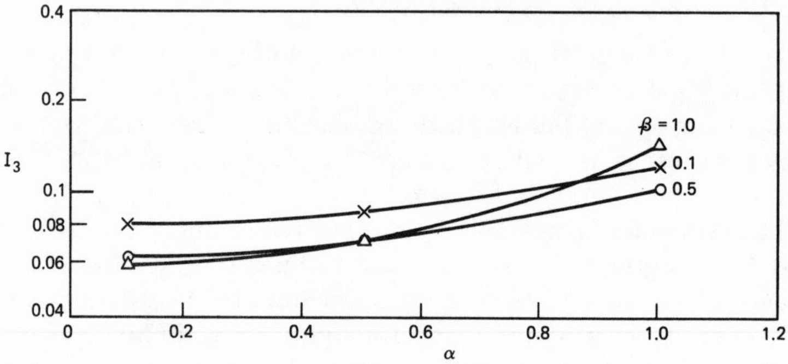


Fig. 10—Rectangular family $I_3$ vs $\alpha$ and $\beta$.

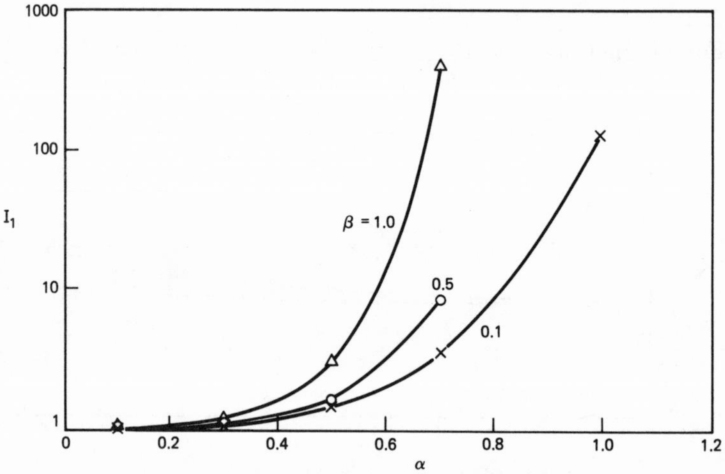


Fig. 11—Gaussian family $I_1$ vs $\alpha$ and $\beta$.

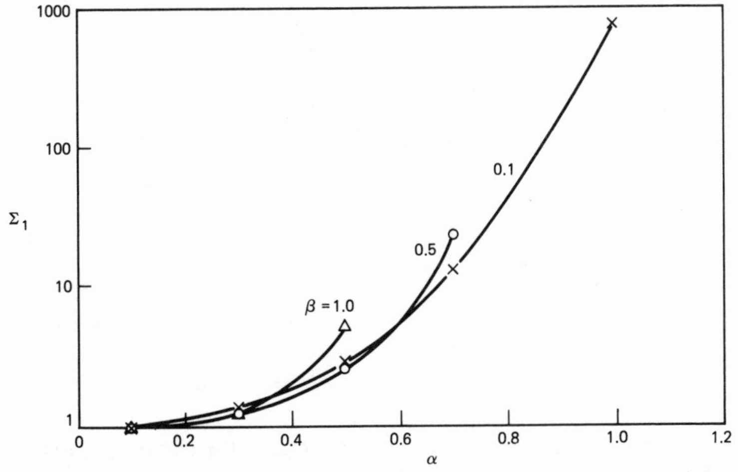


Fig. 12—Gaussian family $\Sigma_1$ vs $\alpha$ and $\beta$.

pulse width, but that these sensitivities imply a practically useful tradeoff in required optical power vs allowable bit rate. That is, one might take a certain power penalty to allow equalization which can substantially increase the usable bit rate on a channel having a fixed optical output pulse width. The sensitivity of $I_2$ and $I_3$ to the optical pulse width is similar to that of $\sum_1$ and less significant because in-

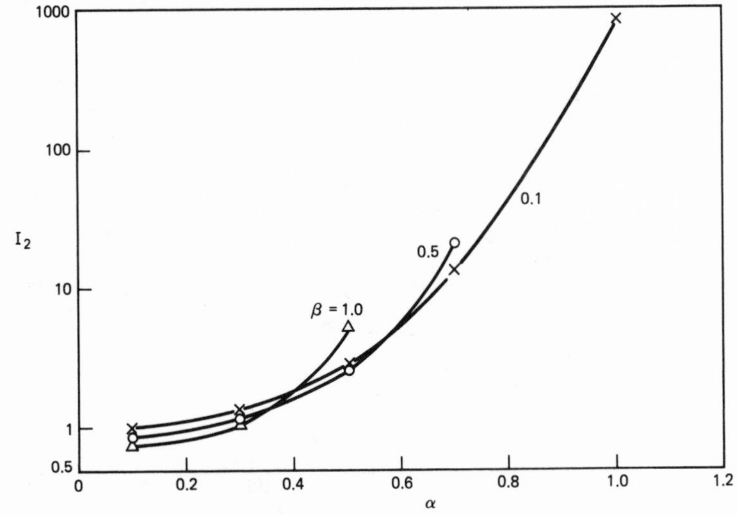


Fig. 13—Gaussian family $I_2$ vs $\alpha$ and $\beta$.

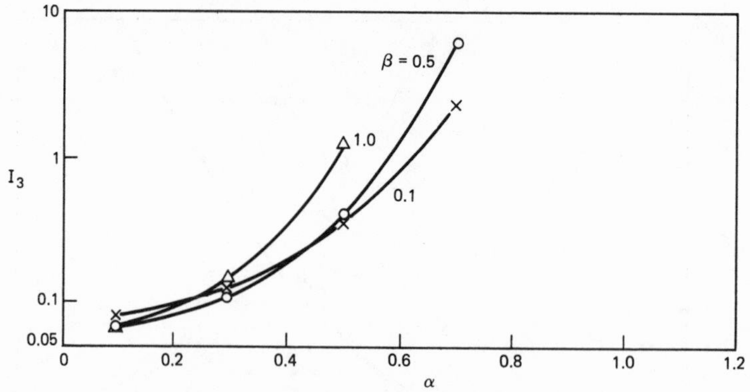


Fig. 14—Gaussian family $I_3$ vs $\alpha$ and $\beta$.

creases in the thermal noises of the receiver are for the most part compensated for by adjustment of the avalanche gain, with only a small penalty in excess shot noise. The above statements will be made quantitative in Section VI.

## VI. OBTAINING THE RELATIONSHIPS FOR FIXED ERROR RATE BETWEEN THE REQUIRED ENERGY PER PULSE, OPTIMAL AVALANCHE GAIN, AND OTHER PARAMETERS

Suppose that in (23) all parameters are fixed except $\langle g \rangle$, $\langle g^2 \rangle$, $b_{\min}$, and $b_{\max}$.

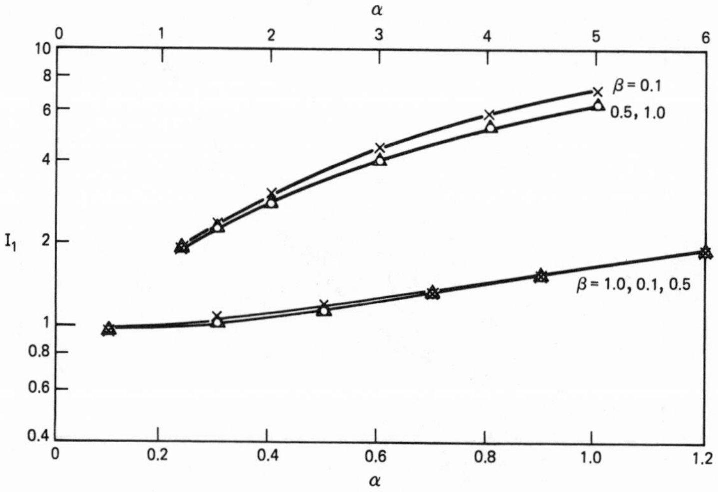


Fig. 15—Exponential family $I_1$ vs $\alpha$ and $\beta$.

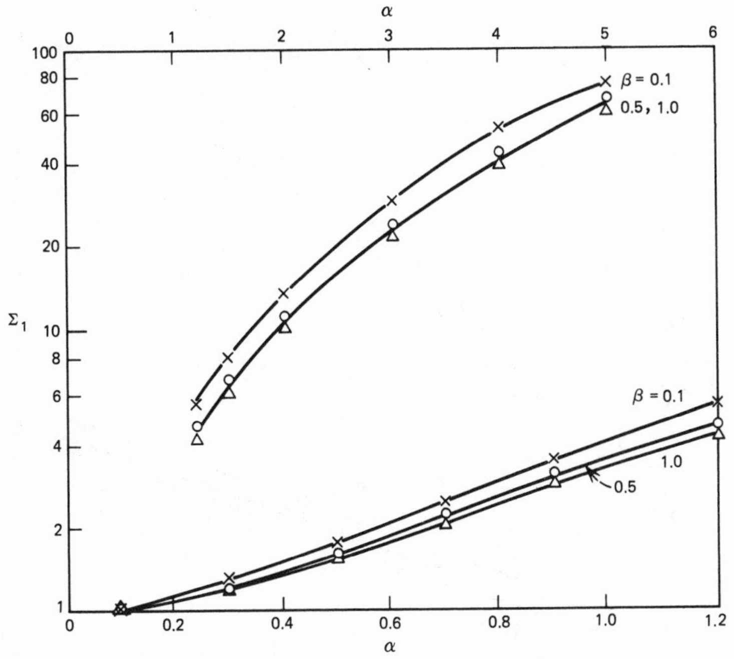


Fig. 16—Exponential family $\Sigma_1$ vs $\alpha$ and $\beta$.

The receiver equalized output at the sampling time, due to an optical pulse of energy $b_0$, is $b_0$.

When $b_0 = b_{\min}$, we must be sure that the probability that noise drives the receiver output $v_{\text{out}}(t)$ at the sampling time above the threshold $D$ is less than $10^{-9}$.† Using the signal-to-noise ratio approximation,‡ we require the noise variance, $NW(b_{\min})$, to be less than $\{\frac{1}{6}[D - b_{\min}]\}^2$.

Therefore, we require that

$$NW(b_{\min}) \leqq \frac{1}{36}[D - b_{\min}]^2. \tag{26}$$

Furthermore, when $b_0 = b_{\max}$ we must be sure that the probability that the noise drives the receiver output below the threshold is less than $10^{-9}$. Therefore, we require that

$$NW(b_{\max}) \leqq \frac{1}{36}[b_{\max} - D]^2. \tag{27}$$

† An error rate of $10^{-9}$ is arbitrarily chosen here. Dependence of required optical power on error rate is discussed in Part II of this paper.

‡ See Appendix A.

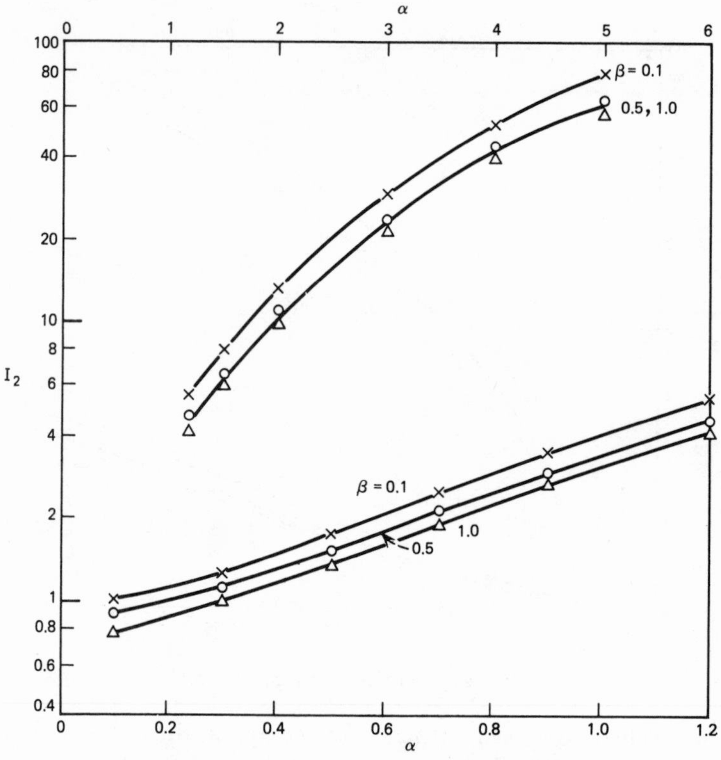


Fig. 17—Exponential family $I_2$ vs $\alpha$ and $\beta$.

Using equality in (26) and (27), we require for a $10^{-9}$ error rate

$$\sqrt{NW(b_{\max})} + \sqrt{NW(b_{\min})} = \tfrac{1}{6}(b_{\max} - b_{\min}). \tag{28}$$

Very often we have a fixed ratio $(b_{\min}/b_{\max}) = \rho$.

Rearranging (28) we obtain

$$b_{\max} = \frac{6}{1-\rho}\left[\sqrt{NW(b_{\max})} + \sqrt{NW(\rho b_{\max})}\right]. \tag{29}$$

In order to obtain numerical results, we shall make the following reasonable assumptions. Let the dark current be negligible and let $b_{\min}/b_{\max}$ be much less than unity. Therefore we shall set $\lambda_0 = 0$, $b_{\min} = 0$.† We obtain from (23)

† Quantitative discussion of the consequences of these approximations are given in Part II.

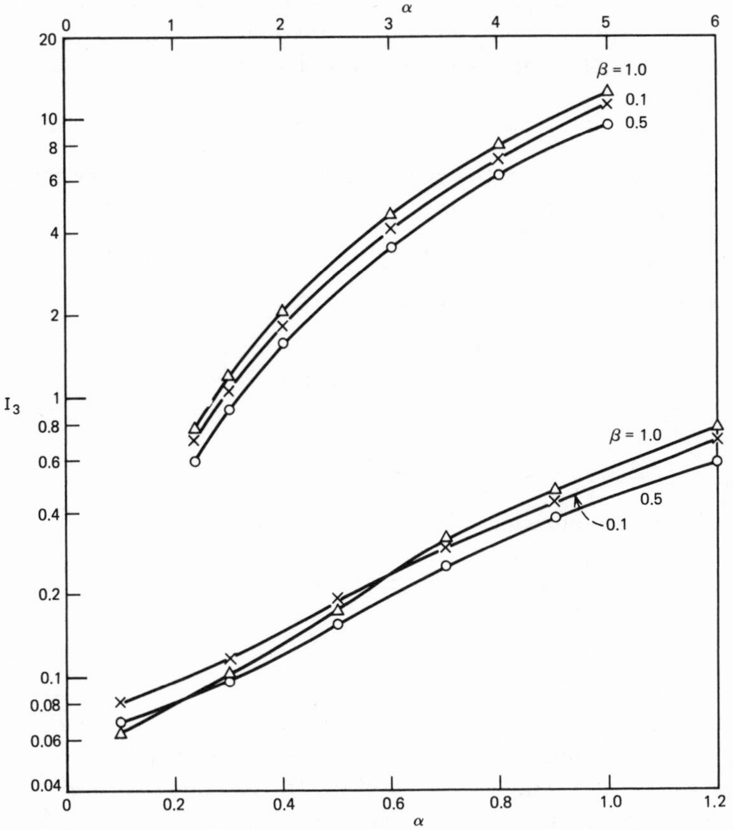


Fig. 18—Exponential family $I_3$ vs $\alpha$ and $\beta$.

$$NW(b_0) \cong \left[\frac{\hbar\Omega}{\eta}\right]^2 \left\{\frac{\langle g^2\rangle}{\langle g\rangle^2}\frac{\eta}{\hbar\Omega}\left[b_0 I_1 + b_{\max}\left(\textstyle\sum_1 - I_1\right)\right] + \frac{1}{\langle g\rangle^2}[Z]\right\},$$

where

$$Z \triangleq \left\{\frac{T}{e^2}\left[S_I + \frac{2k\theta}{R_b} + \frac{S_E}{R_T^2}\right] I_2 + \frac{(2\pi C_T)^2}{Te^2} S_E I_3\right\}. \tag{30}$$

In (30), $Z$ includes all the thermal noise terms of (23).

From (29), taking the limit as $\rho \to 0$ ($b_{\min} \to 0$), we obtain the conditions to achieve a $10^{-9}$ error rate as follows.

*Case I*: Thermal noise ($Z$) dominates (i.e., little or no avalanche gain).

$$b_{\max} = \frac{12\hbar\Omega}{\eta\langle g\rangle} Z^{\frac{1}{2}}. \tag{31}$$

*Case II*: Optimal gain (i.e., $\langle g \rangle$ adjusted to minimize the required optical energy in an "on" pulse $b_{\max}$).

Let the relationship between $\langle g^2 \rangle$ and $\langle g \rangle$ be specified in the usual way:

$$\langle g^2 \rangle = \langle g \rangle^{2+x}, \tag{32}$$

where $x$ depends upon the type of detector. We obtain the following formula for the optimal gain:

$$\langle g \rangle_{\text{optimal}} = (6)^{-1/(1+x)}(Z)^{1/(2+2x)}(\gamma_1)^{1/(2+2x)}(\gamma_2)^{-1/(1+x)}, \tag{33}$$

where defining $I_5 = \sum_1 - I_1$ [see eq. (23)]

$$\gamma_1 \triangleq \frac{-[\sum_1 + I_5] + \sqrt{(\sum_1 + I_5)^2 + \dfrac{16(1+x)}{x^2}\sum_1 I_5}}{2\sum_1 I_5} \tag{34}$$

$$\gamma_2 \triangleq \sqrt{1/\gamma_1 + I_5} + \sqrt{1/\gamma_1 + \textstyle\sum_1}.$$

We obtain the following formula for $b_{\max}$:

$$b_{\max} = \frac{\hbar\Omega}{\eta}(6)^{(2+x)/(1+x)}(Z)^{x/(2+2x)}(\gamma_1)^{x/(2+2x)}(\gamma_2)^{(2+x)/(1+x)}. \tag{35}$$

That is,

$$b_{\max} \propto [Z]^{x/(2+2x)}. \tag{36}$$

We therefore see that for these assumptions and $x = 0.5$ corresponding to a silicon avalanche detector the minimum required energy per pulse varies as the one-half power of the thermal noise term, $Z$, without avalanche gain, and as the one-sixth power of the thermal noise term, $Z$, with optimal gain.

However, this does not mean that at optimal gain the value of $Z$ is unimportant. By reducing $Z$ (the thermal noise terms) through proper choice of biasing and amplifier circuitry, we still minimize the optimizing avalanche gain [see (33)] and obtain some reduction in the required energy per pulse (see Part II).

### 6.1 *Example*

From eqs. (23), (30), (34), and (35) we can calculate, for various shaped optical pulses, the effect of intersymbol interference on the required energy per "on" pulse ($b_{\max}$) and therefore on the required average optical power needed for a $10^{-9}$ error rate.† We shall assume

† That is, if pulses are "on" half the time, the required optical power equals $b_{\max}/2T$.

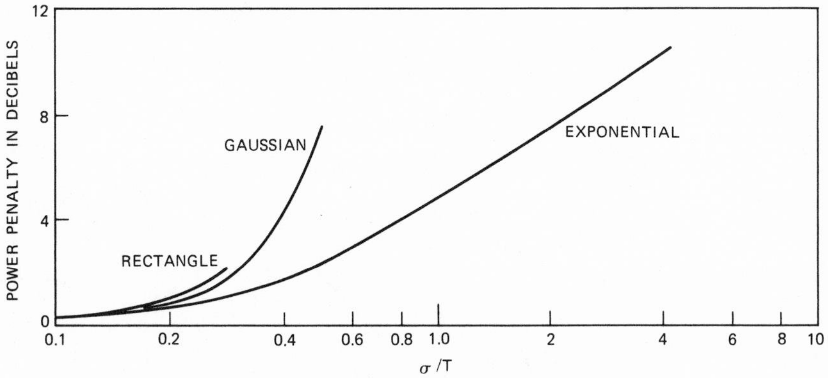


Fig. 19—No avalanche gain.

that the detector amplifier shunt resistance $R_T$ is sufficiently large so that the term $((2\pi C_T)^2/Te^2)S_E I_3$ dominates the thermal noise in (23) and (30).

The minimal required optical power is obtained for very narrow optical input pulses.† For other pulse shapes, the *excess* required optical power can be defined as a *penalty* in dB for not using narrow pulses. This penalty is plotted in Figs. 19 and 20 for the case of no avalanche gain and optimal avalanche gain using the pulse shapes of (25), assuming a silicon detector ($x = 0.5$). In those figures, the abscissa is the normalized rms optical pulse width defined as follows:

$$\frac{\sigma^2}{T^2} = \frac{\left(\int t^2 h_p(t)dt\right) - \left(\int th_p(t)dt\right)^2}{T^2}, \tag{37}$$

where $T$ = time slot width.

## VII. CONCLUSIONS

### 7.1 *Conclusion on Choosing the Biasing Circuitry*

From the results of Sections IV and VI, and from (23), it is clear that, to minimize the thermal noise degradations introduced by the amplifiers following the detector, it is necessary to make the amplifier input resistance and the biasing circuit resistance sufficiently large so that the amplifier series noise source dominates the Johnson noise of these parallel resistances. When designing the amplifier, one should keep in mind that for a silicon avalanche detector the required optical

† See Appendix B.

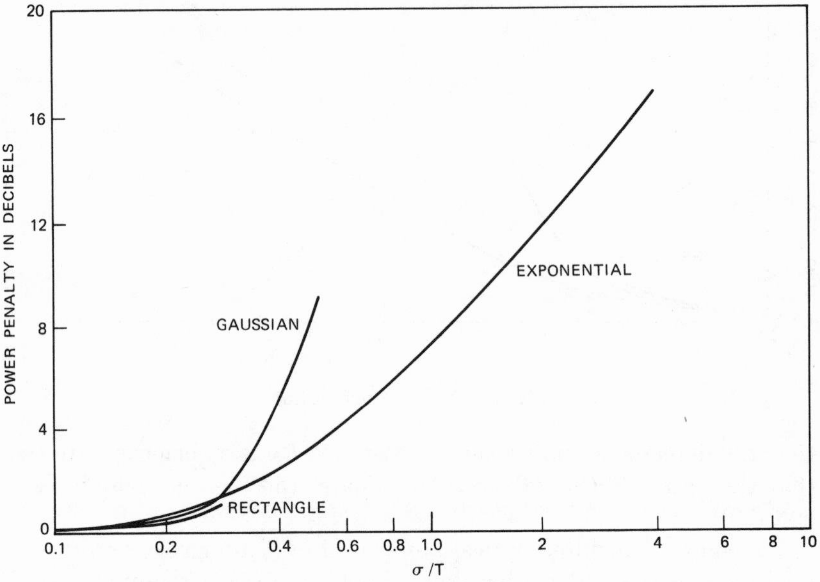


Fig. 20—Optimal gain.

energy per pulse at optimal gain varies roughly as the one-sixth power of the thermal noise variance at the receiver output, and therefore it is not wise to spend too much money on thermal noise reduction. On the other hand, if one is not using avalanche gain, the required energy per pulse varies roughly as the one-half power of the thermal noise variance at the receiver output.

In order to minimize the effects of the thermal noise, the total capacitance shunting the detector should be as small as possible and the equivalent series thermal noise source of the amplifier should also be as small as possible.

### 7.2 *The Effect of Bit Rate on Required Energy Per Pulse*†

The effect of bit rate on the required energy per pulse is small if the received pulses remain well confined to a time slot. In (23), assume $I_1$, $\sum_1$, $I_2$, and $I_3$ are fixed corresponding to a fixed received pulse width relative to a time slot. Then the shot noise terms due to the signal are independent of the bit rate $1/T$, and the shot noise due to the dark current decreases with increasing bit rate. If the series noise from the amplifier dominates, then the thermal noise increases with increasing

† This subject will be discussed in more detail in Part II.

bit rate, but is for the most part compensated for by the avalanche gain with little penalty in required energy per pulse.

If considerable equalization is being used, then the required energy per pulse increases with the bit rate (because a higher bit rate necessitates greater equalization). For the equalization assumed above, where the equalized pulses are forced to go to zero at all sampling times except one, the required energy per pulse is a strong function of the bit rate. For example, with exponential-shaped received pulses, the required optical power at optimal avalanche gain was roughly 6 dB higher for a pulse 1 time slot wide to the $1/e$ point compared to a pulse only 0.25 time slot wide to the $1/e$ point (see Fig. 20).

On the other hand, it is clear that zero-forcing-type equalization is not optimal, particularly for received pulses whose spectra fall off rapidly with frequency. It is more likely that some compromise between eye opening and output noise variance results in minimum required energy per pulse.

For the assumed zero-forcing equalization, we still can conclude that a usable tradeoff exists between required energy per pulse and bit rate, and this will allow some extension of the usable rate on "dispersion-limited" fibers.

### 7.3 *Comments on Previous Work*

The purpose of this paper has been to illustrate the application of the "high-impedance" front-end design to optical digital repeaters, to take into account precisely the input pulse shape and the equalizer-filter shape, and to obtain explicit formulas for the required optical power to achieve a desired error rate as a function of the other parameters.

Previous authors[12,13] working in the areas of particle counting and video amplifier design have recognized that a high-impedance front end followed by proper equalization in later stages provides low noise and adequate bandwidth. However, optical communication theorists[5,6,14,15] have in the past often used the criterion "$RC \leqq T$"–loading down the front-end amplifier so as to have adequate bandwidth without equalization–therein incurring an unnecessary noise penalty. Some optical experimenters[16,17] have recognized the high-impedance design for observing isolated pulses or single frequencies, but failed to recognize the use of equalization.

Many previous authors[3,4,6,15] have used simple formulas (which usually assume isolated rectangular input pulses and a front-end bandwidth of the reciprocal pulse width) to obtain the required power in optical communication systems for a desired signal-to-noise ratio. Often these formulas average out the signal-dependent nature of the shot noise. If modified to include the high-impedance design concept, such formulas are very useful for obtaining "ball park" estimates of optical power requirements. Such formulas are, in general, special cases of the formulas described here.

### 7.4 *Experimental Verification*

In work recently reported,[18] J. E. Goell has shown that, in a 6.3-Mb/s repeater operating at an error rate of $10^{-9}$, agreement of experimentally determined power requirements and the above theory were within 1 dB (0.25 dB in cases without avalanche gain). In particular, using an FET front end and the "high-impedance" design, the optical power requirement without avalanche gain was 8 dB less than with the front end loaded down to the "$RC = T$" design.

## APPENDIX A

### *Signal-to-Noise Ratio Approximation*

In this paper we have calculated the mean voltage ($b_{max}$ or $b_{min}$) and the average-squared deviation from the mean voltage ($NW(b_{max})$ or $NW(b_{min})$) at the receiver output at the sampling times. In order to calculate error rates, we shall assume that the output voltage is approximately a Gaussian random variable. This is the signal-to-noise ratio approximation. Thus if the threshold, to which we compare the output voltage, is $D$, and if the desired error probability is $P_e$, we have

$$\frac{1}{\sqrt{2\pi\sigma_o^2}} \int_D^\infty \exp\left[-(v - b_{min})^2/2\sigma_o^2\right] dv = P_e, \tag{38}$$

where

$$\sigma_o^2 = NW(b_{min})$$

and

$$\frac{1}{\sqrt{2\pi\sigma_1^2}} \int_{-\infty}^D \exp\left[-(v - b_{max})^2/2\sigma_1^2\right] dv = P_e,$$

where

$$\sigma_1^2 = NW(b_{max}).$$

Changing the variables of integration we obtain the following expressions, equivalent to (38):

$$\frac{1}{\sqrt{2\pi}} \int_Q^\infty e^{-x^2/2} dx = P_e, \tag{39}$$

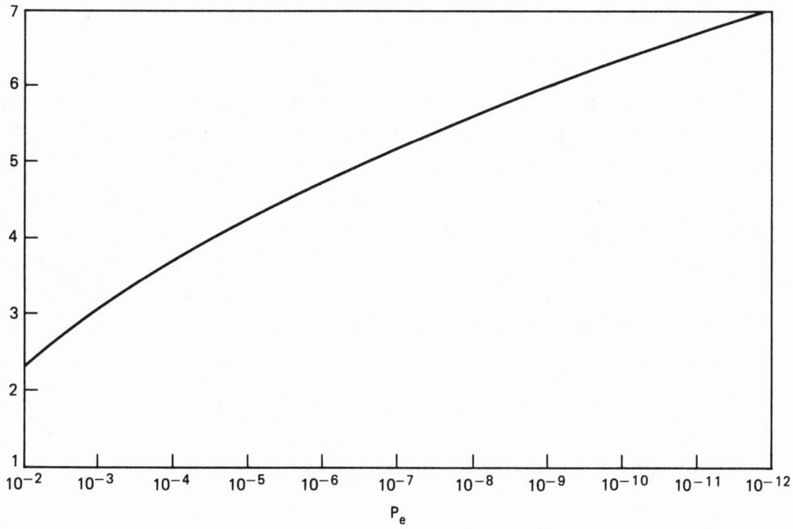


Fig. 21—$Q$ vs $P_e$, $P_e = \frac{1}{\sqrt{2\pi}} \int_Q^\infty e^{-x^2/2} dx$.

where

$$Q = (D - b_{\min})/\sigma_o$$

and also

$$Q = (b_{\max} - D)/\sigma_1.$$

Thus we must have

$$\sigma_o = \sqrt{NW(b_{\min})} = (D - b_{\min})/Q$$

and

$$\sigma_1 = \sqrt{NW(b_{\max})} = (b_{\max} - D)/Q.$$

Therefore we must also have (eliminating $D$)

$$\sqrt{NW(b_{\max})} + \sqrt{NW(b_{\min})} = (b_{\max} - b_{\min})/Q.$$

The value of $Q$ is determined by the error rate through (39) above. Figure 21 shows a plot of $Q$ vs $P_e$ which can be obtained from standard tables.

Equation (39) states that the threshold must be $Q$ standard deviations (of the noise at $b_{\min}$) above $b_{\min}$, and also must be $Q$ standard deviations (of the noise at $b_{\max}$) below $b_{\max}$ to insure the desired error rate. For an error rate of $10^{-9}$ ($P_e = 10^{-9}$) $Q$ is roughly 6 (5.99781).

APPENDIX B

*Optimal Input Pulse Shape*

We now wish to show that the optimal input pulse, $h_p(t)$ shape (which minimizes the required average optical power) is ideally an impulse; and for practical purposes a pulse which is sufficiently narrow so that its Fourier transform is almost constant for all frequencies passed by the receiver. To do this, we shall show that such a narrow pulse minimizes the noises $NW(b_{\max})$ and $NW(b_{\min})$ defined in (23).

We begin with the already established condition that the area of $h_p(t)$ is equal to unity and that $h_p(t)$ is positive (power must, of course, be positive).

$$\int h_p(t)dt = 1; \qquad h_p(t) > 0. \tag{40}$$

These conditions imply the following weaker condition:

$$|H_p'(f)| = \left|\int h_p(t)e^{-i2\pi ft/T}dt\right|$$
$$\leqq \int |h_p(t)|\,|e^{-i2\pi ft/T}|\,dt = \int h_p(t)dt = H_p'(0) = 1. \tag{41}$$

Consider first the thermal noise terms of (23) involving the integrals $I_2$ and $I_3$:

$$I_2 = \int \frac{|H_{\text{out}}'(f)|^2}{|H_p'(f)|^2}\,df; \qquad I_3 = \int \frac{|H_{\text{out}}'(f)|^2}{|H_p'(f)|^2}\,f^2df. \tag{42}$$

Using (41) in (42) we see that these terms $I_2$ and $I_3$ are minimized for any desired output pulse $H_{\text{out}}'(f)$ by setting $|H_p'(f)| = H_p'(0) = 1$ for all frequencies, $f$, for which $|H_{\text{out}}'(f)| > 0$. Thus, ideally, to minimize $I_2$ and $I_3$, $h_p(t)$ is an impulse of unit area which also satisfies the conditions (40).

We must now show that the shot noise terms of (23), $I_1$ and $\sum_1 - I_1$, are minimized by a very narrow pulse $h_p(t)$.

First recall that $(\sum_1 - I_1)b_{\max}(\hbar\Omega/\eta)\langle g^2\rangle/\langle g\rangle^2$ is the worst-case, mean-square shot noise at the sampling time due to all other pulses except the one under decision, and assuming all of those pulses are "on" ($b_k = b_{\max}$ for $k \neq 0$). Thus, from (17), we obtain

$$\textstyle\sum_1 - I_1 \geqq 0, \tag{43}$$

where

$$\sum{}_1 - I_1 = \int \Big(\sum_{k\neq 0} h_p(t' - kT)\Big)h_I^2(-t')dt'$$

and where $h_I(t)$ is the overall receiver impulse response relating $h_p(t)$ to $h_{\text{out}}(t)$.

Now let the optical pulse $h_p(t)$ be an impulse of unit area. Then the overall impulse response $h_I$ must be equal to $h_{\text{out}}(t)$ and therefore using (43) and (9) we obtain

$$\begin{gathered}\textstyle\sum_1 - I_1 = \sum_{k \neq 0} h_{\text{out}}^2(-kT) = 0 \\ (\text{for } h_p(t) = \delta(t)).\end{gathered} \tag{44}$$

Because condition (9) requires zero-crossing equalization, we have shown that an impulse shape for $h_p(t)$ minimizes (removes) the shot noise from pulses other than the one under decision.

Finally, consider the shot noise from the pulse under decision given by $I_1(\hbar\Omega/\eta)b_o\langle g^2\rangle/\langle g\rangle^2$ where

$$I_1 = \int h_p(t')h_I^2(-t')dt' > 0. \tag{45}$$

We already have the condition (9)

$$h_{\text{out}}(0) = \int h_p(t')h_I(-t')dt' = 1. \tag{46}$$

We can next use the Shwarz inequality on (46)

$$\begin{aligned}(h_{\text{out}}(0))^2 = 1 &= \left(\int h_p^{\frac{1}{2}}(t)h_p^{\frac{1}{2}}(t)h_I(-t)dt\right)^2 \\ &\leqq \int h_p(t)dt \int h_p(t)h_I^2(-t)dt.\end{aligned} \tag{47}$$

Since $\int h_p(t)dt = 1$, we have from (47) and (45)

$$I_1 \geqq 1. \tag{48}$$

Now set $h_p(t)$ equal to a unit area impulse. It then must follow from (46) that $h_I(0) = 1$. We finally obtain

$$\int h_p(t)h_I^2(t)dt = h_I^2(0) = 1. \tag{49}$$

From (48) and (49) we see that an impulse-shaped $h_p(t)$ makes $I_1$ achieve its minimum value of unity.

Summarizing, an impulse-shaped optical input pulse $h_p(t)$ (for practical purposes a sufficiently narrow pulse so that its Fourier transform is approximately constant for all frequencies passed by the receiver) minimizes all the pulse-shape-dependent coefficients ($I_1$, $\sum_1 - I_1$, $I_2$, and $I_3$) in the noise expression (23) and thereby minimizes the required average optical power to achieve a desired error rate (using the signal-to-noise ratio approximation of Appendix A).

REFERENCES


1. Personick, S. D., "Baseband Linearity and Equalization in Fiber Optic Communication Systems," to appear in B.S.T.J., September 1973.
2. Personick, S. D., "Statistics of a General Class of Avalanche Detectors with Applications to Optical Communication," B.S.T.J., *50*, No. 10 (December 1971), pp. 3075–3096.
3. Melchior, H., et al., "Photodetectors for Optical Communication Systems," Proc. IEEE, *58*, No. 10 (October 1970), pp. 1466–1486.
4. Pratt, W. R., *Laser Communication Systems*, New York: John Wiley and Sons, 1969.
5. Hubbard, W. M., "Comparative Performance of Twin-Channel and Single-Channel Optical Frequency Receivers," IEEE Trans. Commun. *COM20*, No. 6 (December 1972), pp. 1079–1086.
6. Anderson, L. K., and McCurtry, B. J., "High Speed Photodetectors," Proc. IEEE, *54* (October 1966), pp. 1335–1349.
7. McIntyre, R. J., "Multiplication Noise in Uniform Avalanche Diodes," IEEE Trans. Electron Devices, *ED-13*, No. 1 (January 1966), pp. 164–168.
8. Melchior, H., and Lynch, W. T., "Signal and Noise Response of High Speed Germanium Photodiodes," IEEE Trans. Electron Devices, *ED-13* (December 1966), pp. 829–838.
9. Klauder, J. R., and Sudarshan, E. C. G., *Fundamentals of Quantum Optics*, New York: W. A. Benjamin, Inc., 1968, pp. 169–178.
10. Parzen, E., *Stochastic Processes*, San Francisco: Holden-Day, 1962, p. 156.
11. Figure 5b is from *Transmission Systems for Communication*, Bell Telephone Laboratories, 1970, p. 651.
12. Gillespie, A. B., *Signal, Noise, and Resolution in Nuclear Particle Counters*, New York: Pergamon Press, Inc., 1953.
13. Schade, O. H., Sr., "A Solid-State Low-Noise Preamplifier and Picture-Tube Drive Amplifier for a 60 MHz Video System," RCA Rev., *29*, No. 1 (March 1968), p. 3.
14. Chown, M., and Kao, K. C., "Some Broadband Fiber-System Design Considerations," ICC 1972 Conf. Proc., June 19–21, 1972, Philadelphia, Pa., pp. 12-1, 12-5.
15. Ross, M., *Laser Receivers*, New York: John Wiley and Sons, 1967, p. 328.
16. Edwards, B. N., "Optimization of Preamplifiers for Detection of Short Light Pulses with Photodiodes," Appl. Opt. *5*, No. 9 (September 1966), pp. 1423–1425.
17. Mathur, D. P., McIntyre, R. J., and Webb, P. P., "A New Germanium Photodiode with Extended Long Wavelength Response," Appl. Opt., *9*, No. 8 (August 1970), pp. 1842–1847.
18. Goell, J. E., work to be presented at the Conference on Laser Engineering and Applications (CLEA) Washington, D.C., May 30–June 2, 1973.

# 16B



Reprinted from *Bell. Syst. Tech. J.* **52**(6):875–886 (1973)

# Receiver Design for Digital Fiber Optic Communication Systems, II

By S. D. PERSONICK

(Manuscript received January 15, 1973)

*This paper applies the results of Part I to specific receivers in order to obtain numerical results. The general explicit formulas for the required optical average power to achieve a desired error rate are summarized. A specific receiver is considered and the optical power requirements solved for. The parameters defining this receiver (e.g., bit rate, bias resistance, dark current, etc.) are then varied, and the effects on the required optical power are plotted.*

## I. INTRODUCTION

This paper will apply the theory of Part I to illustrate in detail how the required received optical power in a digital fiber optic repeater varies with the parameters such as the desired error rate, the thermal noise sources, the bit rate, detector dark current, imperfect modulation, etc. We shall begin by first applying the formulas of Part I to a specific realistic example to obtain reference point. We shall then derive curves of how the required power varies around this point as we vary the system parameters.

## II. REVIEW OF RESULTS OF PART I

In Part I we derived explicit formulas for the required optical power at the input of a digital fiber optic communication system repeater to achieve a desired error rate. One formula was applicable when little or no internal (avalanche) detector gain was used, so that thermal noise from the amplifier dominated. The other formula was applicable when optimal gain was being used. These formulas are repeated below:

$$p_{\text{required}} = \frac{QZ^{\frac{1}{2}}}{GT}\frac{\hbar\Omega}{\eta}, \qquad \text{(Thermal Noise Dominates)} \qquad (1)$$

where

$$Z = \left\{ \frac{T}{e^2} \left[ S_I + \frac{2k\theta}{R_b} + \frac{S_E}{R_T^2} \right] I_2 + \frac{(2\pi C_T)^2 S_E I_3}{Te^2} \right\}; \tag{1a}$$

$$p_{\text{required}} = \frac{1}{2T} (Q)^{(2+x)/(1+x)} \left[ (Z)^{x/(2+2x)} (\gamma_1)^{x/(2+2x)} (\gamma_2)^{(2+x)/(1+x)} \right] \frac{\hbar\Omega}{\eta},$$

(Optimal Avalanche Gain) (2)

where

$$G_{\text{optimal}} = (Q)^{-1/(1+x)} \left[ (Z)^{1/(2+2x)} (\gamma_1)^{1/(2+2x)} (\gamma_2)^{-1/(1+x)} \right],$$

where (referring to Fig. 1)

$\eta/\hbar\Omega$ = detector quantum efficiency/energy in a photon
$T$ = interval between bits = 1/bit rate
$G$ = average detector internal gain
$G^x$ = detector random internal gain excess noise factor
$Q$ = number of noise standard deviations between signal and threshold at receiver output. $Q = 6$ for an error rate of $10^{-9}$. (See Fig. 21 in Part I for a graph of error rate vs $Q$.)
$e$ = electron charge
$k\theta$ = Boltzman's constant · the absolute temperature
$R_T$ = total parallel resistance in shunt with the detector including the physical biasing resistor and the amplifier input resistance
$R_b$ = value of physical detector biasing resistor
$C_T$ = total shunt capacitance across the detector including the shunt capacitance of the detector and that of the amplifier
$S_I$ = amplifier shunt noise source spectral height (two-sided) in amperes²/Hz
$S_E$ = amplifier series noise source spectral height (two-sided) in volts²/Hz.

$I_2$, $I_3$, $\gamma_1$, and $\gamma_2$ are functions only of the shapes of the input optical pulses and the equalized repeater output pulses, where the length of a time slot has been scaled out. These functions are defined in eqs. (23) and (34) of Part I.

Formulas (1) and (2) neglect dark current and assume perfect modulation (received optical pulses completely on or off). We shall investigate deviations from these idealizations later in the paper. For silicon detectors and bit rates above a few megabits per second, these idealizations are reasonable approximations.

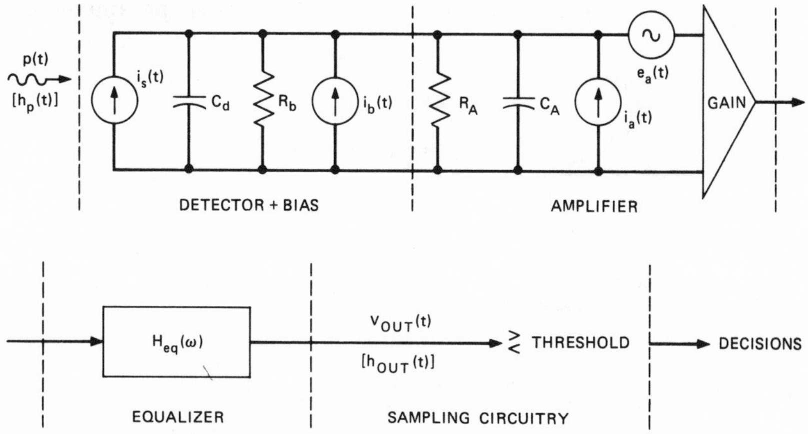

Fig. 1—Receiver.

## III. A TYPICAL OPTICAL REPEATER

Consider the following practical optical repeater, operating at a bit rate of $2.5 \times 10^7$ bits per second and an error rate of $10^{-9}$. The detector is a silicon device with excess noise exponent $x = 0.5$, quantum efficiency 75 percent, dark current before avalanche gain of 100 picoamperes, and an operating wavelength of 8500 angstroms. The front-end amplifier is a field-effect transistor in a common-source configuration. The total shunt capacitance across the detector is 10 pF. The detector biasing resistor is 1 megohm. The amplifier input resistance is 1 megohm. The amplifier shunt-current noise-source spectral height is equal to the thermal noise of a 1-megohm resistor. The amplifier series-voltage noise-source spectral height is equal to the thermal noise of a conductance with a value equal to the transistor transconductance, $g_m$, which is 5000 micromhos. The received optical pulses are half-duty-cycle rectangular pulses. The desired equalized output pulse is a raised cosine pulse [see Part I, eq. (25)] with parameter $\beta = 1$.

We must first calculate the value of $Q$ which depends only upon the desired error rate. From Part I, Fig. 21, we see that for an error rate of $10^{-9}$, $Q = 6$.

Next we must obtain the constants $I_2$, $I_3$, $\gamma_1$, and $\gamma_2$. These depend only upon the input optical pulse shape and the equalized output pulse shape. From (23) and (34) of Part I we obtain

$$I_2 = 0.804046, \qquad I_3 = 0.071966, \qquad \gamma_1 = 21.4106, \qquad \gamma_2 = 1.25424. \tag{3}$$

Using the above data we obtain the thermal noise parameter $Z$ as follows:

$$Z = \left\{ \frac{\overset{T}{4 \times 10^{-8}}}{(\underset{e}{1.6 \times 10^{-19}})^2} \left[ 8.28 \overset{2k\theta}{10^{-21}} \left( 10^{-6} + 10^{-6} + \frac{4 \times 10^{-12}}{5 \times 10^{-3}} \right) \overset{I_2}{0.804046} \right] + \frac{(2\pi \times 10^{-11})^2 \left( \frac{8.28 \times 10^{-21}}{5 \times 10^{-3}} \right) (\overset{I_3}{0.071966})}{(1.6 \times 10^{-19})^2 (4 \times 10^{-8})} \right\} = 4.8027 \times 10^5. \quad (4)$$

From the data we have $\hbar\Omega/\eta = 3.117 \times 10^{-19}$ joules.

We obtain from (1), at unity internal gain (no avalanche), $p_{\text{required}} = 3.25 \times 10^{-8}$ watts $= -44.89$ dBm (no gain).

We obtain from (2), at optimal avalanche gain, $p_{\text{required}} = 1.6409 \times 10^{-9}$ watts $= -57.85$ dBm, $G_{\text{optimal}} = 56.89$.

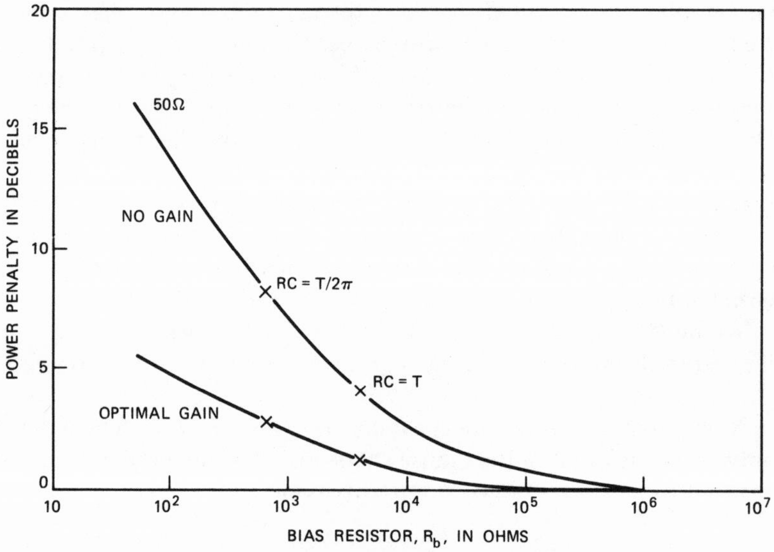


Fig. 2—Required power penalty vs $R_b$.

We therefore observe that optimal avalanche gain buys a 13-dB reduction in required optical power in this example. Before proceeding, we can check the validity of neglecting dark current. The average number of primary photoelectrons produced by the signal per pulse interval $T$ is the required optical power multiplied by $\eta T/\hbar\Omega$. When shot noise is important (with avalanche gain) this number is 210 primary signal counts per interval $T$. The number of dark current counts per interval $T$ is the dark current in amperes multiplied by $T/e$, which in this example is 25 primary dark current counts. Thus, the shot noise due to the dark current is about 10 percent of the signal shot noise. It is therefore a reasonable approximation to neglect this dark current noise. In Section VI we shall calculate precisely the effect of dark current upon the required optical power.

## IV. VARYING THE PARAMETERS

In this section, we shall calculate the effect of varying parameter values used in the example of Section III.

### 4.1 *Biasing Resistor Value*

It was pointed out in Part I that the biasing resistor $R_b$ should be sufficiently large so that the amplifier series noise source $S_E$ dominates in the expression for $Z$ of (1a). This was in fact the case in the example of Section III. We can calculate the penalty in required optical power for using a smaller biasing resistor. This penalty is plotted in Fig. 2 in dB with zero dB being the penalty associated with an infinitely large biasing resistor. The exact penalty of Fig. 2 is applicable with the other relevant parameters (which make up $Z$) given in the example above. However, the qualitative conclusions are that significantly more optical power is needed if one adheres to the "$RC = T$" design rather than the "large $R$" (high-impedance) design, in the absence of avalanche gain. Figure 3 shows how the optimal avalanche gain varies when $R_b$ is changed. The qualitative conclusion is that the "$RC = T$" design requires significantly more avalanche gain that the "large $R$" (high-impedance) design. It should be pointed out that, for lower bit rates and/or a smaller capacitance $C_T$, the improvement associated with use of a large $R_b$ rather than a value to keep $R_bC_T = T$ is more pronounced.

### 4.2 *Desired Error Rate*

As mentioned before, the error rate is coupled to the parameter $Q$ in (1) and (2). Figures 4a and 4b show plots of the variation in the re-

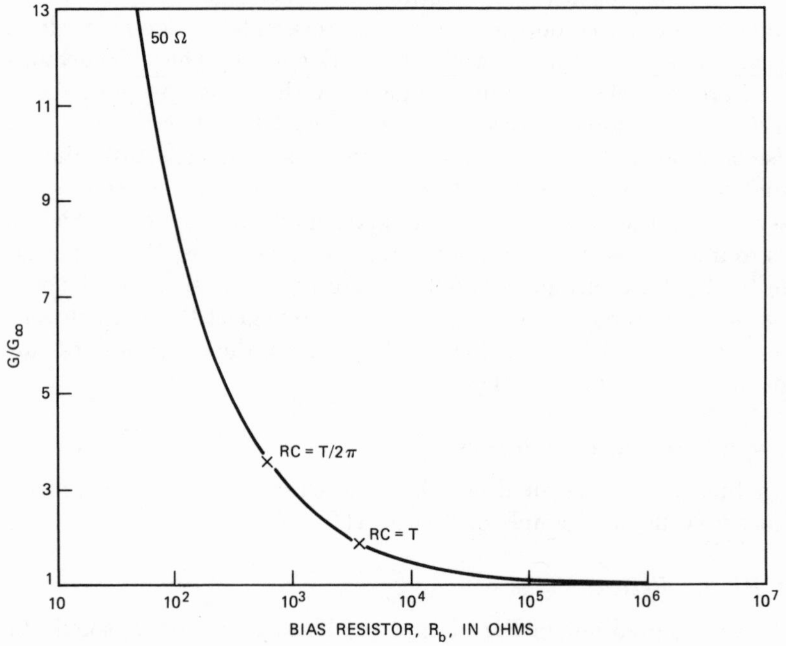


Fig. 3—Optimal gain penalty vs $R_b$, $G_\infty$ = optimal gain at $R_b = \infty$.

quired power in dB with the desired error rate without gain and with optimal gain. The absolute power in dBm is only applicable to the example of Section III above. However, the difference in required power in dB between any two error rates is applicable in general, as should be apparent from (1) and (2), provided a silicon detector ($x = 0.5$) is being used.

### 4.3 *Bit Rate* ($1/T$)

As mentioned before, the pulse spacing $T$ is scaled out of $I_2$, $I_3$, $\gamma_1$, and $\gamma_2$. These numbers depend only upon the input and output pulse *shapes* (e.g., half-duty-cycle rectangular input pulse, raised-cosine equalized output pulse). Therefore, the effect of the parameter $T$ is explicitly given in (1) and (2) without any hidden dependencies. (This of course assumes that the input pulse shape is not limited by dispersion in the transmission medium and can therefore be held to a half-duty-cycle rectangle.) If we assume that the high-impedance design is being used and that this dominance of the term proportional to $1/T$ in $Z$ of (1a) can be maintained as the bit rate is varied (becomes difficult

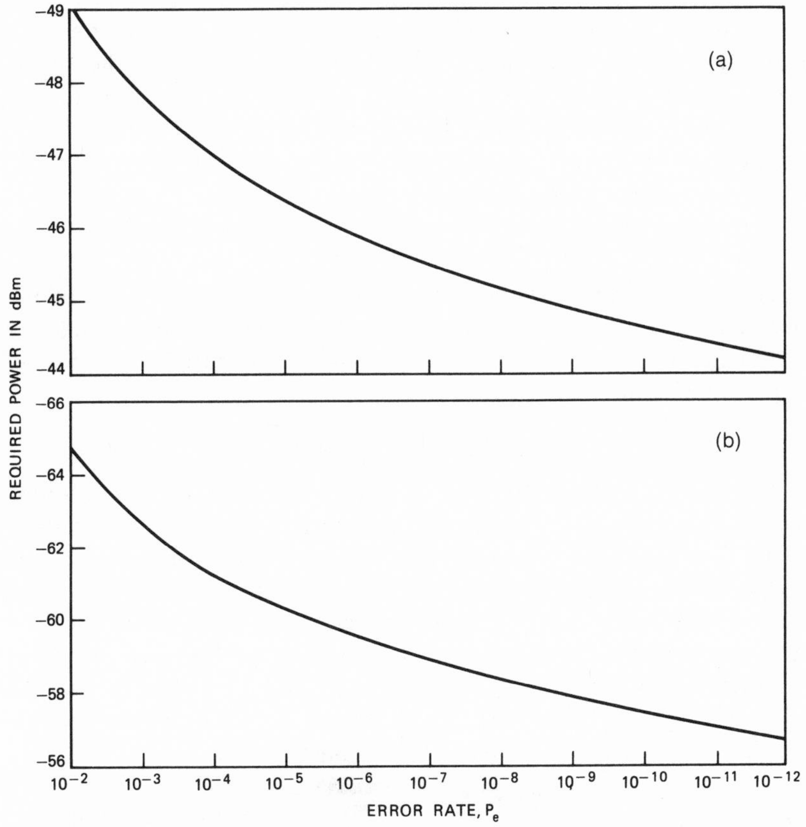


Fig. 4—(a) Required power vs error rate (no avalanche gain). (b) Required power vs error rate (optimal gain).

at low bit rates), then we have the following dependence of the required optical power upon the bit rate $1/T$ without gain and with optimal gain:

$$p_{\text{required}} \propto T^{-3/2} \quad \text{(no gain)} \quad \text{(4.5 dB/octave of bit rate)} \tag{5a}$$

$$p_{\text{required}} \propto T^{-7/6} \quad \text{(optimal silicon gain)} \quad \text{(3.5 dB/octave of bit rate)} \tag{5b}$$

$$G_{\text{optimal}} \propto T^{-1/3} \quad \text{(1 dB/octave of bit rate).}$$

One should be careful extrapolating (5a) and (5b) to very low bit rates. First, the shot noise is no longer negligible compared to the thermal noise at bit rates where the optimal gain is low. Thus (5a) loses validity at very low bit rates. Further, (5b) is only valid for optimal gains greater than unity. Near unity optimal gain, the silicon excess noise factor departs from $G^{.5}$. In addition, at low bit rates, dark current may not be negligible. It is reasonable to use (5a) and (5b) to extrapolate the results of the example in Section III to bit rates between 5 and 300 Mb/s.

## V. THE EFFECT OF IMPERFECT MODULATION

The above formulas (1) and (2) assume that there is perfect modulation. That is, it was assumed that each optical pulse is either completely on or completely off. In this section we shall investigate two versions of imperfect modulation.

### *Case 1: Pulses Not Completely Extinguished*

This case is illustrated in Fig. 5. In each time slot the optical pulse is either completely or partly on. The partly on pulse has the same shape as a completely on pulse, but has area $EXT$ times the area of a completely on pulse. This may correspond to an externally modulated mode-locked laser source. Thus the ratio of the power received when a sequence of all "off" pulses is transmitted to the power received when a sequence of all "on" pulses is transmitted is $EXT$. Using the results of Part I eqs. (23) and (34), we obtain the following power requirements which are modifications of (1) and (2) above:

$$p_{\text{required}} = \left(\frac{1 + EXT}{1 - EXT}\right) \frac{QZ^{\frac{1}{2}}}{GT} \frac{\hbar\Omega}{\eta}, \qquad \text{(Thermal Noise Dominates)} \quad (6)$$

$$p_{\text{required}} = \frac{1 + EXT}{2T} \left(\frac{Q}{1 - EXT}\right)^{(2+x)/(1+x)} \times \left[(Z)^{x/(2+2x)} (\gamma_1')^{x/(2+2x)} (\gamma_2')^{(2+x)/(1+x)}\right] \frac{\hbar\Omega}{\eta}, \qquad \text{(Optimal Gain)} \quad (7)$$

where defining from Part I (23) and (34)

$$I_6 = \Sigma_1 - (1 - EXT) I_1$$

we have

$$\gamma_1' = \frac{-(\Sigma_1 + I_6) + \sqrt{(\Sigma_1 + I_6)^2 + \dfrac{16(1+x)}{x^2} \Sigma_1 I_6}}{2 \Sigma_1 I_6}$$

$$\gamma_2' = \sqrt{1/\gamma_1' + \Sigma_1} + \sqrt{1/\gamma_1' + I_6}.$$

[Compare (6) and (7) to (1) and (2).]

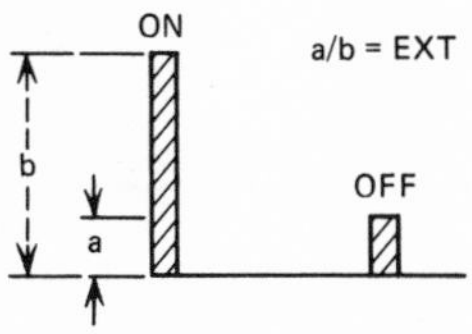


Fig. 5—Imperfect modulation, pulses not completely extinguished.

Using (1), (2), (7), and (8), we can calculate the extra required optical power due to a nonzero value of $EXT$ with and without avalanche gain. When avalanche gain is being used, this power penalty depends upon the input and output pulse shapes. We plot in Fig. 6 the power penalty vs $EXT$, assuming the pulse shapes of the example in Section III above for the avalanche gain case.

*Case 2: Pulses on a Pedestal*

This case is illustrated in Fig. 7. The received optical pulses arrive on a pedestal, which may correspond to inability to completely extinguish the light from a modulated source which is not in a pulsing (mode-locked) condition. We set the ratio of average received optical power when all pulses are "off" to average received optical power when all

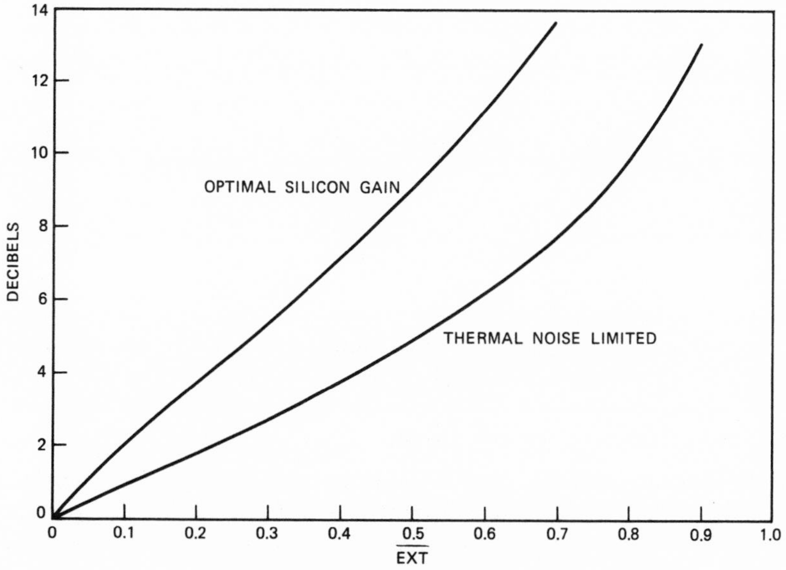


Fig. 6—$EXT$ penalty (dB) vs $EXT$.

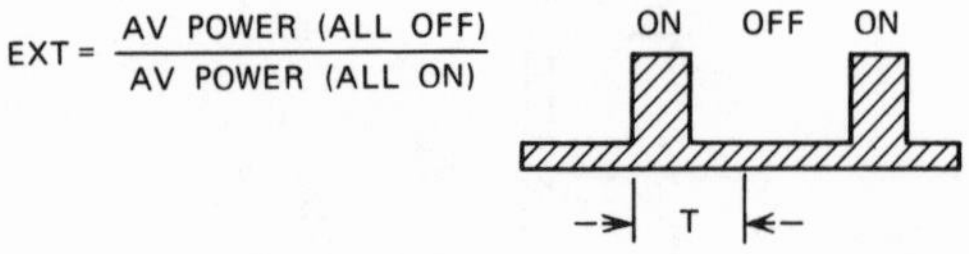


Fig. 7—Imperfect modulation, pulses on pedestal.

pulses are "on" to be $EXT$ in analogy to Case 1 above. This ratio will remain fixed if the pulse changes in propagation from transmitter to receiver. Using the results of Part I we obtain the following formulas for the required optical power:

$$p_{\text{required}} = \frac{1+EXT}{1-EXT}\frac{QZ^{\frac{1}{2}}}{GT}\frac{\hbar\Omega}{\eta}, \qquad \text{(Thermal Noise Dominates)} \qquad (8)$$

$$p_{\text{required}} = \frac{1+EXT}{1-EXT}\frac{(Q)^{(2+x)/(1+x)}}{2T} \times \left[(Z)^{x/(2+2x)}(\gamma_1'')^{x/(2+2x)}(\gamma_2'')^{(2+x)/(1+x)}\right]\frac{\hbar\Omega}{\eta}, \qquad \text{(Optimal Gain)} \qquad (9)$$

where defining from Part I (23) and (34)

$$\Sigma_1' = \Sigma_1 + \left(\frac{EXT}{1-EXT}\right) I_2$$

$$I_7 = \Sigma_1 - I_1 + \left(\frac{EXT}{1-EXT}\right) I_2$$

we have

$$\gamma_1'' = \frac{-(\Sigma_1' + I_7) + \sqrt{(\Sigma_1' + I_7)^2 + \frac{16(1+x)}{x^2}(\Sigma_1')I_7}}{2(\Sigma_1')I_7}$$

$$\gamma_2'' = \sqrt{1/\gamma_1'' + \Sigma_1'} + \sqrt{1/\gamma_1'' + I_7}.$$

Once again we can use (1), (2), (8), and (9) to calculate the penalty for nonzero extinction. This penalty is plotted in Fig. 8 vs $EXT$ where we assume the input and output pulse shapes of the example in Section III when there is optimal avalanche gain.

## VI. THE EFFECT OF DARK CURRENT

In order to allow for dark current, we must solve the following set of simultaneous equations which treat the dark current as an equivalent pedestal-type nonzero extinction. (When thermal noise dominates, dark current is either negligible or its shot noise can be added trivially to the amplifier parallel current noise source $S_I$.)

$$p_{\text{required}} = \frac{Q^{(2+x)/(1+x)}}{2T} (Z)^{x/(2+2x)} (\gamma_1''')^{x/(2+2x)} (\gamma_2''')^{(2+x)/(1+x)} \frac{\hbar\Omega}{\eta},$$

(At optimal avalanche gain) (10)

where defining from Part I (23) and (34)

$$\Sigma_1'' = \Sigma_1 + \delta I_2$$
$$I_8 = \Sigma_1 - I_1 + \delta I_2$$

we have

$$\gamma_1''' = \frac{-(\Sigma_1'' + I_8) + \sqrt{(\Sigma_1'' + I_8)^2 + \dfrac{16(1+x)}{x^2} \Sigma_1'' I_8}}{2 \Sigma_1'' I_8}$$

$$\gamma_2''' = \sqrt{1/\gamma_1''' + \Sigma_1''} + \sqrt{1/\gamma_1''' + I_8}$$

$$i_d = (2p_{\text{required}}) \frac{\eta e \delta}{\hbar\Omega}, \tag{11}$$

where $i_d$ = primary dark current in amperes.

There are various ways to solve (10) and (11) simultaneously. One way is to solve (10) first with $\delta = 0$ for $p_{\text{required}}$. Then one can solve

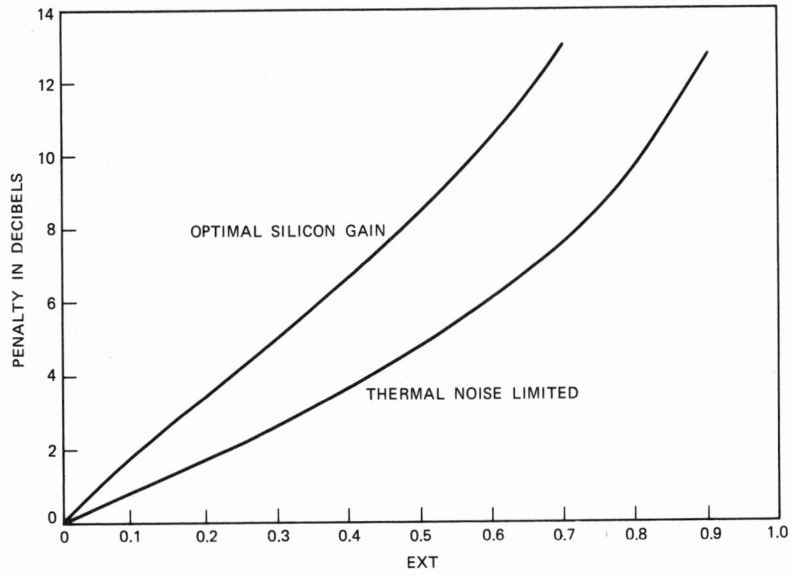


Fig. 8—Power penalty vs $EXT$.

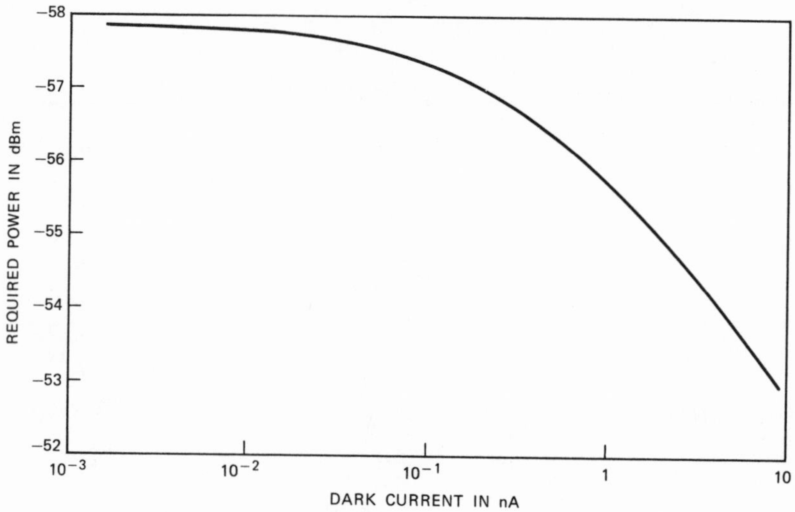


Fig. 9—Required power vs dark current.

(11) for a new value of $\delta$. One then resolves (10) and then (11), etc.–repeating the iterations until satisfactory convergence is obtained. Figure 9 shows a plot of the required power in dBm for the example in Section III vs dark current in nanoamperes. We see that a dark current of 100 picoamperes results in an optical power requirement which is about 0.5 dB more than that which would be required with zero dark current. Thus it was reasonable to neglect dark current when calculating the required power in Section III. Dark current will result in even less of a penalty at higher bit rates. Although the curve of Fig. 9 is applied to the specific example of Section III, it is apparent in general that, at bit rates above a few megabits per second and with primary dark currents less than 0.1 nanoampere, dark current will have a small effect upon the required optical power.

Part IV

# QUANTUM COMMUNICATION THEORY AFTER 1971

# Editor's Comments on Papers 17 Through 21



The resolution of the problem of defining a quantum measurement in sufficient generality to base a theory of statistical inference was resolved in the work of Alexander Holevo, beginning in the early seventies and culminating in his brilliant "Statistical Decision Theory for Quantum Systems" in 1973 (Paper 17). It placed in a mathematical context of vast generality previously partially understood notions of approximate measurement of noncommuting observables and use of adjunct apparatus, which had been adumbrated in the previously cited work of Arthurs and Kelly, Gordon and Louisell, Personick, and in Yuen, Kennedy, and Lax [1] and others.

One might be led to this required generalization in the following way. For commuting measurements, represented by their common projection-valued measure (p.v.m.) $M(\cdot)$[2, p. 249], the average risk assumes the form $R(M) = Tr\int \mathscr{F}(a)M(da)$, where $\mathscr{F}(a) = E_\Omega\{\int W(\theta, a)\rho(\theta)\}$: the optimum quantum measurement is represented by that projection-valued measure $\hat{M}(\cdot)$ that achieves the minimum (Bayes) risk. It is readily shown that the set of all projection-valued measures is not convex, a convenient property to have for an optimization problem.

One might then be led (as one sometimes is led in optimal control theory) to consider a larger convex set, which includes projection-valued measures. One might then perform the optimization over this set. It turns out the desired set is the set of "positive (or probability) operator measures" (p.o.m.'s). Give a measurable space $(U, \mathcal{B})$, a p.o.m. $X(\cdot)$ maps the Borel sets $\mathcal{B}$ of $U$ into the algebra $\mathcal{B}(\mathcal{H})$ of all bounded operators on $\mathcal{H}$ such that (1) $X(B) \geq 0$ for any $B \in \mathcal{B}$ and (2) if $\{B_i\}$ is a partition of $U$, $\Sigma_i X(B_i) = I$, the identity on $\mathcal{H}$ (weak convergence). (If, as usual, the complex field underlies $\mathcal{H}$, (i) implies that $X(B)$ is self-adjoint for any $B \in \mathcal{B}$.) The optimization problem now becomes more tractable, although still very difficult; e.g., the Lagrange duality theory [3, p. 224] can be applied to obtain necessary and sufficient conditions but explicit solutions are rare. Holevo offered the first example [4] that showed that a p.o.m. could produce a smaller Bayes risk than a p.v.m.

For the concept of a p.o.m. to be useful, however, it must have a realization: this was in effect provided by a theorem due to Naimark that asserted that every p.o.m. had an extension as a p.v.m. on a larger Hilbert space, which could be taken as a cross-product of an adjunct Hilbert space and the given Hilbert space and hence was physically interpretable as the adjoining of an adjunct apparatus and (commuting) measurement on the combined systems. More precisely, slightly rephrasing Proposition 3.1 in Holevo's article, for every p.o.m. $X(\cdot)$ there exists a Hilbert space $\mathcal{H}_0$, a pure state (density operator) $\rho_0$, and a p.v.m. $E(\cdot)$ in $\mathcal{H} \otimes \mathcal{H}_0$ such that

$$Tr\{\rho \cdot X(B)\} = Tr\{\rho \otimes \rho_0 \cdot E(B)\}$$

for any Borel set $B$. That is, "measuring" $X(\cdot)$ is statistically identical to measuring $E(\cdot)$. Such a triple, $(\mathcal{H}_0, \rho_0, E)$ is termed a *realization* of $X(\cdot)$.*

A special type of p.o.m., called a "p.o.m. with a base ($\mu$)," has the form $X(B) = \int_B P(u)\mu(da)$ where $P(u) = E_{\phi(u)}$, a projection onto the subspace spanned by $\phi(u)$, a member of an "over-complete" family of vectors. Thus in the Dirac notation, for example, the relation

$$X(B) \equiv \int_B |\alpha >< \alpha|\, d^2\alpha \quad (d^2\alpha \equiv d\alpha_R\, d\alpha_1, \quad \alpha \equiv \alpha_R + i\alpha_I)$$

where $|\alpha>$ is a characteristic function of the annihilation operator

* Holevo [4] discusses the underlying "quantum logic" that replaces the Boolean algebra of the classical (Kolmogoroff) probability theory.

**a** associated with the harmonic oscillator, defines a p.o.m. that is particularly useful in quantum optics [6].

The basic notions of this generalized quantum measurement are discussed in Sections 2 and 3 of Holevo's article. Note that Proposition 3.2 gives still another plausible reason to introduce p.o.m.'s. Section 4 considers the special case of a finite number of decisions—i.e., $M$-ary detection—for a "quality function" $Q$ and establishes existence under rather general conditions on $Q$. Application of Lagrange duality theory gives a necessary and sufficient condition for the optimal generalized quantum measurement $\hat{X}(\cdot)$ that does not generally provide an explicit solution for $\hat{X}(\cdot)$. (See also Yuen's thesis [7], Yuen, Kennedy, and Lax [1], and Holevo [8], especially Theorem 4.) Holevo concludes this section with a specific example in which a p.o.m. achieves an average risk strictly less than that achievable by any p.v.m.

Section 5 introduces the general case treated in Sections 6–9, namely, establishing the form and minimizing the average risk

$$R(X) = Tr \int_U \mathcal{F}(u)X(du)$$

over all p.o.m. Section 6 establishes the required integration theory for p.o.m.'s and Section 7 gives conditions for the existence of an optimal generalized quantum measurement. Section 8 discusses the special commutative case. Section 9 establishes necessary and sufficient conditions for optimal measurements.

The remainder of Holevo's paper specializes in the important case of Gaussian states. We elide this material in favor of Holevo's "Some Statistical Problems for Quantum Gaussian States," another masterful contribution. After a concise referencing of earlier work on the estimation problem (Section I), the author reviews briefly (Section II) the important technique of treating a finite number of quantized modes of an electromagnetic field with a finite dimensional real vector space $Z$ on which is defined a skew-symmetric bilinear form $\{\cdot,\cdot\}$—a "symplectic space." For each $z \in Z$, $R(Z)$ is a self-adjoint operator, called a "canonical observable," satisfying the canonical commutation relation (CCR) $[R(Z), R(W)] = i\{z, w\}$. "Gaussian states" (density operators, $\rho$) have the characteristic function $E\{\exp iR(z)\} = Tr\{\rho \exp iR(z)\}$ of the form $\exp[i\theta(z) - \frac{1}{2}\langle z, z\rangle]$ where $\theta(z) = E\{R(z)\}$ is the "mean value" and $\langle z, w\rangle = E\{[R(z) - \theta(2)]\circ[R(w) - \theta(w)]\}$, where $T\circ S = \frac{1}{2}(TS + ST)$, is the "correlation function" of the state.

The important concept of "wide-sense canonical measurements" is defined in Section III in terms of "operator moments." A condition, imposed by the CCR, is given for their existence; if met, an operator characteristic function defines a generalized quantum measurement (p.o.m.) termed "(strictly) canonical", and Holevo cites its realization. The p.o.m. is a "p.o.m. with a base" associated with a family of coherent states. (An adumbrative special case of this result had been given by Personick [9].) Though terse, this section unifies remarkably a large number of ideas.

In Sections V–VII, optimal quantum measurements are found for the following problem. For a fixed correlation function, the mean value is assumed to be of the form $\theta(z) = \alpha_1\theta^1(z) + \ldots + \alpha_m\theta^m(z)$, where the $\{\alpha_i\}$ are jointly Gaussian, zero mean random variables and the $\{\theta^i(z)\}$ are linear in $Z$. The average risk, with a weighting matrix $[g^{ik}]$ corresponding to a quadratic loss function, is minimized. The problem is solved—in the se e of necessary and sufficient conditions obtainable from Lagrange duality theory—by first finding the optimal measurement over the class of canonical measurements and then showing no improvement in average risk is possible over all p.o.m.

Holevo's ideas had an immediate effect on other researchers, of course, and not unexpectedly, their novelty caused some initial difficulties. For example, one fact apparently was not always properly accounted for: that the realization $(\mathcal{H}_0, \rho_0, E)$ of a p.o.m. $X(\cdot)$ in fact depends on the specific p.o.m. $X(\cdot)$—in particular the Hilbert space $\mathcal{H}_0$ itself depends on $X(\cdot)$ [10, p. 124]. Thus any optimization problem formulated on the extended space would seem in general quite complicated.

Paper 20, "Optimum Testing of Multiple Hypotheses in Quantum Detection Theory" by Horace Yuen, Robert Kennedy, and Melvin Lax also reviews from the authors' vantage point the development of the idea of quantum measurement and the formulation of the $M$-ary quantum detection problem. Some simplifications are made in the paper's body for accessibility; necessary and sufficient conditions (Theorem I) are established and discussed interestingly. Application is made (Section V) to $M$-ary communication of orthogonal and simplex signals (in the absence of thermal noise and any bandwidth restraint), where it is shown that capacity becomes infinite as $M \to \infty$. That is, "quantum noise" in itself does not limit capacity. Asymptotically the optical receiver is realized by photon counters in each mode, and the optimal receiver, under broad conditions, is better "by 3 dB" over the homodyne receiver.

The $M$-ary detection problem has also been considered by Belavkin [14] who gives further references to parallel work in the USSR.

The next paper in this collection is "Noncommuting Observables in Quantum Detection and Estimation Theory" by Carl Helstrom and Robert Kennedy (Paper 19). The paper begins (Section I) with the authors' brief review of the development of the concept of quantum measurement and introduces the detection problem (Section II), reviewing Helstrom and Liu's earlier finding that the Bayes risk is independent of the time of measurement for a quantum system with conservative dynamics and pointing out known cases where any p.o.m. cannot decrease the Bayes risk below that achieved by a p.v.m. on the original system. The authors next consider the estimation problem (Section III) and derive Cramer–Rao bounds; the formulation is bothersome for the reason mentioned in the paragraph above, but the type of bounds derived turn out not to depend on the realization at all (p. 00, Eq. 43). The estimation of the in-phase and quadrature amplitudes of a laser signal in thermal noise (Section IV) and the estimation of delay and Doppler are studied (Section V)—the classical range–Doppler ambiguity function puts in an appearance. A curious interplay between "right" and "symmetrized" logarithmic derivatives and risk function suggests that further study would be rewarding. In their concise conclusion, the authors do state: "The minimization of the Bayes cost can, therefore, be carried out over the class of such noncommuting operators [i.e, p.o.m.] in $\mathcal{H}_s$, which having been found can be extended [to a p.v.m.] in an encompassing Hilbert space $\mathcal{H}_s \otimes \mathcal{H}_A$. . . ." The finding of such extensions and their physical realizations are open problems. A closely related paper is [11]; see also [12] and [13].

A central theme in communication theory—and more broadly still, in electrical engineering—is signal filtering; many of the most celebrated results in these fields concern filtering theory. It is natural to seek extensions that incorporate quantum mechanical restraints on measurements, or observations; it is also natural to extend the quantum estimation theory developed thus far to include dynamics and repeated measurements. To our knowledge, there exists no quantum measurement theory for "continuous observation" and indeed it would seem to require a complete revamping of the nonrelativistic theory of measurement that has been relied on thus far [15, p. v]. There also appear to be fundamental problems concerning whether the observation uniquely defines the system's quantum state subsequent to measurement [16].

These problems were avoided in the formulation of the filtering problem in the final paper, "Quantum-Mechanical Linear Filtering of Random Signal Sequences" by John Baras, R. O. Harger, and Young Park, by assuming discrete time measurements, independent in a prescribed sense. Also, a scalar signal process was assumed, allowing more explicit characterization of solutions; the more interesting (and difficult) vector signal case will appear in Baras and Harger [17] (see also Belavkin [18]). The filter weights and optimum contemporary quantum measurement are determined by applying the projection theorem. (In the vector case Lagrange duality theory gives a necessary and sufficient condition.) From the practical viewpoint it is important to know when the optimal quantum measurement does not depend on past optimal measurements and on time in an important structural way. When the signal sequence is pairwise Gaussian and when a certain linearity condition holds, the problem separates in the sense that the optimal quantum measurement is the optimal measurement without regard to past data, and the past and present observations are processed classically. In an optical communication application, with a coherent wave received with thermal noise in a single mode cavity and the signal sequence satisfying a linear recursion, the optimal estimate can be calculated efficiently using a homodyne detector—whose structure does not depend on time—followed by classical Kalman–Bucy filtering. [Similar results in the vector signal case were obtained with certain diagonality assumptions. The "separation" is impeded by the fact that the optimal quantum estimate of $(CX)$, where $C$ is a constant matrix, is not generally $C$ times the optimal measurement of $X$.] In an example in a different direction, a one-step memory signal sequence, it was shown that the optimal observable differs from the optimal observable disregarding the past and a recursive calculation for it and the optimal quantum measurement is given. The filtering of signals has also been considered in the quantum mechanical setting by Belavkin [18] and by Grishanin and Stratonovich [19].

The area of quantum communication theory is a rich area for further study. Obviously one can attempt to carry over many topics of classical statistical inference: these are especially interesting to optical communication theory when one keeps a careful eye on physics. As mentioned severally, there is a paucity of realizations of mathematically characterized solutions and, of course, no known "synthesis" procedure of even fair generality. When the optimal measurement is not related to photon counting (the number operator $\mathbf{aa}^{+}$), or homodyning [the operator $(\mathbf{a} + \mathbf{a}^{+})/2$] or heterodyning (the operator $\mathbf{a}$), original invention is required. In this regard Dolinar's thesis work [20] is interesting; he utilizes a feedback arrangement with a local oscillator signal that is modulated by an ideal photon counter output and shows that specific optimal quantum measurements can be realized in binary, coherent state detection and discusses generalizations. It is possible to realize a quantum measurement corresponding to a p.o.m. as the limit of a sequence of measurements corresponding to a sequence of p.v.m.'s [21] and such measurements have been discussed by Chan [22] in the context of optical communication.

As mentioned at the outset, quantum communication theory has concentrated on the receiver and generally ignored the optimum selection of transmitted quantum state. Yuen [23], however, has considered this problem and established that "under suitable conditions" significant performance improvement can be obtained using "generalized coherent states." Again, the relation to physics is interesting, and Yuen discusses how such states might be generated by stimulated two-photon emissions and degenerate parametric amplification. (Note that the Bayes risk is linear in the density operator $\rho$, a positive definite, unit trace operator on $\mathscr{H}$.)

## REFERENCES


1. Yuen, H. P., R. S. Kennedy, and M. Lax. "On Optimal Quantum Receivers for Digital Signal Detection." *IEEE Proc.* **58**:1770–1773 (Oct. 1970).
2. Jauch, J. M. *Foundations of Quantum Mechanics*. Reading, Mass." Addison-Wesley, 1968.
3. Luenberger, D. G. *Optimization by Vector Space Methods*. New York: John Wiley & Sons, 1969.
4. Holevo, A. S. "Statistical Problems in Quantum Physics." *Proc. Second Japan–USSR Symp. Prob. Theo. Kyotv.* **1**:22–40 (1972). Also in *Lecture Notes in Mathematics*, vol. 330. Providence: Amer. Math. Soc., pp. 104–119.
5. Holevo, A. S. "An Analog of the Theory of Statistical Decisions in Noncommutative Probability Theory." *Moscow Math. Soc. Trans.* **26**:133–149 (1972).
6. Glauber, R. J. "Coherent and Incoherent States of the Radiation Field." *Phys. Rev.* **131**:2766–2788 (1963).
7. Yuen, H. P. H., "Communication theory of quantum systems." Cambridge, Mass.: MIT RLE Tech. Rep. 482 (Aug. 1971).
8. Holevo, A. S. "The Theory of Statistical Decisions on an Operator Algebra." *Sov. Math. Dokl.* **15**(5):1276–1281 (1974).
9. Personick, S. D. "An Image-band Interpretation of Optical Heterodyne Noise." *Bell Syst. Tech. J.* **50**:213–216 (1971).
10. Akhiezer, N. I., and I. M. Glazman. *Theory of Linear Operators in Hilbert Space*. New York: Frederick Ungar, 1963.
11. Helstrom, C. W. "Cramer–Rao Inequalities for Operator-Valued Measures in Quantum Mechanics." *Int. J. Theor. Phys.* **8**(5):361–376 (1973).

12. Helstrom, C. W. "Estimation of a Displacement Parameter of a Quantum System." *Int. J. Theor. Phys.* **11**(6):357–378 (1974).
13. Helstrom, C. W. "Simultaneous Measurement from the Standpoint of Quantum Estimation Theory." *Found. Phys.* **4**(4): 453–463 (1974).
14. Belavkin, V. P. "Optimal Multiple Quantum Statistical Hypothesis Testing." *Stochastics* **1**:315–345 (1975).
15. Davies, E. B., and J. T. Lewis. "An Operational Approach to Quantum Probability." *Commun. Math. Phys.* **17**:239–260 (1970).
16. Baras, J. S., and R. O. Harger. "Quantum Mechanical Linear Filtering of Vector Signal Processes," to appear in *IEEE Trans. Inf. Theory*, (Nov. 1977).
17. Baras, J. S., and R. O. Harger. "Multiparameter Filtering with Quantum Measurements." *Proc. 1975 Conf. Inform. Sci. and Syst.*, Johns Hopkins University (April 1975), pp. 178–184.
18. Belavkin, V. P. "Optimal Linear Randomized Filtration of Quantum Boom Signals." *Probl. Control and Inf. Theory* **3**(1):47–62 (1974).
19. Grishanin, B. A., and R. L. Stratonovich. "Optimal Filtering of Quantum Variables for Quadratic Quality Function" [in Russian]. *Probl. Peredach. Inf.* **6**:15–25 (1970).
20. Dolinar, S. J. Jr. "A Class of Optical Receivers Using Optical Feedback." *Proc. 1975 Conf. Inform. Sci. and Syst.*, Johns Hopkins University (April 1975), p. 193.
21. Benioff, P. A. "Operator Valued Measures in Quantum Mechanics: Finite and Infinite Processes." *J. Math. Phys.* **13**(2):231–242 (1972).
22. Chan, V. W. S. "Two Realizations of Quantum Measurements Characterized by General Operator-Valued Measures." *IEEE Proc. Intern. Symp. Inf. Theory*, South Bend, Ind. (1974), p. 4.
23. Yuen, H. P. "Generalized Coherent States and Optical Communications." *Proc. 1975 Conf. Inform. Sci. and Syst.*, Johns Hopkins University (April 1975), pp. 171–177.

# 17



Reprinted from pp. 337–366, 368–372, 392–394 of *J. Multivar. Anal.* **3**(4):337–394 (1973)

## Statistical Decision Theory for Quantum Systems

A. S. HOLEVO

*Steklov Mathematical Institute, Academy of Sciences of the U.S.S.R., Moscow, U.S.S.R.*

*Communicated by Yu. A. Rozanov*

Quantum statistical decision theory arises in connection with applied problems of optimal detection and processing of quantum signals. In this paper we give a systematic treatment of this theory, based on operator-valued measures. We study the existence problem for optimal measurements and give sufficient and necessary conditions for optimality. The notion of the maximum likelihood measurement is introduced and investigated. The general theory is then applied to the case of Gaussian (quasifree) states of Bose systems, for which optimal measurements of the mean value are found.

### 1. INTRODUCTION

In the classical formulation of statistical decision theory due to Wald [1] one has the parameter space $\Theta$, the space of observations $\Omega$, the family $\{P_\theta; \theta \in \Theta\}$ of probability distributions on $\Omega$ and the space of decisions $U$. The problem is to find the optimal, in a sense, decision procedure, i.e., the rule of choosing a decision $u \in U$ given an observation $\omega \in \Omega$.

In many cases $\Omega$ may be considered as the phase space of a physical system $\mathscr{A}$ and the distribution $P_\theta$ may then be regarded as giving the statistical description of the state of $\mathscr{A}$.

In the present paper we consider the following modification of the picture just described. We still have the parameter space $\Theta$ and the space of decisions $U$, but now to each $\theta \in \Theta$ corresponds the state $\boldsymbol{\rho}_\theta$ of a *quantum* system $\mathscr{A}$ (yet to be defined). A decision is to be chosen on the basis of a measurement over $\mathscr{A}$, and the problem is to find the optimal quantum measurement.

The need for such generalization of the classical statistical theory arose in

Received July, 1973.

AMS 1970 subject classifications: Primary 62C10, 62H99, 82A15; Secondary 46G10, 49A35.

Key words and phrases: Quantum measurement, positive operator-valued measure, Gaussian state, coherent state, canonical measurement.

connection with the study of communication systems based on quantum-mechanical devices such as lasers, etc. In this context $\theta$ is the signal transmitted, $\rho_\theta$ is the state of quantum electromagnetic field $\mathscr{A}$ at the input of the receiver and the optimal measurement corresponds to the optimal reception of the signal in quantum noise.

Although in some cases valuable recommendations may be obtained on the basis of classical methods of statistics (see, for example, [2–4]), in general the problem of optimal quantum reception does not reduce to a problem of classical statistical theory (the reason for this is, in brief, that quantum system cannot be described in terms of phase space). This point of view was clearly expressed in the work of Helstrom [5], and a number of interesting results in this direction was obtained (in particular, quantum analogues of Rao–Cramer inequality). For the survey of these results as well as for physical motivation of the theory we refer the reader to [6] and [17].

All this work was based substantially on the assumption, generally accepted in quantum theory [7, 24], according to which quantum measurements are described by projection-valued measures (orthogonal resolutions of the identity) in underlying Hilbert space. However, there have been indications in physical literature [15, 31] that some statistical measuring procedures would require rather nonorthogonal resolutions for their description. It seems that the first explicit use of general resolutions of the identity or positive operator-valued measures (p.o.m.) in quantum theory was made by Davies and Lewis [8], in connection with the problem of repeated measurements. On the other hand, the need for this generalization in quantum statistical and information theory has been suggested and substantiated [9–11]. As noticed in [9], p.o.m. in a way correspond to randomized decision procedures in classical theory, making the set of all measurements convex, but there is no full analogy; the systematic use of p.o.m. not only allows unified treatment for different problems about optimal measurements and gives to them useful geometric interpretation but also makes possible further progress in the solution of multivariate problems. The fact is that the optimal measurement for these problems is often described by a non-orthogonal resolution of the identity.

In this work we give a detailed account of results summarized partly in earlier works [11–14]. The theory is by no means complete, and we do not attempt here to achieve the natural degree of generality. The exposition is destined for a probabilist familiar with the operator theory in Hilbert space. In Section 2 we give a brief survey of the "noncommutative probability theory" needed in the sequel. Section 3 is devoted to quantum measurements and their description in terms of p.o.m. In Section 4 the problem of optimal quantum measurements is treated for the finite number of decisions. Mathematically this case is much simpler than the general one and may serve as a motivation for the latter. Results for the general case are briefly discussed in Section 5, and in Sections 6–9 the case where the space of decisions is a region in finite-dimensional space is considered. Here we study the existence problem and give conditions for optimality, using integration theory for p.o.m. developed in Section 6. Applications to the important "Gaussian" case are given in Section 10–14.

## 2. Quantum States and Observables

It is accepted in quantum theory [24, 25] that the set of events (or propositions) related to a given quantum system may be described as a family $\mathfrak{E}$ of all orthogonal projections in a separable Hilbert space $H$ (corresponding to the quantum system under consideration). Thus in contrast to the classical probability theory where events form a Boolean $\sigma$-algebra, here the set of events is a complete lattice with the orthocomplementation [25].

A *state* is a function $\boldsymbol{\rho}$ on $\mathfrak{E}$ possessing the usual properties of probability

(1) $\boldsymbol{\rho}(E) \geqslant 0,\ E \in \mathfrak{E}$;

(2) $\sum_i \boldsymbol{\rho}(E_i) = 1$ for any countable orthogonal resolution of identity $\{E_i\}$ in $H$ (i.e., $E_iE_j = \delta_{ij}E_i$ and $\sum_i E_i = \mathrm{I}$ in the sense of weak (or strong) operator topology, where I is the identity operator in $H$).

Gleason's theorem [24] asserts that each state on $\mathfrak{E}$ is of the form

$$\boldsymbol{\rho}(E) = \operatorname{Tr} \rho E \qquad \text{(Tr denotes trace)},$$

where $\rho$ is nonnegative trace-class operator in $H$ such that $\operatorname{Tr} \rho = 1$. It is called the *density operator* (d.o.) of the state $\boldsymbol{\rho}$.

In particular, let $\varphi$ be a unit vector of $H$ and $E_\varphi$ be the projection on $\varphi$. Then

$$\boldsymbol{\rho}(E) = (\varphi, E\varphi) = \operatorname{Tr} E_\varphi E \tag{2.1}$$

is a state on $\mathfrak{E}$. This state is *pure*, which means that it cannot be represented as a convex combination of some other states.

By analogy with the classical probability theory one may introduce observables (the term corresponding to classical "random variables") with finite number of values $\{x_i\}$ as

$$X = \sum_i x_i E_i ,$$

where $\{E_i\}$ is a finite orthogonal resolution of the identity in $H$; some more elaborate consideration [24] lead one to define an *observable* as an arbitrary self-adjoint operator in $H$

$$X = \int xE(dx), \tag{2.2}$$

where $E(dx)$ is a projection-valued measure on $(R, \mathscr{B}(R))$, called the spectral measure of the operator $X$ (here $(R, \mathscr{B}(R))$ is the real line with the $\sigma$-algebra of Borel sets).

If $\rho$ is a state then the relation

$$P_X(B) = \rho(E(B)), \qquad B \in \mathscr{B}(R),$$

defines a probability distribution (p.d.) on $(R, \mathscr{B}(R))$ which is called the p.d. of the observable $X$ with respect to (w.r.t.) the state $\rho$. Thus, the mean value of $X$, if it exists, is equal to $\int x P_X(dx)$. If $X$ is bounded then the last is equal to $\mathrm{Tr}\, \rho X$ and putting

$$\rho(X) = \mathrm{Tr}\, \rho X$$

we obtain the extension of the state $\rho$ to a linear functional on the algebra of all bounded operators $\mathfrak{B}(H)$ possessing the following properties:

(1) $\rho(X^*X) \geqslant 0$;

(2) if $X_1 \geqslant \cdots \geqslant X_n \geqslant \cdots$ is a decreasing sequence of Hermitean operators weakly converging to zero then

$$\lim_n \rho(X_n) = 0;$$

(3) $\rho(\mathrm{I}) = 1$.

In quantum theory one usually starts with $\mathfrak{B}(H)$ and state is defined as a functional on $\mathfrak{B}(H)$, satisfying conditions of the type (1)–(3). More generally, one can consider states on a *von Neumann algebra* $\mathfrak{B} \subset \mathfrak{B}(H)$. Let $M$ be arbitrary set of bounded operators in $H$ and denote by $M'$ the collection of all bounded operators commuting with all operators in $M$, i.e., the commutant of $M$. The set $M$ is called a von Neumann algebra if $(M')' = M$. In general, $(M')'$ is the least weakly closed self-adjoint algebra of bounded operators which contains $M$ and the identity operator I (see [19, p. 41]). It is called the von Neumann algebra generated by $M$.

If we start with an arbitrary von Neumann algebra $\mathfrak{B}$ we would obtain a statistical theory which includes both the "pure quantum case" ($\mathfrak{B} = \mathfrak{B}(H)$) and the classical case (when $\mathfrak{B}$ is Abelian). Moreover, one could cover more complicated cases arising in the study of infinite systems such as fields (in this connection see [9, 15]). In this paper we concentrate our attention on pure quantum case, though occasionally we shall make use of some von Neumann subalgebras of $\mathfrak{B}(H)$. We now want to discuss the noncommutative version of conditional expectation [26–28]. Let $\mathfrak{B}$ be a von Neumann subalgebra of $\mathfrak{B}(H)$, and $\sigma$ be a state on $\mathfrak{B}(H)$. The linear mapping $\epsilon$ from $\mathfrak{B}(H)$ onto $\mathfrak{B}$ is called *the conditional expectation* onto $\mathfrak{B}$ w.r.t. $\sigma$ [26] if

(1) $\epsilon$ is a projection ($\epsilon \circ \epsilon = \epsilon$) of norm one;

(2) for any uniformly bounded sequence $\{X_n\}$, weakly converging to zero, $\epsilon(X_n)$ weakly converges to zero;

(3) $\sigma(\epsilon(X)) = \sigma(X)$, $X \in \mathfrak{B}(H)$.

As shown by Tomiyama [26] every projection of norm one possesses the properties

(4) $\epsilon(X^*X) \geqslant 0$;

(5) $\epsilon(YXZ) = Y\epsilon(X)Z$, $X \in \mathfrak{B}(H)$, $Y, Z \in \mathfrak{B}$.

The necessary and sufficient condition for the existence of conditional expectation was given by Takesaki [26] for faithful states. Here we consider an important example (cf. [27]).

If there are two quantum systems, described by Hilbert spaces $H$ and $H_0$, then the totality of these two systems is described by the tensor product $H \otimes H_0$ (see e.g. [19, p. 21]). For any two operators $X \in \mathfrak{B}(H)$, $Y \in \mathfrak{B}(H_0)$ the operator $X \otimes Y \in \mathfrak{B}(H \otimes H_0)$ is defined and $\mathfrak{B}(H \otimes H_0)$ is just the von Neumann algebra generated by such operators [19, p. 26]. If $\rho$ is a state on $\mathfrak{B}(H)$, $\rho_0$ is a state on $\mathfrak{B}(H_0)$ then there is a unique state $\rho \otimes \rho_0$ on $\mathfrak{B}(H \otimes H_0)$ such that

$$(\rho \otimes \rho_0)(X \otimes Y) = \rho(X)\, \rho_0(Y),$$

and it is called a product state.

Fix $\rho_0$, and put

$$\epsilon(X \otimes Y) = X\rho_0(Y). \tag{2.3}$$

Then $\epsilon$ is uniquely extended to the linear mapping from $\mathfrak{B}(H \otimes H_0)$ onto $\mathfrak{B}(H)$ satisfying the conditions (1)–(3) for any state $\sigma$ of the form

$$\sigma = \rho \otimes \rho_0\,, \tag{2.4}$$

where $\rho$ is an arbitrary state on $\mathfrak{B}(H)$. Thus, $\epsilon$ is the conditional expectation onto $\mathfrak{B}(H)$ w.r.t. any state $\sigma$ of the form (2.4).

Let $\Sigma = \{\sigma\}$ be a family of states; we say that a von Neumann subalgebra $\mathfrak{B}$ is *sufficient* for $\Sigma$ if there exists a conditional expectation onto $\mathfrak{B}$ w.r.t. any $\sigma \in \Sigma$ which does not depend on $\sigma$. In particular we see that the subalgebra $\mathfrak{B}(H) \subset \mathfrak{B}(H \otimes H_0)$ is sufficient for the family of states of the form (2.4), where $\rho_0$ is a fixed state on $\mathfrak{B}(H_0)$ and $\rho$ is an arbitrary state on $\mathfrak{B}(H)$.

## 3. Quantum Measurements

Let $(U, \mathscr{B})$ be a measurable space. We call *U-measurement* any $\mathfrak{B}(H)$-valued function $X(B)$, $B \in \mathscr{B}$, such that

(1) $X(B) \geqslant 0$, $B \in \mathscr{B}$;

(2) if $U = \sum_i B_i$ is a decomposition of $U$ into countable sum of disjoint measurable sets $B_i$, then

$$\sum_i X(B_i) = I,$$

where the series converges weakly in $H$.

In other words, $\mathbf{X} = \{X(\cdot)\}$ is a resolution of the identity [18] or a positive operator-valued measure on $(U, \mathscr{B})$, such that $X(U) = I$. In condition (2) weak convergence may be replaced by strong convergence [22].

If $\mathbf{X}$ is an orthogonal resolution, i.e., $BC = \varnothing$ implies $X(B)\,X(C) = 0$ then $\mathbf{X}$ is projection-valued [22] and in this case the measurement is called *simple*. Particularly, the relation (2.2) shows that there is a one-to-one correspondence between observables and simple $R$-measurements.

Probability distribution of the measurement $\mathbf{X}$ w.r.t. the state $\rho$ is defined by the relation

$$P_{\mathbf{X}}(B) = \rho(X(B)), \qquad B \in \mathscr{B}.$$

Suppose that a simple measurement $\mathbf{E} = \{E(\cdot)\}$ is performed over the composite system which consists of two independent systems described by Hilbert spaces $H$ and $H_0$. If $\rho_0$ is a fixed state on $\mathfrak{B}(H_0)$ and $\epsilon$ is defined by (2.3) then the relation

$$X(B) = \epsilon(E(B)), \qquad B \in \mathscr{B}$$

defines a measurement $\mathbf{X}$ (which is, in general, not simple). For any state $\rho$ on $\mathfrak{B}(H)$ we have

$$P_{\mathbf{X}}(B) \equiv P_{\mathbf{E}}(B),$$

where $P_{\mathbf{X}}$ is the p.d. of $\mathbf{X}$ w.r.t. $\rho$ and $P_{\mathbf{E}}$ is the p.d. of $\mathbf{E}$ w.r.t. $\rho \otimes \rho_0$. In this sense the description of measuring procedure in terms of p.o.m. $\mathbf{X}$ and that of a triple $(H_0, \rho_0, \mathbf{E})$ are "statistically equivalent." On the other hand, as shown in [8], each *sequential* measuring procedure can be also "statistically equivalently" described by a p.o.m. (It should be noted, however, that the state of the system after actual measuring procedure cannot be reconstructed from $\mathbf{X}$).

The question arises whether arbitrary measurement may be implemented by a measuring procedure involving only simple measurements. The next proposition [11] gives an answer to this question.

PROPOSITION 3.1. *Let* $\mathbf{X}$ *be a* $U$*-measurement. Then there exist a Hilbert space* $H_0$, *a pure state* $\rho_0$ *on* $\mathfrak{B}(H_0)$ *and a simple* $U$*-measurement* $\mathbf{E}$ *in* $H \otimes H_0$ *such that*

$$\rho(X(B)) = (\rho \otimes \rho_0)(E(B)), \qquad B \in \mathscr{B},$$

*for any state* $\rho$ *on* $\mathfrak{B}(H)$, *or equivalently*

$$X(B) = \epsilon(E(B)), \qquad B \in \mathscr{B}.$$

Any such triple $(H_0, \rho_0, \mathbf{E})$ is called a *realization* of the measurement $\mathbf{X}$.

*Proof.* By Naimark's theorem [18, p. 393] one can construct an orthogonal resolution of identity $\tilde{\mathbf{E}}$ in a Hilbert space $\tilde{H} \supset H$ such that

$$X(B) = \tilde{P}\tilde{E}(B)\tilde{P}, \qquad B \in \mathscr{B}, \tag{3.1}$$

where $\tilde{P}$ is the orthogonal projection from $\tilde{H}$ onto $H$.

Evidently, one can embed $\tilde{H}$ in the direct orthogonal sum

$$\mathscr{H} = \bigoplus_{i \in \mathrm{I}} H^i,$$

where each $H^i$ is isomorphic with $H$, and, moreover, $H^{i_0} = H$ for some $i_0 \in \mathrm{I}$. Let $\hat{\mathbf{E}}$ be an arbitrary orthogonal resolution of the identity in $\mathscr{H} \ominus \tilde{H}$. Then $E(B) = \tilde{E}(B) + \hat{E}(B)$ is an orthogonal resolution of the identity in $\mathscr{H}$ such that

$$X(B) = PE(B)P, \qquad B \in \mathscr{B}, \tag{3.2}$$

where $P$ is the projection from $\mathscr{H}$ onto $H$.

Denote by $H_0 = L^2(\mathrm{I})$ the Hilbert space of complex functions $(c_i)_{i \in \mathrm{I}}$ satisfying $\sum_i |c_i|^2 < \infty$, and put $\varphi_0 = (\delta_{ii_0})_{i \in \mathrm{I}}$, where $\delta_{ij}$ is Kronecker's delta. Then $\mathscr{H}$ may be identified with $H \otimes H_0$ in such a way that $H$ corresponds to $H \otimes \varphi_0$ [19, p. 22]. Every $Z \in \mathfrak{B}(H \otimes H_0)$ is then represented by the block operator $(Z_{ij})$ in $\mathscr{H}$ $(Z_{ij} \in \mathfrak{B}(H))$ in such a way that $X \otimes Y$ is represented by $(y_{ij}X)$, where $(y_{ij})$ is the matrix of the operator $Y$ in canonical basis of $L^2(\mathrm{I})$. Since $(\varphi_0, Y_{\varphi 0}) = y_{i_0 i_0}$ then we see by (2.3) that

$$\epsilon(X \otimes Y) = P(X \otimes Y)P;$$

hence,

$$\epsilon(Z) = PZP, \qquad Z \in \mathfrak{B}(H \otimes H_0).$$

From (3.2) it follows that $X(B) = \epsilon(E(B))$, and the result is proved.

The introduction of p.o.m. is plausible in many respects. Denote by $\Sigma$ the set of all states on $\mathfrak{B}(H)$ and by $S$ the set of all p.d. on $(U, \mathscr{B})$. Then the relation

$$K\rho(B) = \rho(X(B)), \qquad B \in \mathscr{B}, \tag{3.3}$$

defines the affine mapping $K$ from $\Sigma$ to $S$. This means that for any $\lambda$, $0 \leqslant \lambda \leqslant 1$,

$$K(\lambda\rho_1 + (1 - \lambda)\,\rho_2) = \lambda K(\rho_1) + (1 - \lambda)\,K(\rho_2). \tag{3.4}$$

As pointed out in [29], such mappings describe "decodings" in the theory of quantum channels. We now show that (3.3) establishes a one-to-one correspondence between decodings and measurements.

PROPOSITION 3.2. *Let $K$ be an affine mapping from $\Sigma$ to $S$. Then there exists a (unique) measurement* $\mathbf{X}$ *for which* (3.3) *holds.*

We shall denote by $\mathfrak{T}_h$ the set of all Hermitean trace-class operators in $H$ (see [20, 21]). The norm of an operator $\sigma$ in $\mathfrak{T}_h$ will be denoted by $|\sigma|$.

*Proof.* Fix $B \in \mathscr{B}$ and consider a functional

$$F_B(\rho) = K\boldsymbol{\rho}(B),$$

defined on the set of all density operators. It extends uniquely to the linear positive functional on the real ordered Banach space $\mathfrak{T}_h$, satisfying

$$|F_B(\sigma)| \leqslant |\sigma|.$$

Then by a slight modification of the representation theorem [20, p. 47] there is a Hermitean nonnegative operator $X(B)$, such that

$$F_B(\sigma) = \operatorname{Tr} X(B)\sigma.$$

In particular,

$$K\boldsymbol{\rho}(B) = \operatorname{Tr} \rho X(B).$$

Let $U = \bigcup_i B_i$, where $B_i$ are disjoint. For any fixed $\boldsymbol{\rho} \in \Sigma$

$$1 = \sum_i K\boldsymbol{\rho}(B_i) = \sum_i \operatorname{Tr} \rho X(B).$$

Putting $\rho = E_\varphi$ we get

$$(\varphi, \varphi) = \sum_i (\varphi, X(B_i)\varphi),$$

from which it follows that $\sum_i X(B_i) = I$ in the weak sense.

In the next section we present the statistical decision theory for finite number of decisions. Let $U$ be a finite set. Then a $U$-measurement is a collection of nonnegative operators $\mathbf{X} = \{X_u; u \in U\}$ such that

$$\sum_u X_u = I. \tag{3.5}$$

If $\boldsymbol{\rho}$ is a state on $\mathfrak{B}(H)$ then the probability of getting a decision $u$ is equal to $\boldsymbol{\rho}(X_u)$.

It is instructive to discuss the classical case, when we have the space of observations $\Omega$ with a measure $\mu$. Then we have the Abelian von Neumann algebra $\mathfrak{B}$ in $H = L_\mu^2(\Omega)$, consisting of "multiplication operators" of the form

$$(X_f\varphi)(\omega) = f(\omega)\,\varphi(\omega), \qquad \varphi \in L_\mu^2(\Omega),$$

where $f$ is an essentially bounded measurable function on $(\Omega, \mu)$. Let $\{X_u\}$ be a family of nonnegative operators in $\mathfrak{B}$ satisfying (3.5), and let $P(u \mid \omega)$ be a function defining operator $X_u$. Then $P(u \mid \omega) \geqslant 0$, $\sum_u P(u \mid \omega) = 1$; if $\mathfrak{p}$ is a "state" (probability distribution) on $\mathfrak{B}$, defined by a density $\rho(\omega) = d\rho/d\mu$ then the probability of getting a decision $u$ is equal to

$$\mathfrak{p}(X_u) = \int P(u \mid \omega)\,\rho(\omega)\,\mu(d\omega).$$

Thus, $P(u \mid \omega)$ may be considered as the conditional probability of getting a decision $u$ given an observation $\omega \in \Omega$. We see that in classical statistics measurements introduced in the beginning of this section reduce to randomized decision procedures; simple measurements correspond to pure decision procedures.

Returning to the quantum case we may call a measurement $\mathbf{X} = \{X_u\}$ randomized if

$$X_u X_v = X_v X_u; \qquad u, v \in U.$$

For the general consideration of randomized measurements, see [9].

## 4. Optimal Quantum Measurements with Finite Number of Decisions

Let $\Theta = \{\theta\}$ be a finite set and $\{\mathfrak{p}_\theta; \theta \in \Theta\}$ a family of states on $\mathfrak{B}(H)$. Let $U = \{u\}$ be a finite set of decisions and $\mathbf{X} = \{X_u)$ be some $U$-measurement. Then the probability of choosing a decision $u$, given the parameter value $\theta$, is equal to

$$P_{\mathbf{X}}(u \mid \theta) = \mathfrak{p}_\theta(X_u). \tag{4.1}$$

Denote by $\mathscr{P}$ the set of all transition probabilities $\mathbf{P} = \{P(u \mid \theta); \theta \in \Theta, u \in U\}$ from $\Theta$ to $U$, and assume that a quality function $Q(\mathbf{P}), \mathbf{P} \in \mathscr{P}$ is prescribed. Then the problem is to find a measurement $\mathbf{X}$ which maximizes the function

$$Q(\mathbf{P}_{\mathbf{X}}), \qquad \mathbf{X} \in \mathfrak{X},$$

where $\mathfrak{X}$ is the set of all $U$-measurements.

The following quality functions are of the main interest. Let $\{\pi_\theta\}$ be some a priori distribution on $\Theta$ and $W_\theta(u)$; $\theta \in \Theta$, $u \in U$ be a loss function. Put $Q(\mathbf{P}) = -R(\mathbf{P})$, where

$$R(\mathbf{P}) = \sum_\theta \pi_\theta \sum_u W_\theta(u)\, P(u \mid \theta) \tag{4.2}$$

is Bayes risk. If there exists a measurement minimizing $R(\mathbf{P_X})$ then it is called an optimal Bayes measurement. Another important case is $Q(\mathbf{P}) = I(\mathbf{P})$, where

$$I(\mathbf{P}) = \sum_\theta \pi_\theta \sum_u P(u \mid \theta) \ln \Big(P(u \mid \theta)\Big/\sum_\lambda \pi_\lambda P(u \mid \lambda)\Big), \tag{4.3}$$

is Shannon's information. If in this case there exists a measurement maximizing $I(\mathbf{P_X})$ then we call it information-optimal. In the general case we speak of $Q$-optimal measurement.

Now we turn to the existence of the optimal measurement. For two $U$-measurements $\mathbf{X} = \{X_u\}$ and $\mathbf{Y} = \{Y_u\}$ and a number $\lambda$, $0 \leqslant \lambda \leqslant 1$ put

$$\lambda\mathbf{X} + (1 - \lambda)\mathbf{Y} = \{\lambda X_u + (1 - \lambda)\, Y_u\}.$$

Then $\mathfrak{X}$ is a convex set. We say that a sequence of measurements $\mathbf{X}^{(i)} = \{X_u^{(i)}\}$ converges to a measurement $\mathbf{X} = \{X_u\}$ if $X_u^{(i)} \to X^{(i)}$, $i \to \infty$, weakly for each $u \in U$. Since $X_u^{(i)}$ are in the unit ball of $\mathfrak{B}(H)$ which is weakly compact [18, p. 105] then $\mathfrak{X}$ is compact, i.e., any sequence of $U$-measurements contains a converging subsequence. Denote by $T$ the mapping from $\mathfrak{X}$ to $\mathscr{P}$ defined by (4.1).

The mapping $T$ is an affine continuous mapping from convex compact set $\mathfrak{X}$ to $\mathscr{P}$.

The continuity of $T$ follows from the next lemma (see [19, p. 38]).

LEMMA 4.1. *If the sequence of operators $\{X^{(i)}\}$ in the unit ball of $\mathfrak{B}(H)$ converges weakly to an operator $X$ then*

$$\lim_i \rho(X^{(i)}) = \rho(X)$$

*for each state $\rho$ on $\mathfrak{B}(H)$.*

PROPOSITION 4.1. *Let $Q(P)$ be upper semicontinuous on $\mathscr{P}$. Then the $Q$-optimal measurement exists. If, moreover, $Q(P)$ is a convex function on $\mathscr{P}$ then it assumes the maximum at an extremal point of $T(\mathfrak{X})$.*

For the definitions and results of convex analysis the reader may refer to [30] and [51].

*Proof.* The set $T(\mathfrak{X})$ is an affine continuous image of the convex compact set $\mathfrak{X}$. Therefore, $T(\mathfrak{X})$ is a convex compact subset of $\mathscr{P}$. Hence, the result follows [30, p. 273].

Now we give some optimality conditions [14].

THEOREM 4.1. *Let* $\mathbf{X} = \{X_u\}$ *be a* $Q$*-optimal measurement, and let* $Q$ *be differentiable at the point* $\mathbf{P} = \mathbf{P}_\mathbf{X}$. *Put*

$$F_u = \sum_\theta \rho_\theta(\partial Q/\partial P(u \mid \theta)) \mid_{\mathbf{P}=\mathbf{P}_\mathbf{X}} . \tag{4.4}$$

*Then the two equivalent conditions hold*

(1) $X_u(F_u - F_v) X_v = 0;\ u, v \in U;$

(2) *The operator* $\Lambda = \sum_u F_u X_u$ *is Hermitean and*

$$(F_u - \Lambda) X_u = 0, \qquad u \in U.$$

Notice that for Bayes risk

$$F_u = \sum_\theta \pi_\theta W_\theta(u)\, \rho_\theta \tag{4.5}$$

and for information

$$F_u = \sum_\theta \pi_\theta \ln \left[\left(P(u \mid \theta)\Big/\sum_\lambda \pi_\lambda P(u \mid \lambda)\right)\right] \rho_\theta .$$

*Proof.* Let $H_n = H \oplus \cdots \oplus H$ be the direct orthogonal sum of $n$ copies of the Hilbert space $H$ and $S = (s_{ij})_{i,j=1}^n$ be a unitary operator in $H_n$. Then it is easy to see that the relation

$$\tilde{X}_u = \sum_{ij} (X_i)^{1/2}\, s_{ui}^* s_{uj} (X_j)^{1/2}, \qquad u \in U, \tag{4.6}$$

defines a $U$-measurement $\tilde{\mathbf{X}} = \{\tilde{X}_u\}$. (The converse is also true: For any two $U$-measurements $\mathbf{X}, \tilde{\mathbf{X}}$ there exists a unitary operator $S = \{s_{ij}\}$, such that (4.6) holds [14].)

To prove (1) we fix $u, v \in U$ and consider the operator of "elementary rotation" $S_\epsilon$ with the matrix $(s_{ij})$ of the form

$$s_{ij} = \delta_{ij}\,; \qquad i, j \neq u, v,$$

$$\begin{pmatrix} s_{uu} & s_{uv} \\ s_{vu} & s_{vv} \end{pmatrix} = \exp \epsilon \begin{pmatrix} 0 & -A^* \\ A & 0 \end{pmatrix},$$

where $A$ is an arbitrary bounded operator in $H$, $\epsilon$-real number. Let $\mathbf{X}^\epsilon$ be the measurement, obtained from $\mathbf{X}$ through (4.6) with the operator $S_\epsilon$. Then we have for small $\epsilon$

$$P_{\mathbf{X}^\epsilon}(u \mid \theta) = P_{\mathbf{X}}(u \mid \theta) + \epsilon \operatorname{Re} \operatorname{Tr}(X_u)^{1/2} \rho_\theta (X_v)^{1/2} A + o(\epsilon),$$

$$P_{\mathbf{X}^\epsilon}(u \mid \theta) = P_{\mathbf{X}}(u \mid \theta) - \epsilon \operatorname{Re} \operatorname{Tr}(X_u)^{1/2} \rho_\theta (X_v)^{1/2} A + o(\epsilon),$$

$$P_{\mathbf{X}^\epsilon}(i \mid \theta) = P_{\mathbf{X}}(i \mid \theta); \qquad i \neq u, v,$$

hence,

$$Q(\mathbf{P}_{\mathbf{X}^\epsilon}) = Q(\mathbf{P}_{\mathbf{X}}) + \epsilon \operatorname{Re} \operatorname{Tr}(X_u)^{1/2} (F_u - F_v)(X_v)^{1/2} A + o(\epsilon).$$

Since $\mathbf{X}$ is optimal then

$$\operatorname{Re} \operatorname{Tr}(X_u)^{1/2}(F_u - F_v)(X_v)^{1/2} A = 0$$

for any bounded $A$, and (1) follows.

Summing (1) by $v \in U$ we obtain

$$X_u(F_u - \Lambda) = 0, \qquad u \in U,$$

and summing by $u \in U$ we get $\Lambda^* = \Lambda$. On the other hand, multiplying (2) by $X_v$ from the left we have $X_u F_u X_v = X_u \Lambda X_v = (X_v \Lambda X_u)^* = (X_v F_v X_u)^* = X_u F_v X_v$, hence the condition (1).

In the Bayesian case (4.2) there is a simple sufficient condition of optimality. In this case one must minimize

$$R(\mathbf{X}) = \operatorname{Tr} \sum_u F_u X_u, \tag{4.7}$$

where the $F_u$ are given by (4.5).

*Let* $\Lambda = \sum_u F_u X_u$ *be Hermitean and*

$$F_u \geqslant \Lambda, \qquad u \in U. \tag{4.8}$$

*Then* $\mathbf{X} = \{X_u\}$ *is a Bayes optimal measurement.*

*Proof.* For any other measurement $\tilde{\mathbf{X}} = \{\tilde{X}_u\}$

$$R(\tilde{\mathbf{X}}) = \operatorname{Tr} \sum F_u \tilde{X}_u \geqslant \operatorname{Tr} \Lambda \sum \tilde{X}_u = \operatorname{Tr} \Lambda = R(\mathbf{X}).$$

Conditions of this type were formulated in the paper of Yuen, Kennedy, and Lax [31] and independently by the author [11] in a more general case. Moreover, it was pointed out in [31] that these conditions are also necessary. We shall not discuss this result here because it will not be needed in the sequel.

One way of approaching the problem of optimal measurement is the reduction of the set of possible measurements. We say that a subset $\mathfrak{M}$ of $U$-measurements is *essential* if

$$\sup_{\mathbf{X}\in\mathfrak{M}} Q(\mathbf{P_X}) = \sup_{\mathbf{X}\in\mathfrak{X}} Q(\mathbf{P_X}).$$

Let $\mathfrak{B}$ be a von Neumann algebra sufficient for the family $\{\rho_\theta;\ \theta \in \Theta\}$ (see the end of Section 2), and denote by $\mathfrak{X}_\mathfrak{B}$ the subset of $U$-measurements $\mathbf{X} = \{X_u\}$ with the property

$$X_u \in \mathfrak{B}, \qquad u \in U.$$

*Then* $\mathfrak{X}_\mathfrak{B}$ *is essential.* Indeed for any $\mathbf{X} \in \mathfrak{X}$ the measurement $\epsilon(\mathbf{X}) = \{\epsilon(X_u)\}$ is such that $\rho_\theta(X_u) = \rho_\theta(\epsilon(X_u))$; hence,

$$Q(\mathbf{P_X}) = Q(\mathbf{P}_{\epsilon(\mathbf{X})}).$$

PROPOSITION 4.2. *Let* $\mathfrak{B}$ *be the von Neumann algebra generated by the family* $\{\rho_\theta;\ \theta \in \Theta\}$. *Then* $\mathfrak{B}$ *is sufficient and, hence,* $\mathfrak{X}_\mathfrak{B}$ *is essential.*

*Proof.* $\mathfrak{B}$ is generated by the family of trace-class operator; hence, the restriction of the trace to $\mathfrak{B}$ is semifinite and the main result of [26] says that there exists a linear mapping $\epsilon$ from $\mathfrak{B}(H)$ onto $\mathfrak{B}$ satisfying the properties (1) and (2) of the conditional expectation and such that

$$\operatorname{Tr} Y = \operatorname{Tr} \epsilon(Y)$$

for any trace-class operator $Y$. From (5) we have $\epsilon(\rho_\theta X) = \rho_\theta \epsilon(X)$ for $X \in \mathfrak{B}(H)$; hence,

$$\rho_\theta(X) = \rho_\theta(\epsilon(X));\ \theta \in \Theta,$$

which means that $\epsilon$ is an expectation w.r.t. any $\rho_\theta$, i.e., $\mathfrak{B}$ is sufficient for $\{\rho_\theta;\ \theta \in \Theta\}$.

If $Q$ is affine (Bayes problem) then $\mathfrak{X}_\mathfrak{B}$, where $\mathfrak{B}$ is the von Neumann algebra generated by the family $\{\rho_\theta - \rho_\lambda;\ \theta \in \Theta\}$, $\lambda$ fixed, is essential. We shall show this in Section 8 in a more general situation.

In some cases symmetry considerations may help with finding the optimal measurement. We assume for simplicity that $\Theta = U$. Let $G$ be a permutation group of $U$ and $g \to V_g$ a unitary representation of $G$ in $H$. We say that the family of states $\{\rho_u;\ u \in U\}$ is *invariant* if

$$\rho_{gu} = V_g \rho_u V_g^*, \qquad u \in U, \qquad g \in G.$$

Let the quality function be also invariant, i.e.,

$$Q(\{P(g\theta \mid gu)\}) = Q(\{P(\theta \mid u)\}).$$

We put

$$\mathbf{X}^{(g)} = \{V_g{}^* X_{gu} V_g\}$$

for each $U$-measurement $\mathbf{X}$. Evidently $\mathbf{X}^{(g)}$ is also a $U$-measurement. We say that a measurement $\mathbf{X}$ is *covariant* (cf. [32]) if $\mathbf{X}^{(g)} = \mathbf{X}$ for each $g \in G$. Denote by $\mathfrak{X}^G$ the (convex) subset of all covariant measurements.

PROPOSITION 4.3. *Let $Q$ be an invariant concave quality function. Then $\mathfrak{X}^G$ is an essential set of measurements.*

*Proof.* For each $\mathbf{X} \in \mathfrak{X}$ the relation

$$\bar{\mathbf{X}} = N^{-1} \sum_{g \in G} \mathbf{X}^{(g)},$$

where $N$ is number of elements in $G$, defines a covariant measurement. Since $Q$ is concave,

$$Q(\mathbf{P}_{\bar{\mathbf{X}}}) \geqslant N^{-1} \sum_g Q(\mathbf{P}_{\mathbf{X}^{(g)}}).$$

However,

$$P_{\mathbf{X}^{(g)}}(u \mid \theta) = \operatorname{Tr} \rho_\theta V_g{}^* X_{gu} V_g = \operatorname{Tr} \rho_{g\theta} X_{gu} = P_{\mathbf{X}}(gu \mid g\theta);$$

hence, by invariance of $Q$, we have $Q(\mathbf{P}_{\mathbf{X}^{(g)}}) = Q(\mathbf{P}_{\mathbf{X}})$ and

$$Q(\mathbf{P}_{\bar{\mathbf{X}}}) \geqslant Q(\mathbf{P}_{\mathbf{X}}),$$

which implies that $\mathfrak{X}^G$ is essential.

Assume that $gu_0 = u_0$, where $u_0$ is a fixed element of $G$, implies $g = e$, where $e$ is identity of $G$. Then for each $u \in U$ there is a unique $g_u \in G$ such that $u = g_u u_0$. Assume, moreover, that $\dim H = h < \infty$ and the representation $g \to V_g$ is irreducible. Then it is easy to describe all covariant measurements.

Each covariant measurement $\mathbf{X} = \{X_u\}$ is of the form

$$X_u = (h/N)\, V_{g_u} \rho V_{g_u}^* \tag{4.10}$$

where $\rho$ is a d.o. in $H$.

This follows directly from the definition of covariant measurement and the classical relation of group representation theory

$$N^{-1} \sum_g V_g \rho V_g{}^* = (\operatorname{Tr} \rho / h) \mathrm{I}. \tag{4.11}$$

Using these results we can give a complete solution of the problem in the case of invariant concave quality function $Q$.

THEOREM 4.2. *Let* $\{\rho_u;\, u \in U\}$ *be an invariant family of states,* $Q$ *an invariant concave differentiable quality function. Then the maximum of* $Q(\mathbf{P}_X)$ *is achieved on a covariant measurement of the form* (4.10), *where* $\rho$ *is a d.o. satisfying*

$$E\rho = \rho \tag{4.12}$$

*for a spectral projection* $E$ *of the operator* $F_{u_0}$.

*If* $Q$ *is affine then* $E$ *corresponds to the maximal eigenvalue* $\lambda$ *of* $F_{u_0}$ *and*

$$\max Q(\mathbf{P}_X) = \lambda h.$$

*Proof.* From the invariance conditions it follows that

$$F_{gu} = V_g F_u V_g{}^*,$$

where $F_u$ are defined by (4.4). By Proposition 4.3 we may restrict ourselves to measurements of the form (4.10). Using (4.11) we obtain

$$\Lambda = \sum_u F_u X_u = (h/N) \sum_g V_g F_{u_0} \rho V_g{}^* = \lambda I,$$

where $\lambda = \operatorname{Tr} F_{u_0}\rho$. From the condition (2) of Theorem 4.1 we get

$$F_{u_0}\rho = \lambda\rho;$$

hence, (4.12).

For affine $Q$ we have $Q(\mathbf{P}_X) = \operatorname{Tr} \Lambda = \lambda h$, and the last statement of the theorem follows.

EXAMPLE 4.1. Assume that the linearly polarized photon is observed [41, p. 110] and that the polarization angle is equal to

$$2\pi u/n; \qquad u = 0, \ldots, n-1$$

with equal probabilities $\pi_u = 1/n$. We shall find the optimal measurement of the polarization angle.

Let $H$ be the two-dimensional unitary space and $E_u$; $u = 0, \ldots, n-1$ be the projections on $n$ directions of polarization. Assume that

$$W_\theta(u) = 1 - \delta_{\theta u}.$$

Then we must minimize

$$R(\mathbf{X}) = n^{-1}\,\mathrm{Tr}\sum_{\theta\neq u}\sum E_\theta X_u \qquad (4.13)$$

over all measurements $\mathbf{X} = \{X_0,..., X_{n-1}\}$, or maximize

$$\mathrm{Tr}\sum_u E_u X_u = \mathrm{Tr}\sum_u E_u - \mathrm{Tr}\sum_{u\neq\theta}\sum E_\theta X_u .$$

Let $V$ be the rotation of $H$ with the angle $2\pi/n$. Then $\{V^K; K = 0,..., n-1\}$ is an irreducible representation of the cyclic group of $n$th order and the function $\mathrm{Tr}\sum_u E_u X_u$ satisfies the conditions of Theorem 4.2. Hence, the optimum is achieved on the covariant measurement

$$X_u = (2/n)\, V^u E_0 (V^u)^* = (2/n)\, E_u .$$

The minimum of $R(\mathbf{X})$ is equal to $1 - (2/n)$.

Denote by $\hat{\mathfrak{X}}$ the set of all simple measurements. Then, even in the case $n = 3$ we have [9]

$$\min_{\mathbf{X}\in\mathfrak{X}} R(\mathbf{X}) < \min_{\mathbf{X}\in\hat{\mathfrak{X}}} R(\mathbf{X}) = (2 - \sqrt{3}/2)/3.$$

## 5. Optimal Quantum Measurements in the General Case—Introduction

Here we discuss briefly the results which will be obtained rigorously in Sections 6–9. To be definite we restrict ourselves to the Bayesian problem, though many results of Section 4 for arbitrary quality function $Q$ are transferable to this more general situation.

Let $\Theta$ be an arbitrary parameter space and $\{\rho_\theta; \theta \in \Theta\}$ a family of states on $\mathfrak{B} = \mathfrak{B}(H)$; let $(U, \mathscr{B})$ be a measurable space of decisions and $W_\theta(u)$; $\theta \in \Theta$, $u \in U$ a loss function. The role of decision procedures is now played by $U$-measurements. The risk corresponding to the parameter value $\theta$ and the measurement $\mathbf{X}$ is

$$R_\theta(\mathbf{X}) = \int_U W_\theta(u)\, \rho_\theta(X(du)).$$

If $\pi(d\theta)$ is a prior distribution on $\Theta$ then Bayes risk is given by

$$R(\mathbf{X}) = \int_\Theta R_\theta(\mathbf{X})\, \pi(d\theta).$$

A formal computation shows that

$$R(\mathbf{X}) = \operatorname{Tr} \int_U F(u)\, X(du), \tag{5.1}$$

where $F(u) = \int W_\theta(u)\, \rho_\theta \pi(d\theta)$.

Thus, formally, the problem of the Bayes optimal measurement reduces to the minimization of the affine functional of type (5.1) over the convex set $\mathfrak{X}$ of all $U$-measurements.

Of course, first we must give some rigorous meaning to the expressions of type (5.1) and to the formal computations that have led to it. Integration with respect to an operator-valued measure was developed in several papers [33–37], but none of these works seem to be directly applicable in our case. The reason for this is that we need to integrate rather restricted class of functions with respect to an arbitrary operator-valued measure, while in the papers just mentioned somewhat opposite problem of constructing the natural class of integrable functions for restricted classes of operator-valued measures was considered. In Section 6 we propose a Riemann–Stieltjes type integral for the case where $U$ is a region in finite dimensional case, which is quite sufficient for our purpose. This construction may be considerably generalized, but this will be done elsewhere.

In Section 7 we give conditions under which the functional (5.1) achieves the minimum on $\mathfrak{X}$. In Section 9 we give the optimality conditions analogous to the results of Section 4 for the finite case. In particular we show that for the measurement $\mathbf{X}$ to be optimal it is necessary that the operator $\Lambda = \int F(u)\, X(du)$ be Hermitean and satisfy a condition of the type

$$(F(u) - \Lambda)\, X(du) = 0,$$

and sufficient that $F(u) \geqslant \Lambda$, $u \in U$.

We discuss also "maximum likelihood measurements." In classical statistics the maximum likelihood estimate of the parameter $\theta = (\theta_1, \ldots, \theta_n)$ may be regarded formally as a Bayes estimate corresponding to the a priori distribution $\pi(d\theta) = d\theta_1 \cdots d\theta_n$ and the loss function $W_\theta(u) = -\delta(\theta - u)$, where $\delta$ is delta-function (see, e.g., [17, p. 360]). Thus, the maximum likelihood measurement could be defined formally as a measurement maximizing the functional

$$\operatorname{Tr} \int_\Theta \rho_\theta X(d\theta). \tag{5.2}$$

If $\Theta$ is bounded then this may be taken for the rigorous definition but otherwise the expression (5.2) is divergent. At the end of Section 9 we show how to avoid this difficulty and give the condition for a measurement to be one of a maximum likelihood type.

## 6. Riemann–Stieltjes Type Integral with Respect to an Operator-Valued Measure

We adopt the following notations. Let $\mathfrak{B}(\mathfrak{B}_+)$ be the set of all bounded (Hermitean nonnegative) operators in $H$. The norm of $T$ in $\mathfrak{B}$ will be denoted by $\| T \|$. By $\mathfrak{T}$, $\mathfrak{T}_h$, $\mathfrak{T}_+$ we denote, respectively, the set of all trace-class, Hermitean trace-class, nonnegative trace-class operators in $H$. The norm in $\mathfrak{T}$ will be denoted $| T |$. We put $| T | = (T^*T)^{1/2}$, $T \circ S = \frac{1}{2}(TS + ST)$. By $\mathfrak{S}$ we shall denote the set of all Hilbert–Schmidt operators in $H$.

Let $\mathbf{U}$ be a real $n$-dimensional space. We denote by $\mathscr{A}_0$ the class of all bounded $n$-dimensional intervals in $\mathbf{U}$ (it is supposed that a coordinate system is chosen in $\mathbf{U}$). Let $X(B)$, $B \in \mathscr{A}_0$ be a $\mathfrak{B}$-valued function, satisfying the conditions

(1) $X(B) \geqslant 0$; $B \in \mathscr{A}_0$;

(2) if $B = \bigcup_i B_i$ is a partition of an interval into finite sum of intervals, then

$$X(B) = \sum_i X(B_i).$$

Consider a $\mathfrak{T}_h$-valued function $F(u)$, $u \in \mathbf{U}$. Fix a $B \in \mathscr{A}_0$ and let $\tau = \{B_i\}$ be an arbitrary finite partition of $B$ and $\delta_\tau$ be the size of the partition, i.e., maximum of diameters of $B_i$. Introduce an integral sum

$$\sigma_\tau = \sum_i F(u_i)\, X(B_i),$$

where $u_i \in B_i$. Evidently $\sigma_\tau \in \mathfrak{T}$. If the limit of this expression exists in $\mathfrak{T}$ as $\delta_\tau \to 0$ (and does not depend on the choice of $u_i \in B_i$) then $F$ is called *left integrable* with respect to $X(du)$ over $B$ and the limit, called the *left integral*, is denoted by

$$\int_B F(u)\, X(du).$$

The right integral is similarly defined. It is evident that right integrability is equivalent with left integrability and

$$\int_B X(du)\, F(u) = \left[\int_B F(u)\, X(du)\right]^*.$$

We say that $F$ is trace-integrable if there exists

$$\lim_{\delta_\tau \to 0} \operatorname{Tr} \sigma_\tau = \langle F, \mathbf{X} \rangle_B$$

We now introduce an important class of $\mathfrak{T}_h$-valued functions. We say that *$F(u)$, $u \in U$ is of class $\mathfrak{C}$ if for any $B \in \mathscr{A}_0$ there is an operator $K \in \mathfrak{T}_h$ and a real-valued function $\omega(\delta)$, $\delta \in R$, such that $\omega(\delta) \to 0$, as $\delta \to 0$* and

$$-K\omega(| u - v |) \leqslant F(u) - F(v) \leqslant K\omega(| u - v |), \qquad u, v \in B. \tag{6.1}$$

The class $\mathfrak{C}$ is a linear space; an example of a function from $\mathfrak{C}$ is given by

$$F(u) = \sum_{i=1}^{N} K_i g_i(u), \tag{6.2}$$

where $K_i \in \mathfrak{T}_h$ and $g_i(u)$ are continuous real-valued functions. Moreover, each function of $\mathfrak{C}$ may be in a sense approximated by functions of the form (6.2).

LEMMA 6.1. *Let $F$ satisfy* (6.1). *Then for each $\epsilon > 0$ there is $F_\epsilon$ of the form* (6.2) *such that*

$$-\epsilon K \leqslant F(u) - F_\epsilon(u) \leqslant \epsilon K, \qquad u \in B.$$

*Proof.* To simplify notations we assume that $B = [0, 1]^n$. Fix an integer $M$ and introduce following continuous functions of one variable $t$, $0 \leqslant t \leqslant 1$.

$$h_m(t) = \max\{0, 1 - M \mid t - m/M \mid\}; \qquad m = 0,..., M.$$

We have

$$\sum_{m=0}^{M} h_m(t) \equiv 1,$$

$h_m(t) = 0$ for $\mid t - m/M \mid > 1/M$. Put $\mathbf{m} = (m_1 ,..., m_n)$ and

$$h_{\mathbf{m}}(u) = h_{m_1}(u_1) \cdots h_{m_n}(u_n).$$

Then $h_{\mathbf{m}}$ are nonnegative continuous functions on $B$ such that

$$\sum_{\mathbf{m}} h_{\mathbf{m}}(u) \equiv 1, \tag{6.3}$$

$$h_{\mathbf{m}}(u) = 0 \qquad \text{for} \quad \mid u - u_{\mathbf{m}} \mid > \sqrt{n}\, M^{-1}, \tag{6.4}$$

where $u_{\mathbf{m}} = (m_1/M,..., m_n/M)$. Using (6.3) we get

$$F(u) - \sum_{\mathbf{m}} h_{\mathbf{m}}(u) F(u_{\mathbf{m}}) = \sum_{\mathbf{m}} h_{\mathbf{m}}(u)(F(u) - F(u_{\mathbf{m}})),$$

therefore, by (6.4) and (6.1)

$$-K\omega(\sqrt{n}\, M^{-1}) \leqslant F(u) - \sum_{\mathbf{m}} h_{\mathbf{m}}(u) F(u_{\mathbf{m}}) \leqslant K\omega(\sqrt{n}\, M^{-1}).$$

Thus, we can take for $F_\epsilon$ the function $\sum_{\mathbf{m}} h_{\mathbf{m}}(u) F(u_{\mathbf{m}})$ with $M$ large enough

THEOREM 6.1. *Each function of the class $\mathfrak{C}$ is trace-integrable with respect to any $X(du)$ satisfying the conditions* (1) *and* (2) *over* $B \in \mathscr{A}_0$.

*Proof.* Let $\tau_1 = \{B_i\}$, $\tau_2 = \{B_{iK}\}$ be two partitions of $B$, such that $\tau_2$ is a subpartition of $\tau_1$. Using (6.1),

$$|\operatorname{Tr} \sigma_{\tau_1} - \operatorname{Tr} \sigma_{\tau_2}| \leqslant \sum_i \sum_K |(F(u_i) - F(u_{iK}))\, X(B_{iK})| \leqslant \omega(\delta_{\tau_1}) \operatorname{Tr} KX(B)$$

The existence of $\lim \operatorname{Tr} \sigma_\tau$ follows from this inequality.

In particular the function $F(u) = \sum_i K_i g_i(u)$ is trace-integrable and

$$\langle F, \mathbf{X} \rangle_B = \sum_i \int_B g_i(u) \operatorname{Tr} K_i\, X(du).$$

Let $\mu(du)$ be a real positive measure on $\mathscr{A}_0$ and $P(u)$ be a measurable [38] $\mathfrak{B}_+$-valued function on $\mathbf{U}$ such that

$$\int_B \| P(u) \|\, \mu(du) < \infty \tag{6.5}$$

for any $B \in \mathscr{A}_0$. This means that $P(u)$ is Bochner $\mathfrak{B}$-integrable over $B$[38] and the relation

$$X(B) = \int_B P(u)\, \mu(du), \tag{6.6}$$

where the integral is Bochner's $\mathfrak{B}$-integral, defines positive operator-valued measure on $\mathscr{A}_0$. Each measure $X(du)$, representable in the form (6.6), will be called a *measure with the base* $\mu(du)$; $P(u)$ will be called the density of $X(du)$ with respect to $\mu(du)$ and denoted by $X(du)/\mu(du)$.

P.o.m. (6.6) has finite variation, i.e.

$$\sup \sum_i \| X(B_i) \| \leqslant \infty$$

where the supremum is taken over all partitions $\{B_i\}$ of a set $B \in \mathscr{A}_0$.

LEMMA 6.2. *If $X(du)$ has finite variation and $F(u)$ is $\mathfrak{T}$-continuous* (*i.e. continuous as a function with values in Banach space* $\mathfrak{T}$), *then $F$ is* (*left or right*) *integrable.*

The proof is simple and is omitted.

LEMMA 6.3. *Let $X(du)$ be a positive operator-valued measure with the base $\mu(du)$, and let $F$ be $\mathfrak{T}$-continuous. Then the operator-valued function $F(u)\,P(u)$, $u \in \mathbf{U}$, is Bochner $\mathfrak{T}$-integrable w.r.t. $\mu(du)$ over each $B \in \mathscr{A}_0$ and*

$$\int_B F(u)\,X(du) = \int_B [F(u)\,P(u)]\,\mu(du),$$

*where on the right is the Bochner's $\mathfrak{T}$-integral.*

*Proof.* Since $F$ is $\mathfrak{T}$-continuous then $|F(u)|$ is bounded on $B$. We have

$$|F(u)\,P(u)| \leqslant |F(u)|\,\|P(u)\|,$$

therefore, from (6.5)

$$\int_B |F(u)\,P(u)|\,\mu(du) < \infty,$$

i.e., $F(u)\,P(u)$ is Bochner $\mathfrak{T}$-integrable.

Let $P^n(u) = \sum_i P_i^n \mathbf{1}_{B_i^n}(u)$, where $\mathbf{1}_B(u)$ is the characteristic function of the set $B$, be a sequence of step functions such that

$$\int \|P^n(u) - P(u)\|\,\mu(du) \to 0. \tag{6.7}$$

Without loss of generality we may assume that the size of the partition $\tau^n = \{B_i^n\}$ tends to zero as $n \to \infty$. Then it is easy to show that

$$\int |G_n(u) - F(u)\,P(u)|\,\mu(du) \to 0,$$

where

$$G_n(u) = \sum_i F(u_i^n)\,P_i^n \mathbf{1}_{B_i^n}(u); \quad u_i^n \in B_i^n.$$

It follows that

$$\int G_n(u)\,\mu(du) \to \int [F(u)\,P(u)]\,\mu(du).$$

It remains to show that

$$\int G_n(u)\,\mu(du) \to \int F(u)\,X(du).$$

Denoting by $\sigma_n$ the integral sum corresponding to the partition $\tau_n$ and $u_i^n \in B_i^n$ we have

$$\left|\sigma_n - \int G_n(u)\,\mu(du)\right| = \left|\sum_i F(u_i^n)(P_i^n\mu(B_i^n) - X(B_i^n))\right|.$$

From (6.5) we get

$$\sum_i \left\| \int_{B_i^n} (P^n(u) - P(u))\,\mu(du) \right\| \leqslant \int_B \| P^n(u) - P(u)\|\,\mu(du) \to 0,$$

or

$$\sum_i \| P_i^n\mu(B_i^n) - X(B_i^n)\| \to 0.$$

Thus,

$$\left|\sigma_n - \int G_n(u)\,\mu(du)\right| \leqslant \max_{u \in B} |F(u)| \sum_i \| P_i^n\mu(B_i^n) - X(B_i^n)\| \to 0,$$

and the lemma is proved.

Denote by $\mathscr{A}$ the class of all intervals (not necessarily bounded) in $\mathbf{U}$. Now we are going to define the integral over a set $U \in \mathscr{A}$. We say that $F$ is *locally trace-integrable* if it is trace-integrable over any $B \in \mathscr{A}_0$. Let $B_1 \subset \cdots \subset B_n \subset \cdots$ be a nondecreasing sequence of bounded intervals $B_i \subset U$ and $\bigcup_i B_i = U$. Then we write $B_i \uparrow U$. If the limit

$$\lim_{B_i \uparrow U} \int_{B_i} F(u)\,X(dn)$$

exists in $\mathfrak{T}$, which does not depend on the choice of the sequence $\{B_i\}$, then we say that $F$ is *integrable* over $U$ and the limit is denoted $\int_U F(u)\,X(du)$. In the case that $U = \mathbf{U}$ we write $\int F(u)\,X(du)$. The right integral is similarly defined.

Let $F$ be locally trace-integrable w.r.t. $\mathbf{X} = \{X(du)\}$. (In particular $F \in \mathscr{L}$). For $U \in \mathscr{A}$ we put

$$\langle F, \mathbf{X}\rangle_U = \lim_{B_i \uparrow U} \langle F, \mathbf{X}\rangle_{B_i}$$

if the limit exists, finite or infinite. We put $\langle F, \mathbf{X}\rangle_{\mathbf{U}} = \langle F, \mathbf{X}\rangle$. The expression $\langle F, \mathbf{X}\rangle_U$ will be called traced integral of $F$ w.r.t. $X(du)$ over $U$. Evidently, if $F$ is left or right integrable over $U$ then

$$\langle F, X\rangle_U = \operatorname{Tr} \int_U F(u)\,X(du) = \operatorname{Tr} \int_U X(du)\,F(u).$$

Following properties of the traced integral are easily established.

PROPOSITION 6.1. (1) *If at least one of the expressions* $\langle F_1, \mathbf{X}\rangle_U$, $\langle F_2, \mathbf{X}\rangle_U$ *is finite then*

$$\langle c_1F_1 + c_2F_2, \mathbf{X}\rangle_U = c_1\langle F_1, \mathbf{X}\rangle_U + c_2\langle F_2, \mathbf{X}\rangle_U .$$

(2) *If $F$ is locally trace-integrable nonnegative operator-valued function then the traced integral $\langle F, \mathbf{X}\rangle_U$ is defined for any $U \in \mathscr{A}$ and*

$$0 \leqslant \langle F, \mathbf{X}\rangle_U \leqslant +\infty.$$

(3) *If $X(du)$ is a positive operator-valued measure with base $\mu(du)$* (*see* (6.6)) *then*

$$\langle F, \mathbf{X}\rangle_U = \int_U \mathrm{Tr}[F(u)\, P(u)]\, \mu(du).$$

Now we are in a position to prove the representation (5.1) for Bayes risk.

PROPOSITION 6.2. *Let $\pi(d\theta)$ be a p.d. on a measurable space $(\Theta, \mathscr{T})$, $\{\rho_\theta;\, \theta \in \Theta\}$ be a measurable family of density operators and $W_\theta(u)$, $\theta \in \Theta$, $u \in U$; $(U \in \mathscr{A})$ be a nonnegative real function satisfying*

(1) *$W_\theta(u)$ is measurable function of $\theta$ for each $u \in U$;*
(2) *$\int W_\theta(u)\, \pi(d\theta) < \infty$ for each $u \in U$;*
(3) *for any $B \in \mathscr{A}_0$ there are real functions $\Phi$, $\omega$ such that*

$$| W_\theta(u) - W_\theta(v)| \leqslant \Phi(\theta)\, \omega(u - v); \qquad u, v \in B,$$

*where $\omega(u) \to 0$ as $u \to 0$ and*

$$\int \Phi(\theta)\, \pi(d\theta) < \infty.$$

*Then the nonnegative operator-valued function*

$$F(u) = \int_\Theta W_\theta(u)\, \rho_\theta \pi(d\theta),$$

*which is well defined as Bochner's $\mathfrak{T}$-integral due to the conditions* (1) *and* (2), *belongs to the class $\mathfrak{C}$ and*

$$\langle F, \mathbf{X}\rangle_U = \int_\Theta \int_U W_\theta(u)\, \rho_\theta(X(du))\, \pi(d\theta).$$

*Proof.* From condition (3) it follows that $F \in \mathfrak{C}$ and we can take $K = \int \Phi(\theta)\, \rho_\theta \pi(d\theta)$ in (6.1). Since $F$ is nonnegative then it is sufficient to prove that

$$\langle F, \mathbf{X} \rangle_B = \int_\Theta \pi(d\theta) \int_B W_\theta(u)\, \mathsf{p}_\theta(X(du)) \tag{6.8}$$

for any $B \in \mathscr{A}_0$. Let $\{\tau_i\}$ be a partition of $B$ and $u_i \in B_i$. Then

$$\operatorname{Tr} \sigma_\tau = \operatorname{Tr} \Big( \sum_i \int W_\theta(u_i)\, \rho_\theta \pi(d\theta)\, X(B_i) \Big) = \int \pi(d\theta) \sum_i W_\theta(u_i)\, \mathsf{p}_\theta(X(B_i));$$

hence,

$$\begin{aligned} &\Big| \operatorname{Tr} \sigma_\tau - \int_\Theta \pi(d\theta) \int_B W_\theta(u)\, \mathsf{p}_\theta(X(du)) \Big| \\ &\quad = \Big| \int_\Theta \pi(d\theta) \sum_i \int_{B_i} [W_\theta(u_i) - W_\theta(u)]\, \mathsf{p}_\theta(X(du)) \Big| \\ &\quad \leqslant \omega(\delta_\tau) \int \Phi(\theta)\, \pi(d\theta), \end{aligned}$$

where condition (3) was used. Tending $\delta_\tau$ to zero we obtain (6.8).

COROLLARY 6.1. *Let $F(u) = \rho W(u)$ where $\rho \in \mathfrak{T}_+$ and $W$ is a real nonnegative continuous function. Then*

$$\langle F, \mathbf{X} \rangle_U = \int_U W(u) \operatorname{Tr} \rho X(du).$$

For the proof it is sufficient to apply Proposition 6.2 in the case where $\Theta$ consists of one point.

EXAMPLE 6.1. Let $\Theta = \mathbf{U}$, $W_\theta(u) = |\,\theta - u\,|^2$ be a positive definite quadratic form in $\theta - u$, and let $\pi(d\theta)$ have second moments

$$\int |\,\theta\,|^2\, \pi(d\theta) < \infty.$$

Then the conditions of Proposition 6.2 are fulfilled; hence, the representation (5.1) holds with

$$F(u) = \int |\,\theta - u\,|^2\, \rho_\theta \pi(d\theta).$$

EXAMPLE 6.2. An observable $X$ has second moment w.r.t. the state $\rho$ if

$$\int x^2 P_X(dx) < \infty,$$

where $P_X(dx) = \rho(E(dx))$ is the p.d. of $X$ w.r.t. $\rho$.

We shall need the following simple result.

LEMMA 6.4. *The necessary and sufficient condition for $X$ to have second moment is that the range of $\rho^{1/2}$ is in the domain of $X$ and $X\rho^{1/2} \in \mathfrak{S}$, where $\mathfrak{S}$ is the space of Hilbert–Schmidt operators.*

The proof is based on the relation

$$\int x^2 P_X(dx) = \sum_i \rho_i \| X\varphi_i \|^2,$$

where $\rho_i$ are eigenvalues, $\varphi_i$ are eigenvector of d.o. $\rho$.

Now let $X_1, \ldots, X_n$ be some observables which have second moments w.r.t. the state $\rho$, then by Lemma 6.4 $\sigma_i = X_i\rho^{1/2} \in \mathfrak{S}$. Consider the nonnegative operator-valued function

$$F(u_1, \ldots, u_n) = \sum_{K=1}^{n} (u_K \mathrm{I} - X_K)\,\rho(u_K \mathrm{I} - X_K)$$

$$= \Big(\sum_K u_K{}^2\Big)\,\rho - 2\sum_K u_K\,\rho^{1/2} \circ \sigma_K + \sigma_0\,;$$

here $\rho^{1/2} \circ \sigma_K \in \mathfrak{T}$, $\sigma_0 = \sum \sigma_K \sigma_K{}^* \in \mathfrak{T}$, hence, $F \in \mathfrak{C}$. By Proposition 6.1 the traced integral

$$\langle F, \mathbf{X}\rangle = \lim_{B_i \uparrow \mathrm{U}} \mathrm{Tr} \int_{B_i} \sum_K (\mathrm{I}u_K - X_K)\,\rho(\mathrm{I}u_K - X_K)\,X(du) \tag{6.9}$$

is well defined. As shown in [11] this expression gives the total mean-square error of the joint measurement of observables $X_1, \ldots, X_n$.

## 7. EXISTENCE OF THE OPTIMAL MEASUREMENT

In this section we give conditions sufficient for the functional $\langle F, \mathbf{X}\rangle_U$, $\mathbf{X} \in \mathfrak{X}$, to achieve the minimum. Here $U \in \mathscr{A}$, and $\mathfrak{X}$ is the convex set of all $U$-measurements.

THEOREM 7.1. *Let $U$ be a closed interval, $F \in \mathfrak{C}$ and, if $U$ is unbounded,*

$$F(u) \geqslant \rho g(u) + \sigma, \tag{7.1}$$

*where $\rho$ is a nondegenerate operator from $\mathfrak{T}_+$, $\sigma \in \mathfrak{T}_h$ and $g$ is a continuous real function such that*

$$\lim_{u\to\infty} g(u) = +\infty,$$

*Then $\langle F, \mathbf{X}\rangle_U$ achieves the minimum on $\mathfrak{X}$ and the minimum is achieved at an extremal point.*

COROLLARY 7.1. *Let $\Theta = \mathbf{U}$, the loss function $W_\theta(u)$ be a positive definite quadratic form in $\theta - u$ and the a priori distribution $\pi(d\theta)$ has second moments (see Example 6.1). Then the Bayes optimal measurement of $\theta = (\theta_1, ..., \theta_n)$ exists and may be chosen to be an extremal point of the set of all measurements*

*Proof.* For any real $\alpha$

$$W_\theta(u) \geqslant (1 - \alpha^2) \mid u \mid^2 + (1 - \alpha^{-2}) \mid \theta \mid^2;$$

hence,

$$F(u) \geqslant (1 - \alpha^2) \mid u \mid^2 \rho + (1 - \alpha^{-2})\sigma,$$

where

$$\rho = \int \rho_\theta \pi(d\theta), \qquad \sigma = \int \mid \theta \mid^2 \rho_\theta \pi(d\theta).$$

If $\rho$ is nondegenerate then we can directly apply Theorem 7.1 and the result follows. In general, let $E_0$ be the projection on the null subspace of $\rho$, then $E_0 F(u) = 0$. Indeed $0 = (\varphi, \rho\varphi)$ means that $(\varphi, \rho_\theta\varphi) = 0$ a.e. with respect to $\pi(d\theta)$; hence, $(\varphi, F(u)\varphi) = \int \mid \theta - u \mid^2 (\varphi, \rho_\theta\varphi) \cdot \pi(d\theta) = 0$ and $F(u)\varphi = 0$. Therefore, putting $E = I - E_0$, we get

$$F(u) = F(u)E = EF(u)E,$$

from which we conclude that $\langle F, \mathbf{X}\rangle_U = \langle F, E\mathbf{X}E\rangle_U$. Thus, the problem in $H$ may be reduces to the problem in $EH$ where the operator $E\rho E$ is nondegenerate.

COROLLARY 7.2 [11]. *Let $\rho$ be a nondegenerate d.o. and observables $X_1, ..., X_n$ have second moment w.r.t. the state $\rho$. Then the joint optimal measurement of $X_1, ..., X_n$ exists and may be chosen to be an extremal point of the set of all measurements.*

*Proof.* The total mean-square error of joint measurement is given by (6.9). For any $T, S \in \mathfrak{B}$ and real $\alpha$ we have

$$(S - T)(S - T)^* \geqslant (1 - \alpha^2)\, SS^* + (1 - \alpha^{-2})\, TT^*.$$

Applying this inequality to $S = u_K \rho^{1/2}$, $T = X_K \rho^{1/2}$ and summing we get

$$F(u) \geqslant (1 - \alpha^2) \mid u \mid^2 \rho + (1 - \alpha^{-2})\, \sigma_0\,,$$

where $\mid u \mid^2 = \sum_K u_K^2$. Taking $\mid \alpha \mid < 1$ we obtain an estimate (7.1) for $F(u)$ and the result follows.

To prove Theorem 7.1 we shall establish a number of intermediate results. We say that a sequence of measurements $\mathbf{X}^{(n)} = \{X^{(n)}(du)\}$ *converges* if for any $\varphi \in H$ the sequence of scalar measures $\mu_\varphi{}^n(du) = (\varphi, X^{(n)}(du)\varphi)$ weakly converges i.e., the limit

$$\lim_{n\to\infty} \int g(u)\, \mu_\varphi{}^n(du)$$

exists for any bounded continuous $g(u)$. If this limit is equal to $\int g(u)\, \mu_\varphi(du)$, where $\mu_\varphi(du) = (\varphi, X(du)\varphi)$, then $X^{(n)}(du)$ converges to $X(du)$.

If $U$ is closed then $\mathfrak{X}$ is closed, i.e., any converging sequence of measurements converges to some measurement. Indeed, this result is known for scalar measures [39]; hence, there exists a family $\{\mu_\varphi; \varphi \in H\}$ of scalar measures such that

$$\lim_{n\to\infty} \int g(u)\, \mu_\varphi{}^n(du) = \int g(u)\, \mu_\varphi(du).$$

It is easy to verify that the family $\{\mu_\varphi\}$ satisfies the conditions of Theorem 2 [22, p. 9] and, thus, defines measurement $X(du)$ such that $\mu_\varphi(du) = (\varphi, X(du)\varphi)$.

Lemma 7.1. *Let* $T_i \in \mathfrak{T}_h$, $\mu_i(du) = \operatorname{Tr} T_i X(du)$, $i = 1, 2$. *Then*

$$\operatorname{var}(\mu_1 - \mu_2) \leqslant \| T_1 - T_2 \|.$$

*In particular*

$$\operatorname{var}(\mu_\varphi - \mu_\psi) \leqslant \| \varphi - \psi \| \, \| \varphi + \psi \|.$$

The proof is easy, and we omit it.

Lemma 7.2. *Let* $X^{(n)}(du)$ *converge to* $X(du)$. *Then for each* $K \in \mathfrak{T}_h$ *the sequence of scalar measures* $\mu_n(du) = \operatorname{Tr} KX^{(n)}(du)$ *weakly converges to* $\mu(du) =$ $\operatorname{Tr} KX(du)$.

*Proof.* If $K$ is finite dimensional then the assertion follows directly from the definitions. For any $K \in \mathfrak{T}_h$ and $\epsilon > 0$ there is a finite dimensional $K_\epsilon$ such that $\| K - K_\epsilon \| < \epsilon$ [21]. Putting $\mu_n^\epsilon(du) = \operatorname{Tr} K_\epsilon X^{(n)}(du)$, $\mu^\epsilon(du) = \operatorname{Tr} K_\epsilon X(du)$, we get from Lemma 7.1

$$\operatorname{var}(\mu_n^\epsilon - \mu_n) < \epsilon, \qquad \operatorname{var}(\mu^\epsilon - \mu) < \epsilon.$$

Since $\mu_n^\epsilon$ weakly converges to $\mu^\epsilon$ for any $\epsilon$ then $\mu_n$ weakly converges to $\mu$.

A set $\mathfrak{M} \subset \mathfrak{X}$ is *relatively compact* if each sequence $X^{(n)}(du)$ contains a converging subsequence; it is *compact* if the limit belongs to $\mathfrak{M}$.

LEMMA 7.3. *The set of measurements $\mathfrak{M}$ is relatively compact if and only if there is a dense countable subset $\mathscr{F} = \{\varphi_K\} \subset H$ such that for any $\varphi_K$ the set of scalar measures*

$$\mathfrak{M}_K = \{\mu \mid \mu(du) = (\varphi_K, X(du)\, \varphi_K); \mathbf{X} \in \mathfrak{M}\}$$

*is relatively compact.*

*Proof.* The necessity is trivial. To prove the sufficiency we take $\{\mathbf{X}^{(n)}\} \subset \mathfrak{M}$ and apply the diagonal process. Since $\mathfrak{M}_1$ is relatively compact one can choose a subsequence $\{\mathbf{X}_1^{(n)}\}$ such that the scalar measures $(\varphi_1, X_1^{(n)}(du)\, \varphi_1)$ weakly converge. Since $\mathfrak{M}_2$ is relatively compact one can choose a subsequence $\{\mathbf{X}_2^{(n)}\}$ of $\{\mathbf{X}_1^{(n)}\}$ such that scalar measures $(\varphi_2, X_2^{(n)}(du)\, \varphi_2)$ weakly converge. Thus, we construct the countable family of sequences $\{\mathbf{X}_1^{(n)}\}, \{\mathbf{X}_2^{(n)}\},\ldots, \{\mathbf{X}_K^{(n)}\},\ldots$ each of which is a subsequence of the foregoing. Consider the "diagonal" sequence $\{\mathbf{X}_n^{(n)}\}$. For each $\varphi_K \in \mathscr{F}$ scalar measures $\{\varphi_K, X_n^{(n)}(du)\, \varphi_K)$ weakly converge. We now show that for any $\varphi \in H$ scalar measures

$$\mu_\varphi^n(du) = (\varphi, X_n^{(n)}(du)\varphi)$$

weakly converge and the result will follow. Fix a bounded continuous $g(u)$ and $\epsilon > 0$. By Lemma 7.1 we can find $\varphi_K \in \mathscr{F}$ such that $\operatorname{var}(\mu_\varphi - \mu_{\varphi_K}) < \epsilon$. Then

$$\left| \int g(u)\, \mu_\varphi^n(du) - \int g(u)\, \mu_\varphi^m(du) \right| \leqslant \left| \int g(u)\, \mu_{\varphi_K}^n(du) - \int g(u)\, \mu_{\varphi_K}^m(du) \right| + 2\epsilon \max | g |.$$

The first term in the right converges to zero as $n, m \to \infty$ since $\mu_{\varphi_K}^n$ weakly converge, therefore the same is true for left side since $\epsilon$ is arbitrary. Thus, $\mu_\varphi^n$ weakly converge for any $\varphi \in H$.

LEMMA 7.4. *Let $F$ satisfy the conditions of the Theorem 7.1. Then for any real $c$ the set*

$$\mathfrak{X}_c = \{\mathbf{X} \mid \langle F, \mathbf{X}\rangle_U \leqslant c\}$$

*is relatively compact.*

*Proof.* Let $U$ be unbounded. If $\psi$ is a finite linear combination of eigenvectors of the d.o. $\rho$ then

$$|(\varphi, \psi)|^2 \leqslant c_\psi(\varphi, \rho\varphi), \qquad \varphi \in H,$$

with some $c_\psi > 0$. From the properties (1) and (2) of Proposition 6.1 and from Corollary 6.1 we get

$$\langle F, \mathbf{X}\rangle_U \geqslant c_\psi^{-1} \int g(u)(\psi, X(du)\psi) + \operatorname{Tr} \sigma.$$

Thus, for $\mathbf{X} \in \mathfrak{X}_c$

$$\int g(u)(\psi, X(du)\psi) \leqslant d,$$

where $d$ is some constant. For any $B \in \mathscr{A}_0$ we have

$$(\psi, X(B^c)\psi) \leqslant d/\min_{u \in B^c} g(u).$$

But $g(u) \to +\infty$ as $u \to \infty$; hence, the condition of weak compactness holds for the family of scalar measures $\{\mu \mid \mu(du) = (\psi, X(du)\psi); \mathbf{X} \in \mathfrak{X}_c\}$ [39].

Consider now the set $\mathscr{F}$ of vectors $\psi$ which are finite linear combinations of eigenvectors of $\rho$ with rational coefficients. This is a countable set, and since $\rho$ is nondegenerate, $\mathscr{F}$ is dense in $H$. Thus, $\mathscr{F}$ satisfies the conditions of Lemma 7.3, and $\mathfrak{X}_c$ is relatively compact. The consideration is much simpler when $U$ is bounded (in fact, then $\mathfrak{X}$ is compact).

LEMMA 7.5. *If $U$ is bounded and $F \in \mathfrak{C}$ then the functional $\langle F, \mathbf{X}\rangle_U$ is continuous on $\mathfrak{X}$.*

*If $U \in \mathscr{A}$, $F \in \mathfrak{C}$ and $F$ is nonnegative then $\langle F, \mathbf{X}\rangle_U$ is lower semicontinuous on $\mathfrak{X}$.*

*Proof.* Let us show that the functional $\langle F, \mathbf{X}\rangle_U$ where $U \in \mathscr{A}_0$ is continuous on $\mathfrak{X}$. Let $F_\epsilon(u) = \sum_i K_i g_i(u)$ be the function from Lemma 6.1, approximating $F(u)$. Then

$$|\langle F, \mathbf{X}\rangle_U - \langle F_\epsilon, \mathbf{X}\rangle_U| \leqslant \epsilon \operatorname{Tr} KX(B) \leqslant \epsilon \operatorname{Tr} K.$$

Thus $\langle F, \mathbf{X}\rangle_U$ is uniformly approximated by functionals of the form $\langle F_\epsilon, \mathbf{X}\rangle_U$. Therefore, it is sufficient to show the continuity of the functional

$$\int_U g_i(u) \operatorname{Tr} K_i X(du)$$

and this follows from Lemma 7.2.

Now let $U$ be unbounded and $U_i \uparrow U$, $U_i \in \mathscr{A}_0$. Then for each $\mathbf{X} \in \mathfrak{X}$ the sequence $\langle F, \mathbf{X}\rangle_{U_i}$ converges to $\langle F, \mathbf{X}\rangle_U$. Thus, $\langle F, \mathbf{X}\rangle_U$ is the limit of a nondecreasing sequence of continuous functionals and hence is lower semicontinuous.

*Proof of Theorem* 7.1. It is sufficient to show that $\langle F, \mathbf{X}\rangle_U$ achieves the minimum on $\mathfrak{X}_c$ where $c > \inf_{\mathfrak{X}}\langle F, \mathbf{X}\rangle_U$. By Lemma 7.4 $\mathfrak{X}_c$ is relatively compact and by Lemma 7.5 it is closed; hence, it is compact. It is known [51] that a lower semicontinuous functional achieves its minimum on a compact set and the minimum is achieved at an extremal point. The theorem is proved.

[*Editor's Note:* Material has been omitted at this point.]

## 9. Optimality Conditions

Theorem 9.1. *Let $F$ be a nonnegative function of class $\mathfrak{C}$ and let $\mathbf{X}_*$ be a measurement such that*

(1) *$F$ is integrable w.r.t. $X_*(du)$ over $U$ and the operator $\Lambda = \int_U F(u)\, X_*(du)$ is Hermitean;*

(2) *$F(u) \geqslant \Lambda$ for all $u \in U$.*

*Then $\mathbf{X}_*$ is optimal.*

*Proof.* By Proposition 6.1 we have $\langle F, \mathbf{X}\rangle_U \geqslant \langle \Lambda, \mathbf{X}\rangle_U$ for any $\mathbf{X} \in \mathfrak{X}$. By Corollary 6.1

$$\langle \Lambda, \mathbf{X}\rangle_U = \int_U \operatorname{Tr} \Lambda\, X(du) = \operatorname{Tr} \Lambda.$$

Since $\operatorname{Tr} \Lambda = \operatorname{Tr} \int_U F(u)\, X_*(du) = \langle F, \mathbf{X}_*\rangle_U$, the theorem is proved.

Theorem 9.2. *Let $\langle F, \mathbf{X}\rangle_U$, where $F \in \mathfrak{C}$, has an extremum at $X_*$, where the p.o.m. $X_*(du)$ has the base $\mu(du)$ (see(6.6)) and let $P(u) = X_*(du)/\mu(du)$. Then*

(1) *$P(u)(F(u) - F(v))\, P(v) = 0$ $\mu$ a.e.;*

(2) *If $F$ is integrable then $\Lambda = \int_U F(u)\, X_*(du)$ is Hermitean and*

$$(F(u) - \Lambda)\, P(u) = 0 \quad \mu \text{ a.e.};$$

(3) *If $P$ is $\mathfrak{B}$-continuous (i.e., continuous as a function with values in the Banach space $\mathfrak{B}$) and $F$ is $\mathfrak{T}$-differentiable then*

$$P(u)(\partial F/\partial u_i)\, P(u) = 0, \qquad u \in U.$$

*Note.* An important role in applications is played by measurements, determined by the so called "overcomplete" families of vectors [16]. A measurable family of unit vectors $\{\varphi(u); u \in U\}$ in $H$ is called overcomplete if for some scalar measure $\mu(du)$

$$\int_U E_{\varphi(u)}\mu(du) = \mathrm{I}$$

in the weak sense. Given such a family we can construct a measurement with the base $\mu$ by the formula

$$X(B) = \int_B E_{\varphi(u)}\mu(du), \qquad B \in \mathscr{A}_0,$$

(here the integration may be understood in Bochner's sense). For such a measurement the condition (1) becomes

$$(\varphi(u), F(u)\,\varphi(v)) = (\varphi(u), F(v)\,\varphi(v)) \quad \mu \text{ a.e.}$$

and the condition (3)

$$(\varphi(u), (\partial F/\partial u_i)\,\varphi(u)) = 0 \quad \mu \text{ a.e.}$$

*Proof of the Theorem* 9.2. Fix two arbitrary points $u, v \in U$. Let $B_0$ be an interval containing $u$ in its interior. Put $\Delta = u - v$ and define a transformation $g$ by

$$gw = \begin{cases} w + \Delta, & w \in B_0, \\ w - \Delta, & w \in gB_0, \\ w, & w \,\bar{\in}\, B_0, gB_0. \end{cases}$$

We suppose that $B_0$ is small enough such that $B_0 \cap gB_0 = \varnothing$. Evidently $g^2 = e$, where $e$ is the identity transformation, and $gu = v$. Let $\mu_g(du)$ be the image of measure $\mu(du)$ under $g$. Put

$$\nu(dw) = \mu(dw) + \mu_g(dw),$$
$$q(w) = [\mu(dw)/\nu(dw)]^{1/2},$$
$$q_g(w) = [\mu_g(dw)/\nu(dw)]^{1/2}.$$

Let $A$ be a bounded operator in $H$. Then for any real $\epsilon$

$$\exp \epsilon \begin{pmatrix} 0 & -A \\ A^* & 0 \end{pmatrix} = \begin{pmatrix} s_{11} & s_{12} \\ s_{21} & s_{22} \end{pmatrix}$$

is a unitary operator in $H \oplus H$ (cf. proof of Theorem 4.1). Put

$$s_1(w) = \begin{cases} s_{11}, & w \in B_0, \\ s_{22}, & w \in gB_0, \\ \mathrm{I}, & w \bar{\in} B_0, gB_0, \end{cases} \qquad s_2(w) = \begin{cases} s_{12}, & w \in B_0, \\ s_{21}, & w \in gB_0, \\ 0, & w \bar{\in} B_0, gB_0, \end{cases}$$

and consider the function

$$\tilde{P}(w) = Q(w)\, Q(w)^*,$$

where

$$Q(w) = (P(w))^{1/2} q(w)\, s_1(w) + (P(gw))^{1/2} q_g(w)\, s_2(w).$$

A direct computation shows that

$$\int_B \tilde{P}(w)\, \nu(dw) = \int_B P(w)\, \mu(dw)$$

for any interval $B$ containing both $B_0$ and $gB_0$. Hence, the relation

$$X(B) = \int_B \tilde{P}(w)\, \nu(dw), \qquad B \in \mathscr{A}_0$$

defines a new measurement with base $\nu(dw)$.

Calculations which we omit show that

$$\langle F, \mathbf{X} \rangle_U - \langle F, \mathbf{X}_* \rangle_U = \epsilon \int_{B_0} \operatorname{Re} \operatorname{Tr}(P(w))^{1/2} [F(w) - F(w + \Delta)](P(w + \Delta))^{1/2} A$$
$$\cdot\, q(w)\, q_g(w)\, \nu(dw) + o(\epsilon).$$

Since $\langle F, \mathbf{X} \rangle_U$ has an extremum at $\mathbf{X}_*$ then the coefficient of $\epsilon$ must be equal to zero for any small enough interval $B_0$ containing $u$; hence,

$$\operatorname{Re} \operatorname{Tr}(P(u))^{1/2}[F(u) - F(v)](P(v))^{1/2} A = 0 \quad \mu \text{ a.e.}$$

Since this is true for any bounded $A$ then the condition (1) must hold.

Integrating (1) w.r.t. $\mu(du)$, $\mu(dv)$ over $B \in \mathscr{A}_0$ we have

$$\left[\int_B X_*(du) F(u)\right] X_*(B) - X_*(B) \left[\int_B F(u)\, X_*(du)\right] = 0.$$

Let $F$ be integrable over $U$; taking the limit as $B_i \uparrow U$ we obtain

$$\Lambda^* = \int_U X_*(du) F(u) = \int_U F(u) X_*(du) = \Lambda.$$

Integrating (1) w.r.t. $\mu(du)$ for a fixed $v$ we obtain (2). Finally let $P(u)$ be $\mathfrak{B}$-continuous and let the partial $\mathfrak{T}$-derivatives $\partial F/\partial u_i$ exist. Then dividing (1) by $u_i - v_i$ and taking the limit as $u \to v$ we obtain (3).

Now we shall discuss the noncommutative analogue of maximum likelihood. Let $\Theta \in \mathscr{A}$ and $\{\rho_\theta;\, \theta \in \Theta\}$ be a family of d.o. which is locally integrable w.r.t. any measurement (for example, $\rho_{(\cdot)} \in \mathfrak{C}$). We say that $X_*(d\theta)$ is a *maximum likelihood measurement* (m.l.m.) for the family $\{\rho_\theta\}$ if

$$\langle \rho, \mathbf{X}_* \rangle_B \geqslant \langle \rho, \mathbf{X} \rangle_B \tag{9.3}$$

for any bounded interval $B$ and any measurement $\mathbf{X}$ satisfying $X(B) = X_*(B)$.

LEMMA 9.1. *Let* (9.3) *be satisfied for some* $B \in \mathscr{A}_0$. *Then it is satisfied for any* $\tilde{B} \subset B$, $\tilde{B} \in \mathscr{A}_0$.

*Proof.* Let $X(\tilde{B}) = X_*(\tilde{B})$. Then the relation

$$\tilde{X}(A) = X(A\tilde{B}) + X_*(A\tilde{B}^c)$$

defines a new measurement satisfying

$$\tilde{X}(B) = X_*(B);$$

hence,

$$\langle \rho, \mathbf{X}_* \rangle_B \geqslant \langle \rho, \tilde{\mathbf{X}} \rangle_B .$$

On the other hand,

$$\tilde{X}(A) = X(A), \qquad A \subset \tilde{B},$$
$$\tilde{X}(A) = X_*(A), \qquad A\tilde{B} = \varnothing;$$

therefore,

$$\langle \rho, \tilde{\mathbf{X}} \rangle_B = \langle \rho, \mathbf{X} \rangle_{\tilde{B}} + \langle \rho, \mathbf{X}_* \rangle_{B\tilde{B}^c}$$

and

$$\langle \rho, \mathbf{X}_* \rangle_{\tilde{B}} \geqslant \langle \rho, \mathbf{X} \rangle_{\tilde{B}} .$$

COROLLARY 9.1. *Let $\Theta$ be bounded and $\langle \rho, \mathbf{X} \rangle_\Theta$ achieve the maximum at $\mathbf{X}_*$. Then $\mathbf{X}_*$ is m.l.m.*

COROLLARY 9.2. *If (9.3) is satisfied only for some sequence $\{B_i\} \in \mathscr{A}_0$, $B_i \uparrow \Theta$, then $\mathbf{X}_*$ is m.l.m.*

The proof of the following theorem is similar to those of Theorems 9.1 and 9.2.

THEOREM 9.3. *Let the measurement $\mathbf{X}_*$ be such that*

(1) *for some sequence $\{B_i\} \in \mathscr{A}_0$, $B_i \uparrow \Theta$ the operators*

$$\Lambda_i = X_*(B_i) \int_{B_i} \rho_\theta X(d\theta)$$

*are Hermitean and*

(2) $X_*(B_i)\, \rho_\theta X_*(B_i) \leqslant \Lambda_i$, $\theta \in B_i$;

*Then $\mathbf{X}_*$ is m.l.m. for the family $\{\rho_\theta\}$.*

*Let $\mathbf{X}_*$ be the m.l.m.; assume that $X_*(d\theta)$ has the base $\mu(d\theta)$. Then*

$$(P(\theta))^{1/2}(\rho_\theta - \rho_\lambda)(P(\lambda))^{1/2} = 0 \quad \mu \text{ a.e.}$$

*If, moreover, $P$ is $\mathfrak{B}$-continuous and $\rho_\theta$ be $\mathfrak{T}$-differentiable then*

$$P(\theta)(\partial\rho_\theta/\partial\theta_i)\, P(\theta) = 0. \tag{9.4}$$

[*Editor's Note:* Material has been omitted at this point.]

## References

[1] Wald, A. (1939). Contributions to the theory of statistical estimation and testing hypotheses. *Ann. Math. Stat.* **10** 299–326.

[2] Lebedev, D. S. and Levitin, L. B. (1964). *Information Transmission by Electromagnetic Field—Information Transmission Theory*, pp. 5–20 (In Russian). Nauka, Moscow.

[3] Bakut, P. A. et al. (1966). Some problems of optical signals reception. *Problems of Information Transmission* **2**, No. 4, 39–55 (In Russian).

[4] Stratonovich, R. L. (1966). Rate of information transmission in some quantum communication channels. *Problems of Information Transmission* **2** 45–57 (In Russian).

[5] Helstrom, C. W. (1967). Detection theory and quantum mechanics. *Information and Control* **10** 254–291.

[6] Helstrom, C. W., Liu, J., and Gordon, J. (1970). Quantum mechanical communication theory. *Proc. IEEE* **58** 1578–1598.

[7] von Neumann, J. (1955). *Mathematical Foundations of Quantum Mechanics*. Princeton Univ. Press, Princeton, NJ.

[8] Davies, E. B. and Lewis, J. T. (1970). An operational approach to quantum probability. *Commun. Math. Phys.* **17** 239–260.

[9] Holevo, A. S. (1972). The analogue of statistical decision theory in the noncommutative probability theory. *Proc. Moscow Math. Soc.* **26** 133–149 (In Russian).

[10] Holevo, A. S. (1973). Information theory aspects of quantum measurement. *Problems of Information Transmission* **9** 31–42 (In Russian).

[11] Holevo, A. S. (1972). Statistical problems in quantum physics. *Proceedings of the Second Japan-USSR Symposium on Probability Theory*, Kyoto 1 22–40; *Lecture Notes in Mathematics*, Vol. 330, pp. 104–119. American Mathematical Society, Providence, RI.

[12] Holevo, A. S. (1973). Optimal measurements of parameters in quantum signals. *Proceedings of the 3d International Symposium on Information Theory*, Part I, pp. 147–149 (In Russian). Tallin, Moscow.

[13] Holevo, A. S. (1973). On the noncommutatuve analogue of maximum likelihood. *Proc. Int. Conf. Prob. Theory Math. Statist. Vilnius* **2** 317–320 (In Russian).

[14] Holevo, A. S. (1973). Statistical decisions in quantum theory. *Theory Prob. Appl.* **18** 442–444 (In Russian).

[15] Holevo, A. S. (1972). Some statistical problems for quantum fields. *Theory Prob. Appl.* **17** 360–365.

[16] Gordon, J. P. and Louisell, W. H. (1966). Simultaneous measurement of noncommuting observables. *Physics of Quantum Electronics*, pp. 833–840. New York, McGraw–Hill.

[17] Helstrom, C. W. (1972). Quantum detection theory. *Progress in Optics* **10** 291–369

[18] Achiezer, N. I. and Glazman, I. M. (1966). *Theory of Operators in Hilbert Space* (In Russian). Nauka, Moscow.

[19] Dixmier, J. (1969). *Les Algèbres d'opérateurs dans l'espace Hilbertien.* Gauthier-Villars, Paris.

[20] SHATTEN, R. (1960). *Norm Ideals of Completely Continuous Operators.* Springer, Berlin.
[21] GELFAND, I. M. AND VILENKIN, N. YA. (1961). *Generalized Functions, Applications of Harmonic Analysis,* Vol. 4, (In Russian). Fizmatgiz, Moscow.
[22] BERBERIAN, S. K. (1966). *Notes on Spectral Theory.* Van Nostrand-Reinhard, New York.
[23] SEGAL, I. E. (1963). *Mathematical Problems of Relativistic Physics.* American Mathematical Society, Providence, RI.
[24] MACKEY, G. (1963). *The Mathematical Foundations of Quantum Mechanics.* Benjamin, New York.
[25] VARADARAJAN, V. S. (1962). Probability in physics and a theorem on simultaneous observability. *Comm. Pure Appl. Math.* **15** 169–217.
[26] TAKESAKI, M. (1972). Conditional expectations in von Neumann algebras. *J. Functional Analysis* **9** 306–321.
[27] UMEGAKI, H. (1954). Conditional expextation in an operator algebra. *Tohoku Math. J.* **6** 177–181.
[28] NAKAMURA, M. AND UMEGAKI, H. (1962). On von Neumann's theory of measurement in quantum statistics. *Math. Japan* **7** 151–157.
[29] HOLEVO, A. S. (1972). Towards the mathematical theory of quantum channels. *Problems of Information Transmission* **8** 63–71 (In Russian).
[30] CHENTSOV, N. N. (1972). *Statistical Decision Rules and Optimal Inference* (In Russian). Nauka, Moscow.
[31] YUEN, H. P., KENNEDY, R. S., AND LAX, M. (1970). On optimal quantum receivers for digital signal detection. *Proc. IEEE* **58** 1770–1773.
[32] DAVIES, E. B. (1970). On the repeated measurements of continuous observables in quantum mechanics. *J. Functional Analysis* **6** 318–346.
[33] DAY, M. M. (1942). Operators in Banach spaces. *Trans. Amer. Math. Soc.* **51** 583–608.
[34] BARTLE, R. G. (1956). A general bilinear vector integral. *Studia Math.* **15** 337–352.
[35] DOBRAKOV, I. (1970). On integration in Banach spaces, I. *Czech. Math. J.* **20** 511–536.
[36] MASANI, P. (1968). Orthogonally scattered measures. *Adv. Math.* **2** 61–117.
[37] MANDREKAR, V. AND SALEHI, H. (1970). The square-integrability of operator-valued functions with respect to a nonnegative operator-valued measure and the Kolmogorov isomorphism theorem. *Indiana Univ. Math. J.* **20**, 545–563.
[38] HILLE, E. AND PHILLIPS, R. S. (1957). *Functional Analysis and Semigroups.* American Mathematical Society, Providence, RI.
[39] ALEXANDROV, A. D. (1943). Additive set functions in abstract spaces. *Mat. Sb.* **13** 169–238.
[40] GLAUBER, R. J. (1963). Coherent and incoherent states of the radiation field. *Phys. Rev.* **131** 2766–2788.
[41] KLAUDER, J. R. AND SUDARSHAN, E. (1968). *Fundamentals of Quantum Optics.* Benjamin, New York.
[42] LOUISELL, W. H. (1964). *Radiation and Noise in Quantum Electronics.* McGraw-Hill, New York.
[43] MANUCEAU, J. AND VERBEURE, A. (1968). Quasi-free states of the CCR. *Commun. Math. Phys.* **9** 293–302.
[44] HOLEVO, A. S. (1970). On quantum characteristic functions. *Problems of Information Transmission* **6** 44–48 (In Russian).
[45] HOLEVO, A. S. (1971). Generalized free states of the $C^*$-algebra of CCR. *Theoret. Math. Phys.* **6** 3–20 (In Russian).

[46] Holevo, A. S. (1972). On quasiequivalence of locally-normal states. *Theoret. Math. Phys.* **13** 184–199.

[47] Loupias, G. and Miracle-Sole, S. (1966). $C^*$-algebras des systèmes canoniques. *Commun. Math. Phys.* **2** 31–48.

[48] Pool, J. C. T. (1966). Mathematical aspects of Weyl correspondence. *J. Math. Phys.* **7** 66–76.

[49] Personick, S. D. (1971). An image band interpretation of optical heterodyne noise. *Bell Syst. Tech. J.* **50** 213–216.

[50] Rocca, F. (1966). La $P$-représentation dans la formalisme de la convolution gauche. *C. R. Acad. Sci. Ser. A* **262** 547–549.

[51] Bauer, H. (1958). Minimalstellen von Funktionen und Extremalpunkte. *Arch. Math.* **9** 389–393.

[52] Miller, M. M. (1968). Convergence of the Sudarshan expansion for the diagonal coherent-state weight functional. *J. Math. Phys.* **9** 1270–1274.

## ERRATUM

Page 348, line 4: Interchange $u$ and $v$. Page 352, line 5: The representation $\{V^K\}$ is reducible and the reference to Theorem 4.2 in line 7 is not valid. The proof follows directly from (4.8). (This note was stimulated by comments of C. W. Helstrom.) Page 366, line 6: For functionals $\langle F, \mathbf{X}\rangle_{U_i}$ to be continuous in $\mathbf{X}$, the $U_i$ must be chosen such that their boundaries have zero $\mathbf{X}$-measure. Page 374, line 17: Replace $\mathrm{Tr}X\rho Y$ by Re Tr $X\rho Y$. Page 374, line 27: Replace $\langle z, w\rangle$ by $\{z, w\}$. Page 392, line 2: Replace $M$ by $M'$ or the whole formula by $M = (A + B + K/2)^{-1}B$. In the Notes, pages 387 and 388: $\Theta_A$ must be an invariant subspace of the operator $A$.

# 18



Reprinted from *IEEE Trans. Inf. Theory* **IT-21**(5):533–543 (1975)

# Some Statistical Problems for Quantum Gaussian States

ALEXANDER S. HOLEVO

*Abstract*—**Optimal quantum measurements of regression coefficients in the presence of quantum Gaussian noise are considered. The best unbiased measurements are found in a particular case. General solutions for the multimode Bayes problem and the problem of optimal joint measurement of canonical observables are obtained, including explicit characterization of the optimal measurement.**

## I. Introduction

RECENTLY MUCH attention has been paid to the problems of optimal reception and the processing of signals transmitted by quantum channels. Mathematical methods for the solution of such problems constitute what may be called quantum estimation theory. An important role in applications of this theory is played by Gaussian states (which are known also as quasi-free in quantum field theory). It is suggested that these states give a satisfactory description for the radiation field of real sources [1]–[3]; on the other hand, they are analytically tractable and provide a good illustration to the general theory.

In the present paper we consider the quantum-mechanical counterpart of the classical multiple regression problem; we assume that the mean value of a Gaussian state (i.e., the signal transmitted by quantum Gaussian channel) is a linear combination of known functions with unknown coefficients $\alpha_j$, $j = \overline{1,n}$, and we look for the optimal joint measurement of $\alpha_j$. As in classical statistics we may treat $\alpha_j$ either as deterministic or random parameters and correspondingly look for the best unbiased or the optimal Bayes measurements.

The best unbiased estimate (= measurement) for a single parameter $\alpha_j$ and for the finite number degrees of freedom $N$ has been found in the pioneering work of Helstrom [4] by means of a noncommutative extension of the Cramér–Rao inequality. Corresponding results for the Bayes and filtering problems were obtained by Personick [6] and Stratonovich and Grishanin [5]. For the general Bose field ($N = \infty$) this range of problems has been treated in the author's paper [7]; it was shown that they reduce to a solution of a regularized version of the Wiener–Hopf type integral equation. Estimates for several parameters $\alpha_j$, $j = \overline{1,n}$, found in that way separately for each parameter generally do not commute and hence do not constitute a joint measurement of $\alpha_j$, $j = \overline{1,n}$.

This new difficulty is closely related to the problem of the joint measurement of several noncommuting observables in quantum theory [8], [9], which has no analogy in classical statistics. A mathematical approach to the problems of optimal joint measurement of several observables or several parameters of quantum states has been proposed in [10] and worked out in detail in [16]; in particular, it was pointed out that the optimal joint measurement of the canonical observables-momentum $p$ and position $q$ is given by the commuting observables

$$c(p \otimes I_0 + I \otimes p_0) \qquad c(q \otimes I_0 - I \otimes q_0) \qquad \text{(I.1)}$$

where $c$ is a constant, $p_0,q_0$ are momentum and position of an auxiliary independent system in the gauge invariant Fock state (it is supposed that $p,q$ are described by a gauge invariant Gaussian state and optimality means the minimum of the total mean-square error (mse)). The observables (I.1) have been introduced earlier by Personick [11] who showed that measuring them is statistically equivalent to physical heterodyning. It was also shown by different methods that the measurement of type (I.1) is the best unbiased and optimal Bayes for the mean value of the Gaussian state in the gauge invariant case with $N = 1$ (Holevo [12], Yuen and Lax [13], Helstrom and Kennedy [14]).

Passage to the case $N > 1$ and rejection of gauge invariance involves new analytical difficulties. Roughly speaking, gauge invariance means the possibility of reducing the problem to a simpler problem in terms of creation-annihilation operators (for precise definition see Section II). Reduction to the case $N = 1$ is possible only in particular cases since three matrices—correlation, commutation, and weight—which generally cannot be simultaneously diagonalized, enter in computations.

For an arbitrary Bose field measurements of the type (I.1) were introduced by the author [15]; for finite $N$ they were studied in [16]. As in [16] we shall call them canonical measurements since they are evidently closely related to the canonical position-momentum or field observables.

The results for $N = 1$ suggest that the optimal measurements for the mean value of a Gaussian state must generally be canonical measurements. So far some partial results in this direction were known. The author showed [16] that the best unbiased measurement is canonical under the restriction that the weight matrix is gauge invariant (in which case the measurement does not depend on the weight matrix and coincides with the maximum likelihood measurement). General Bayes and filtering problems were considered by Belavkin and Grishanin [18], [19], who obtained some lower bounds for weighed mse, but the ultimate solution for the Bayes problem was given only in the gauge invariant case (for unit weight matrix) by Stratonovich [17].

In this paper we present the following new results.

1) In Section IV we show that the best unbiased measurement is canonical without assuming the weight matrix to be gauge invariant. The proof utilizes the Yuen–Lax

Manuscript received April 11, 1974; revised January 1, 1975.
The author is with Steklov Mathematical Institute, Academy of Sciences of the USSR, Moscow, USSR.

inequality [13] that, as we show, may be used to obtain a general lower bound for the weighted mse of unbiased measurements. However, we had to retain a weaker restriction (IV.2), and the problem of the best unbiased measurement in the general case is still left open.

2) In Sections V–VII we give a general solution for the Bayes problem, based on a special parametrization of canonical measurements introduced in Section VI. We show that the optimal measurement is canonical and give an explicit characterization for parameters of this measurement.

3) In Section VIII we give an analogous solution for the problem of optimal joint measurement of several canonical observables.

The specific feature of the solutions for problems 1)–3) is their dependence of the weight matrix, which is not even smooth in cases 2), 3).

A brief introduction is given in Sections II, III. For a more detailed description of the mathematics involved the reader may refer to [16] and to other references given there.

## II. Gaussian States and Connected Classes of Operators in Symplectic Space

Let $\mathcal{Q}$ be the space region where the receiver is located and let $\mathcal{T}$ be the time interval of reception, then $\mathcal{X} = \mathcal{Q} \times \mathcal{T}$ is the space–time region available for observation. The field in the region is described by the operator-valued function

$$R(x,k), \qquad x \in \mathcal{X} \tag{II.0}$$

where $k$ are parameters specifying the components if (II.0) is a vector field. The field operators (II.0) must satisfy the canonical commutation relation (CCR)

$$[R(x,k),R(x',k')] = -i\Delta(x,k;x',k')$$

where $\Delta$ is a scalar (generalized) function, antisymmetric in the pair of arguments $(x,k),(x',k')$ (we take $\hbar = 1$).

Assume that in the absence of a signal the field has zero mean and correlation function $B(x,k;x',k')$. A fixed source produces a signal that results in the nonzero mean value of the field $\theta_{\alpha_1,\cdots,\alpha_n}(x,k)$, where $\alpha_j$ are unknown parameters. The correlation function is assumed to be unaffected by the signal and remains the same for all values of $\alpha_j$. The problem is to describe optimal, in a sense, quantum measurement of $\alpha_j$.

It has been stressed (see, e.g., [20]) that the field operators (II.0), both mathematically and physically, are rather meaningless objects and that one should start with "smeared" or "smoothed" operators

$$R(z) = \int \sum_k R(x,k)z(x,k)\, dx$$

where $z$ are "test functions" running over a rich enough space of real-valued functions $K$. The CCR becomes

$$[R(z),R(w)] = -i\{z,w\} \tag{II.1}$$

where

$$\{z,w\} = \iint \sum_{k,k'} \Delta(x,k;x',k')z(x,k)w(x',k')\, dx\, dx'$$

is a bilinear skew-symmetric form on $K$; the correlation function gives rise to the positive definite symmetric bilinear form

$$\langle z,w\rangle = \iint \sum_{k,k'} B(x,k;x',k')z(x,k)w(x',k')\, dx\, dx'$$

on $K$ and the mean value—to the linear functional

$$\theta_{\alpha_1,\cdots,\alpha_n}(z) = \int \sum_k \theta_{\alpha_1,\cdots,\alpha_n}(x,k)z(x,k)\, dx$$

on $K$. In the following we shall assume that the $\alpha_j$ enter linearly, that is

$$\theta_{\alpha_1,\cdots,\alpha_n}(z) = \alpha_1\theta^1(z) + \cdots + \alpha_n\theta^n(z)$$

where $\theta^j$ are linearly independent linear functions on $K$. It is, of course, a strong restriction, but this is the first and yet a difficult enough problem to be resolved.

The space $K$ has infinite dimension, however, by choosing an appropriate basis in $K$ and selecting only those modes that are substantially affected by the signal one may often reduce to a finite-dimensional subspace $Z \subset K$. The restriction to the finite number degrees of freedom is by no means necessary from a mathematical point of view, but it considerably simplifies treatment of the problem.

Thus we assume that we are given a *symplectic space*, i.e., finite-dimensional real vector space $Z$ and a skew-symmetric bilinear form $\{z,w\}$ on $Z$. We assume $\{z,w\}$ to be nondegenerate on $Z$, i.e., that $\{z,w\} = 0$, for all $w \in Z$ implies $z = 0$ (this, of course, need not be fulfilled for the arbitrary choice of $Z$). In the present paper we shall not specialize the form of $\{z,w\}$ so that the results are applicable to any Bose system with the finite number degrees of freedom.

By the Baker–Hausdorff formula (see, e.g., [2, sec. III.3.2]) the relation (II.1) is formally equivalent to the Weyl–Segal relation

$$V(z)V(z') = \exp\left[\frac{i}{2}\{z,z'\}\right] V(z+z') \tag{II.2}$$

with $V(z) = \exp[iR(z)]$ [20]. Mathematically the last one is more convenient since it is concerned with bounded operators. Thus we postulate that there is a continuous representation $z \to V(z)$ of the CCR (II.2) in the Hilbert space $H$. Then by Stone's theorem $V(z) = \exp[iR(z)]$, where $R(z)$ are selfadjoint operators satisfying (II.1) on a common dense domain. The $R(z)$, $z \in Z$, are called *canonical observables*.

Without loss of generality we may assume that $V(z)$, $z \in Z$, act irreducibly in $H$ [20], so that each bounded operator in $H$ belongs to the weak closure of the set of finite linear combinations $\sum_k c_k V(z_k)$. If $\rho$ is a density operator, then $\rho$ will denote the corresponding state

$$\rho(T) = m(\rho T), \qquad m \text{ denotes trace in } H.$$

This relation is defined for any operator $T$ such that $\rho T$ is a trace-class operator.

We shall consider *Gaussian states* that are defined by the characteristic function

$$\rho(V(z)) = \exp\left[i\theta(z) - \tfrac{1}{2}\langle z,z\rangle\right] \tag{II.3}$$

where $\theta(z) = \rho(R(z))$ is the *mean value* and $\langle z,w\rangle = \rho((R(z) - \theta(z)) \circ (R(w) - \theta(w)))$ is the *correlation function* of the state. Here $T \circ S = \frac{1}{2}(TS + ST)$ is the symmetrized product of $T$ and $S$.

The CCR imply the following restriction on the correlation function of a state, which is a generalization of the Heisenberg inequality [21]

$$\langle z,z\rangle\langle w,w\rangle \geq \tfrac{1}{4}\{z,w\}^2. \qquad \text{(II.4)}$$

This is equivalent to the following [16]

$$\langle z,z\rangle + \langle w,w\rangle \geq \{z,w\}. \qquad \text{(II.5)}$$

Indeed, substituting $tw$ in place of $w$, one sees that (II.4) is equivalent to the nonnegativity of the resulting polynomial in $t$.

Let $(z,w)$ be an inner product in $Z$ and consider $Z$ as an Euclidean space with this inner product. Then the relations

$$(z,\mathscr{D}w) = \{z,w\} \qquad (z,Aw) = \langle z,w\rangle \qquad \text{(II.5a)}$$

define a skew-symmetric *commutation operator* $\mathscr{D}$ and a symmetric *correlation operator* $A$ in $Z$, and (II.5) may be rewritten as

$$\begin{pmatrix} A & 0 \\ 0 & A \end{pmatrix} \geq \frac{1}{2}\begin{pmatrix} 0 & \mathscr{D} \\ -\mathscr{D} & 0 \end{pmatrix}, \qquad \text{in } Z \times Z. \qquad \text{(II.6)}$$

Introduce the complexification $\boldsymbol{Z}$ of $Z$ as the space of formal combinations $z + iw$; $z, w \in Z$ with natural linear operators and the inner product (antilinear in the second argument). Then (II.6) is equivalent to

$$A \geq (i/2)\mathscr{D}, \qquad \text{in } \boldsymbol{Z} \qquad \text{(II.7)}$$

(cf. [18]). In particular, setting $(z,w) = \langle z,w\rangle$ we obtain $1 + (i/2)\mathscr{D} \geq 0$ (where one is the identity operator in $\boldsymbol{Z}$), hence $(1 - (i/2)\mathscr{D}) = (1 + (i/2)\mathscr{D})' \geq 0$ and

$$1 + \tfrac{1}{4}\mathscr{D}^2 = (1 - (i/2)\mathscr{D})(1 + (i/2)\mathscr{D}) \geq 0.$$

In the following we shall assume for simplicity that $1 + \frac{1}{4}\mathscr{D}^2 > 0$.

We shall denote by $S(Z)$ the class of all bilinear symmetric forms $\langle z,w\rangle$ (or symmetric operators $A$) in $Z$, satisfying one of the equivalent restrictions (II.4)–(II.7).

The operator $\mathscr{J}$ is a *complex structure* in the symplectic space $Z$, if $\mathscr{J}^2 = -1$, and the bilinear form

$$\langle z,w\rangle = \tfrac{1}{2}\{\mathscr{J}z,w\} \qquad \text{(II.8)}$$

is positive definite (and hence belongs to $S(Z)$). We mention in passing that the necessary and sufficient condition for a Gaussian state to be pure is that its correlation function has the form (II.8) [21], [16].

Since $\mathscr{D}$ is skew symmetric in Euclidean space $Z$ it is normal and admits *polarization*

$$\mathscr{D} = |\mathscr{D}|\mathscr{J} = \mathscr{J}|\mathscr{D}|$$

where $|\mathscr{D}|$ is positive symmetric and $\mathscr{J}$ is a unitary operator in $Z$ [22]. It is easily seen that $\mathscr{J}$ is necessarily a complex structure in $Z$ [21].

If a priviledged complex structure $\mathscr{J}$ is distinguished in $Z$, then operators commuting with $\mathscr{J}$ are called *gauge invariant*.

As an illustration consider the case $N = 1$. Then for each $\langle z,w\rangle$ there is a basis $z_1,z_2$ in $Z$ such that

$$\{z,z'\} = x'y - xy'$$
$$\langle z,z'\rangle = a(xx' + yy')$$

where $x,y$ $(x',y')$ are the components of the vector $z(z')$ in the basis $z_1,z_2$. The restriction (II.4) reduces to $a \geq \frac{1}{2}$.

Vectors $e_j = a^{-1/2}z_j$, $j = 1,2$, constitute an orthonormal basis with respect to the inner product $\langle z,w\rangle$. In this basis $\mathscr{D}$ has the matrix

$$\mathscr{D} = \begin{bmatrix} 0 & -a^{-1} \\ a^{-1} & 0 \end{bmatrix} = \begin{bmatrix} a^{-1} & 0 \\ 0 & a^{-1} \end{bmatrix}\begin{bmatrix} 0 & -1 \\ 1 & 0 \end{bmatrix} = |\mathscr{D}|\mathscr{J}$$

where the right side shows the polarization of $\mathscr{D}$.

An example of a nongauge invariant (with respect to the $\mathscr{J}$) operator is given by matrix

$$\begin{bmatrix} 0 & -g_1 \\ g_2 & 0 \end{bmatrix} = \begin{bmatrix} \sqrt{g_1g_2} & 0 \\ 0 & \sqrt{g_1g_2} \end{bmatrix} \cdot \begin{bmatrix} 0 & -(g_1/g_2)^{1/2} \\ (g_2/g_1)^{1/2} & 0 \end{bmatrix}, \quad g_1 \neq g_2 \qquad \text{(II.9)}$$

where the right side again shows the polarization of the left side.

## III. Canonical Measurements

In the present paper we shall deal with the families of Gaussian states $\{\rho_\alpha;\ \alpha = [\alpha_j]_{j=\overline{1,n}} \in R^n\}$ with unknown mean value

$$\theta(z) = \alpha_1\theta^1(z) + \cdots + \alpha_n\theta^n(z)$$

where $\alpha_j$, $j = \overline{1,n}$, are unknown parameters, $\theta^j(z)$ are prescribed linear functions on $Z$ (which are linearly independent), and with the prescribed correlation function $\langle z,w\rangle$. We shall look for the optimal joint measurement of $\alpha_j$, $j = \overline{1,n}$.

According to [10], [16] any joint measurement may be described by a positive operator-valued measure $X(d\alpha_1,\cdots,d\alpha_n)$ on $R^n$ such that $X(R^n) = I$ ($I$ is the identity operator in $H$); if $\rho$ is a state then the probability distribution of possible outcomes of the measurement is equal to $\rho(X(d\alpha_1,\cdots,d\alpha_n))$.

By analogy with scalar measures we may introduce the *operator characteristic function*

$$\Phi(t_1,\cdots,t_n) = \int\left[\exp i \sum_j t_j\alpha_j\right] X(d\alpha_1,\cdots,d\alpha_n)$$

and *operator moments* of the measurement

$$M_{i_1,\cdots,i_k} = \int \alpha_{i_1},\cdots,\alpha_{i_k} X(d\alpha_1,\cdots,d\alpha_n)$$

which may be expressed in the usual way through the partial derivatives of $\Phi$.

The first operator moments

$$M_j = \int \alpha_j X(d\alpha_1\cdots d\alpha_n)$$

and central second operator moments

$$M_{kj}^0 = \iint \alpha_k\alpha_j X(d\alpha_1,\cdots,d\alpha_n) - M_k \circ M_j$$

are of main interest for us, since the first and second moments of the resulting probability distribution with respect to the state $\rho_\alpha$ depend on the $X(d\alpha)$ through $M_j, M_{kj}^0$

$$m_j(\alpha) = \int \beta_j \rho_\alpha(X(d\beta)) = \rho_\alpha(M_j)$$

$$s_{jk}(\alpha) = \iint (\beta_j - \alpha_j)(\beta_k - \alpha_k)\rho_\alpha(X(d\beta))$$
$$= \rho_\alpha(M_{jk}^0 + (M_j - \alpha_j) \circ (M_k - \alpha_k)).$$

Thus the problems with quadratic loss functions involve only the first and the second operator moments of the measurement. We mention in passing that these moments should satisfy the constraint

$$\sum_j \sum_k c_j\bar{c}_k M_{jk}^0 \geq \frac{i}{2} \sum_j \sum_k c_j\bar{c}_k [M_j, M_k]$$

for any complex $c_j$, as it follows from the operator Schwarz inequality

$$\int \overline{\left(\sum_j c_j\alpha_j\right)} X(d\alpha) \cdot \int \left(\sum_j c_j\alpha_j\right) X(d\alpha) \leq \int \left|\sum_j c_j\alpha_j\right|^2 X(d\alpha)$$

(see, e.g., [16, sec. 13]).

We say that the measurement is *wide-sense canonical* if

$$M_j = R(\hat{z}_j) \qquad M_{jk}^0 = \kappa_{jk} \cdot I, \qquad j,k = \overline{1,n}$$

for some $\hat{z}_j \in Z$ and real numbers $\kappa_{jk}$. Let $\hat{Z}$ be the subspace of $Z$ generated by $\hat{z}_j$, $j = \overline{1,n}$, and $L$ be the operator in $\hat{Z}$ defined by

$$(\hat{z}_j L \hat{z}_k) = \kappa_{jk}. \tag{III.1}$$

The canonical measurement with the prescribed first and second operator moments exists if and only if $L \in S(\hat{Z})$, or in the matrix form

$$[\kappa_{jk}]_{j,k=\overline{1,n}} \geq i/2[\{\hat{z}_j,\hat{z}_k\}]_{j,k=\overline{1,n}} \tag{III.2}$$

(cf. (II.7)). If this is the case then the operator characteristic function

$$\exp\left[i \sum_j t_j R(\hat{z}_j) - \tfrac{1}{2} \sum_j \sum_k \kappa_{jk} t_j t_k\right] \tag{III.3}$$

defines the measurement with these moments. Its realization is the measurement of commuting observables

$$R(\hat{z}_j) \otimes I_0 + I \otimes R_0(\Lambda \hat{z}_j), \qquad j = \overline{1,n}$$

where $R_0(z)$ are the canonical observables of an auxiliary independent system in the Gaussian state with zero mean and the correlation function $(\hat{z},L\hat{z}')$, and $\Lambda$ is an involution [16] in $Z$ such that $(\Lambda\hat{z},L\Lambda\hat{z}') = (\hat{z},L\hat{z}')$. If the commutation matrix $[\{z_j,z_k\}]$ is nondegenerate, then $X(d\alpha)$ is the resolution of identity associated with a family of coherent states. For a more complete treatment see [16].

Of course, first and second operator moments do not determine the measurement uniquely; the measurement defined by the operator characteristic function (III.3) may be termed strictly *canonical.*

## IV. Best Unbiased Measurement

In this section we shall consider $Z$ as Euclidean space with the inner product $(z,w) = \langle z,w\rangle$. Denote by $z^k$ the element of $Z$ defined uniquely by the equation

$$\theta^k(z) = \langle z^k, z\rangle, \qquad z \in Z. \tag{IV.1}$$

Denote by $\Theta$ the subspace of $Z$ spanned by $z^k$, $k = \overline{1,n}$, and let $z_j$, $j = \overline{1,n}$, be the biorthogonal basis in $\Theta$

$$\langle z_j, z^k\rangle = \sigma_{jk}.$$

Note that $R(z_j)$ is the best unbiased estimate of $\alpha_j$ [7]. Since $R(z_j)$, $j = \overline{1,n}$, commute only if $\{z_j,z_k\} \equiv 0$, they do not give joint measurement of $\alpha_j$, $j = \overline{1,n}$.

We fix some weight matrix $[g^{jk}]$ and say that $X(d\alpha)$ is the *best unbiased measurement* for $\alpha_j$, $j = \overline{1,n}$, if it minimizes the weighted mse

$$\Sigma_\alpha = \sum_j \sum_k g^{jk} s_{jk}(\alpha)$$

under the condition of unbiasedness

$$m_j(\alpha) = \alpha_j, \qquad j = \overline{1,n}.$$

We shall obtain the best unbiased measurement under the restriction that $\Theta$ is invariant under the operator $\mathcal{D}$, defined in (II.5a)

$$\mathcal{D}(\Theta) \subset \Theta. \tag{IV.2}$$

In fact this condition reduces the problem to the case $\Theta = Z$. Introduce the *weight operator* $\mathcal{G}$ in $\Theta$ defined by

$$(z,\mathcal{G}w) = \sum_j \sum_k g^{jk}(z_j,z)(z_k,w). \tag{IV.3}$$

Due to (IV.2) and the results of Appendix A the operator $\mathcal{G}\mathcal{D}$ admits polarization in $\Theta$,

$$\mathcal{G}\mathcal{D} = |\mathcal{G}\mathcal{D}|\mathcal{J} = \mathcal{J}|\mathcal{G}\mathcal{D}|$$

where $\mathcal{J}$ is the complex structure commuting with $\mathcal{G}\mathcal{D}$.

*Theorem 1:* Let the condition (IV.2) be satisfied. Then the wide-sense canonical measurement with

$$M_j = R(z_j) \qquad M_{jk}^0 = \tfrac{1}{2}\{\mathcal{J}z_j, z_k\}$$

is the best unbiased measurement for $\alpha_j$, $j = \overline{1,n}$. For each $\alpha$

$$\min \Sigma_\alpha = \operatorname{tr}(\mathcal{G} + \tfrac{1}{2}|\mathcal{G}\mathcal{D}|).$$

Before the proof we shall illustrate this result with two examples.

1) Let $N = 1$ and $z = xz_1 + yz_2$ as at the end of Section II. Let $\rho_{\alpha\beta}$ be the family of Gaussian states with the mean $\theta(z) = \alpha x + \beta y$ and correlation function $\langle z,z'\rangle = a(xx' + yy')$. Then if $g^{jk} = \delta_{jk}g_j$, the operator $\mathcal{G}\mathcal{D}$ has the matrix (II.9) in the basis $e_j = a^{-1/2}z_j$, $j = 1,2$.

According to Theorem 1 the minimal mse is

$$a(g_1 + g_2) + \sqrt{g_1 g_2}$$

and the optimal measurement has $p = R(z_1)$, $q = R(z_2)$, as the first operator moments and

$$a^{-1/2}\begin{bmatrix}(g_2/g_1)^{1/2} & 0\\ 0 & (g_1/g_2)^{1/2}\end{bmatrix}$$

as the matrix of second operator moments. The realization of this measurement is (I.1) with $c = 1$, and the state of the auxiliary independent system has zero mean and the correlation function of the form

$$\tfrac{1}{2}[(g_2/g_1)^{1/2}xx' + (g_1/g_2)^{1/2}yy'].$$

2) *Gauge Invariant Case:* As pointed out in Section II $\mathcal{D}$ admits polarization $\hat{\mathcal{D}} = |\mathcal{D}|\mathcal{J}$. Assume that $\mathcal{G}$ is gauge invariant, i.e., commutes with the $\mathcal{J}$. Then $\mathcal{G}\mathcal{D}$ also commutes with the $\mathcal{J}$, and the polarization of $\mathcal{G}\mathcal{D}$ is

$$\mathcal{G}\mathcal{D} = (\mathcal{G}|\mathcal{D}|)\mathcal{J} = \mathcal{J}(\mathcal{G}|\mathcal{D}|).$$

Thus the minimal mse is $\operatorname{tr}\mathcal{G}(1 + \tfrac{1}{2}|\mathcal{D}|)$, and we obtain the results in [16, sec. 13]. If $N = 1$ then gauge invariance implies $g_1 = g_2$, the situation considered in [12]–[14].

*Proof of Theorem 1:* We shall use the inequality obtained in [13], [14] that says that for any unbiased measurement

$$\mathcal{S}_\alpha \ge \mathcal{S}_+, \qquad \text{in } C^n \tag{IV.4}$$

where $\mathcal{S}_\alpha = [s_{jk}(\alpha)]$ is the correlation matrix of the measurement $\mathcal{S}_+^{-1} = [\rho_\alpha((L_+^k)^* L_+^j)]$, $L_+^k$ being the *left logarithmic derivative* of $\rho_\alpha$

$$\frac{\partial\rho_\alpha}{\partial\alpha_k} = \rho_\alpha L_+^k. \tag{IV.5}$$

It is convenient to write $R(z) = R(z_1) + iR(z_2)$, $\theta(z) = \theta(z_1) + i\theta(z_2)$, for $z = z_1 + iz_2 \in Z$. Then for Gaussian states

$$L_+^k = R((1 + (i/2)\mathcal{D})^{-1}z^k) - \theta((1 + (i/2)\mathcal{D})^{-1}z^k) \tag{IV.6}$$

if $(1 + \tfrac{1}{4}\mathcal{D}^2) > 0$, which we assumed. Indeed, one may show that

$$\frac{\partial\rho_\alpha}{\partial\alpha_k} = (R(z^k) - \theta(z^k)) \circ \rho_\alpha \tag{IV.7}$$

(see [16, sec. 12]); if we use the relation

$$(R(z) - \theta(z))\rho_\alpha = \rho_\alpha[R((1 + (i/2)\mathcal{D})^{-1}(1 - (i/2)\mathcal{D})z) - \theta((1 + (i/2)\mathcal{D})^{-1}(1 - (i/2)\mathcal{D})z)] \tag{IV.8}$$

which is proved in Appendix B, we obtain (IV.5) with $L_+^k$ given by (IV.6).

Using the relation

$$\rho_\alpha(R(z) - \theta(z))\cdot(R(\bar{w}) - \theta(\bar{w})) = (z,(1 + (i/2)\mathcal{D})w)$$

we obtain $\mathcal{S}_+^{-1} = [(z^k,(1 + (i/2)\mathcal{D})^{-1}z^j)]$. Under the condition (IV.2) we have

$$\mathcal{S}_+ = [(z_j,(1 + (i/2)\mathcal{D})z_k)].$$

Indeed

$$\sum_j (z^k,(1 + (i/2)\mathcal{D})^{-1}z^j)(z_j,(1 + (i/2)\mathcal{D})z_l) = (z^k,(1 + (i/2)\mathcal{D})^{-1}P(1 + (i/2)\mathcal{D})z_l)$$

where $P$ is the orthogonal projection on $\Theta$. The condition (IV.2) implies that $P$ commutes with $\mathcal{D}$; hence the right side is equal to $(z^k,Pz_l) = (z^k,z_l) = \delta_{kl}$. Thus we obtain

$$\mathcal{S}_\alpha \ge [(z_j,(1 + (i/2)\mathcal{D})z_k)] = [(z_j,z_k) + i/2\{z_j,z_k\}].$$

Introducing the operator $S_\alpha$ in $\Theta$ by

$$(z,S_\alpha w) = \sum_j\sum_k s_{jk}(\alpha)(z^k,z)(z^j,w)$$

we may rewrite the last inequality as

$$S_\alpha \ge I + (i/2)\mathcal{D}, \qquad \text{in } \Theta \tag{IV.9}$$

i.e., $L \equiv S_\alpha - I \in S(\Theta)$. Since $\Sigma_\alpha = \operatorname{tr}\mathcal{G}S_\alpha$ then

$$\Sigma_\alpha \ge \operatorname{tr}\mathcal{G} + \min_{L\in S(Z)} \operatorname{tr}\mathcal{G}L.$$

As shown in Appendix A the minimum is equal to $\tfrac{1}{2}\operatorname{tr}|\mathcal{G}\mathcal{D}|$ and is achieved for $L_0 = -\tfrac{1}{2}\mathcal{D}\mathcal{J}$.

For the wide-sense canonical measurement introduced in Theorem 1 we have

$$\begin{aligned}\Sigma_\alpha &= \sum_j\sum_k g^{jk}\rho_\alpha(M_{jk}^0 + (M_j - \alpha_j)\circ(M_k - \alpha_k))\\ &= \sum_j\sum_k g^{jk}(z_j,(1 - \tfrac{1}{2}\mathcal{D}\mathcal{J})z_k) = \operatorname{tr}\mathcal{G}(1 + \tfrac{1}{2}L_0)\\ &= \min\Sigma_\alpha\end{aligned}$$

and the theorem is proved.

*Note:* The inequality (IV.4) enables us to obtain a general lower bound for the weighted mse. Since $\mathcal{S}_\alpha$ is real then (IV.4) implies

$$\mathcal{S}_\alpha \ge \mathcal{S}_\pm, \qquad \text{in } C^n \tag{IV.10}$$

where $\mathcal{S}_- = \mathcal{S}_+'$. Let $\mathcal{S}_\pm = \mathcal{R} \pm (i/2)\mathcal{T}$, where $\mathcal{R} = [r_{jk}]$ is the real symmetric matrix, $\mathcal{T}$ is the real skew-symmetric matrix. Introducing the Euclidean space $Z$ of vectors $z = [u_j]_{j=\overline{1,n}}$ with the inner product $(z,z') = \sum_j\sum_k r_{jk}u_j u_k'$, and the symmetric in $Z$ operator $S_\alpha$ with the matrix $\mathcal{R}^{-1}\mathcal{S}_\alpha$, we may rewrite (IV.10) in the operator form as $S_\alpha \ge 1 \pm (i/2)T$, where $T$ is a skew-symmetric operator in $Z$ with the matrix $\mathcal{R}^{-1}\mathcal{T}$. Introducing the weight operator $\mathcal{G}$ with the matrix $G\mathcal{R}$ we have as in Theorem 1

$$\Sigma_\alpha \ge \operatorname{tr}(\mathcal{G} + \tfrac{1}{2}|\mathcal{G}T|).$$

## V. Bayes Measurements

We assume now that $\alpha = [\alpha_j]_{j=\overline{1,n}}$ is a random Gaussian vector parameter with zero mean and (nondegenerate) correlation matrix $[b_{jk}] = [E\alpha_j\alpha_k]$, and we want to minimize the Bayes risk

$$R\{X(d\alpha)\} = E\left[\sum_j\sum_k g^{jk}s_{jk}(\alpha)\right]$$

where $E$ denotes expectation with respect to $\alpha$.

As in Section IV, introduce the subspace $\Theta$ spanned by $z^k$, $k = \overline{1,n}$, which are defined by (IV.1). Introduce the bilinear form

$$\langle z,w\rangle_B = \sum_j \sum_k b_{jk}\theta^k(z)\theta^j(w) = \sum_j \sum_k b_{jk}\langle z^k,z\rangle\langle z^j,w\rangle.$$

We choose the inner product in $Z$ to be

$$(z,w) = \langle z,w\rangle + \langle z,w\rangle_B. \quad \text{(V.1)}$$

We shall consider $Z$ as Euclidean space with the scalar product (V.1) and define the *correlation operator $B$ of $\alpha_j$* by

$$(z,Bw) = \langle z,w\rangle_B.$$

It is easily seen that $B$ is symmetric with the range $\mathscr{R}(B) = \Theta$.

Introduce the weight operator $\mathscr{G}$ by (IV.3) *where* $(z,w)$ *is defined by* (V.1). We have $\mathscr{R}(\mathscr{G}) = \Theta$. Let $\mathscr{D}$ be the commutation operator, $(z,\mathscr{D}w) = \{z,w\}$; we assume again for simplicity that $1 + \frac{1}{4}\mathscr{D}^2 > 0$. Introduce the symmetric operator

$$\hat{\mathscr{G}} = (1 + \tfrac{1}{4}\mathscr{D}^2)^{-1/2}B\mathscr{G}B(1 + \tfrac{1}{4}\mathscr{D}^2)^{-1/2}$$

with $\mathscr{R}(\hat{\mathscr{G}}) = (1 + \frac{1}{4}\mathscr{D}^2)^{-1/2}\Theta$. Now we formulate the main result which will be proved in the following sections.

*Theorem 2:* The minimal Bayes risk is equal to

$$\min R\{X(d\alpha)\} = \operatorname{tr}(\mathscr{G}B - \hat{\mathscr{G}}) + \min\{\operatorname{tr}\hat{\mathscr{G}}L: L \in S(Z), L \leq 1\}. \quad \text{(V.2)}$$

The wide-sense canonical measurement with

$$M_j = R(F_*Bz_j) \qquad M_{jk}{}^0 = (Bz_j,F_*(1 - F_*)Bz_k) \quad \text{(V.3)}$$

where

$$F_* = (1 + \tfrac{1}{4}\mathscr{D}^2)^{-1/2}(1 - L_*)(1 + \tfrac{1}{4}\mathscr{D}^2)^{-1/2}$$

$L_*$ being the solution of the minimization problem in the right side of (V.2), is the optimal Bayes measurement.

We shall discuss some particular cases.

1) First we shall consider the *regular* case when the skew-symmetric form $\{z,w\}$ is nondegenerate on $(1 + \frac{1}{4}\mathscr{D}^2)^{-1/2}\Theta$ (which holds, in particular, if $Z = \Theta$). Then according to Lemma 6 of Appendix A the operator $\hat{\mathscr{G}}\mathscr{D}$ admits polarization

$$\hat{\mathscr{G}}\mathscr{D} = |\hat{\mathscr{G}}\mathscr{D}|\mathscr{J} = \mathscr{J}|\hat{\mathscr{G}}\mathscr{D}|$$

and the problem

$$\inf_{L \in S(Z)} \operatorname{tr}\hat{\mathscr{G}}L$$

has the solution $L = -\frac{1}{2}\mathscr{D}\mathscr{J}$. Assume that

$$-\tfrac{1}{2}\mathscr{D}\mathscr{J} < 1. \quad \text{(V.4)}$$

Then by (V.2) the minimal Bayes risk is equal to

$$\operatorname{tr}(\mathscr{G}B - \hat{\mathscr{G}} + \tfrac{1}{2}|\hat{\mathscr{G}}\mathscr{D}|)$$

and the optimal measurement is given by (V.3) with $L_* = -\frac{1}{2}\mathscr{D}\mathscr{J}$.

2) Consider the situation of the Example 1, Section IV, and let $E\alpha\beta = 0$, $E\alpha^2 = E\beta^2 = b$. The inner product in $Z$ is $(z,z') = (a + b)(xx' + yy')$. The orthonormal basis is $e_j = (a + b)^{-1/2}z_j$, $j = 1,2$. In this basis

$$\mathscr{G} = (a + b)\begin{bmatrix} g_1 & 0 \\ 0 & g_2 \end{bmatrix} \qquad \mathscr{D} = (a + b)^{-1}\begin{bmatrix} 0 & -1 \\ 1 & 0 \end{bmatrix}$$

$$B = (a + b)^{-1}\begin{bmatrix} b & 0 \\ 0 & b \end{bmatrix} \qquad 1 + \tfrac{1}{4}\mathscr{D}^2 = (1 - \tfrac{1}{4}(a + b)^{-2})1$$

hence

$$\hat{\mathscr{G}} = (1 - \tfrac{1}{4}(a + b)^{-2})^{-1}(a + b)^{-1}b^2\begin{bmatrix} g_1 & 0 \\ 0 & g_2 \end{bmatrix}$$

and by (II.9) we have

$$|\hat{\mathscr{G}}\mathscr{D}| = ((a + b)^2 - \tfrac{1}{4})^{-1}b^2\sqrt{g_1g_2}\,1$$

$$\mathscr{J} = \begin{bmatrix} 0 & -(g_1/g_2)^{1/2} \\ (g_2/g_1)^{1/2} & 0 \end{bmatrix}.$$

Then

$$-\tfrac{1}{2}\mathscr{D}\mathscr{J} = [2(a + b)]^{-1}\begin{bmatrix} (g_2/g_1)^{1/2} & 0 \\ 0 & (g_1/g_2)^{1/2} \end{bmatrix} \quad \text{(V.5)}$$

and (V.4) reduces to

$$[2(a + b)]^{-1} < (g_1/g_2)^{1/2} < 2(a + b). \quad \text{(V.6)}$$

If $g_1,g_2$ satisfy this restriction then $L_*$ is given by (V.5). In general

$$L_* = [2(a + b)]^{-1}\begin{bmatrix} l((g_2/g_1)^{1/2}) & 0 \\ 0 & l((g_1/g_2)^{1/2}) \end{bmatrix}$$

where $l(x) = \max[[2(a + b)]^{-1}, \min(2(a + b),x)]$ and the minimal Bayes risk is equal to

$$(g_1 + g_2)b[(a + b)^2 - \tfrac{1}{4}]^{-1}[a(a + b) - \tfrac{1}{4}] + \tfrac{1}{2}b^2[(a + b)^2 - \tfrac{1}{4}]^{-1} [g_1l((g_2/g_1)^{1/2}) + g_2l((g_1/g_2)^{1/2})].$$

We omit the explicit formulas for the optimal measurement since they are rather cumbersome (analogous formulas for the problem of optimal joint measurement of $p,q$ are given in [12]), but we want to draw attention to the following feature that was first observed in [12]. Let the ratio $g_1/g_2$ be such that $[2(a + b)]^{-1} > (g_1/g_2)^{1/2}$. Then (V.7) and Theorem 2 give the following optimal estimates for $\alpha$ and $\beta$:

$$\alpha_* = 0 \qquad \beta_* = (a + b)^{-1}bq.$$

Thus if the ratio $g_1/g_2$ is small enough, one must measure only the parameter with the larger weight $g_2$; for the estimate of the parameter with the smaller weight one must take its *a priori* mean value (which is zero in our case).

3) *Gauge Invariant Case:* Assume that a complex structure $\mathscr{J}$ exists that commutes with $\mathscr{D}$, $B$, and $\mathscr{G}$. Then

$$\mathscr{D} = |\mathscr{D}|\mathscr{J} = \mathscr{J}|\mathscr{D}|$$

$$\hat{\mathscr{G}} = (1 - \tfrac{1}{4}|\mathscr{D}|^2)^{-1/2}B\mathscr{G}B(1 - \tfrac{1}{4}|\mathscr{D}|^2)^{-1/2}$$

and $\hat{\mathscr{G}}\mathscr{D}$ commutes with $\mathscr{J}$. Thus $\hat{\mathscr{G}}\mathscr{D}$ polarizes, $\hat{\mathscr{G}}\mathscr{D} = (\hat{\mathscr{G}}|\mathscr{D}|)\mathscr{J}$, and we have the regular case with $|\hat{\mathscr{G}}\mathscr{D}| = \hat{\mathscr{G}}|\mathscr{D}|$.

The condition (V.4) is automatically fulfilled since

$$-\tfrac{1}{2}\mathscr{D}\mathscr{J} = \tfrac{1}{2}|\mathscr{D}| < 1.$$

Thus $L_* = \frac{1}{2}|\mathscr{D}|$ and the minimal Bayes risk reduces to

$$\operatorname{tr}(\mathscr{G}B - B\mathscr{G}B(1 + \tfrac{1}{2}|\mathscr{D}|)^{-1}).$$

The optimal measurement is defined by (V.3) with

$$F_* = (1 - \tfrac{1}{4}|\mathscr{D}|^2)^{-1/2}(1 - \tfrac{1}{2}|\mathscr{D}|)(1 - \tfrac{1}{4}|\mathscr{D}|^2)^{-1/2}$$
$$= (1 + \tfrac{1}{2}|\mathscr{D}|)^{-1}.$$

For $N = 1$ and in the situation of Example 2 gauge invariance reduces to $g_1 = g_2$; the solution for this case has been obtained in [12], [13]. For $N > 1$ with unit weight matrix ($g^{jk} = \delta_{jk}$), the solution was obtained in [17].

4) Let us check the result of Theorem 2 by considering the case $n = 1$. Then the mean value is $\alpha\theta(z)$, where $\alpha$ is a Gaussian parameter with zero mean and variance $b$. If $z^1$ is defined by

$$\theta(z) = \langle z^1,z\rangle$$

then $z_1 = z^1 \cdot a$, where $a = \langle z^1,z^1\rangle^{-1}$. We shall deduce from Theorem 2 that the optimal estimate is

$$\alpha_* = (a + b)^{-1}bR(z_1)$$

and the minimal risk is equal to $(a + b)^{-1}ab$ (with unit weight), which agrees with the result of [6].

In the case here

$$(z,w) = \langle z,w\rangle + a^{-1}b\langle z_1,z\rangle\langle z_1,w\rangle$$

hence $(z_1,w) = (1 + a^{-1}b)\langle z,w\rangle$, in particular, $(z_1,z_1) = a + b$. In view of this relation we obtain, in Dirac's notation

$$B = (a + b)^{-2}b|z_1)(z_1|, \mathscr{G} = |z_1)(z_1|.$$

Setting $\hat{z}_1 = (1 + \frac{1}{4}\mathscr{D}^2)^{-1/2}z_1$, we get

$$\hat{\mathscr{G}} = (a + b)^{-2}b^2|\hat{z}_1)(\hat{z}_1|.$$

Now we evaluate

$$\min \operatorname{tr} \hat{\mathscr{G}}L = (a + b)^{-2}b^2 \min(\hat{z}_1L\hat{z}_1)$$

over all $L$ satisfying

$$(z,Lz) + (w,Lw) \geq \{z,w\}, \qquad (zLz) \leq (z,z).$$

Putting $w = \mathscr{D}z$ in the first inequality and taking the second inequality into account, we have

$$(z,Lz) \geq \tfrac{1}{4}(\mathscr{D}z,\mathscr{D}z), \qquad z \in Z.$$

Hence $\min(\hat{z}_1,L\hat{z}_1) = \frac{1}{4}(\mathscr{D}\hat{z}_1,\mathscr{D}\hat{z}_1)$, and the equality is achieved if $L_*\hat{z}_1 = -\frac{1}{4}\mathscr{D}^2\hat{z}_1$. Since $\operatorname{tr}\hat{\mathscr{G}} = (a + b)^{-2}b^2 \cdot (\hat{z}_1,\hat{z}_1)$, then

$$\min R\{X(d\alpha)\} = b - (a + b)^{-2}b^2(z_1,z_1) = (a + b)^{-1}ab$$

and the optimal estimate is

$$\alpha_* = (a + b)^{-1}bR((1 + \tfrac{1}{4}\mathscr{D}^2)^{-1/2}(1 - L_*)\hat{z}_1)$$
$$= (a + b)^{-1}bR(z_1)$$

which is required.

## VI. Optimum in Class of Canonical Measurements

In this section we shall find the optimal among the wide-sense canonical measurements. The method is based on the following result.

*Lemma 1:* The canonical measurement with

$$M_j = R(\hat{z}_j) \qquad M_{jk}{}^0 = \kappa_{jk}, \qquad j,k = \overline{1,n}$$

exists if and only if there exist the symmetric operator $F$ in $Z$ such that

$$0 \leq F \leq (1 + (i/2)\mathscr{D})^{-1}, \qquad \text{in } Z \qquad \text{(VI.1)}$$

and the elements $z_j{}^0 \in Z$ satisfying $\hat{z}_j = Fz_j{}^0$ and

$$\kappa_{jk} = (z_j{}^0,F(1 - F)z_k{}^0).$$

*Proof:* Let $F$ and $z_j{}^0$ satisfy the conditions of the lemma. Then (III.2) may be rewritten as

$$[(z_j{}^0,F(1 - F)z_k{}^0)]_{j,k=\overline{1,n}} \geq i/2[(Fz_j{}^0,\mathscr{D}Fz_k{}^0)]_{j,k=\overline{1,n}}.$$

We shall establish it by proving that

$$F(1 - F) \geq (i/2)F\mathscr{D}F, \qquad \text{in } Z$$

or equivalently, $F \geq F(1 + (i/2)\mathscr{D})F$ in $Z$. Using the relation

$$(z,T^{-1}z) = \max_w [2 \operatorname{Re}(z,w) - (w,Tw)]$$

(see [23, exercise 6.5.13]) we have

$$(z,F(1 + (i/2)\mathscr{D})Fz)$$
$$= \max_w [2 \operatorname{Re}(Fz,w) - (w,(1 + (i/2)\mathscr{D})^{-1}w)]$$
$$\leq \max_w [2 \operatorname{Re}(Fz,w) - (w,Fw)] = (z,Fz)$$

which proves the inequality.

To prove the necessity denote by $\hat{Z}$ the subspace spanned by $\hat{z}_j$, $j = \overline{1,n}$ and let $L$ defined by (III.1) belong to $S(Z)$. Put $F = (1 + L)^{-1}$ on $\hat{Z}$, $F = 0$ on $\hat{Z}^\perp$, with $\mathscr{R}(F) = \hat{Z}$. Therefore, we can find $z_j{}^0 \in \hat{Z}$ such that $\hat{z}_j = Fz_j{}^0$. We have

$$\kappa_{jk} = (\hat{z}_j,L\hat{z}_k) = (z_j{}^0,FLFz_k{}^0) = (z_j{}^0,F(1 - F)z_k{}^0)$$

and we need to check (VI.1). Denoting by $\hat{z}$ the orthogonal projection of $z \in Z$ onto $\hat{Z}$ we have

$$(z,Fz) = (\hat{z},(1 + L)^{-1}\hat{z}) = \max_{w \in \hat{Z}} \frac{|(\hat{z},w)|^2}{(w,(1 + L)w)}$$
$$= \max_{w \in Z} \frac{|(z,w)|^2}{(w,(1 + L)w)}.$$

Since $L \in S(\hat{Z})$ then $(wLw) \geq i/2(w\mathscr{D}w)$, $w \in \hat{Z}$, hence

$$(z,Fz) \leq \max_{w \in Z} \frac{|(z,w)|^2}{(w,(1 + (i/2)\mathscr{D})w)} \leq \max_{w \in Z} \frac{|(\hat{Z},w)|^2}{(w,(1 + (i/2)\mathscr{D})w)}$$
$$= (w,(1 + (i/2)\mathscr{D})^{-1}w).$$

and the lemma is proved.

*Lemma 2:* The quantity (V.2) gives the minimal risk in the class of wide-sense canonical measurements; the optimal canonical measurement is given by (V.3).

*Proof:* Simple calculation shows that the Bayes risk, corresponding to the wide-sense canonical measurement with

$$M_j = R(Fz_j^0) \qquad M_{jk}^0 = (z_j^0, F(1 - F)z_k^0)$$

is equal to

$$R\{X(d\alpha)\} = \sum_j \sum_k g^{jk}[((z_j^0 - Bz_j), F(z_k^0 - Bz_k)) + (z_j, Bz_k) - (Bz_j, FBz_k)].$$

The first term in the sum is nonnegative; choose $z_j^0 = Bz_j$ to make it equal to zero. Then it remains to minimize

$$\sum_j \sum_k [(z_j, Bz_k) - (Bz_j, FBz_k)] \qquad \text{(VI.2)}$$

over all $F$ satisfying (VI.1). Introduce

$$L = 1 - (1 + \tfrac{1}{4}\mathcal{D}^2)^{1/2} F (1 + \tfrac{1}{4}\mathcal{D}^2)^{1/2}.$$

Then (VI.1) is equivalent to

$$1 \geq L \geq 1 - (1 + \tfrac{1}{4}\mathcal{D}^2)^{1/2}(1 + i/2\mathcal{D})^{-1}(1 + \tfrac{1}{4}\mathcal{D}^2)^{1/2} = (i/2)\mathcal{D}$$

i.e., $L \leq 1$, $L \in S(Z)$. The quantity (VI.2) is tr $(\mathcal{G}B - \mathcal{G})$ + tr $\mathcal{G}L$, hence the lemma is proved.

We shall need the relation

$$\min \{\text{tr } \mathcal{G}L: L \in S(Z), L \leq 1\} = \max_{\Lambda \geq 0} \Big[ \inf_{L \in S(Z)} \text{tr } (\mathcal{G} + \Lambda)L - \text{tr } \Lambda \Big]. \qquad \text{(VI.3)}$$

To prove it note that tr $\mathcal{G}L$ is an affine function on the convex set $S(Z)$. The restriction $L \leq 1$ is also of affine nature and may be rewritten as $L - 1 \leq 0$. The relation (VI.3) is then an application of the Lagrange duality theorem ([24, p. 224]).

Note also that the minimum on the left side of (VI.3) is indeed achieved since the set $\{L: L \in S(Z), L \leq 1\}$ is a compact subset of the space of all symmetric operators in the finite-dimensional $Z$.

## VII. Optimum over All Joint Measurements

According to [10], the Bayes risk, corresponding to the measurement $X(d\alpha)$ may be written as

$$m\left(\int F(\alpha)X(d\alpha)\right) \qquad \text{(VII.1)}$$

where

$$F(\alpha) = \int \sum_j \sum_k g^{jk}(\alpha_j - \beta_j)(\alpha_k - \beta_k)\rho_\beta \mu(d\beta)$$

$\mu$ being an *a priori* distribution of $\alpha$. It follows [16] from the properties of the traced integral (VII.1) that

$$\inf_{X(d\alpha)} m\left(\int F(\alpha)X(d\alpha)\right) \geq \sup \{m(T): T \leq F(\alpha), \forall \alpha\}. \qquad \text{(VII.2)}$$

To accomplish the proof of Theorem 2 it is sufficient to show that the right side is no less than the quantity (V.2) that, as it was shown in the Section VI, is equal to the minimum over all canonical measurements.

We shall give an explicit formula for $F(\alpha)$ by considering the identity

$$\hat{\rho}_\alpha = \int \rho_\beta \mu_\alpha(d\beta) \qquad \text{(VII.3)}$$

where $\mu_\alpha$ is a Gaussian distribution on $R^n$ with the mean vector $\alpha$ and the correlation matrix $[b_{jk}]$, and $\hat{\rho}_\alpha$ is a Gaussian density operator with mean value $\sum \alpha_j \theta^j(z)$ and correlation function $(z,w) = \langle z,w \rangle + \langle z,w \rangle_B$. The relation may be proved using the characteristic functions of $\rho_\alpha, \hat{\rho}_\alpha$ (cf. [16, sec. 14]). Taking the derivative of (VII.3) with respect to $\alpha_j$ and using the identity (IV.7), we have

$$\int \beta_j \rho_\beta \mu(d\beta) = \hat{\rho} \circ R(z_j^0)$$

$$\int \beta_j \beta_k \rho_\beta \mu(d\beta) = [\hat{\rho} \circ R(z_j^0)] \circ R(z_k^0) + \hat{\rho}(z_j, B(1 - B)z_k)$$

where $\mu = \mu_0$, $\hat{\rho} = \hat{\rho}_0$, and $z_j^0 = Bz_j$. Hence

$$F(\alpha) = \sum_j \sum_k g^{jk}\{[(R(z_j^0) - \alpha_j) \circ \hat{\rho}] \circ (R(z_k^0) - \alpha_k) + \hat{\rho}(z_j, B(1 - B)z_k)\}.$$

Now we transform this expression to the form close to what was suggested in [19]. Using the relation

$$R(z)\hat{\rho}^{1/2} = \hat{\rho}^{1/2} R((1 + \tfrac{1}{4}\mathcal{D}^2)^{-1/2}(1 + (i/2)\mathcal{D})z) \qquad \text{(VII.4)}$$

which is proved in Appendix B, we get

$$F(\alpha) = \hat{\rho}^{1/2} \left\{\sum_j \sum_k g^{jk}(R(\hat{z}_j) - \alpha_j)(R(\hat{z}_k) - \alpha_k)\right\} \hat{\rho}^{1/2} + \hat{\rho} \text{ tr } (\mathcal{G}B - \mathcal{G}) \qquad \text{(VII.5)}$$

where $\hat{z}_j = (1 + \tfrac{1}{4}\mathcal{D}^2)^{-1/2} z_j^0$.

Now we establish the basic inequality. Let $z_j^0$, $j = \overline{1,N}$, be a basis in $Z$, containing $z_j^0$; $j = \overline{1,n}$, as its first $n$ elements. For each matrix $[\lambda^{jk}]_{j,k=\overline{1,N}}$ define the operator $\Lambda$ by

$$(z, \Lambda w) = \sum_{j=1}^N \sum_{k=1}^N \lambda^{jk}(z_j^0, z)(z_k^0, w)$$

and put $\hat{\Lambda} = (1 + \tfrac{1}{4}\mathcal{D}^2)^{-1/2}\Lambda(1 + \tfrac{1}{4}\mathcal{D}^2)^{-1/2}$. We have

$$(z, \hat{\Lambda} w) = \sum_{j=1}^N \sum_{k=1}^N \lambda^{jk}(\hat{z}_j, z)(\hat{z}_k, w)$$

$$\text{tr } \hat{\Lambda} = \sum_{j=1}^N \sum_{k=1}^N \lambda^{jk}(\hat{z}_j, \hat{z}_k).$$

*Lemma 3:* For any nonnegative matrix $[\lambda^{jk}]$

$$F(\alpha) \geq T_{\hat{\Lambda}}, \qquad \alpha \in R^n$$

where

$$T_{\hat{\Lambda}} = -\hat{\rho}^{1/2} \sum_{j=1}^N \sum_{k=1}^N \lambda^{jk} R(\hat{z}_j) R(\hat{z}_k) \hat{\rho}^{1/2} + \hat{\rho}[\text{tr } (\mathcal{G}B - \mathcal{G}) + \inf_{L \in S(Z)} \text{tr } (\mathcal{G} + \hat{\Lambda})L].$$

*Proof:* We shall adopt the convention $g^{jk} = 0$, for $j$ or $k > n$. Define $\hat{\alpha}_j$, $j = \overline{1,N}$, as the solution of the (compatible) system

$$\sum_{j=1}^{N} (g^{jk} + \lambda^{jk})\hat{\alpha}_j = \sum_{j=1}^{N} g^{jk}\alpha_j, \qquad j = \overline{1,N}.$$

Then

$$\sum_{j=1}^{n}\sum_{k=1}^{n} g^{jk}(R(\hat{z}_j) - \alpha_j)(R(\hat{z}_k) - \alpha_k)$$
$$\geq \sum_{j=1}^{N}\sum_{k=1}^{N} (g^{jk} + \lambda^{jk})(R(\hat{z}_j) - \hat{\alpha}_j)(R(\hat{z}_k) - \hat{\alpha}_k)$$
$$- \sum_{j=1}^{N}\sum_{k=1}^{N} \lambda^{jk}R(\hat{z}_j)R(\hat{z}_k).$$

According to (A.7) the first term is greater than or equal to

$$\inf \{\mathrm{tr}\,(\hat{\mathscr{G}} + \hat{\Lambda})L\colon L \in S(Z)\}.$$

Taking (VII.5) into account we prove the lemma.

Now we can complete the proof of the Theorem 2. We have

$$m(T_{\hat{\Lambda}}) = -\mathrm{tr}\,\hat{\Lambda} + \mathrm{tr}\,(\mathscr{G}B - \hat{\mathscr{G}}) + \inf_{L \in S(Z)} \mathrm{tr}\,(\hat{\mathscr{G}} + \hat{\Lambda})L.$$

By (VII.2) and Lemma 3

$$\inf_{X(d\alpha)} R\{X(d\alpha)\} \geq \max_{\hat{\Lambda}\geq 0} m(T_{\hat{\Lambda}})$$

and by (VI.3), the right side coincides with the minimum of $R\{X(d\alpha)\}$ over the canonical measurements. The theorem is proved.

## VIII. Joint Measurement of Several Canonical Observables

In this section we describe the optimal (in the sense of weighted mse) joint measurement for the canonical observables $R(z_1),\cdots,R(z_n)$, where $z_j$ are some elements of $Z$. Fix a weight matrix $[g^{jk}]$; as shown in [10] the weighted mse of the measurement $X(d\alpha)$ may be written in the form (VII.1) with

$$F(\alpha) = \sum_{j=1}^{n}\sum_{k=1}^{n} g^{jk}(R(z_j) - \alpha_j)\rho(R(z_k) - \alpha_k)$$

$\rho$ being the density operator describing the state of the system.

Assume that $\rho$ is the Gaussian density operator with mean zero and correlation function $\langle z,w\rangle$. Introduce the inner product $(z,w) = \langle z,w\rangle$ and the operator $\mathscr{G}$ by (IV.3). Put $\hat{\mathscr{G}} = (1 + \frac{1}{4}\mathscr{D}^2)^{-1/2}\mathscr{G}(1 + \frac{1}{4}\mathscr{D}^2)^{-1/2}$.

*Theorem 3:* The minimum weighted mse is equal to

$$\tfrac{1}{4}\,\mathrm{tr}\,\hat{\mathscr{G}}\mathscr{D}^2 + \min\{\mathrm{tr}\,\hat{\mathscr{G}}L\colon L \in S(Z),\, L \leq 1\}. \quad \text{(VIII.1)}$$

The optimal measurement is the wide-sense canonical measurement with

$$M_j = R(F_* z_j) \qquad M_{jk}^{0} = (z_j, F(1 - F)z_k)$$

where

$$F_* = (1 + \tfrac{1}{4}\mathscr{D}^2)^{-1/2}(1 - L_*)(1 + \tfrac{1}{4}\mathscr{D}^2)^{-1/2}$$

$L_*$ being the solution of the minimization problem in (VIII.1).

It is easily seen that the result of Theorem 3 coincides with that of Theorem 2 if we put $B = 1$. The proof also follows the same lines, and we omit it.

In the gauge invariant case (VIII.1) reduces to

$$\tfrac{1}{2}\,\mathrm{tr}\,\mathscr{G}|\mathscr{D}|(1 + \tfrac{1}{2}|\mathscr{D}|)^{-1}$$

where $|\mathscr{D}|$ is defined from the polarization $\mathscr{D} = |\mathscr{D}|\mathscr{J}$, and the optimal measurement is given by (V.3) with $B = 1$. In particular, for $N = 1$ this reduces to the result of [10], [12].

## IX. Discussion

In Sections V–VII we gave a general solution for the Gaussian Bayes problem. In the case of the best unbiased measurements we had to be restricted by condition (IV.2), which is a rather strong restriction (in particular, it excludes the case $n = 1$, though this case may be treated separately by Helstrom's inequality [4] involving the symmetric logarithmic derivative). Thus there is an open question, whether the best unbiased measurement of regression coefficient is wide-sense canonical for arbitrary $\Theta$ (i.e., $\theta^j(z)$).

As a first step one may try to find the optimum in the class of wide-sense canonical measurements using the parametrization of Section VI. We shall look for the optimal canonical measurement with

$$M_j = R(Fz_j^{0}) \qquad M_{jk}^{0} = \langle z_j^{0}, F(1 - F)z_k^{0}\rangle$$

where $F$ satisfies (VI.1). Then

$$\Sigma_\alpha = \sum_j\sum_k g^{jk}\langle z_j^{0}, Fz_k^{0}\rangle$$

and the unbiasedness condition takes the form

$$\langle z^k, Fz_j^{0}\rangle = \delta_{jk}, \qquad j,k = \overline{1,n}.$$

First fix $F$ and find the minimum over $z_j^{0}$. According to the classical theory of regression (see, e.g., [24, pp. 82–101]) the minimum, equal to

$$\sum_j\sum_k g^{jk}[\langle z^j, Fz^k\rangle]^{-1} \quad \text{(IX.1)}$$

is achieved for

$$z_j^{0} = \sum_k [\langle z^j, Fz^k\rangle]^{-1} z^k.$$

Thus the problem is reduced to minimization of (IX.1) over all $F$ satisfying (VI.1). However, is it possible to obtain further information about the optimal $F$ as in the Bayes problem?

One can see that formally putting $\mathscr{D} = 0$ in the results here one obtains the corresponding classical results. Indeed, the theorems of this paper are valid without the assumption that $\{z,w\}$ is nondegenerate (in this case regularity should be understood in the sense of (A.3)). However, careful treatment of this case requires use of mathematical concepts that are beyond the scope of this paper. Let $V(z)$, $z \in Z$, be a family of unitary operators in $H$, satisfying (II.2). Then one has to consider the von Neumann algebra $\mathfrak{B}$ generated by $V(z)$ [25]. If $\{z,w\}$ is degenerate, then $\mathfrak{B} \neq \mathfrak{B}(H)$, the algebra of all bounded operators in $H$. The relation (II.3) defines a state on $\mathfrak{B}$, the trace $m$ is also defined only on $\mathfrak{B}$ and, of course, does not coincide with the usual trace on $\mathfrak{B}(H)$. The density operator should be defined as the Radon–Nikodym derivative of the state with respect to $m$ [25] etc. A detailed treatment of this case will be given elsewhere.

In conclusion we discuss briefly the case of infinitely many degrees of freedom. To any symplectic space $Z$ describing the classical object (field) corresponds with the CCR algebra $\mathfrak{A}(Z)$ generated by unitary elements, satisfying (II.2), which describes the quantized object [20], [21]. The relation (II.3) defines the states $\rho_\alpha$ on $\mathfrak{A}(Z)$. The results will be essentially the same, however, now one must postulate the representation (IV.1) for the "regression functions" $\theta^j(z)$. This condition, closely related to the classical equivalence condition for Gaussian distributions, ensures unitary equivalence of states $\rho_\alpha$ [27] that enables us to build (according to Gelfand–Naimark–Segal construction [20]) a Hilbert space $H$, one and the same for all $\alpha$, and consider $\rho_\alpha$ as normal states on a von Neumann algebra $\mathfrak{B}$ in $H$. For concrete fields the condition (IV.1), as in the classical case, leads to an integral equation similar to a Wiener–Hopf type, the examples of which may be found in [7]. If the condition (IV.1) is violated then some parameters $\alpha_j$ will admit errorless estimation. Further detail will be given elsewhere.

## Appendix A
### Polarization of Operators in Symplectic Space

Let $A$ be an operator in symplectic space $Z$ such that $\langle z,w\rangle_A = \{Az,w\}$ is a nonnegative symmetric form in $Z$. Assume first that $\langle z,w\rangle_A$ is nondegenerate on $Z$. Then $Z$ may be considered as a Euclidean space $Z_A$ with the inner product $\langle z,w\rangle_A$. The operator $A$ is skew symmetric, hence normal in $Z_A$ and admits unique polarization

$$A = |A|\mathscr{J} = \mathscr{J}|A| \tag{A.1}$$

where $\mathscr{J}$ is a complex structure in $Z$, $|A|$ is the positive square root of $A'A = -A^2$ in $Z_A$, i.e.,

$$|A|^2 = -A^2 \qquad \langle z,|A|z\rangle_A \geq 0 \tag{A.2}$$

(see [21]). Evidently $|A|$ and $\mathscr{J}$ commute with $A$.

In general, we say that $A$ admits polarization if there exists a complex structure $\mathscr{J}$ commuting with $A$. Setting $|A| = -A\mathscr{J}$ we obtain (A.1), where $|A|$ satisfies (A.2). A subspace $\mathscr{M}$ is called *regular* if $\{z,w\}$ is nondegenerate on $\mathscr{M}$.

*Lemma 4:* $\mathscr{M}$ is regular if and only if

$$\mathscr{D}(\mathscr{M}) \cap \mathscr{M}^\perp = 0 \tag{A.3}$$

(in particular, $\mathscr{D}(\mathscr{M}) \subset \mathscr{M}$ implies regularity of $\mathscr{M}$).

*Proof:* The relation (A.3) means that $z \in \mathscr{M}$ and $\mathscr{D}z \in \mathscr{M}^\perp$ implies $\mathscr{D}z = 0$ and, since $\mathscr{D}$ is nondegenerate, $z = 0$. On the other hand, $\mathscr{D}z \in \mathscr{M}^\perp$ means that

$$0 = (\mathscr{D}z,w) = \{z,w\}, \qquad w \in \mathscr{M}. \tag{A.4}$$

Thus (A.3) holds if and only if from (A.4) and $z \in \mathscr{M}$, it follows that $z = 0$, i.e., $\{z,w\}$ is nondegenerate on $\mathscr{M}$.

The condition (A.3) may be rewritten as

$$Z = \mathscr{M} + \mathscr{D}(\mathscr{M})^\perp. \tag{A.5}$$

Notice that $\{z,w\} = 0$, if $z \in \mathscr{M}$, $w \in \mathscr{D}(\mathscr{M})^\perp$. hence (A.5) is a direct sum.

*Lemma 5:* The operator $A$ admits polarization, if and only if its range $\mathscr{R}(A)$ is regular.

*Proof:* Let $\mathscr{J}$ commute with $A$, then $\mathscr{J}(\mathscr{R}(A)) \subset \mathscr{R}(A)$. Since $\mathscr{J} \in S(Z)$, then $\{\mathscr{J}z,z\} > 0$, for $z \neq 0$. In particular, this is valid for $z \in \mathscr{R}(A)$ with $\mathscr{J}z \in \mathscr{R}(A)$, hence $\{z,w\}$ is nondegenerate on $\mathscr{R}(A)$.

To prove sufficiency consider the decomposition of $Z$ in the direct sum (A.5) with $\mathscr{M} = \mathscr{R}(A)$. We have $\mathscr{D}(\mathscr{R}(A))^\perp = \mathscr{N}(A)$ (null subspace of $A$) since $z \in \mathscr{N}(A)$ is equivalent to

$$0 = \{Az,w\} = -\{z,Aw\} = -(z,\mathscr{D}Aw), \qquad w \in Z.$$

Thus $Z$ is the direct sum of invariant subspaces of $A$

$$Z = \mathscr{R}(A) + \mathscr{N}(A).$$

Denote by $A_{\mathscr{R}}$ the restriction of $A$ onto $\mathscr{R}(A)$. Since $\mathscr{R}(A)$ is regular and $\langle z,w\rangle_A$ is nondegenerate on $\mathscr{R}(A)$, then $A_{\mathscr{R}}$ polarizes in $\mathscr{R}(A)$: $A_{\mathscr{R}} = |A|\mathscr{J}_{\mathscr{R}}$. Let $\mathscr{J}_{\mathscr{N}}$ be a complex structure in $\mathscr{N}(A)$. Putting $\mathscr{J} = \mathscr{J}_{\mathscr{R}} + \mathscr{J}_{\mathscr{N}}$ we obtain the required polarization (A.1) of $A$ in $Z$. Notice that in this polarization only $|A|$ is defined uniquely.

Let $(z,w)$ be an inner product in $Z$ and $\mathscr{G}$ be a nonnegative operator in $Z$. Then for $A = \mathscr{G}\mathscr{D}$ the bilinear form $\{\mathscr{G}\mathscr{D}z,w\} = (\mathscr{G}\mathscr{D}z,\mathscr{D}w)$ is symmetric and nonnegative hence all the preceding applies to the operator $\mathscr{G}\mathscr{D}$. In particular $\mathscr{G}\mathscr{D}$ polarizes, if and only if the subspace $\mathscr{R}(\mathscr{G}) = \mathscr{R}(\mathscr{G}\mathscr{D})$ is regular.

Consider the problem

$$\inf \{\operatorname{tr} \mathscr{G}L: L \in S(Z)\}. \tag{A.6}$$

A solution for a similar matrix problem for nondegenerate $\mathscr{G}$ was obtained in [18] in terms of complex matrices. We give a different general solution for (A.6) based on polarization in the real space $Z$.

*Lemma 6:* Let $\mathscr{R}(\mathscr{G})$ be regular. Then the infimum in (A.6) is achieved for $L = -\frac{1}{2}\mathscr{D}\mathscr{J}$ and is equal to $\frac{1}{2} \operatorname{tr} |\mathscr{G}\mathscr{D}|$.

*Proof:* It is sufficient to prove that $\operatorname{tr} \mathscr{G}L \geq \frac{1}{2} \operatorname{tr} |\mathscr{G}\mathscr{D}|$. Consider $Z$ as an Euclidean space $Z_{\mathscr{J}}$ with the inner product $\langle z,w\rangle_{\mathscr{J}} = \{\mathscr{J}z,w\}$. Putting $Q = \mathscr{J}\mathscr{D}^{-1}L$ we have $(z,Lw) = \langle z,Qw\rangle_{\mathscr{J}}$. Thus $L \in S(Z)$ reduces to

$$\langle z,Qz\rangle_{\mathscr{J}} + \langle w,Qw\rangle_{\mathscr{J}} \geq \{w,z\}.$$

Putting $w = \mathscr{J}z$ we obtain $Q - \mathscr{J}Q\mathscr{J} \geq I$. Noticing that $|\mathscr{G}\mathscr{D}|$ is a nonnegative operator in $Z_{\mathscr{J}}$ commuting with $\mathscr{J}$ we have

$$\operatorname{tr} \mathscr{G}L = \operatorname{tr} |\mathscr{G}\mathscr{D}|Q = \tfrac{1}{2}(\operatorname{tr} |\mathscr{G}\mathscr{D}|Q - \operatorname{tr} |\mathscr{G}\mathscr{D}|\mathscr{J}Q\mathscr{J})$$

$$\geq \tfrac{1}{2} \operatorname{tr} |\mathscr{G}\mathscr{D}|$$

which is required.

Let $[g^{jk}]$ be a nonnegative matrix, $z_j \in Z$ and $\mathscr{G}$ is defined by (IV.3). Notice that $\mathscr{R}(\mathscr{G})$ coincides with the linear span of $z_j$, $j = \overline{1,n}$. Let us show that for any real $\alpha_j$

$$\sum_j \sum_k g^{jk}(R(z_j) - \alpha_j)(R(z_k) - \alpha_k) \geq \inf_{L \in S(Z)} \operatorname{tr} \mathscr{G}L. \tag{A.7}$$

It is sufficient to show that for any state $\rho$

$$\rho\left(\sum_j \sum_k g^{jk}(R(z_j) - \alpha_j)(R(z_k) - \alpha_k)\right) \geq \inf_{L \in S(Z)} \operatorname{tr} \mathcal{G}L.$$

However, the right side is greater or equal to $\sum_j \sum_k g^{jk}\langle z_j, z_k\rangle = \operatorname{tr} \mathcal{G}L$, where $\langle z,w\rangle = (z,Aw)$ is the correlation function of $\rho$; since $A \in S(Z)$ then (A.7) is proved.

## Appendix B

### Proof of Relations (IV. 8), (VII. 4)

For each trace class operator $T$ in $H$ the *Weyl transform* $\mathcal{F}_z(T) = m(TV(z))$, $z \in Z$, is defined. It is easy to see that $\mathcal{F}_z(T^*) = \overline{\mathcal{F}_{-z}(T)}$. The Weyl transform of the density operator $\rho_\alpha$ is equal to its characteristic function (II.3). From the properties of Weyl transform [26] one deduces the following result.

Let $T$, $TR(w)$ be trace class operators, then

$$\mathcal{F}_z(R(w)T) = -i\frac{d}{dt}\mathcal{F}_{(z+tw)}(T)\bigg|_{t=0} + \tfrac{1}{2}\{w,z\}\mathcal{F}_z(T)$$

$$\mathcal{F}_z(TR(w)) = i\frac{d}{dt}\mathcal{F}_{(z-tw)}(T)\bigg|_{t=0} - \tfrac{1}{2}\{w,z\}\mathcal{F}_z(T).$$

In particular, for $\rho_\alpha$ we have

$$\mathcal{F}_z(R(w)\rho_\alpha) = [\theta(w) - i\langle z,w\rangle + \tfrac{1}{2}\{z,w\}]\mathcal{F}_z(\rho_\alpha)$$

with the analogous relation for $\rho_\alpha R(w)$. This leads to (IV.8).

Consider $\hat{\rho}^{1/2}$. As shown in [27] its Weyl transform is proportional to $\exp(-\frac{1}{2}(z,z)_1)$, where

$$(z,z)_1 = (z,(1 + (1 + \tfrac{1}{4}\mathcal{D}^2)^{1/2})z).$$

Thus $\{z,w\} = (z\mathcal{D}_1 w)$, where $\mathcal{D}_1 = \mathcal{D}(1 + (1 + \frac{1}{4}\mathcal{D}^2))^{-1}$. Taking it into account and putting $\rho_\alpha = \hat{\rho}$ in (IV.8) we obtain (VII.4).

## References


[1] R. J. Glauber, "Coherent and incoherent states of the radiation field," *Phys. Rev.*, vol. 131, pp. 2766–2788, 1963.

[2] W. H. Louisell, *Radiation and Noise in Quantum Electronics.* New York: McGraw-Hill, 1964.

[3] J. R. Klauder and E. Sudarshan, *Fundamentals of Quantum Optics.* New York: Benjamin, 1968.

[4] C. W. Helstrom, "The minimum variance of estimates in quantum signal detection," *IEEE Trans. Inform. Theory*, vol. IT-14, pp. 234–242, Mar. 1968.

[5] B. A. Grishanin and R. L. Stratonovich, "Optimal filtering of quantum variables for quadratic quality function" (in Russian), *Probl. Peredach. Inform.*, vol. 6, pp. 15–25, 1970.

[6] S. D. Personick, "Application of quantum estimation theory to analog communication over quantum channels," *IEEE Trans. Inform. Theory*, vol. IT-17, pp. 240–246, May 1971.

[7] A. S. Holevo, "Some statistical problems for quantum fields" (in Russian), *Theor. Verojatn. Primen.*, vol. 17, pp. 360–365, 1972.

[8] E. Arthurs and J. L. Kelly, Jr., "On the simultaneous measurement of a pair of conjugate observables," *Bell Syst. Tech. J.* (Briefs), vol. 44, pp. 725–729, 1965.

[9] J. P. Gordon and W. H. Louisell, "Simultaneous measurements of noncommuting observables," in *Physics of Quantum Electronics*, P. L. Kelley, B. Lax, and P. E. Tannenwald, Eds. New York: McGraw-Hill, 1966, pp. 833–840.

[10] A. S. Holevo, "Statistical problems in quantum physics," in *Proc. 2nd Japan–USSR Symp. Probability Theory*, vol. 1, 1972, pp. 22–44; reproduced in Lecture Notes in Mathematics, vol. 330, pp. 104–119, 1973.

[11] S. D. Personick, "An image-band interpretation of optical heterodyne noise," *Bell Syst. Tech. J.* (Briefs), vol. 50, pp. 213–216, 1971.

[12] A. S. Holevo, "Optimal quantum measurements" (in Russian), *Theor. i. Matem Fiz.*, vol. 17, pp. 319–326, Dec. 1973.

[13] H. P. Yuen and M. Lax, "Multiple-parameter quantum estimation and measurement of nonselfadjoint observables," *IEEE Trans. Inform. Theory*, vol. IT-19, pp. 740–750, Nov. 1973.

[14] C. W. Helstrom and R. S. Kennedy, "Noncommuting observables in quantum detection and estimation theory," *IEEE Trans. Inform. Theory*, vol. IT-20, pp. 16–24, Jan. 1974.

[15] A. S. Holevo, "Towards the mathematical theory of quantum communication channels" (in Russian), *Probl. Peredach. Inform.*, vol. 8, no. 1, pp. 63–71, 1972.

[16] ——, "Statistical decision theory for quantum systems," *J. Multiv. Anal.*, vol. 3, pp. 337–394, 1973.

[17] R. L. Stratonovich, "Optimal dequantization at the output of quantum channels in Gaussian case" (in Russian), in *Proc. 3rd Int. Symp. Inform. Theory*, abstracts, part I, 1973, pp. 104–108.

[18] V. P. Belavkin and B. A. Grishanin, "Investigation of the problem of optimal estimation in quantum channels via method of generalized Heisenberg inequality" (in Russian), *Probl. Peredach. Inform.*, vol. 9, pp. 44–52, 1973.

[19] B. A. Grishanin, "Some methods of solution of quantum detection and measurement problems" (in Russian), *Tech. Cybern.* (USSR), no. 5, pp. 127–137, 1973.

[20] I. E. Segal, "Mathematical problems of relativistic physics," *Amer. Math. Soc.*, Providence, R.I., 1963.

[21] J. Manuceau and A. Verbeure, "Quasi-free states of the CCR," *Commun. Math. Phys.*, vol. 9, pp. 293–302, 1968.

[22] F. R. Gantmacher, "The Theory of Matrices," vols. I, II. New York: Chelsea, 1959.

[23] R. Bellman, *Introduction to Matrix Analysis.* New York: McGraw-Hill, 1960.

[24] D. G. Luenberger, *Optimization by Vector Space Methods.* New York: Wiley, 1969.

[25] I. E. Segal, "A non-commutative extension of abstract integration," *Ann. Math.*, vol. 57, pp. 401–457, 1953.

[26] A. S. Holevo, "On quantum characteristic functions" (in Russian), *Probl. Peredach. Inform.*, vol. 6, pp. 44–48, 1970.

[27] ——, "On quasiequivalence of locally-normal states" (in Russian), *Theor. Math. Phys.*, vol. 13, pp. 184–189, 1972.

# 19



Reprinted from *IEEE Trans. Inf. Theory* **IT-20**(1):16–24 (1974)

# Noncommuting Observables in Quantum Detection and Estimation Theory

CARL W. HELSTROM, FELLOW, IEEE, AND ROBERT S. KENNEDY, MEMBER, IEEE

***Abstract*—Basing decisions and estimates on simultaneous approximate measurements of noncommuting observables in a quantum receiver is shown to be equivalent to measuring commuting projection operators on a larger Hilbert space than that of the receiver itself. The quantum-mechanical Cramér–Rao inequalities derived from right logarithmic derivatives and symmetrized logarithmic derivatives of the density operator are compared, and it is shown that the latter give superior lower bounds on the error variances of individual unbiased estimates of arrival time and carrier frequency of a coherent signal. For a suitably weighted sum of the error variances of simultaneous estimates of these, the former yield the superior lower bound under some conditions.**

## I. Quantum Measurement

QUANTUM detection theory has been developed within the conventional framework of quantum mechanics, one of the principal tenets of which is that only observables associated with commuting operators can be simultaneously measured on the same system [1]–[3]. It has been suggested that this formulation is too restrictive, that noncommuting operators can be at least approximately measured on the same system, and that to include this possibility may permit more effective detection, appraised at a lower average Bayes cost [4], [5]. An explication of this proposal requires prior discussion of quantum measurement in general. A more thorough treatment can be found in many a textbook on quantum mechanics [6]–[8].

In quantum mechanics an observable is associated with an Hermitian operator, say $F$, which possesses an array of orthonormal eigenstates $|f_n\rangle$ and eigenvalues $f_n$, defined by

$$F|f_n\rangle = f_n|f_n\rangle. \tag{1}$$

The operator $|f_n\rangle\langle f_n|$ projects an arbitrary state vector onto the eigenvector $|f_n\rangle$, and these projection operators $|f_n\rangle\langle f_n|$ commute for different indices $n$ and sum to the identity operator,

$$\sum_n |f_n\rangle\langle f_n| = 1; \tag{2}$$

we say that they form a complete, commuting resolution of the identity.

The primary measurement concept of quantum mechanics envisions the measurement of an observable $F$ as performed by an ideal apparatus that applies to the system such a resolution of the identity. The state of the system, originally —let us say—described by a density operator $\rho$,[1] is projected onto one and only one eigenstate $|f_n\rangle$, and the apparatus registers the associated eigenvalue $f_n$, which is termed the outcome of the measurement of $F$; the probability of this event is

$$\Pr(f_n) = \mathrm{Tr}\,[\rho|f_n\rangle\langle f_n|] = \langle f_n|\rho|f_n\rangle, \tag{3}$$

where "Tr" stands for the trace of an operator. Because $\mathrm{Tr}\,\rho = 1$, (2) shows that the probabilities $\Pr(f_n)$ sum to 1. (An operator may be "degenerate," possessing a set of several eigenstates for each eigenvalue $f_n$. A practical measurement of $F$ may then project the initial state onto the subspace spanned by that set.)

More generally, any finite or infinite resolution of the identity into commuting projection operators $E_n$,

$$\sum_n E_n = 1, \qquad E_nE_m = E_n\delta_{nm}, \tag{4}$$

is in principle measurable by some apparatus. A projection operator has eigenvalues 0 and 1, and the apparatus measuring the set $\{E_n\}$ will register the value 1 for one of them, say $E_k$, and the value 0 for the rest; the probability that this happens is $\mathrm{Tr}\,(\rho E_k)$. The fundamental role of projection operators in quantum measurement was emphasized by von Neumann [9].

The apparatus effects the measurement by first interacting with the system; during the interaction both system and apparatus change in a manner described by the Schrödinger equation. The apparatus afterward is in a state or a mixture of states that manifests itself, for instance, through the position of a meter needle or the number shown on a counter. The meter or the counter could then be read automatically and, perhaps after some computation, a particular one of the projection operators $\{E_n\}$ would be identified and assigned the value 1. The measurement is consummated when an observer looks to see which of the $E_n$ was thus selected. Whether this final act of registration and perception is also governed by the Schrödinger equation is a controversial question, but the only aspect that concerns us here is that for some resolution of the identity (4) depending on the structure of the apparatus and its inter-

Manuscript received November 9, 1972; revised July 20, 1973. The research of C. W. Helstrom was supported by NASA under Grant NGL 05-009-079 and by the National Science Foundation under Grant GK-33811. The research of R. S. Kennedy was supported by NASA under Grant 22-009-013.

C. W. Helstrom is with the Université de Paris-Sud, Orsay, France, on leave from the Department of Applied Physics and Information Science, University of California at San Diego, La Jolla, Calif. 92037.

R. S. Kennedy is with the Department of Electrical Engineering and Research Laboratory of Electronics, Massachusetts Institute of Technology, Cambridge, Mass. 02139.

[1] On the subject of density operators, see Dirac [6, p. 132], or Louisell [8, ch. 6, pp. 220–228].

action with the system, the probability that a particular projection operator $E_k$ is identified is given by Tr $(\rho E_k)$.

Commuting operators share a common resolution of the identity into commuting projection operators, and to say that commuting operators are being measured simultaneously on a system is only to assert that the apparatus is applying to it their common resolution of the identity. The eigenstates composing the resolution bear multiple parameters, each of which is associated with one of the commuting operators [6, pp. 49–52]. The simultaneous eigenstates $|xyz\rangle$ of the operators $X$, $Y$, and $Z$ corresponding to the three rectilinear coordinates provide one example; another is the set of simultaneous eigenstates of the energy $H$, the total angular momentum $L$, and the component $L_z$ of angular momentum along an arbitrary axis, for a particle in a spherically symmetrical potential. The observables $X$, $Y$, and $Z$—or $H$, $L$, and $L_z$—are said to be simultaneously measurable or compatible. The simultaneous measurement of noncommuting observables has no meaning in the sense of this primary concept of measurement.

Gordon and Louisell have advanced a secondary concept of measurement that may lend meaning to the at least approximate simultaneous measurement of noncommuting observables [10]. They remind us that there exist overcomplete resolutions of the identity in terms of noncommuting operators. The most familiar example involves the coherent states $|\alpha\rangle$, which are the right eigenstates of the annihilation operator $a$ that plays an important role in the quantum theories of harmonic oscillators and boson fields [11], [8, §3.7],

$$a|\alpha\rangle = \alpha|\alpha\rangle, \qquad a = a_x + ia_y. \tag{5}$$

The real part $a_x$ of $a$ is proportional to the coordinate operator, the imaginary part $a_y$ to the momentum operator, and these do not commute, nor does the non-Hermitian operator $a$ commute with its conjugate $a^+$, the creation operator,

$$aa^+ - a^+a = [a,a^+] = 1. \tag{6}$$

The eigenvalues $\alpha = \alpha_x + i\alpha_y$ are complex, and the states $|\alpha\rangle$ are overcomplete in the sense that when integrated over the entire complex $\alpha$-plane,

$$\pi^{-1}\int |\alpha\rangle\langle\alpha|\, d^2\alpha = \mathbf{1}, \qquad d^2\alpha = d\alpha_x\, d\alpha_y. \tag{7}$$

As these states are not orthogonal,

$$\langle\alpha \mid \beta\rangle = \exp(\alpha^*\beta - \tfrac{1}{2}|\alpha|^2 - \tfrac{1}{2}|\beta|^2), \tag{8}$$

the projection operators $|\alpha\rangle\langle\alpha|$ do not commute. Because of (7) it is tempting to assert that the quantity $P(\alpha_x,\alpha_y) = \pi^{-1}\langle\alpha|\rho|\alpha\rangle$ represents the joint probability density function (p.d.f.) of the outcomes $\alpha_x$ and $\alpha_y$ of simultaneous approximate measurements of the noncommuting operators $a_x$ and $a_y$ when the system has the density operator $\rho$, for

$$\iint P(\alpha_x,\alpha_y)\, d\alpha_x\, d\alpha_y = 1. \tag{9}$$

A physical interpretation of this concept was provided by Arthurs and Kelly [12] and developed further by She and Heffner [13].

Generalizing to arbitrary multiparameter noncommuting resolutions of the identity, Gordon and Louisell [10] defined an *ideal* measurement on $S$ as one yielding outcomes having a joint p.d.f. calculated in this way, and the nonorthogonal states corresponding to the coherent states $|\alpha\rangle$ were termed *measurement states*. They showed how such an ideal measurement can be carried out on a system $S$ by causing it to interact for a time with an auxiliary system $A$. After the interaction, commuting observables are measured on the system $A$, or more generally on both $S$ and $A$, by applying a commuting resolution of the identity as described earlier. From the outcomes of these measurements, values of what correspond to $\alpha_x$ and $\alpha_y$ are deduced that have the joint p.d.f. required.

## II. Detection

Let us apply to quantum detection the scheme of allowing the system $S$, which is now our ideal receiver, to interact with a suitable auxiliary system, which for brevity we shall call the *ancilla*. The decision about the received signal will be based on the outcome of measuring commuting projection operators on the combined system $S + A$. We suppose that an observer is to decide among $M$ hypotheses $H_1$, $H_2,\cdots,H_M$ about the state of the receiver. It interacts with the ancilla for a while, and at a later time $t$ the density operator for the combined system under hypothesis $H_j$ is $\rho_j^{S+A}(t)$. Let $\{\Pi_j\}$ be a set of commuting projection operators forming an $M$-fold resolution of the identity,

$$\sum_{i=1}^{M} \Pi_i = \mathbf{1}_{S+A}. \tag{10}$$

On the combination $S + A$ we are to measure these $M$ projection operators at time $t$, and if the $k$th yields the value 1, hypothesis $H_k$ is selected as true. The average cost is then [1]

$$\bar{C} = \sum_{i=1}^{M}\sum_{j=1}^{M} \zeta_j C_{ij} \operatorname{Tr}[\rho_j^{S+A}(t)\Pi_i], \tag{11}$$

where $\zeta_j$ is the prior probability of hypothesis $H_j$ and $C_{ij}$ is the cost of choosing $H_i$ when $H_j$ is true. Let $\{\Pi_j(t)\}$ be the projection operators that minimize $\bar{C}$ when the system $S + A$ is observed at time $t$; we call these optimum.

In the Schrödinger picture the density operator $\rho_j^{S+A}(t)$ is related to the density operator $\rho_j^{S+A}(t_0)$ at an earlier time $t_0$ by

$$\rho_j^{S+A}(t) = U(t,t_0)\rho_j^{S+A}(t_0)U^+(t,t_0), \tag{12}$$

with $U(t,t_0)$ a unitary operator obeying the Schrödinger equation

$$i\hbar\frac{\partial}{\partial t}U(t,t_0) = HU(t,t_0), \qquad U(t_0,t_0) = \mathbf{1}, \qquad UU^+ = \mathbf{1}, \tag{13}$$

where $H$ is the Hamiltonian (energy) operator for the combined system $S + A$ and $\hbar$ is Planck's constant $h/2\pi$ [8, p. 225].

As the set $\{\Pi_i(t)\}$ of projection operators minimizes the Bayes cost $\bar{C}$ when measured at time $t$, by (12) the operators

$$\Pi_j(t_0) = U^+(t,t_0)\Pi_j(t)U(t,t_0) \quad (14)$$

minimize $\bar{C}$ when $S + A$ is observed at time $t_0$. Because of the unitarity of $U(t,t_0)$, the set $\{\Pi_j(t_0)\}$ also forms an $M$-fold resolution of the identity into commuting projection operators, and the $\Pi_j(t_0)$ are optimum at time $t_0$. Since the minimization is carried out over all possible $M$-fold resolutions of the identity, the minimum Bayes cost $\bar{C}_{\min}$ must be independent of the observation time $t$. To this independence Helstrom [14] and Liu [15] have previously adverted.

Now let us roll time back to an epoch $t_0$ before the system $S$ has come into contact with the ancilla $A$. In the Schrödinger picture this amounts to applying the inverse unitary transformation $U^+(t,t_0)$ to the state vectors of the combined system $S + A$. Because $S$ and $A$ are independent at this time $t_0$, the density operators $\rho_j^{S+A}$ must now have the factored form

$$\rho_j^{S+A}(t_0) = \rho_j^S(t_0) \otimes \rho^A(t_0), \qquad j = 1,2,\cdots,M, \quad (15)$$

on the product of the Hilbert spaces for system $S$ and ancilla $A$. Furthermore, as the ancilla $A$ before the interaction has no information about which hypothesis is true, $\rho^A(t_0)$ in (15) must be independent of $j$. The Bayes cost is now

$$\bar{C} = \mathrm{Tr}\left\{\sum_{i=1}^{M}\sum_{j=1}^{M}\zeta_j C_{ij}[\rho^A(t_0)\otimes\rho_j^S(t_0)]\Pi_i\right\}. \quad (16)$$

Let us define nonnegative-definite Hermitian operators $Q_i$ acting on the Hilbert space $\mathscr{H}_S$ of the system $S$ alone by

$$Q_i = \mathrm{Tr}_A[\rho^A(t_0)\Pi_i(t_0)], \quad (17)$$

where $\mathrm{Tr}_A$ indicates a trace with respect to the Hilbert $\mathscr{H}_A$ of the ancilla $A$. Then the Bayes cost can be written

$$\bar{C} = \mathrm{Tr}_S \sum_{i=1}^{M}\sum_{j=1}^{M}\zeta_j C_{ij}\rho_j^S Q_i. \quad (18)$$

We consider henceforth only the epoch $t_0$ and dispense with labeling our operators therewith. The operators $Q_i$ form a resolution of the identity $\mathbf{1}_S$ for the system $S$,

$$\sum_{i=1}^{M} Q_i = \mathrm{Tr}_A\left[\rho^A \sum_{i=1}^{M}\Pi_i\right] = \mathrm{Tr}_A[\rho^A \mathbf{1}_{S+A}]$$

or

$$\sum_{i=1}^{M} Q_i = \mathbf{1}_S, \quad (19)$$

but they do not necessarily commute and thus may not be measurable on system $S$ alone.

Although it is not immediately obvious, any set of suitably well-behaved nonnegative-definite Hermitian operators that satisfy (19) can be expressed in the form of (17) [16], [17]. Specifically, it is possible to find a Hilbert space $\mathscr{H}_A$ and a density operator $\rho^A$ such that in the product space $\mathscr{H}_S \otimes \mathscr{H}_A$ there exists a set $\{\Pi_i\}$ of commuting projectors that when substituted into (17) yield the given $Q_i$. There is considerable arbitrariness in the choice of $\rho^A$; the space $\mathscr{H}_A$ must in general have infinite dimension. The density operator $\rho^A$ may be taken as representing a pure state of the ancilla

$$\rho^A = |\Psi_A\rangle\langle\Psi_A|. \quad (20)$$

Let $|w_i\rangle$ be a complete orthonormal set spanning the Hilbert space $\mathscr{H}_S$. The vectors $|w_i\rangle|\Psi_A\rangle$ then span a linear manifold in $\mathscr{H}_S \otimes \mathscr{H}_A$, within which the operators $Q_i \otimes \rho^A$ form a noncommuting resolution of the identity. By virtue of a theorem of Naĭmark's [17], this resolution can be extended to a resolution of the identity into commuting projection operators satisfying (10) and (17). That the optimum strategy might require measuring commuting operators on a Hilbert space larger than $\mathscr{H}_S$ was adumbrated by Personick [18].

The equivalence of the constraints provided by (17) and (19) allows us to view the optimization problem as one of minimizing (18) over all sets of nonnegative-definite Hermitian operators that satisfy (19). If the $Q_i$ that minimize the Bayes cost $\bar{C}$ in (18) do happen to commute, they must possess at least one common set of eigenstates $|v_j\rangle$ and can be written

$$Q_i = \sum_j q_{ij}|v_j\rangle\langle v_j|, \qquad 0 \le q_{ij} \le 1, \qquad \sum_{i=1}^{M} q_{ij} = 1. \quad (21)$$

Then the optimum strategy is to measure the projection operators $|v_j\rangle\langle v_j|$ in $\mathscr{H}_S$ and to choose hypothesis $H_i$ with probability $q_{ik}$ when the measurement of $|v_k\rangle\langle v_k|$ yields the outcome 1. This would in general be a randomized strategy. However, once the set $\{|v_k\rangle\langle v_k|\}$ has been specified, the decision process can be treated by classical decision theory in terms of the probabilities $\Pr\{v_k \mid H_j\} = \langle v_k|\rho_j^S|v_k\rangle$ and the likelihood ratios formed from them. As we know that the minimum Bayes cost can be attained by a pure strategy, the $q_{ik}$ must be either 0 or 1, and the $Q_i$ must be projection operators. If we then take $\Pi_i = Q_i \otimes \mathbf{1}_A$ as the decision operators in the product space of $S + A$, we can attain the same minimum Bayes cost $\bar{C}_{\min}$. Furthermore, $\bar{C}_{\min}$ will be independent of the density operator $\rho^A$ of the ancilla, and measurements on both system and ancilla cannot lead to a lower Bayes cost than measurements made on the system $S$ alone.

There are three cases in which the optimum Bayes stragey is known to require measuring commuting projection operators on the space $\mathscr{H}_S$ of the receiver alone: a) binary decisions ($M = 2$)[1], b) decisions among $M$ commuting density operators [1], and c) decisions among $M$ linearly independent pure states. A proof of c) in the framework of general noncommuting resolutions of the identity has been discovered by Kennedy [19]. In general, however, there is no guarantee that the nonnegative-definite Hermitian operators $Q_i$ that minimize the Bayes cost $\bar{C}$ of (18) subject to (19) will commute. To the contrary, Holevo [16] has shown, by an example involving three linearly dependent pure states, that minimum Bayes cost may sometimes be attained by a set of nonnegative-definite noncommuting operators $Q_i$ in the Hilbert space $\mathscr{H}_S$. Necessary and sufficient conditions for the operators $Q_i$

that minimize (18) subject to (19) were first derived by Yuen [20], [5], although the equivalence of this problem to the quantum optimization problem was not then recognized. The necessary and sufficient conditions for the minimizing operators are

$$(K_i - \Lambda)Q_i = 0, \qquad K_i - \Lambda \geq 0, \qquad i = 1,2,\cdots,M, \tag{22}$$

where

$$K_i = \sum_{j=1}^{M} \zeta_j C_{ij} \rho_j^S, \tag{23}$$

and the operator

$$\Lambda = \sum_{i=1}^{M} K_i Q_i \tag{24}$$

must be Hermitian. Holevo [16] demonstrated the equivalence of the quantum optimization problem to the problem of minimizing (18) subject to (19). Independently of Yuen, and by different methods, he obtained (22) through (24) as sufficient conditions for the minimizing operators and showed that, without the condition that $K - \Lambda_i$ be nonnegative-definite, (22)–(24) are necessary.

If the minimizing operators $Q_i$ turn out to commute, they can be measured on the receiver itself. Otherwise an extension to a set of commuting projection operators $\Pi_i$ in a product space $\mathscr{H}_S \otimes \mathscr{H}_A$ must be determined, and if the minimum Bayes cost is to be actually attained, some way of measuring them must be invented.

## III. Estimation

Determining the values of signal parameters such as amplitude, carrier frequency, and time of arrival corresponds in quantum theory to estimating the parameters $\theta_1,\theta_2,\cdots,\theta_m$ of the density operator $\rho^S(\theta_1,\theta_2,\cdots,\theta_m)$ of a receiver of the signal. Parameter estimation is a continuous version of multiple hypothesis testing; costs of errors as functions of the true values and the estimates lead to an average cost similar to $\bar{C}$ in (11); and by an argument like that in §2 the minimum cost can be shown to be independent of the epoch at which the receiver is measured. One can again expect that attaining the minimum cost may require measurements of commuting operators in a product Hilbert space $\mathscr{H}_S \otimes \mathscr{H}_A$ of the receiver $S$ and an ancillary system $A$. Holevo [16] has treated both estimation and detection from this point of view. In general, the operators that must be measured in order to minimize an arbitrary cost function will be difficult to calculate. The minimization of a quadratic cost function in estimating a single parameter $\theta$ has been achieved by Personick [21], and Yuen and Lax have similarly derived the optimum estimates of a pair of parameters combined into a complex number, the cost being the sum of the mean-square errors in each [22].

Bounds can be set below the mean-square errors of unbiased estimates of parameters of an ordinary probability density function by means of the Cramér–Rao inequality of statistics. A quantum-mechanical counterpart to it has been formulated in terms of the symmetrized logarithmic derivatives of the density operator $\rho^S$ [3]. Yuen and Lax have produced a similar inequality for the simultaneous estimates of pairs of parameters combined into complex numbers, one pair for each mode of a multimode quantum receiver [22]. We wish to show how their method can be applied to setting bounds below the variances of unbiased estimates of arbitrary real parameters of a density operator. The role of noncommuting observables measured on the receiver itself will become apparent, and we shall see that sometimes the one, sometimes the other type of bound is superior.

A quantum-mechanical system $S$ is in a state described by a density operator $\rho^S(\boldsymbol{\theta})$ that is a function of a number $m$ of unknown real parameters $\boldsymbol{\theta} = (\theta_1,\theta_2,\cdots,\theta_m)$, whose values are to be estimated. The procedure for doing so may require creating an auxiliary system $A$, which will be called the ancilla and which is in a state described by the density operator $\rho^A$ independent of $\boldsymbol{\theta}$; the density operator for the combination of system and ancilla is the tensor product

$$\rho(\boldsymbol{\theta}) = \rho^S(\boldsymbol{\theta}) \otimes \rho^A. \tag{25}$$

On this combination a set of commuting Hermitian operators $\Theta_1,\Theta_2,\cdots,\Theta_m$ are measured, and the outcomes $\hat{\theta}_1,\hat{\theta}_2,\cdots,\hat{\theta}_m$ of the measurement are taken as the estimates of the parameters $\boldsymbol{\theta}$. These estimates are simultaneously eigenvalues of the $m$ operators $\Theta_j$ with eigenstates $|\hat{\boldsymbol{\theta}}\rangle$ defined in the product space of $S + A$,

$$\Theta_j|\hat{\boldsymbol{\theta}}\rangle = \hat{\theta}_j|\hat{\boldsymbol{\theta}}\rangle, \qquad \hat{\boldsymbol{\theta}} = (\hat{\theta}_1,\hat{\theta}_2,\cdots,\hat{\theta}_m), \qquad j = 1,2,\cdots,m. \tag{26}$$

We postulate that the estimates are unbiased,

$$\mathrm{Tr}\,(\rho\Theta_j) = \theta_j, \qquad j = 1,2,\cdots,m. \tag{27}$$

An inequality of the Cramér–Rao type is now derived by a method used by Yuen and Lax [22]. The right-logarithmic-derivative (r.l.d.) operators $L_j$ are defined by

$$\frac{\partial\rho}{\partial\theta_j} = \rho L_j = L_j^{+}\rho. \tag{28}$$

Equation (27) and the fact that $\mathrm{Tr}\,\rho = 1$ give as usual

$$\mathrm{Tr}\,\frac{\partial\rho}{\partial\theta_k}(\Theta_j - \theta_j) = \mathrm{Tr}\,\rho(\Theta_j - \theta_j)L_k^{+} = \delta_{kj} = \begin{cases}1, & k = j,\\ 0, & k \neq j.\end{cases} \tag{29}$$

Multiplying by the complex numbers $y_j^*$ and $z_k$ and summing we get

$$\mathrm{Tr}\sum_{j=1}^{m}\sum_{k=1}^{m} y_j^*\rho(\Theta_j - \theta_j)L_k^{+}z_k = \sum_{k=1}^{m} y_k^* z_k, \tag{30}$$

which can be written

$$Y^{+}Z = \mathrm{Tr}\,PQ^{+},$$

where $Y$ and $Z$ are column vectors of the $y_j$ and $z_j$, respectively, and $P$ and $Q$ are the operators

$$P = \rho^{1/2}\sum_{j=1}^{m} y_j^*(\Theta_j - \theta_j), \tag{31}$$

$$Q = \rho^{1/2}\sum_{j=1}^{m} z_j^* L_j. \tag{32}$$

The Schwarz inequality for traces,

$$|\mathrm{Tr}\, PQ^+|^2 \le \mathrm{Tr}\, PP^+\, \mathrm{Tr}\, QQ^+, \tag{33}$$

yields

$$|Y^+Z|^2 \le (Z^+AZ)(Y^+BY), \tag{34}$$

where $A$ and $B$ are Hermitian matrices whose elements are

$$A_{ij} = \mathrm{Tr}\, \rho L_i L_j^+ = \mathrm{Tr}\left(\frac{\partial \rho}{\partial \theta_i} L_j^+\right) = \mathrm{Tr}\left(L_i \frac{\partial \rho}{\partial \theta_j}\right), \tag{35}$$

$$\begin{aligned} B_{ij} &= \mathrm{Tr}\, \rho(\Theta_i - \theta_i)(\Theta_j - \theta_j) \\ &= \mathrm{cov}\,(\hat{\theta}_i,\hat{\theta}_j). \end{aligned} \tag{36}$$

The diagonal element $B_{ii}$ is the variance var $\hat{\theta}_i$ of the estimate $\hat{\theta}_i$; "cov" stands for covariance. Equality holds in (33) if $P$ and $Q$ are proportional, that is if

$$\rho \sum_{j=1}^{m} y_j^*(\Theta_j - \theta_j) = k(\theta)\rho \sum_{j=1}^{m} z_j^* L_j, \tag{37}$$

where we have multiplied both sides by $\rho^{1/2}$ for later use. Here $k(\theta)$ is a $c$-number function, not an operator.

If we put $Y = B^{-1}Z$, we obtain from (34)

$$Z^+B^{-1}Z \le Z^+AZ, \tag{38}$$

the left-hand side of which, when the $z_j$ are real variables, is a quadratic form that when set equal to a constant $(m + 2)$ specifies the concentration ellipsoid of the estimates [23]; and (38) states that that concentration ellipsoid lies outside the ellipsoid specified by the equation $Z^+AZ = m + 2$. Alternatively we can put $Z = A^{-1}Y$ to obtain the multivariate Cramér–Rao inequality

$$Y^+BY \ge Y^+A^{-1}Y, \tag{39}$$

which for various choices of the $y_j$ yields inequalities among linear combinations of the variances and covariances of the estimates. Furthermore, a quadratic risk function can be set up in terms of a positive-definite matrix $G$ as

$$R = \mathrm{Tr}\, GB, \tag{40}$$

and by writing $G$ in terms of its eigenvalues and eigenvectors one can show that the risk $R$ must exceed Tr $GA^{-1}$.

Because the density operator $\rho$ has the product form in (25) with $\rho^A$ independent of $\theta$, we can write the matrix element in (35) as

$$\begin{aligned} A_{ij} &= \mathrm{Tr}\, \frac{\partial \rho^S}{\partial \theta_i} \otimes \rho^A L_j^+ = \mathrm{Tr}\, \rho^S L_i^S \otimes \rho^A L_j^+ \\ &= \mathrm{Tr}\, L_i^S \otimes 1_A L_j^+ \rho = \mathrm{Tr}\, L_i^S \otimes 1_A \frac{\partial \rho}{\partial \theta_j} \\ &= \mathrm{Tr}\, (L_i^S \otimes 1_A)(L_j^S \otimes 1_A)(\rho^S \otimes \rho^A), \end{aligned} \tag{41}$$

where the r.l.d. operators $L_j^S$ defined by

$$\partial \rho^S / \partial \theta_j = \rho^S L_j^S \tag{42}$$

act only on the Hilbert space of the system $S$, and $1_A$ is the identity operator for the Hilbert space of the ancilla $A$.[2]

[2] We are indebted to Dr. H. P. H. Yuen for remarks leading to the simplification of the argument at this point.

Thus the matrix elements $A_{ij}$ needed in the inequality (39) become

$$A_{ij} = \mathrm{Tr}_S\, (\rho^S L_i^S L_j^{S+}) \tag{43}$$

and are independant of the density operator $\rho^A$ for the apparatus. These bounds, therefore, have a universal validity in the sense that they hold no matter what ancillary system $A$ is brought up and no matter what the density operator $\rho^A$ is. They apply also to measurements of commuting estimators on the system $S$ alone.

If we put into (37) $Z = A^{-1}Y$, we find that equality in (39) is attained if there is a set of commuting estimating operators $\Theta_j$ such that

$$\rho \sum_{j=1}^{m} y_j^*(\Theta_j - \theta_j) = k(\theta)\rho \sum_{j=1}^{m}\sum_{k=1}^{m} y_j^*(A^{-1})_{jk} L_k$$

or

$$\begin{aligned} &\rho^S \otimes \rho^A \sum_{j=1}^{m} y_j^*(\Theta_j - \theta_j) \\ &= k(\theta) \sum_{j=1}^{m}\sum_{k=1}^{m} y_j^*(A^{-1})_{jk}(\rho^S L_k^S) \otimes \rho^A. \end{aligned} \tag{44}$$

Now, following Holevo, [16] we suppose that there exists a mapping of the parameter space $\mathbf{\Theta}$ into a set of nonnegative Hermitian measurement operators $X(F)$ in the Hilbert space $\mathscr{H}_S$ of the system $S$ such that $F \to X(F)$, where $F$ is any region of the space $\mathbf{\Theta}$, $\mathbf{\Theta} \to 1_S$, and

$$\sum_i X(F_i) = X\left(\sum_i F_i\right) \tag{45}$$

when $\{F_i\}$ is a countable measurable decomposition of the space $\mathbf{\Theta}$ into disjoint regions $F_i$. Let $X(\theta;d^m\theta)$ be the operator corresponding to the differential region of volume $d^m\theta$ in the neighborhood of the point $\theta$ of the parameter space, and define the operators

$$\Theta_j^S = \int_{\mathbf{\Theta}} \theta_j X(\theta; d^m\theta), \qquad \theta = (\theta_1,\cdots,\theta_m). \tag{46}$$

The operators $\Theta_j^S$ may not commute, but suppose they satisfy the equation

$$\sum_{j=1}^{m} y_j^*(\Theta_j^S - \theta_j) = k(\theta) \sum_{j=1}^{m}\sum_{k=1}^{m} y_j^*(A^{-1})_{jk} L_k^S. \tag{47}$$

Then one can interpret the results of Holevo's work as asserting the existence of an ancilla $A$, a product space $\mathscr{H}_S \otimes \mathscr{H}_A$, a pure state $\rho^A = |\Psi_A\rangle\langle\Psi_A|$ of the ancilla, and a set of commuting estimators $\{\Theta_j\}$ in $\mathscr{H}_S \otimes \mathscr{H}_A$ such that (44) holds and the equality in (39) is attained. This set of estimators is constructed by starting with the set of operators $X(F) \otimes \rho^A$ acting in the subspace $\mathscr{H}_S \otimes |\Psi_A\rangle$ of $\mathscr{H}_S \otimes \mathscr{H}_A$ that is spanned by the tensor products $|w_i\rangle|\Psi_A\rangle$ of $|\Psi_A\rangle$ and each of a complete orthonormal set of vectors $|w_i\rangle$ spanning $\mathscr{H}_S$. By using Naĭmark's procedure [17] this noncommuting set of operators can be extended to a commuting resolution of the identity in $\mathscr{H}_S \otimes \mathscr{H}_A$,

$$X(F) \otimes \rho^A \to X'(F),$$

where

$$\sum_i X'(F_i) = X'\left(\sum_i F_i\right) \tag{48}$$

for any countable measurable decomposition of the parameter space $\Theta$ into disjoint regions $F_i$. Projection of the operators $X'(F)$ into the subspace $\mathscr{H}_S \otimes |\Psi_A\rangle$ yields the operators $X(F) \otimes \rho^A$. Then the estimators defined by

$$\Theta_j = \int_{\Theta} \theta_j X'(\theta; d^m\theta) \tag{49}$$

will commute and satisfy (44), for

$$(\rho^S \otimes \rho^A)\Theta_j = \rho^S \int_{\Theta} \theta_j X(\theta; d^m\theta) \otimes \rho^A$$
$$= \rho^S \Theta_j^S \otimes \rho^A, \tag{50}$$

which when applied to (47) yields (44). In order to carry out this extension a product space $\mathscr{H}_S \otimes \mathscr{H}_A$ of infinite dimension is required. As Holevo pointed out, the state $\rho^A$ and the ancilla are not necessarily unique; many such states in many such product spaces $\mathscr{H}_S \otimes \mathscr{H}_A$ may exist that permit achieving equality in (39).

## IV. Estimation of Complex Mode Amplitudes

As an example we use the well-worn problem of estimating the real and imaginary parts of the complex amplitude $\mu = \mu_x + i\mu_y$ of a coherent signal in a harmonic oscillator representing a single mode of a quantum receiver with thermal noise. The density operator is, in the $P$-representation [11],

$$\rho^S(\mu) = (\pi N)^{-1} \int \exp(-|\alpha - \mu|^2/N)|\alpha\rangle\langle\alpha|\, d^2\alpha, \tag{51}$$

where $|\alpha\rangle$ is a coherent state, $\alpha = \alpha_x + i\alpha_y$, $d^2\alpha = d\alpha_x d\alpha_y$, integration is taken over the entire complex $\alpha$-plane, and $N$ is the mean number of thermal photons in the mode. The normalization is such that $|\mu|^2$ is the mean number of photons contributed by the signal.

By (28) and (3.20) of [1] the r.l.d. operators corresponding to $\partial\rho^S/\partial\mu_x$ and $\partial\rho^S/\partial\mu_y$ are

$$L_x^S = \frac{a'^+}{N} + \frac{a'}{N+1}, \qquad L_y^S = i\left(\frac{a'^+}{N} - \frac{a'}{N+1}\right), \tag{52}$$

where $a' = a_S - \mu$ and $a_S$ is the annihilation operator for the mode, obeying the usual commutation rule $a_S a_S^+ - a_S^+ a_S = \mathbf{1}_S$. Using this and

$$\operatorname{Tr} \rho^S a'^+ a' = N,$$

we can easily derive the matrix $A$ of (35) and its inverse,

$$A = \frac{1}{N(N+1)}\begin{bmatrix} 2N+1 & -i \\ i & 2N+1 \end{bmatrix},$$
$$A^{-1} = \frac{1}{4}\begin{bmatrix} 2N+1 & i \\ -i & 2N+1 \end{bmatrix} \tag{53}$$

and

$$A^{-1}\begin{bmatrix} L_x^S \\ L_y^S \end{bmatrix} = \begin{bmatrix} Q_S - \mu_x \\ P_S - \mu_y \end{bmatrix}, \tag{54}$$

where

$$Q_S = \tfrac{1}{2}(a_S + a_S^+), \qquad P_S = \tfrac{1}{2}i(a_S^+ - a_S) \tag{55}$$

are proportional to the coordinate and momentum operators for the mode. If we now take $y^+ = [1\ 0]$ and $y^+ = [0\ 1]$ we obtain from the inequality (39) the bounds [3]

$$\operatorname{var} \hat{\mu}_x \quad \text{and} \quad \operatorname{var} \hat{\mu}_y \ge \tfrac{1}{2}(N + \tfrac{1}{2}). \tag{56}$$

By (47) the operator achieving the minimum value of the variance $\operatorname{var} \hat{\mu}_x$ is $Q_S$, and the operator minimizing $\operatorname{var} \hat{\mu}_y$ is $P_S$. These do not commute and cannot be measured simultaneously on the same system $S$ in such a way that both attain the minimum variance $\tfrac{1}{2}(N + \tfrac{1}{2})$.

If on the other hand we take $y^+ = [1\ i]$, we find from (39) for simultaneous measurement of the commuting estimators $M_x$ of $\mu_x$ and $M_y$ of $\mu_y$

$$\operatorname{var} \hat{\mu}_x + \operatorname{var} \hat{\mu}_y$$
$$= \operatorname{Tr} \rho[(M_x - \mu_x)^2 + (M_y - \mu_y)^2] \ge N + 1, \tag{57}$$

an inequality discovered by Yuen and Lax [22]. If we use (54) with $y^+ = [1\ i]$ in (47) we find that inequality is achieved in (57) by the noncommuting operators $M_x' = Q_S$, $M_y' = P_S$. The noncommuting resolution of the identity corresponding to (45) is provided by the operators

$$X(\mu; d^2\mu) = |\mu\rangle\langle\mu|\, d^2\mu/\pi, \tag{58}$$

in terms of the coherent states $|\mu\rangle$, and the real and imaginary parts of

$$Q_S + iP_S = a_S = \int \mu|\mu\rangle\langle\mu|\, d^2\mu/\pi \tag{59}$$

correspond to (46).

It is known that equality in (57) is achieved by measuring the commuting operators [24]

$$M_x = Q_S + Q_A, \qquad M_y = P_S - P_A \tag{60}$$

on a combination of the system $S$ and another harmonic oscillator $A$ in the ground state $|0_A\rangle$, the density operator being now

$$\rho = \rho^S \otimes |0_A\rangle\langle 0_A|. \tag{61}$$

Here $Q_A$ and $P_A$ are coordinate and momentum operators for $A$. Equation (44) requires, with $k(\mu_x,\mu_y) = 1$, $y^+ = [1\ i]$,

$$(\rho^S \otimes \rho^A)(M_x + iM_y) = \rho^S a_S \otimes \rho^A,$$

which is satisfied by (60) because

$$\rho^A(Q_A - iP_A) = \rho^A a_A^+ = |0_A\rangle\langle 0_A|a_A^+ = 0.$$

## V. Estimation of Essential Signal Parameters

By essential signal parameters we mean those intrinsic to the form of the signal, as distinct from its complex amplitude; the arrival time $\tau$ and carrier frequency $\Omega$ are the essential parameters we shall deal with here. We shall see that when these are measured separately, the Cramér–Rao inequality based on the symmetrized logarithmic derivatives [3] (s.l.d.) $\mathscr{L}_j$ yields greater lower bounds on the error variances than does the inequality (34) based on the right logarithmic derivatives (r.l.d.) $L_j$.

The s.l.d. $\mathscr{L}_j$ is an Hermitian operator defined by

$$\frac{\partial\rho}{\partial\theta_j} = \frac{1}{2}(\rho\mathscr{L}_j + \mathscr{L}_j\rho). \tag{62}$$

The corresponding Cramér–Rao inequality has the form [3]

$$\tilde{Y}B'Y \geq YA'^{-1}Y, \tag{63}$$

where the column vector $Y$ has real elements and $\tilde{Y} = (y_1, y_2, \cdots, y_m)$. The elements of the matrices $A'$ and $B'$ are

$$A_{ij}' = \frac{1}{2}\operatorname{Tr}\rho(\mathscr{L}_i\mathscr{L}_j + \mathscr{L}_j\mathscr{L}_i) = \operatorname{Tr}\left(\frac{\partial\rho}{\partial\theta_i}\right)\mathscr{L}_j, \tag{64}$$

$$B_{ij}' = \frac{1}{2}\operatorname{Tr}\rho(\Theta_i'\Theta_j' + \Theta_j'\Theta_i');\ \Theta_i' = \Theta_i - \theta_i. \tag{65}$$

If one goes through the derivation of (63) as in reference [3], one sees that it does not require that the estimating operators $\Theta_i$ commute. Furthermore, the density operator $\rho$ may have the product form $\rho^S(\theta) \otimes \rho^A$ corresponding to a combination of the receiver $S$ and an ignorant ancilla $A$. The matrix element $A_{ij}'$, by an analysis like that leading to (43), will then take the form

$$A_{ij}' = \operatorname{Tr}_S \frac{\partial\rho^S}{\partial\theta_i}\mathscr{L}_j^S = \frac{1}{2}\operatorname{Tr}_S \rho^S(\mathscr{L}_i^S\mathscr{L}_j^S + \mathscr{L}_j^S\mathscr{L}_i^S), \tag{66}$$

where the s.l.d. operators $\mathscr{L}_j^S$ are given by (62) with $\rho$ replaced by $\rho^S(\theta)$. The matrix $A'$ then depending only on $\rho^S$, the bound in (63) has a universal validity, applying no matter what ancilla $A$ is used nor what its density operator $\rho^A$ is.

We consider estimates of parameters $\theta$ of a coherent signal with complex envelope

$$g(\theta,t) = \beta f(t-\tau)e^{i\Omega(t-\tau)}, \quad \beta = \beta_x + i\beta_y, \quad \theta = (\beta_x,\beta_y,\tau,\Omega), \tag{67}$$

$\tau$ being the arrival time and $\Omega$ the deviation from a reference carrier frequency $\Omega_0$. The signal field is spatially coherent over the aperture of the observing instrument, so that (67) represents the amplitude of a single spatial mode [25]. The signal occupies such a narrow band of frequencies that the thermal noise can be considered to have a spectral density independent of frequency, and the observation interval $(-\frac{1}{2}T, \frac{1}{2}T)$ is assumed so long that the possibility that the signal overlaps either end of it can be disregarded. We then expand the signal into temporal modes

$$\gamma_k(t) = T^{-1/2}\exp i\omega_k t, \qquad \omega_k = 2\pi k/T, \tag{68}$$

whose amplitudes are

$$\mu_k(\theta) = \int_{-T/2}^{T/2} g(\theta,t)\gamma_k^*(t)\,dt$$

$$\doteq \beta T^{-1/2}\exp(-i\omega_k\tau)F(\omega_k - \Omega), \tag{69}$$

where

$$F(\omega) = \int_{-\infty}^{\infty} f(s)e^{-i\omega s}\,ds \tag{70}$$

is the spectrum of the signal. The density operator $\rho^S(\theta)$ now has a Gaussian $P$-representation, and as in (38) of reference [3],

$$\partial\rho/\partial\theta_j = \sum_k N^{-1}\left[\frac{\partial\mu_k^*}{\partial\theta_j}(a_k - \mu_k)\rho + \rho\frac{\partial\mu_k}{\partial\theta_j}(a_k^+ - \mu_k^*)\right], \tag{71}$$

where $N$ is the mean number of background photons per mode and $a_k$ and $a_k^+$ are the annihilation and creation operators for the $k$th mode. The right logarithmic derivative is now

$$L_j = \sum_k\left[N^{-1}\frac{\partial\mu_k}{\partial\theta_j}(a_k^+ - \mu_k^*) + (N+1)^{-1}\frac{\partial\mu_k^*}{\partial\theta_j}(a_k - \mu_k)\right], \tag{72}$$

as can be shown by using (3.47a) and (3.47b) of [8, p. 111]. From this, with

$$\operatorname{Tr}\rho a_k'^+ a_k' = N, \qquad a_k' = a_k - \mu_k,$$

we find for the matrix $A$ of (35) the elements

$$A_{ij} = \sum_k\left[N^{-1}\frac{\partial\mu_k}{\partial\theta_i}\frac{\partial\mu_k^*}{\partial\theta_j} + (N+1)^{-1}\frac{\partial\mu_k^*}{\partial\theta_i}\frac{\partial\mu_k}{\partial\theta_j}\right]$$

$$= \left[N^{-1}\frac{\partial^2 G}{\partial\theta_{1i}\,\partial\theta_{2j}} + (N+1)^{-1}\frac{\partial^2 G}{\partial\theta_{2i}\,\partial\theta_{1j}}\right], \qquad \theta_1 = \theta_2 = \theta \tag{73}$$

where

$$G(\theta_1,\theta_2) = \sum_k \mu_k(\theta_1)\mu_k^*(\theta_2)$$

$$= \beta_1\beta_2^*\int_{-\infty}^{\infty} F(\omega - \Omega_1)F^*(\omega - \Omega_2)\cdot\exp[-i\omega(\tau_1 - \tau_2)]\,d\omega/2\pi \tag{74}$$

in the limit $T \to \infty$. This is conveniently written in terms of the ambiguity function as [26, p. 354]

$$G(\theta_1,\theta_2) = \beta_1\beta_2^*\exp[-\tfrac{1}{2}i(\Omega_1 + \Omega_2)(\tau_1 - \tau_2)]\lambda(\tau_1 - \tau_2, \Omega_2 - \Omega_1). \tag{75}$$

By using (2.11) of ch. X of [27], we find the derivatives

$$\begin{aligned}
\partial^2G/\partial\beta_{1x}\partial\beta_{2x} &= \partial^2G/\partial\beta_{1y}\partial\beta_{2y} = 1,\\
\partial^2G/\partial\beta_{1x}\partial\beta_{2y} &= -\partial^2G/\partial\beta_{1y}\partial\beta_{2x} = -i,\\
\partial^2G/\partial\tau_1\partial\tau_2 &= |\beta|^2\,\Delta\omega^2,\\
\partial^2G/\partial\tau_1\partial\omega_2 &= -|\beta|^2[\Delta(\omega t) + \tfrac{1}{2}i],\\
\partial^2G/\partial\tau_2\partial\omega_1 &= -|\beta|^2[\Delta(\omega\tau) - \tfrac{1}{2}i],\\
\partial^2G/\partial\omega_1\partial\omega_2 &= |\beta|^2\,\Delta\tau^2,
\end{aligned} \tag{76}$$

where we have set $\theta_1 = \theta_2 = \theta$ and used the definitions of the mean-square duration $\Delta t^2$, mean-square bandwidth $\Delta\omega^2$, and mean duration-frequency product $\Delta(\omega t)$ as given in [26], ch. I. §5, and we have taken

$$\bar{t} = 0, \qquad \bar{\omega} + \Omega = 0, \tag{77}$$

where $\bar{t}$ is the mean epoch and $\bar{\omega}$ the mean frequency deviation of the signal. The matrix $A$ now has the block form

$$A = \begin{bmatrix} A_1 & 0 \\ 0 & A_2 \end{bmatrix}, \tag{78}$$

with $A_1$ given by (53); the elements of $A_2$ are

$$A_{2\tau\tau} = (2N + 1)|\beta|^2\Delta\omega^2/N(N + 1), \tag{79}$$

$$A_{2\tau\Omega} = A^*_{2\Omega\tau} = -|\beta|^2[(2N + 1)\Delta(\omega t) + \tfrac{1}{2}i]/N(N + 1), \tag{80}$$

$$A_{2\Omega\Omega} = (2N + 1)|\beta|^2\Delta t^2/N(N + 1). \tag{81}$$

Thus the bounds on the error variances as given by the Cramér–Rao inequality (39) based on the r.l.d.s $L_j$ depend on the matrix $A_2^{-1}$, whose elements are

$$(A_2^{-1})_{\tau\tau} = \mathscr{F}(2N + 1)\,\Delta t^2, \tag{82}$$

$$(A_2^{-1})_{\tau\Omega} = (A_2^{-1})_{\Omega\tau}^* = \mathscr{F}[(2N + 1)\,\Delta(\omega t) + \tfrac{1}{2}i], \tag{83}$$

$$(A_2^{-1})_{\Omega\Omega} = \mathscr{F}(2N + 1)\,\Delta\omega^2, \tag{84}$$

where

$$\mathscr{F} = |\beta|^{-2}N(N + 1)[(2N + 1)^2D - \tfrac{1}{4}]^{-1}, \quad D = \Delta\omega^2\,\Delta t^2 - [\Delta(\omega t)]^2. \tag{85}$$

In particular, (82) and (84) give the lower bounds on var $\hat{\tau}$ and var $\hat{\Omega}$, respectively.

From the symmetrized logarithmic derivative $\mathscr{L}_j$ as given by (39) of [3] we obtain, as in (43) therein, the matrix elements of $A'$ in (64),

$$A_{ij}' = 4(2N + 1)^{-1}\,\mathrm{Re}\,[\partial^2 G/\partial\theta_{1i}\,\partial\theta_{2j}]_{\theta_1=\theta_2=\theta}, \tag{86}$$

where Re indicates the real part. From (76) this yields the matrix $A'$ in block form

$$A' = \begin{bmatrix} A_1' & 0 \\ 0 & A_2' \end{bmatrix} \tag{87}$$

where $A_1'^{-1}$ is diagonal with diagonal elements $\tfrac{1}{4}(2N + 1)$, and the elements of $A_2'$ are

$$A'_{2\tau\tau} = 4(2N + 1)^{-1}|\beta|^2\Delta\omega^2, \tag{88}$$

$$A'_{2\tau\Omega} = A'_{2\Omega\tau} = -4(2N + 1)^{-1}|\beta|^2\Delta(\omega t), \tag{89}$$

$$A'_{2\Omega\Omega} = 4(2N + 1)^{-1}|\beta|^2\Delta\tau^2. \tag{90}$$

The elements of the matrix $A_2'^{-1}$ needed in (63) are now

$$(A_2'^{-1})_{\tau\tau} = \tfrac{1}{4}(2N + 1)|\beta|^{-2}\Delta t^2/D, \tag{91}$$

$$(A_2'^{-1})_{\tau\Omega} = \tfrac{1}{4}(2N + 1)|\beta|^{-2}\Delta(\omega t)/D, \tag{92}$$

$$(A_2'^{-1})_{\Omega\Omega} = \tfrac{1}{4}(2N + 1)|\beta|^2\Delta\omega^2/D, \tag{93}$$

with $D$ given in (85). In particular, (91) and (93) give lower bounds on the variances var $\hat{\tau}$ and var $\hat{\Omega}$ of estimates of arrival time $\tau$ and carrier-frequency shift $\Omega$. These bounds are larger than those given by (82) and (84), except when $D = \tfrac{1}{4}$. The minimum value $\tfrac{1}{4}$ is attained by $D$ when the signal has a Gaussian envelope [26, p. 20]; the s.l.d.s and the r.l.d.s then yield equal lower bounds.

If, on the other hand, we invent a risk function of the form

$$R = \frac{\mathrm{var}\,\hat{\tau}}{\Delta t^2} + \frac{\mathrm{var}\,\hat{\Omega}}{\Delta\omega^2}, \tag{94}$$

we find, upon using (39), (79)–(81), and $y^+ = [\Delta\omega\; i\Delta t]$, that when the operators estimating the arrival time $\tau$ and the frequency shift $\Omega$ commute,

$$R \geq \frac{2N(N + 1)}{|\beta|^2\Delta\omega\Delta t[(2N + 1)\Delta\omega\Delta t - \tfrac{1}{2}]} = R_1; \tag{95}$$

here we assumed for simplicity that $\Delta(\omega t) = 0$. The s.l.d. bounds in (91) and (93) yield, on the other hand,

$$R \geq \tfrac{1}{2}(2N + 1)|\beta|^{-2}\Delta\omega^{-2}\Delta t^{-2} = R_2, \tag{96}$$

and $R_1 \geq R_2$ for $\tfrac{1}{2} \leq \Delta\omega\Delta t \leq N + \tfrac{1}{2}$. Thus if the arrival time and carrier frequency of the signal are to be measured in the same receiver, the r.l.d. Cramér–Rao inequality (39) sometimes yields a superior lower bound on a weighted sum of the error variances to that provided by the s.l.d. inequality (63).

Efficient estimators for essential parameters such as arrival time and carrier-frequency do not exist, and the lower bounds derived here and in [3] have only an asymptotic significance. Both sets go into the classical forms in the limit $N \gg 1$.

For simultaneous estimation of the complex amplitude $\beta = \beta_x + i\beta_y$ the r.l.d. bound on var $\hat{\beta}_x$ + var $\hat{\beta}_y$ is, as we have seen, greater than the s.l.d. bound, and from this we gain an instructive insight into the role of noncommuting observables. A similar result was found for the special risk function in (94). For single measurements of other parameters than the amplitude, however, the s.l.d. bound may be superior.

## Conclusion

In order to realize minimum Bayes cost in quantum detection and estimation by measurements of commuting operators it may be necessary to couple the receiver $S$ with an ancillary system $A$ and perform the measurements on the combination. The resulting Bayes cost is the same as if commuting operators were somehow measured on the pair $S + A$ before they interacted, and the optimum strategy is equivalent to a resolution of the identity into possibly noncommuting, nonnegative-definite Hermitian operators acting in the Hilbert space $\mathscr{H}_S$ of the receiver alone. The minimization of the Bayes cost can, therefore, be carried out over the class of such noncommuting operators in $\mathscr{H}_S$, which having been found can be extended to a resolution of the identity into commuting projection operators in an encompassing Hilbert space $\mathscr{H}_S \otimes \mathscr{H}_A$ characterizing a combination of the receiver $S$ with some ancillary system $A$ initially ignorant of the state of the receiver. Minimum Bayes cost can be attained without violating the quantum-mechanical restriction of simultaneous measurement to the class of commuting Hermitian operators.

There are two types of Cramér–Rao inequalities setting lower bounds to mean-square errors and quadratic loss functions in unbiased estimates of parameters of the density operator of a quantum-mechanical receiver. Sometimes one, sometimes the other yields the superior bound. The difference between them lies not in how they handle the commutativity of the estimating operators, but in their definitions in terms of right-hand or symmetrized logarithmic derivatives. Both can be applied to a combination of the receiver $S$ with an arbitrary ignorant ancillary system $A$, on which combination $S + A$ commuting observables are measured. The lower bounds they assert depend only on the parameters of the receiver $S$. Because commuting estimators on $S + A$ can be reduced to possibly noncommuting estimators on the receiver $S$ alone, both inequalities apply to these as well.

## Acknowledgment

We are grateful to A. S. Holevo and H. P. H. Yuen for sending us preliminary copies of their papers, and to E. A. Bishop, H. P. H. Yuen, and S. D. Personick for enlightening discussions of these matters.

## References

[1] C. W. Helstrom, "Detection theory and quantum mechanics," *Inform. Contr.*, vol. 10, pp. 254–291, Mar. 1967.
[2] ——, "Detection theory and quantum mechanics, II," *Inform. Contr.*, vol. 13, pp. 156–171, Aug. 1968.
[3] ——, "The minimum variance of estimates in quantum signal detection," *IEEE Trans. Inform. Theory*, vol. IT-14, pp. 234–242, Mar. 1968.
[4] C. W. Helstrom, J. W. S. Liu, and J. P. Gordon, "Quantum mechanical communication theory," *Proc. IEEE*, vol. 58, pp. 1578–1598, Oct. 1970.
[5] H. P. Yuen, R. S. Kennedy, and M. Lax, "On optimal quantum receivers for digital signal detection," *Proc. IEEE*, vol. 58, pp. 1770–1773, Oct. 1970.
[6] P. A. M. Dirac, *The Principles of Quantum Mechanics*, 3rd ed, London: Oxford, chs. 1–3, pp. 1–83.
[7] D. Bohm, *Quantum Theory*. Englewood Cliffs, N.J.: Prentice-Hall, 1951.
[8] W. H. Louisell, *Radiation and Noise in Quantum Electronics*. New York: McGraw-Hill, 1964, ch. 1, pp. 1–68.
[9] J. von Neumann, *Mathematische Grundlagen der Quantenmechanik*. Berlin: Springer, 1932, ch. III, sect. 5, pp. 130–134.
[10] J. P. Gordon and W. H. Louisell, "Simultaneous measurement of noncommuting observables," in *Physics of Quantum Electronics*, P. L. Kelley, B. Lax, and P. E. Tannewald, Eds. New York: McGraw-Hill, 1966, pp. 833–840.
[11] R. J. Glauber, "Coherent and incoherent states of the radiation field," *Phys. Rev.*, vol. 131, pp. 2766–2788, Sept. 15, 1963.
[12] E. Arthurs and J. L. Kelly, Jr., "On the simultaneous measurement of a pair of conjugate observables," *Bell Syst. Tech. J.*, vol. 44, pp. 725–729, Apr. 1965.
[13] C. Y. She and H. Heffner, "Simultaneous measurement of noncommuting observables," *Phys. Rev.*, vol. 152, pp. 1103–1110, Dec. 23, 1966.
[14] C. W. Helstrom, "Fundamental limitations on the detectability of electromagnetic signals," *Int. J. Theor. Phys.*, vol. 1, pp. 37–50, May 1968.
[15] J. W. S. Liu, "Reliability of quantum-mechanical communication systems," Res. Lab. Electron., M.I.T., Cambridge, Mass., Tech. Rep. 468, Dec. 31, 1968, p. 22.
[16] A. S. Holevo, "Statistical problems in quantum physics," in *Proc. Soviet-Japanese Symp. Probability and Statistics*, vol. 1, 1968, p. 22–40.
——, "An analog of the theory of statistical decisions in a noncommutative theory of probability," *Tr. Mosk. Mat. Obshchesoyuz.* (in Russian), vol. 26, pp. 133–149, 1972.
[17] M. A. Naĭmark, "Spectral functions of a symmetric operator," *Izv. Akad. Nauk USSR*, Math. Ser., vol. 4, no. 3, pp. 277–318, 1940.
M. A. Neumark, "On a representation of additive operator set functions," *Comptes Rendus (Doklady) de l'Acad. des Sci. de l'URSS*, vol. 41, pp. 359–361, 1943.
[18] S. Personick, "Efficient analog communication over quantum channels," Ph.D. dissertation, Dep. Elec. Eng., M.I.T., Cambridge, Mass., Dec. 1969; also, Res. Lab. Electron., M.I.T., Cambridge, Mass., Tech. Rep. 477, May 15, 1970.
[19] R. S. Kennedy, "On the optimum receiver for the *M*-ary linearly independent pure state problem," M.I.T. Res. Lab. Electron, Cambridge, Mass., Quarterly Progress Rep. 110, July 15, 1973.
[20] H. P. H. Yuen, "Communication theory of quantum systems," Ph.D. dissertation, Dep. Elec. Eng., M.I.T., Cambridge, Mass., June 1970; also, M.I.T. Res. Lab. Electron., Cambridge, Mass., Tech. Rep. 482, Aug. 30, 1971, p. 124.
[21] S. D. Personick, "Application of quantum estimation theory to analog communication over quantum channels," *IEEE Trans. Inform. Theory*, vol. IT-17, pp. 240–246, May 1971.
[22] H. P. H. Yuen and M. Lax, "Multiple parameter quantum estimation and measurement of nonselfadjoint operators," presented at the IEEE Int. Symp. on Information Theory, Asilomar, Calif., Jan. 31, 1972; also, *IEEE Trans. Inform. Theory*, vol. IT-19, pp. 740–750, Nov. 1973. (In the newer version, the restriction to one pair of operators per mode has been removed.)
[23] L. Schmetterer, *Mathematische Statistik*. New York: Springer, 1966, p. 63.
[24] S. Personick, "An image-band interpretation of optical heterodyne noise," *Bell Syst. Tech. J.*, vol. 50, pp. 213–216, Jan. 1971.
[25] C. W. Helstrom, "Quantum detection theory," in *Progress in Optics*, vol. 10, E. Wolf, Ed. Amsterdam: North-Holland, 1972, pp. 289–369.
[26] ——, *Statistical Theory of Signal Detection*, 2nd ed. Oxford: Pergamon, 1968.

# 20



Reprinted from *IEEE Trans. Inf. Theory* **IT-21**(2):125–134 (1975)

# Optimum Testing of Multiple Hypotheses in Quantum Detection Theory

HORACE P. YUEN, MEMBER, IEEE, ROBERT S. KENNEDY, MEMBER, IEEE, AND MELVIN LAX

***Abstract*—The problem of specifying the optimum quantum detector in multiple hypotheses testing is considered for application to optical communications. The quantum digital detection problem is formulated as a linear programming problem on an infinite-dimensional space. A necessary and sufficient condition is derived by the application of a general duality theorem specifying the optimum detector in terms of a set of linear operator equations and inequalities. Existence of the optimum quantum detector is also established. The optimality of commuting detection operators is discussed in some examples. The structure and performance of the optimal receiver are derived for the quantum detection of narrow-band coherent orthogonal and simplex signals. It is shown that modal photon counting is asymptotically optimum in the limit of a large signaling alphabet and that the capacity goes to infinity in the absence of a bandwidth limitation.**

## I. Introduction

THE GENERAL mathematical specification of the optimal detector in multiple hypotheses testing is a well-known result in classical decision theory [1]–[3]. In this paper we will derive the corresponding optimal detector in quantum detection theory.

The development of quantum detection theory was initiated by Helstrom [4], who first formulated and solved the quantum binary decision problem. In that work the class of quantum measurements was taken to be those described by self-adjoint operators defined on the original receiver field. While this class is sufficient for the binary problem, more general quantum measurements may be needed in the $M$-ary case. Moreover, even among the class of self-adjoint operators the optimum $M$-ary quantum receiver was yet to be found. Previously, we formulated several problems related to the $M$-ary quantum detection problem [5], [6]. Although the formulation allowed for quantum measurements of nonselfadjoint operators, a complete solution of the detection problem was prevented by the lack of a mathematical characterization of all the quantum measurements that can be carried out in principle.

Recently, a generalized characterization of quantum measurement by probability operator measures was discovered in the mathematics literature [7]–[10]. In particular, Holevo [8]–[10] explicitly developed a generalized quantum measurement description and applied it in quantum detection theory. It turns out that one of the problems solved in [5], [6] is indeed the general $M$-ary quantum detection problem for probability operator measures. Holevo [8], [9] also treated this problem and independently derived the sufficient condition for the optimal Bayesian quantum detector by a different method, but he did not establish that it was also a necessary condition. The results presented here were first given in [5], [6] before Holevo's work appeared.

In the following section we will formulate the $M$-ary quantum detection problem in terms of probability operator measures. To demonstrate the essential simplicity of our major result, the necessary and sufficient condition on the optimal detector is derived for the case of a finite-dimensional space in Section III. The infinite-dimensional proof is given in the Appendix. In Section IV we discuss the optimality of self-adjoint operator measurements together with some examples. In Section V we discuss the structure and performance of the optimal receiver in the quantum detection of narrow-band coherent orthogonal and simplex signals.

## II. Formulation

We wish to consider the quantum correspondent of the following classical decision problem. Let $\{H_j\}$ be a finite set of $M$ hypotheses indexed by the set $J$ of integers, $J = \{1,\cdots,M\}$. An observation of a random variable $\tilde{X}$ is made, which is defined on a measurable space $(\Omega,A)$ with measurable sets $\mathscr{A}$, $\mathscr{A} \in A$. The elements of $\Omega$ are points in an Euclidean $k$-space, $\Omega \subseteq R^k$. The range $\tilde{X}$ is also taken to be $\Omega$ so that $x \in \Omega$, where $x$ denotes the value of $\tilde{X}$. The *a priori* probability $p_j$ on $J$ and the conditional density functions $p_j(x)$ are given. An optimal set of decision functions $\{\pi_j(x)\}$ is sought, which minimizes the Bayes cost

$$\bar{C} = \sum_{i=1}^{M} \sum_{j=1}^{M} p_j C_{ij} \int \pi_i(x) p_j(x)\, dx \tag{II.1}$$

where $C_{ij}$ is the cost of choosing $H_i$ when $H_j$ is true, $C_{ij} \in R$ a real number.[1] For each $x$, $\pi_j(x)$ is the probability of

Manuscript received February 15, 1974; revised September 6, 1974. This work was supported in part by NASA under Grant NGL 22-009-013 and in part by the Office of Naval Research under Grant N00014-73-C-0407.

H. P. Yuen is with the Research Laboratory of Electronics, Massachusetts Institute of Technology, Cambridge, Mass. 02139.

R. S. Kennedy is with the Department of Electrical Engineering and the Research Laboratory of Electronics, Massachusetts Institute of Technology, Cambridge, Mass. 02139.

M. Lax is with Bell Laboratories, Murray Hill, N.J., and the City College of the City University of New York, N.Y.

[1] More generally when conditional distribution functions $P_j(x)$ are given that may not possess a density function, the Bayes cost can be written as a Lebesgue–Stieltjes integral

$$\bar{C} = \sum_{i=1}^{M} \sum_{j=1}^{M} p_j C_{ij} \int \pi_i(x)\, dP_j(x). \tag{II.1n}$$

This will not affect our results, and only simple notational modifications are needed for proper interpretation in the later development.

deciding on $H_j$ given the observation $x$, so that

$$1 \geq \pi_j(x) \geq 0, \qquad j \in J \tag{II.2}$$

$$\sum_j \pi_j(x) = 1. \tag{II.3}$$

In a quantum formulation of the multiple hypotheses testing problem, the observation $x$ is obtained by a quantum measurement of a physical variable of the system under consideration. The quantum system is described by a separable Hilbert space $\mathscr{H}$ over the complex field $\mathbb{C}$ [11], [12]. Possible states (or mixed states) of the system are characterized by density operators [11], [12], which take the role of the distribution functions in the classical problem; to each hypothesis $H_j$, there corresponds a different density operator $\rho_j$. Each physical variable is represented by a probability operator measure[2] on $\mathscr{H}$ [7]–[10], [13]–[16].

A quantum measurement at the receiver can be characterized by a probability operator measure $X(A)$ defined on a certain measurable space $(\Omega,A)$. The measurement will yield some vector value $x \in \Omega \subseteq R^k$, and if $H_j$ is true, the probability distribution describing the observed $x$ is given by [7], [8]

$$P_j(x) = \text{tr } \rho_j X(\mathscr{A}_x) \tag{II.4}$$

$$\mathscr{A}_x = \{x' \in \Omega \mid x_i' \leq x_i\}. \tag{II.5}$$

Here the $x_i$ are the components of $x$ in $R^k$, and the trace operation tr applies to the complete expression that follows it.

We will, for simplicity, suppose that the measured random vector $x$ possesses a probability density. That density is given by

$$p_j(x) = \frac{dP_j}{dx} \equiv \text{tr } \rho_j X(x). \tag{II.6}$$

From the definition of a probability operator measure, $X(x)$ is a positive semidefinite self-adjoint operator on $\mathscr{H}$ for each $x$, with the property

$$\int X(x)\, dx = I \tag{II.7}$$

where $I$ is the identity operator on $\mathscr{H}$.

The measurements represented by probability operator measures on $\mathscr{H}$ can be interpreted as the ordinary quantum measurements of commuting observables on an extension space $\mathscr{H}^e$ of $\mathscr{H}$ [7]–[10]. Specifically, given a probability operator measure $X(\mathscr{A})$ on $(\Omega,A)$ and a density operator $\rho$ on $\mathscr{H}$, there exist a space $\mathscr{H}^A$, a tensor product density operator $\rho^e = \rho \otimes \rho^A$ on $\mathscr{H}^e = \mathscr{H} \otimes \mathscr{H}^A$, and a spectral measure[3] $E(\mathscr{A})$ on $\mathscr{H}^e$ and $(\Omega,A)$ such that the density function describing the measurement of the self-adjoint operator $X^e$ corresponding to $E(\mathscr{A})$ is given by (II.6). Mathematically, this is a consequence of Naimark's theorem on the equivalence of probability operator measures on $\mathscr{H}$ and spectral measures on some $\mathscr{H}^e$ [8], [17]. Physically, a measurement represented by a probability operator measure can be interpreted as a conventional quantum measurement on the composite system formed by adjoining an apparatus to the original system [11], [15], [16], [18], [19].

By choosing different quantum measurements corresponding to different $X(\mathscr{A})$, we have infinitely many different possible conditional probability densities $p_j(x)$ from (II.6) in contrast to a fixed given $p_j(x)$ in the classical problem. For a fixed $X(\mathscr{A})$, the average Bayes cost is of the same form as (II.1). The quantum decision problem consists in the choice of a measurable space $(\Omega,A)$, an $X(\mathscr{A})$, and a set of $\{\pi_j(x)\}$, which together yield the minimum Bayes cost $\bar{C}$.

Specifically, given that the random vector $x$ possesses a probability density (II.6), we can write (II.1) in the form

$$\bar{C} = \sum_i \sum_j p_j C_{ij} \text{ tr } \pi_i \rho_j \tag{II.8}$$

where we have defined the detection operators[4]

$$\pi_j = \int \pi_j(x) X(x)\, dx, \qquad j \in J. \tag{II.9}$$

The quantity $\text{tr } \pi_i \rho_j$ is the probability of choosing $H_i$ when $H_j$ is true. Since $X(x)$ is a positive semidefinite operator for each $x$, we see from (II.7) that the $\pi_j$ must obey

$$I \geq \pi_j \geq 0, \qquad j \in J \tag{II.10a}$$

and

$$\sum_j \pi_j = I \tag{II.10b}$$

where $\lambda_1 \geq \lambda_2$ ($\lambda_1 > \lambda_2$) denotes that $\lambda_1 - \lambda_2$ is a positive semidefinite (definite) operators. These operators $\{\pi_j\}$ of

[2] The definition of a probability operator measure is as follows.

Let $\Omega$ be a set and $A$ a $\sigma$-field of subsets of $\Omega$ with elements $\mathscr{A} \in A$. Let $B_+$ be the set of all bounded positive semidefinite linear operators on a Hilbert space $\mathscr{H}$. Then a probability operator measure $X(\mathscr{A})$ on $\mathscr{H}$ is defined to be a mapping with domain $A$ and range in $B_+$ such that

$$X(\mathscr{A}') = \sum_n X(\mathscr{A}_n) \tag{N.1}$$

for each sequence $\{\mathscr{A}_n \mid n = 0,1,\cdots\}$ of pairwise disjoint sets in $A$ with $\mathscr{A}' = \cup_n \mathscr{A}_n$, and that

$$X(\Omega) = I, \tag{N.2}$$

the identity operator.

Sometimes the term operator-valued measure is used when the condition (N.2) is omitted. Sometimes the term operator-valued measure is used including (A.2). Since we always include (N.2) in our discussion, we use the more accurate term probability operator measure throughout.

As a consequence of Naimark's theorem [17, p. 5], a probability operator measure on $\mathscr{H}$ can always be extended to become a spectral measure on an extension space $\mathscr{H}^e$ of $\mathscr{H}$. For further discussion of probability operator measures and its importance in quantum mechanics, see [7]–[10] and [13]–[14].

[3] A spectral measure on $\mathscr{H}$ is a probability operator measure on $\mathscr{H}$ with the additional condition that the range in $B$ is a set of mutually commuting projection operators. The spectral theorem of Von Neumann [42, p. 320], [11], [12] establishes the one-one correspondence of spectral measures and self-adjoint operators on a Hilbert space. Measurements of self-adjoint operators as discussed in ordinary quantum theory [11], [12], [27] are, therefore, measurements of spectral measures, a subset of the measurements of probability operator measures.

[4] More generally if $x$ does not possess a density we would write

$$\pi_j = \int \pi_j(x)\, dX(\mathscr{A}_x) \tag{II.9n}$$

with the probability operator measure $X(\mathscr{A}_x)$. This integral with respect to an operator-valued measure can be defined through its action of generating ordinary measures [13, p. 27].

(II.9) incorporate all the freedom in our optimization; hence the minimization may be formulated in terms of them.

Note that a set $\pi_j$ obeying (II.10) is a probability operator measure on $\Omega = J$, and hence represents a quantum measurement. The measurement outcome in this case will be an integer $j$, $j \in J$, with probability distribution tr $\rho\pi_j$ for a given density operator $\rho$. Thus we may either minimize $\bar{C}$ with respect to the probability operator measure $X(x)$ satisfying (II.7) and the decision probabilities $\pi_j(x)$ satisfying (II.2), (II.3), or we may minimize it with respect to the $\pi_j$ satisfying (II.10). The former approach allows the "measurement" to be followed by "data processing"; the latter approach incorporates this processing into the description of the measurement. The latter approach is more direct for the purposes of this paper.

As a final preliminary we define

$$\rho_j' = \sum_{i=1}^{M} p_i C_{ji} \rho_i, \qquad j \in J. \tag{II.11}$$

The $\rho_j'$ will be trace class (or nuclear) self-adjoint operators on $\mathscr{H}$ since $\rho_j$ are positive semidefinite operators with unit trace. We can then summarize our problem as follows.

Let $B$ be the Banach space over $R$ of bounded self-adjoint operators on $\mathscr{H}$. Let $\rho_j' \in T$ be given, where $T$ is the Banach space of trace class self-adjoint operators. (For a discussion of operator theory and operator spaces, consult [39]–[42].) We wish to consider the minimization problem

$$\min_{\pi_j \in B} \sum_{j=1}^{M} \text{tr } \pi_j \rho_j', \qquad \text{given } \rho_j' \in T \tag{II.12}$$

under the constraint

$$\pi_j \geq 0, \qquad j \in J \tag{II.13a}$$

$$\sum_{j=1}^{M} \pi_j = I. \tag{II.13b}$$

## III. Optimum Detector

The preceding minimization problem is a linear programming problem on an infinite-dimensional normed space. Although it is not usually done, the classical decision problem can also be phrased as a linear programming problem by considering the decision functions $\pi_j(x)$ as elements of an appropriate space. The solutions of both problems can be obtained by a general duality theorem for linear programs.

The derivation of the general solution to the problem we have posed involves, and is to some extent obscured by, the subtleties of infinite-dimensional spaces. Therefore, it is relegated to the Appendix. On the other hand, the nature of the proof is instructive in itself and elucidates the character of the result. To exhibit this nature in the simplest context we derive here the optimal detector for a finite-dimensional space $H$. This restricted derivation involves more familiar concepts than does the general one given in the Appendix. Moreover, the finite-dimensional result is of independent interest since it includes the important example of detecting $M$ pure quantum states.

The problem now becomes the following, from (II.12)–(II.13). Let $H_D$ be a finite $D$-dimensional space over $\mathbb{C}$. Let $T_D$ be the linear space over the real numbers $R$, whose elements consist of self-adjoint linear transformations on $H_D$, or equivalently of $D \times D$ Hermitian matrices. The problem is

$$\min_{\pi_j \in T_D} \sum_{j=1}^{M} \text{tr } \pi_j \rho_j', \qquad \text{given } \rho_j' \in T_D \tag{III.1}$$

subject to the constraints

$$\pi_j \geq 0, \qquad j \in J \qquad \text{(III.2)}^5$$

$$\sum_{j=1}^{M} \pi_j = I_D \tag{III.3}$$

where $I_D$ is the identity on $H_D$. This is now a finite-dimensional linear programming problem.

Before proceeding we note a property of $T_D$ that will be heavily exploited in subsequent development. Specifically, upon defining an inner product in $T_D$ by

$$(\lambda_1,\lambda_2) = \text{tr } \lambda_1\lambda_2 \tag{III.4}$$

the space $T_D$ becomes a $D^2$ dimensional inner-product space over $R$. It is, therefore, isometrically isomorphic to $R^{D^2}$, the $D^2$-dimensional Euclidean space [20, pp. 166, 186]. This means that $T_D$ and $R^{D^2}$ are completely equivalent, both algebraically and topologically. Thus any result in $R^{D^2}$ whose validity depends only on the inner-product structure of $R^{D^2}$ is equally valid on $T_D$.

The optimum quantum detector can be determined by employing the following linear programming duality theorem [21, p. 126].

*Duality Theorem*

Let $y,u,b,c$ be column vectors in an Euclidean space $R^k$ and let $A$ be a $k \times k$ matrix on $R^k$. Let the corresponding row vectors be denoted by $y',u',b',c'$ and the transpose matrix by $A'$. Then

$$\min_{\substack{Au=c \\ u\geq 0}} b'u = \max_{A'y\leq b} c'y. \tag{III.5}$$

Furthermore, a solution to the left or the right problem in (III.5) exists if and only if a solution exists for both problems.

To apply this theorem to the problem of interest, (III.1)–(III.3), we consider the direct-product space

$$T_D{}^M = \underbrace{T_D \times T_D \times \cdots \times T_D}_{M} \tag{III.6}$$

which is of dimension $MD^2$. An element of $T_D{}^M$ is of the form

$$\boldsymbol{\lambda}' = (\lambda_1,\cdots,\lambda_M) \tag{III.7}$$

where $\boldsymbol{\lambda}$ is in the form of a column vector. The inner product in $T_D{}^M$ is, naturally,

$$(\boldsymbol{\lambda}^a,\boldsymbol{\lambda}^b) = \boldsymbol{\lambda}^{a\prime}\boldsymbol{\lambda}^b \tag{III.8}$$

$$= \text{tr} \sum_{j=1}^{M} \lambda_j{}^a\lambda_j{}^b. \tag{III.9}$$

[5] Recall that $\pi_j \geq 0$ means $\pi_j$ is positive semidefinite.

In this notation, the problem (III.1)–(III.3) can be written as

$$\min_{\substack{\tilde{A}u=c \\ u\geq 0}} b'u \tag{III.10}$$

with

$$u' = (\pi_1,\cdots,\pi_M) \tag{III.11}$$

$$c' = (I_D,0,\cdots,0) \tag{III.12}$$

$$b' = (\rho_1',\cdots,\rho_M') \tag{III.13}$$

$$\tilde{A} = \begin{pmatrix} I_D & \cdots & I_D \\ 0 & \cdots & 0 \\ \vdots & \cdots & \vdots \\ 0 & \cdots & 0 \end{pmatrix}. \tag{III.14}$$

By virtue of the previously noted equivalence between $T_D{}^M$ and $R^{MD^2}$, the duality theorem (III.5) can be used to yield, with $\lambda' = (\lambda,0,\cdots,0)$,

$$\max_{\substack{\lambda-\rho_j'\leq 0 \\ \lambda\in T_D}} \operatorname{tr}\lambda = \min_{\substack{\pi_j\geq 0 \\ \Sigma_j\pi_j=I_D \\ \pi_j\in T_D}} \sum_j \operatorname{tr}\pi_j\rho_j'. \tag{III.15}$$

The left-side problem,

$$\max_{\lambda\in T_D} \operatorname{tr}\lambda \tag{III.16}$$

subject to the constraint

$$\lambda \leq \rho_j', \qquad j\in J \tag{III.17}$$

is the dual problem to (III.1)–(III.3), its right-side. Equation (III.15) is the foundation of our derivation, which will be given after the following two lemmas.

*Lemma 1:* A solution to problem (III.1)–(III.3) exists.

*Proof:* The set of elements $\pi$ obeying (III.2), (III.3) is closed and bounded and, therefore, compact. The existence of a solution follows from the Weierstrass theorem [20, p. 140] since the function is continuous.

With some change of terminology this proof is valid in the infinite-dimensional case, which was first given by Holevo [9].

The following lemma is required in the proof of our theorem. It will also be useful in our later applications. We prove the infinite-dimensional version here since it requires no extra effort.

*Lemma 2:* Let $\lambda_1 \in B$ and $\lambda_2 \in T$ be two positive semidefinite self-adjoint operators. Then

$$\operatorname{tr}\lambda_1\lambda_2 \geq 0. \tag{III.18}$$

Equality in (III.18) holds if and only if

$$\lambda_1\lambda_2 = \lambda_2\lambda_1 = 0. \tag{III.19}$$

*Proof:* Every $\lambda_1 \geq 0$ admits a unique positive semidefinite square root $\lambda_1{}^{1/2}$ such that $\lambda_1 = (\lambda_1{}^{1/2})^2$, $\lambda_1{}^{1/2} \geq 0$. Let also $\lambda_2 = (\lambda_2{}^{1/2})$, we have

$$\begin{aligned}\operatorname{tr}\lambda_1\lambda_2 &= \operatorname{tr}(\lambda_1{}^{1/2})^2(\lambda_2{}^{1/2})^2 \\ &= \operatorname{tr}(\lambda_1{}^{1/2}\lambda_2{}^{1/2})^\dagger(\lambda_1{}^{1/2}\lambda_2{}^{1/2}) \geq 0 \end{aligned}\tag{III.20}$$

where $\dagger$ denotes the adjoint of an operator. It also follows from (III.20) that $\operatorname{tr}\lambda_1\lambda_2 = 0$, if and only if $\lambda_1{}^{1/2}\lambda_2{}^{1/2} = 0$.

If $\lambda_1{}^{1/2}\lambda_2{}^{1/2} = 0$, $\lambda_1{}^{1/2}\lambda_1{}^{1/2}\lambda_2{}^{1/2}\lambda_2{}^{1/2} = \lambda_1\lambda_2 = 0$. On the other hand, $\lambda_1\lambda_2 = 0$ implies $\lambda_2\lambda_1 = 0$ so that $[\lambda_1,\lambda_2] = 0$. This in turn implies $[\lambda_1{}^{1/2},\lambda_2] = 0 = [\lambda_1{}^{1/2},\lambda_2{}^{1/2}]$. Thus $\lambda_1{}^{1/2}\lambda_2{}^{1/2}\lambda_1{}^{1/2}\lambda_2{}^{1/2} = 0$ implies $\lambda_1{}^{1/2}\lambda_2{}^{1/2} = 0$, and the proof is completed.

We are now prepared to prove the following fundamental theorem.

*Theorem I:* There exists a set $\{\pi_j\}$ that solves (III.1)–(III.3). A necessary and sufficient condition for this optimum set, in addition to the constraint (III.2), (III.3), is

$$\sum_{i=1}^{M} \pi_i\rho_i' = \sum_{i=1}^{M} \rho_i'\pi_i \tag{III.21a}$$

$$\sum_{i=1}^{M} \pi_i\rho_i' \leq \rho_j', \qquad j\in J. \tag{III.21b}$$

*Proof:* The existence of a solution to (III.1)–(III.3) has already been proved in Lemma 1. It remains to establish (III.21) from (III.15).

Let $\{\pi_j{}^\circ\}$ and $\lambda^\circ$ solve the right and left problems of (III.15), respectively. Then (III.15) gives

$$\sum_j \operatorname{tr}\pi_j{}^\circ(\lambda^\circ - \rho_j') = 0. \tag{III.22}$$

By Lemma 2, (III.22) yields

$$\pi_j{}^\circ(\lambda^\circ - \rho_j') = (\lambda^\circ - \rho_j')\pi_j{}^\circ = 0, \qquad j\in J. \tag{III.23}$$

Summing (III.23) over $j$, we obtain

$$\lambda^\circ = \sum_j \pi_j{}^\circ\rho_j' = \sum_j \rho_j'\pi_j{}^\circ. \tag{III.24}$$

Therefore, (III.24) together with the constraint $\lambda^\circ \leq \rho_j'$ show that (III.21) are necessary conditions on $\{\pi_j{}^\circ\}$.

To show sufficiency, we note from Lemma 2 that any set $\{\pi_j\}$ obeying (III.2), (III.3) implies, for any $\lambda \in T_D$ obeying (III.17),

$$\operatorname{tr}\lambda \leq \operatorname{tr}\sum_j \pi_j\rho_j'. \tag{III.25}$$

However, for a set $\{\pi_j{}^\circ\}$ satisfying (III.21), (III.25) will hold with equality for $\lambda = \sum_j \pi_j{}^\circ\rho_j'$. Hence $\operatorname{tr}\sum_j \pi_j\rho_j'$ is indeed minimized by the set $\{\pi_j{}^\circ\}$. The proof of our theorem is completed.

It should be observed that Lemma 1 is needed only in establishing the existence of a solution to our detection problem. From the duality theorem (III.5), (III.21) always provides a necessary and sufficient condition on the optimum $\{\pi_j\}$ independent of whether a solution exists.

A result identical to Theorem I can be developed for the infinite-dimensional case, using the same conceptual approach. The only complication arises from the mathematical technicalities of an infinite-dimensional space. In the Appendix, the proof of this general case is given in detail. For the purpose of emphasizing its general validity, we state here the general version of Theorem I.

*Theorem IA:* There exists a set $\{\pi_j\}$ that solves the problem (II.12)–(II.13). A necessary and sufficient condition for this optimum set, in addition to the constraint (II.13), is

$$\sum_{i\in J} \pi_i\rho_i' = \sum_{i\in J} \rho_i'\pi_i \tag{III.26a}$$

$$\sum_{i\in J} \pi_i\rho_i' \leq \rho_j', \qquad j\in J. \tag{III.26b}$$

We note in passing that the optimum set $\{\pi_j^\circ\}$ is not, in general, unique. To see this, suppose that the $\rho_j$ commute among themselves so that the $\pi_j$ are commuting projection operators [4], [22]. If there exists an element $l \in \mathscr{H}$ for which

$$\operatorname{tr} \rho_i' P_l = \operatorname{tr} \rho_k' P_l < \operatorname{tr} \rho_j' P_l, \qquad j \neq i \neq k \qquad \text{(III.27)}$$

where $P_l$ is the projection operator onto $l$, then $P_l$ can be incorporated into either $\pi_i$ or $\pi_k$ with the same final cost. Thus the optimum set $\{\pi_j\}$ is not unique in general.

A different form of the conditions (III.26) was given in our previous work [5], [6]. Defining

$$\rho_j'' = \sum_i p_i(1 - C_{ji})\rho_i, \qquad j \in J \qquad \text{(III.28)}$$

the necessary and sufficient conditions on the optimum $\pi_j$ are [5], [6],

$$\sum_{j \in J} \pi_j \rho_j'' = \sum_{j \in J} \rho_j'' \pi_j \qquad \text{(III.29a)}$$

$$\sum_{i \in J} \pi_i \rho_i'' \geq \rho_j'', \qquad j \in J. \qquad \text{(III.29b)}$$

It is obvious that (III.29) is identical to (III.26). The additional condition

$$\pi_j \left( \sum_{i \in J} \pi_i \rho_i'' - \rho_j'' \right) = 0, \qquad j \in J \qquad \text{(III.30)}$$

reported in [5], [6] is redundant,[6] given (III.29), the constraint (II.13), and Lemma 2.

Equation (III.26a) and (III.30) were given by Holevo [8], [9] as necessary conditions on the optimal $M$-ary quantum detector. He also showed that (III.26) provide a sufficient condition but did not show that they were necessary.

In general, one cannot expect an analytic solution to the set (III.26) of linear equations and inequalities on $\pi_j$, just as one cannot for the familiar finite-dimensional linear programming problem. Some approximation method will usually be needed to obtain a usable form of $\{\pi_j\}$. The dual problem (A.1)–(A.2) may be easier to handle in this regard, because the operators $\pi_j$ are not even generally compact. Of course, one may always attempt to guess the solution of (III.26) and then verify that it satisfies the conditions. The situation is not unlike that of computing channel capacity. Some simple examples on the use of (III.26) are considered in the following section.

## IV. Discussions

A solution of the quantum detection problem was previously found [4], [22] under the condition that the density operator $\rho_j$ obey

$$[\rho_i - \rho_j, \rho_k - \rho_l] = 0, \qquad i,j,k,l \in J. \qquad \text{(IV.1)}$$

Equation (IV.1) includes the binary case and the situation where the $\rho_j$ commute among themselves as special cases. Under (IV.1), there is a complete orthonormal sequence of vectors $l_n \in \mathscr{H}$, which are simultaneous eigenvectors of $\rho_i - \rho_j$ [11], [12]. The optimum quantum detector measures a commuting set of $\pi_j$, which are simultaneously diagonal in the $l_n$-representation. A decision is then made in the usual way by maximizing the *a posteriori* probability. We have shown [5], [6] that such a set $\{\pi_j\}$ obeys our condition (III.29). Another important situation in which the optimum $\pi_j$ are commutative occurs when the given $\rho_j$ are one-dimensional projection operators into $M$ linearly independent vectors [23].

With these examples in mind, the question arises as to when the optimum $\pi_j$ are commutative, i.e., when does the optimal detector measure a self-adjoint operator on $\mathscr{H}$ directly?

One approach to this question would be to derive the necessary and sufficient condition on the optimum detector among those characterized by commutative $\pi_j$, and then compare the result to (III.26). Indeed, since there is no loss of optimality in adapting a nonrandom strategy after the choice of a quantum measurement, the $\{\pi_j\}$ may be taken to be commuting projecting operators. Therefore, it suffices to consider the problem (II.12)–(II.13) with the additional constraint [5], [6]

$$\pi_j^2 = \pi_j, \qquad j \in J. \qquad \text{(IV.2)}$$

This nonlinear equality constraint precludes a direct use of the techniques applied in Section III. However, one can apply the general Lagrange theorem [24, p. 243] to obtain a necessary condition, which turns out to be the same as (III.26) [5, p. 166], [6]. Unfortunately, it is more difficult to obtain a necessary and sufficient condition, and it is not yet known when the optimum $\pi_j$ will be commutative, except for the situations discussed previously.

That such measurements are not always optimum has been demonstrated by example. For the parameter estimation problem the first example in which the optimum receiver cannot be realized by a self-adjoint operator was given in [25], [16]. Holevo [8] gave the first such example for the discrete decision problem. The following is a generalization of that example. Although not of great practical interest, it does demonstrate that the optimum detection performance cannot always be achieved by self-adjoint operators defined on the original space.

Consider the problem of minimizing the probability of error with $p_j = 1/M$, so that $C_{ij} = 1$, $i \neq j$; $C_{ij} = 0$, $i = j$. We will use (III.29) with $\rho_j'' = (1/M)\rho_j$. Let each $\rho_j$ be a one-dimensional projection operator onto $l_j \in \mathscr{H}$,

$$\rho_j = P_{l_j}, \qquad j \in J. \qquad \text{(IV.3)}$$

From the problem formulation (II.12)–(II.13), it is easy to see that $\mathscr{H}$ can be restricted to the $D$-dimensional space $\mathscr{H}_D$ generated by $\{l_j\}$, $D \leq M$.

If there exists a set of real numbers $\alpha_j \geq 0$ such that

$$\sum_{j=1}^{M} \alpha_j \rho_j = I_D \qquad \text{(IV.4)}$$

where $I_D$ is the identity in the $D$-dimensional space, the optimum $\pi_j$ are given by

$$\pi_j = \alpha_j \rho_j, \qquad j \in J. \qquad \text{(IV.5)}$$

[6] This redundancy was brought to our attention by Holevo.

In particular, we have $\lambda = (1/M)I_D$, and the constraint (II.13) and the condition (III.29) are obeyed by the $\pi_j$ given by (IV.5). It is also easy to show that the resulting minimized error probability is

$$P(\varepsilon) = 1 - \frac{D}{M}. \qquad \text{(IV.6)}$$

We next observe that when the $\rho_j$ are one-dimensional projectors, as in (IV.3), the probability of error is always bounded below by

$$P(\varepsilon) \geq 1 - \frac{D}{M} \qquad \text{(IV.7)}$$

where $D$ is the dimension of the space spanned by the $\rho_j$. This follows from

$$I_D \geq P_{l_j}, \qquad j \in J \qquad \text{(IV.8)}$$

$$\sum_j \pi_j = I_D \qquad \text{(IV.9)}$$

so that

$$\sum_j \operatorname{tr} \rho_j P_{l_j} \leq \sum_j \operatorname{tr} \pi_j = D. \qquad \text{(IV.10)}$$

Equality in (IV.7) occurs when and only when (IV.4) is satisfied. Indeed, from (IV.10)

$$\sum_j \operatorname{tr} \pi_j (I_D - P_{l_j}) = 0. \qquad \text{(IV.11)}$$

Using (IV.8) and (III.18), we see

$$\operatorname{tr} \pi_j (I_D - P_{l_j}) \geq 0, \qquad j \in J. \qquad \text{(IV.12)}$$

Together with (IV.11) and (III.19) this implies the following

$$\pi_j = \pi_j P_{l_j} = P_{l_j} \pi_j, \qquad j \in J. \qquad \text{(IV.13)}$$

Equation (IV.13) shows that (IV.5) must hold for some $\alpha_j \geq 0$. With the constraint (IV.9), (IV.4) therefore follows. We have proved the following lemma.

*Lemma 3:* Let $M$ given $\rho_j$ be one-dimensional projection operators $P_{l_j}$ that span a $D$-dimensional space. Then the probability of detection error is bounded below by (IV.7), and equality is achieved if and only if (IV.4) is satisfied for some $\alpha_j \geq 0$. Furthermore, the $\pi_j$ achieving the minimum error probability must be of the form (IV.5) when (IV.4) is satisfied.

It follows from this lemma that when $D < M$, the minimum error probability cannot be achieved by measurement of commuting $\pi_j$ under the situation (IV.4) since it is achieved by (IV.5) uniquely. This shows that measurements of general probability operator measures may be needed in $M$-ary quantum detection.

As an aside, we note that (IV.4) is satisfied when the vectors $l_j$ in the range of $P_{l_j}$ are distributed in a properly symmetric fashion on the surface of a unit $D$-dimensional sphere. For example, in two-dimensions any number of $M(M > D)$ vectors on the perimeter of a circle such that the length of arc between two nearest neighbors is a constant obey (IV.4) with $\alpha_j = D/M$. We omit the proof of this fact here for brevity.

## V. Quantum Noise in Orthogonal and Simplex Signals

We now discuss the structure and performance of the optimum receiver in the quantum detection of coherent orthogonal and simplex signals. Consider a given classical signal set $\{S_i(t), i = 1, \cdots, M\}$. It is well known that each of the waveforms $\{S_i(t)\}$ is completely determined by the vector of its coefficients

$$S_j = (S_{j_1}, \cdots, S_{j_N}), \qquad j \in J \qquad \text{(V.1)}$$

in an orthonormal set of basic functions $\{\phi_i(t)\}$

$$S_j(t) = \sum_{i=1}^{N} S_{ji}\phi_i(t), \qquad j \in J \qquad \text{(V.2)}$$

with $N \leq M$, [26, p. 225]. We consider the narrow-band orthogonal signal set

$$\begin{aligned} S_1 &= \underbrace{(\beta, 0, \cdots, 0)}_{M} \\ S_j &= (\underbrace{0, \cdots, 0}, \beta, \underbrace{0, \cdots, 0}) \quad j\text{th} \\ S_M &= (0, \cdots, 0, \beta) \end{aligned} \qquad \text{(V.3)}$$

where $\beta$ is a known real constant so that $hf\beta^2$ represents the identical energy in each of the signals. Here $h$ is Planck's constant, and $f$ is the nominal frequency of the narrow-band signal. This set of signals is coherent since the phase of $\beta$ is known exactly.

The density operators representing such coherent narrow-band orthogonal signals at a quantum receiver can be written as a projection operator whose range is a direct product of state vectors. These state vectors are defined in individual Hilbert spaces describing the different "modes." Using the Dirac notation [27], we can write

$$\rho_j = |j\rangle\langle j| \qquad \text{(V.4)}$$

$$\begin{aligned} |1\rangle &= |\beta\rangle_1 |0\rangle_2 \cdots |0\rangle_M \\ |j\rangle &= |0\rangle_1 \cdots |0\rangle_{j-1} |\beta\rangle_j |0\rangle_{j+1} \cdots |0_M\rangle \\ |M\rangle &= |0\rangle_1 \cdots |0\rangle_{M-1} |\beta\rangle_M. \end{aligned} \qquad \text{(V.5)}$$

The notation $|\alpha\rangle_j$ indicates the coherent state vector of the $j$th mode with eigenvalue $\alpha$ for the photon destruction operator of that mode [28], [29, ch. 7]. The detailed justification for (V.4) will not be discussed here. The reader is referred to [5], [30].

The coherent orthogonal signals (V.3) can be transformed to the following coherent simplex signals in the standard way [26, p. 259],

$$\begin{aligned} S_1 &= \left(\beta\left(1 - \frac{1}{M}\right), -\frac{\beta}{M}, \cdots, -\frac{\beta}{M}\right) \\ &\vdots \\ S_j &= \left(\underbrace{-\frac{\beta}{M}, \cdots, -\frac{\beta}{M}}, \beta\left(1 - \frac{1}{M}\right), \underbrace{-\frac{\beta}{M}, \cdots, -\frac{\beta}{M}}\right) \quad j\text{th} \\ &\vdots \\ S_M &= \left(-\frac{\beta}{M}, \cdots, -\frac{\beta}{M}, \beta\left(1 - \frac{1}{M}\right)\right). \end{aligned} \qquad \text{(V.6)}$$

The density operator representation of (V.5) is accordingly of the form (V.4) with

$$|1\rangle = \left|\beta\left(1-\frac{1}{M}\right)\right\rangle_1 \left|-\frac{\beta}{M}\right\rangle_2 \cdots \left|-\frac{\beta}{M}\right\rangle_M$$
$$\vdots$$
$$|j\rangle = \left|-\frac{\beta}{M}\right\rangle_1 \cdots \left|-\frac{\beta}{M}\right\rangle_{j-1} \left|\beta\left(1-\frac{1}{M}\right)\right\rangle_j \cdot \left|-\frac{\beta}{M}\right\rangle_{j+1} \cdots \left|-\frac{\beta}{M}\right\rangle_M$$
$$\vdots$$
$$|M\rangle = \left|-\frac{\beta}{M}\right\rangle_1 \cdots \left|-\frac{\beta}{M}\right\rangle_{M-1} \left|\beta\left(1-\frac{1}{M}\right)\right\rangle_M. \tag{V.7}$$

The set of pure states (V.5) or (V.7) obeys the following special property:

$$\langle i \mid j\rangle = \gamma, \qquad i \neq j \tag{V.8}$$

for a real constant $\gamma$ independent of $i$ and $j$. In this case we have $\gamma = e^{-\beta^2}$. Of course, we always have from normalization

$$\langle j \mid j\rangle = 1, \qquad j \in J. \tag{V.9}$$

The optimum quantum receiver for such states (V.4), (V.8), has been briefly described previously [5], [6]. We now give a more complete description with particular reference to orthogonal and simplex signals.

We will show that the optimum receiver measures a set of commuting projection operators $\pi_j$

$$\pi_j = |\alpha_j\rangle\langle\alpha_j|, \qquad j \in J \tag{V.10a}$$

$$|\alpha_i\rangle = \sum_{j=1}^{M} \alpha_{ij}|j\rangle, \qquad i \in J \tag{V.10b}$$

$$\alpha_{ii} = \frac{a + (M-2)b}{(a-b)[a + (M-1)b]}, \qquad i \in J \tag{V.10c}$$

$$\alpha_{ij} = \frac{-b}{(a-b)[a + (M-1)b]}, \qquad i \neq j \tag{V.10d}$$

where

$$a = b + \sqrt{1-\gamma} \qquad b = \frac{-\sqrt{1-\gamma} + \sqrt{1 + (M-1)\gamma}}{M}. \tag{V.11}$$

These values of $a$ and $b$ provide a solution to the equations

$$a^2 + (M-1)b^2 = 1 \tag{V.12a}$$

$$2ab + (M-2)b^2 = \gamma. \tag{V.12b}$$

It is easy to show directly from (V.8)–(V.10) and (V.12) that the states $|\alpha_j\rangle$ obey

$$\langle \alpha_j \mid j\rangle = a \tag{V.13a}$$

$$\langle \alpha_i \mid j\rangle = b, \qquad i \neq j. \tag{V.13b}$$

Equation (V.12) also implies, with (V.8)–(V.10) and (V.13)

$$\sum_{i=1}^{M} |\alpha_i\rangle\langle\alpha_i| = I_M \tag{V.14}$$

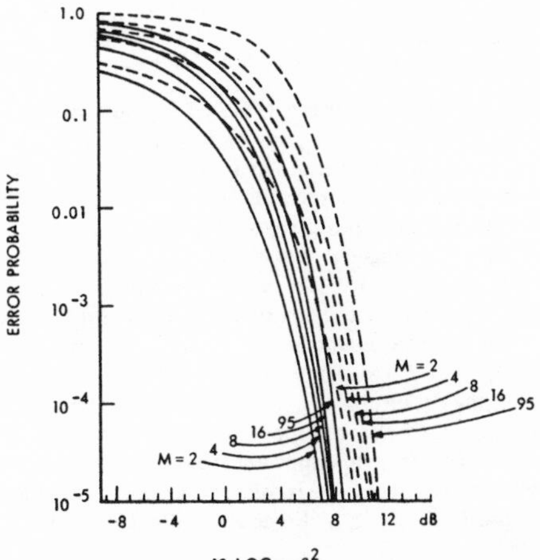


Fig. 1. Behavior of error probability as function of signal energy for coherent orthogonal and simplex signals. Solid lines are obtained from (V.17), representing optimum error behavior; dotted lines result from homodyne receiver and are adopted from [26, p. 259].

in the $M$-dimensional space spanned by the $M$ vectors $|j\rangle$. Equation (V.14) implies

$$\langle \alpha_i \mid \alpha_j\rangle = \delta_{ij}. \tag{V.15}$$

The necessary condition (III.21a) is satisfied from (V.15) and (V.13). The additional condition (III.21b) will also be satisfied if

$$a^2 > ab, \qquad ab > b^2. \tag{V.16}$$

Equation (V.16) is indeed valid for $(a,b)$ given by (V.11). Therefore, (V.10)–(V.11) provide an optimal receiver to the cases of orthogonal and simplex signals. It can also be shown that the optimum set of $\pi_j$ is unique in this case [31].

The optimal probability of correct detection is given by $a^2$ or

$$P[C] = \left\{\frac{(M-1)(1-e^{-\beta^2})^{1/2} + [1 + (M-1)e^{-\beta^2}]^{1/2}}{M}\right\}^2. \tag{V.17}$$

Similar to the classical case, the performance expression for the orthogonal and simplex signals are the same, but the simplex signals have their energies reduced by the factor $[1 - (1/M)]$ from that required for the orthogonal signals. The error probability from (V.17) is plotted in Fig. 1 as a function of $\beta^2$ for the cases $M = 2, 4, 8, 16, 95$. The performance of a homodyne receiver for these signals is also plotted in the dotted lines. The quantum noise in the homodyne receiver is an additive white Gaussian noise with two-sided spectral density $\frac{1}{4}hf$. It can be seen that over a wide range of $M$ and $\beta^2$, the optimal receiver has approximately a 3 dB improvement over the homodyne receiver.

However, one can also observe the tendency of the error probability to converge to a fixed limit independent of $M$

as $M$ increases. This is apparent from (V.17), where

$$P[C] \rightarrow 1 - e^{-\beta^2} \text{ as } M \rightarrow \infty. \qquad (V.18)$$

This error performance is achieved asymptotically in $M$ by a receiver that counts photons in the individual modes for the coherent orthogonal signal set. We restrict ourselves to orthogonal signals for simplicity in this case, since there is little energy saving in using simplex signals for large $M$. With these orthogonal signals (V.4)–(V.5) and photon counting on each mode, it is easy to see that an error occurs if and only if no photon count is registered in the receiver. This no photon count event occurs with probability $|\langle 0 \mid \beta\rangle|^2 = e^{-\beta^2}$ independently of which signal was actually sent. In the equiprobable signal case we, therefore, get the performance (V.18) by modal photon counting when $M \rightarrow \infty$. This is a quantum analog of the classical result that envelope detection is asymptotically optimum for orthogonal signals in additive white Gaussian noise [32, p. 247].

Equation (V.18) implies that reliable communication is possible at an arbitrarily high rate for any given fixed power, if an arbitrarily large amount of bandwidth is available. In other words, the capacity of this signal set with a photon counting receiver goes to infinity when the bandwidth goes to infinity. In contrast, the capacity of an infinite bandwidth classical additive white Gaussian noise channel is finite, being proportional to the signal-to-noise ratio. This infinite capacity conclusion can also be drawn from the result of some previous work [33] and is also observed in a recent note by Helstrom [34].

It is important to emphasize the infinite bandwidth condition for the attainment of infinite capacity in the preceding manner. For any finite bandwidth, the information rate for orthogonal signal transmission would approach zero even though vanishing probability of error is still obtained for a large time interval. The situation here can be compared to the influence of fading on classical channels [35]. Therefore, one should not draw the conclusion that quantum noise poses no fundamental limitation on the transmission capacity of optical channels, because infinite bandwidth is not a physically meaningful condition in this sensitive situation. One should also recall that the narrowband or constant frequency $f$ (white) condition breaks down for large bandwidth.

With a finite bandwidth, the problems of finding optimum or good signal sets are both important and interesting.

## VI. Conclusions

We have presented a rigorous derivation of the optimum quantum detector in multiple hypotheses testing. The quantum detection problem is solved in the sense that the optimum detector is given as the solution of a set of linear operator equations and inequalities. A great deal of effort may be required to determine the optimal detector in any specific problem, but in some instances the conditions are useful for checking the optimality of intuitively conjectured detectors.

## Acknowledgment

The authors wish to thank Dr. Jane W. S. Liu for helpful discussions on this problem. They also benefited from discussions with Dr. Holevo concerning his work on this topic.

## Nomenclature

| | |
|---|---|
| $H_j$ | $j$th hypothesis. |
| $J$ | Set of $M$ integers. |
| $j$ | $j$th integer. |
| $\tilde{X}$ | Vector-valued random variable. |
| $x$ | Value of the random variable $\tilde{X}$. |
| $R$ | Real numbers. |
| $R^k$ | Euclidean space of $k$ dimensions. |
| $\mathbb{C}$ | Complex numbers. |
| $(\Omega,A)$ | Measurable space with set $\Omega$ and $\sigma$-field $A$ of subsets of $\Omega$. |
| $\mathscr{A}$ | Element of $A$ (a measurable set). |
| $\mathscr{A}_x$ | Measurable set of $\{x' \in \Omega \mid x_i' \leq x_i,\ x_i$ components of $x$ in $R^k$, $\Omega \subseteq R^k\}$. |
| $p_j$ | *A priori* probability of the $j$th hypothesis. |
| $C_{ij}$ | Cost of choosing $H_i$ when $H_j$ is true. |
| $\bar{C}$ | Average Bayes cost. |
| $p_j(x)$ | Density function for $\tilde{X}$ conditioned on the $j$th hypothesis. |
| $P_j(x)$ | Distribution function for $\tilde{X}$ conditioned on the $j$th hypothesis. |
| $\pi_j(x)$ | Probability of deciding $H_j$ given the observation $x$. |
| $\mathscr{H}$ | Separable Hilbert space over $\mathbb{C}$. |
| $\mathscr{H}^e$ | Extension Hilbert space of $\mathscr{H}$. |
| $\mathscr{H}_D$ | Finite $D$-dimensional linear space over $\mathbb{C}$. |
| $\rho_j$ | Density operator on $\mathscr{H}$ conditioned on the $j$th hypothesis. |
| $\rho_j'$ | Trace class operator defined by (II.11) in terms of the $\rho_j$. |
| $\rho_j''$ | Another trace class operator defined in (III.28) in terms of the $\rho_j$. |
| $\rho^e$ | Extension density operator on $\mathscr{H}^e$. |
| $X(\mathscr{A})$ | Probability operator measure on $(\Omega,A)$. |
| $E(\mathscr{A})$ | Spectral measure on $(\Omega,A)$. |
| $X(x)$ | Operator function defined in (II.4)–(II.6)—it generates probability density functions whose corresponding distribution functions are generated in the same way from $X(\mathscr{A})$. |
| $\otimes$ | Tensor product. |
| $I$ | Identity operator on $\mathscr{H}$. |
| $I_D$ | Identity operator on $\mathscr{H}_D$. |
| $\pi_j$ | Detection operators defined in (II.9) or (II.9n). |
| tr | Trace. |
| $\times$ | Direct product. |
| $\lambda$ | Bounded linear operator on $\mathscr{H}$. |
| $\lambda_1 \geq \lambda_2$ | Operator $\lambda_1 - \lambda_2$ is positive semidefinite (self-adjoint). |
| $B$ | Space of bounded self-adjoint operators on $\mathscr{H}$. |
| $T$ | Space of trace class self-adjoint operators on $\mathscr{H}$. |
| $T_D$ | Space of $D \times D$ Hermitian matrices. |
| $(\lambda)^{1/2}$ | Positive semidefinite square root operator of $\lambda$. |

| | |
|---|---|
| max | Maximum. |
| min | Minimum. |
| $\in$ | Element inclusion. |
| $\subset$ | Set inclusion. |
| $\cup$ | Set union. |
| $\rightarrow$ | Limiting operation. |
| $(\cdot,\cdot)$ | Inner product in a Hilbert space. |
| $[\cdot,\cdot]$ | Commutator of two operators. |
| $P_l$ | Projection operator to $l \in \mathscr{H}$. |
| $P(\varepsilon)$ | Probability of error. |
| $P[C]$ | Probability of correct detection. |
| $\|i\rangle$ | Dirac notation for a vector $l_j$ indexed by $j$ in a Hilbert space $\mathscr{H}$. |
| $\|j\rangle\langle j\|$ | Dirac notation for the projection operator $P_{l_j}$. |
| $\langle i \| j\rangle$ | Dirac notation for the inner product $(i,j)$. |
| $A^\dagger$ | Adjoint transformation of $A$. |
| inf | Infumum, or greatest lower bound. |
| sup | Supremum, or least upper bound. |

## APPENDIX

*Proof of Theorem IA*

We prove here the infinite-dimensional version of Theorem I, i.e., Theorem IA, which states that (III.34) provides the necessary and sufficient condition on the optimal $M$-ary quantum detector in general. The derivation parallels that of the finite-dimensional case with the introduction of some further technical points. Whenever possible we will make use of the finite-dimensional development by merely indicating the modifications required in the infinite-dimensional situation in order to avoid repetitions.

The derivation in [5] utilizes the Lagrange duality theorem [24, p. 224] for convex programs. As Holevo[7] pointed out to us, the original proof is not valid in the infinite-dimensional case, but he was able to deduce (III.34) from the Lagrange duality theorem in a different way. His proof will be forthcoming. Since the problem (II.12)–(II.13) is actually a linear programming problem, we will derive (III.26) by a linear programming duality theorem that is parallel with the derivation in Section III.

The dual problem of (II.12)–(II.13) is

$$\max_{\lambda \in T} \operatorname{tr} \lambda \tag{A.1}$$

subject to the constraint

$$\lambda \le \rho_j', \qquad j \in J \tag{A.2}$$

for given $\rho_j' \in T$. Instead of the duality theorem (III.5), we will employ the following duality theorem that is valid for infinite-dimensional linear programs.

*General Duality Theorem (Linear Programming)*

Let $X$ and $Y$ be locally convex linear Hausdorff topological spaces, $c(x)$ a continuous linear functional on $X$, $b$ a given element of $Y$, $A$ a continuous linear operator from $X$ to $Y$, and $L$ a closed convex cone in $X$ defining the partial order $\ge$. Let $A^\dagger$ be the continuous adjoint transformation of $A$ from $Y^*$ to $X^*$, the topological duals of $Y$ and $X$. Let $L^*$ be the conjugate cone of $L$ in $X^*$. Then

$$\inf_{\substack{Ax=b\\ x\ge 0}} c(x) = \sup_{A^\dagger y^* \le c} y^*(b) \tag{A.3}$$

and a solution to both the inf and sup problems exist under the following conditions:

i) the inf and sup problems have finite values;

ii) the set $\tilde{\mathscr{C}}$ is closed in $R \times Y$ with respect to the natural product topology

$$\tilde{\mathscr{C}} = \{(r,y) \mid r = c(x),\, y = Ax \text{ for some } x \in L\}; \tag{A.4}$$

iii) the set $\tilde{D}$ is closed in $R$

$$\tilde{D} = \{r \mid r = -y^*(b) \text{ for some } y^* \text{ satisfying } A^\dagger y^* \le c\}. \tag{A.5}$$

This theorem is contained in the results of Van Slyke and Wets [36]. The particular form we give here is adopted for convenience in the following application. For the definition of various terms and the treatment of general optimization theory, consult [24], [36]–[38].

To put the prime problem (II.12)–(II.13) in the form of the minimum problem of (A.3), we first let

$$X = B^M, \qquad Y = B \tag{A.6}$$

where $B^M$ is the direct product of $M$ spaces $B$ with elements

$$\pi = (\pi_1,\cdots,\pi_M), \qquad \pi_j \in B. \tag{A.7}$$

The positive cone $L$ in $X$ is taken to be

$$L = \{\pi \mid \pi_j \ge 0,\, \pi \in B^M\}. \tag{A.8}$$

The topology in $B(B^M)$ is chosen to be the weak-star topology [24, p. 126], [38, p. 92]. The topological dual space of $B(B^M)$ is, therefore, $T(T^M)$ [39, p. 48], [40]. A linear continuous map $c(\pi)$ can thus be represented by $\lambda \in T^M$ in the form

$$c(\pi) = \operatorname{tr} \sum_j \pi_j \lambda_j = \operatorname{tr} \pi\lambda, \qquad \lambda \in T^M. \tag{A.9}$$

By choosing $\lambda = \rho' = (\rho_1',\cdots,\rho_M')$ to represent $c(\pi)$ and letting

$$b = I, \qquad A\pi = \sum_j \pi_j. \tag{A.10}$$

The minimum problem in (A.3) with (A.6)–(A.10) becomes the prime problem (II.12)–(II.13) if $A$ is continuous.

Note that $B$ is reflexive under the weak-star topology so that $(B,T)$ form a dual pair [38, p. 183]. The adjoint transformation (transpose) [24, p. 150], [38, p. 254] of $A$ is the diagonal imbedding [41, p. 39] of $T$ to $T^M$

$$A^\dagger \lambda = \{\lambda,\cdots,\lambda\}. \tag{A.11}$$

Since the diagonal imbedding is continuous, $A$ is also continuous and $(A^\dagger)^\dagger = A$ [38, p. 255]. Furthermore, the maximum problem of (A.3) becomes our dual problem (A.1), (A.2). If conditions i)–iii) of the preceding general duality theorem are satisfied, we would have established the relation

$$\max_{\substack{\lambda-\rho_j'\le 0\\ \lambda\in T}} \operatorname{tr}\lambda = \min_{\substack{\pi_j\ge 0\\ \Sigma_j\pi_j=I\\ \pi_j\in B}} \sum_j \operatorname{tr} \pi_j\rho_j'. \tag{A.12}$$

The proof of Theorem IA can then be completed like that of Theorem I. Thus it remains to establish i)–iii).

Condition i) is satisfied because $|\operatorname{tr} \pi_j\rho_j'| \le |\operatorname{tr} \rho_j'|$ and $\operatorname{tr}\lambda \le \operatorname{tr}\rho_j'$.

To show that condition ii) is satisfied, we first write

$$\tilde{\mathscr{C}} = \{(r,y) \mid r = \operatorname{tr} \pi\rho',\, y = A\pi, \text{ for some } \pi \in L\}. \tag{A.13}$$

Note that $A$ is a topological homomorphism because $A^\dagger$ has a closed range [38, p. 263].

[7] Private communication; we would like to thank Dr. Holevo for bringing this to our attention.

*Lemma 4:* The set $\mathscr{C}$ of (A.13) is closed.

*Proof:* Let $(r_n, y_n) \in \mathscr{C}$ such that $r_n \to r$, and $y_n \to y$ in the sense of weak-star convergence. From $A\pi_n \to y$ and the topological homomorphism properties of $A$, it follows that there are sets $S_n \subset L$, $AS_n = y_n$, such that $S_n \to S \subset L$ with $AS = y$. From $r_n = \operatorname{tr} \pi_n \rho'$, it follows that there are subsets $S_n'$ of $S_n$ such that $\pi_n \in S_n'$. Therefore, the limit set $S'$ of $S_n'$ contains $\pi'$ with the properties $\pi_n \to \pi'$, $A\pi_n \to A\pi'$, and $\operatorname{tr} \pi_n \rho' \to \operatorname{tr} \pi' \rho'$. This shows that $r = \operatorname{tr} \pi' \rho'$ and $y = A\pi'$ so that $(r,y) \in \mathscr{C}$. The closure proof is then completed.

Condition iii) follows in a similar way. Writing

$$\tilde{D} = \{r \mid r = -\operatorname{tr} \lambda \text{ for some } \lambda \in T \text{ with } \lambda \leq \rho_j'\} \quad (A.14)$$

and noting that $-\operatorname{tr} \lambda$ is a topological homomorphism defined on the closed set $\lambda \leq \rho_j'$, the closure of $D$ results as in Lemma 4.

We have now established the existence of a solution to (II.12), (II.13) as well as (A.12). Theorem IA follows in a way identical to Theorem I.

## References


[1] A. Wald, *Statistical Decision Functions.* New York: Wiley, 1950.
[2] D. Middleton, *An Introduction to Statistical Communication Theory.* New York: McGraw-Hill, 1960, ch. 23.
[3] H. L. Van Trees, *Detection, Estimation, and Modulation Theory: Part I.* New York: Wiley, 1968, ch. 2.
[4] C. W. Helstrom, "Detection theory and quantum mechanics," *Inform. Contr.*, vol. 10, pp. 254–291, Mar. 1967.
[5] H. P. Yuen, "Communication theory of quantum systems," Res. Lab. Electron., M.I.T., Cambridge, Mass., Tech. Rep. 482, Aug. 1971 (Ph.D. dissertation submitted to the Dep. Elec. Eng., M.I.T., June 1970), pp. 116–129.
[6] H. P. Yuen, R. S., Kennedy, and M. Lax, "On optimal quantum receivers for digital signal detection," *Proc. IEEE* (Lett.), vol. 58, pp. 1770–1773, Oct. 1970.
[7] E. B. Davies, "On the repeated measurement of continuous observables in quantum mechanics," *J. Functional Anal.*, vol. 6, pp. 318–346, 1970, see in particular pp. 340–343.
[8] A. S. Holevo, "Statistical problems in quantum physics," in *Proc. Soviet-Japanese Symp. Probability and Statistics*, vol. 1, 1972, pp. 22–40.
[9] ——, "Statistical decision theory for quantum systems," *J. Multivariate Analysis*, vol. 3, pp. 337–394, 1973.
[10] ——, "Optimal quantum measurement," (in Russian) *Theoreticheskayer i Matematicheskaya Fizika*, vol. 17, pp. 319–326, Dec. 1973.
[11] J. Von Neumann, *Mathematical Foundations of Quantum Mechanics.* Princeton, N.J.: Princeton Univ. Press, 1955.
[12] E. Prugovechi, *Quantum Mechanics in Hilbert Space.* New York: Academic, 1971.
[13] S. K. Berberian, *Notes on Spectral Theory.* New York: Van Nostrand-Reinhold, 1966.
[14] P. A. Benioff, "Operator valued measures in quantum mechanics: Finite and infinite processes," *J. Math. Phys.*, vol. 13, pp. 231–242, 1972.
[15] C. W. Helstrom and R. S. Kennedy, "Noncommuting observables in quantum detection and estimation theory," *IEEE Trans. Inform. Theory*, vol. IT-20, pp. 16–24, Jan. 1974.
[16] H. P. Yuen and M. Lax, "Multiple parameter quantum estimation and measurement of nonselfadjoint observables," *IEEE Trans. Inform. Theory*, vol. IT-19, pp. 740–750, Nov. 1973.
[17] B. Sz-Nagy, "Transformations in Hilbert space which extend beyond this space," Appendix to F. Riesz and B. Sz-Nagy, *Functional Analysis.* New York: Ungar, 1960.
[18] E. Arthurs and J. L. Kelly, Jr., "On the simultaneous measurement of a pair of conjugate observables," *Bell Syst. Tech. J.*, (Briefs), vol. 44, pp. 725–729, Apr. 1965.
[19] J. P. Gordon and W. H. Louisell, "Simultaneous measurements of noncommuting observables," in *Physics of Quantum Electronics*, P. L. Kelly, B. Lax, and P. E. Tannenwald, Eds. New York: McGraw-Hill, 1966. pp. 833–840.
[20] H. L. Royden, *Real Analysis.* New York: MacMillian, 1965.
[21] O. L. Mangasarian, *Nonlinear Programming.* New York: McGraw-Hill, 1969.
[22] J. W. S. Liu, "Reliability of quantum-mechanical communication systems," Res. Lab. Electron., M.I.T., Cambridge, Mass., Tech. Rep. 468, Dec. 1968. See also *IEEE Trans. Inform. Theory*, vol. IT-16, pp. 319–329, May 1970.
[23] R. S. Kennedy, Res. Lab. Electron., M.I.T., Cambridge, Mass., Q.P.R. 110, July 15, 1973, pp. 142–146.
[24] D. G. Luenberger, *Optimization by Vector Space Methods.* New York: Wiley, 1969.
[25] H. P. Yuen and M. Lax, "Multiple parameter quantum estimation with applications to radar and analog communications," presented at IEEE Int. Symp. Information Theory, Asilomar, Calif., Jan. 31, 1972.
[26] J. M. Wozencraft and I. M. Jacobs, *Principles of Communication Engineering.* New York: Wiley, 1965.
[27] P. A. M. Dirac, *The Principles of Quantum Mechanics*, 4th ed. New York: Oxford Univ. Press, 1958.
[28] R. J. Glauber, "Optical coherence and photon statistics," in *Quantum Optics and Electronics.* C. M. De Witt *et al.*, Eds. New York: Gordon and Breach, 1965.
[29] J. R. Klauder and E. C. G. Sudarshan, *Fundamentals of Quantum Optics.* New York: Benjamin, 1968.
[30] C. W. Helstrom, J. W. S. Liu, and J. P. Gordon, "Quantum-mechanical communication theory," *Proc. IEEE*, vol. pp. 1578–1598, Oct. 1970.
[31] R. S. Kennedy, Res. Lab. Electron, M.I.T., Cambridge, Mass., Q.P.R. 112, Jan. 1974.
[32] A. J. Viterbi, *Principles of Coherent Communication.* New York: McGraw-Hill, 1966.
[33] J. P. Gordon, "Quantum effects in communication systems," *Proc. IRE*, vol. 50, pp. 1898–1908, Sept. 1962.
[34] C. W. Helstrom, "Capacity of the pure-state quantum channel," *Proc. IEEE* (Lett.), vol. 62, pp. 139–140, Jan. 1974.
[35] J. N. Pierce, "Ultimate performance of *M*-ary transmissions on fading channels," *IEEE Trans. Inform. Theory*, vol. IT-12, pp. 2–5, Jan. 1966.
[36] R. M. Van Slyke and R. J. B. Wets, "A duality theory for abstract mathematical programs with applications to optimal control theory," *J. Math. Anal. Appl.*, vol. 22, pp. 679–706, 1968.
[37] L. Hurwicz, "Programming in linear spaces," in *Studies in Linear and Nonlinear Programming*, K. J. Arrow *et al.*, Eds. Stanford, Calif., Stanford Univ. Press, 1958, pp. 38–102.
[38] J. Horvath, *Topological Vector Spaces and Distributions*, vol. 1, Reading, Mass.: Addison-Wesley, 1966.
[39] R. Schatten, *Norm Ideals of Completely Continuous Operators.* Berlin: Springer-Verlag, 1970.
[40] I. M. Gelfand and N. Y. Vilenkin, *Generalized Functions*, vol. 4, New York: Academic, 1964.
[41] S. T. Hu, *Elements of General Topology.* San Francisco: Holden-Day, 1964.
[42] F. Riesz and B. Sz-Nagy, *Functional Analysis.* New York: Ungar, 1955.


# AUTHOR'S NOTE

The claim in our paper that (III.15) follows from a duality theorem on (III.10) that is in the same form as (III.5), which is indeed correct, is nevertheless misleading as kindly pointed out to us by Professor Sanjoy K. Mitter. This is due to the general possibility of duality gaps even on finite dimensional linear programs in partially ordered spaces so that the validity of (III.15) depends on more than the mere "equivalence" between $T_D{}^M$ and $R^{MD2}$ as implied in the paper. We observe here that a proof of (III.15) can be given in many ways, for example by using the Lagrange duality theorem originally employed in [5]. This follows from the obvious existence of an interior point in the constraint set (III.17), and the existence of a solution to (III.16)-(III.17) similar to lemma 1 when we further constrain (III.17) to $\rho_j' \geq \lambda \geq [D\gamma_m - (D-1)\gamma_M]I_D$ without loss of optimality, where $\gamma_m$ and $\gamma_M$ are the smallest and largest eigenvalues of the $\rho_j'$s respectively.

# 21



Reprinted from *IEEE Trans. Inf. Theory* **IT-22**(1):59–64 (1976)

# Quantum-Mechanical Linear Filtering of Random Signal Sequences

JOHN S. BARAS, MEMBER, IEEE, ROBERT O. HARGER, MEMBER, IEEE, AND YOUNG H. PARK

***Abstract*—The problem of estimating a member of a scalar random signal sequence with quantum-mechanical measurements is considered. The minimum variance linear estimator based on an optimal present quantum measurement and optimal linear processing of past measurements is found. When the average optimal measurement without post-processing, for a fixed signal, is linear in the random signal and the signal sequence is pairwise Gaussian, the optimal processing separates: the optimal measurement is the same as the optimal measurement without regard to past data, and the past and present data are processed classically. The results are illustrated by considering the estimator of the real amplitude of a laser signal received in a single-mode cavity along with thermal noise; when the random signal sequence satisfies a linear recursion, the estimate can be computed recursively. For a one-step memory signal sequence it is shown that the optimal observable generally differs from the optimal observable disregarding the past; the optimal measurement can be computed recursively.**

Manuscript received February 7, 1975; revised August 1, 1975. This work was supported in part by the National Science Foundation under Grant GK-14920.

J. S. Baras and R. O. Harger are with the Electrical Engineering Department, University of Maryland, College Park, Md. 20742.
Y. H. Park is with Bendix Corporation, Columbia, Md.

## I. INTRODUCTION

DETECTION and estimation problems have recently been studied [1]–[3] employing measurement models correctly incorporating quantum mechanics. Such work applies directly, e.g., to establishing fundamental limitations in optical communication systems [4]. More recently, the analog of filtering a random signal sequence has been considered [5], [6], [13]. Here the problem of estimating $x_k$, a member of a "signal" sequence $\{x_0,x_1,\cdots,x_k,\cdots\}$ of scalar random variables, is considered; the parameter $k$ is conveniently regarded as discrete time. To be chosen are the optimal measurements at time $k$ and the optimal linear combination of present and past measurements at times $j = 0, 1,\cdots, k - 1$. The random sequence so obtained is defined precisely below, but it is simply described in the optical communication setting as follows.

At time $k$ a laser signal modulated in some fashion by $x_k$ is received in a cavity containing otherwise only an electromagnetic field due to thermal noise; the total field is in a state described by a density operator $\rho(x_k)$ that depends on $x_k$ (but not otherwise on $k$). If $x_k$ is a scalar, the measurement at time $k$, whose outcome is denoted by $v_k$, will correspond to a self-adjoint operator $V_k$ [7, p. 192]. If $x_k$ is a vector the essentially quantum problem of simultaneous measurement arises, and a more general concept of measurement [1], [2], [8], [9] must be resorted to [14].

By optimal is meant *minimum mean-square error*; the implied average is over the classical distributions of $\{x_k\}$ and the distributions due to quantum-mechanical measurement.

An ultimate objective would include efficient computation; e.g., suppose that $x_k$ is a scalar "dynamical state" generated by the recursive equation

$$x_{k+1} = \phi_k x_k + w_k \tag{1}$$

where $\{\phi_k\}$ is a sequence of scalars and $\{w_k\}$ is a sequence of independent Gaussian random variables with zero mean and variance $Q_k$. Solutions in a form that recursively compute the optimal estimate and measurement at time $k$ would be highly desirable. In specific situations below, this is achieved.

## II. Filtering Problem

The customary formulation of quantum mechanics [10, sec. 8.5] associates a self-adjoint operator $V$ on a Hilbert space $\mathscr{H}$ with each measurement and incorporates *a priori* statistical information with a density operator $\rho$ on $\mathscr{H}$ ($\rho$ a self-adjoint, positive semidefinite operator with unit trace). The measurement represented by $V$ produces a real number $v$ (the outcome) whose expectation is

$$E_v\{v\} = \mathrm{tr}\,\{\rho V\}$$

where $\mathrm{tr}\,\{\cdot\}$ denotes trace.[1] In case the density operator $\rho$ depends on a random variable $x$ with distribution function $F_x$, $E_v$ should be replaced with the conditional expectation $E_{v|x}$. The unconditional expectation is then

$$E\{v\} = \int \mathrm{tr}\,\{\rho(x)V\}F_x(dx). \tag{2}$$

Here the following sequence of measurements is of interest. At each time $j$, $j = 0,1,\cdots$, a measurement represented by the self-adjoint operator $V_j$ is made, with outcome $v_j$. The state of the system prior to the measurement is described by $\rho(x_j)$. The outcomes $v_j$ are classical random variables which, conditioned upon a fixed signal sequence $\{x_j\}$, are independent.[2] This conditional independence of the measurement outcomes implies[3] that for any multinomial of $\{v_0,\cdots,v_k\}$

$$E_{v|x}\{v_0^m\cdots v_k^n\} = \mathrm{tr}\,\{\rho(x_0)V_0^m\}\cdots \mathrm{tr}\,\{\rho(x_k)V_k^n\}$$

for any integers $m,\cdots,n$. The unconditional expectation is then

$$E\{v_0^m\cdots v_k^n\} = \int \mathrm{tr}\,\{\rho(x_0)V_0^m\} \cdots \mathrm{tr}\,\{\rho(x_k)V_k^n\}F_{x_0,\cdots,x_k}(dx_0,\cdots,dx_k). \tag{3}$$

The linear filtering problem is the following. At time $k$, $k = 0,1,\cdots$, the previous outcomes $\{v_j,\ j = 0,1,\cdots, k-1\}$ and the present measurement outcome $v_k$ are used to form a linear estimate

$$\hat{x}_k = \sum_{j=0}^{k} c_j(k)v_j \tag{4}$$

of $x_k$. Then the $\{c_j(k), j = 0,\cdots,k\}$ and the present measurement represented by $V_k$ are to be chosen to minimize the mean-square error $E\{\mathscr{E}_k^2\}$, where $\mathscr{E}_k \equiv x_k - \hat{x}_k$ and the expectation is as in (3). Clearly one may set $c_k(k) = 1$.

Explicitly writing out that part of $E_{v|x}$ for the $k$th stage yields

$$E\{\mathscr{E}_k^2\} = E_x E_{v|x}\,\mathrm{tr}\left\{\rho(x_k)\left[x_k I - V_k - I\sum_{j=0}^{k-1} c_j(k)v_j\right]^2\right\} \tag{5}$$

where $I$ is the identity operator on $\mathscr{H}$. It is also convenient to note that

$$E\{\mathscr{E}_k^2\} = E\{x_k^2\} - 2\sum_{j=0}^{k} c_j(k)\,\mathrm{tr}\,(\delta_{kj}V_j) + \sum_{i,j=0}^{k} c_i(k)c_j(k)\,\mathrm{tr}\,\{\zeta_{ji}V_j\} \tag{6}$$

where

$$\delta_{kj} \equiv E_x\{x_k\rho(x_j)\} \tag{7}$$

$$\eta_k \equiv E_x\{\rho(x_k)\} \tag{8}$$

and

$$\zeta_{ij} \equiv \begin{cases} E_x\{(\mathrm{tr}\,\rho(x_j)V_j)\rho(x_i)\}, & i \neq j; \\ \eta_i V_i, & i = j. \end{cases} \tag{9}$$

In the sequel, $\hat{V}_k$ will denote the optimal observable and $\{\hat{c}_j(k),\ j = 0,\cdots,k-1\}$ the optimal processing coefficients at the $k$th stage. Applying the calculus of the variations argument of [12] to $[V_k + I\sum_{j=0}^{k} c_j(k)v_j]$ in (5) formally gives a necessary condition for $\hat{V}_k$ to minimize separately $E\{\mathscr{E}_k^2\}$

$$\eta_k\hat{V}_k + \hat{V}_k\eta_k = 2\delta_{kk} - 2\sum_{j=0}^{k-1}\hat{c}_j(k)\zeta_{kj}. \tag{10}$$

Simple differentiation on (6) shows that a necessary and sufficient condition that the $\{\hat{c}_j(k)\}_{j=0}^{k-1}$ minimize separately

[1] It is worthwhile to note the distribution function $F_v$ of the classical random variable $v$. The spectral theorem [7, p. 249] associates with each self-adjoint operator $V$ on $\mathscr{H}$ a unique spectral measure $M_V$, a mapping of Borel sets of the real line into projection operators on $\mathscr{H}$. Then the distribution function is $F_v(\nu) = \mathrm{tr}\,\{\rho M_V(-\infty,\nu]\}$. The spectral theorem also yields the moments of the random variable $v$ via $E_v(v^m) = \mathrm{tr}\,\{\rho V^m\}$, $m = 1,2,\cdots$.

[2] In the optical communication example cited above, this conditional independence corresponds to "clearing" the receiver cavity prior to each reception.

[3] The conditional independence assumed here is best described by stating that the joint distribution function $F_{v|x}$ is the product $F_{v_0|x_0}\cdots F_{v_k|x_k}$, where each $F_{v_j|x_j}$ has already been described.

$E\{\mathscr{E}_k^2\}$ is

$$\sum_{j=0}^{k-1} \hat{c}_j(k) \operatorname{tr}\{\zeta_{ji}V_j\} = \operatorname{tr}\{\delta_{ki}V_i\} - \operatorname{tr}\{\zeta_{ki}\hat{V}_k\}, \quad i = 0, 1, \cdots, k-1. \tag{11}$$

It is important for the subsequent results of this paper to establish necessary and sufficient conditions for $\hat{V}_k$ and $\{\hat{c}_j(k), j = 0, \cdots, k-1\}$ to minimize jointly $E\{\mathscr{E}_k^2\}$. This is done in the following theorem which employs the projection theorem [11, p. 49]. It also settles the question of the existence of optimal $V_k$ and $\{c_j(k)\}$.

*Theorem 1:* There exists an optimum observable $\hat{V}_k$ and optimal processing coefficients $\hat{c}_j(k)$, $j = 0, 1, \cdots, k-1$, if and only if there exists a solution to (10) and (11).

*Proof:* Let $\mathscr{L}$ be the set of operator-valued functions of the form

$$f(x) \equiv \beta x I + I \sum_{j=0}^{k-1} \alpha_j v_j + V_k$$

where $x$ is a random variable, $\beta$ and $\{\alpha_i\}$ are real scalars, and $V_k$ is a self-adjoint operator on $\mathscr{H}$. With the ordinary addition of scalars and operators and the multiplication by scalars, $\mathscr{L}$ is seen to be a linear space. For $f,g \in \mathscr{L}$, define the form

$$(f,g) \equiv E_x E_{v|x} \operatorname{tr}\{\rho(x_k) \cdot [f(x_k)g(x_k) + g(x_k)f(x_k)]\}.$$

Let $\mathscr{L}' \subset \mathscr{L}$ be the subspace of elements $f$ such that $(f,f)$ is finite. Then $(\cdot,\cdot)$ is a degenerate inner product on $\mathscr{L}'$ in the sense that $\|\cdot\| \equiv (\cdot,\cdot)^{1/2}$ is a seminorm [11, p. 45]. It is not a norm since $\|f\| = 0$ does not imply $f = 0$.

Let $\mathscr{L}'' \subset \mathscr{L}'$ be the subspace of operator-valued functions of the form

$$h \equiv I \sum_{j=0}^{k-1} \alpha_j v_j + D_k.$$

Then (see (5)) the problem of minimizing the mean-square error is a minimum norm problem, and the projection theorem [11, p. 44] provides necessary and sufficient conditions for a solution. $\{\hat{c}_j(k), j = 0, 1, \cdots, k-1\}$ and $\hat{V}_k$ are the solution if and only if, for any real scalars $\alpha_j$, $j = 0, \cdots, k-1$, and self-adjoint operator $D_k$ on $\mathscr{H}$,

$$0 = E_x E_{v|x} \operatorname{tr}\left[\rho(x_k) \cdot \left\{\left[x_k I - I \sum_{j=0}^{k-1} \hat{c}_j(k) v_j - \hat{V}_k\right] \cdot \left[I \sum_{j=0}^{k-1} \alpha_j v_j + D_k\right] + \left[I \sum_{j=0}^{k-1} \alpha_j v_j + D_k\right] \cdot \left[x_k I - I \sum_{j=0}^{k-1} \hat{c}_j(k) v_j - \hat{V}_k\right]\right\}\right]. \tag{12}$$

Two necessary conditions, which together are sufficient, may be obtained from (12), the first by setting the $\{\alpha_j\} \equiv 0$ and the second by setting $D_k \equiv 0$.

Setting the $\{\alpha_j\} \equiv 0$ and interchanging the trace over $\mathscr{H}$ with expectation $E_x E_{v|x}$, one obtains

$$0 = \operatorname{tr}\left\{D_k \left[2\delta_{kk} - 2 \sum_{j=0}^{k-1} \hat{c}_j(k)\zeta_{kj} - \eta_k \hat{V}_k - \hat{V}_k \eta_k\right]\right\}$$

for any self-adjoint operator $D_k$. The arbitrariness of $D_k$ implies this last equality holds if and only if

$$\eta_k \hat{V}_k + \hat{V}_k \eta_k = 2\delta_{kk} - 2 \sum_{j=0}^{k-1} \hat{c}_j(k)\zeta_{kj}.$$

Setting $D_k \equiv 0$, one is similarly led to the condition

$$\sum_{j=0}^{k-1} \hat{c}_j(k) \operatorname{tr}\{\zeta_{ji}V_j\} = \operatorname{tr}\{\delta_{ki}V_i\} - \operatorname{tr}\{\zeta_{ki}\hat{V}_k\}, \quad i = 0, 1, \cdots, k-1.$$

Q.E.D.

Equations (11) are the normal equations [11, p. 56] for the $\{\hat{c}_j(k)\}$. A redundant equation may be obtained from (10) by multiplying through by $\hat{V}_k$ and tracing; adding it to the above set, one has the complete set of normal equations. It is special in that necessarily $\hat{c}_k(k) \equiv 1$

$$\sum_{j=0}^{k} \hat{c}_j(k) E\{v_i v_j\} = E\{v_i x_k\}, \qquad i = 0,1,\cdots,k \tag{11a}$$

where the expectation is as in (3) and $v_k = \hat{v}_k$, the outcome of the optimal measurement. The equations (10) and (11) can be cast in a more convenient form.

*Corollary 1:* The optimal observable $\hat{V}_k$ and processing coefficients $\{\hat{c}_j(k)\}$ satisfy the equations

$$\hat{V}_k = T_k - \sum_{j=0}^{k-1} \hat{c}_j(k)\sigma_{kj} \tag{13}$$

and

$$\sum_{j=0}^{k-1} \hat{c}_j(k) \operatorname{tr}\{\zeta_{ji}V_j - \zeta_{ki}\sigma_{kj}\} = \operatorname{tr}\{\delta_{ki}V_i - \zeta_{ki}T_k\}, \quad i = 0, 1, \cdots, k-1 \tag{14}$$

where $T_k$ and $\sigma_{kj}$ are such that

$$\eta_k T_k + T_k \eta_k = 2\delta_{kk} \tag{15}$$

and

$$\eta_k \sigma_{kj} + \sigma_{kj} \eta_k = 2\zeta_{kj}. \tag{16}$$

*Proof:* Substituting (15) and (16) into (10) immediately yields (13). Multiplying (13) on the right by $\zeta_{ki}$, $i = 0, 1, \cdots, k-1$, tracing over $\mathscr{H}$, and substituting for $\operatorname{tr}\{\zeta_{ki}\hat{V}_k\}$ in (11) yields (14). Q.E.D.

Equations (13) and (14) are "decoupled" in the sense that, after solving (15) and (16), the $\{\hat{c}_j(k)\}$ are found via (14); then $\hat{V}_k$ is found via (13). Note also that conditions for existence of solutions in (10) imply existence of solutions for (15) and (16), and conversely.

It is remarked that (13) and (14) apply for any set of $k+1$ jointly distributed random variables $\{x_0, x_1, \cdots, x_k\}$ and for any set of $k$ prior measurements represented by $\{V_0, V_1, \cdots, V_{k-1}\}$. If, additionally, the $\{x_j\}$ satisfy a recursion such as (1) there is the hope that a recursive determination of $\hat{V}_k$ and, at least implicitly, of the $\{\hat{c}_j(k)\}$ could be obtained, especially if the $\{V_j\}$ are chosen optimally at each time $j$. This would avoid a calculation of growing complexity at each time $k$. It is also of interest to know when

$\hat{V}_k$ depends in a significant structural way, on $k$—for then a new measuring device is required at each time $k$! We now turn to examples that partially answer such questions.

## III. Filter Separation

Assume the $\{x_j, j = 0,1,\cdots,k\}$ are pairwise Gaussian random variables and that the observables $\{V_j, j = 0,1 \cdots,k\}$ have each been chosen optimally according to (13) and (14); suppose further

$$\operatorname{tr}\{\rho(x_j)T_j\} = \Gamma_j x_j, \qquad j = 0,1,\cdots,k \tag{17}$$

where $\Gamma_j$ is a scalar, that is, the average optimal measurement without postprocessing (see [12]), for a fixed signal, is proportional to said signal.

*Theorem 2:* If $\{x_j, j = 0,1,\cdots,k\}$ are pairwise Gaussian random variables, if measurements $\{\hat{V}_j, j = 0,1,\cdots,k\}$ are optimally chosen (according to (13) and (14)), if $\{T_j, j = 0,1,\cdots,k\}$ are given by (15), and if (17) holds, then

$$\hat{V}_k = B_k T_k \tag{18}$$

where

$$B_k = 1 - \sum_{j=0}^{k-1} \hat{c}_j(k) B_j \Gamma_j A_{jk}, \qquad B(0) = 1 \tag{19}$$

and $A_{jk}$ is such that $E(x_j \mid x_k) = A_{jk}x_k$.

*Proof:* Trivially, (18) holds at $k = 0$. At time $k = 1$, $\hat{V}_1 = T_1 - \hat{c}_0(1)\sigma_{10}$; to find $\sigma_{10}$ by (16) note that (using (17))

$$\begin{aligned} \zeta_{10} &= E_x\{\operatorname{tr}\{\rho(x_0)T_0\} \cdot \rho(x_1)\} \\ &= E_x\{\Gamma_0 x_0 \rho(x_1)\} \\ &= \Gamma_0 E_x\{\rho(x_1)E(x_0 \mid x_1)\}. \end{aligned}$$

Since $x_0$ and $x_1$ are jointly Gaussian random variables there exists a constant $A_{01}$ such that $E(x_0 \mid x_1) = A_{01}x_1$, therefore,

$$\begin{aligned} \zeta_{10} &= \Gamma_0 A_{01} E_x\{\rho(x_1)x_1\} \\ &= \Gamma_0 A_{01} \delta_{11}. \end{aligned}$$

Using this result in (16) and comparing to (15), one sees that $\sigma_{10} = \Gamma_0 A_{01} T_1$. So (13) yields

$$\hat{V}_1 = B_1 T_1$$

where

$$B_1 \equiv 1 - \hat{c}_0(1) B_0 \Gamma_0 A_{01}.$$

Assuming (18) and (19) hold at time $k - 1$, again one finds

$$\begin{aligned} \zeta_{kj} &\equiv E_x\{\operatorname{tr}\{\rho(x_j)V_j\} \cdot \rho(x_k)\} \\ &= E_x\{\operatorname{tr}\{\rho(x_j)B_jT_j\} \cdot \rho(x_k)\} \end{aligned}$$

using the induction hypothesis,

$$\zeta_{kj} = B_j \Gamma_j A_{jk} \delta_{kk}$$

where $E(x_j \mid x_k) = A_{jk}x_k$. Using this result in (16) and comparing to (15), one sees $\sigma_{kj} = B_j \Gamma_j T_k$, thus (13) gives

$$\hat{V}_k = B_k T_k$$

where

$$B_k = 1 - \sum_{j=0}^{k-1} \hat{c}_j(k) B_j \Gamma_j A_{jk}.$$

Q.E.D.

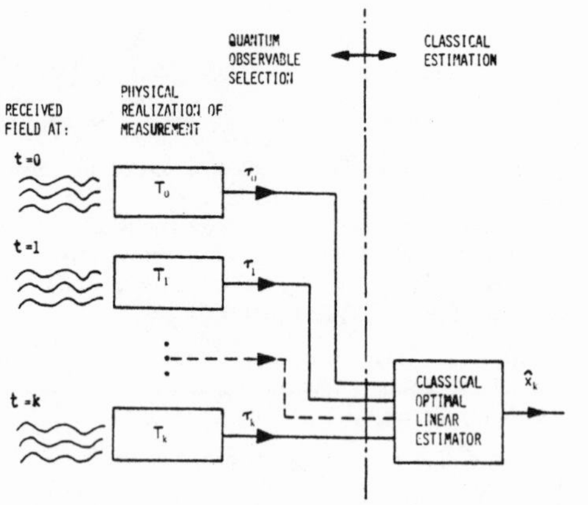


Fig. 1. Separation of optimal filter when signal sequence is pairwise Gaussian and average optimal measurement without postprocessing, for fixed signal, is linear in signal.

Note that the observable $\hat{V}_k$ of (18) is proportional to $T_k$, *the optimal measurement if the past measurements are disregarded (proof: set $k = 0$).* This $\hat{V}_k$ is greatly simpler than that of (13) and yields the following "separation." *The optimal quantum observables are chosen separately from the optimal classical postprocessing of the measurement outcomes.* This is illustrated in Fig. 1.

Note that the left side of (17) is $E(\tau_j \mid x_j)$, where $\tau_j$ is the outcome of the measurement represented by $T_j$, which is, therefore, linear in $x_j$—as is true if $\tau_j$ and $x_j$ are jointly Gaussian when necessarily $\Gamma_j = E(\tau_j x_j)/E(x_j^2)$.

*Lemma 1:* If (17) holds then i) $\Gamma_j = E(\tau_j x_j)/E(x_j^2)$ and ii) $0 \le \Gamma_j \le 1$.

*Proof:* Multiplying (17) through by $x_j$ and taking $E_x\{\cdot\}$, one finds $E(x_j\tau_j) = \Gamma_j E(x_j^2)$ establishing i). However, $E(x_j\tau_j) = \operatorname{tr}\{\delta_{jj}T_j\}$, which by (15) is $\operatorname{tr}\{\eta_j T_j^2\} = E\{\tau_j^2\}$, thus

$$\Gamma_j = \frac{E(x_j\tau_j)}{E(x_j^2)} = \frac{E(\tau_j^2)}{E(x_j^2)} \ge 0.$$

However, $[E(x_j\tau_j)]^2 \le E(x_j^2)E(\tau_j^2)$ so that

$$\Gamma_j = \frac{E(\tau_j^2)}{E(x_j^2)} \le 1.$$

Q.E.D.

In view of (18) the optimal estimate is

$$\begin{aligned} \hat{x}_k &\equiv \hat{v}_k + \sum_{j=0}^{k-1} \hat{c}_j(k)\hat{v}_j \\ &= B_k\tau_k + \sum_{j=0}^{k-1} B_j\hat{c}_j(k)\tau_j. \end{aligned} \tag{20}$$

The normal equations (11a) become

$$B_i \sum_{j=0}^{k} B_j \hat{c}_j(k) E\{\tau_i \tau_j\} = B_i E\{\tau_i x_k\}, \qquad i = 0,1,\cdots,k.$$

Without loss of generality one can assume each $B_j \neq 0$, for if $B_j = 0$, for any $j$, $\hat{c}_j(k)$ is indeterminate but does not affect $\hat{x}(k)$; thus the $j$th equation can be deleted along with the $j$th column of the matrix of elements $B_i B_j E(\tau_i \tau_j)$, and this reduced matrix equation can be solved instead. Dividing $B_j$ out of the $j$th equation, one has

$$\sum_{j=0}^{k} B_j \hat{c}_j(k) E\{\tau_i \tau_j\} = E\{\tau_i x_k\}, \qquad i = 0,1,\cdots,k. \quad (21)$$

Comparing equations (20) and (21), one has the following.

*Theorem 3:* If $\{x_j, j = 0,1,\cdots,k\}$ are jointly Gaussian random variables, if measurements $\{\hat{V}_j, j = 0,1,\cdots,k\}$ are optimally chosen (according to (10) and (11)), and if $\mathrm{tr}\,\{\rho(x_j)T_j\} = \Gamma_j x_j$, $j = 0,1,\cdots,k$, then the $\{\tau_j, j = 0,1,\cdots,k\}$ are a sufficient statistic for $\hat{x}_k$.

Theorem 3 makes it clear that the estimator including the past measurements will perform at least as well as an estimator using only the present measurement. Also, if the measurement outcomes $\{\tau_j, j = 0,1,\cdots,k\}$ allow a (classical) recursive estimate of $\hat{x}_k$, the quantum filtering problem will have a recursive solution, such an example follows.

*Example:* Suppose that $x_k$ is a Gaussian random variable and is transmitted as the real amplitude of a laser signal (assumed monochromatic) and received, along with thermal noise, in a single-mode cavity upon which an optimal measurement is to be made. The density operator in the coherent state or $P$-representation is then [4]

$$\rho(x_k) = \frac{1}{\pi N} \int \exp\left(-\frac{|\alpha - x_k|^2}{N}\right) |\alpha\rangle\langle\alpha| d^2\alpha$$

and the solution to (15) is known [12] to be

$$T_k = D_k \cdot \frac{a + a^+}{2} \qquad D_k \equiv \frac{2\lambda_k}{N + 2\lambda_k + \frac{1}{2}}$$

here $N$ defines the thermal noise level and $\lambda_k \equiv E(x_k^2)$. A measurement of $(a + a^+)/2$, assuming fixed $x_k$, results in a Gaussian random variable with mean $x_k$ and variance $(N/2 + 1/4)$ and is realized by homodyning [12].

Thus $x_k$ and $\tau_k$ are jointly Gaussian random variables and $E\{\tau_k \mid x_k\} = \mathrm{tr}\,\{\rho(x_k)T_k\} = D_k x_k$. Theorem 3 applies here with $\Gamma_j = D_j$. Moreover, in this case $T_k$ is proportional to an observable $(a_k + a_k^+)/2$ that is structurally independent of $k$, only one type of device is required—a simplification of great practical importance. Clearly the $(k + 1)$ measurements of $Y_j \equiv (a_j + a_j^+)/2$ at the times $j = 0,1,\cdots,k$ gives a sufficient statistic for the optimal estimate $\hat{x}_k$. Now

$$\hat{x}_k = B_k \Gamma_k y_k + \sum_{j=0}^{k-1} B_j \Gamma_j \hat{c}_j(k) y_j \quad (20a)$$

where the $\{y_j\}$ are the $(k + 1)$ outcomes of the measurements represented by $\{Y_k\}$, and the normal equations (21)

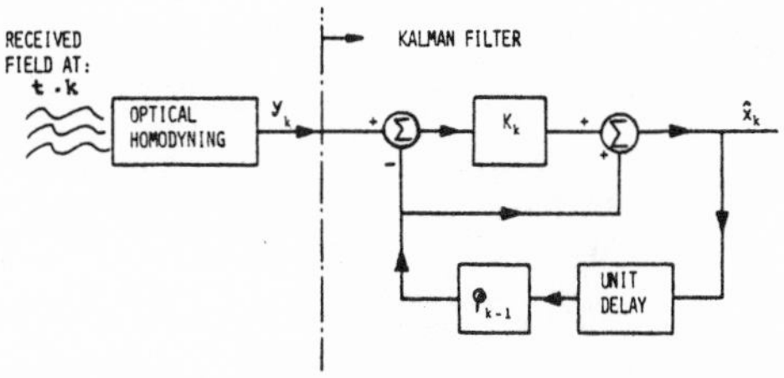


Fig. 2. Optimal filter for signal sequence of (1) when received as amplitude of a laser signal in single-mode cavity along with thermal noise.

become

$$\sum_{j=0}^{k} \Gamma_j B_j \hat{c}_j(k) E\{y_i y_j\} = E\{y_i x_k\}, \qquad i = 0,1,\cdots,k. \quad (21a)$$

Equations (20a) and (21a) describe an equivalent, although fictitious, classical estimation problem. Estimate $x_k$ given a sequence of observations

$$y_k = x_k + u_k$$

where $\{u_j, j = 0,1,\cdots,k\}$ is a sequence of independent zero-mean identically distributed Gaussian random variables with variance $(N/2 + 1/4)$.

Furthermore, if the sequence $\{x_j, j = 0,1,\cdots,k,\cdots\}$ satisfies the recursion (1), then $\hat{x}_k$ can be recursively calculated by the Kalman–Bucy filtering equations [11, p. 96]

$$\hat{x}_k = \phi_{k-1}\hat{x}_{k-1} + K_k[y_k - \phi_{k-1}\hat{x}_{k-1}]$$

where the so-called Kalman gain is

$$K_k = P_k \left[P_k + \left(\frac{N}{2} + \frac{1}{4}\right)\right]^{-1}$$

and

$$P_k = \phi_{k-1}^2\{P_{k-1}[1 - K_{k-1}]\} + Q_{k-1}$$

is the error variance based on the past $k$ observations. See Fig. 2.

## IV. Finite-Memory Signal Process

As an example in a different direction, suppose $\{x_j, j = 0,1,\cdots,k,\cdots\}$, a sequence of zero-mean random variables, is such that $x_j$ and $x_i$ are independent if $|j - i| > 1$. Such a random sequence is said to have a "one-step memory."

*Theorem 4:* If $\{x_j, j = 0,\cdots,k,\cdots\}$ has a one-step memory and each observable $\hat{V}_j$, $j = 0,1,\cdots,k$, is chosen optimally according to (13) and (14), then

$$\hat{V}_k = T_k - \hat{c}_{k-1}(k)\sigma_{k,k-1}, \qquad k \geq 1, \quad \hat{V}_0 = T_0. \quad (22)$$

*Proof:* For $k = 1$, trivially, the relation is true. For time $k + 1 > 2$, by (13)

$$\hat{V}_{k+1} = T_{k+1} - \sum_{j=0}^{k} \hat{c}_j(k + 1)\sigma_{k+1,j} \quad (23)$$

where $\sigma_{k+1,j}$ is determined by (16); in turn, by (9),

$$\zeta_{k+1,j} \equiv E_x\{\mathrm{tr}\,[\rho(x_j)\hat{V}_j]\rho(x_{k+1})\}. \tag{24}$$

For $j < k$, using the assumption of pairwise independence, $\zeta_{k+1,j} = [\mathrm{tr}\,\eta_j\hat{V}_j]\eta_{k+1}$ implying that $\sigma_{k+1,j} = [\mathrm{tr}\,\eta_j\hat{V}_j]I$. However, using the induction hypothesis,

$$\begin{aligned}\mathrm{tr}\,\eta_j\hat{V}_j &= \mathrm{tr}\,\eta_j\{T_j - \hat{c}_{j-1}(j)\sigma_{j,j-1}\}\\ &= \mathrm{tr}\,\delta_{jj} - \hat{c}_{j-1}(j)\,\mathrm{tr}\,\zeta_{j,j-1}\end{aligned}$$

(using (15) and (16)); as $\mathrm{tr}\,\delta_{jj} = E(x_j) = 0$, using (24) gives

$$\mathrm{tr}\,\eta_j\hat{V}_j = -\hat{c}_{j-1}(j)\,\mathrm{tr}\,\eta_{j-1}\hat{V}_{j-1}.$$

Iterating this procedure, eventually a product with the factor $\mathrm{tr}\,\eta_0\hat{V}_0 = \mathrm{tr}\,\delta_{00} = E(x_0) = 0$ appears. Thus $\zeta_{k+1,j}$ and $\sigma_{k+1,j} \equiv 0$, $j < k$. Q.E.D.

Note (22) may be written (using (9), (15), and (16))

$$\eta_k\hat{V}_k + \hat{V}_k\eta_k = 2\delta_{kk} - 2\hat{c}_{k-1}(k)E_x\{\mathrm{tr}\,[\rho(x_{k-1})\hat{V}_{k-1}]\rho(x_k)\}$$

which, knowing $\hat{c}_{k-1}(k)$, gives $\hat{V}_k$ recursively in terms of $\hat{V}_{k-1}$. Recursive calculations of $\hat{c}_{k-1}(k)$, the mean-square error at time $k$, and $\hat{x}_k$ can also be given, and these results extend to the "$n$-step memory" case for $n > 1$ [15].

## Acknowledgment

The authors wish to thank an anonymous reviewer for suggestions simplifying the original version of this paper.

## References

[1] C. W. Helstrom, "Detection theory and quantum mechanics," *Inform. Contr.*, vol. 10, pp. 254–291, Mar. 1967.
[2] A. S. Holevo, "Statistical problems in quantum physics," in *Proc. Soviet–Japanese Symp. on Probability and Statistics*, vol. 1, pp. 22–40, 1972.
[3] ——, "Statistical decision theory for quantum systems," *J. Multivariate Analysis*, vol. 3, pp. 337–394, 1973.
[4] C. W. Helstrom, J. W. Liu, and J. P. Gordon, "Quantum-mechanical communication theory," *Proc. IEEE*, vol. 58, pp. 1578–1598, Oct. 1970.
[5] Y. H. Park, "Quantum linear recursive minimum mean-square error estimation," Ph.D. dissertation, Dep. Elec. Eng., Univ. Md., College Park, Aug. 1974.
[6] J. S. Baras, R. O. Harger, and A. Ephremides, "Recursive filtering of operator-valued processes in quantum estimation," in *Proc. 1974 Int. Symp. on Information Theory*, Notre Dame, Ind., Oct. 1974, p.5.
[7] E. Prugovečki, *Quantum Mechanics in Hilbert Space*. New York: Academic, 1971.
[8] H. P. Yuen and M. Lax, "Multiple-parameter quantum estimation and measurement of nonselfadjoint observables," *IEEE Trans. Inform. Theory*, vol. IT-19, pp. 740–750, Nov. 1973.
[9] C. W. Helstrom and R. S. Kennedy, "Noncommuting observables in quantum detection and estimation theory," *IEEE Trans. Inform. Theory*, vol. IT-20, pp. 16–24, Jan. 1974.
[10] J. M. Jauch, *Foundations of Quantum Mechanics*. Reading, Mass.: Addison-Wesley, 1968.
[11] D. G. Luenberger, *Optimization by Vector Space Methods*. New York: Wiley, 1969.
[12] S. D. Personick, "Application of quantum estimation theory to analog communication over quantum channels," *IEEE Trans. Inform. Theory*, vol. IT-17, pp. 240–246, May 1971.
[13] J. S. Baras and Y. H. Park, "Estimation of random signals based on quantum mechanical measurements," in *Proc. 8th Asilomar Conf. on Circuits, Systems, and Computers*, 1974, pp. 533–539.
[14] J. S. Baras and R. O. Harger, "Multiparameter filtering with quantum measurements," in *Proc. Johns Hopkins Conf. on Information Sciences and Systems*, 1975, pp. 178–184.
[15] R. O. Harger and L. Wilhelm, "Quantum mechanical filtering of finite memory signal sequences," in *Proc. Johns Hopkins Conf. on Information Sciences and Systems*, 1975, (Abstract), p. 185.

# AUTHOR CITATION INDEX

# SUBJECT INDEX